Films that Work

Charles Seale-Hayne Library
University of Plymouth
(01752) 588 588
LibraryandITenquiries@plymouth.ac.uk

Films that Work

Industrial Film and the Productivity of Media

Edited by Vinzenz Hediger and Patrick Vonderau

AMSTERDAM UNIVERSITY PRESS

This publication was made possible through a generous grant from the Alfried Krupp von Bohlen und Halbach Foundation, Essen.

Front cover illustration: Car promotion for Renault, 1934
Back cover illustration: Buster Keaton in a commercial for PURE OIL (USA 1965)

Cover design: Kok Korpershoek, Amsterdam
Lay-out: JAPES, Amsterdam

ISBN   978 90 8964 013 0 (paperback)
ISBN   978 90 8964 012 3 (hardcover)
e- ISBN   978 90 4850 226 4
NUR   674

Contents

Introduction   9
    Vinzenz Hediger and Patrick Vonderau

I   NAVIGATING THE ARCHIVE

Archives and Archaeologies   19
The Place of Non-Fiction Film in Contemporary Media
    Thomas Elsaesser

Record, Rhetoric, Rationalization   35
Industrial Organization and Film
    Vinzenz Hediger and Patrick Vonderau

Vernacular Archiving   51
An Interview with Rick Prelinger
    Patrick Vonderau

II   VISUALITY AND EFFICIENCY

Early Industrial Moving Pictures in Germany   65
    Martin Loiperdinger

Layers of Cheese   75
Generic Overlap in Early Non-Fiction Films on Production Processes
    Frank Kessler and Eef Masson

Images of Efficiency   85
The Films of Frank B. Gilbreth
    Scott Curtis

**"What Hollywood Is to America, the Corporate Film Is to
    Switzerland"**   101
Remarks on Industrial Film as Utility Film
    Yvonne Zimmermann

POUSSIÈRES   119
Writing the Real vs. the Documentary Real
    Gérard Leblanc

Thermodynamic Kitsch   127
Computing in German Industrial Films, 1928/1963
    Vinzenz Hediger

III FILMS AND FACTORIES

Touring as a Cultural Technique   153
Visitor Films and Autostadt Wolfsburg
    Patrick Vonderau

Corporate Films of Industrial Work   167
Renault (1916-1939)
    Alain P. Michel

Filming Work on Behalf of the Automobile Firm   187
The Case of Renault (1950-2002)
    Nicolas Hatzfeld, Gwenaële Rot and Alain P. Michel

Eccentricity, Education and the Evolution of Corporate Speech   211
Jam Handy and His Organization
    Rick Prelinger

Centron, an Industrial/Educational Film Studio, 1947-1981   221
A Microhistory
    Faye E. Riley

Films from Beyond the Well   243
A Historical Overview of Shell Films
    Rudmer Canjels

IV SEE, LEARN, CONTROL

The Personnel Is Political   259
Voice and Citizenship in Affirmative-Action Videos in the Bell
    System, 1970-1984
    Heide Solbrig

Behaviorism, Animation, and Effective Cinema   283
The McGraw-Hill INDUSTRIAL MANAGEMENT Film Series and the Visual
    Culture of Management
    Ramón Reichert

Technologies of Organizational Learning   303
Uses of Industrial Films in Sweden during the 1950s
  Mats Björkin

The Central Film Library of Vocational Education   315
An Archeology of Industrial Film in France between the Wars
  Valérie Vignaux

"Reality Is There, but It's Manipulated"   329
West German Trade Unions and Film after 1945
  Stefan Moitra

V URBANITY, INDUSTRY, FILM

Modernism, Industry, Film   349
A Network of Media in the Baťa Corporation and the Town of Zlín
  in the 1930s
  Petr Szczepanik

A Modern Medium for a Modern Message   377
Norsk Jernverk, 1946-1974, Through the Camera Lens
  Bjørn Sørenssen

Harbor, Architecture, Film   391
Rotterdam, 1925-1935
  Floris Paalman

Industrial Films   405
An Analytical Bibliography
  Anna Heymer and Patrick Vonderau

The Desiderata of Business-Film Research   463
  Ralf Stremmel

Contributors   471

Index of Names   477

Index of Film Titles   480

Index of Subjects   485

Introduction

Vinzenz Hediger and Patrick Vonderau

Reminiscing about his days as a union organizer, David McDonald, the former president of the United Steel Workers of America, relates the following anecdote. According to McDonald, in order to get steel workers to join the union, the union organizers used a technique

> which we called ... visual education, which was a high-sounding label for a practice much more accurately described as dues picketing. It worked very simply. A group of dues-paying members selected by the district director (usually more for their size than their tact) would stand at the plant gate with pick handles or baseball bats and confront each worker as he arrived for his shift.[1]

"Visual education" here serves as a euphemism for the ostentatious threat of physical violence against workers unwilling to join the union. What is more, "visual education" is put on display at the factory gate, which is, of course, a key site of industrial culture, but also of film history. Workers leaving the factory have been a staple of industrial photography since its introduction in the second half of the 19th century, and workers leaving the factory, plus a dog, were the subject of the first Lumière film. However, the anecdote deals with workers arriving at the factory rather than leaving; apparently, changing the direction of the worker's physical movement and moving the time of the observation to the beginning of the shift rather than its end reveals something that is not quite as obvious in either the photographs of workers leaving the factory or the Lumière film.

The story highlights a relationship between visuality, power, and industrial organization that in one form or another may well have run through a good part of the history of modern industrial societies. Unions, for one, became a fact of life throughout these societies in the second half of the 19th century, which coincidentally is about the same time that the workers leaving the factory started appearing in photographs. Certainly, the story does not involve the use of film but rather another visual medium, the *tableau vivant*, albeit one formed by a troupe of thugs armed with bats and pick handles rather than a group of ladies and gentlemen styled in the fashion of old paintings. Moreover, its purpose is not primarily aesthetic in nature. The visuality of the display, however, is still indispensable to its effect, which, together with its organizational purpose, makes it relevant to the present undertaking. Tracing and analyzing films in and on industrial organizations is the main concern of this volume.

In terms of output, industrial and commissioned films are definitely among the most prolific formats or genres in film history. Still, little scholarship has been devoted to this corpus of films, and almost none of it with a view to the field of knowledge and power evoked in McDonald's anecdote. Most studies on industrial films come from social historians and historians of technology, who tend to value moving images as source material rather than objects worthy of interest on their own. In cinema studies, the criteria employed for selecting worthy objects of study seem to preclude any prolonged engagement with utility films, with the exception of the early films of canonical directors such as Alain Resnais or Jean-Luc Godard. However, relative to the wealth of material in industrial film archives that apparently lacks artistic distinction, such specimens are in short supply. Accordingly, any attempt to use the holdings of the industrial film archive as raw material for the production of academic auteur criticism will lead to a trickle rather than a stream of exciting scholarship.[2] Assuming, as this volume does, that films made by and for the purposes of industrial and social organizations constitute the next big chunk of uncharted territory in cinema studies,[3] one cannot but agree with collector-archivist Rick Prelinger, a pioneer in the field of industrial-film research, when he states that "it would be a great leap forward for cinema studies if we were able to avoid the auteur theory this time."[4]

But how, indeed, if not through the auteurist lens, should the film scholar approach such films? What, if anything, can film scholarship contribute to an understanding of this material? What kinds of questions that images of and for industry pose can cinema studies help to answer with its particular set of analytical tools? And if the purpose of industrial and other utility films is not to provide, first and foremost, an aesthetic experience of the artistic kind, which theoretical models and frameworks should be employed in examining these films in order to explain why they look the way they do and better understand their purpose?

In various ways, these are the questions that the contributions in this volume address. If there is one common answer to be found in the essays that follow, it is the assumption that the films discussed here cannot be divorced from the conditions of their production and the contexts of their use. Far from constituting self-sufficient entities for aesthetic analysis, industrial and utility films have to be understood in terms of their specific, usually organizational, purpose, and in the very context of power and organizational practice in which they appear. As Thomas Elsaesser points out in his contribution (as well as in his other work on industrial films), all industrial films have an occasion, a purpose, and an addressee, or an *Auftrag, Anlass,* and *Adressat,* rather than an auteur. Furthermore, as the editors of this volume propose in their joint contribution, there are the "three Rs" or areas of purpose that media in general and films in particular can serve in industrial organizations: *record* (institutional memory), *rhetoric* (governance) and *rationalization* (optimizing process).

A good part of the film scholar's work when addressing industrial films, one might argue, lies in the search for the three As and the three Rs to complement the actual film. As found in the archive, the films constitute traces of the forms of social and industrial organization which they once served, and, more often than not, their intelligibility depends on the degree to which a reconstruction of these frames of organization is possible. Of necessity, then, as objects of knowledge, industrial films transcend the boundaries of the material object of film found in the archive and refer to a *dispositif*, a complex constellation of media, technology, forms of knowledge, discourse, and social organization.[5]

But, if production histories have long been part and parcel of film analysis, particularly for approaches such as the Bordwellian "historical poetics" of film, industrial films call for a different kind of approach. Production histories of fiction films reveal the situations that produced the films. What is at stake in industrial and utility film research is not just the institutional framework in which the film was produced, but also, and perhaps first and foremost, the situation or constellation that the film produces. Assuming that films, like other media at work in social and industrial organization, from writing and graphics to the telephone and the computer, provide the condition sine qua non for the emergence of certain types of social practice such as large-scale industrial production and globalized financial markets,[6] industrial films are perhaps best understood as *interfaces* between discourses and forms of social and industrial organization.

Industrial organizations, like all forms of organization, are based on knowledge and its transferability. Some kinds of knowledge, such as an experienced worker's specific skills, remain implicit and are not transferable.[7] Technical and administrative knowledge, however, is eminently transferable and allows for the emergence of functional hierarchies and the differentiation of professional roles and the division of labor. Furthermore, control in organizations, and particularly large organizations in competitive markets, depends on knowledge in the sense of informational feedback about specific operations and their success. If we thus understand organizations as systems of knowledge and knowledge transfer aimed at creating certain kinds of outputs, their emergence in turn depends on the availability of technical media that store and transmit information and thus allow for the transfer of knowledge, such as the telephone, the computer, or film.

More often than not, industrial films are supposed to directly translate discourse into social practice, which is particularly obvious in training and educational films, such as the management films discussed by Ramón Reichert in his contribution to this volume, but also in the union films discussed by Stefan Moitra, whose visual strategies provide guidelines for political action. At the same time, industrial films, like other media, document social practice and create feedback for social and industrial organizations, thus facilitating their operation and their adaptation to changing environments. What is at stake in industrial film research, then, is the complex interrelationship of visuality, power, and organization, and specifically how film as a medium creates the preconditions for forms of knowledge and social practice.

In that sense, industrial film research might best be understood as part of an epistemology of media in a broader sense, a project guided by a set of questions that have thus far been most prominent in certain areas of the history of science. At the same time, industrial film research points to a domain circumscribed by Foucault's concept of governmentality, i.e., the dependence of modern forms of governance on certain types of knowledge, particularly statistical knowledge concerning entire populations. If the contributions in this volume provide a survey of relevant topics in industrial film research and, through what they discuss as much as through what they omit, create a map of possible topics for future research, they also provide the outlines of a field of research in which epistemological questions related to media and political questions concerning governance, knowledge, and power can be brought together in a new form of inquiry with a potential to impact both film and media studies and political and social science. For, if epistemological inquiries into the role of media in science tend to neglect the social realm beyond the space of the lab and the scientific community, governmentality studies, closely following the lead of Foucault himself, are generally oblivious to the role that media, and particularly technical media, play in constituting the power relationships that they analyze and discuss.

In that sense, the essays in this volume may also be read as contributions towards the project of a *historical epistemology of media in social and industrial organizations* that translates specific historical findings into a systematic framework that helps us better understand how social practice emerges from certain forms of knowledge and their configuration with (technical) media.[8] If film scholars tend to be sensitive to ideology in representations but rarely say much about social practice beyond the screen, sociologists and political scientists care only about social practice and tend to neglect how much of it is mediated, not least through the cinema screen. Industrial film research, this volume would like to show, provides a chance for both to overcome the specific limitations of their methodologies and mindsets. It may help the social scientist understand just how carefully chosen a euphemism "visual education" is in our introductory anecdote, and it may help the film scholar better comprehend the impact of visual displays, even when there is not a single frame of film in sight.

The contributions in this volume are divided into six sections. Section I, "Navigating the Archive," brings together three contributions of a methodological nature. In "Archives and Archaeologies: The Place of Non-Fiction Film in Contemporary Media" Thomas Elsaesser situates industrial films within a broader research agenda concerned with non-fiction film and provides a series of theoretical handles that may prove useful in future research. In "Record, Rhetoric, Rationalization: Industrial Organization and Film" Vinzenz Hediger and Patrick Vonderau propose a framework of analysis that differentiates between the film medium's specific organizational functions. And finally, in "Vernacular Archiving," a conversation with Patrick Vonderau, Rick Prelinger discusses some of the issues involved in the archiving of industrial and other "ephemeral" films, as he proposes to call them.

Section II, "Visuality and Efficiency," brings together a series of case studies that discuss issues of knowledge, visuality, and efficient industrial organization, with most of the six contributions focusing on early cinema and paracinematic visual practices such as the slide show. In "Early Industrial Moving Pictures in Germany," film historian Martin Loiperdinger provides a survey of the representation of industrial production in early German cinema. In "Layers of Cheese: Generic Overlap in Early Non-Fiction Films on Production Processes," Frank Kessler and Eef Masson discuss process films in terms of their strategies of address and visual representation, demonstrating the extent to which the visual vernacular of the industrial film was formed outside organizational discourse in popular film forms, only to be imported into the rhetoric of industrial organization later on. Scott Curtis proposes a new perspective on the work-study films of Frank Gilbreth in "Images of Efficiency," highlighting their formal strategies as part of the discourses of contemporary management theory rather than taking the films and their claims of improved efficiency at face value. In " 'What Hollywood Is to America, the Corporate Film Is to Switzerland': Remarks on Industrial Film as Utility Film," Yvonne Zimmermann proposes a post-auteurist approach to industrial films, arguing from the wealth of such material in Swiss film archives. Gérard Leblanc discusses the complex web of relationships that condition the work of the industrial filmmaker in "Poussières: Writing the Real vs. the Documentary Real," taking a film by Georges Franju on the prevention of health hazards in postwar France as his example. In "Thermodynamic Kitsch: Visuality, Computing, and Industrial Organization in German Industrial Films, 1928/1963," Vinzenz Hediger discusses the introduction of computing technology in German industrial production and its representation in industrial films, arguing that computing technologies induce a specific crisis of visibility in the representational strategies of industrial films.

Section III, "Films and Factories," comprises case studies of the use of film in specific corporations. In "Touring as a Cultural Technique: Visitor Films and Autostadt Wolfsburg," Patrick Vonderau discusses film and the visual strategies of the guided tour of Volkswagen's main factory in Wolfsburg, Germany, and proposes an analysis of the factory visit as a specifically modern "cultural technique," i.e., a technique that transforms unproductive resources into productive ones. In "Corporate Films of Industrial Work: Renault (1916-1939)," Alain P. Michel traces the uses of photography and film at the Renault car factory, while Michel and his co-authors Nicolas Hatzfeld and Gwenaële Rot provide a companion piece to cover the rest of Renault's company history in "Filming Work in the Name of the Automobile Firm: The Renault Case (1950-2002)." Together, these two essays represent one of the very first comprehensive company histories with regard to the use of photography or film available to date. In "Eccentricity, Education, and the Evolution of Corporate Speech: Jam Handy and His Organization," Rick Prelinger traces the company history of one of the most prolific North American producers of industrial films, while Faye Riley's "Centron, an Industrial/Educational-Film Studio, 1947-1981: A Microhistory" provides another company history of a particularly tenacious provider of industrial-film services based on first-hand accounts and archival research. And finally, in "Films from Beyond the Well: A Historical Overview of Shell Films" Rudmer Canjels studies the relationship between film work and company policies of the Royal Dutch Shell corporation, one of the main energy corporations in the world, in a historical perspective.

Section IV, "See, Learn, Control," brings together five contributions that focus on aspects of film and governance. In "The Personnel Is Political: Voice and Citizenship in Affirmative-Action Videos in the Bell System, 1970-1984" Heide Solbrig analyzes the strategies of address employed by the educational films a major American telecommunications company produced with regard to a key policy issue of the past few decades, affirmative action. Ramón Reichert's essay, "Behaviorism, Animation, and Effective Cinema: The McGraw-Hill INDUSTRIAL MANAGEMENT Film Series and the Visual Culture of Management," discusses the visual strategies of postwar US management-education films in light of ideologies of governance and control. In "Technologies of Organizational Learning: Uses of Industrial Films in Sweden during the 1950s" Mats Björkin shows how industrial lobby organizations used film to attune Swedish corporations to the new teachings of cybernetic management theory, while Valérie Vignaux traces the work of an industrial-education cinémathèque in France in "The Central Film Library of Vocational Education: An Archeology of Industrial Film in France between the Wars." Stefan Moitra dissects an important corpus of the film work of West German labor unions, a major factor in the Germany's postwar "economic miracle," in " 'Reality Is There, But It's Manipulated.' West German Labor Unions and Film after 1945."

Section V, "Urbanity, Industry, Film," contains three essays that explore the relationship between film, urban planning, and industrial development. In his contribution on the city of Zlín and the Bat'a shoe factory in the Czech Republic Petr Szczepanik demonstrates how city planning, industrial organization, and media use, from telephone to film, were intricately intertwined in this model city built in the Moravian countryside in the 1920s. In "A Modern Medium for a Modern Message: Norsk Jernverk, 1946-1974, Through the Camera Lens," Bjørn Sørenssen discusses the Norwegian mining and steel town Mo i Rana, a key example of state planning in the postwar era and a prestige project whose changing fortunes can be traced through the film work devoted to the project. And finally, in "Harbor, Architecture, Film: Rotterdam, 1925-1935," a study of an early case of city branding, Floris Paalman shows how film played a major role in providing the port city of Rotterdam with a modernist self-image and implementation of the relevant architectural policies. Concluding the volume, the last section of our book combines an essay by historian and archivist Ralf Stremmel on potential future avenues of industrial film research with an annotated international bibliography of industrial film scholarship by Anna Heymer and Patrick Vonderau.

Finally, one omission in this volume needs to be addressed: The collection does not include an essay on Sovjet industrial films or from a socialist country. Being at the stage that it is, this area has as yet to be addressed in industrial film research. While we purposely wanted to avoid an auteurist approach to industrial rhetoric in classical Sovjet cinema, few if any scholars at this point have developed a sustained interest in the archival holdings of industrial films in the former Sovjet republics and former socialist countries of central Europe beyond the auteurist canon. At least judging from the case of the National Film Archive in Prague, these holdings are considerable and promise to be rewarding for future research.

For the English translations and revisions of the manuscript, our gratitude goes to David Hendrickson and especially to Steve Wilder for his many helpful suggestions.

Translations were made possible through a generous grant from the Alfried Krupp von Bohlen und Halbach foundation.

Notes

1. Quoted in Mancur Olson, *The Rise and Decline of Nations: Economic Growth, Stagflation, and Social Rigidities* (New Haven and London: Yale University Press, 1982), p. 21.
2. But how exciting such scholarship can be. See, for instance, Edward Dimendberg's detailed analysis of Alain Resnais' LE CHANT DU STYRÈNE, which, for reasons of space, could not be reprinted here but should be consulted by the interested reader. Edward Dimendberg, "'These Are Not Exercises in Style': *Le Chant du Styrène*," *October*, 112 (Spring 2005), pp. 63-88.

3. "Uncharted Territory" was, of course, the title of a pioneering workshop organized by Daan Hertogs and Nico de Klerk at the Nederlands Filmmuseum in 1996 which set the pace and the agenda for the study of early non-fiction film. See Daan Hertogs, Nico de Klerk, *Uncharted Territory: Essays on Early Non-Fiction Film* (Amsterdam: Stichting Nederlands Filmmuseum, 1997).

4. See the conversation between Patrick Vonderau and Rick Prelinger in this volume.

5. We are referring to the notion of *dispositif* proposed by Michel Foucault rather than the *dispositif* of 1970s film theory, which refers to the material and technological conditions of film screenings and aims at a critique of the ideological implications of the screening.

6. For a detailed discussion of media as a prerequisite for the emergence of large-scale industrial production from the 19th century onward, see JoAnne Yates, *Control Through Communication: The Rise of System in American Management* (Baltimore: Johns Hopkins University Press, 1989).

7. For the concept of implicit knowledge see Michael Polanyi, *Personal Knowledge: Towards a Post-Critical Philosophy* (New York: Harper, 1962).

8. The term "historical epistemology" is borrowed from Georges Canguilhem.

I
Navigating the Archive

Archives and Archaeologies

The Place of Non-Fiction Film in Contemporary Media

Thomas Elsaesser

I am not a specialist on industrial film. However, I decided to accept the invitation to make this contribution because I realized that there are at least three, possibly even four distinct areas of work that I am currently engaged in that touch upon – and indeed intersect with – the *Gebrauchsfilm* or utility film, of which the industrial film forms such an important corpus. My motto in this respect is that "there are many histories of the moving image, only some of which belong to the movies."[1]

Media archaeology

First of all, there is a broad historiographic project I have been involved with. Its aim is to try to identify the different genealogies that make up the histories of the moving image in order to come to a fuller understanding of the different cultural logics and technological dynamics that both unite and separate film, television, video-installation work, and the digital media. Under the general title of *Film History as Media Archaeology*, I have been especially focused on isolating particular moments of media transfer and media convergence. The key ones we eventually selected are the period of early cinema from the 1890s to 1910, the coming of sound in the late 1920s and early 1930s, the emergence of television and video in the 1950s and early 1960s, and finally, the transfer from photographic to digital images in the 1980s and 1990s.

In each case – whether generically identified as actuality or travel film, current-events film or documentary, or still oscillating around more unstable classifications such as avant-garde, advertising, experimental, educational, propaganda, public-service film, or promo spot – the non-fiction film seems to have played either the role of *intermedia*, as appetizer, trial balloon, and lightning fuse, or it has existed as a legitimate but parallel cinematic universe – sometimes also called "Expanded Cinema," about which film history so far has been largely ignorant or deliberately silent.[2]

Another way of approaching this truly vast and uncharted corpus, to which the industrial film centrally belongs, would be to speak about the non-entertainment uses of the cinematic apparatus over the past hundred years. The Amsterdam project has been inventorying some of these non-entertainment histories of the moving image under what I have called the *three S/M practices* of the cinematic machine: *surveillance and military applications, surgery and medicine, and sensoring and monitoring*. I recently edited a book on Harun Farocki, where notably the first S/M practice, i.e., surveillance and military uses, is being extensively thematized.[3] Farocki, an increasingly well-known German media artist and theorist, has – in addition to his recent installations relating to the notion of surveillance (*Ich glaubte, Gefangene zu sehen, Die Schöpfer der Einkaufswelten*) – a long and exemplary filmography dealing with industrial films, training films, procedurals, test films, and aerial reconnaissance photography.[4] A colleague of mine, Jose van Dijck, has written on surgery and medicine, in a study called *The Transparent Body* (2005).[5] Together with Lev Manovich I am also working on a project dealing with *Augmented Space and Intelligent Surfaces*, which will look at embedded information in our built urban and domestic environment, that is, the increasing presence of sensors and interactive devices which passively register our presence or provide information when actively accessed.[6] Although none of these media archaeologies or S/M practices is specifically focused on the industrial film, I see our endeavor in this direction to offer potentially interesting insights and fruitful cross-referencing with scholars and archivists working on the industrial film.

Cinema Europe

Another line of inquiry that has already obliged me to engage with the industrial film proper comes out of a four-year funded doctoral research project I set up for some 12 Ph.D. candidates, called Cinema Europe. Of the various subprojects, at least three are directly relevant to our topic. One is concerned with *Architecture, Urbanism and Cinematic City* in Europe. Floris Paalman's doctoral thesis is centered on the mediatization of Rotterdam over the past 60 to 80 years. Here, hitherto barely identified and virtually anonymous creators of the photographic and cinematic iconography of the city such as Andor von Barsy are given their due, e.g., for industrial films featuring the harbor, bridges across the Maas, and other public works. However, the point is not to unearth forgotten "auteurs" of the art of cinema, but to make a city the central reference point, indeed the veritable "auteur" of a body of work that crosses the media (film, photography, audio records) and genres (documentary, fiction, training, industrial, advertising), while providing something like a living memory and neural network for a major European city's changing self-image and media self-presentation. A second sub-project concerns the intersection of industry, technology and the cinematic avant-garde during the period of the coming of sound. On this topic, Malte Hagener has completed a comprehensive re-examination of the leading avant-garde filmmakers' involvement with, among other things, commissioned films for large-scale engineering projects; political parties; companies in steel production, electrical appliances, shipping, tourism, radio, and other consumer goods and services.

The third project was a study that I myself conducted – in connection with the DFG research project *Geschichte des Dokumentarfilms in Deutschland* – of the nonfiction films made in connection with modern architecture in the 1920s, notably films associated with *Das Neue Bauen* and in particular, *Das Neue Frankfurt*.[7] Again, the chief aim was to put a strategically located city – known for shipping, aviation, architecture, and finance – at the center of audiovisual production during a specific period of rapid growth and urban renewal. The somewhat surprising realization I came to was that conventional wisdom, namely that the architectural avant-garde and the cinematic avant-garde were natural allies and made for each other, turned out to be in need of some historical revision. When I looked at the (rather meager) result of this alliance, and began to speculate on the reasons for it, I realized that two assumptions were mistaken. One was that architects saw film as the most avant-garde and most appropriate medium to promote and propagate their ideas and work. It turned out that they invariably seemed to prefer still photography, well-designed books and pamphlets with modern typography, industrial catalogues and trade publications over cinema films. Even postcards seemed to have been a more congenial and certainly more popular advertising medium for modern architecture than film.[8]

The other assumption I had to question was that, if architects looked to the cinema as a medium, they would naturally prefer avant-garde film forms, such as Russian montage cinema or Dada collage films to the sober and conventional formats of the documentary or educational film. However, many of the films made about *Das Neue Bauen* fit much better into the then prevalent formats of the industrial film, the training film or possibly the Ufa Kulturfilm than the avant-garde or experimental film, with the exception perhaps of a film by Hans Richter, DIE NEUE WOHNUNG (1930). However, one of the films, DIE STADT VON MORGEN, an internationally very well-known film made in 1929/1930 and usually credited to one Dr. Max von Goldeck, turns out, on closer inspection, to owe its fame more to the animation work of the once more well-known though also notorious Svend Noldan than to the direction of the otherwise totally unknown Goldeck.

The case of Noldan, a brilliant animator of maps and graphics and a key figure in the history of the industrial film, the newsreel, and the propaganda film (who threw in his lot with the Nazi Party before continuing his career after the war with BASF, the successor of IG Farben), somewhat recalls the situation of both Walter Ruttmann and of Andor von Barsy. But he also reminds me of another figure, featured in a study done some years back by Martin Loiperdinger, around a symptomatic misunderstanding between an avant-garde filmmaker and his corporate client. The filmmaker was Willy Zielke, the client the Deutsche Reichsbahn, and the film was DAS STAHLTIER (1934). The direction of the Reichsbahn in Munich had wanted a film that celebrated the centenary of the German railway's achievements and advertised the amenities and comforts of modern rail travel. Zielke, a former cameraman with Leni Riefenstahl, on the other hand, saw it as his chance to make an avant-garde masterpiece, in the tradition of the Russian masters Eisenstein and Vertov, or inspired by the Bolshevik agit-prop trains that had pioneered new concepts of film projection, education, and display. The film, not surprisingly, was refused by the Reichsbahn, and for many decades all but disappeared. However, rather than the misunderstanding being one of politics – here the National Socialist Reichsbahn, there a crypto-Bolshevik filmmaker – I tend to think the clash was one of culture, between two kinds of modernism: between an avant-garde high-art modernism, of revolt and revolution, and an avant-garde of industrial modernism or commercial modernization, of advertising and design, serviced more by filmic modes modeled on industrial films than experimental style and formally innovative technique.

The conclusion I drew from my study of *Bauen und Wohnen* films was that, in examining a particular corpus of non-fiction films, it is perhaps advisable to suspend all pre-existing categorizations, such as they have evolved in film history around "documentary," "avant-garde," or "experimental," just as much as "advertising film," "fascist propaganda film," or "politically progressive" filmmaking. Rather, it is better to assume, in the first instance, that non-fiction filmmaking (but many fiction films as well), especially during the 1920s and 1930s, but possibly at other times as well, functioned as part of a *Medienverbund*. By *Medienverbund* I mean, in the first instance, a network of competing, but also mutually interdependent and complementary media or media practices, focused on a specific location, a professional association, or even a national or state initiative. In my case, the location for such a *Medienverbund* was the city of Frankfurt (or, in Floris Paalman's project, Rotterdam), but the Bauhaus can also best be understood as a *Medienverbund*, as can the agit-prop initiatives of the Russian Revolution. In the 1930s, the German Propaganda Ministry was an example of a state-controlled *Medienverbund*, since Goebbels had clearly studied the principles of the earlier (left-wing) media networks.

In other words, if today the political labels left and right have become questionable, so has the traditional avant-garde argument around media-specificity. Both seem unhelpful at best, if they are not revised in the direction of factoring in the question of technological constraints and possibilities on the one hand, and the issue of institutions – industrial, party political, or governmental – acting as funding bodies on the other, in broadly conceived media offensives, aimed at influencing the newly mediatized public spheres. Networks of artists are, of course, familiar from avant-garde movements, such as Futurism, Expressionism, Dadaism, Surrealism. Its members often not only had close personal ties with each other (shared schools, shared wars, shared women), but especially in Europe, they tended to congregate or converge in nodal cities, notably Paris, Zurich, and Berlin, with the possible addition of Rotterdam, Frankfurt, Stuttgart, Dessau, and Vienna in the case of architects and designers. But what I understand by network and node in the concept of the *Medienverbund* would also include the creative energies bundled in company towns such as Eindhoven (headquarters of Philips), Jena (Zeiss), Zlín (Baťa works) and no doubt Essen, Bochum, and Wuppertal as well. There, filmmakers often found work in the areas of research and development, as well as in the design and advertising departments. Avant-garde directors like Walter Ruttmann, Joris Ivens, George Pal, Alexander Hackenschmidt were able – through company commissions – to make use of the latest technical equipment and the resources, and to develop new film forms, for instance, in the fields of animation, the combination of live action and trick photography, or special effects. In addition, once one adds some of the other S/M practices I mentioned, such as the use of film/moving images for recording processes and documenting phenomena of the natural sciences, such as biology and zoology, then other networks and nodes become visible. For instance, once one locates some of the films made at the intersection of science, entertainment, and education (as represented in Germany by the Ufa Kulturfilm), then filmmakers such as Jean Painlevé in France, J.C. Mol in the Netherlands, Martin Rikkli, and Svend Noldan in Germany emerge as auteurs, part of another avant-garde in their crucial role as formal innovators, but also as pioneers in extending the uses and applications of the cinematic apparatus.

In this more historio-pragmatic, as opposed to essentialist, perspective I tried to summarize in the rule of the three A's that need to be applied to a non-fiction film when trying to classify it, but also when attempting to read and interpret it. These A's are "wer war der *Auftraggeber*" (who commissioned the film), "was war der *Anlass*" (what was the occasion for which it was made), and "was war die *Anwendung* oder der *Adressat*" (to what use was it put or to whom was it addressed). These are, you will have realized, precisely the questions avant-garde artists or documentary filmmakers do not wish to be asked or routinely refuse to answer, since they fear it compromises their standing as auteurs and artists. Histories of the documentary film have often in the past been motivated by a desire to carefully write out of their accounts of auteurs, of styles and movements, any evidence of the industrial or commercial sponsorship, institutional or governmental funding, even though these commissions were largely responsible for making the work of these auteurs possible.

For the scholar or student, however, the three A's are the first line of inquiry. They are not always easy to identify, and often require extensive research in film archives, government agency records, and also company files, publicity material of trade fairs, Werkbund exhibitions, or professional conferences. I remember a student of mine a few years back, whom I had shown a Messter film from 1916, called DAS STAHLWERK DER POLDIHÜTTE WÄHREND DES WELTKRIEGS (*The Steel Foundries of Poldihütte During the Great War*), of which, at that time, the Netherlands Filmmuseum possessed the only copy. She became so fascinated by the film that she undertook a six-month, ruinously expensive research tour, which finally led her to a small mining town in Silesia and extensive studies of the Wittgenstein family archives in Vienna.[9] Even so, she only scratched the surface. We know next to nothing about what the film was used for: to advertise the precision ordinance produced there, as propaganda intended to impress the enemy, or as birthday present to Leopoldine Wittgenstein, after whom the steelworks were named. Thus, there is much about this extraordinary industrial film focusing on the steel production of the Austro-Hungarian Empire and its temporary conversion into a munitions plant during World War I that still awaits clarification, before we can do more than note that the narrative follows the standard trajectory or process-as-progress, from raw material to finished product, with the intended irony that the finished products are mortar shells and grenades, rather than kitchen utensils or machine tools.

Similarly, a barely nine-minute film about the famous Frankfurter Küche from 1927 not only led me to a little-known film company in Berlin, the Humboldt Film AG, which specializes in the compilation of industrial films or demonstration films of new building materials or techniques into feature-length programs, for distribution to specialized exhibition venues, it also made me review the relation between the media hype of this particular prototype and its actual success or failure on site and in use. Again, I realized that while the film – commissioned by the then chief city architect Ernst May to promote *Das Neue Frankfurt* – was hardly seen or distributed other than as part of a traveling exhibition, following a screening at a CIAM conference held in Frankfurt for international architects, urbanists, and town planners, a particular photo of the Frankfurt Küche appeared in every architectural journal. The photo, not the film, is now immortalized in scores of architectural histories – so much so that museums all over the world have begun to feature replicas of the Frankfurt kitchen, as if it was a Duchamp ready-made or had always been intended mainly as a piece of installation art.[10]

Preservation and presentation of the moving image

The third Amsterdam project through which I encountered the industrial film is a new graduate program I initiated in 2003, called the Professional Master in Preservation and Presentation of the Moving Image, which is taught at the University in conjunction with the Nederlands Filmmuseum, the Hilversum Television Archive, and the Rotterdam International Film Festival (as well as involving professional placements or internships at six to eight other museums, archives, and festivals in the Amsterdam-Utrecht-Rotterdam region).

Without wishing to blow our own trumpet, it should be pointed out just how unusual such an academic program still is in Europe, and how difficult it has been to initiate active cooperation between professional archives and universities. For me, it symbolically signals an end – at least at the local level of Amsterdam – to some 60 years of suspicion, distrust, and downright hostility that existed between archivists and academics. Legion and legendary are the stories of scholars being refused access even to official film archives, funded by taxpayer money, presided over by archivists who guard their treasures with a compulsive obsession worthy of Alberich of the Nibelungen and who surround their holdings with the secrecy worthy of the KGB. Two factors have begun to change this situation. One is that, since the mid-1970s, archives have realized that, faced with the increasingly desperate situation around their nitrate holdings and the lack of funds for preserving them adequately on safety stock, they are in need of wider public support. One source of such support was the new generation of film historians, interested especially in early cinema and the origins of the medium, which I have already referred to. The so-called New Film History not only brought into the archives experts that could help identify, classify, and catalogue hitherto anonymous or fragmentary material, it also – via the scholars and students becoming actively engaged in this filmic heritage through annual festivals such as those at Pordenone and Bologna – brought the archives new audiences, new users, and new international prestige, themselves factors vital for increasing their state subsidies or generating special task operational funds.

The other key factor in opening up the archives, not only to individual scholars, but to structural cooperation with institutions such as universities, was the fact that, during the 1980s, a new generation of archivists had assumed positions of leadership and influence. Many of these Young Turks had graduated from university film courses or had been involved in independent filmmaking, film festivals, or the avant-garde. The climate since the 1990s was thus more favorable for new types of cooperation between archives and the academy. And yet, the course I was eventually able to set up in Amsterdam was itself the result

of a failed initiative to establish a Europe-wide Masters Degree in Archiving
and Curatorship on the part of Archimedia, a subdivision of the European Union Media Programme in Brussels. I participated in Archimedia for six years,
until it, for all intents and purposes, came to an end in 2002. But for the last two
years of its existence – together with Leonardo Quaresima, from the University
of Udine – I was charged with working out a plan for such a master's program.
Archimedia's loss was Amsterdam's gain, and since 2003, the Professional Master's course P&P is now admitting up to 15 students per year, for a three-seme-
ster program, of which the last is an internship or placement.

When setting up the curriculum and thinking about the individual modules, I
had to consider not only the mix of academic and professional courses, but also
what kind of academic work could prepare students for their future professions
as curators, archivists, or programmers of the moving image. Especially tricky
were traditional subjects such as film history and film theory, for which I felt a
new approach was necessary. For instance, I was confronted with the fact that
most film archives, and even the most prestigious ones, have vast amounts of
material among their holdings that has no canonical status whatsoever, and are
made up of films from the most diverse sources and provenance, the so-called
"bits and pieces," sometimes also known as "orphan films."[11] What then is the
point of talking about Eisenstein's BATTLESHIP POTEMKIN (1925) or Renoir's LA
REGLE DU JEU (1939) to students faced with the task of identifying 50 feet of a
Western drama from the late teens or a home movie made by a Dutch colonial
officer as he left Jakarta/Batavia in 1947?

This embarrassment of riches of the un-canonized, the inconsequential, and
the overlooked was a particular burden for the Netherlands Filmmuseum,
which in the 1970s and 1980s became vulnerable to government cuts because
its holdings consisted mainly of discarded prints of commercial films that had
been distributed in the Netherlands, along with huge amounts of non-fiction
material, shot when the Dutch still had overseas colonies and dominions, as
well as much early fiction and non-fiction material from the Desmet collection.[12]
The core task of most other national archives, i.e., the preservation of domestic
film production in the form of safeguarding the national cinematic patrimony,
played a comparatively minor role, seeing how the Netherlands could not boast
of a particularly vibrant or internationally recognized filmmaking tradition,
even compared with other smaller European countries, such as Denmark or
Sweden, Poland or the Czech Republic.

However, it was precisely through the rediscovery of early cinema and the
professional interest in the non-canonized, broad spectrum of international
filmmaking from the first decades of cinema, sparked off by the New Film History and the Italian Silent Cinema festivals, that the holdings of the Nederlands
Filmmuseum suddenly acquired worldwide fame and status. It thereby at-

tracted fresh government funds, but also brought to Amsterdam scores of international scholars working on early French, German, Danish, or Russian cinema, on the early Western or slapstick comedy, on Oskar Messter or Asta Nielsen, on Italian diva films, as well as on early non-fiction film, on color in early cinema, on colonial film, or the history of early cinema programming. (Heide Schluepmann, Martin Loiperdinger, Richard Abel, Yuri Tsivian, Caspar Tybjerg, Tom Gunning, Angela della Vacche, Charles Musser, Antonia Lant – to name only a few whom I know personally).

Thus, in order to prevent the cooperation between the University of Amsterdam and the Netherlands Filmmuseum from becoming a one-way street, and ensure that it was based instead on a recognition of mutual interests, I tried to address in my academic courses what I perceived to be one of the needs of the archives in general, and the Amsterdam Filmmuseum in particular. The principle I tried to reflect as much as possible was that of valorization, of how the core activity of the university – research, teaching, and the generation of discourses – could add specific kinds of value to an archive or a collection. What I mean by this concept of valorization is that the University should not simply endorse as educational and validate academically some of the specialized work done in an archive, such as cataloguing or conducting historical research on programming, exhibition, and audience reception via their paper and non-filmic documents.

Given that, besides transmitting historical scholarship and philological methods, the University also has a key role to play in formulating new research paradigms and circulating new discourses relating to specific disciplines as well as to public debates, it must also seek – with courses such as those I was involved in creating – new ways to help archives highlight the cultural significance or contemporary uses of their holdings in innovative and productive contexts. In other words, rather than simply combining graduate courses on film aesthetics or media history ("theory") with courses on film registration and identification, conservation and restoration, accessibility and public presentation ("practice"), the two sides of the course had to be brought into some sort of dialogue. For instance, by tapping into the broad general discussion around cultural memory and the specific controversies regarding the media representations of particular moments of the national past, the course can generate specific projects and allow its students to work with specific institutions, such as the National Centre for War Studies (NIOD), or the Amsterdam Historical Museum. General debates about the national heritage are usually sparked by historical compilation programs on television (in Germany Guido Knopp's programs for ZDF, in the Netherlands a program called *Andere tijden*), but they can also be part of the "fall-out" of controversial feature films on historical figures and events (SCHINDLER'S LIST, 1993; DER UNTERGANG, 2004*)*. Specific scholarly tasks can arise from the work of the International Court of Justice at The Hague, or the use of video and photography at sites of public commemoration, national days of remembrance, anniversary exhibitions, or centenaries.

But cultural memory restricted to World War II, Hitler, and the Holocaust is itself a somewhat slender basis on which to build a reorientation or revalorization of a moving-image heritage that now spans a hundred years. It brings me back to the special historiographical project with which I began: the course on Media Archaeology. As indicated, its main aim is to also make the insights and methods derived over the past 20 years from the study of the so-called "origins of the cinema" (Early Cinema, *le cinema des premiers temps, cinema muto*) fruitful for the history of television and the digital media, and to indicate how closely linked but also how complexly differentiated the technical developments, cultural histories, and mutual interferences of these media are, once one studies them from an "archaeological," as opposed to a single-strand, linear, chronological perspective. Topics include the archaeology of projection, the archaeology of the camera, the archaeology of the screen, the archaeology of recorded sound. Cultural practices range from the so-called prehistory of the cinema (phantasmagorias, dioramas, stereoscopy, optical toys), to the contemporary use of the moving image in galleries, museums and as installation art. They include the medical uses of the cinematographic apparatus, the importance of military vision machines, as well as the various *dispositifs* of surveillance, from Jeremy Bentham's panopticon to closed-circuit television in shopping malls at traffic intersections. Attention is also given to the history of popular (literary and filmic) fantasies around these various deployments ("the history of futures past": different kinds of futurisms, man-machine scenarios, the history of failed and successful inventions, and urbanist imaginaries), and the formation of a media memory in the realms of public history (the already mentioned television series on the First or Second World War) as well as private histories (home movies, autobiography, video diaries, and weblogs).

At the graduate level, this approach has a distinct advantage for all students over more conventional film histories, but seems especially suitable for those who in their careers may want to compile or curate programs that are alternatives to the traditional mainstream programming according to stars, national cinemas, genres, or recognized masterpieces of the auteur or avant-garde cinema. Media Archaeology also helps them to think about the audiovisual media "laterally," that is, thematically and by *topoi*, i.e., not only as a chronological succession of movements and new waves, but as parallel or parallax histories, or co-extensive practices that form recurring kinds of cultural genealogies, linked by network structures as well as the clustering of clichés, around certain nodes. Thus, the work of Harun Farocki on certain filmic tropes, such as "workers leaving the factory," "the expression of hands," and "prison surveillance," as well as Wolfgang Ernst's work on the development of pictorial search algorithms for accessing and retrieving digitally stored still- and moving-image archives would also be of central relevance to such an approach to film history from a media-archaeological perspective.[13] It goes without saying that material relating to industrial films would have a central place in a project involving a transversal history of the moving image and its cultural contents, recontextualizing it and thereby also revalorizing its significance in the history of film.

Most archives are confronted with often stark alternatives, either taking over existing classifications of what is considered culturally important and aesthetically canonized, or – realizing the mutability of these criteria of value – trying to preserve everything, however haphazardly and unsystematically it had found its way into the archive in the first place. If, in order to protect themselves from the anger and contempt of future generations, they choose the latter path, labeling everything culturally valuable and part of the national patrimony, they of course risk drowning in the sheer amount of material, or quickly running out of the resources required to maintain this material at even the minimal level of physical survival.

The dilemma reminds us of the fact that the film archive was itself born of contradictory impulses. The major film archives – the Cinémathèque in Paris, the British Film Institute, the Museum of Modern Art in New York, and the Reichsfilmarchiv Berlin – owe their existence to the fact that, with the coming of sound, a whole world of cinema was going to disappear, but also the gradual realization of what an extraordinary treasure of factual, historical, social, and material information lay buried in the moving image.

Henri Langlois of the Cinémathèque Française and his mania for collecting everything is perhaps the best example of this double impulse of the archive: to protect the cinema as an art form, and to discover it as the richest source of information about material culture: As is well-known, not André Bazin or Francois Truffaut, but Langlois, with his retrospectives, is the real father of auteur theory, which was so crucial in revalorizing the American cinema in the 1950s and 60s. However, as is becoming increasingly evident, Langlois was also the father of all the specialized archives that now collect films on different subjects, such as the University of Nebraska archives, for instance, on American pornographic films, which was apparently established in order to study the history of middle-class domestic furniture and interior design, or the somewhat better-known archive of ephemeral films, put together by Rick Prelinger.[14]

How can an archive intervene in the cycle that affects all commodities – going from commercial uselessness, via their non-status as junk, to a new life as cult objects, as collectible and once more valuable antiques (or classics) – and how can such processes of cultural capital be adapted to the life and value cycles of the commodity film? If the idea of a Media Archaeology at present does not yet constitute by and of itself sufficient ground for determining an archive's criteria for selection and de-selection, there is no reason why such exercises in classification and categorization, necessary in the age of ubiquity and the myth of total availability, should not be able to set out some of the terms of the debate, some of the parameters of curatorial practice, and the historical conditions of discursive (re-)valorization, on the strength of which archivists can make informed decisions about the presentation of their holdings.

It is here that I see a particular opportunity for a university-based course, as a site that analyzes, debates, and also launches new discourses, by adapting existing ones from within the field, or by initiating a dialogue with adjacent disciplines. For instance, what is emerging among several of my colleagues is an intensified reflection – surely not unrelated to such practices as zapping, sampling, or web-surfing – about a new poetics of the fragment and the different "evidentiary fictions of the real," about the status of the found object, and about the aesthetics of repetition and seriality, of the migration of motifs and the transfer of tropes. Of course, this is not in itself very new: these topics have preoccupied various disciplines in the humanities for at least the last two decades, and within film history they have led to seminars on the "essay film," reflecting a new interest in documentary genres, in family films and home movies, but also leading to an interest among students in the pragmatics and poetics of the film material we are concerned with here: the utility film (*Gebrauchsfilm*) in all its genres, sub-genres, and variants.

What is relatively new is an alliance of sorts that seems to have emerged between the archive and the filmic avant-garde, as well as between the cinema library and installation artists. Besides Harun Farocki, who makes frequent trips to film museums and more specialized archives, there are filmmakers such as Peter Delpeut (who for a decade worked as deputy director of the Nederlands Filmmuseum) who have used found footage (LYRICAL NITRATE, 1991; DIVA DOLOROSA, 1999), and Peter Forgacs from Hungary (who specialized in working with home movies, e.g., THE MAELSTROM, 1997; THE DANUBE EXODUS, 1998) or Gustav Deutsch from Austria (FILM IST, 2002). They and many others have also begun to show to a wider public what this kind of collaboration between the archive and the practicing filmmaker can yield. Other filmmakers one could name are Mark Rappaport, Martin Arnold, and Matthias Mueller, who have recycled, re-edited, and re-worked found footage from feature films, rather than non-fiction films. Taken together, such creative networks and curatorial practices suggest that the history of the avant-garde film can in the future no longer be written without reference to the history of the *Gebrauchsfilm*, which appropriately mirrors and repeats their mutual involvement in the 1920s and 30s already alluded to.

However, found-footage material seems to have gradually entered the documentary mainstream as well. If one takes the recent International Documentary

Festival in Amsterdam as a test case, one will be surprised by how "natura-lized" this use of stock footage had become. Checking at random, I immediately found three very different films, Werner Herzog's THE WHITE DIAMOND (2004); a student film from the Potsdam Film Academy, TECHNIK DES GLÜCKS (2000-2003); and a new Danish film by Max Kestner, MAX BY CHANCE (2004), all work-ing industrial films, old newsreels, and scientific films into the texture of their respective arguments and reflection. This new status of archival footage as a universally convertible currency of sound and image material raises questions of access and availability, of copyright and intellectual property that have thus far not even been near to being resolved. I noted, for instance, that two of the three films just named had a discrete acknowledgement to the (by now partly on-line) image databank of the already mentioned Rick Prelinger.

This last point, perhaps, also highlights another paradox: that of the asymme-try inherent to the value generation and valorization I have been speaking about. The images and artefacts of the audiovisual heritage are exceptionally fragile, perishable, and even materially unstable. They need substantial re-sources for their conservation and restoration, for the most part provided by the shrinking budgets of state and local authorities, or private sponsors and foundations. At the same time, the demand for pristine, well-kept and perfectly preserved moving images of "the past" continues to increase, led by the insati-able appetite of television, but also fed by the advertising industries and other parts of the commercial sector.

Thus, another apparently still growing market for the use and display of non-fiction material are the bonus packages of DVDs. Problematic as a tool of pre-servation and maybe even research, the DVD has become a popular and profit-able resource, whose "bundling" of added material poses challenges to the film historian about the nature of our film culture, but it also opens up new opportu-nities for the archivist and programmer. Altogether, moving images increas-ingly represent commercially valuable assets. How should this gap between the social costs of keeping these images alive and the commercial benefits that can be drawn from them be bridged? Should archives be asked to finance them-selves and their work by realizing these assets commercially, possibly at the ex-pense of the archives' cultural function and institutional autonomy? If they price their work competitively, do they not price themselves out of other "mar-kets," such as that of education, as well as risk redefining what is heritage and patrimony in direct proportion to their institutional and commercial clients' in-terests? Perhaps it is here that the new alliance that is being struck between the archives and the universities will, in the long run, bear fruit as important as that of training a new generation of professionals: maintaining an independence of inquiry and openness of debate that makes "preservation and presentation" not just the service provider of the experience economy, but also its conscience and

site of critical reflection? Let me conclude with three methodological points and
a programmatic one:

- In view of current archival practices and in order to contribute to the future
  valorization of archival holdings, an international research project such as
  the one currently envisaged by a number of participating institutions needs
  to reexamine existing classifications of non-fiction materials in order to agree
  on a number of new research parameters. This will involve extending, revis-
  ing, and opening up traditional categories around non-fiction, documentary,
  industrial film, advertising film, training film, but also *Gebrauchsfilm* in its
  broadest sense, including family film, amateur film, and similar practices.
  One of the premises for such a reexamination must be to look at the industrial film from a pragmatic premise, which is to say: within the context of my
  three A's: commissioning client, concrete occasion, and target use or target
  audience.
- To facilitate this shift, a notion of *film as event* is preferable to the traditional
  idea of *film as text*. The event has its own temporal and spatial coherence, but
  as a process and usually tied to a site; an event is linked to a time structure
  not as a continuum like narrative, but as pulsed, intermittent, and shaped by
  intervals. Events as spaces tend to be centrifugal, multi-layered, and heterogeneous in their consistency and materiality; an event implies the notion of
  programming and planning, but also of accident and coincidence. All these
  associations are useful for rethinking non-fiction films in terms of an event
  scenario, in which the actual film is only one piece of the evidence and resi-
  due to be examined and analyzed. To think of film as an event is furthermore
  to prefer a network model, in order to determine the relation of one film to
  another, and to understand its place within wider histories. Event and network also help to overcome traditional binaries, such as the left-right, pro-
  gressive-reactionary division that has marked the history of documentary
  film, notably for the interwar period, 1920-1940, and the Cold War period,
  1950-1990.
- For the last decade or so, the situation presents itself as a kind of inverse
  mirror to the relation between the avant-garde, industry, and technology,
  which I sketched for the 1920s and 1930s, where the avant-garde artist found
  in the industrial, corporate or government client the commission that permitted him to experiment in form and technique, at a time when these spaces
  no longer existed either in the art world or in the culture of the politicized-
  polarized public spheres. Today, given an art world that has itself become a
  corporate player, while liberal democracies use culture as a political tool, it
  seems that design studios and architectural offices have become the spaces
  where the media avant-garde finds commercial or institutional commissions,
  pilot projects, and feasibility studies that allow it to push the formal envel-

ope, use cutting-edge technology, and promote social and political scenarios. It is this new context for invention, innovation, and acceptance that I also want to bear in mind as my conceptual horizon, when formulating my final, programmatic point, which is to suggest that:

–   We need to forge a bond between another set of A's: the study of the industrial film will find appropriate genealogies and histories, but also its platform for reaching new audiences, I believe, when it has succeeded in making the most of the new alliances between the archive and the academy, on one side, and between the archive and the avant-garde on the other. All three participants can benefit from such a partnership, to create and to sustain a public sphere for the industrial film as one of the very special resources for our knowledge about the forces that have shaped the 20th century.

Notes

1.   Thomas Elsaesser (ed.), *Harun Farocki: Working on the Sight-Lines* (Amsterdam: Amsterdam University Press, 2004), p. 12.

2.   A pioneering work was Gene Youngblood's *Expanded Cinema* (London: Studio Vista, 1970). Since then there have been a number of exhibition catalogues, notably *X-Screen* (Vienna), *Control Screen* (ZKM Karlsruhe), and *Future Cinema* (ZKM Karlsruhe), that retrace the interface between avant-garde art practice and contemporary imaging technologies.

3.   See note 1.

4.   www.farocki-film.de.

5.   Jose van Dijck, *The Transparent Body: A Cultural Analysis of Medical Imaging* (Seattle: University of Washington Press, 2005).

6.   See Lev Manovich, "The Poetics of Augmented Space," at www.manovich.net.

7.   Thomas Elsaesser, "Die Stadt von Morgen: Filme zum Bauen und Wohnen," in K. Kreimeier, A. Ehmann, J. Goergen (eds.), *Geschichte des dokumentarischen Films in Deutschland* (Stuttgart: Reclam, 2005), pp. 381-409.

8.   See Kisten Baumann, Rolf Sachsse (eds.), *Moderne Gruesse/Modern Greetings* (Stuttgart: Arnoldsche Verlagsanstalt, 2004).

9.   Kimberly O'Quinn, "The Reason and Magic of Steel: Industrial and Urban Discourses in Die Poldihütte," T. Elsaesser (ed.), *A Second Life: German Cinema's First Decades* (Amsterdam: Amsterdam University Press, 1996), pp. 192-201.

10.   Thomas Elsaesser, "Die Kamera in der Küche: Werben für das Neue Wohnen," in G. Koch (ed.), *Umwidmungen* (Berlin: Vorwerk 8, 2005), pp. 36-56.

11.   The American scholar Dan Streible regularly organizes festivals devoted to Orphan Films, see http://www.sc.edu/filmsymposium/index.html.

12.   On the Desmet collection and its unique status as a historical resource, see Ivo Blom, *Jean Desmet and the Early Film Trade* (Amsterdam: Amsterdam University Press, 2003).

13. Wolfgang Ernst and Harun Farocki, "Towards an Archive for Visual Concepts," in T. Elsaesser (ed.), *Harun Farocki: Working on the Sight-Lines* (Amsterdam: Amsterdam University Press, 2004), pp. 261-286.

14. Rick Prelinger's collection is now mostly on-line and can be accessed via http://www.panix.com/~footage.

Record, Rhetoric, Rationalization

Industrial Organization and Film

Vinzenz Hediger and Patrick Vonderau

Corporate archives store the traces of corporate decision-making processes and their consequences. They contain minutes, memos, balance sheets, and other written and printed materials that document what has gone well and what has gone wrong during a company's history. Among other things, they allow the prospective historian to write a history in the event that a company should come to the conclusion that it needs one, which usually happens for one of two reasons: out of a sense of pride in a tradition of excellence and success, or because a company bows to external pressure to shed light on the darker sides of its past, which was, and still is, the case with many German firms in the 21st century. But corporate archives are also image archives. In any given major corporate archive in Germany, for instance – say in the corporate archives of Krupp in Essen, Thyssen Steel in Duisburg, or Bayer Chemicals in Leverkusen – one will find an average of several hundred films and a collection of photographs that number literally in the hundreds of thousands. The photographs show factory buildings, machines, products, or employees; they document factory visits, company reunions, shareholder meetings, fairs, or, as in the case of the Krupp archive, cannon-shooting exercises for representatives of foreign and domestic governments, who are among the potential buyers of the devices on display.[1] The films cover similar ground: factory visits, company trips, machines and products in action, buildings. They include process films that tell a product's story from the delivery of raw materials to the shipping of the finished product; education films that train workers in new production processes; crash-test and shooting-exercise films that record and document product characteristics; etc.

Industrial production as image production

Considering the immense amounts of technically generated images in these archives, one cannot but conclude that industrial production always also involves the production of photographs and films. As indeed it does. Many large companies operated their own photography departments in the classic factory period, with Krupp being one of the first companies on the continent to do so. At the behest of the company's head, Alfred Krupp, it opened its own photography department as part of the Graphische Abteilung, the printing office centrally located on the factory lot, in 1860. As found in the archive today, however, the images these departments produce are largely obsolete. They represent a significant investment, yet the companies that ordered and paid for them store them without exhibiting or otherwise exploiting them. These images are not integrated into digital databases or transferred to art museums either, a reliable indicator of their status as surplus materials in a time in which digital image databases constitute a significant source of revenue for media companies.

Perhaps more than other photographic archives, corporate archive collections of photographs seem to confirm Hubert Damisch's view that photographs – because they are technically produced and reproduced – are typically overabundant rather than scarce and therefore are condemned to a fate of devaluation.[2] Company histories are indeed one of the few places where such photographs gain visibility. All of which suggests, among other things, that the value of industrial photographs, other than the value of recognized works of art, is limited not only in terms of money but also, and more fundamentally, in terms of time. In fact, rather than outlast the time of their production, industrial images are part and parcel of the production process, which means that they are supposed to organize time and contribute to the attainment of specific goals within a given time period. Their use is their essence (to the extent that use can even be considered to be a form of essence), i.e., a set of externally defined purposes for which they are produced, but which also render them useless and superfluous once these purposes are attained.[3]

Serially produced images and serial analysis

Assuming that images without viewers are as much the media historian's concern as those that do attain visibility and secure their place in what you might call a culture's pictorial memory, the millions of photographs and hundreds of thousands of films in corporate archives the world over raise a challenge that may be answered with an inquiry into the principle of their production. In dealing with utility films, of which industrial films form a subcategory,[4] film historian Thomas Elsaesser proposes the approach of the so-called three A's. In order to account for any given utility film found in an archive Elsaesser argues that the film historian and/or media archaeologist should reconstruct the occasion, or *Anlass*, for which the film was produced; the *Adressat* or audience to which it was destined; and the *Auftraggeber* or commissioning body that financed and ordered the film's production.[5] This approach is particularly apt for a microanalysis of individual films, especially in cases where sufficient archive materials survive to provide the basis for a detailed account of individual production and distribution histories. In many corporate archives, however, few if any paper materials pertaining to films and photographs survive. Where documenting commissions and addressees is impossible, methods of film and image analysis may provide clues as to the purpose and occasion of a given film or photograph. Formal devices in industrial films are highly standardized and relate to the contexts of use, making it relatively easy to identify whether a film was made for a trade fair or a shareholder meeting. Not least because these films are so standardized, however, it is sometimes difficult to determine for which particular fair or meeting the film was made. If the specific occasion is of interest, one can of course always rely on the image itself and use a historian's approach to image materials, studying dress styles, technical gear, etc. From a media historian's point of view, however, it is not the film's content but the fact of the film's existence that is of interest. In this perspective, it is again the high degree of standardization and the virtual seriality of industrial films that become important. The industrial film is a format that, by its very nature, demands serial analysis as proposed by Michèle Lagny,[6] i.e., comparative analysis of a large corpus of film materials.

Among other things, such an analysis can yield insight into possible stylistic and rhetorical patterns and parameters that are used recursively, i.e., that reappear regularly with only minor variations. Only through comparative analysis of large amounts of image material can we determine whether, for instance, the camera pan that provides a full panoramic view of a factory lot or the inside of a factory hall is indeed a convention of the industrial film and to what extent the same goes for the structure and argument of the before-and-after narrative that industrial films use so often to illustrate the advantages of a new product or the innovation of a new method of production. Serial analysis will also provide insights into strategies and styles of corporate communications and their changes over relatively long periods of time.[7] But while serial analysis as a method remains limited to the level of film style, its results may constitute a stepping stone for a more comprehensive understanding of the visual practices of industry, i.e., they can help us understand why industrial concerns produce, and later store, so many photographs and films in the first place. If the recursive patterns of style that a serial analysis focuses on turn out to be conventionalized in the sense that they occur regularly and reliably in different industries, places, and time periods, they can then be analyzed with regard to what you might call their organizational functionality.

Organization as communication

In order to understand that functionality or to understand why industrial organizations produce images and what they use them for, the serial analysis of films and photographs needs to be coupled with a theoretical understanding of the company or corporation as an organizational entity. One such understanding may be drawn from Luhmannian systems theory, which has a particular affinity to questions of communication. According to Niklas Luhmann and his disciple Dirk Baecker, industrial organization does not only imply communication, but actually results from communication. Organizations establish and maintain themselves by constantly marking out the difference between inside and outside, i.e., through a constant process of communication about who belongs to a given organization and to what ends, and who does not.[8] According to organizational sociologists, a company is a unit of action that accomplishes a transformation of reality on two levels. On a first level, that of basic transformation, the company transforms raw materials and other input into marketable goods through production processes. On a second level, that of reflexive transformation, the company transforms reality, and more specifically its own reality, through recursive – i.e., regular and incessant – processes of reflecting and deciding upon what to produce how for whom.[9]

Media communication first comes into play on the basic level. Handling input and organizing production processes presupposes constant communication about the availability and allocation of resources. Decisions are made on the basis of available information and have to be communicated in order to make a difference. More fundamentally, decisions only become possible once a survey – one that is as complete as possible – of the available resources and the other parameters of the production process exists. Furthermore, decisions only become effective once they are converted into information, i.e., something that will make a difference in the later development of the organization, by setting a specific process of production into motion, for instance. But if modern industrial organizations are based on communication, this communication is, in turn, based on the availability of specific media technologies. As JoAnne Yates[10] has shown, the modern corporation depends on the emergence of new media such as the telegraph, the telephone, the typewriter, and the tabulation machine, as well as through the coordination of these media in a *Medienverbund*, i.e., the coordination of several media in a media setup.

Film and the *Medienverbund* of industry

Film has figured in the *Medienverbund* of organizational practice since the early 1910s. In 1911, Frank Bunker Gilbreth published his book *Motion Study*.[11] Gilbreth, who refined the Taylorist concept of scientific management by using film as a tool for the study and improvement of the worker's physical movements on the factory floor, had a significant impact on industrial production both in the US and Europe, and particularly in Germany. At around the same time, major corporations started their own in-house film production units. Thus, Krupp opened its own film department for the production of research, training, and advertising films in 1913 (1908 according to some accounts),[12] while Ford in Detroit followed suit in 1914. In conjunction, the various technical media provided the means for a regime of "control through communication," to cite JoAnne Yates's phrase, which led to the emergence of systematic management in industrial organizations the world over after 1850. Generally speaking, industrial organizations constantly face the double task of maintaining their own stability and improving their structure and operations in the face of the competition. In a historical perspective, the conjunction of media and industrial organizations develops along the fault lines of any organization's twin goals of maintaining its stability and improving its structure.

If a new medium such as film enters the scene it will be adopted into the fold of organizational media if and when its use promises to make specific contributions toward the attainment of those two goals. Since competing organizations continually observe not only themselves (through media, one might add) but also each other, they will tend to emulate competitors and integrate technologies and media that have proven to be successful elsewhere into their own operations – as long as that technology is readily available and economically viable. It is only through this dynamic of mutual observation, copying, and adaptation that one can understand the quick and thorough spread of film as a medium of industry after 1910. At the same time it is important to note that the implementation of new media technologies relies on factors that go beyond technological innovation. Industrial organizations took more than a decade after the invention of film to systematically integrate the new medium into their operations, while the "informatization of work," i.e., the adoption of the computer for industrial production and corporate logistics, only really began in the mid 1960s and only became a fact of life in the 1970s, i.e., almost 30 years after the "invention" of the computer as it is commonly understood. Innovation alone, then, does not guarantee the spread and implementation of a technology.

Accordingly, in order to study and explain the complex interactions and interpenetrations of media and industrial organizations one has to take into account factors that lie outside the technological structure of the media as such.[13] None-theless, it is safe to assume, as did Karl Knies in his pioneering 1857 work on the "Telegraph als Verkehrsmittel"[14] (the telegraph as a means of communication and economic exchange), that media, and *Medienverbunde*, constitute what, in Friedrich Kittler's sense, you might call a technological a priori, a prerequisite for modern industrial production. If communication is key to the establishment and governance of industrial organizations, the availability of the media technology necessary for that communication is crucial to their success.[15] In that sense, then, organizational practice is always already media practice.

Record, rhetoric, rationalization

Within this field of organizational practice as media practice, three major areas may be determined in which media – and film among them – contribute to the establishment and governance of industrial organizations. For the sake of convenience, these areas could be labeled *record, rhetoric,* and *rationalization.* "Record" means that media provide industrial organizations with an institutional memory, i.e., an archive of their operations on all levels of activity. "Rhetoric" means that media are used to induce workers and employees to share the company's stated goals and collaborate toward attaining those goals. And finally, "rationalization" means that media are used not only to sustain, but also improve organizational performance on all levels, from administration to product development to production and marketing.

Record. The fact that all companies maintain some kind of corporate archive seems to indicate that institutional memory is among the prerequisites for the successful operation of any industrial organization. Historically speaking, writing and tabulating are the primary media of this institutional memory. Double bookkeeping, which was based on the use of ink, paper, and handwriting, emerged as a key innovation of early capitalism because it was a form of institutional memory that delivered a survey of day-to-day operations and therefore provided a foundation for solid short- and long-term business decisions.[16] Photography and film obviously figure among the media of industry's institutional memory as well. In their major study on private uses of photography from the 1960s, Pierre Bourdieu and his collaborators defined photography as a *"technique de fête,"* as a technology of celebration – a term that aptly defines one of the key uses of industrial photography and film as well.[17] Photographs and films and media record company events and celebrations in the "life" of a company, such as factory openings, factory visits by important guests, company outings, presentations of new product lines, company events at trade fairs, and the like. As in the case of private photography, the celebration takes place in front of and for the camera, and the camera's presence elevates the event to its significant status. Beyond these festive uses, photography and film also document development and production processes. Thus, for instance, research films provide a record of product development and testing processes, information that later generations of engineers may turn to in order better to understand previous development processes. Moreover, photography and film are used to record and register workers and employees. A significant, albeit singular example of such uses may be found in the Krupp company archive. In celebration of the company's 60th anniversary the photography department set out to photograph every single one of the several thousand men then employed by the company. The idea was to create a family album of sorts, to be presented to the company head, Alfred Krupp, for the official celebration of the company's anniversary.[18] The project was never finished, but the company archive contains several volumes of a work that, by taking the form of a family album, speaks quite unmistakably of the parentage of private and industrial uses of photography. On the other hand, the Krupp corporate family album also bears a relation to another contemporary archive of photographically stored data, Bertillon's image archive of criminals, which was meant to provide the police with physiognomic profiles of potential delinquents.[19] By photographing all its employees, Krupp created an instrument of control that could potentially be used to identify unruly individuals in a time when much of the company's policies were aimed at keeping the workforce from joining unions or other social movements.

As the example of the company outing film shows, institutional memory has its official and unofficial, or private, layers. Along with company-produced photographs and films, corporate archives quite often contain private films in Super-8 and other formats. Many of these films are intimate records of the company owner's family life, but others were made by employees and later given to the archives. Among other things, these films are an important source for studies in social history. Private films from the ThyssenKrupp corporate archives in Duisburg show scenes from a company outing to Berlin in the late 1930s, where company employees dress up as women for a late-night dance event.[20] While such films have little direct impact on or importance for the company's performance, it is quite clear that, by fostering cohesion among employees through a celebration of shared experience, these films contribute to the organization's stability and thus affect performance, however indirectly. Much like conventional family films, which "create" the family in and through the acts of filming and viewing the film record in the family group, such film records of company outings create and reaffirm the company as a community.[21]

Rhetoric. According to Kenneth Burke, rhetoric is "the use of language as a symbolic means of inducing cooperation."[22] Assuming that film and photography may be used for the purposes of argument – which means accepting one of the basic assumptions of documentary film theory since Grierson – one can easily extend Burke's notion of rhetoric to (audio)visual media. Companies use film systematically to project a certain image and create what is usually known as a corporate identity, i.e., a company's internal and external symbolic and social cohesion. Films that record and document company events and celebrations are meant to foster the company's cohesion and induce in their audience a spirit of cooperation, particularly if and when they are shown at other company events that serve that same purpose.

Again, the Krupp archive contains a striking example for this use of film. From 1953 through 1967 – the year Alfried Krupp von Bohlen und Halbach, the last Krupp to run the 150-year-old family business that was converted into a foundation upon his death, died – Krupp produced so-called *Jahresfilme*, i.e., films that reviewed the past year. These films, composed of short segments documenting major events in a year of the company's "life," were shot by outside teams or the remaining film crew in the company's information department. The *Jahresfilme* were produced specifically for company events such as the factory Christmas celebrations. In their form, they very much resemble year-in-review compilations of family films that can be found in many collections of private and home movies. Sampling and joining short home movies is indeed a standard way of archiving and performing family films.[23] Just as in the case of the family album mentioned above, the formal analogy of private films and the Krupp *Jahresfilm* is not coincidental. Krupp was family owned when founded in 1812 and never went public. It was a family business in the most emphatic sense imaginable, with the company head and his wife acting as "patrons," or surrogate fathers and mothers to their workers, even after Krupp had emerged in the second half of the 19th century as the largest producer of steel in the world and one of the largest corporations, not only in Germany but in the world. For a company that had always defined itself in this way, it seems perfectly fitting to use film in a way that is reminiscent of the repertory of media techniques that bourgeois families use to reaffirm their cohesion.

But film also serves the purpose of inducing cooperation from outside the organization. In particular, film has been used to recruit workers and employees since the early 1910s in Europe as well as in the United States. In 1914, an American trade paper reported that a tobacco company building a new factory in the Southern United States faced recruiting problems. Rural workers in the region where the factory was built were not interested in signing up for factory work, which they apparently deemed noisy, dirty, and detrimental to their overall well-being. According to the trade-paper report, the company solved the problem by shooting a film at one of its existing factories in the northern United States. The company took this film, which shed a favorable light on the factory's working conditions, to the new factory's location and showed it to the local population, apparently with great success:

> [The film] was an entertainment and the workers thereabouts flocked to be entertained. But they went away persuaded. And when the new factory opened, the films had brought about a complete reversal of local opinion on the factory question. Instead of the dreaded dearth of workers, by far more workers applied for jobs than were required and the new institution started off with flying colors, a success from the very start.[24]

"They flocked to be entertained. But they went away persuaded." Thus the entertainment value of film proves to be an asset for the company's bank, yielding a return in terms of the workers' willingness to cooperate. A similar analysis pertains to a film produced by Thyssen Steel and directed by veteran union film director Robert Menegoz in 1965 with camerawork by Sacha Vierny, NUR DER NEBEL IST GRAU (*The Fog Alone Is Grey*). The film, produced for the opening of a new, ultra-modern steel factory on the Rhine, shows an elegantly utilitarian, modernist factory building that does not look anything like the traditional steel works so dramatically aestheticized in the photographs of Rodchenko or Charles Sheeler taken in the 1920s. As the film shows, the factory's interior offers safe workplaces for everyone. Rather than manually handling the steel slabs freshly cast of liquid metal, the workers operate remote-controlled machines and robots by means of joysticks in a cockpit-like setting. Striking incarnations of the *kybernetes*, the man at the helm of a complex system that gave the modern science of cybernetics its name, the men working in the factory are technicians rather than traditional steel workers. While injury rates at traditional steel mills were high and health problems the rule rather than the exception, the workers shown in the Menegoz film enjoy a relatively safe and sane working environment, with the possible exception of the men working the blast furnace (where high and low temperatures alternate and pose a health hazard no matter how technologically advanced the furnace is). But then, in an act of blatant disregard for the established conventions of the steel-mill process film, Menegoz's film does not contain any images of the blast furnace in operation. This is all the more remarkable because images of liquid metal spouting spectacular rays of sparks as it is being poured into molds constitute one of the main visual attractions available to the industrial filmmaker when shooting inside a steel mill.[25] About the workers we learn that they previously worked in other professions. One is a former baker (which meant he had to get up in the middle of the night) while another worked in construction (which meant he was exposed to bad weather most of the time). Now they are enjoying the advantages of civilized regular work hours inside a clean, safe factory. In addition, the film points out that in the Germany of the "economic miracle" of the 1950s and 1960s everyone had a job and workers were in such high demand that they could freely chose their area of employment. The film was actually shot in color and widescreen format with a 1:1.85 ratio, with a modernist score and visually stunning traveling shots that stressed surface effects and graphic structures as against depth of field. Clearly intended for the large screen, it was shown in German cinemas in the *Kulturfilm* program, as an educational short that, by law, preceded every commercial film running in Germany until the late 1960s. If screened before a Hollywood spectacle of the time, it probably would have made a discerning audience find the latter quaint and old-fashioned, wanting in both style and execution. Nur der Nebel ist Grau, which was produced partly in response to an article in *Der Spiegel* decrying the working and living conditions in West Germany's key industrial area, the Ruhr Valley, the seat of both Krupp and Thyssen, not only emblematizes the company's innovative business strategy through its advanced – and visibly expensive – (audio)visual style, it also serves up a rather tempting invitation to prospective employees who might want to join the company.

Production histories are also part of "rhetoric" in the Burkean sense of inducing cooperation proposed here. One of the standard forms of the industrial film is the process film, which tells the story of the production of a specific ware, from the acquisition of the raw materials through testing, shipping, and sometimes even marketing. Not counting the illustrations in Georg Agricola's scientific works on mining and mineralogy from the 17th century, the predecessors of the process film date back to the 18th century. Diderot and d'Alembert's *Encyclopédie* contained numerous articles on specific trades and industries like printing and mining. Profusely illustrated, these articles were not intended for practical purposes, i.e., they were educational in approach but for an audience that had no intention of working in the trades presented there.[26] One could not learn how to make a glove by reading the *Encyclopédie*, but as someone who owned and used gloves one could learn how they were made. While the illustrations in the *Encyclopédie* were part of an enlightenment project of making the material world transparent to an educated audience, representations of production processes became part and parcel of trade and thus, by extension, of industrial organization in the 19th century. In the course of early 19th century industrialization, trade became increasingly internationalized, and trade relations became more abstract. Because personal face-to-face relationships between producers and buyers could no longer be relied on as a guarantee of quality, product quality became a problem in the process. Under these conditions, representations of production processes acquired a new level of importance. As William Reddy has shown in his study of sample books and prospects from the French cloth industry of the 18th and 19th centuries, visual representations of production processes provide vital information about the quality of the marketed goods from the mid-19th century onward.[27] The process films of the 20th century continued both traditions, the educational and the mercantile. Early non-fiction films about the production of Swiss cheese or French bottle corks extend the educational ambition of the *Encyclopédie* into the age of moving-image entertainment, while process films produced for trade fairs and other trade occasions continue in the footsteps of the 19th-century prospectus, supplying information about the product's qualities. The latter will usually contain a section on quality testing towards their end, a clear indication of their rhetorical function as these scenes are unmistakably meant to attest to the quality of the product whose production history the films tell.

   Another part of rhetoric in the sense proposed here are the shareholder films, i.e., films that are specifically produced for screenings at annual shareholder meetings. These films highlight the company's performance and its potential for continuous innovation, thus reassuring the shareholders that the prospects are good and the company will continue to make money for them. This is another way of inducing cooperation, this time from outside the company, but from people who, in a way, are the real insiders in the sense that they bankroll the company's operations.

Rationalization. Rationalization is a term for a key principle of industrial organization and designates all practices aimed at improving performance. Rationalization either leads to higher output with the same input, or to the same output with lower input or, better still, it leads to a simultaneous reduction in input and increase in output. Traditionally, rationalization was driven by technological innovation, i.e., by new machines that enhanced and extended the performance of the individual worker and/or made parts of the workforce superfluous to what was required. In that sense, at least for traditional industries that transform energy into performance, the machine industry is the industry of industries because its innovations drive industrial development as a whole. In today's "information age" and "information societies" the IT industry has now assumed that role. As JoAnne Yates and Knies have pointed out, communication and media technologies are key among the engines of rationalization: first the telegraph, then the telephone, the tabulating machine, the computer, but also the technical image media such as photography and film. Film may be used for the purposes of rationalization in all phases of the development and production process. Film serves research and documentation purposes[28] in the development of new products and services, which includes material testing and crash tests for automobiles, for instance (even though the traditional crash test film has increasingly been replaced by computer simulations of late). An early example for such uses of film can be seen in the shooting-exercise films for which Krupp developed, or had developed, a high-speed camera capable of shooting more than 300 frames per second as early as 1913. Other examples of rationalization through film include the already mentioned work-study films of Frank Gilbreth, which were aimed at increasing productivity by optimizing worker's body movements, as well as instructional films that introduce workers to new and improved modes of production or handling new machines. And finally, advertising films too may be seen as part of what we propose to call the "rationalization" aspect of the mutual interpenetration of technical image media and industrial organization, at least to the extent they are meant to improve sales and thus also enhance productivity.

In conclusion, it is important to note that the three R's – *record, rhetoric, rationalization* – are not genre terms in the sense that they do not describe inherent qualities specific to the industrial film as a genre. In fact, we would argue that the industrial film is a not a genre in the accepted sense of the term at all. Rather, it is a strategically weak and parasitic form. Certain conventions exist that make a film recognizable as an industrial film, but they are pliable to whatever organizational purpose the filmmaker has to meet. It is a strategically weak and parasitic form in the sense that it can assume the appearance of other, more stable genres and formats and pass as a scientific film, an educational film, or a documentary for specific strategic reasons. To the media historian, the common trait of all the shapes and forms that the industrial film can assume lies in their organizational purpose. Not only have the countless numbers of industrial films in corporate archives all been commissioned (*Auftraggeber*) for a specific occasion (*Anlass*) and a specific audience (*Adressat*), they also serve, or have served, one or more of the three purposes of record, rhetoric, and rationalization. Most of these films may not be works of art on their own, but clearly they had a job to do.

Notes

1.   Alfred Krupp invited political dignitaries and prospective buyers to shooting trials at the company's testing fields in Emden. On these occasions, a company photographer would be present to take a group portrait of the visitors, usually in front of the equipment. Large-scale prints of these photographs were later sent to the guests as a souvenir of their experience. In the 1860s and 1870s, before the introduction of the Kodak camera, these photographs were considered valuable gifts. Cf. Barbara Wolbring, *Krupp und die Öffentlichkeit im 19. Jahrhundert. Selbstdarstellung, öffentliche Wahrnehmung und gesellschaftliche Kommunikation* (Munich: C.H. Beck Verlag, 2000);

Klaus Tenfelde, *Bilder von Krupp. Fotografie und Geschichte im Industriezeitalter* (Munich: C.H. Beck, 2000).

2. Hubert Damisch, "Fünf Anmerkungen zu einer Phänomenologie des fotografischen Bildes," in Herta Wolf (ed.), *Paradigma Fotografie. Fotokritik am Ende des fotografischen Zeitalter* (Frankfurt am Main: Suhrkamp, 2002), pp. 135-139.

3. See Vinzenz Hediger, " 'Dann sind Bilder also *nichts!*' Vorüberlegungen zur Konstitution des Forschungsfeldes 'Gebrauchsfilm'", *Montage AV* 14, 2 (2005), pp. 11-22; and Patrick Vonderau's contribution in this volume.

4. On the notion of the utility film, see Hediger, op. cit.

5. Thomas Elsaesser, "Die Stadt von morgen: Filme zum Bauen und Wohnen," in Klaus Kreimeier, Antje Ehmann and Jeanpaul Goergen (eds.), *Geschichte des dokumentarischen Films in Deutschland. Band 2: Weimarer Republik 1918-1933* (Stuttgart: Reclam, 2005), pp. 381-409.

6. Michèle Lagny, "Film History: or History Expropriated," *Film History* 6, 1 (1994), pp. 26-44.

7. One of the striking patterns in industrial film production is the use of the musical term "symphony" in film titles, particularly regarding the steel industry, from the 1930s through the 1950s. This was probably adapted from the avant-garde films of directors like Walter Ruttmann, whose oeuvre includes several industrial films for Mannemann steel and others, the notion of a symphony obviously served the purpose of elevating and dignifying industrial production processes through their association with one of the most prestigious compositional forms of European art music.

8. Dirk Baecker, *Die Form des Unternehmens* (Frankfurt am Main: Suhrkamp, 1999).

9. Ludger Pries, *Betrieblicher Wandel in der Risikogesellschaft. Empirische Befunde und konzeptionelle Überlegungen* (Munich and Mering: Rainer Hampp Verlag, 1998).

10. JoAnne Yates, *Control Through Communication: The Rise of System in American Management* (Baltimore: Johns Hopkins University Press, 1989).

11. Cf. Ramón Reichert, "Der Arbeitsstudienfilm. Eine verborgene Geschichte des Stummfilms," *Medien und Zeit*, 4 (2002), pp. 29-43; Philipp Sarasin, "Die Rationalisierung des Körpers. Über 'Scientific Management' und 'biologische Rationalisierung,' " *Geschichtswissenschaft und Diskursanalyse* (Frankfurt am Main: Suhrkamp, 2002), pp. 61-99.

12. Manfred Rasch et al. (eds.), *Industriefilm – Medium und Quelle: Beispiele aus der Eisen- und Stahlindustrie*, (Essen: Klartext, 1997).

13. When analyzing the interaction and interpenetration of media and industrial organization, an approach that focuses on technology alone and systematically excludes social aspects – such as the one proposed by Friedrich Kittler and others who were inspired by Heidegger's philosophy of technology – will have its limits, not least since it cannot explain why new technologies can take so long to take root, and sometimes disappear. The sociology of technology instead proposes reading technological innovation as a "process of conflict between social actors and of translation between politics, the economy, and science." Technological change, much like economic development, does not follow any preordained patterns, and because they are heavily determined by social actors and their respective interests they should be analyzed accordingly. Cf. Werner Rammert, *Technik aus soziologischer Perspektive 2. Kultur, Innovation, Virtualität* (Opladen: Westdeutscher Verlag, 2000), p. 61; and Patrick Vonderau in this volume.

14. Karl Knies, *Der Telegraf als Verkehrsmittel. Mit Erörterungen über den Nachrichtenver-kehr überhaupt* (Tübingen: Laupp, 1857).

15. The same goes for social organizations, as Klaus Tenfelde convincingly shows in a study of the emergence of social movements in the Ruhr Valley in the 19th century. In his study, Tenfelde assesses the impact of communication media on the formation of social movements in a fashion reminiscent of the work of Harold Innis. Cf. Klaus Tenfelde, "Arbeiterschaft, Arbeitsmarkt und Kommunikationsstrukturen im Ruhr-gebiet in den 50er Jahren des 19. Jahrhunderts," *Archiv für Sozialgeschichte*, 16 (1976), pp. 1-59.

16. Bernhard Siegert, *Passage des Digitalen. Zeichenpraktiken der neuzeitlichen Wissenschaf-ten* (Berlin: Brinkmann und Bose, 2003), p. 32 ff.

17. Pierre Bourdieu, *Eine illegitime Kunst. Die sozialen Gebrauchsweisen der Fotografie* (Hamburg: Europäische Verlagsanstalt, 1982).

18. Tenfelde, *Bilder von Krupp,* op. cit.

19. Allan Sekula, "Der Körper und das Archiv," in Herta Wolf (ed.), *Diskurse der Foto-grafie. Fotokritik am Ende des fotografischen Zeitalters* (Frankfurt am Main: Suhrkamp, 2003), pp. 269-334.

20. Thanks to Professor Manfred Rasch for this information.

21. Alexandra Schneider, *Die Stars sind wir. Familienfilm als mediale Praxis* (Marburg: Schüren, 2004).

22. Kenneth Burke, *A Rhetoric of Motives* (Berkeley: University of California Press, 1969).

23. Schneider, op. cit., 219 ff.

24. "The Play Is the Thing. Motion Picture Uses," *Motography: Exploiting Motion Pictures* 12, 7 (August 15, 1914), pp. 245-248. A methodological caveat is in order here: To varying degrees, motion-picture trade papers carry stories manufactured by com-pany publicists from the film and other industries (*Variety,* first published in New York in 1905, and the *Hollywood Reporter*, published in Los Angeles since the early 1930s, being among the few publications that do not routinely bend their editorial standards to accommodate advertisers). While the article cited here may not have been directly written by a company agent but rather someone from the editorial staff of the paper – it contains examples from various industries and companies, without naming the companies in question – it is far from being dryly informa-tional. Instead, its tone is motivational. As such, this text is typical for a type of article that appeared regularly in trade papers in the 1910s: news about the med-ium's achievements in and contributions to culturally legitimate areas of society and the economy. These articles were also meant to boost the morale of small-town exhibitors and provide them with ammunition for debates with the forces of reform, who considered the cinema to be an evil to society. As such, these motivational arti-cles belong to a larger discourse in and through which the film industry struggled to achieve cultural legitimacy in the 1910s.

25. Cf. Bjørn Sørenssen's contribution in this volume.

26. John R. Pannabecker, "Printing technology in the *Encyclopédie*. Constructing sys-tematic knowledge," *Journal of Industrial Teacher Education* 29, 4 (1992), pp. 73-91; John R. Pannabecker, "Mechanical Arts in Diderot's *Encyclopédie,*" *Technology and Culture* 39, 1 (1998), pp. 33-73.

27. William R. Reddy, "The Structure of a Cultural Crisis: Thinking About Cloth in France Before and After the Revolution," in Arjun Appadurai (ed.), *The Social Life of*

Things: Commodities in Cultural Perspective (Cambridge: Cambridge University Press, 1986), pp. 261-284.

28. The difference between research and documentation films was introduced by Gotthard Wolf, who specified two qualities of scientific films: Research films are merely records of experiments, while documentation films reveal new problems and raise questions that the researcher was previously unaware of. The difference is not one of essence, but of performance: research films can turn into documentation films the minute they start to raise new questions. Wolf's notion of the documentation films bears a strong similarity to the notion of the experimental system as proposed by Hans-Jörg Rheinberger in his work on the history of molecular biology. An experimental system, which is composed of a set of technical equipment and a number of theories that coalesce in order to define a specific object of knowledge, may be seen as productive to the extent that it is capable of raising questions of which the research was previously unaware, and which can guide his research in an entirely new direction. See Gotthard Wolf, *Der wissenschaftliche Dokumentationsfilm und die Encyclopaedia Cinematographica* (Munich: Barth, 1967); and Hans-Jörg Rheinberger, "Experimental Complexity in Biology. Some Epistemological and Historical Remarks," *Philosophy of Science*, 64 (Dec. 1997), pp. 245-254.

Vernacular Archiving

An Interview with Rick Prelinger

Patrick Vonderau

Rick Prelinger (www.prelinger.com), an archivist, writer and filmmaker, founded the Prelinger Archives in 1982. This collection of 51,000 advertising, educational, industrial, and amateur films was acquired by the Library of Congress in 2002. Rick has partnered with the Internet Archive to make 2,500 films from Prelinger Archives available online for free viewing, downloading, and reuse. With the Voyager Company, a pioneer new-media publisher, he produced 14 laserdiscs and CD-ROMs with material from his archives, including *Ephemeral Films*, the *Our Secret Century* series and *Call It Home: The House That Private Enterprise Built*, a laserdisc on the history of suburbia and suburban planning (co-produced with Keller Easterling). Rick has taught in the MFA Design program at New York's School of Visual Arts and lectured widely on American cultural and social history and issues of cultural and intellectual property access. He sat on the National Film Preservation Board (2002-2005) as a representative of the Association of Moving Image Archivists and is currently Board President of the Internet Archive. His feature-length film Panorama Ephemera, depicting the conflicted landscapes of 20th-century America, premiered in summer 2004. He is the co-founder (with Megan Shaw Prelinger) of the Prelinger Library (www.prelingerlibrary.org), an appropriation-friendly reference library located in San Francisco.

Maybe we could start by discussing the notion of "ephemeral films"?

Ephemeral films was an anti-definition, an oppositional definition, because in 1982, when I first thought of calling sponsored films ephemeral films, I took the definition from the antiques or book business, where ephemera is used for things like paper documents that were short-lived. They might be bus schedules or maps, or a blotter with advertising on it. And it seemed to me that these films constituted ephemera, but within the broader context of film. A lot of ephemera isn't ephemeral anymore because now it's seen as a primary historical resource, it isn't an afterthought. So maybe the ephemera definition is short-lived. I used it very loosely and in a sloppy way because I said industrial, educational, advertising, and amateur. I couldn't stand up before hundreds of people and successfully argue that amateur films are ephemeral, but in some cases they really are. They come and go quickly and nobody bothers to save them systematically.

But I don't think the idea of ephemeral films has anything in particular to do with aesthetics, or with style. It's much more about the conditions of appreciation and whether they're in the cultural foreground. And now I think they are. I think that's one thing that I helped accomplish, which was to move this material from the periphery somewhere closer to the center. The fan culture thing is double edged. It's absolutely necessary. It's a good thing. Every "genre" needs fan culture. Experimental and avant-garde film desperately needs fan culture if it's going to survive and not become some arcane museum piece. But fan culture is weird. To many people ephemeral films are things that are goofy and funny. When I made my feature film PANORAMA EPHEMERA a few years ago, a lot of people who saw it said, "Rick, why didn't you put in all the old campy kitsch about dating and romance and washing your hands?" And I had stayed away from those on purpose. The Internet Archive has a rating system, and you're supposed to rate a film on a five-star scale. Until recently, in order to post a comment you had to give it a rating. I complained about this for years and finally they made the ratings optional. But what does a rating mean? That it's a valuable historical document? That I liked it? And as ephemeral films get a lot of fans, you have to ask the question, what are people responding to? But at the same time there are many serious people who are not scholars or academics who look at these films as complex objects and have made many contributions towards understanding them better. So it's double edged.

What makes an ephemeral film a document?

I think it's always been a document of value. It may not be so ephemeral anymore. To speak in general about these films, they can be very precise documentation. Alternatively, they may be imprecise documentation. That is, they are not simply documents of how things looked or how people behaved, but they're documentation of how it was wished that people would behave. In other words they're normative, they document the worldview of influential groups. They're a very good way to begin to understand the history of persuasion. A lot of scholars treat films as secondary documents. They've got to find some print resource, and they either don't look at the films or they don't listen to the films very seriously. And part of that has been that most of the work about ephemeral films until very recently has been mostly about inventory taking.

Somebody will say, as an afterthought, General Electric had an active film program. They made hundreds of films. Then the next move, which is what I did in *Our Secret Century*, is to move towards the sociocultural, to understand these films contextually in the light of movements happening in other realms and sectors. And now what we begin to see is a real focus on what the economy of representation is in these films, how styles, techniques, strategies of rhetoric are mobilized by these films. I think whole new areas of study will evolve, just as semiotics, or gender studies, or psychoanalysis came up in relation to film.

From your point of view, what has been done in research on this issue so far?

There was some interest in the 1950s and 1960s, but not very much. There were a few dissertations written, but part of the problem was that scholars did not have access and part of it was that this material was exclusively claimed by fans, playing on late-night TV. I've talked about how there's been a real gentrification of ephemeral films because now they're seen as fit topics for scholars. So maybe it's not ephemeral anymore and maybe the films have moved to the inside. That's fine. It's going to get complicated though, because there's such a mass of material. If we talk about industrial films in the United States before the end of film, we have to be talking about 400,000 works. And when you begin to talk about corporate video, which almost nobody's done serious work on, you're talking about millions of works. And you get to the point where, yes, you can pick out examples, but the field is so diverse it's almost fruitless. It's like understanding the Web. You can pick some sites and talk about them, but it's very hard to understand all the different strains of vernacular that are going on.

You were just giving an estimation about the number of works. But much of the material is being reused under different titles all the time.

Yes, that's very true.

So therefore I wonder ...

... what is a work? Yes, I think that's very true. And I also think that there are many works made for one-time use, which were maybe shown once. Perhaps there was a negative response, perhaps not. If we ever try to do a filmography, it will be based on information that has different levels of quality. Some of it might be a lab inventory, but when you see something coming out of a lab, unclaimed material, it's very hard to understand for whom it was produced and in what context. And what is a work? Sometimes raw footage was cut together to be presented, and I guess that constitutes a work.

That's the reason why the work approach is not so productive. This is more about practices, isn't it?

Right, the only thing is, you need to have some tentative definition of what a work is so you know what kind of record to make in a database.

Are there any archival restraints on research from your experience?

In the United States, there are many records and private archives, business archives, for example, and there's no accountability, there's no openness. Records are only really available by the grace of the company. Some companies are very open about their history, others are not so open, but typically it's a lack of funding and a lack of interest rather than a wish to hide or censor. What I'm a little more concerned about is that the vast majority of industrial and sponsored films that survive are held in a wide variety of public and private collections and the access situation to archival film is still very poor in the United States. We've developed unprecedented means to access archival material and distribute it at very low cost, and now that digitizing technology has become a commodity, it's quite simple. But the disjunction between our ability to provide access and our will and capability to do so, that disjunction is growing. And I'm quite concerned about that.

In the United States, historically, there's been a difference between archives and libraries, although many libraries are privately held by research institutions, universities, and so on. There's also a long and very honorable tradition of public libraries. Archives have a lot to learn from that. I think that archives are beginning to realize that, although they may have been founded as a department of an organization or a university or a corporation or a government agency, in reality they derive their existence and their legitimacy from an implicit social contract between themselves and the public, and a very important part of that social contract is the provision of access. This is where archives meet the public. Archives define their public mandate through access. This was an arcane issue a few years ago because archives typically dealt with intermediaries. You could call them wholesale entities. The archive user was somebody that was making a product that would then be used by the public or by scholars or by students. But now archives have gone retail. Ordinary people are very interested in the contents of archives, and there's a whole history to this. This goes back to genealogists. Amateur genealogists have been important, as has been the growth of fan culture around many archival films, and a growing interest in moving-image genres that were very obscure. Moving-image archives in the States don't have a very good record or a good tradition of access. We have the opportunity to change that right now, but there's so much inertia.

At the same time that we have the means to provide access much more easily, our will to do so seems to be falling short. There are a few key digitization projects that have happened, but most moving image material is still under a kind of quiet embargo. You hear many things: it's too expensive to digitize, we should not digitize before we preserve. Although we may digitize and we may preserve, we shouldn't provide public access because we don't know what the rights situation is. Of course, although copyright is very complicated in the United States, we have hundreds of thousands of films in the public domain, unlike Europe, and archives control many of their holdings. A lot of archives don't want to put material out into the world without full cataloging, full description, full contextualization.

How would you describe your role as a collector? Are you still collecting?

We call ourselves a foster archive. We copy things when we can to work with them personally or to sell stock footage, but then we try to find a long-term home for the material. At the moment we have about 40,000 cans of material that we acquired after the Library of Congress deal and that's also going to go to the Library of Congress, probably in 2008. And yes, we do still collect. Although I would love not to be a moving-image archivist, but it's hard not to jump on things when they are made available.

How about your plans for the Internet Archive?

At the moment we have just under 2,000 films. We are now starting to transfer more films to video and I think that we'll put up at least 500 more items. There are some materials that it isn't terribly meaningful to put up. Perhaps they're poor condition, sometimes if we just have pre-print elements on a film, like A and B rolls, I don't put them up because it doesn't represent the film very well.

What about the costs of digitization?

At the Internet Archive we digitize video for between 15 and 20 dollars an hour, which is a very modest investment. Literally, if you were to spend a 100,000 dollars, you could digitize 5,000 hours of video, you could do a hundred hours of video from 50 archives. A little bit less, obviously, but you could build a very strong representation that was pluralistic, that showed many different traditions and collections. There are many thoughtful and intelligent and forward-looking people in moving image archives right now, but typically the people who have the vision don't have the power, and they don't have the freedom to sign the checks. There's a real generational issue. I don't know if this is so in

Europe, but we have a lot of younger and emerging archivists who understand that the economy of cultural distribution has changed as production has changed. Unfortunately, they're not running the institutions yet.

How about your view on copyright infringements in relation to video-sharing sites?

There's no question that people are infringing on copyright law, but we need to stop thinking about copyright and more about access. What we do as archivists isn't the same as the people that sit outside on the sidewalk selling bootleg DVDs. Archives function as a gigantic legitimation and preview apparatus for the entertainment industry. Archives are never going to put the entertainment industry out of business. Archives do what the entertainment industry isn't able to do itself. And we constantly add value to work that's privately owned. And archives need to continue to do that. And in the same way, YouTube adds value to copyrights that are owned and that were maybe not exploited previously. You know about our experience selling stock footage. We still survive and fund almost all of our activities from selling stock footage. Shortly after we put up almost 2,000 of our films online for free, our income doubled. It isn't all because of putting things up for free, but a large percentage of the increase is a result of the exposure and the fact that our images are so much more propagated. And it was absolutely life changing to do that. We entered into a collaboration with tens of thousands of people, most of whom we don't know, and a tremendous number of new works were made possible. I think tens of thousands of new works. And other archives can do this if they choose.

I would like to discuss the online presentation of archived materials in the Internet Archive.

There's not a clear strategy behind the way that the Internet Archive is organized and how it presents itself. The user interface is designed by geeks. It's a techy thing. It doesn't come out of any sensitivity for the material. But the good news about the Internet Archive is that anybody can design a front end to it. So you could harvest metadata and build a much better and more coherent index for a category if you wanted. That's completely open and I hope people do that. I have a real issue, and I think this is an important question. The portal right now to our film collection is completely fan oriented. And this is fine, but we need a window into that database that's more suited to research and education, and that's maybe moderated, so that if a scholar puts up a note or a question, it isn't just, "I like the film." I think we need an educational journal.

There have been numerous attempts to make historical-critical editions of feature-film classics in the last years, but most of them have been based on rather traditional concepts of work and authorship, supplementing an authored "original" with what is regarded as mere contextual material, i.e., production notes. How would such an approach work for sponsored films?

It would be a great leap forward for cinema studies if we were able to avoid the auteur theory this time. But it is possible to speak of auteurs and individual authorship with many sponsored films. It's just that the information is so often lacking. But I think that there are clear, not simply categories, but clear voices within many of these films. Geoff Alexander, who founded the Academic Film Archive of North America, has done a lot of work on educational films that were seen as works of art. He has done important work on many filmmakers who did have a distinct vision that comes through. But context of presentation. Why do we have to have just one context? Why can't we have a whole number of them? I resist any assertion that there's only one way to present these films. I think it would be wonderful, and in fact I've done it with my CD-ROMs, where films are presented with a great deal of contextual material, with essays, with period evidence, with collateral, printed visual materials that explain the conditions around which the film was produced. It's great but it's not an obligation. The point is, every generation needs to reinterpret the cultural heritage over again. And it isn't just the substance of the interpretation but the form in which it's interpreted that's going to change.

Will there be cross-references between the Prelinger Archive and the Prelinger Library?

I started collecting books to contextualize the films, and now my spouse and I collect books for many other reasons, but there are many connections back and forth. Somebody, and I don't know if it's me because I don't have any time right now, should draw the links between films and contextualization elsewhere linked to the books. That's a lifelong project. It's like the Warburg Library, drawing hyperlinks between different areas of knowledge. Another way to do that might be to use Wikipedia.

Speaking about the contexts of sponsored films, one often has the problem that there are virtually no sources beyond the film itself.

For years I've been interested in doing something on Jam Handy and the Jam Handy organization. We had many of the films, about 1,600 items, and some historical material that we had found, mostly through people in Detroit who had picked it out of the trash when the company closed, and then we had some of the published material, but there's not much. I thought I'd love to do a biography or a film about this person. And one of the points of this approach would be the scarcity of information and how that forces you to imagine a great deal. I knew that his papers were at the Detroit Public Library, but I didn't think there was very much. I went to visit the library a couple of years ago, and what I found was that there are actually quite a lot of papers. And there was a great deal of documentation about the legendary or mythical parts of his life, like getting kicked out of university and some of his personal peculiarities, like not wearing jackets with pockets so he couldn't put his hands in his pockets. There were a tremendous number of personal letters, many of which dealt with difficult episodes in his life, such as his divorce from his first wife, his relationship with his children and other family members. I realized that there was an abundance of material, and that it would completely change the nature of anything that I might do.

Jam Handy seems to be a unique case of sponsored filmmaking in the United States. Are there other companies fostering a house style like the Jam Handy organization did?

There are usually no director's credits on Handy's films, except for a few that are dramatic, little dramas about automobiles and the farm, etc. But he looked at all the important work and had a great deal of authorial control. I think the Jerry Fairbanks films represent a merger of early television dramatic technique and Hollywood musical technique. They have a cloudy gender orientation. I think they have kind of a queer sensibility. They tend to play fast and loose with reality. There's the suspension of disbelief that you would see in musicals. There are the Calvin films, and many other directors. But there's a house style that traffics in surrealism, in surprise, in a visual demonstration technique that's very didactic but also filled with tricks. There are the industrial films made by Centron in Lawrence, Kansas. I think the key author there is Margaret Carlile Travis, known as Trudy Travis, who was their scriptwriter, one of the only women who worked in that field. She has a very interesting sensibility. She's a true democrat, she has a real sense of people meeting cooperatively to solve problems together that's very interesting. A company that somebody needs to do serious work on is the company called On Film Inc. in Princeton, New Jersey. This was, as some people have written, a hotbed of creativity. Stan Brakhage worked with them, Stan Vanderbeek. That's a company where the values of avant-garde art and avant-garde film are very much part of these corporate productions. And Virginia Bell, who was known professionally by the name Tracy Ward, a gender-neutral pseudonym, was an incredibly important person in this area and her films are very distinctive works. That company also worked in sort of a quasi-collective manner, and everybody who's been involved with it has always said it was very exciting.

I was also thinking about Herk Harvey.

Herk Harvey is credited with a lot of films that I don't think he made. One of the drawbacks of fan culture is that they get a lot of things wrong. There's an urban legend that DATING DO'S AND DON'TS (1949), the educational film, was directed by Ed Wood, which is completely not true. I've only seen Herk Harvey's educational films, which aren't that different from the other films that Centron was making. We also don't know a lot yet about some of the broader movements. I think there was kind of a New York School in the late 1950s and early 1960s. I relate to the whole upswell of postwar artistic activity in New York, and On Film was certainly part of that. A lot of people who we would now think of as avant-garde or experimental, or also documentarians, worked with On Film, and we've hardly begun to look at these films yet. One of them is Henry Strauss, who Heide Solbrig has written about.

How about Jam Handy's relation to the car industry? There seems to be more than one connection between the making of films and the making of cars.

Picture Detroit at the beginning in the 1920s. It's not just cars. Within a 400-mile radius of Detroit is most of the industrial production in the United States, so Detroit is a very logical place to build an industrial-film company. It's been rumored, and I don't know if this is true, that Jam Handy married the daughter of the national sales manager for Chevrolet and that he had this connection. Typically, industrial-film companies would work exclusively for one car company for competitive reasons. So Jam Handy had Chevrolet, one division of General Motors, he did a little work for Pontiac, for Buick, for Cadillac, and General Motors trucks. But, for example, Wilding did work for Ford and Chrysler Plymouth. Jam Handy did Ford trucks, but not Ford cars. There was a kind of competitive carving up. I think Chevrolet was the number one automotive brand, it was the top-selling suite of models for years, and they had a huge film program. So did everybody else. It's important not to take the Chevy film program as typical, because in some ways I think it was very influenced by Ford. Ford himself was in the film production business, and a lot of the Jam Handy films, although they're very beautifully executed, are derivative. Goodyear Rubber had a weekly newsreel. Jam Handy made newsreels for Chevrolet, but it was years after Ford had been doing so. So I don't think he was the first to come up with a lot of these ideas, I think it was really his execution and his visual style that mattered.

How does the product affect style?

It isn't just the situation in which the film was to be used. The Jam Handy organization analyzed the use situation very closely. We have two binders of notes that were issued to salespeople for the company. Their job was to go to corporations and say, here, these are our capabilities, you're in the electric-accessories business, let me show you another film we've made for another company. What these memoranda show is that the films are targeted very specifically to situations. Some of the Jam Handy films were made for just one person to see. Maybe you're trying to sell a vice president on making a big equipment purchase, perhaps you're talking to the employees of some large company about economic issues. They were targeted in that sense. I don't think that it has as much to do with specific products. In the United States there are many different subsectors of industrial films: there are training films for workers, there are management-training films, there are sales-training films, and one very interesting group that not a lot of work has been done on is what's called institutional advertising. Rather than promoting the products of the company, these films are about promoting the corporate view, or promoting the corporation as an entity. Jam Handy was very good at those. The classic example is the American series, made for Chevy, which are AMERICAN HARVEST (1955), AMERICAN ENGINEER (1956), AMERICAN LOOK (1958), AMERICAN MAKER (1960), and AMERICAN THRIFT (1962). AMERICAN CHOICE was the last one, but it wasn't finished. They just shot it and then the project was cancelled. And it would be well worth somebody's time to do close textual and visual analysis of these films. For example, AMERICAN HARVEST is about all the different raw materials that go into making a car. That film is a response to a concern over the control of raw materials during the Korean War. There was a President's Materials Policy Commission, and the notion was that, since we no longer directly controlled many resources around the world and the British Empire was gone, what could we do to ensure that there was a continuous supply of raw materials, especially things like rare metals and certain commodities? The notion of a government stockpile was introduced in this way. AMERICAN HARVEST is a corporate intervention, saying, we actually have many things here that we can work with, and in the automobile we use mostly United States products. In some respects it was an anti-cosmopolitan or anti-globalist film. A large percentage of General Motors stock was owned by the Dupont family and the Dupont corporation. In fact, an analysis that nobody has done is that Handy worked for a lot of companies that had Dupont and Rockefeller money in them, RCA, General Motors, even a small company called the Ferry Morris Seed Company. Jam Handy made films for them in the late 1930s and early 1940s. That's a Rockefeller-owned company. You may also have this in Germany, because you also had big family monopolies, but then you had more in-house and less private production. There was also a General Motors in-house production, GM Photographic, which still exists today, and they did a lot of things that Handy could not or did not do.

To conclude this interview, I would like to ask you about your view on the prospects for online archiving projects.

I think it will be an uneven development. I think we'll see more digitization projects, and I hope that they will become interoperable. In other words, the Internet Archive films will interoperate with other material, they can be edited with public-television material, with UCLA, Hearst newsreels that are going to be digitized, and that it won't be a series of walled gardens. I think that there will also be a lot of private digitization projects. The fans have moved way ahead of archives in this respect. In less than a year, YouTube built an online collection of about 11 million videos. In spring 2008, their collection will have over 80 million videos. Many of these are commercially produced or orphan materials that are not available through the DVD or Video-on-Demand distribution apparatus, and although it's only for access and the quality is terrible, this is a real case of popular, vernacular archival activity that's outstepped anything that established archives have done. And it poses a tremendous challenge because now public expectations are that, number one, moving-image archives should be accessible, number two, that they should be universal, number three, that they should be participatory, in other words I can post my own material into this big repository. Number four, that there's some kind of social networking involved. Number five, that it's segmented, in other words, a moving-image object like a Monty Python program isn't 56 minutes long, but each individual sketch is accessible. All these things that archivists have been talking about forever and haven't been able to do have been done by YouTube, and now public expectations are so increased that whatever we do may seem inadequate by comparison.

This interview was conducted by Patrick Vonderau in Pordenone, Italy, in October 2007.

II
Visuality and Efficiency

Early Industrial Moving Pictures in Germany[1]

Martin Loiperdinger

Numerous subjects in the areas of business and commerce provide the film camera with attractive views. As long as the cinematograph was presented as "the latest technological wonder," cameramen focused less on the activities of workers than on the effect of "true-to-life" photographic reproductions of the powerful yet fleeting rise of steam and smoke (for example in Défournage du coke, 1896). Even the shots of locomotives rushing toward the camera, so popular in the early years, were less interesting because of their depiction of a technical wonder than the spatial effect they produced when projected onto the two-dimensional screen.[2]

Such surprise effects, however, wore off very quickly. Even before 1900, trains rushing toward the camera had lost their appeal and were seldom shot from this perspective again. Instead, cameras were placed on locomotives to obtain "Ghost rides", travelling shots of landscape panoramas. When the train drove past spectacular stretches or elaborate bridge structures, these "travel pictures" accentuated industrial technology as a part of the landscape. As a subject for non-fiction film shots, locomotives and trains were only rediscovered in the 1920s and 1930s because of the avant-garde's fascination with technology. Due to its idiosyncratic technical structure, the suspension railway in Wuppertal maintained a certain attraction, and it found a large audience with the Flying Train (1901), which was produced by the German subsidiary of the Mutoscope and Biograph Company.[3]

Traveling with industrial moving pictures

The term *Industriebild* was used in German trade press ads starting in 1907. In the UK, we usually find the expression "industrial moving pictures." The Pathé catalog uses the term *scènes d'art et d'industrie*. This was meant to indicate films that showed the public various kinds of work and manufacturing processes. The bulk of industrial films available prior to 1914 as part of short-film programs in German commercial cinemas came from the French manufacturers Pathé, Gaumont, Eclipse, and Raleigh & Robert. Industrial moving pictures had a status in the programming similar to that of "travel pictures": they showed technical phenomena and work processes from agriculture, trade, and industry that, like tropical regions or Swiss vacation spots, were not generally accessible.

The similarity to travel films sometimes resulted in film titles that suggest a combination of travel and industrial imagery. For instance, Gaumont advertised its APFELSINEN-INDUSTRIE (*Orange Industry,* 1906) under the series title PANORAMA VON ALGIERS (*Panorama of Algiers*). Eclipse offered INDUSTRIE IN VENEDIG (*Industry in Venice,* 1909) as well as INDUSTRIE UND SPORT IN BURMA (*Industry and Sport in Burma,* 1909). Likewise, Pathé released exotic shorts like DIE HERSTELLUNG VON BAMBUSHÜTTEN (*The Manufacture of Bamboo Huts,* 1909), ARBEITENDE ELEPHANTEN (*Working Elephants,* 1909), and DIE ERNTE DES ZUCKERROHRS (*Harvesting Sugar Cane,* 1910), which could all be seen as industrial or travel pictures. This was equally true for films on handcrafts like DIE HERSTELLUNG KÜNSTLICHER ROSEN (*The Manufacture of Artificial Roses,* 1910), FABRIKATION VON KUNSTBLUMEN (*Making Artificial Flowers,* 1911), as well as the manufacture of products typical of certain regions such as FABRIKATION VENETIANISCHER SPITZEN (*Manufacturing Venetian Lace,* 1906) and FÄCHERINDUSTRIE IN JAPAN/INDUSTRIE DES ÉVENTAILS AU JAPON (*The Fan Industry in Japan,* 1907).

In many of these films the country and the people merge with the regional products to become a folkloristic stereotype. This is, above all, "a production strategy of the firm Pathé frères. With its high-grade, thoroughly organized international network Pathé consistently focused on the manufacture of films distinguishable by national characteristics, in the areas of both fiction and non-fiction film."[4] Examples of this can be seen in the films that Alfred Machin directed for Pathé in the Netherlands in 1909 and 1910. HERSTELLUNG VON HOLLÄNDISCHEM KÄSE/COMMENT SE FAIT LE FROMAGE DE HOLLANDE (*The Production of Dutch Cheese,* 1909), for instance, features a dual form of presentation:

> On the one hand, it presents the process of cheese making in an instructional mode (which, in this case, could be referred to as turning it into a museum object), on the other hand, it presents the inhabitants of Holland as exotic and picturesque. As such, a peculiar image of a national culture is created that makes relative geographical proximity appear foreign.[5]

As late as 1950, this film was included in an anthology of educational films published by the German Institut für Film und Bild in Wissenschaft und Unterricht (FWU).[6]

The presentation of the unknown or quaint sometimes resulted in unavoidable similarities with the world of entertainment: A work elephant carefully picking up a block of wood and laying it on a pile in Rangoon demonstrates as much training as the elephant in the staggeringly funny number in THOMPSON'S

DRESSIERTE ELEFANTEN (*Thompson's Trained Elephants*, 1908), shot at Berlin's Wintergarten. This similarity to contemporary entertainment can be seen even more clearly in the shots of work processes in handcrafts or the construction of housing in African or Asian colonial territories. They are so similar to the supposedly authentic processes of handcrafts and home building seen in the then-popular human zoos that Lumière cameramen shot many of these scenes in Paris or Lyon rather than Africa.

Unusual visual attractions were occasionally shot in Germany, such as WAS GESCHIEHT MIT ALTEN EISEN- UND BLECHABFÄLLEN? (*What Happens to Iron and Metal Waste?*, 1911):

> A highly engrossing film, shot in one of the largest iron works in Saxony, the Lauchhammer Works, thanks to the kind permission of the factory's management. We see how waste iron and metal is collected from the factory by giant, electromagnetic cranes and pressed into huge blocks, which is then brought to the smelting oven where it is smelted and purified into raw iron, then made available for further use.[7]

Views of production

Industrial views, in the strictest sense, like those that were available for short-film programs between 1907 and 1912, concentrate on the more or less thorough demonstration of manufacturing processes for various consumer articles. They show industrial production of food products or everyday consumer goods such as light bulbs or paper, but also luxury goods like cameras and automobiles. Relevant titles include DIE TOMATEN (*Tomatoes*, 1908), SARDINENINDUSTRIE (*The Sardine Industry*, 1909), ERNTE UND ZUBEREITUNG DER ANANAS ZUR HERSTELLUNG VON KONSERVEN (*Harvesting and Preparing Pineapples for Canning*, 1910), or FABRIKATION DES PAPIERS (*Manufacturing Paper*, 1911). In January 1911, the first two titles of the series RALEIGH & ROBERT'S INDUSTRIELLE BILDER (*Raleigh & Robert's Industrial Scenes*) appeared: WIE EINE ELEKTRISCHE GLÜHBIRNE ENTSTEHT (*How an Electric Light Bulb Is Made*, 1911) and DIE HERSTELLUNG EINER WACHSFIGUR (*The Manufacture of a Wax Figure*, 1911), the latter "a glimpse into the workshops of Parisian bust manufacturing."[8]

Food manufacturers were happy to use industrial moving pictures to inform consumers about their products. DIE FABRIKATION DER SCHWEIZERKÄSE (*The Manufacture of Swiss Cheese*, 1913) shows the basic production steps, from the cows being taken out to pasture and milked to the transport of the finished cheeses to the "export house" (title card), and further provides explanations through the extensive use of title cards through which the audience discovers that 1,000 to 1,300 liters of milk are necessary to make a wheel of cheese weighing 80 to 110 kilograms, which, when heated to 33 degrees Celsius after the addition of enzymes, coagulates "into a uniform gelatinous mass within 30 minutes" (title card). This can all be followed in detail from a position above the action, such as how four dairy workers use a pulley to hoist the mass of cheese gathered in a cloth from a large copper cauldron and pour it into shallow, round containers, where it is pressed into rounds. Finally, there is a demonstration of how the holes are made in Swiss cheese. In a similarly extensive way, MILCHERZEUGUNG IN DER SCHWEIZ/PRÉPARATION ET EXPORTATION DU LAIT PAR LA STÉ LAITIÈRE DES ALPES BERNOISES (*Milk Production in Switzerland*, 1909) shows the production of condensed milk and gives precise information about the heating process that pasteurizes the milk: "The milk is heated to 100 degrees Celsius, mixed with six percent sugar, and reduced in volume by half through evaporation of its liquid content" (title card).

Figures 1 and 2 MILCHERZEUGUNG IN DER SCHWEIZ *(1909)*

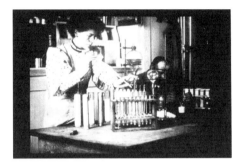

Photo: Marian Stefanowski

Industrial films as we now know them were made for exhibitions and trade fairs. They were geared not to commercial use, but a professional audience. This did not exclude their being used as training and educational films, serving as a kind of cinematic replacement for factory visits by schools and associations, or as "business propaganda" abroad. For instance, the Ernemann company, which manufactured photography and film equipment in Dresden, shot WER-DEGANG EINER KAMERA (*Development of a Camera*, 1909) for the International Photographic Exhibition in Dresden. In 1911, a film series from the Siemens-Schuckert Works drew visitors' attention to the company's exhibition stand at the Turin World's Fair. The small-engine factory was shown along with the cable workshop of the Siemens-Schuckert Werke, the manufacture of tantalum lamps as well as the use of electricity for smelting ore in the furnaces at Gute-hoffnungshütte. In the summer of 1912, its main competitor AEG followed suit and commissioned the Messter company to film the manufacture of electric cable and wire at the Oberspree Cable Factory. The Messter company also shot DER WERDEGANG EINES DAIMLERMOTORS (*The Development of a Daimler Engine*, 1912) for Daimler. The international Building Trade Exhibition in Leipzig impressed visitors in 1913 with a specially installed cinema in which, among other things, gigantic excavators could be seen digging the Panama Canal.

Compressing time

In contrast to the travel pictures, whose individual *views* or *vues* usually did not reproduce the temporal course of a trip, their progression loosely organized around a named place or region, industrial pictures take the temporally predetermined process of production from raw material to finished product as their dramatic framework. The spatial "from . . . to . . ." of travel films is here a temporal succession, and just as the travel films shrink the distances from one place to the next through their choice of excerpts, the industrial pictures shrink the production time necessary for the processing of raw materials or the assembly of ready-made parts: fresh milk is ready for consumption as condensed milk or cheese in a matter of minutes. Even an Opel car is assembled in its entirety within three minutes. BLICK IN EINE AUTOMOBILFABRIK (*A Look into a Car Factory*, 1910) makes this feat possible, in which the cameraman stops his camera 22 times while four workers from the Opel Factory in Rüsselsheim reenact the "complete assembly of an automobile" (title card). The film's title does indeed presume an observer or a visitor looking around the Opel Factory while production goes on as usual. But the film is in no way a documentation of an actual production process, compressed in time, but a reenactment: in the interest of better lighting conditions, assembly was temporarily shifted from the factory hall outside, enabling clear shots of the process. In contrast to the typical assembly process in the factory hall, the demonstration in the factory courtyard had to be done without technical aids. This does not create an impression of highly technical work, and has an improvised, non-professional effect. The cameraman makes the best of this adversity by stressing speed: at the film's end a worker pumps up a tire with slapstick-like swiftness – and suddenly the car is being taken for a test drive (though not the car shown, but a showpiece: the Kaiser's car painted white).

Product and image advertising

Industrial moving pictures speak to an audience in various ways. Only in the course of such a film, sometimes not until the end, is it made clear that it is all about a certain brand-name product, and not simply about how cheese, condensed milk, pralines, or cars are produced: initially – in a more or less strictly arranged chronological order – "views" of various steps in the industrial manufacturing process are shown. Only during the latter stages of packaging and shipping is the brand or company name of the product revealed, ultimately serving as an explicit advertisement. In the case of food, the final product is presented at the film's end being consumed with great relish – frequently facing the camera directly. These final appellative images, staged in the style of a contemporary humoresque, are aesthetically set off from the sober presentation of manufacturing and packaging with the audience being addressed without mediation. The contrast inspires laughter and creates a smooth transition to the following section of the short-film program – for instance a comedy.

Product and image advertising do not appear to be distinctly separate. The brand is presented more or less casually – albeit as a special example or even exemplary for a category of products: Bärenmarke stands for condensed milk, Othello Wafers stands for cookies, Opel stands for cars.

Industrial films that convey information about the manufacturing process and in doing so demonstrate the hygiene and care taken during the manufacture of food products entirely serve the function of advertising. Exporting the products functions as a mark of quality that boosts the company's image further: sales success is meant here to be taken as shorthand for the quality of the product. The sense of wonder that the audience experiences when faced with big machines being used to produce a brand-name product also serves to boost the company's image.

Industrial films about the manufacture of luxury articles were always used as image advertising. The distribution of BLICK IN EINE AUTOMOBILFABRIK was not meant to speak to a target audience of potential buyers, who were in any case scarce in German cinemas in 1910. Thus, the assembly of an Opel car did not have to succeed as product information in any authentic sense, but could be improvised for the camera in the factory courtyard. It was enough to give an approximate idea of how an Opel was put together. The sheer presentation of the product is what boosts the image here: The Opel automobile functions as a technical marvel that, as if it went without saying, can drive off by itself.

The visible and the invisible

The various assembly processes are spread out in space and time in a variety of ways. They take place outdoors or in closed spaces, near the film producer's laboratory or far away in the tropics. This very diversity is what makes industrial topics so appealing as subjects for richly varied, impressive, or just instructive cinematic views. Spacious industrial facilities can form a landscape of their own and at the same time make details of production processes available for closeups. On the other hand, there are certain processes in industrial production that the camera lens cannot capture. For instance, the brewing process cannot be represented well by shooting in a brewery: HOPFEN UND MALZ, GOTT ERHALT'S! EIN RUNDGANG DURCH DIE BRAUEREI BINDING IN FRANKFURT AM MAIN (*God Save Hops and Malt! A Tour of the Binding Brewery in Frankfurt*, 1910) merely shows large containers in dark corridors, with title cards indicating "The Mashhouse" and "In the Fermenting Cellar." After the title card "The Manufacture of Ice" the camera travels down a wall with pipes. No more information is given, or if so, it is left to the film commentators.

As in most film genres, the human body is the most important reference point for industrial moving pictures. Technical work processes in which a single worker or a few workers can be clearly seen working on specific objects are the most appropriate for cinematic views. They show the human worker in direct physical relation to the material or in the process of turning raw materials into finished products. Workers are always shown as being highly focused on their work. Distinctions between manual and industrial work processes are rarely made. Although the beer barrels at the Frankfurt Binding Brewery were still assembled by hand, HERSTELLUNG VON FÄSSERN DURCH MASCHINEN/LA FABRICATION MÉCANIQUE DES TONNEAUX À CETTE (*The Production of Barrels by Machines*, 1911) showed the mechanical replacement of human skills. In the same year, Eclipse started distributing the Urban film SEILFABRIKATION IN KENT (*Rope Manufacturing in Kent*, 1911), in which it is explained that "the machine continually encroaches on the territory of the human hand. For this reason it's even more interesting to show activities where the skilled hand of a human being is still at work."[9]

Direct comparisons of handcraft and mechanization are quite rare: in HOPFEN UND MALZ, after the title card "The Filling Machine," a medium shot shows a worker attaching a filling mechanism to a beer keg, pulling a lever to fill it, removing it, rolling the keg away with his foot, and then repeating this process several times. After this, with the title card "Filling Bottles," several shots from various perspectives show the finishing and disconnecting of bottles from the filling machine, all of which is done by hand. It is immediately clear that the work rhythm is determined by the speed of the filling machine. The workers conform to the machine.

Industrial moving pictures are not in a position to document actual human labor. They cannot show the performance of tasks as they would occur without the presence of the film camera. There are two primary reasons for this: The production of goods usually takes place on private company grounds and is not accessible to the general public. The cameramen of industrial moving pictures can only shoot there on commission or with the owners' support. At the very least, they need permission to shoot, which always entails certain conditions. Therefore, their choice of subjects is limited. Secondly, the manufacturing processes shown are practically always set up for the film camera. Workers function as actors or presenters of the work they perform on a daily basis: They do their work for the camera – knowing very well that they are not simply being observed at work, but that their performance and actions are being recorded for screening before a general audience. They do their work carefully and with full concentration. Spontaneous movement is generally suppressed when presenting the work process for the film camera. In this way, the workers shown in industrial moving pictures always appear to be fulfilling their function in the working process – they do not yawn; they do not sweat, laugh, or joke; they do not swear, take breaks, or eat or drink.

Industrial images always present disciplined, ambitious, and hard-working people at work in the production of useful things (quite in keeping with the original sense of the term *industria*). The paying of wages is not shown. Neither supervisors nor inspectors are shown. Ultimately, the entire economics of production are excluded from these moving pictures.

Notes

1. This is a slightly shortened version of Martin Loiperdinger's "Industriebilder," in Martin Loiperdinger, Uli Jung (eds.); *Geschichte des dokumentarischen Films in Deutschland. Band 1: Kaiserreich 1895-1918* (Stuttgart: Reclam, 2005), pp. 324-332.
2. Cf. Martin Loiperdinger, "Lumière's Arrival of the Train: Cinema's Founding Myth," *The Moving Image* 4, 1 (spring 2004), pp. 89-113.

3. Kemp R. Niver, *Early Motion Pictures: The Paper Print Collection in the Library of Congress* (Washington, DC, 1985); on p. 108, the location of shooting is falsely identified as Bremen.

4. Cf. Frank Kessler, "Wie der Käse in Holland gemacht wird. Anmerkungen zum frühen nonfiction-Film," in Malte Hagener, Johann N. Schmidt, Michael Wedel (eds.), *Die Spur durch den Spiegel. Der Film in der Kultur der Moderne* (Berlin: Bertz, 2004), pp. 159-166.

5. Kessler 2004, p. 165. The film is available on the DVD Exotic Europe under the original title Comment se fait le fromage de Hollande.

6. Cf. Roland Cosandey, *Welcome Home, Joye! Film um 1910* (Basel and Frankfurt am Main: Stroemfeld and Roter Stern, 1993), pp.138-140.

7. *Der Kinematograph*, no. 249 (October 4, 1911).

8. Ibid., no. 213 (January 25, 1911).

9. Ibid., no. 264 (January 17, 1911).

Layers of Cheese

Generic Overlap in Early Non-Fiction Films on Production Processes[1]

Frank Kessler and Eef Masson

While defining genres and sub-genres may be one of the most difficult tasks of film scholarship in general, it seems an almost hopeless endeavor for those studying non-fiction cinema.[2] Approaching the largely uncharted territory of industrial and business films, authors such as Thomas Elsaesser, Yvonne Zimmermann, Vinzenz Hediger and Patrick Vonderau have suggested taking into account paratextual discourses as well as the institutional contexts of films in order to establish, or reconstruct, the generic divisions structuring the industrial uses of cinematography.[3] While we agree with the general line of their argument (which one could characterize as a "historical pragmatics" approach[4]), their focus on organizational functionality fails to address the fact that many of the generic markers that they rely on do in fact originate outside the context of industrial organization, and, in some cases, predate the systematic use of film by industry by years, if not decades. Fully accounting for the generic subdivisions of industrial film also requires a look into the past – and more particularly, a consideration of the emergence of what has retrospectively been termed "process films" in early non-fiction film.

In this article we argue that the generic labels of non-fiction cinema always overlap with others in terms of the formal, thematic, structural, institutional, or pragmatic dimensions that constitute genre definitions. In the specific case that we shall analyze – (pre)industrial films depicting the process of cheese making – the rendering of the different production stages closely resembles the way such practices are represented in travelogues and educational films. Genres should therefore be seen as complex and multi-layered configurations demanding to be understood in terms of historically specific, pragmatic contexts. The latter, in turn, offer functional frameworks for textual structures, which both constrain the construction of meaning and are open enough to allow a variety of readings.

Generic differentiation in non-fiction cinema

One of the best ways to understand how generic subdivisions are established in the vast domain of non-fiction film is to analyze the criteria according to which such labels were discursively constructed over time. Arguably, the most important distinction in the field of factual filmmaking is the one that differentiates the documentary, as a specific type of non-fiction film, from other types, such as the travelogues of early cinema, newsreels, and scientific or instructional films. John Grierson's famous and often quoted definition of documentary as "the creative treatment of actuality" is a case in point here, as Grierson implicitly opposes two types of practice: one that is content to record actuality, and another one – namely that which Grierson associates with the work of Robert Flaherty – that creatively shapes actuality.[5] In his 1935 essay "Some Principles of Documentary," Paul Rotha elaborates on this opposition in the following terms:

> It is often suggested that documentary has close similarity to the newsreel. By the trade they are naturally confused because they both, in their respective ways, deal with natural material. But there the likeness ends. Their approach to and interpretation of that material are widely different. The essence of the documentary method lies in its dramatization of actual material. The very act of dramatization causes a film statement to be false to actuality. ... To be truthful within the technical limits of the camera and microphone demands description, which is the aim of the instructional film, and not dramatization, which is the qualification of the documentary method.[6]

What Grierson and Rotha describe as different practices or methods ultimately refers to a difference with regard to *style*: the opposition between recording and creatively treating actuality, between description and dramatization, implies a distinction between downplaying the expressive possibilities of the medium on the one hand, and foregrounding them on the other. One could indeed state that, within the logic of the distinction proposed by Grierson and Rotha, documentary filmmakers, as opposed to those producing other types of non-fiction films, need to make explicit stylistic choices, whereas, in these other cases, style is determined by the obligation "to be truthful within the technical limits of the camera and microphone."

Further differentiation in the field of non-fiction cinema is often based upon the criterion of the *purpose* or *function* a film is supposed to serve. Denominations such as instructional, educational, scientific, ethnographic, etc. films, and also terms like newsreel or propaganda, refer to the uses these films are being put to, or to the institutional domain in which they are employed. Here, the formal characteristics are more or less irrelevant, the basic assumption being generally that form will just have to follow function. Closely related to this perspective are categorizations centered on *thematic* issues, that is, the content matter of the films. Examples are generic labels such as travelogues, military scenes, colonial films, sports films, wildlife films, etc. Such a thematic approach is, in fact, often connected to distribution categories, which materialize in the form of subdivisions in catalogues, especially in the early period. And last but not least, there are generic subsets constructed in terms of *production* or *exhibition*: the *Kulturfilm*, for instance, as well as the amateur film, as made by and shown to the members of clubs [men indentation]. It is important to note that the above labels originate from practitioners' discourses. When taken up by film historians or genre theorists they tend to be used as analytical categories and thus must be defined in a relatively strict and stable manner. This tension between the rough-and-ready labeling by film producers or distributors and the scholarly demand for precision is arguably one of the reasons why genre is such a notoriously complex field.

Consequently, as even such a rapid sketch demonstrates, none of these criteria can serve as a basis for clear-cut definitions. Most types of films will fall into several categories, and individual films can be grouped together in various ways. In spite of these difficulties, an analysis of generic categories can be useful in order to understand the complexity of the phenomenon of genre in (early) non-fiction.

Industrial film as a genre category

When looking at the generic label "industrial film," we may find the complexity of such a category discouraging at first sight, but mapping out its different layers of meaning may eventually be helpful in gaining a better understanding of the broad range of potential meanings that it covers.

The first, and most obvious, criterion here is the depiction of industrial work processes, and thus, directly or indirectly, the presentation of factories. But several possible distinctions come into play here. Does the label only concern so-called "heavy" industries, or other branches of production as well, such as, for instance, the industrial processing of food? And is drawing a line between crafts or manufacturing and industry possible? To what degree must production processes be automated or at least mechanized? In the early 1900s, the Pathé company's distribution catalogues included the category *scènes (d'art et) d'industrie*, which covers a variety of subjects, from the oil industry in Baku to the snake-skin industry of Java, and the wooden-shoe industry in Brittany (in all of these cases, and in many similar ones, the word *industrie* appears in the title of the films). From this point of view, almost all the various types of what Tom Gunning has called "process films" would fall within the genre.[7]

A somewhat narrower criterion would limit the category to those films produced or commissioned by the industry itself. This, again, leaves open the question as to which types of enterprises qualify as "industrial". Furthermore, it is possible to distinguish between a number of purposes such films fulfill: they can serve the interests of public relations, aim at attracting clients, help market the product, provide information or training for employees, instruct them about company policies with regard to security, address matters of health and safety related to the production process, etc. The question of the specific purposes of the films is also linked to issues of exhibition, as there can be an enormous difference between images made for public screenings, either in commercial cinema or in other, specialized venues (trade fairs, conventions, but also classrooms), and those that are produced to address a select and predefined group of viewers only (business partners, the workers), which are produced to be screened exclusively within the factory walls.

In 1904, for instance, the American Mutoscope and Biograph Company shot more than twenty films for the Westinghouse Corporation, showing aspects of the production process or parts of the company's facilities. They were projected at the 1904 Louisiana Purchase Exhibition in St. Louis. This is an example of a company commissioning films for public relations purposes. However, what gets lost when we compare them to "process films" is the intelligibility of the production process. "Instead," Wiatr argues, "the films offered a panorama of visual instants that unfold across time."[8] The Westinghouse films, in other words, differ from Pathé's *scènes (d'art et) d'industrie* in that they provide a much more general view of industrial work. Rather than describing the different stages of a specific production process, they present an overall corporate image – or maybe even an emblematic image of American industry – to visitors of the St. Louis Fair.

Finally, in a much broader conception of the genre, the so-called "factory-gate films," and in fact any film concerned with aspects of industrial labor, would also be included. Several company archives contain images of workers that are not related to their professional activities, showing instead more leisurely gatherings such as a collective day out or some festivity. The existence of different versions of Lumière's SORTIE D'USINE is an interesting case in point, as they may at one time have served a promotional function when used to demonstrate the origins of the miracle of living pictures, but, over time, also became social and cultural documents as representations of workers in France at the turn of the century. The factory-gate films produced by the English firm Mitchell & Kenyon are also promotional, but more specifically for the traveling showmen who commissioned them to incite the filmed workers to come and see the show in the hopes of recognizing themselves on the screen.[9] In addition, they are also important social and cultural documents, as visual records of turn-of-the-century industrial Britain.

Whichever approach one chooses, it should be clear that the category of industrial film always and necessarily is a constructed one, functioning in view of implicit or explicit purposes, leading to inclusions and exclusions, drawing boundaries, and establishing discursive fields. In what follows we shall limit the scope of our analyses to one type of process film in order to demonstrate how a given structural pattern can function in different pragmatic contexts.

Cheese making as a production process

Early non-fiction films about the way cheese is made are probably not among the first examples that come to mind when we talk about industrial films. However, as members of the larger category of "process films," they are, at least in a structural sense, hardly any different from films depicting the various stages of an industrial production process. The examples we want to discuss, in spite of their obvious similarities, present interesting variations that point to differences in the way they were intended to address audiences, while at the same time the multiple layers of meaning contained in their structural organization turn them into "open" texts that can fit into a variety of contexts.

The 1909 Pathé film COMMENT SE FAIT LE FROMAGE DE HOLLANDE (*How Dutch Cheese Is Made*) depicts the process of cheese making as a pre-industrial one, where traditional wooden tools are used by people wearing traditional costumes, working in a stereotypical Dutch environment of pastures and windmills.[10] The film begins and ends with shots of a girl in traditional dress holding a block of cheese up to the camera; in the final shot, the cheese carries a Pathé frères rooster logo. Because of the strong presence of "typically Dutch" imagery, COMMENT SE FAIT LE FROMAGE DE HOLLANDE is in fact not only a "process film," but also a "place film"[11] which creates a picturesque image of the Netherlands. In contrast, the 1920 British film CHEDDAR, produced by Ideal, presents the same process as an industrialized one, stressing the efficiency and modernity of British cheese making, while at the same time insisting on its quality, as the opening shot presents a prize-winning cheddar. In this respect, the film can be situated at the other end of the spectrum, almost at the antipode of COMMENT SE FAIT LE FROMAGE DE HOLLANDE.

Both films, however, show more or less the same sequence of stages in the cheese making process: the milking of the cows, curdling the milk by adding rennet, stirring the curd, cutting the solid curd, packing it into vats and pressing it, and weighing the cheese and transporting it to the market (the Pathé film also shows the salting and washing of the cheese, sales on the market, and preparation for export). Following the (sub)generic convention of the "process film," they depict the transformation of the raw material into a finished product.

The structure of both films – at a syntagmatic level – thus shows important similarities, but at the same time, each approaches its subject matter from a different angle. The Pathé production, by focusing on the traditions of Dutch cheese farmers as much as on the production process itself, and by emphasizing the picturesque aspects of the environment, overlaps in these respects with the travelogue (note that the title already stresses the location, in contrast to that of CHEDDAR). The British film takes more interest in the efficiency of the production chain, and therefore has more in common with films presenting modernization processes in rural areas.

Figures 1 and 2 KAAS (1943)

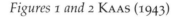

NOF/NIAM collection, Nederlands Insituut voor Beeld en Geluid

These differences, however, are not necessarily very revealing with regard to how either film functioned. Both may have taken on a variety of meanings, depending on the audience they were shown to. While a screening of the film about Dutch cheese making for a general French public quite probably foregrounded its "exotic" or "idyllic" aspects, an audience of schoolchildren may have been encouraged instead to focus on the procedures involved in the production of a type of food they ate on a daily basis. In the UK, the film about cheddar cheese production may have served to demonstrate the advanced level of automation in the countryside to a general public. Yet one can also imagine that it would have been used as a means of instruction with a more restricted audience of factory employees.

That either or even both of the films would have been used in an educational context seems particularly plausible when one considers another title dealing with the same subject, part of a Dutch collection of classroom films. The film KAAS (*Cheese*, 1943), produced by the Stiching Nederlandse Onderwijs Film (N. O.F.), also shows how cheese is made, from the milking of the cows onward. Even though KAAS was made considerably later, its textual strategies hardly differ from those used in the two earlier films. Like CHEDDAR, it focuses on the genesis of a product rather than picturing an average day on a busy family farm. Like the Pathé film, it shows procedures that seem to be based on experience and skill rather than an automated production chain. In its final scene the film briefly assumes the character of an advertising short. A close-up of a label with the cheese's brand name (reminiscent of the rooster emblem at the end of the Pathé film) is followed by a shot of a family enjoying the featured product at dinner time, thus explicitly reproducing the common structure of early "process films" that usually end with the consumption of the goods produced.

However, as opposed to both CHEDDAR and COMMENT SE FAIT LE FROMAGE DE HOLLANDE, KAAS was made especially – and exclusively – for a school audience. The film was distributed with a set of teachers' notes advising educators on how it should be used. At the time it was made, the N.O.F. was engaging in the production of a series of films based on what it termed *centres d'intérêt*. This concept was borrowed from the Belgian pedagogue Ovide Decroly, who advocated "global learning," a teaching method that was considered to value the pupils' "natural" interest in their immediate surroundings.[12] Each series was a combination of a so-called "foundation film" that documented the geographical characteristics of a particular region, and a few titles dealing with local activities that were supposed to be relevant to the children since they related to their everyday needs – for instance, the production of a particular type of food or a tool.[13] This production strategy not only strengthened the filmmakers in their belief in the purposefulness of their activities, but also allowed them to build on non-fiction traditions that had been developed in previous decades.

In most European countries the institutionalization of teaching films coincided with the expansion of the non-theatrical film circuit during and after the Second World War. Considering the relatively sudden increase in screening opportunities,[14] it is hardly surprising that films shown in 1940s classrooms and earlier non-fictional forms display a remarkable amount of continuity. Not only industrial and other production processes were depicted in great number: films with biological subjects took up the tradition of early scientific experimentation and relied on techniques such as time-lapse photography and microphotography to produce images of flowering plants and growing embryos. Films catalogued as "social geography" tended to focus on the way people in particular children lived elsewhere (doing the same things, but in slightly different ways) – thus continuing a long-standing tradition of (pseudo)ethnographic films.

Throughout the years and decades, teaching films certainly did develop their own particular features – characteristics by which they can be identified more easily as targeting a school audience. Efforts were taken to simplify what was being shown and structure it visually, as an aid to the pupils' memory. Even KAAS, produced in the early 1940s, is slower in pace and contains more repetition than industrial films on the same topics that were made at the time. In films with similar subjects, live-action images were sometimes alternated with schematic representations of crucial stages in the production process. In addition, written captions were used to introduce relevant terminology. In the film about cheese, for instance, pieces of paper are attached to containers to identify their contents, or the functions of specific ingredients. None of these properties, however, are exclusive to teaching films, nor can they be generalized as "typical" of all.

In addition, not all films used in classrooms were produced with a specific purpose in mind. The N.O.F.'s distribution catalogue, for instance, also contains items that were intended for specialized technical education. Such films were often straightforward training films, made by the companies that manufactured the featured products. Although some of the pupils to whom they were projected in schools may subsequently have been hired by those same enterprises, they were intended primarily for the instruction of current personnel. In addition, the institute also distributed award-winning Dutch documentaries that were valued for their artistic qualities at least as much as for what they might pass on in terms of actual subject knowledge.[15] Yet the question is exactly how much it matters whether or not films shown in classrooms were made with that specific audience in mind. In a school setting, after all, they would have functioned as teaching films, even if they had been "recycled" from very different prior contexts.

The example of the films about cheese making discussed above suggests that similar structures can serve a variety of ends, and, inversely, a variety of textual structures can function within the same institutional contexts. More precisely, the film texts are organized in ways sufficiently open to make them usable for different purposes.

Conclusions

In early non-fiction films, generic patterns overlap in many ways, regardless of the definition of genre used. Textual definitions have limited validity due to the fact that no type of patterning is exclusive to one genre; functional or institutional ones because of the migration of films from one context to another. Generic labeling tends to create a problematic illusion of coherence and clarity in an unstable and protean field. Similarly, talking about industrial films as a coherent genre conveniently hides the multiple forms, purposes, user contexts, and audiences that are linked to such a category.

Comprehending the potential complexity of seemingly simple and straightforward non-fiction films is facilitated by taking into account their textual openness, or "strategic weakness of form" (Hediger and Vonderau), with regard to the variety of institutional contexts in which they can be employed. Between entertainment and instruction, between the picturesque and the informative, between demonstration and attraction, between the cliché and the surprising, (early) industrial films, just like all other types of non-fictional views, can serve multiple purposes. In other words, there may be more to cheese making than meets the eye.

Notes

1.   This article was written as part of the Utrecht Media Research Program.
2.   For an overview of problems concerning genre definitions see Rick Altman, *Film/Genre* (London: BFI, 1999).
3.   Thomas Elsaesser, "Die Stadt von morgen: Filme zum Bauen und Wohnen," in Klaus Kreimeier, Antje Ehmann and Jeanpaul Goergen (eds.), *Geschichte des dokumentarischen Films in Deutschland. Band 2: Weimarer Republik 1918-1933* (Stuttgart: Reclam, 2005), pp. 381-409. See also Hediger and Vonderau as well as Zimmermann in this volume.
4.   See Frank Kessler, "Historische Pragmatik," *Montage/AV* 11, 2 (2002), pp. 104-112.
5.   John Grierson, *Grierson on Documentary* (London: Faber and Faber, 1966), p. 13. This is, at least, one of the ways to read the phrase. See the critical discussion of it by Brian Winston, *Claiming the Real: The Documentary Film Revisited* (London: BFI, 1995), pp. 11-14.

6.   Paul Rotha, "Some Principles of Documentary" [1935], in Richard M. Barsam (ed.), *Nonfiction Film Theory and Criticism* (New York: Dutton, 1978), p. 53.

7.   See Tom Gunning, "Before Documentary: Early nonfiction films and the 'view' aesthetic," in Daan Hertogs, Nico de Klerk (eds.), *Uncharted Territory: Essays on Early Nonfiction Film* (Amsterdam: Stichting Nederlands Filmmuseum, 1997), pp. 9-24.

8.   Elizabeth Wiatr, "Between Word, Image, and the Machine: visual education and films of industrial process," *Historical Journal of Film, Radio and Television* 22, 3 (2002), p. 338.

9.   On the Mitchell & Kenyon factory-gate films, see Tom Gunning, "Pictures of Crowd Splendor: The Michtell and Kenyon Factory Gate Films," in Vanessa Toulmin, Patrick Russell, Simon Popple (eds.), *The Lost World of Mitchell and Kenyon: Edwardian Britain on Film* (London: BFI, 2004), pp. 49-58.

10. For a detailed discussion of this film, see Frank Kessler, "Wie der Käse in Holland gemacht wird. Anmerkungen zum frühen *nonfiction*-Film," in Malte Hagener, Johann N. Schmidt, Michael Wedel (eds.), *Die Spur durch den Spiegel. Der Film in der Kultur der Moderne* (Berlin: Bertz Verlag, 2004), pp. 159-166.

11. See Tom Gunning, "Before Documentary," op. cit.

12. For more on Decroly's doctrine and its value to his contemporaries, see Marc Depaepe et al., "The Canonization of Ovide Decroly as a 'Saint' of the New Education," *History of Education Quarterly* 43, 2, pp. 224-249.

13. See Bert Hogenkamp, " 'De onderwijsfilm is geen Duitsche uitvinding.' A.A. Schoevers, Ph.A. Kohnstamm en de Nederlandse Onderwijs Film, 1941-1949," in *Stichting Film en Wetenschap – Audiovisueel Archief Jaarboek 1996* (Amsterdam: Stichting Film en Wetenschap/Nederlands Audiovisueel Archief, 1997), p. 66.

14. See, for instance, Andrew Buchanan, *The Film in Education* (London: Phoenix House, 1951), p. 80.

15. Cf. N. Crama, "Drie Nederlandse documentaires," *Mededelingen van de Stichting Nederlandse Onderwijs Film* 1, 1 (1958), pp. 4-6.

Images of Efficiency

The Films of Frank B. Gilbreth

Scott Curtis

From 1912 to his death in 1924, Frank B. Gilbreth – a disciple of Frederick W. Taylor and, with his wife, Lillian, one of the most prolific popularizers of scientific management – made hundreds of films designed to document, analyze, and correct worker movements in a "quest for the one best way" to do any given job.[1] Scientific management, of course, swept through the American workplace at the turn of the 20th century as Progressive ideals of reform and uplift joined forces with industrial trends toward increased specialization and rationalization of labor.[2] Reformers and industrialists alike could agree that "efficiency" and the elimination of "waste" (economic for the industrialist, social for the reformer) were vitally important to the moral and productive longevity of the nation.[3] This social and economic agenda attempted to assuage or solve bitter struggles between management and labor, especially as workers protested – by forming unions, among other tactics – the increased centralization of power in the hands of managers.[4] Taylor's management system appropriated the rhetoric of scientific objectivity and neutrality while regulating worker productivity. His method of regulation, which he dubbed "time study" (essentially measuring worker efficiency with a stopwatch), often drew protests from both workers and managers for its inaccuracy and reliance on the "subjective" skills of whoever happened to be holding the stopwatch.[5] Designed to be an improvement on Taylor's methods and thus to garner cooperation from worker and manager alike, Gilbreth's method of "motion study" via motion pictures and other visual technologies promised an even more thoroughly "scientific" and "objective" solution. Frank and Lillian Gilbreth succeeded in promoting motion study to industry as an essential tool for designing and measuring work. Together, time and motion studies are still used today as a means of finding the "methods of greatest economy and for measuring labor accomplishment."[6]

Exactly what kind of work did these images do? On the one hand, these images remind us of the work of Etienne-Jules Marey or others like him, who used filmic and photographic technology to measure human locomotion in order to understand the origins and limits of human fatigue.[7] But Gilbreth did not use his films in this way; his method of extracting data from the films, as we shall see, was positively crude compared to Marey's, or especially compared to the sophisticated photogrammetry of Wilhelm Braune and Otto Fischer of Germany in the 1880s.[8] On the other hand, some have argued that Gilbreth's films do not do much work at all. Brian Price, one of the leading experts on the Gilbreths and their legacy, maintains that their films were primarily promotional tools for selling the Gilbreth package: "That their strategies and techniques survived and prospered is testimony less to their intrinsic worth as they practiced them than to the image of their worth which the Gilbreths carefully cultivated."[9]

Both of these positions are true, in their own way, but both overstate their case. The Gilbreth films belong fully neither to the tradition of Marey nor of P. T. Barnum. There is a little bit of both Marey and Barnum in Gilbreth; we need to look closely at the Gilbreth films and their application in order to sort out the kinds of work they accomplished. I suggest that we analyze the way Gilbreth used his images in much the same way that he analyzed the motions of workers. For example, after Gilbreth had filmed, say, a worker assembling something, he would submit this film to repeated viewings, indicating on a data sheet the kinds and duration of each movement made by the worker's left hand. Then he would do the same for the right hand. This he called "micromotion study." (Mere "motion study," by contrast, involves documentation and measurement of the task without detailed, frame-by-frame extraction of data.) He would then translate this data into what he called a "simultaneous motion chart" (or SIMO chart), which would graphically compare the kind and amount of work of each hand. The right hand, for example, might be doing more work than the left. From this, Gilbreth would figure out a way to distribute the work equitably and symmetrically, hence efficiently, thus decreasing worker fatigue and increasing productivity.

We can do the same for the Gilbreth films themselves. What kind of work do they do? I submit that they do two kinds: productive and promotional. Only by carefully charting out the uses to which a Gilbreth film is put can we understand the relationship between these two kinds of work, the "right hand" and the "left hand." It may turn out that the distribution of work is asymmetrical, but it is important to note that whatever the distribution, Gilbreth is deriving significant productivity from his films by giving them multiple, simultaneous tasks. Indeed, in this sense, Gilbreth's visual technologies are incredibly efficient images. They provide, at once, documentation of processes that the analyst can study and improve on, as well as images of efficiency for workers to study and to assimilate. Because the films both document and promote, they are exemplary industrial films; they demonstrate a process while promoting that process as "the one best way," much like all sponsored films. Here, however, the process they document (the worker assembling something) is not the primary product. Instead, the product is the process of filming, or the image of efficiency that the documentation represents. In other words, Gilbreth was not promoting any spe-

Figure 1 Motion-study experts still use Gilbreth's simultaneous motion (SIMO) charting system to display graphically the work of each hand for a given task

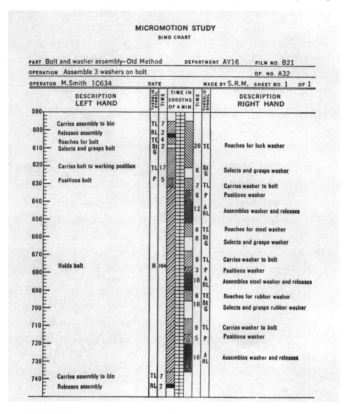

Ralph M. Barnes, *Motion and Time Study* (New York 1980)

cific process that he filmed so much as the films themselves as a process. The act of filming itself becomes the product.

However, that product is careful not to disturb class relations. In fact, those relations are built into the process, even into our generic distinctions between scientific and educational film. For if we inspect his method closely, we also find that the films reveal interesting "right-hand, left-hand" dualities within documentary practice, especially regarding the relationship between science ("objectivity") and spectacle ("subjectivity"). And this relationship between science and spectacle arguably rehearses or reinforces the relationship between "manager" and "worker." That is, the line between them is inscribed not only in how workers are filmed, but how the films are viewed and how they are used to persuade viewers. I would therefore argue that the difference between "science" and "spectacle" aligns neatly with class divisions. This essay, then, will perform something of a "micromotion study" of the Gilbreth films and photographs in order to chart out exactly the kind of work they did; this will then provide the data necessary to assess their legacy and their significance to an understanding of industrial film theory and practice.

Efficient images

It is perhaps misleading to call Frank Gilbreth a "disciple" of Taylor. Certainly, by the time they actually met in 1907 Gilbreth was an ardent admirer of Taylor and his system; Gilbreth had already established himself as a successful contractor who had won wide acclaim for his innovative and efficient approaches to bricklaying. Taylor, for his part, was well-known for his "scientific" approach to management and considered himself a patriarch and protector of the system bearing his name. But for some reason Taylor did not adopt Gilbreth into his inner circle of experts, whom he trained and considered the only rightful heirs to scientific management.[10] The Taylorites were cautious towards Gilbreth, but willing to use his skills for self-promotion to their ends: with Taylor's blessing and encouragement, Gilbreth often made public presentations on behalf of scientific management. Gilbreth's wife, Lillian, was a full partner in her husband's endeavors; her degree in psychology proved invaluable for public discussions of the benefits of scientific management for workers. But when Frank and Lillian decided to quit construction and start consulting, the Taylorites saw them as competitors rather than collaborators, and a rift developed that by 1914 was unbridgeable. Gilbreth's use of film and photography must thus be seen as first an improvement on Taylor's methods, but ultimately as a means of differentiating the Gilbreths from Taylor. Specifically, while Taylor employed a stop watch in order to speed up worker productivity, Gilbreth used photographs and films to find alternative work methods; whereas Taylor concentrated on *speed*, Gilbreth concentrated on *efficiency*.

Gilbreth first started using motion picture technology in 1912 for his installation of scientific management at the New England Butt Company in Providence, Rhode Island, "a small foundry and factory employing about three hundred men in the production of braiding machines for making shoe laces, women's dress trimmings and electrical wire insulation."[11] To achieve his stated goal of "out-Tayloring Taylor,"[12] Gilbreth employed a motion picture camera to record the motions, duration, and conditions surrounding a job. However, on the factory floor the "conditions" of a job – especially the lighting conditions –

were not easily filmed, so Gilbreth built a "Betterment Room" on the site, specifically constructed so that worker motions could be filmed. The worker and his or her working area or machine were brought from the factory floor and set up in the room; Gilbreth continued to use this approach for all his films. Two elements of the "mise-en-scène" of these films are noteworthy. First, we see that each worker and his or her station is placed against a white background with a four-inch grid pattern.

Figure 2 A typical shot from one of Gilbreth's motion study films. Note the chronometer, the grid, and the camera angle
THE QUEST OF THE ONE BEST WAY *(USA 1968)*

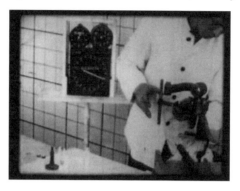

The grid is ostensibly designed for easy measurement of worker movements; when the film is examined slowly or under the magnifying glass, the analyst can determine the length of a movement against the grid.

I say "ostensibly," however, because close inspection of the films reveals that only the crudest estimates of distance could be made with this system – the angle of the camera is almost always completely inappropriate for this kind of detail work. That is, Gilbreth only rarely filmed his subjects from an appropriate angle and height if he were indeed interested in taking accurate measurements from the photogram. Instead, the grid more likely serves other purposes: the white background provides contrast and extra light, and the grid, while giving a rough estimate of distance, also gives the *impression* of "scientificity." Like Muybridge's grid background, which is useful as a guide if not a precision instrument, it provides a fig leaf of objectivity.

Yet Gilbreth repeatedly relies on proclamations of precision. The second notable element of the image is the chronometer – a clock, placed in view of the camera, with a second hand that moves 20 times a minute. Given a steady frame rate and an accurate chronometer, Gilbreth could reliably measure the duration of any given movement. Gilbreth boasted, "Our latest microchronometer records intervals of time down to any degree of accuracy required. We have made, and used, in our work of motion study investigations of hospital practice and surgery, one that records times to the millionth of an hour."[13] This, I believe, is bluster. In research films for which measurement is crucial it would be incongruous, to say the least, to find such extraordinarily precise measurements of time alongside such a disregard for accurate measurements of distance.[14] Moreover, given the methodological constraints of micromotion study, nothing could be gained by such small increments. Clearly, we cannot compare Gilbreth's motion pictures with bona fide research films; precision – or even measurement – was not the primary goal in Gilbreth's motion studies. True enough, not all research films measure, but my point here is that the grid and the chronometer in Gilbreth's films are more *promotional* than productive. The instruments do a different kind of work than that claimed by their accompanying rhetoric. But this is not to say that they are completely unproductive. So what information is the image under motion study expected to reveal? What work, other than promotional, is the film expected to perform?

The answers to these questions depend less on the content of the images than who is looking at them. That is, the work the films perform – productive and promotional – is divided between two kinds of viewers: managers and workers, broadly speaking. The films do one kind of work for experts with a trained eye and another kind of work for laymen with an untrained eye. This division of labor is not unusual; we find it precisely at the difference between research films and educational films. Scientists make research films in order to document phenomena or processes. Research films can, on the one hand, document aspects of the object that the researcher has already observed and confirmed; in this case, the film is not the primary object of observation, it is merely a confirmation or illustration of it. Or, on the other hand, the motion picture can be used to reveal new aspects of the object unavailable to normal observation (as in time-lapse cinematography, for example); in this case, the film itself is the primary object of observation, a substitute for the object – the film is the ground for exploration and discovery. In the first kind of research film, questions have already been asked and answered. In the second kind, the film prompts entirely new questions. Both versions of the research film, however, presume an expert eye.[15] Both versions are predicated on a particular mode of viewing, namely, the kind of close, undistracted observation that is associated with scientific method. We can see this as well in the actual form of a typical research film: unedited footage, nearly always without sound (even in the sound era), and without explanatory captions or narrative. If any explanations are given, they are usually in accompanying articles or lectures. By studiously avoiding the structures of identification and the techniques of emotional involvement entailed in most documentary editing patterns, for example, the *form* of the films implies the objective, distanced, expert gaze of a scientific observer.

Educational films, on the other hand, presume an untrained eye. Often, the raw footage of the research film is edited, explained, and packaged for a lay audience. Sometimes material is photographed specifically for the film in an easy-to-understand form and then edited into a story structure or similar rhetorical approach. Here we can make a useful distinction based on modes of viewing: if the research film presumes "observation," the educational film presumes "spectatorship." The first presumes "contemplation," while the second presumes "distraction." The distinction depends not only on the difference between the attentive gaze of the scientist and the distracted gaze of the layperson, but also on the presumed *direction of knowledge* in relation to spectator and screen. In the research film, the knowledge of the scientist flows toward the image, thereby framing the phenomenon depicted. In the educational film, the knowledge represented on screen flows toward the spectator.

Let me put it another way. Scientific observation connotes an attentive, measuring gaze, but the most important aspect of scientific observation is the context the scientist brings to it; the researcher assimilates observed data into an existing framework of knowledge. What the scientific observer already knows frames what he or she observes, thus incorporating or juxtaposing new data with old and thereby generating new insights. "Observation" therefore implies the *production* of knowledge. On the other hand, the lay spectator learns from the educational film, but does not bring new knowledge to it. (Structurally speaking, the position of "spectator" precludes that possibility because he or she cannot enter the conversation among experts who produce knowledge.) "Spectatorship" therefore implies the *consumption* of knowledge. The division of labor between these two kinds of "useful" film therefore echo in their presumed mode of viewing a hierarchy (even a class system) between experts and laymen – or between managers and workers.

For the present discussion, however, the distinction between research and educational films is less important than their presumptive modes of viewing. Even so, the boundary between observation (with its connotations of expertise, objectivity, and productivity) and spectatorship (inexperience, subjectivity, consumption) is by no means crystal clear. Any given viewer may occupy either position at any given time, even alternating positions in the course of a single film. But the presumed modes of viewing – the viewer to whom the films address themselves – allows us to see clearly the different kinds of work the Gilbreth films are expected to perform. Specifically, I find four kinds of work: On the one hand (say, the "right" hand), there is the work of *standardization* and *problem-solving*. On the other ("left") hand, we can see the work of *visualization* and *promotion*.

What kind of productive work did the films do for Gilbreth and his band of experts? First, they *standardized* the object of investigation. Taylor's method of time study required the expert to time the worker, as many times as needed, as he or she performed the task. Each performance was different, of course, not only in terms of the worker, but also in terms of the expert's "performance" of the timing itself. Instead, Gilbreth filmed the worker's best performance and that record served as the standard and object of study. Gilbreth thereby eliminated the variables of human interaction while simultaneously standardizing the worker (this one performance becoming the exemplar of all who perform the task) and the work (both the task under observation and the observation itself). Moreover, because film decomposes and recombines movement into standardized, individual units (the film frames, the shot), it was the perfect tool for Gilbreth's similar analysis and synthesis of the worker's body.[16] As Elspeth Brown notes,

> The filming of repetitive industrial labor encapsulates the logic of the industrializing process... The ways in which Gilbreth saw the working body had already been structured by an industrialized consciousness predicated on decomposition, interchangeability, standardization, and kineticism. Film presented itself in 1912 as a logical methodological culmination of Gilbreth's already fully industrialized visuality.[17]

Second, the films performed *problem-solving* tasks. With the film in hand, Gilbreth reviewed the film, looking for ways to improve the efficiency of the worker's performance. In this respect, the films functioned as research films in that close observation by an expert eye could reveal information not normally available.[18] Micromotion study – the minute recording of worker movements via photographic and cinematographic technology – is also an important part of the problem-solving process, according to Gilbreth. "From the data on the film and the observations of the observer, can be formulated an improved method."[19] But we should be cautious about assigning micromotion study too large a role in the problem-solving process. It is important to note that neither Gilbreth nor future motion-study experts regularly used this form of analysis. Because it requires a considerable amount of detail work from highly paid experts, it is a very expensive process; one expert even notes that "a micromotion study is often the last resort."[20] Then there is the fact that, in Gilbreth's case at least, it was apparently not very necessary. Brian Price argues persuasively that the improvements that Gilbreth made at his factory installations were not the result of motion study, but due instead to efficient work design and the application of basic principles of scientific management.[21]

This is not to discount the continuing significance of motion studies for the field of work measurement. I do not want to characterize motion studies as an empty gesture; a simultaneous motion chart does the important work of vividly displaying problems in work design. But this is exactly my point. Motion studies are only secondarily a problem-solving technique. It is primarily a process that translates a film's data into graphic terms. It is a means for rendering one kind of image (detailed, moving) into another (simplified, still) in order to visualize more clearly the essential elements of the task. Once these elements are identified, alternative solutions can be proposed. But more importantly, this rendering process provides a graphic image of *what efficiency and inefficiency look like*. Motion and micromotion studies can undoubtedly solve problems. But there is evidence to indicate that, for Gilbreth, the educational aspects of this technique were more significant than its problem-solving capacity. Motion studies have not been used primarily for measurement or for work design; they were used first and foremost to visualize an image of efficiency.

Images of efficiency

Visualization was absolutely crucial to the Gilbreth program, but it also replicated the manager-worker hierarchy. According to the Gilbreths, to visualize is to plan, to imagine a future solution based on observation of present details. But not everyone is equipped to observe and to visualize; only the trained eye could be expected to do both. In fact, the ability to observe and to visualize is precisely what distinguishes a manager from a worker or, more broadly, an expert from a layman. In *The Psychology of Management* (1914), Lillian Gilbreth describes visualization in exactly these terms:

> The best planner is he who – other things being equal – is the most ingenious, the most experienced and the best observer. It is an art to observe; it requires persistent attention. The longer and the more the observer observes, the more details, and variables affecting details, he observes. The untrained observer could not expect to compete with one of special natural talent who has also been trained. It is not every man who is fitted by nature to observe closely, hence to plan. To observe is a condition precedent to visualizing. Practice in visualizing makes for increasing the faculty of constructive imagination. He with the best constructive imagination is the master planner.[22]

What role, then, do the films and photographs play for the expert? Certainly, they are an aid to visualization: Gilbreth's images helped the specialist in planning the most efficient work design by serving as a document of the problem from which to visualize the solution. Yet the importance of images as an aid to visualization is different for the expert and the worker. In fact, there is the im-

plication that the expert is not tied to these technologies in the same way that
the worker is:

> It is not always recognized that some preliminary motion study and time study can
> be done without the aid of any accurate devices. It is even less often recognized that
> such work, when most successful, is usually done by one thoroughly conversant
> with, and skilled in, the use of the most accurate devices... With this training and
> equipment, a motion- and time-study expert can obtain preliminary results without
> devices, that, to the untrained or uninformed, seem little short of astounding.[23]

The expert can visualize on his own, without the aid of images. This is not the
case, however, for the worker, who needs an image in order to visualize.

> The average engineer, who becomes, through his training and the necessity of his
> work, a good visualiser, even though he is not one by nature, often fails to realize the
> small capacity for visualisation possessed by the average person. A long experience in
> teaching in the industries made this fact impressive and led to the invention of the
> cyclegraph, and, later, the chronocyclegraph method of recording, in order to aid the
> non-visualising worker to grasp motion economy easily.[24]

Experts (*cum* managers) can see the solution in their heads; they can visualize.
Workers cannot, so they must rely on visual aids. Only the lack of a little imagi-
nation holds the worker back, apparently. Cyclegraphs are the best example of
Gilbreth's use of images to aid visualization.

These were still photographs of workers as they performed their task with a
small incandescent bulb on their fingers. The shutter would remain open for the
duration of the task, so that the resulting photograph would show the path the
worker's movements had taken as bright, white lines. By interrupting the light
at regular intervals, these continuous bright lines would become discontinuous
dashes of light that indicated the duration, as well as the direction of the movement; Gilbreth called these photographs "chronocyclegraphs." (Gilbreth also
experimented with stereoscopic versions, which he of course dubbed "stereo-
chronocyclegraphs.") Mimicking Marey's use of similar devices to capture the
variables of human locomotion, the cyclegraphs were, according to Gilbreth,
crucial for demonstrating the "paths of least waste."[25] Gilbreth even crafted
wire models of these paths of light in order to provide a "tactile" display of the
one best way. (These models were originally developed to help the blind, bringing to mind Kittler's dictum that "media begin with a physiological defi-
ciency."[26]) Whether these photographs and models actually worked as training
aids is another question entirely. Price shows that Gilbreth's systems unraveled
– the improvements in worker efficiency lost – as soon as he left the factory.[27]
Even if their effectiveness as educational tools is in doubt, they provided a compelling image of efficiency – compelling enough that Gilbreth continued to get

Figure 3 To create his "cyclegraphs", Gilbreth attached small lights to the worker's hand, photographed the path the hands took during task, then created three-dimensional wire models for instruction

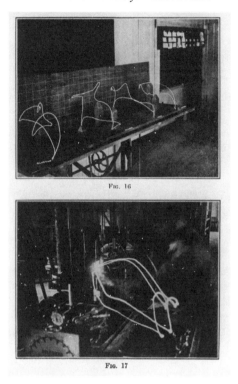

F.B. and L.M. Gilbreth, *Applied Motion Study* (New York 1917)

work. What does efficiency look like? It has smooth lines, simplified design, and standardized geometries. We can even see this aesthetic in the simultaneous motion charts: Efficiency is here clearly symmetrical and consists of geometrical units, like bricks, recalling Gilbreth's first career. (As Sharon Corwin has argued, this set of choices eventually found its way into American art, especially the work of such Precisionists as Charles Sheeler.[28]) The aesthetic of cleanliness and order – the very picture of efficiency – pervades Gilbreth's images; this is arguably their most effective instructional technique.

This presentation of efficiency may also be the true function of these images. For if Gilbreth's films and photographs did not function primarily to measure, to provide solutions, or to instruct, what were they really meant to do? Who were they really for? Neither experts nor workers, but *owners*. Gilbreth often boasted to his wife about the rhetorical power of his images, their ability to "chloroform" potential clients into procuring his services.[29] And, as Richard Lindstrom has demonstrated, Gilbreth used the seductive lure of "being in the movies" to coax cooperation from otherwise recalcitrant workers and managers.[30] Gilbreth's films and photographs were like a calling card, a snappy, eye-catching technique that was instantly attached to his name.[31] For example, after developing the cyclegraph, Gilbreth envisioned applications in a variety of fields, especially sports, the publicity from which he hoped would gain him a larger audience. He teamed up with Walter Camp, the famous Yale football coach, to make a series of motion studies of athletes. His first in the series – cyclegraphs of a number of champion golfers – received national coverage in *Golf Illustrated* and *Vanity Fair* in 1916. The images illustrated the path of the golfers' swing and the articles held out the promise of greater golfing "efficiency."[32] It is not clear, however, what information a golfer could glean from the article – or the technique – in order to improve his or her swing. Of course, this is exactly the issue: Gilbreth's images are not about information; they are about the process itself. Gilbreth appears to be selling solutions (and there may be some in the back somewhere), but he is really selling a process of visualizing an *imagined* solution, a utopian efficiency. He is mostly selling the technique and wonder of the camera. In this respect, Gilbreth's legacy is aligned less with Marey than with Muybridge, or especially with Harold Edgerton, the MIT engineer whose high-speed photographs received much attention and acclaim, but revealed very little scientifically.

This emphasis on promoting the process while giving the impression of objectivity and utility seems to also be the defining feature of the industrial or sponsored film. Industrial films usually follow a documentary format while serving as an advertisement or promotional spot for a product, process, or company. As Vinzenz Hediger and Patrick Vonderau argue, the industrial film contributes to the establishment and maintenance of organizations in three ways: it provides a "record" of industry events and practice, induces employees and others to share goals through its "rhetoric," and adheres to the principles of "rationalization" that aim at improving performance.[33] We can see clearly how Gilbreth's films fit into this scheme, and how they seamlessly do all three things at once. Indeed, Gilbreth's films are incredibly efficient in that they serve multiple functions simultaneously: they standardize the object of study, provide the ground for solutions to problems in work design, visualize the solutions for workers, and promote the solutions to managers and owners. But they ultimately promote more than a workplace solution – they promote themselves as images of efficiency and as the proprietary process of Frank B. Gilbreth.

Notes

My thanks to John Carnwath for valuable research assistance.

1.   This phrase, the motto of the Gilbreth family, is strewn throughout their work, but see especially Lillian Moller Gilbreth, *The Quest of the One Best Way: A Sketch of the Life of Frank Bunker Gilbreth* (Easton, PA: Hive Publishing Co., 1973 [1954]).

2.   On Taylor and scientific management, see Monte A. Calvert, *The Mechanical Engineer in America, 1830-1910: Professional Cultures in Conflict* (Baltimore: Johns Hopkins Press, 1967); Daniel Nelson, *Frederick W. Taylor and the Rise of Scientific Management* (Madison: University of Wisconsin Press, 1980); Daniel Nelson (ed.), *A Mental Revolution: Scientific Management since Taylor* (Columbus: Ohio State University Press, 1992); and Robert Kanigel, *The One Best Way: Frederick Winslow Taylor and the Enigma of Efficiency* (New York: Viking, 1997).

3.   On efficiency as a cultural phenomenon, see Samuel P. Hays, *Conservation and the Gospel of Efficiency: The Progressive Conservation Movement, 1890-1920* (Cambridge, MA: Harvard University Press, 1959); Samuel Haber, *Efficiency and Uplift: Scientific Management in the Progressive Era, 1890-1920* (Chicago and London: University of Chicago Press, 1964); Cecelia Tichi, *Shifting Gears: Technology, Literature, Culture in Modernist America* (Chapel Hill: University of North Carolina Press, 1987); and Ed Andrew, *Closing the Iron Cage: The Scientific Management of Work and Leisure* (Montreal and New York: Black Rose Books, 1999).

4.   For more on scientific management and its history with labor unions, see Milton J. Nadworny, *Scientific Management and the Unions, 1900-1932: A Historical Analysis* (Cambridge, MA: Harvard University Press, 1955); and Lizabeth Cohen, *Making a New Deal: Industrial Workers in Chicago, 1919-1939* (Cambridge and New York: Cambridge University Press, 1990).

5.   For his own explication, see Frederick Winslow Taylor, *Scientific Management; Comprising Shop Management, the Principles of Scientific Management [and] Testimony before the Special House Committee* (Westport, CN: Greenwood Press, 1972). For more on Taylor and his legacy, see the volumes by Daniel Nelson above.

6.   Ralph Mosser Barnes, *Motion and Time Study*, 2nd ed. (New York and London: J. Wiley & Sons, 1937), vii.

7.   On the science of work in Europe, see Anson Rabinbach, *The Human Motor: Energy, Fatigue, and the Origins of Modernity* (New York: Basic Books, 1990). On Marey, see Marta Braun, *Picturing Time: The Work of Etienne-Jules Marey (1830-1904)* (Chicago: University of Chicago Press, 1992), esp. Chapter 8. For more on Gilbreth's relation to Marey's legacy, see Ramón Reichert, "Der Arbeitsstudienfilm: Eine verborgene Geschichte des Stummfilms," *Medien & Zeit: Kommunikation in Vergangenheit und Gegenwart*, 5 (2002): pp. 46-57; Philipp Sarasin, "Die Rationalisierung des Körpers: Über 'Scientific Management' und 'biologische Rationalisierung,' " in *Geschichtswissenschaft und Diskursanalyse* (Frankurt am Main: Suhrkamp, 2003); and Florian Hoof, " 'The One Best Way': Bildgebende Verfahren der Ökonomie und die Innovation der Managementtheorie nach 1860," *Montage AV: Zeitschrift für Theorie und Geschichte audiovisueller Kommunikation* 15, 1 (2006), pp. 123-38.

8.   Wilhelm Braune and Otto Fischer, *The Human Gait*, trans. Paul Maquet and Ronald Furlong (Berlin and New York: Springer, 1987).

9.   Brian Price, "Frank and Lillian Gilbreth and the Manufacture and Marketing of Motion Study, 1908-1924," *Business and Economic History*, 18 (1989), p. 88.

10. The best presentation of the often troubled relationship between Taylor and Gilbreth is Milton J. Nadworny, "Frederick Taylor and Frank Gilbreth: Competition in Scientific Management," *Business History Review* 31, 1 (1957), pp. 23-34.

11. Brian Charles Price, *One Best Way: Frank and Lillian Gilbreth's Transformation of Scientific Management, 1885-1940* (Dissertation, Purdue University, 1987), p. 153.

12. Ibid., p. 154.

13. Frank Bunker Gilbreth and Lillian Moller Gilbreth, *Applied Motion Study: A Collection of Papers on the Efficient Method to Industrial Preparedness* (Easton, PA: Publishing Co., 1973 [1917]), p. 66.

14. Unless, of course, distance isn't an issue, as in the time-lapse films of Jean Comandon, for example.

15. Gotthard Wolf makes a similar distinction, calling the first kind a "Dokumentationsfilm" (documentary film) and the second a "Forschungsfilm" (research film). But since I am focusing here on a distinction based on mode of observation, I will group them both in the same camp. Gotthard Wolf, *Der Wissenschaftliche Dokumentationsfilm und die Encyclopedia Cinematographica* (Munich: Johann Ambrosius Barth, 1967).

16. Gilbreth notes that the combination of motions "can never be considered standardized till each separate motion is a standard." Frank Bunker Gilbreth, *Motion Study: A Method for Increasing the Efficiency of the Workman* (New York: D. Van Nostrand Co., 1911), p. 70.

17. Elspeth H. Brown, *The Corporate Eye: Photography and the Rationalization of American Commercial Culture, 1884-1929* (Baltimore: Johns Hopkins University Press, 2005), p. 84.

18. The expertise required at this stage is underlined by Gilbreth's habit of reviewing negatives rather than making positive prints. See Gilbreth, *Applied Motion Study*, p. 81.

19. Ibid., p. 46.

20. Ralph Mosser Barnes, *Motion and Time Study: Design and Measurement of Work*, 7th ed. (New York: Wiley, 1980), p. 111.

21. As Price explains, "Gilbreth estimated that by February 1913 word of his invention had been broadcast in at least two million individual copies of periodicals alone. Of course, Gilbreth did not publicize the facts that the development of the basic packet and bench braider assembly method at the Butt Company preceded the installation of micro-motion study equipment; that because of the limitations of his artificial lights he was still dependent on stop watch time study for task setting; and that when he attributed the assemblers' increased output to improved, micro-motion studied methods, he subdivided and redistributed the jobs of filing, fitting, and inspecting, and did not discount the possible impetus to higher output of either increased supervision or financial incentives on the performance of the workers. Micro-motion study, as presented, was on the map." Price, *One Best Way* (1987), pp. 206-207.

22. Lillian Moller Gilbreth, *The Psychology of Management: The Function of the Mind in Determining, Teaching and Installing Methods of Least Waste* (Easton, PA: Hive Publishing Company, 1973 [1914]), pp. 76-77.

23. Gilbreth, *Applied Motion Study*, pp. 60-61.
24. Ibid., p. 83.
25. Ibid., figure 16.
26. Frank Bunker Gilbreth and Lillian Evelyn Gilbreth, *Motion Study for the Handicapped* (London: G. Routledge & Sons Ltd., 1920); Friedrich A. Kittler, *Discourse Networks 1800/1900*, trans. Michael Metteer with Chris Cullens (Palo Alto, CA: Stanford University Press, 1990), p. 231.
27. Price, *Frank and Lillian Gilbreth* (1989), pp. 94-95.
28. Sharon Corwin, "Picturing Efficiency: Precisionism, Scientific Management, and the Effacement of Labor," *Representations* 84 (2003), pp. 139-65.
29. Richard Lindstrom, "'They All Believe They Are Undiscovered Mary Pickfords': Workers, Photography, and Scientific Management," *Technology and Culture* 41,4 (2000), pp. 725-51, here 736.
30. Ibid.
31. Brown quotes a letter from Frank to Lillian about the impact of the cyclegraphs: "I have made a decided hit... The cyclegraphs will make anybody sit up and take notice." Quoted in Brown, *Corporate Eye*, p. 101.
32. See Brown, *Corporate Eye*, pp. 102-106.
33. See Vinzenz Hediger and Patrick Vonderau, "Record, Rhetoric, Rationalization: Industrial Organization and Film," in this volume.

"What Hollywood Is to America, the Corporate Film Is to Switzerland"

Remarks on Industrial Film as Utility Film

Yvonne Zimmermann

Until recently, industrial or corporate film has been a neglected category in film studies, despite the often quoted fact that the very first work in film history, the Lumières' SORTIE D'USINE (*Workers Leaving the Factory*, 1895) was an industrial film.[1] This has various causes. Due to the traditional focus of film studies on feature film, interest in non-fiction film, which includes industrial film, developed late and remains comparatively limited even today. In addition, from the perspective of production, industrial film belongs to the category of commissioned or sponsored film, and from a pragmatic perspective, it can be considered a subgenre of the utility film. Both sponsored and utility film contradict the idea of film as the work of an author, of film as art. Therefore, they do not fit into a concept of film studies that is primarily concerned with film art. While this fixation on "art" can be historically understood as an attempt to legitimate the subject as an academic discipline, a wider perspective is necessary today, one that examines the entire field of audiovisual production, dissemination, and consumption of non-fiction films, that looks at amateur film practice in addition to professional, and that examines the whole spectrum of film consumption outside commercial cinemas, which already played an important role well before the introduction of video, DVD, and the Internet.

The exclusion of industrial film from the canon of objects worthy of academic research can be traced back to the *auteur* film movement of the 1950s and 1960s. The establishment of the *auteur* was based on a radical rejection of the sponsored film as an outdated, ideologically and artistically unacceptable form of production: "The sponsored film is a danger to its maker; only the precise awareness of this danger, only the iron will to resist the danger, can save the author,"[2] stated Swiss director Alexander J. Seiler, who himself took the "arduous and artistically dangerous detour through sponsored film" before he made SIAMO ITALIANI (*The Italians*, 1964), one of the first works of the so-called "New" Swiss Film.[3]

Sponsored and *auteur* films seemed to be two incompatible concepts.[4] In a socially and politically radicalized environment that understood film exclusively as a medium of personal artistic expression and social critique the industrial film was doubly frowned upon: as a sponsored film and as a film spon-

sored by the "embodiment of capitalism," the industry. Because of its "advertising function," Seiler denied it any "artistic or intellectual" value. Most film
critics shared this opinion, as did film studies to a large part. Accordingly, the
few industrial films that have been studied more closely are formally ambitious,
avant-garde works that bear the signature of *auteurs* like Walter Ruttmann,
Hans Richter, or Willy Zielke, and can thus be inserted seamlessly into the corpus of art film. Such is the case not only for industrial film, but for non-fiction
film in general: without a recognizable "signature," it remains a neglected category in film historiography.[5]

"What Hollywood is to America, the corporate film is to Switzerland,"
claimed Peter M. Wettler, head of Condor Documentaries in the 1980s, thus underlining the eminent economic importance of industrial film in certain countries such as Switzerland, where, in the past as in the present, it is the backbone
of the domestic film industry.[6] But academic analysis of industrial film, as has
begun in numerous European countries in the last few years, cannot simply
seek to justify or even ennoble the subject by either proving its dominance in
film business or searching for unknown works by various *auteurs*.[7] Evaluating
industrial film in terms of film art makes little sense, and neither does restricting
it to its value as a historical source, which historians – before media studies –
have begun to scrutinize. What seems to be more fruitful is a historical and
theoretical study of industrial film as a media practice that focuses on its function as utility film, a genre that has hardly been researched as yet. Since industrial film incorporates economic interests, analyzing it can produce knowledge
on the significance and functions of media in business. Beyond that, such
knowledge can help us to understand the workings of utility films in political,
social, and cultural contexts.

Serial film analysis and historical analysis of context

In the following essay, I will outline dominant characteristics, basic functions,
and exhibition practices of the industrial film by means of concrete examples.
Thereby, I will suggest a methodological approach to industrial film that proved
of value in a three-and-a-half year research project of the Swiss National Science
Foundation on the *History of Non-Fiction Film in Switzerland (1896 to 1964)*,
which focused on industrial and commissioned film, alongside tourism and
educational film. Most of the following examples are drawn from the corpus of
this project.[8]

In order to come to terms with the types, aesthetics, rhetoric, functions,
and utilization practices relevant to industrial film, I suggest a combination of

Figure 1 The ad promotes performance, the film shows it in
STARR-DREH-MASCHINE SDM *(1943)*

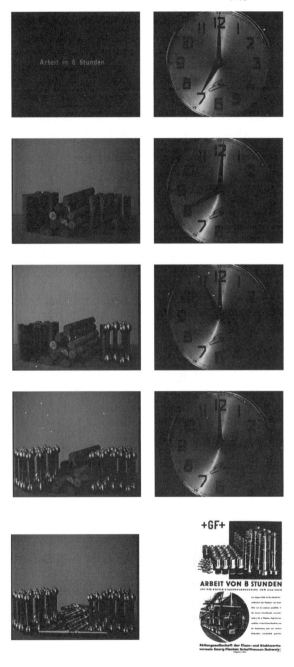

"serial" film analysis and analysis of historical context. By serial film analysis I mean a process in which the largest possible number of films is examined in regard to recurring narratives, motives, and formal and rhetoric patterns. The reason for this is simple: industrial film has not yet been studied systematically.[9] Therefore, whenever a single film is considered, the question of its representativeness remains unanswered. Serial film analysis can provide knowledge on structural, thematic, aesthetic, and rhetorical characteristics and stereotypes that make it possible to distinguish the typical from the atypical, establish coherencies in form and content, and identify continuities and changes. Such an analysis can lay the ground for comparative studies of narratives, styles, arguments, and intertextualities from local, regional, national, and transnational perspectives.

Film analysis alone, however, will not suffice. Context analysis is indispensable for industrial and other kinds of utility films, since they are all highly situational and closely bound to their production and exhibition context. Deprived of context and viewed in retrospect, they can barely be understood adequately. Additionally, film texts hardly tell us about their contemporary function, utilization, or reception. Such crucial information can only be retained from additional research of historical sources. The same is true for other characteristics of industrial film such as seriality and intermediality. As is the case with corporate photography, an industrial film rarely comes alone; it is usually part of a series of films. Furthermore, industrial films are always integrated in an orchestrated media mix (or *Medienverbund*) for corporate communication, and thus not used in isolation, but in correlation with other media.[10]

When studying industrial film one must free oneself from equating "film" with "cinema": The utility film has a wider exhibition frame than that of "film," which is commonly understood as a professionally produced feature-length narrative screened in cinemas. Given the variety of non-theatrical exhibition venues, the terms must be distinguished in regard to industrial and other utility films.

Definitions and classifications

Industrial or corporate films, as they are called in today's business praxis, can be defined as films commissioned and used as a communication tool by corporations and business associations (excluding advertising spots).[11] Industrial films, then, are communicative devices for corporate governance.

Capitalist economy depends on growth, which is achieved by reducing production costs or increasing productivity (or most efficiently, by doing both at the same time). Therefore, rationalization and innovation are the engines of industry, and the rhetoric of rationalization and innovation is inherent to industrial film.

Industrial films come in different types, and specialized encyclopedias list four of them: the representation film (*Repräsentationsfilm*), also called image film, which gives a comprehensive overview of a corporation; the representative film (*Vertreterfilm*), which demonstrates the functioning of products to potential customers; the educational and training film (*Lehr- und Ausbildungsfilm*) used for the instruction of employees, and finally the trade fair and exhibition film (*Messe- und Ausstellungsfilm*).[12] This list must be complemented by the manufacturing or process film (*Fabrikationsfilm*), which shows the step-by-step manufacturing of goods from raw material to consumable product, often including shipping and the joy of consumption. The manufacturing film is the earliest type of industrial film to represent a separate category, possibly due to the fact that it inherited its distinctive narrative from preceding media practices, such as lantern slides, photographs, and prints. From 1907 onwards, process films were included in the programs of stationary cinematograph theaters under the contemporary designation of *Industriebild* (industrial moving picture) or *scène (d'art et) d'industrie*, and by 1910 they had taken on the distinctive narrative and form that would be the norm until the end of the 1930s.[13] The research film (*Forschungsfilm*), which documents academic experiments, could also be added; in contrast to the types mentioned above, however, it served to produce knowledge rather than disseminate it. Not mentioned in secondary literature, but to be considered as a separate type, is the actuality film (*Aktualitätenfilm*), which records important moments in corporate history (anniversaries, receptions, dedications of corporate facilities, social events such as leisure trips of staff and trainees, etc.), thus contributing to the constitution of corporations.

Categories have remained relatively constant over the years. Curt Ascher, general director of the Deutsche Industriefilm-Aktiengesellschaft (German Industrial Film Stock Company), named four types of industrial film in 1924: *Repräsentationsfilm* (representation film), *Fabrikationsfilm* (manufacturing film), *Anwendungsfilm* (use film, which generally shows large-scale tools and machines in action), and *Gebrauchsanweisungsfilm* (instructional film).[14] However, care should be taken, since contemporary designations have been subject to historical shifts in meaning. What Albert Masnata, chairman of the Schweizerische Zentrale für Handelsförderung (Business Network Switzerland), understood in 1929 by the term *film documentaire* (documentary film) – a film that, "for advertising purposes, offers the audience a means to learn about the existence, the fabrication and the application of certain products" – would be called a manufacturing film today.[15] Likewise, in 1949, films that showed "the occupations and activities of corporations, associations, and institutions, perhaps even their historical development," were called documentary films (*Dokumentarfilme*).[16]

Today, they would fall into the category of representation or image film. Both examples provide evidence that those historical terms must be returned to their contemporary meanings. Additionally, it should be noted that in recent research, consistent terminology is generally missing. In the second volume of the *Geschichte des dokumentarischen Films in Deutschland* (2005) alone, the industrial film is either subsumed under the category of *Kulturwerbefilm* (cultural advertising film), reduced to examples from heavy industry, or extended to include films on "housing and construction" (*Wohnen und Bauen*), which were commissioned by public authorities and not by corporations, thus not belonging to the classification of industrial films, although they do qualify as sponsored utility films.[17]

Figure 2 "And will you be there, too?" Industrial films as local films

Source: *La Feuille d'Avis de Neuchâtel* (1929)

The examples accentuate the need for a distinct definition of industrial film in alignment with the sponsoring agencies – corporations and business associations – and with the films' utilization in corporate communication. Such a definition implies a fundamental change in the perspective of research from producer/director to film sponsor and from the film's aesthetic to its function.

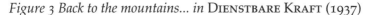

Figure 3 Back to the mountains... in Dienstbare Kraft (1937)

Figure 4 ... with Brown, Boveri & Cie
Schweizerische Privatbahnen (1939)

Industrial films were never produced haphazardly. Instead, they were always commissioned for specific reasons on a specific occasion. Corporate motivation to sponsor films is central to a retrospect understanding of their function. Since they barely left any traces in the films, contemporary motivations have to be reconstructed from historical sources. Generally speaking, there are three basic types of occasions for commissioning corporate films: trade fairs and exhibitions; anniversaries and other corporate festivities, and innovations such as the introduction of new products and the implementation of new organizational structures – especially if the measures taken by a corporation encountered resistance from employees, consumers, or society. The three types justify describing corporate film as a phenomenon of either prosperity or crisis. Whenever public conflicts, for example opposition to exploitation of waterpower or atomic energy, interfered with economic development, corporate films would be used as "troubleshooters" for negotiating between employer and employee, producer and consumer, and industry and society in order to adapt the opposing party to the needs of the industry. Such adaptation processes imply a rhetorical pattern of manufacturing consent that, more or less explicitly, addresses the objections of the opponents and negotiates controversial positions (usually between nature and technology, tradition and progress) in order to conclude with a display of the social benefit that will result from consenting to economic progress. A stereotypical example of such negotiation is DREI IN EINEM BOOT from the early 1950s (director: Victor Borel), sponsored by the electricity company of the canton of Zurich in order to promote the construction of the hydroelectric power station in Rheinau near Schaffhausen, a project that met with fierce social opposition. In a fictional dispute between an environmentalist and an engineer, the film negotiates between environmental protection and industrial modernization, and presents waterpower as clean energy that guarantees both the conservation of the Alpine landscape and the maintenance of national independence. Thus, social consent to industrial exploitation is manufactured on the basis of patriotic feelings.[18]

As elaborate as its argument may be, an industrial film can fulfill its function only if it reaches its target audience. Industrial film addressed a variety of target groups inside and outside corporations (internal and external exhibition), which either consisted of large lay audiences or experts (company employees, engineers, academics, students, etc.). Either way, the audience played *the* decisive role:

> One must therefore always take into account the fact that an industrial film is a *utility film*. Only if it reaches the target audience is its production justified [emphasis in the original].[19]

The Knorr Food Corporation, for example, made the production of a manufacturing film dependent on its use in schools.[20] And management of the Georg Fischer Corporation dropped a film project on the occasion of the company's 150th anniversary in 1952: the range of products that "at the same time speaks to the highly qualified engineer and the ordinary housewife" cast too much doubt on whether the film could really reach such a broad target audience.[21]

Despite the eminent significance of the audience, it would be hasty to draw parallels to commercial film production, which is dependent on a paying audience. Even if the industrial film represents "a commercial deal" between a sponsoring corporation and a commissioned agent (film producer),[22] this is a commercial deal that usually results in non-commercial films. Seen in retrospect, only a very small percentage of industrial films have ever made it into the pre-feature program of commercial cinemas. In 1959, Friedrich Mörtzsch, head of

AEG's marketing department at the time, estimated the portion of West German industrial films distributed commercially at no more than 5%.[23] Exploitation in commercial cinemas played only a marginal role for industrial film. Generally, the audience did not pay to watch an industrial film, the industry paid for the audience. What was significant for the sponsor in the cost-benefit ratio were not the effective costs of production, but the average amount paid per spectator, which correspondingly sank as their number rose.[24] Obviously, large audiences were always desired. In contrast to the commercial film industry, however, film for corporations and business associations was not a trade good with a commercial end in itself, but an investment. Therefore, industrial and other sponsored utility films obey a different logic of economic exploitation than the commercial film industry.

On the use of industrial film

Industrial films would be screened internally and/or externally, that is within the structures of the commissioning body (screenings for the staff, for instance for training and further education or prevention of accidents; at business and general gatherings; for customers and factory visitors; at subsidiaries, etc.), and/or outside the corporation. In 1959, 30% to 40% of all industrial films were screened outside corporations. External dissemination can also be divided into two categories: commercial or trade distribution and non-commercial distribution.[25] In Germany, industrial films made it into the commercial pre-feature program by way of commercial distribution as *Kulturfilme* (cultural advertising films), facilitated by changed regulations for entertainment tax in 1926.[26] In the late 1940s, cinematic exploitation was dependent on a classification from the Film Evaluation Office of Wiesbaden, since a tax break for the entire program was based on classifications of films for the pre-feature program. The usage rights were contractual rights. In general historical practice the rights for commercial use remained with the producers and those for non-commercial use went to the commissioning body. As such, the filmmakers had a financial incentive to get the films screened in cinemas, whereas the sponsor was guaranteed widespread dissemination of its message.

Non-commercial exhibition, which I am concentrating on here, was the dominant practice for disseminating industrial films. Using the companies' own channels of distribution and other non-commercial channels, industrial films were screened nationally and internationally at trade fairs and exhibitions; in schools and universities; at trade, social, economic, church, and other associations, as well as at public and private institutions; in film clubs; at festivals; in mobile cinemas; at trade events and lecture tours; on cruise ships; in consulates and embassies.

The variety of circulation practices and exhibition venues outside commercial cinema makes historical research on industrial film a very time-consuming undertaking. But it is precisely in this pragmatic field that the constitutive characteristics of the utility film are to be found. The different exhibition frames thereby played a decisive role in determining the meaning and reception of a film, as can be exemplified by ALPSEGEN IM GLARNERLAND (1930, Schweizer Schul- und Volkskino), sponsored by the Schweizerische Milchkommission (Swiss Milk Commission). The film about the manufacture of Glarner Schabziger, an herbed cheese with a distinctive smell and taste, took on a different character depending on the context in which it was screened. If shown at an advertising event organized by the Milk Commission, it was seen as a "propaganda film," as promotional films were called at the time; if screened in cinemas, it became a cultural film on life in the Alpine pastures; and when projected in the classroom and commented upon by a teacher, it was an educational film. Screening contexts always influence reception, but in the case of industrial film, the influence is so far reaching that the actual use of a film could change its basic function and generic character. Thus, industrial films are multi-intentional and multifunctional in that they can reach different target groups with different focuses for different purposes (advertising, information, instruction, and education). Depending on the exhibition context, they could be propaganda films, cultural films, educational films, or even local films. Scenes of workers leaving a factory, which belonged to the standard repertory of motifs in industrial films until the 1940s, provide an example: to a large, unspecific audience they demonstrated the economic power of a corporation; to the staff and local inhabitants, however, who recognized themselves and their surroundings on the screen, such scenes had a home-movie quality and served, among other things, to encourage identification with the company by anchoring it in the local.[27]

Furthermore, industrial films correlate with other media used for corporate communication, such as lectures, slides, photographs, brochures, inserts, and objects.[28] The complexity of such media connections is illustrated by the following example: DIENSTBARE KRAFT/FORCES DOMPTÉES (1937, Charles-Georges Duvanel), about the generation, use, and importance of electricity in Switzerland, is a typical film sponsored by Business Network Switzerland in that it promotes an entire economic sector instead of individual corporations. In a particularly emblematic final scene the mountain railway to the Gornergrat can be seen in front of the Matterhorn. As a symbol of technological transformation of nature into industrial culture, the mountain railway leads the spectator back to where the film – and waterpower – started: the mountains. At the opening of the Schweizerische Landesausstellung (Swiss National Exhibition) in 1939 in

Zurich, where DIENSTBARE KRAFT was screened several times, the Brown, Boveri & Cie. corporation used the same motive as the mountain railway to the Gornergrat in front of the Matterhorn to illustrate an ad for its electric locomotives, published in a special issue of the journal *Schweizerische Privatbahnen*.[29] In this case, the motive circulated not only in different media, it was also transferred from the representation of an entire branch into the media mix of an individual corporation, a mix that included a series of individual corporate films such as LOKOMOTIVBAU BROWN, BOVERI & CIE., also screened at the exhibition.[30]

A further constitutive characteristic of both industrial and utility film in general can be outlined by returning to the example of ALPSEGEN IM GLARNERLAND. The fact that the Schweizerische Arbeitsgemeinschaft für Unterrichtskinematographie (Swiss Society for Educational Cinema, SAFU) shortened the film and divided it into two independent parts for screenings in schools (ALPAUFZUG and HERSTELLUNG DES GLARNER ZIGERS) illustrates the common practice of adapting films to conform to a variety of exhibition contexts. This practice not only underlines the necessity of a combination of film and context analysis, it also points to a problematic of multiple versions inherent to the genre of utility film. According to different exhibition frames, films were commissioned in multiple versions and shortened, complemented with new material, newly edited, and given new soundtracks. This also applies, by the way, to the aforementioned electricity film, which is a shortened and newly sound-edited version of UNSICHTBARE KRAFT/PUISSANCE INVISIBLE from 1933. A further common practice was to recycle shots in newly produced films. This practice is responsible for the modular character so typical of the industrial and utility film. Tullberg Film, for example, Sweden's leading industrial film producer in the 1920s, set up a "film archive" with shots from certain places to be reused in new films.[31] And the film theorist Ernst Iros suggested the foundation of a Swiss Central Office for Cultural Film Production in 1942 which would collect all the unused shots from both narrative and documentary films so that new films could draw their material from this "image reservoir." Such a "highly rational" method, which Iros extolled as a "mosaic, modular, or building-block method," perfectly corresponds to the character of the industrial and utility film.[32] As a consequence, designations like original version and final or director's cut become precarious categories. The problematic of multiple versions evidences the fact that an *auteur*-film approach to industrial film is inappropriate. Like utility films in general, industrial films dispense with the enduring, permanent character of a piece of art. Instead, they are provisional assemblages of working material to be (re)used in new combinations according to the needs of the commissioning bodies. Their assignment is "not to serve art, but ... to put art into service."[33] Art in industrial film, then, is functional art.

Whether commercial or non-commercial, whether presented inside or outside a corporation, industrial films were always just one component of a media event and not the event itself. At commercial cinemas they were elements of the short-film program preceding the main feature. As a corporate communication tool the industrial film was particularly efficient at media events that could be governed and controlled. This was the case in non-commercial exhibition venues where industrial films were commentated by lecturers present at the screening, combined with other media (photographs, slides, brochures), and embedded in an event that often drew upon further attractions. For this reason the extant film prints are not to be seen as complete, timeless works, but fragments of ephemeral screening events. These fragments owe their filmic form less to the artistic will of an *auteur* than to exhibition practice. Form, then, always follows function.

Forms and functions

Serial film analysis, as it was performed in the research project in Switzerland mentioned above, brought certain formal features to light that could lead one to describe industrial film as a "residual" category within non-fiction film.[34] Despite the advent of the discursive "documentary film" in Grierson's sense, many films prolonged the tradition of the "aesthetic of the view," the gesture of showing, until the late 1930s.[35] And many remained silent until the 1950s and black and white until the 1960s.[36] Of the 303 films screened at the Swiss National Exhibition held in 1939 in Zurich, 204 were silent.[37]

These observations apply not only to industrial films, but to other forms of utility film as well.[38] In regard to industrial film, however, a paradox results: how does a rhetoric of innovation in content go together with conservative or even anachronistic form? And how can the technically and formally innovative counterexamples, which were well noted in film history, be explained? The push to renew film language made by the avant-garde in the 1920s and 1930s greatly influenced the industrial film, as is manifest in the sponsored films directed by Walter Ruttmann, who was therefore recognized as the "inventor" of industrial film by traditional historiography.[39] There are other instances of industrial films drawing upon the latest techniques and the display of high production values. In German films like Ruttmann's METALL DES HIMMELS (1935) and MANNESMANN (1937) or, to quote an example from Switzerland, HÄNDE UND MASCHINEN/HOMMES ET MACHINES by Werner Dressler and Kurt Früh (1938, Business Network Switzerland), the rhetoric of innovation is reflected stylistically and technically so that innovations in content and form coincide.

Industrial films can be divided into two formally distinct categories: films de-signed for commercial venues and films produced for non-commercial exhibi-tion. Pre-feature films had to meet the contemporary standards of international film production and entertain a large audience. Often such industrial films were designed as prestige objects of the commissioning corporation, which strove to represent its economic power through innovative film form and technique. As important as pre-feature industrial films may be from a perspective of quality, they are far less relevant in terms of quantity.[40]

The second, quantitatively dominant category is formed by industrial films designed for non-commercial exhibition only. For the most part, their "back-wardness" can be explained by the corresponding exhibition practice. The sig-nification of a silent film devoid of explicit rhetoric in the film text that relies upon sheer demonstration was largely undetermined, which made it suitable for use in a variety of contexts (trade fairs, lectures, schools, etc.). Above all, it was the event that attributed the actual meaning to a film – an instance that once more underlines the fragmentary character of most industrial films. Pre-feature films, on the other hand, had to be self-explanatory and communicate their message without a supporting lecturer. Therefore, they are highly deter-mined by diegetic commentary and music, which, on the other hand, limited their usability.[41] Industrial films for commercial and non-commercial use also differ in format: the standard for screening in a cinema was 35mm, for non-theatrical use 16mm.[42] The answer to whether industrial film is an innovative category of film is therefore different depending upon the utilization practices (internal or external, commercial or non-commercial exhibition).

To conclude, I would like to return to the opening quote: "What Hollywood is to America, the corporate film is to Switzerland." Wettler's statement applies not only to the economic significance of industrial film for the domestic film industry, but also to the status of the industrial film as a means of representing a nation. Like Hollywood productions, industrial films have spread national values, characteristics, and worldviews all over the globe. They have coined na-tional images and disseminated national stereotypes. In the case of Switzerland, the films sponsored by the Business Network Switzerland after the 1930s had a great influence in branding Switzerland internationally as a happy fusion of tradition and innovation with mountains, and a guarantee of quality products. Along with the cultivation of national images abroad, industrial films played a crucial role in constructing and reinforcing local, regional, and especially na-tional identities. To which degree this holds true for countries other than Swit-zerland must still be answered by comparative transnational research. What-ever the results, the history of industrial films includes more than business history. It is, in fact, part of cultural history in the largest sense.

Notes

1. It was first screened on March 22, 1895, for the Society for the Promotion of the National Economy in Paris.
2. Alexander J. Seiler as quoted in Martin Schaub, "Die zweiten Solothurner Filmtage: Leistungen und Probleme des Schweizer Films," *Neue Zürcher Zeitung* (midday edition) (January 27, 1967), p. 7.
3. Alexander J. Seiler, "Kurz nach dem Jahre Null: Das Filmschaffen in der deutschen Schweiz," *Jahrbuch der Neuen Helvetischen Gesellschaft*, 39 (1968), p. 192.
4. Cf. Yvonne Zimmermann, "Auftragsfilm versus Autorenfilm: Zur Geschichte einer Beziehungskiste," *Cinema* (special issue *Erotik*), 51 (2006), pp. 109-118.
5. Cf. Roland Cosandey, *Welcome Home, Joye! Film um 1910: Aus der Sammlung Joseph Joye* (Basel and Frankfurt am Main: Stroemfeld and Roter Stern, 1993), p. 114.
6. Since its foundation in 1947, Condor has remained one of the leading Swiss production companies of sponsored films. Peter M. Wettler's quote was taken from Heidi Ungerer, "Hollywood im Wirtschaftsfilm: 27. Internationaler Wirtschaftsfilm- und Video-Kongress," *Schweizerische HandelsZeitung* (September 4, 1986), no. 36, p. 33.
7. Although there are admittedly happy moments when long-forgotten Swiss films are discovered, for instance Hans Richter's WIR LEBEN IN EINER NEUEN ZEIT! (1938) about the production of Ovomaltine (Ovaltine) in the Swiss Cinémathèque. Cf. Pierre-Emmanuel Jaques, "L'Ovomaltine et un cinéaste d'avant-garde: Hans Richter et le film de commande en Suisse," *Décadrages: Cinéma, à travers champs*, 4/5 (2005), pp. 154-166.
8. The project *Ansichten und Einstellungen: zur Geschichte des dokumentarischen Films in der Schweiz 1896-1964* was conducted by the Department of Film Studies at the University of Zurich under the direction of Margrit Tröhler from 2002 to 2006. Publication of a book is planned for 2009. Further information can be found at http://www.film.unizh.ch/forschung/projekte, last visited on July 10, 2006.
9. This is not the place to go into the concrete workings of the research project mentioned above. Nonetheless, it should be mentioned that over 1,200 non-fiction films from the holdings of national and foreign film archives, corporations, associations, organizations, and government offices were viewed and entered in an electronic database. For every film print the following items were retained: technical details (format, material, length, color, sound, etc.); information on storage location, conservation, and condition; transcriptions of initial titles, credits, and intertitles; a detailed description of the film, and a short summary with keywords on form and content.
10. One example: After the Rauschenbach machine factory was taken over by the Georg Fischer Iron and Steel Corporation in Schaffhausen in 1937, the company launched its new machine tool with the silent film STARR-DREH-MASCHINE SDM (1943, Pro Film, director: Hans Trommer). The core of this representation film, which begins with views of the Rhine Falls and the city of Schaffhausen and ends with a factory exit and the welfare house, consists of thorough instructions for the machine's use and a presentation of its economic efficiency. The target audience is potential customers, that is, business partners in the machine industry. The film is the first of a series of purely instructional films on the use of new types of machines (including

the +GF+ copying turning lathe KDM-P, +GF+ copying turning lathe KDM-7/50 with six cut automation, +GF+ copying turning lathe KDM-automation, +GF+ copying turning lathe KDM-11/70 with ULA universal loading automation). The film's intermediality can be seen in the fact that these machines were being advertised, among other places, in a series of inserts in the *Werkzeitung der schweizerischen Industrie* (e.g., in 11, 4, April 1943, p. 58). On the industrial film of the Swiss iron and steel industry, see Yvonne Zimmermann, "Bilder von Arbeit und Interesse: Zur (Selbst-) Darstellung der Eisen- und Stahlindustrie im Industriefilm aus der Schweiz," *Ferrum: Nachrichten aus der Eisenbibliothek, Stiftung der Georg Fischer AG*, 76 (2004), pp. 60-69.

11. In-house productions can be treated as commissioned films, since they are commissions given to in-house film departments within corporations or associations. In-house productions are internal commissioned films, outside productions are external ones. On the definitions, see http://www.bender-verlag.de/lexikon/suche2.php, last viewed on July 10, 2006, as well as Manfred Rasch, Hans Ulrich Berendes, Peter Döring (eds.), *Industriefilm 1948-1959. Filme aus Wirtschaftsarchiven im Ruhrgebiet* (Essen: Klartext-Verlag, 2003).

12. Cf. http://www.bender-verlag.de/lexikgon/suche2.php, last visited on July 10, 2006.

13. On the emergence of industrial films in the context of lantern slides, see Yvonne Zimmermann, "Vom Lichtbild zum Film: Anmerkungen zur Entstehung des Industriefilms," *Montage/AV* 15, 1 (2006), pp. 74-90 (special issue on utility film II); on industrial moving pictures in Germany, see Martin Loiperdinger in this volume; on the manufacturing film, see Cosandey, op. cit.; as well as Tom Gunning, "Vor dem Dokumentarfilm. Frühe Non-fiction-Filme und die Ästhetik der 'Ansicht,' " *KINtop. Jahrbuch zur Erforschung des frühen Films*, 4 *(Anfänge des dokumentarischen Films)* (1995), pp. 111-123; and Tom Gunning, "Before Documentary: Early Non-Fiction Films and the 'View' Aesthetic," in Daan Hertogs, Nico de Klerk (eds.), *Uncharted Territory: Essays on Early Nonfiction Film* (Amsterdam: Stichting Nederlands Filmmuseum, 1997), pp. 9-24.

14. Curt Ascher, "Der Industriefilm, seine Anwendung und Verbreitung," in Edgar Beyfuss, Alexander Kossowsky (eds.), *Das Kulturfilmbuch* (Berlin: Carl P. Chryselius'scher Verlag, 1924), p. 160 f.

15. Albert Masnata, "Le film – moyen de publicité," *Informations économiques/Wirtschaftliche Mitteilungen* 8, 35 (September 18, 1929), p. 1.

16. Schweizerischer Reklame-Verband SRV (ed.), *Die Grundlagen der Filmwerbung: Eine Wegleitung für Auftraggeber* (Zurich: Schweizerischer Reklame-Verband, 1949), p. 25.

17. Jeanpaul Goergen, "In filmo veritas! Inhaltlich vollkommen wahr: Werbefilme und ihre Produzenten," in Klaus Kreimeier, Antje Ehmann, Jeanpaul Goergen (eds.), *Geschichte des dokumentarischen Films in Deutschland. Band 2: Weimarer Republik 1918-1933* (Stuttgart: Reclam, 2005), pp. 348-363; Elsaesser, op. cit.; Thomas Meyer, "Deutsche Arbeit, deutsche Technik: Aspekte des Industriefilms," op. cit., pp. 364-380.

18. Cf. Yvonne Zimmermann, "Negotiating Landscape: Engineering Consent on the Exploitation of Water Power in Swiss Corporate Films," in Christoph Bartels, Claudia Küpper-Eichas (eds.), *Cultural Heritage and Landscapes in Europe: Landschaften: Kulturelles Erbe in Europa* (Bochum, 2008), pp. 180-191.

19. Balz E. Hatt, "Der Industriefilm: seine Bedeutung im Dienste der Öffentlichkeit," *Industrielle Organisation*, 5 (May 1969), p. 3.

20. Letter from the Knorr Food Corporation to the Education Office of the city of Basel, dated October 17, 1928 (Staatsarchiv Basel Stadt, Erziehung B 73 1926-1928).

21. "Auszug aus Notizen von Herrn Dir. Müller zur kleinen Jubiläumssitzung vom 16. Juli 1948." (+GF+ Werk-Archiv, 0829 / 3.4.1. / anniversary film).

22. Peter M. Wettler, "Was heisst eigentlich 'Auftragsfilm'?," in *Dokumentation des 27th International Industrial Film & Video Congress/Internationaler Wirtschaftsfilm- und Videokongress (iifc), November 8-12, 1986, in Zurich* (Zurich 1986), p. 1.

23. Friedrich Mörtzsch, *Die Industrie auf Zelluloid: Filme für die Wirtschaft* (Düsseldorf: Econ, 1959), p. 66.

24. In 1978 the VW Corporation in Wolfsburg, for example, counted on an average expenditure of 70 pfennigs per spectator per film, based on a running period of three to four years. See Hans Strömel, "Wirtschaftliche Aspekte," in Wilfried von Tresckow (ed.), *Industrie-, Informations-, Wirtschafts-Film im Auftrag: Ein Wegweiser für alle, die mit einem der wirksamsten Kommunikationsmedien arbeiten wollen* (Stuttgart: Kodak, 1978), pp. 146-149.

25. Mörtzsch, op. cit., p. 65.

26. Cf. Goergen, op. cit., p. 357.

27. Industrial film has not yet been examined in light of the local film, whose essential quality is that of self-recognition. This opens up an interesting field of research relating to companies' strategies of social establishment and regional anchoring. On the *local film*, see Uli Jung, "Local Films: A Blind Spot in the Historiography of Early German Cinema," *Historical Journal of Film, Radio and Television* 22,3 (2002), pp. 253-273; as well as Vanessa Toulmin, Martin Loiperdinger, "Is it You? Recognition, Representation and Response in Relation to the Local Film," *Film History* 17, 1 (2005), pp. 7-18.

28. Cf. Elsaesser, op. cit., p. 392.

29. Insert in *Schweizerische Privatbahnen/Les chemins de fer privés suisses/Ferrovie private svizzere. Spezial-Nummer bei Anlass der Eröffnung der Schweizerischen Landesausstellung* 1939, p. 50.

30. The films (in addition to one on locomotive construction, a two-part film on the factory, and a circuitry film) have unfortunately not survived, so further examples of intermediality can be presumed, but not verified. See Schweizerische Landesausstellung (ed.), *Administrativer Bericht. Vorgelegt vom Liquidationskommitee der Schweizerischen Landesausstellung 1939* (Zurich: Schweizerische Landesausstellung, 1942), p. 119.

31. Mats Björkin, Pelle Snickars, "1923/1933: Production, Reception and Cultural Significance of Swedish Non-fiction Film," in Peter Zimmermann, Kay Hoffmann (eds.), *Triumph der Bilder: Kultur- und Dokumentarfilme vor 1945 im internationalen Vergleich* (Konstanz: UVK, 2003), p. 274.

32. Ernst Iros, "Produktionsplanung für die schweizerische Kultur-, Dokumentar-, Propaganda-, Lehr- und Unterrichtsfilm-Produktion ('Baustein-System')," unpublished manuscript (Schweizerisches Bundesarchiv, E 3001(B) -/1: vol. 46 (1942); 14.2.7.3).

33. Gert Rottmann, "Erfahrungen mit industriellen Auftragsfilmen aus unternehmerischer Sicht," in Wilfried von Tresckow (ed.), *Industrie-, Informations-, Wirtschafts-*

Film im Auftrag: Ein Wegweiser für alle, die mit einem der wirksamsten Kommunikations-medien arbeiten wollen (Stuttgart: Kodak, 1978), p. 153.

34. Whether this is a national or transnational phenomenon must be shown through comparative study. Due to screening practices extending beyond the borders which determine form, I tend to discount a national specificity.

35. Cf. Gunning, "Vor dem Dokumentarfilm," op. cit., as well as Gunning, op. cit. On the production of documentary films during World War I see Martin Loiperdinger, "World War I Propaganda Films and the Birth of the Documentary," in Daan Hertogs, Nico de Klerk (eds.), *Uncharted Territory: Essays on Early Nonfiction Film* (Amsterdam: Stichting Nederlands Filmmuseum, 1997), pp. 25-31.

36. The color sound film was established as a standard for industrial films in Switzerland in the early 1960s.

37. Swiss National Exhibition, 1939, Zurich, op. cit., p. 115.

38. Cf. the films on *Bauen und Wohnen* in Frankfurt from the late 1920s/early 1930s, which were created in the context of an architectural avant-garde, but formally bear no avant-garde elements. The fact that they are not industrial films has already been mentioned. Cf. Elsaesser, op. cit.

39. What Flaherty is for documentary film, Ruttmann apparently is for industrial film. His 1927 BERLIN. DIE SINFONIE DER GROSSSTADT is thought to have been the "bridge" "on which film and industry finally found their way to each other." Cf. Mörtzsch, op. cit., p. 17.

40. As a reminder: according to Mörtzsch, in 1959 only 5% of the industrial films produced in West Germany circulated in commercial cinemas.

41. Cf. Yvonne Zimmermann, "Vom Lichtbild zum Film: Anmerkungen zur Entstehung des Industriefilms," *Montage AV* 15,1 (2006, special issue on utility film II).

42. The film format allows one to draw conclusions about the use of a film. Until the introduction of video the cine-film was the dominant format for utility film. The introduction of new techniques is obviously always dependent on economic and practical factors of use also.

POUSSIÈRES

Writing the Real vs. the Documentary Real

Gérard Leblanc

POUSSIÈRES (1954) is the only one of Georges Franju's documentaries for which the screenplay was essentially written before shooting. The title of the present text, with its slogan form, becomes even stronger than it already is if taken literally. Writing before shooting, not in order to create a script but to prefigure cinematic images, sometimes by resting on the power of poetic evocation, while at other times relying on the power of scientific description using verbal language. Cinematic images, once composed, will refer back to verbal language, which, by means of this description, will designate what Franju wanted to see and what he wanted the spectator to see.

Franju, his commissioning body, and the dominant social discourse

But before we enter into the heart of the analysis of Franju's approach and his short film, it is necessary to specify what he understood by the "documentary real." These two terms, for him, far from being related, are actually in radical opposition. In a documentary it is not the real that is manifest, but a preconstituted view of the real, generally that of the commissioning body, the director being the more or less conscious agent of this position.[1] This point of view is not only ideal, it is connected to a form of organization of the real, which the film takes as its goal and which it tends to legitimize and naturalize. In order for another real to have any chance of being manifest in a film, if it is a documentary, it must begin by disassociating the "real" and the "documentary." This is precisely the enterprise that Franju undertook throughout his so-called "documentary" work (from 1948 to 1957), always trying to thwart the traps of the commission.[2]

What is the "documentary real" aimed for by the Institut national de recherche sur la sécurité (INRS) that commissioned POUSSIÈRES? This institution specialized in the prevention of work accidents and work-related illness and commissioned Franju to make a short film to train workers how to protect themselves from industrial dust, which causes numerous work-related illnesses.

The preconsituted point of view of the commissioning body could not be simpler: by properly employing individual and collective measures of protection, it is possible to prevent the majority of these illnesses. This is the point of view that the filmmaker is supposed to relay and reinforce in his film.

The point of view that Franju creates in the course of his approach to this real as desired by the commissioning body is, however, quite different. He formulates it in a note on page six of his shooting notes: "to give the images and the commentary the appearance of engaging in a constant competition between the risk of illness and the preventative measures used."[3] The film subsequently specifies what could be missing in this formulation. The "competition" is decidedly unequal. The protective measures utilized never correspond to the risks run. They are behind even in the evolution of the conditions of production. Dust is ever more fine, invisible, abundant, difficult to neutralize.

While Franju's point of view is in opposition to that of his commissioner, the context of the commission prevents him from showing the relationships between work safety and the organization and goals of the capitalist system. Had he done so, the film would simply have been rejected by the INRS. Did Franju want to show this relationship? There is no evidence to support this. The traces of self-censorship that one finds in the shooting notes only indicate that Franju knew perfectly well how far he could go in his critique. For example, concerning a factory that crushed sea pebbles, he first wrote: "In this factory for the manufacture of dust, man, imitating the sea, makes sand out of pebbles." Later he chose to remove the first clause of the sentence, contenting himself with saying that the production of sand is "useful for industry and dangerous for man." A simple tactical concern can be seen in this cut: not to offend the commissioner too much by attributing an apparently absurd end goal to the factory, namely "the manufacture of dust."

The role that the filmmaker attributes to scientific experimentation appears to be more problematic. This is supposed to "go beyond" nature (which invented the spider's web, "without a doubt the first dust filter") in the daily battle that she wages concerning the different ways that material can be set free, as if Franju were placing all his hopes in scientific discoveries and none in social transformation. This position would have certainly been reassuring to the commissioner. But after this reassurance, the filmmaker stirred up new trouble. At the end of the film he asks: "Man, more powerful than the elements he dominates, will he be safe from the mortal radioactivity of atomic dust ... that threatens the globe...?" The last shot shows an atomic explosion and its formidable dust cloud.

This conclusion is a good example of Franju's strategy. The filmmaker first takes up the socially dominant discourse (to which, of course, the commissioner adheres) in order to undermine it from within. At the same time, this work of destroying the dominant discourse, as stunning as it may sometimes be, remains confined within certain limits that are not to be exceeded. It is man in general that is at stake here and not the social conditions under which he produces and reproduces. If Franju's strategy can have a political effect, it is not political in and of itself, and it can provoke anguished questioning about human nature. It is this possibility that makes it acceptable for the different institutions that Franju collaborated with.

The aesthetics of Franju's cinema are nevertheless aesthetics of destabilization.[4] This destabilization is born of the impossibility of sticking to the commissioner's discourse, the argumentation of which is partially taken up by Franju, even when he finds himself in disagreement with it, with what is shown. The commissioner's discourse, in effect, is always a discourse of normalization. The filmmaker, as he expressed on several occasions, intended to demonstrate the abnormal character of what it habitually presented as normal. He achieves this not only by opposing the verbal and visual discourse, but by first exposing the internal contradictions of the dominant verbal discourse. By contradicting itself, the voice-over gives the spectator the chance to include his or her own voice in the interpretation of the visual discourse. This is what produces the profoundly liberating character of Franju's cinema, which is in sharp contrast to the typical documentary production of the time, in which the off-camera voice tends to impose a one-to-one relationship onto the images.

Poetic and scientific discourse

I would like to return to my point of departure. The primordial importance that Franju gives to the writing of the commentary is first of all a strategy of destabilizing the spectator in his relation to the visual discourse. But there is something more, or rather something else, at work in POUSSIÈRES. Writing precedes the image, and, in a certain sense, creates it.

To begin with, we observe the coexistence of two levels of discourse that ordinarily tend to be mutually exclusive and equally destabilizing for the spectator – which is nothing new with Franju: the poetic and the scientific. These two levels of discourse coexist and overlap without concealing each other. It is not a question of poetically sprucing up scientific discourse to make it easier to consume. Each level of discourse develops according to its own axis, and it is never a question of mistaking the one for the other. Because Franju respects their singularity, the two levels of discourse can meet and interact in a very productive way, for example, concerning the question of the invisible. But first they must be considered separately, since they do not play the same role and do not produce the same effects.

The opening of the film takes up the first level of discourse and leads, by undetectable degrees, to the second. It indicates, in the context of a film that could not be more "objective," the presence of a subjectivity. After all, is it not a training film that takes its arguments from a preconstituted institutional discourse objective? This subjectivity seems to start a daydream about dust, reciting examples of various of kinds of dust. The word "dust" appears in every sentence. This daydream, however, is burdened by the heavy weight of the real. The first shot in the film shows a general view of the city of Leeds blackened by industrial dust. The filmmaker comments: "Dust has covered the city, one of the blackest in the world." This is followed by three sentences (one could very well call them three verses) that, while continuing to play on variations of a single theme – that of dust – seem to snatch the film away from its relation to industry in order to give it over to nature: "living dust of pollen... ancient dust of the Sahara... salty dust released by the waves of the sea..." If the same theme expands from one phrase to the next, the association of blooming trees, of a desert, of the sea, do not obey any logic of argumentation, nor does the order of their succession. It is a question of sensations that seek out and find their poetic formulation.

This poetic formulation is divided up into two stages: that of verbal expression, itself full of imagery, and that of its materialization by the camera. The poetic use of language gives rise to images that the cinema then transforms, interpreting them visually. "Living dust of pollen..." evokes multiple images related to the question: What is alive about the dust of pollen? For the filmmaker-poet Franju – not surprisingly – what brings the dust of pollen to life is the movement of the wind. He then films flowering trees agitated by the wind, which carries off a cloud of pollen. Visual interpretation among a thousand other possibilities. The problem for the filmmaker consists in not taking the spectator's place in the dream. But the cinematic image that Franju has drawn from the verbal image opens up to all sorts of daydreams and excesses. The freedom of the spectator is preserved.

The third sentence introduces a relation of causality that could justify a scientific explanation: "salty dust released by the waves of the sea..." This explanation remains suspended on a shot of high waves breaking and forming foam. But the fourth phrase, aside from its own poetic virtues, indicates the necessity of a scientifically discursive level. "Dust sent by the sun and which, concentrated at the magnetic pole, forms the aurora borealis..." The cinematic image here is made illustrative, even singular. At the words "aurora borealis" we actually see an aurora borealis, as if the image were turning into the objective visual translation of a concept. We therefore pass from one level of discourse to another. It is no longer language's power of evocation that is solicited, but its power of description, taken to a higher level of precision and accuracy. Nevertheless the first level of discourse will not be abandoned and will reappear in the failures of the institutional discourse as it tries to secure its own mastery of images.

The film now leads us back to its starting point. We have left the city of Leeds, blackened by dust. We find ourselves confronted by a more general proposition: "In many industries, the quantity of floating dust is considerable..." The prosaic quality of this sentence is undeniable and leads the listener to wonder if the poetic discourse was not simply a form of evasion that has come to a sudden end. But Franju, by now assigning a descriptive function to language, conserves the fragmentary structure of the poetic phrase, thereby establishing a rhythmic continuity: "big-city train stations... coal mining towns blackened by coal dust ..." The filmmaker makes use of an opposition at equal levels, which is justified at least as much by cinematographic as analytical reasons. The black of the mining towns is opposed to the white of the cemeteries and the limekilns. This is, after all, a film, and a black-and-white film at that, which, starting from this basic opposition, goes on to play on the whole scale of gray.

But it is this connection woven in between the visible and the invisible that will bring the two levels of discourse together through a series of examples. The first case study concerns "a company that produces linen." Franju takes us on a visit to a "faintly lit" threshing workshop. The commentary states what the image confirms: "The threshing machine breaking the linen fibers produces such a quantity of dust that the light of day can only get through with difficulty." A light projector has to be used to "produce a ray of light." The beams go on to reveal an enormous quantity of dust, invisible to the eye in the half-light of the threshing workshop. It is as if the technical means of cinema were coming to the aid of science, and by the same token, releasing a kind of poetry by showing a ray of sunlight.

The level of scientific discourse sometimes takes its authority from the scientific research that Franju integrated into his film. We see, for instance, microscopic images from doctors Policard and Collet showing the destruction of a living cell by a speck of silica dust. "The silica dust, by destroying the living cell, causes the most dangerous type of pneumoconiosis: silicosis... Certain occupations are particularly affected by this illness." Several sequences present a factory that grinds sea pebbles, a Limoges porcelain factory, a mining tunnel in the Alps, a mining pit in Hénin-Liétard, a cemetery, and a sandblasting operation.

In each case presented, the work process is described from the point of view of the "competition" between the risks created for the workers and the technical means utilized to prevent or attenuate these risks. These means are always insufficient. This can be seen in the factory for grinding sea pebbles. After having shown, briefly and precisely, different operations of the work process, after having underlined the dangerous conditions where these operations are put into effect, Franju shows the "powerful air filters" that "reduce" the quantity of silica dust inhaled by the workers. The term "reduce" already indicates that the air filters, as powerful as they may be, do not entirely suffice. But, in the smelting works, the commentary becomes even more unsettling. A worker dressed in a hood (he is therefore provided, as the regulations require, with a means of individual protection) uses a jet of sand to smooth out an object. The sandblasting "loosens particles ... all the more noxious in that they are fine and fresh." For the sandblasting operation, Franju brings in a projector to make "the murderous dust loosened by the smoothing" visible. In his shooting notes he wrote: "Visible and invisible dust. But the source of light, which is mobile, causes the dust that is breathed in to appear under the grinding stone. Repeat this luminous demonstration twice." The sequence concludes: "Collecting all of this invisible dust is the only way to prevent the ever-threatening peril of silicosis."

The visible and the non-visible

The following sequence, located in a porcelain factory, is the longest in this short film, and also constitutes the pivot point (it is in this sequence that Franju expresses his philosophy of film in a note I have transcribed above). The different operations of manufacturing are described in even more detail than before. After a fade to black the border maker appears, whose job, "along with that of the sand blaster, is the most exposed in the porcelain factory." The border maker has no means of individual protection at his disposal. As he blows on the edge of the plate, the commentary underscores the fact that "his breathing fights with the silicon dust for his pulmonary alveolus." After a close-up of the vaporization of dust, we see another of the workers breathing, then an extreme close-up of his mouth. The work of the sandblaster is then broken down into several related shots. At the end of this montage the spectator is invited to leave the terrain of representation in order to come face to face with the opposition between the visible and what the dominant point of view would like to keep hidden in the realm of the invisible. It is not a question here of showing the invisibility of dust, but of showing the invisibility, deliberately sustained, of illness behind the appearance of good health. The commentary, "The living worker in this environment might feel perfectly well, however..." indicates the stereotypical image of a man satisfied with a job well done over a chain of images that undermine the contradiction between the visible and non-visible aspects. When the sandblaster completes his work, he smiles, admiring the results and show-ing them off to the spectator to admire as well. If the transparency of the plate is incontestable, the human transparency suggested by the worker's smile is ideo-logical; it expresses the imaginary relationship it has to the real conditions of work. The film carries out the visual demonstration by showing an x-ray of lungs suffering from silicosis (which could be those of any worker working un-der the same conditions). The suspended sentence is completed in the most im-placable way: "The silicosis is there, detected by the x-ray."

The progression in exposing the danger and the risks is pursued in the fol-lowing sequence, hidden behind a simulacrum of evasion. Here, the film-maker's irony reveals itself to be particularly effective. He knows that it is tradi-tional to follow a dramatic sequence with a more relaxing one, which allows the spectator a little breathing room and time to pull him or herself together before a new dramatic episode begins. At first, it seems that Franju is conforming to this convention. The commentary slips in "Alpine mountains where the pure climate invigorates the diseased lungs...", but then, immediately afterwards, a loud sound makes a group of crows fly away. In the following shot, the specta-tor understands the source of the noise: a detonation that has opened up a mining tunnel in the mountain. Miners are shown leaving the tunnel in the cloud of smoke caused by the explosion. And the commentary explains that the dust is "the most dangerous thing of all." There seems to be no way out of this dilemma.

Thus, the strong interaction that the film constructs between the poetic dis-course and the scientific tends to ruin the representation of appearances and reestablish the unity between the visible and the non-visible. This unity brings out the contradictions that the socially dominant discourse is incapable of con-trolling. While the film does not itself draw out the political consequences, noth-ing prevents the spectator from doing so.

Notes

1. Among the filmmakers of the 1950s whose names have survived as auteurs as well
    as documentary filmmakers – such as Alain Resnais, Chris Marker, and Agnès Var-
    da – Franju was the most insistent about the productive dimension of creation on
    commission.
2. Institutional classifications are as tenacious as the institutions that produce them.
    We would do better to qualify Franju as an essayist-poet, or better yet, a poet-essay-
    ist.
3. A document of 14 typewritten pages, with several handwritten notes by Franju.
    This is not a screenplay but a storyboard consisting of a list of shots numbered from
    1 to 190. Each audiovisual unit is written and described in a very precise manner,

and only minor changes were made during shooting. I was able to consult this document at the Cinémathèque française (dépôt Bjorn Johansen-Franju).

4.   As I have tried to define in a book that bears this title (Maison de la Villette/Créaphis, 1992). See also "L'entre-deux du cinéma de Georges Franju," which appeared in volume II of my *Scénarios du reel* (Paris: L'Harmattan, 1997).

Thermodynamic Kitsch

Computing in German Industrial Films, 1928/1963[1]

Vinzenz Hediger

Markets, according to Joseph Schumpeter, are never stable. Competitive companies are brought to their knees by the sudden appearance of new competitors or products that improve upon existing offerings and can make entire product lines obsolete. Even the most competitive makers of horse carts were doomed once the automobile appeared on the scene and became a fact of life in the early 20th century. Schumpeter's term for this process of constantly punctuated market equilibria is "creative destruction." According to Schumpeter, creative destruction is "the essential fact about capitalism," a "process of industrial mutation ... that incessantly revolutionizes the economic structure *from within*."[2] Creative destruction has something uncanny about it. Those who fall prey to it do not see it coming: It happens from within, as Schumpeter writes. Survival in a market-driven economy depends on being able to avoid the surprise that comes from within, which means being able to anticipate and proactively initiate the process of creative destruction.

The proactive enactment of creative destruction is called "rationalization." "Rationalization" refers to measures taken in order to optimize production processes, or more abstractly speaking, to improve the ratio of input to output. One of the key agents of rationalization and of creative destruction in the 20th century is the computer. Contemporary Western societies like to describe themselves as information societies. There are good reasons for this. Not least among them is the fact that information technology has been driving up productivity and creating entire new industries over the last few decades. Management theorists and economic historians have studied the impact of information technology on productivity and the structure of industrial organizations.[3] This contribution proposes a different approach to gauging the impact of the computer. Assuming that modes of industrial production are tied to specific regimes of knowledge and visibility, this contribution proposes to trace how the creative destruction wrought from within by tabulating machines and computers plays out a level of representation and knowledge.

At stake are issues of work, control, and visibility. Generally speaking, rationalization eliminates input, particularly in terms of physical labor. The computer, however, much like the tabulating machines that preceded it, introduces a new paradigm of productivity. Where productivity was based on the transformation of energy into performance in the thermodynamic age, i.e. the classical age of industrial production, in what may be called the cybernetic age productivity it is primarily based on information processing. In the thermodynamic age work, and the control of work, were essentially tied to visibility. Work is a process in the realm of the visible, and the disappearance of work through rationalization is measurable in term of visible quantities.[4] With the computer, rationalization still results in the disappearance of work, but in the cybernetic age the disappearance of work may no longer be measured relative to the work that remains in the visible realm. Through an analysis of two films from the 1920s and 1960s, I would like to show that the introduction of information technology to the process of industrial production entails a crisis of visibility which profoundly affects the regime of knowledge tied to the traditional, 19th century mode of industrial production. The emergence of information technology provokes a shift in what you might call the visual rhetoric of industrial production, but it also affects the conditions of possibility of, particularly, a Marxist critique of the industrial and capitalist mode of production.

The two films I would like to discuss give us a sense of this crisis both in terms of what they show and in terms of what they fail to represent. The first example is a film produced by Krupp in 1928 concerning the introduction of the Hollerith tabulating machine, a film for internal communication purposes. The second example is a 1963 film produced by the Deutscher Gewerkschaftsbund in order to recruit employees for the union. In both films the effects of information processing on industrial organization are the key issue. Each in its own way deals with the same problem: the separation of visibility and control brought about by the new computing technologies, and the question as to how to represent this shift in a visual medium.

In my first section, I will discuss how industrial production is tied to what I propose calling regimes of knowledge and visibility. In particular, I will discuss how films act to shape and transform these regimes, and what film's role in these regimes entails for film analysis. The second and third sections will be devoted to a discussion of the two examples. In my conclusion, I will bring the results of the analysis together in a discussion of the industrial film as both a medium and a cause of creative destruction.

I

In the introduction to this volume, Patrick Vonderau and I argue that industrial organization, i.e., the activity of coordinating and allocating resources and processes in order to produce goods and services, is based on the production and transmission of knowledge. Three types of knowledge in particular come to mind: First, the skill of workers and technical personnel which may best be characterized as implicit knowledge in the sense of Michael Polanyi; second, the technical and administrative knowledge or transferable know-how that allows for the emergence of differentiated functional hierarchies and the training of workers and employees; and third what one might call feedback knowledge, i.e., information about the organization's overall performance that feeds back into the organization's operation. If industrial organization depends on knowledge, the production and transmission of that knowledge in turn is based on media that collect, store and transmit that knowledge.

Figure 1 The new medium's message: Rise of productivity and loss of manufacturing jobs relative to all jobs since 1950, i.e. concurrent with the spread of information technology

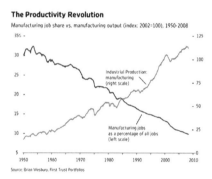

Discussing business practices in terms of regimes of knowledge and media turns the history of industrial production into a subset of media history and opens up the possibility of developing a historical epistemology of industrial organization.[5] Since the mid-19th century three major alignments of knowledge and media seem to have occurred. The introduction of photography in the years after 1850 goes hand in hand with the emergence of what one might call a panoramic-panoptic regime of knowledge and control in the field of industrial organization. Two of the principal genres of early industrial photography were panorama exterior and interior shots of factory buildings and portraits of workers and employees. The panorama shot, usually compiled from several individual photographs smoothly aligned so as to make the transition from one print to the next all but imperceptible, produces the visual image of a coherent space of industrial production and implies that activities occurring in that space are essentially visible.[6] The factory panorama exemplifies, in other words, a panoptic regime of visibility, knowledge and control. Similarly, the introduction of film to the factory floor after 1910 contributed to the emergence of an ergonomic-Taylorist regime of knowledge and control. In this regime, as evidenced in the work-study films of Frank Bunker Gilbreth, attention shifts from control of the worker's minds to control of the body, with the rationalization of movement as the main goal.[7] In this regime, knowledge and control remain tightly linked to visibility. The body of the worker and his observable actions are the locus of rationalization, the key site where to turn in order to increase productivity. Under the ergonomic-Taylorist regime, then, control is still essentially control of visible processes in a homogeneous, continuous space of industrial production. Control and visibility, however, come apart in the cybernetic-systematic regime of knowledge and control that gradually emerges with the introduction of information technology, in particular with the introduction of the computer after 1950. As work ceases to be measurable in terms of visible quantities, the focus of knowledge and control shifts away from the body of the worker to the maintenance of large-scale systems. With that, control no longer plays out on the factory floor, but somewhere beyond the traditional sites of industrial activity.

Film is a visual medium that emerges while the classical regime of industrial production is still in full swing. Accordingly, film is in line with both the panoptic-panoramic and the ergonomic-Taylorist mode and underwrites those regimes' assumptions about the visibility of work. As a consequence, there are certain thresholds of representation that define, and potentially limit, the extent to which film is capable of articulating and shaping changing regimes of knowledge and organization. So far, much of the critical work on industrial film has dealt with strategies of representation. Critical studies of this type ask questions such as: How do individual films represent social and organizational reality? How do representational strategies correspond to what is really there? Implicit in theses studies are certain assumptions about the secondary nature of cinematic representation: They assume that there is such a thing as a reality outside the media, and that cinematic representations must be judged according to the degree of their correspondence to this reality. This is the kind of analysis typically conducted by historians. Historians either treat films as transparent windows on social reality and hence as trustworthy source material (which deserves to be trusted based on an implicit faith in the indexicality of the photogram), or they approach cinematic representations as problematic distortions of social reality which need to be rectified through analysis (a suspicion warranted by the obvious trickery of montage and mise-en-scène). Both approaches, however, assume that out there somewhere reality exists as the ultimate touchstone that defines the status and value of the cinematic image.

More recently, media scholars have started to address films in terms of their value to industrial organizations. This line of inquiry raises questions such as: How does film transmit and implement organizational and procedural knowledge? How do films impact and shape industrial organization? Approaches of this type assume that films do things to and for social organizations. Accordingly, they treat films as agents rather than simply mirrors of what organizations are and do. This is the kind of analysis typically conducted by media historians and media scholars interested in questions of governance and governmentality. They will inquire about the As and the Rs of industrial films and trace the film material back to its organizational origins in an attempt to reconstruct the medium's action on specific organizational contexts. Characteristically, scholars using such an approach trade the ontological realism of representational analysis in for other philosophical frameworks, such as actor-network theory or Foucauldian nominalism.

Drawing on both approaches and addressing the relationship between specific media and historically specific regimes of knowledge, I would like to propose an analysis that focuses on epistemological issues. My approach asks how films produce and convey knowledge and thereby shape and inform the regime of knowledge that prevails in a given industrial organization, but also on how the knowledge available to an organization depends on its use of film. As I stated above my interest is in creative destruction as a crisis of visibility, i.e. in how the creative destruction wrought from within by information technology plays out at the level of cinematic representation and how it affects film's role as an agent in organizational processes. In order to better understand this role, I will focus my analysis on the limits and thresholds of representation and on how these limits define film's impact on regimes of knowledge.

II

In a 1962 article written for the company's in-house magazine Hans-Heinrich Campen, the head of the information department at Krupp Steel works in Essen, Germany, makes the following claim: "film knows no boundaries, no limitations: Everything can be represented cinematically."[8] For the media scholar, this claim resonates with Friedrich Kittler's more recent view of the computer. According to Kittler, the computer is a kind of super-medium, a medium that encompasses all media in that it can represent and perform all other media ("darstellen" is the apparite verb here, and it is important to note that *darstellen* in German means both to represent and to perform). The moving image, the photograph, the sound recording: Everything can be rendered, i.e., represented and performed, in the digital medium of the computer.[9] It is tempting to characterize Kittler's approach as "techno-Hegelianism." In Kittler's view, "history," in the accepted social and cultural understanding of the term, is essentially an afterthought of media technology and its development. Much like the spirit, or *"Geist"*, in Hegel's *Phänomenologie des Geistes*, media technology, pace Kittler, unfolds toward a specific goal in a continuous, steady fashion. For Hegel philosophy develops towards the emergence of the absolute spirit, as exemplified in his philosophy that encompasses and reflects all philosophy that came before it. Techno-Hegelianism holds that the evolution of media technology culminates in the emergence of the computer, the one medium that can simulate all other media (or rather, the medium that can express all other media, or *auf den Begriff bringen*, to phrase it in Hegelian terminology). If for Hegel philosophy is essentially *Darstellung*, i.e., the representation of all philosophy that came before him, in the view of Techno-Hegelianism the computer is a philosophical machine in the sense that it represents and performs all media that came before it with the only difference being that IT hardware takes the place of Hegel's spirit. No longer is "Geist" the medium of philosophy; now information technology takes its place.

What is striking about Campen's euphoric statement concerning film is that he makes the same claim for film that Kittler makes for the computer: Film is the medium that can represent everything. There is an irony to the timing of Campen's claim. 1962 is a time when the computer starts to make inroads into all areas of industrial organization. This is ironic because, as I would like to show, the computer undermines Campen's claim just as he makes it. In fact, the computer creates a problem for corporate communications that is similar to that raised by the emergence of new financial markets in the 1930s, where capital flows clearly affect and determine economic activity but remain all but invisible and difficult to represent.[10] But while financial markets operate outside and, to a certain extent, independently of the core realm of industrial activity, the introduction of the computer creates a problem of visibility at the very heart of industrial production. Information technology fundamentally alters the ontological status of work. It is a process that begins long before 1962, as Hans-Heinrich Campen could have known if he had only taken a look at the history of his own company.

In June of 1927, the top management of Krupp steel in Essen, Germany, embarked on a major overhaul of the company's accounting structure. Handwritten production and sales reports were replaced by mechanical computing, and the thirty accounting offices scattered about the company's multiple lots and factories were abandoned in favor of one central office that gathered and processed all accounting data.[11] The new department was equipped with Hollerith tabulating machines that Krupp acquired from DEHOMAG, the Deutsche Hollerith Maschinen AG, founded in Berlin in 1910 and a full subsidiary of IBM after 1924. Two events prompted Krupp to reform its system of accounting: the Allied occupation of the Ruhr Valley industrial area in 1923 and the financial crisis of 1925,[12] which plunged the region's steel and coal-mining industries into a veritable frenzy of rationalization.[13] When the Hollerith data processing system was introduced in April of 1928, representative of Krupp's legal department had the following to say: "The years of crisis have shown us that our established system of monthly reports, the so-called financial reports, was not sufficient for timely provision of an up-to-date picture of the actual developments at our corporation." Processing the handwritten financial reports had taken up to three months. The old system was replaced by a system of detailed monthly statements that were processed in real time. This created data flows that could only be handled by the Hollerith tabulating machines.

The Hollerith tabulating machine took its name from the German-American engineer Herman Hollerith. Born in 1860 as the son of a political refugee who had left Germany in the wake of the failed 1848 republican revolution, Hollerith worked for the the United States Census in 1879/1880. Based on this experience and anticipating a significant increase in population, Hollerith devised his first mechanical accounting machine for the 1890 census. Hollerith's company merged with a competitor in 1924 to form IBM, the company that was to play a key role in the development of electronic accounting machines in the 1930s and 1940s.[14] By the time of the merger, the name Hollerith was firmly established as a trademark for mechanical accounting and data processing. IBM's German subsidiary, DEHOMAG, retained the name.

Both technologically and in institutional terms, the Hollerith data processor is a predecessor of the modern-day computer. The Hollerith tabulating machine uses punched cards to tabulate statistics from data. Operators generate data sets by punching holes in prescribed areas on the cards. Every hole represents a piece of information – for instance, the gender, profession, residence, or age of a given individual. The punched cards are then stacked in bundles and counted with an electromechanical counting machine. Sensors locate the punched hole. Every sensor that penetrates a punched hole closes an electric circuit and triggers an impulse to calculate a number.

Hollerith adapted the punched-card system from the ticketing system of America's railways at the time. A railway ticket consisted of a card on which punched holes in prescribed areas indicated gender, hair color, and other characteristics of the ticket holder to prevent transfer of tickets. Echoing photography's rendering of real persons in instant portraits, these cards or tickets were called "punchcard photographs." Coincidentally, Hollerith, though a passionate photographer all his life, steadfastly refused to have his picture taken by another photographer.[15] Visual metaphors abound throughout the history of the Hollerith tabulating machine. In the 1920s, DEHOMAG advertised its services with posters showing a factory illuminated by a light source from above, an image suggesting that the Hollerith tabulating machine could cast a light on even the darkest recesses of a company's operations. The copy on the poster used the term *durchleuchten*, i.e., "x-raying," to describe the effect of the Hollerith process, thus establishing an analogy between mechanical tabulation and x-ray photography as invented by Willhelm Röntgen in 1896 (as well as, by implication, an analogy between industrial organization and the human body as potential objects of x-ray scans and *Durchleuchtung*).[16]

The Hollerith data processing system was introduced at the Krupp factory in early 1928. The company's film department, the Kinematographische Abteilung, which had been established as part of the Graphische Abteilung as early as 1908 (1913 according to other sources), making it one of the earliest corporate film departments anywhere in the world, produced a five-part, 90-minute training film which was used mainly for internal communication purposes.[17] Entitled VOM FRÜHEREN UND HEUTIGEN RECHNUNGSWESEN EINES WERKES (*Accounting Then and Now*), the film used the before-and-after rhetoric of run-of-the-mill industrial films to deliver a detailed description of the Hollerith tabulating machine and its effect on business practice and company structure. The original film contains no sound and consists of long, unedited shots. While a viewer watching the film today may consider its pace tedious, the copious use of long, uncut shots points to the way the film was screened. Its style is in fact very much in tune with the style of educational films as used in school and university classrooms in the 1920s and 1930s. Up until the 1950s, many educational films had no sound or commentary whatsoever. Rather, they merely furnished visual materials to accompany the teacher's presentation, i.e., images in motion to be studied by the class according to the teacher's spoken instructions.[18] Similarly, the Krupp film on the Hollerith tabulating machine was clearly designed to illustrate a spoken commentary when shown to company officers and workers alike. While this was standard for educational purposes, it was also commonplace for Krupp's films. Most of the film holdings of the Krupp film archive were destroyed in World War II. Only a very limited number of films produced before 1945 survive. To the extent that they still exist, however, the archive holdings seem to indicate that before the advent of sound most Krupp films produced for public or semi-public screenings closely resembled the Hollerith film. A case in point is a film entitled KRUPP HARTMETALL about the advantages of Widia steel blades, which were invented and introduced to the market in 1926 (Widia was an acronym for *Wie Diamant*, "like diamond").[19] The film consists entirely of long *plan séquences*. In all likelihood, salesmen screened the film at trade fairs to illustrate spoken commentary. For all practical purposes, film presentations of this type were slide shows with moving images. Among other things, these films illustrate the fact that the motion picture was late in being included among the media of internal and business-to-business corporate communications. Films only began to replace the slide in the late 1910s and early

1920s as the primary medium for visual presentations, and even so, the presentational mode of the slide show remained firmly in place until the advent of sound, in some places even later.[20]

The first part of the five-part Krupp film on the Hollerith tabulating machine and its effects on accounting is devoted to the accounting practices of old, beginning with a short resumé of the company's history and its growth during the 19th century. In addition to informing corporate officers and others about a technological innovation, the film also contributed to the company's self-image, reiterating the key points of the standard account of its own origins. The film then moves to old-time accounting practices proper, but not without anchoring the argument in yet another historical reference. We see a portrait of Alfred Krupp, the company founder's son who transformed a precarious family enterprise into the world's most important arms producer within the space of just one generation, and we see a sample of his handwriting.

Figure 2 He saw it all coming: Alfred Krupp in
VOM FRÜHEREN UND HEUTIGEN RECHNUNGSWESEN EINES WERKES *(1928)*

As a title card informs us, these images serve to illustrate the fact that accounting at Krupp, then as now, follows a basic set of principles laid down by the corporate patriarch when the company was still in its infancy. The film then segues into a series of rather nostalgic-looking images of elderly men at large wooden desks copying figures and numbers into folios from paper slips handed them by young pages. The passage ends with a scene showing an impatient phone call to the accounting office from central headquarters. The accounting officer from headquarters inquires about the whereabouts of the monthly balance that has been overdue for several weeks. Clearly frustrated, he hangs up the phone. *"So kann es nicht weitergehen"* ("Things can't go on like this"), he insists, as we learn from a title card. Obviously, something needed to change in the accounting department, and it does in the second part of the film, which is devoted to the introduction of the Hollerith tabulating machine.

Down to the last detail of the title cards, the cinematic description of the Hollerith process follows the outline of the presentation given by a member of the legal department to corporate officers in June 1927 and quoted above. Incidentally, the same text was later recycled in an article published in the Krupp company newspaper *Nach der Schicht* in 1931, which explained the Hollerith data-processing machine to the larger audience of the company's entire workforce.[21] All three versions stress the issue of gender. The film and the two texts discuss at length how the staff of the punched-card department consists of young women supervised by male officers, all the while emphasizing the strict gender differentiation of functional roles. One is tempted to read this emphasis as an indication of a certain uneasiness about the presence of women in the accounting department. Accounting in the old days, as the first part of the film shows, was an all-male business. Under the new accounting structure, the production of the punched cards was done by "young women from 16 to 21 years of age," certainly marriageable ages at the time, while the data processing as such was handled by young men with business diplomas, also highly marriageable, of course.

Figure 3 Marriageable Women learn about information processing in
VOM FRÜHEREN UND HEUTIGEN RECHNUNGSWESEN EINES WERKES (1928)

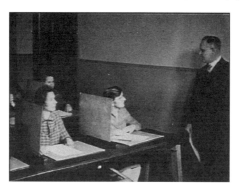

The young women were selected for their tasks by means of tests that employed the methodology of *Psychotechnik*, or "psychotechnology," a branch of applied business psychology pioneered in the early 1910s by Hugo Münsterberg, a German-born professor of psychology at Harvard who coincidentally wrote one of the earliest books on film theory, *The Photoplay*, published in 1916.[22] In view of their tasks as card punchers the "girls ... were tested in groups of twelve to fifteen for roughly four hours: Imagination, memory, attention and alacrity, all qualities that they must possess as card punchers." In this case, then, Psychotechnik involved evaluating the young women's mental affinity to the data-processing apparatus and its use. Such tests had become standard practice in the Ruhr Valley steel and mining industries, with Psychotechnik evaluation successively replacing family ties to former or current factory employees as the key criterion for the selection of trainees and new workers in the 1920s.[23] The widespread use of Psychotechnik by the Ruhr Valley industries corresponded to a general trend in the German economy of the mid- to late 1920s, in which the promise of rationalizing mental processes appealed to actors in all areas of business, from industrial production to distribution and sales.[24] While Psychotechnik was primarily a technique of rationalization and increasing productivity employed for very much the same reasons that led to the introduction of new accounting techniques and the Hollerith tabulating machine by Krupp, there may have been a cultural side to the technique's appeal as well. It would certainly be interesting to study the spread of this particular aspect of business psychology against the background of cultural trends such as Weimar cinema's interest in hypnosis, of which Fritz Lang's 1922 thriller DR. MABUSE, DER SPIELER is a prime example.

  The spiritual makes an appearance in the Hollerith film from the Krupp archives as well. One of the film's key sequences shows the Psychotechnik test, with a group of young women sorting geometric shapes and checking off figures and numbers. While they are at work, the examiner in the back of the room suddenly disappears, then reappears again, all thanks to the magic of double exposure and editing.

Figure 4 Appearance trick: an engineer materializes in
VOM FRÜHEREN UND HEUTIGEN RECHNUNGSWESEN EINES WERKES (1928)

As John Durham Peters points out in his history of the concept of communication, the key problem of technological modernity is not the ghost in the machine, but the body in communication: its seeming presence and factual absence on the telephone, on television, on the Internet, etc.[25] The figure of the male examiner which fades in and out of the room seems to indicate just that: a ghostly presence whose precarious visibility points to a crisis of bodily presence in modern technological communication. What is more, the ghostly examiner is not alone. In a later sequence from the fourth part of the film that explains the workings of the data-processing machine as such, the engineer operating the machine fades in and out of the image in similar fashion. But the ghost in the machine is never far from the scene. As we witness the tabulating machine in action, the contours of a robot appear suddenly, and we see numbers dancing around in circles in the robot's head, with the same speed with which they went through the young card puncher's hands earlier.

Figure 5 Ghost in the machine: A robot, the soul of the tabulating machine in VOM FRÜHEREN UND HEUTIGEN RECHNUNGSWESEN EINES WERKES (1928)

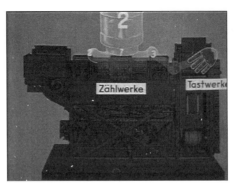

It would certainly be rewarding to further pursue the issue of gender in light of the fact that women's bodies in this film represent a substantial presence in the space of industrial production, while male bodies appear rather insubstantial. My point here is that it seems significant that the male figures performing the Hollerith process are of dubious visibility. One could, of course, argue that it is quite inadmissible to treat an industrial training film such as "Accounting Then and Now" as a coherent and semantically dense text, particularly considering the fact that it is it is not even complete without the presenter's live commentary. I would hold, however, that one should not underestimate the amount of thought and reflection that went into the production of these films. Corporate film departments are usually run on tight budgets, as one can notice from the fact that the Krupp Hollerith film recycled its own footage in several places, thus incorporating the logic of rationalization and cost saving into its own form. Against this backdrop, it seems quite remarkable and indeed significant that the filmmakers should choose to employ a relatively expensive process such as double exposure, which requires twice the amount of film material, just for the sake of creating the ghost-like appearance of the male engineer's body.

So why and whence the vanishing bodies of the data-processing engineers? One possible answer could come from comparing the Krupp Hollerith film and the work-study films produced by Frank Gilbreth in the early 1910s, which were widely used for improving German industrial productivity in the 1920s. As I argued above, the filmed body of the work-study films may be, on the one hand, considered the ergonomic-Taylorist regime's paradigmatic site of knowledge and control: They represent a visible object for study and improvement, making the factory floor the key site where productivity rates are determined. The data-processing engineer's vanishing body, on the other hand, may be considered the paradigmatic figure of a regime in which the privileged form of control is control through communication, and through the processing of large amounts of data in particular, a form of control which by definition is beyond the realm of the visible, and eventually puts the visibility of the body in crisis. It is precisely during the passage of one regime to the other, or at the moment that the new regime is about to become a reality, that the body of the data-processing engineer vanishes in the Krupp film. As I argued above, the Krupp Hollerith film is both an instructional film and a film that serves the purpose of maintaining and fostering the company's self-image, i.e., it is both a medium for transmission of technical knowledge and a medium for the transmission of feedback knowledge. Accordingly, from the point of view of a historical epistemology of media and industrial organization, the figure of the vanishing body may be read as a figure of knowledge in the sense that it dramatizes, or rather renders visible in the film medium, the shift from one regime of knowledge and control to another, but also dramatizes, and renders visible, film's limitations when it comes to the task of representing and performing the new regime of knowledge that comes with information processing as a key means of production. If the vanishing body of the engineer announced the notion of the "disappearance of work," it did so via a visual trick that metaphorically expresses the problem at hand. And the fact that the filmmakers went to such great lengths to make the data-processing engineer's body disappear, and reappear, seems to indicate that they perceived that the vanishing operator represented an important event, or problem.

III

In its imagery and visual effects, the Krupp Hollerith film documents an incipient awareness of the impending shift from a thermodynamic system of production centered on the human body and the transformation of energy into performance to a cybernetic system of production in which the worker no longer makes a personal physical investment in the production process, but is merely at the helm of a complex of machines. Thirty-five years later, the new order was in full swing. A new calculating machine had emerged on the (media) scene and was about to replace the widely used Hollerith tabulating machine, the computer. With the computer, new production technologies were established, not least of which in the steel industry, where much of the dangerous physical work of old is now done by machines and workers who merely push buttons and handle joysticks, steering the production process in truly cybernetic fashion, as if they were *kybernetes*, the pilot of a large ship. This at least is the image of industrial production conveyed by ANGESTELLTE IN UNSERER ZEIT (*Salaried Employees in Our Time*), a film produced by the Deutscher Gewerkschaftsbund in 1963.

Figure 6 Production through thought: Remote control steel production in
ANGESTELLTE UNSERER ZEIT (*1963*)

The film was directed by Rudolf Kipp (1919-1990), a seasoned director of industrial image and advertising films who began his career working for the Ufa Wochenschau during World War II and had more than two hundred commissions from companies such as Volkswagen, Nestlé, British Petroleum, and Ruhrkohle to his name. This 25-minute recruiting film was aimed primarily at administrative employees rather than industrial workers. In the mid-1960s, there were an estimated 4.5 million employees working in corporate administration in Germany, though only a fraction of them were unionized, the majority apparently considering themselves safe from job insecurity thanks to their relatively high degree of education. The DGB's recruiting drive aimed at changing that state of affairs, and ANGESTELLTE IN UNSERER ZEIT was one of their tools.

The film has two protagonists: a generic employee and the electronic calculating machine, or the computer. The time to join the union, the film argues, has come because the advance of the computer is rapidly changing working conditions not only on the factory floor, but in the administrative departments as well. Allowing for important productivity gains, the introduction of the computer was threatening to render a good number of jobs obsolete. In order to avoid being laid off, and to benefit from gains in productivity thanks to the computer – so the argument ran – employees should join the union.

According to the film's argument, salaried employees form a class of dependent workers who are not sufficiently aware of their social and historical situation and, in good Marxist tradition, the film is intended to enlighten its addressees by making them aware of that situation. Once they get the message, they will see the benefit of union membership. It is also a classic case of anticipating creative destruction: There is a threat of obsolescence, but the employees do not see it coming, and the film is supposed to help them recognize it (if it can, of which more later). Technically, the film is rather well made, and its script represents the state of the art in German sociology of the time. Based on a study by Karl Boetticher, a sociologist with ties to the Frankfurt Institut für Sozialforschung who was married to Adorno's former assistant Helge Pross, the film explains the passage from the thermodynamic to the cybernetic age, i.e., that of *Produktion durch Denken*, or production through thought, rather than physical energy, by taking the steel industry as its example. The combination of Frankfurt School social theory and research and the aesthetics of the industrial film alone would make this film a worthwhile object of study. However, I will focus on the way the film represents the computer and its impact on industrial organization. As I would like to argue, ANGESTELLTE IN UNSERER ZEIT is more than just a historical document: Much like the Hollrith film, it represents a media interface of technical and social discourses and organizational form, and it could similarly be said to represent the drama of the separation of control and visibility in industrial organization in the film medium.

It is a commonplace notion of left-wing critiques of industrial film and photography that corporate images cover up the real working conditions and do not represent work in an adequate fashion. Marx himself may have inaugurated that topos in *Das Kapital* when he likened his analysis of the capitalist mode of production to an illicit or illegitimate factory visit that revealed the dirty secrets that company owners, through manifold strategies, tried to keep from the public.[26] A Marxist critique, then, is a critique of political economy in a visual key: It is, if you will, the real factory visit, the one in which *Das Geheimnis der Plusmacherei*, the secret of profiteering, comes to light. It is quite fitting, then, that since the 1970s at least, Marxist critiques have often centered on visual media and their representations of work. There is clearly some substance to the claim, often put forward by social historians, that "real work" is absent from industrial film and photography. Alfred Krupp, for one, ordered that his factories be photographed on Sundays only, and preferably on sunny spring days, in order to create an image of cleanliness and quiet, rather than one of potentially harmful activities. It is important to note, however, that this was partly done for technical reasons. In the early years of industrial photography, exposure times were so long that workers and their work would probably not have shown up very clearly on the photographic plate. Nonetheless, corporate communications tended to play down the potentially harmful impact of working in, for instance, a steel mill. In Angestellte unserer Zeit, however, work is not visible because it is about to cease being so, because in a regime of "production through thought", the essential work is no longer taking place in the visible realm. While industrial films about the steel industry tend to include spectacular footage of liquid steel, the problem with the changes wrought by the computer was that representing the processes that matter in the film medium became difficult. Continuing to focus on imagery of liquid steel would amount to a misrepresentation of the workplace reality and thus repeat the failings of corporate films. Visual effects such as the vanishing body of the data-processing engineer from the Krupp film may work as symptomatic figures of a new regime of knowledge, but would probably not help to convince employees to join the union. But if you are making a film in which the computer and its inner workings is the real protagonist, how do you go about representing that protagonist? What we see instead of the traditional imagery of men at work in factory halls is a huge machine in a room – the "electronic brain" or computer – and a man who manipulates that machine in a rather vague way, pushing buttons and watching a screen. We see him doing something, in other words, but we do not see what he does. After all, pushing a button can trigger all kinds of processes. Controlling a steel press with joysticks, the process that was shown earlier in the film, produces spectacular results, but the actual work that makes the steel move and the machines perform their task, is no longer visible even in that situation. Nor is it in the office space. The protagonist of the film, in other words, remains at least partially intangible.

If a thriller like Jaws builds suspense by withholding the monster's appearance until the very last moment, a recruiting film like Angestellte in unserer Zeit is at a loss when it comes to representing its hero/villain at all. However, it may be precisely the elusiveness of the computer that lends it a certain demonic

Figure 7 Operating beyond the threshold of visibility: IBM hardware in action in ANGESTELLTE UNSERER ZEIT (*1963*)

quality, and it is certainly no coincidence that one of the images of its protagonist the film contains is that of the large, dark, and somewhat deformed looking outer body of the calculating machine, considerably larger than the man in front of it. This imagery of the "electronic brain" remains firmly anchored in the conventions of the thermodynamic age. In terms of the industrial film's visual rhetoric, impact and importance remain directly related to size and volume. An important machine has to look important. In 1963, representing the computer as a small device that takes up almost no space at all but still has a major impact on industrial production would apparently be inconceivable. Furthermore, we see a series of other office machines operated via the computer, a series that carries a clear message of a threat to jobs. And finally, the film eventually does find an image to represent the inner workings of the computer. Luckily for the Marxist paradigm of critique, electronic machines at the time still used transistors and vacuum tubes rather than chips, so that the vacuum tubes could be filmed as they lit up. It is an image that creates a visual formula for the computer's control through communication by breaking it down in the terms of visibility of the thermodynamic age: What we see is an image of energy transformed into performance, i.e., a visual representation of a tangible physical process. Given the advanced stage of the technological and organizational shift to a new mode, this image actually represents a piece of nostalgic thermodynamic kitsch, if you will. Clearly, there is still solace in this imagery of energy being transformed into performance, but it merely provides false solace, and the image itself is actually aporetic: It speaks of film's inability to represent and perform what the computer does, its inherent limits of *Darstellung* in a cybernetic age.[27]

But then, the union film is a political film, produced not by a corporation or an industrial organization, but rather a political organization, for political ends (even though unions and unionizing have been part and parcel of the process of industrial organization ever since the 19th century). Keeping this in mind, the extent to which the film resembles a piece of corporate communication is striking.[28] The carefully crafted visual style and the celebratory mode of showing

advanced machinery in action may come as a surprise when one considers the
director's pedigree as an industrial filmmaker, but some questions arise in light
of who the commissioning body is and for what purpose the film was produced. The real, fully revelatory factory visit as envisioned by Marx himself
this is not. Apparently, the Marxist idea of critique as making the material reality of the capitalist mode of production visible reaches a limit in this film. But
then, one could argue that the DGB film still subscribes to just such a basic concept of critique as visual revelation and representation, in that the union relies
on the visual medium of film to create an awareness among employees of their
historical and social situation. However, the film simultaneously takes a political stance that is typical of the German Social Democratic party and the unions
of post-World War II West Germany. Rather than offering a fundamental critique of capitalism, German Social Democrats and union leaders subscribed to
the idea of technological progress and intended to assure that the workforce
participated in its benefits without fundamental change in the capitalist mode
of production. Indeed, very much in accordance with Mancur Olson's theory of
collective action, German postwar unions were very large and comprehensive
and thus had the critical size necessary for pursuing an increase in economic
output rather than just a policy of redistributing the wealth.[29] The union film's
celebration of steel-making technology, then, may be read as an expression of
ideas and ideals shared by corporate interests; the differences in substance lay
elsewhere. The seeming neutrality of the visual style can, in other words, be
seen as analogous to a certain neutrality in politics, or rather a shared interest
in improving output and performance. Far from opposing rationalization and
creative destruction per se, the union's political work was about redistributing
the increase in returns from these structural changes. But inasmuch as this increase was due to information processing, the union representatives still seemed
to believe that film was the adequate medium for critique and for raising the
consciousness of the salaried employee; otherwise, they would not have commissioned ANGESTELLTE IN UNSERER ZEIT. Even as control became separated
from visibility, the politics of control in and over industrial organizations remained firmly linked to a priority of the visible for union organizers. Which
may help to explain just why German unions have failed to make substantial
inroads into new media industries, particularly IT industries. The classic industries like steel and mining are becoming all but insignificant, and the respective
unions have been conservatively protecting the interests of their ever-dwindling
memberships for several decades now, without really succeeding at branching
out into other and new industries.[30] In particular, while there are spontaneous
forms of unionization and moves toward the creation of *Betriebsräte*, or works
councils, in some IT firms, computer engineers remain largely non-unionized.[31]

From a perspective of a historical epistemology of media and industrial organizations, one wonders if this could have anything to do with the fact that the
traditional unions remained somehow trapped in an outmoded regime of
knowledge based on visibility, trying to sort out, for much longer than was politically useful, the epistemological aporia of thermodynamic kitsch.

Conclusion

An animated graphic in the Krupp Hollerith film shows a map of the company's
Essen factory grounds before and after the introduction of tabulating machines.
In the first stage of the animation sequence, we see icons symbolizing the various accounting offices spread out over the entire space covered by the map.
Then, as if moved by a magic hand, the icons disappear, only to be replaced by
a marker for the new, centralized accounting office. Before and after: a classic
trope in the rhetoric of rationalization. There is nothing easier than visualizing
the changes wrought by creative destruction, it would seem, even those that are
due to advances in information processing. It is enough to show, literally, the
changing landscape of capitalist production, to create a map, a visual model
that allows us to simulate the changes that happen to the economic structure
from within.

But what are we seeing when that landscape changes before our very eyes? A
magic trick of sorts, a disappearing act whose mechanics remain hidden from
our eyes, leaving us with nothing but a sense of astonishment. It is an astonishment quite different from the one produced, say, by the sheer size and volume
of a large, impressive machine battering a block of steel into a certain shape. It is
the astonishment created by a Méliès rather than a Lumière film: a sense of
wonder about the cinematic sleight of hand rather than what film reveals about
the outside world. In tune with the analysis presented here, this may be read as
another sign of crisis. Clearly, the industrial film, itself a medium of rationalization, seems to be one of the casualties left in the wake of the creative destruction
brought about by information processing, reduced, as it is, to the role of purveyor of thermodynamic kitsch and dependent on cinematic tricks that belong
to the fantasy genre rather than the sober discourse of the instructional film.

But then, the Hollerith film's animation may be read in a slightly different
way, as well. It could be viewed as an allegory not of film's demise, but of its
changing role in the new mode of industrial production. Film, the indexical
medium par excellence, the medium of bodily movement that maintains a direct linit of physical causation to the object it represents, is now the imaginary
medium par excellence, illustrating in metaphors, graphs, and visual aporias

what is no longer representable as such, i.e., the new kind of work that has moved from the realm of the visible, of reality, to a kind of Lacanian real, a realm of the unrepresentable. Or, to phrase it in a slightly different way: Rather than indexical images, film now produces epistemic images, images that no longer simply represent, and refer to, reality, but become objects of knowledge in and of themselves. It is not a transition from the medium that can represent and perform everything to purveyor of kitsch, but rather from simile to simulation. Such was the path of creative destruction that the medium of the industrial film took when the computer appeared on the scene of industrial production, a scene that was forever changed by the computer's (non-)appearance. Let us take this as a possible working hypothesis for further research in an area of which my two examples give, at the very best, a preliminary outline.

Notes

1.   Earlier versions of this essay have been published as "Visible Calculations. Computing in German Industrial Films, 1928/1963," *Entreprise et histoire*, 44 (September 2006), pp. 43-54, and "Thermodynamischer Kitsch. Vom Verschwinden der Arbeit im Film," in Freunde der deutschen Kinemathek (ed.), *Work in Progress. Kinematografien der Arbeit* (Berlin: b_books, 2007), pp. 37-43. Illustrations with kind permission of Historisches Archiv Krupp, Essen (fig. 1-4) and Institut für soziale Bewegungen, Bochum (fig. 5-6).
2.   The reference to evolutionary theory is intentional, as Schumpeter himself acknowledges the impact of biological thought on his model: "Creative destruction" is "the ... process of industrial mutation – if I may use that biological term – that incessantly revolutionizes the economic structure *from within*, incessantly destroying the old one, incessantly creating a new one. This process of Creative Destruction is the essential fact about capitalism. It is what capitalism consist in [sic] and what every capitalist concern has got to live in." Joseph Schumpeter, *Capitalism, Socialism and Democracy* (New York: Harper & Row, 1975 [1942]), p. 83.
3.   For the transformation of an IT driven information society see Krishan Kumar, *From Post-Industrial to Post-Modern Society* (Oxford: Blackwell, 1995). For an overall assessment of the impact of IT technology on organizational structure and business performance in the last two decades see Erik Brynjolfsson and Lorin M. Hitt, "Beyond Computation: Information Technology, Organizational Transformation and Business Performance", in: Thomas W. Malone, Robert Laubacher, Michael S. Scott Morton, *Inventing the Organizations of the 21st Century* (Cambridge MA: MIT Press), pp. 71-99. For an early assessment of how IT changes organizational structures towards flat hierarchies and flexible specialization see Erik K. Clemons, Reddi P. Sashidhar, Michael C. Row, "The impact of information technology on the organization of economic activity: the 'Move to the middle' hypothesis", in: *Journal of Management Information System,* Vol. 10 , No. 2 (September 1993), pp. 9-35. Comparable in terms of impact is the introduction of in logistics after 1960. In New York

City alone, due to the relocation of the textile industry and its commercial harbor, more than 700,000 jobs were lost in the wake of the container ship's introduction. See Marc Levinson, *The Box: How the Shipping Container Made the World Smaller and the World Economy Bigger* (Princeton: Princeton University Press, 2006), pp. 76-78.

4. See Anson Rabinbach, *The Human Motor: Energy, Fatigue, and the Origins of Modernity* (Berkeley: University of California Press), particularly chapters 2, 4, and 7.

5. Regarding the notion of historical epistemology, see Georges Canguilhem, *Wissenschaftsgeschichte und Epistemologie. Gesammelte Aufsätze* (Frankfurt am Main: Suhrkamp, 1979).

6. Regarding the cultural and political history of the panorama as a medium and a mode of vision in Germany in the 19th century, see Dolf Sternberger, *Panorama, oder Ansichten vom 19. Jahrhundert* (Frankfurt am Main: Suhrkamp, 1974).

7. Philip Sarasin points out that while Gilbreth based his work on the theories and models of F.W. Taylor, a major difference separated the two. Taylor was interested in solving what he considered to be essentially a moral problem, i.e., the presumed laziness of the industrial worker. Gilbreth, meanwhile, only cared about improving the worker's physical performance without giving much thought to morale, or morals for that matter. In terms of their mentality and attitude, then, it could be argued that Taylor belonged to an older regime of knowledge, i.e., the panoramic-panoptic, whereas Gilbreth initiated a new regime through his work-study films, Taylorist in letter, but not in spirit, if you will. See Philip Sarasin, "Die Rationalisierung des Körpers. Über 'Scientific Management' und 'biologische Rationalisierung'," in Philip Sarasin (ed.), *Geschichtswissenschaft und Diskursanalyse* (Frankfurt am Main: Suhrkamp, 2002), pp. 61-99 .

8. "Für den Film gibt es keine Beschränkungen, keine Fesseln; alles lässt sich filmisch darstellen." Hans-Heinrich Campen, "Industriefilm als wirksames Mittel der Information," *Krupps Mitteilungen*, 46 (1962), pp. 179-180.

9. See Norbert Bolz, Friedrich A. Kittler, Georg Christoph Tholen, *Computer als Medium* (Munich: Fink, 1994).

10. See Urs Stäheli, Dirk Verdicchio, "Das Unsichtbare sichtbar machen. Hans Richters 'Die Börse als Barometer der Wirtschaftslage,' " *Montage AV* 15, 1 (2006), pp. 108-122.

11. "Das Hollerithverfahren, seine Einführung und Durchführung im Stahlwerk der Fried. Krupp A.G.," presentation for the "Studienausschuß für industrielle Verwaltung" (April 25, 1928). Historisches Archiv Krupp, Essen, Werkarchiv, VII f 1583, V. 5102.

12. Cf. Lothar Gall, *Krupp im 20. Jahrhundert* (Berlin: Siedler 2002), pp. 118-120 and 181-183.

13. On the rationalization of the steel industry in the Ruhr Valley in the 1920s, see Christian Kleinschmidt, *Rationalisierung als Unternehmensstrategie. Die Eisen- und Stahlindustrie des Ruhrgebiets zwischen Jahrhundertwende und Weltwirtschaftskrise* (Essen: Klartext, 1993), 116-118.

14. Cf. Emerson W. Pugh, *Building IBM: Shaping and Industry and Its Technology* (Cambridge, MA: MIT Press, 1995).

15. Geoffrey Austrian, *Hermann Hollerith: Forgotten Giant of Information Processing* (New York: Columbia University Press, 1982), p. 145.

16. Cf. Monika Dommann, *Durchsicht, Einsicht, Vorsicht. Eine Geschichte der Röntgenstrahlen, 1896-1963* (Zurich: Chronos, 2003).

17. Cf. the contribution of Herwig Müther in Manfred Rasch, Karl-Peter Ellenbrock, Renate Köhne-Lindenlaub, *Industriefilm als Medium und Quelle* (Essen: Klartext, 1999).

18. On the aesthetics and pragmatics of the educational film see Anita Gertiser, "Domestizierung des bewegten Bildes. Vom dokumentarischen Film zum Lehrmedium," *Montage AV* 15,1 (2006), pp. 59-73; and Eef Masson, "Didaktik vs. Pädagogik. Ein kontextueller Ansatz für die Untersuchung von Unterrichtsfilmen," *Montage AV* 15,1 (2006), pp. 10-25.

19. Krupp Archive, videocassette K1/917VHST1.

20. On the transition from slide presentation to film presentation in industrial and marketing contexts see Yvonne Zimmermann, "Vom Lichtbild zum Film. Anmerkungen zur Entstehung des Industriefilms," *Montage AV* 15, 1 (2006), pp. 74-88.

21. "Das Hollerith-Lochkartenverfahren," *Nach der Schicht (Kruppsche Mitteilungen)*, 12th edition, 1 (July 1931), pp. 4-7.

22. Cf. Matthew Hale Jr., *Human Science and Social Order: Hugo Münsterberg and the Origins of Applied Psychology* (Philadelphia: Temple University Press, 1980).

23. Kleinschmidt (1993), pp. 180-181 and 270.

24. For a survey of the applications of Psychotechnik in the 1920s see Fritz Giese, *Psychotechnik* (Breslau: Hirt, 1928).

25. John Durham Peters, *Speaking into the Air: A History of the Idea of Communication* (Chicago: Chicago University Press, 1999).

26. Karl Marx, *Das Kapital. Kritik der politischen Ökonomie. Der Produktionsprozess des Kapitals* [1872] (Cologne: Parkland, 2003), p. 177.

27. Digitizing the image does not change this basic aporia, by the way: Even in a pixilated version, the image still represents a false concept of how the computer works, and what it does to work in a thermodynamic sense. In that sense, the computer as a medium cannot visually perform the creative destruction it wreaks on the economic structure. This is another way of saying that it cannot "perform" itself in another medium and hence cannot perform itself at all. On the whole, then, the computer-based techno-Hegelianism of the Kittler school is quite as aporetic as the cinematographic techno-Hegelianism proposed by Krupp's erstwhile chief of corporate communications.

28. When I showed an excerpt of the film – the sequence set in the steel mill – to an audience of historians at the University of Frankfurt in May of 2006, one of the professors asked me if I was sure that this was a union film, since it looked so much like a conventional industrial film. I had to refer to the credits to answer the question.

29. "Encompassing organizations have some incentive to make the society in which they operate more prosperous, and an incentive to redistribute income to their members with as little excess burden as possible, and to cease such redistribution unless the amount redistributed is substantial in relation to the social cost of the redistribution." Mancur Olson, *The Rise and Fall of Nations: Economic Growth, Stagflation and Social Rigidities* (New Haven and London: Yale University Press, 1982), p. 53. The Deutscher Gewerkschafts Bund, or DGB, an umbrella organization for major German unions, covers about 85% percent of the unionized German workforce.

30. As part of this strategy, IG Bergbau, formerly one of the most powerful independent unions in Germany, merged with IG Chemie in 1997, to create a membership that was large enough to maintain its bargaining power, one of many such mergers that have taken place in Germany and other European countries over the last 20 years.

31. See, for instance, Jörg Abel, Ludger Pries, "Shifting patterns of labor regulation: Highly qualified knowledge workers in German new media companies," *Critical Sociology,* 33 (2007), pp. 101-125.

III
Films and Factories

Touring as a Cultural Technique

Visitor Films and Autostadt Wolfsburg

Patrick Vonderau

As an umbrella term for films made or commissioned by companies or business associations, "industrial film" stands for a wide array of audiovisual products that are used in the most varied of contexts. This essay concerns a variety of the *process film* that features the assembly of vehicles, namely films made for factory tours that were produced for Volkswagen AG in Wolfsburg and also used there. The commissioned films produced for the Volkswagen Group encompass a broad spectrum of safety films, internal research films, advertising and product films, informational films for schools, and films on traffic education, motor sports, the history of the factory, and environmental protection. The factory-tour or visitor film therefore constitutes only a small segment of the company's film production, which furthermore is largely limited to the years between 1980 and 1992.[1] I am interested here in the visitor film as one element within a larger ensemble of representational processes which served and still serve to show the manufacturing of cars and its results to potential customers. During the 1980s and early 1990s, factory-tour films were screened for guests before the tour; to-day, shorter product and advertising films are integrated into the commercialized tour of Autostadt Wolfsburg.

It would be appropriate – and this is my point of departure – not to view past and present film production in isolation, but as part of an all-encompassing practice of touring. I intend to speak here of a *Kulturtechnik* (cultural technique), understanding the term as a technique in the original sense, by means of which a natural landscape is reshaped into a cultural landscape, altered by man and adapted for human use, or to put it more generally: making something productive which was previously unproductive.[2] The cultural techniques of touring seek to take advantage of previously unused resources by opening up industrial spaces or "landscapes." "Touring," then, has nothing in common with sightseeing or factory inspection as it relates to worker protection, for instance. It has much more to do with regulated action in semiotic arrangements toward a concrete economic result. What is made productive in the cultural technique of the tour is less the factory than the visitor him- or herself: as will be shown, Autostadt Wolfsburg and the media integrated into it can be seen as part of a streamlining measure involving the customer, a measure which has a long prehistory, not only in the history of the visitor film, but equally so in the field of exhibition and finally in the history of marketing initiatives, whose ideas can be traced back to the 1930s. My conclusion will argue for an understanding of industrial film itself as only one of many representational techniques thanks to which, particularly in economic crisis situations, the exchange between producer and consumer is coordinated. Industrial films, and this is the main point of my essay, serve to create conventions for this exchange.

Figure 1 Production of a Volkswagen Beetle in Wolfsburg

Photo by Paul Wolff Tritschler, 1949 (Bildarchiv preussischer Kulturbesitz, Berlin)

Exhibitions, films, and factory tours

The representation of automotive manufacturing is almost as old as the automobile itself. Such presentations were initially made in the framework of industrial exhibitions, for example, the *Erste deutsche Motorwagen-Ausstellung* (First German Motor Vehicle Exhibition) in 1899 in Berlin, which was then repeated nearly annually. In 1913, the Verein Deutscher Motorfahrzeugindustrieller (German Association of Motor Vehicle Industrialists) and the Kaiserliche Automobilclub (Imperial Automobile Club), on the occasion of the planned *Internationale Automobilausstellung* (International Automobile Exhibition), had a special trade fair center built. About 20 years later, it would be here that a *"Kraft durch Freude-Wagen"* from the Volkswagen factory would be presented to a wide public for the first time. At the International Automobile and Motorcycle Exhibition

in 1939, a model of the Volkswagen factory and a model of the vehicle itself
were put on display, accompanied by graphically arranged tables that explained
the manufacturing process from molding to construction of the frame, and then
to the final painting. As an exhibition object, this first Volkswagen also became
the object of a media campaign organized by the Reichsverband der Automobilindustrie (National Association of the Automobile Industry) which encompassed posters, bulk mailings, and slides in addition to film and radio an-
nouncements.[3] Contemporary newsreels present the construction of the factory,
the automobile, and the Autobahn as being related, an attempt to coordinate the
automobile conceived by Porsche at "Führergeheiß" ("the behest of the
Führer") with the presumed leisure needs of wide segments of the population.
In the Third Reich's film PR, the KdF-Wagen was presented as the guarantor of
private mobilization, since it was seen as affordable, reliable and economical.[4]

This advertising campaign of the prewar period, in which "the automobile
became the Volkswagen" (literally, people's car),[5] can be seen in the framework
of National Socialist propaganda about full employment and mobilization, but
also in the context of American marketing-management methods, which German business had been following since the early 1930s. Of particular importance were Earnest Elmo Calkins' ideas of Consumer Engineering.[6] At the time,
marketing and market-research initiatives were intended to control the increasing mobility of consumers by isolating consumption practices and taste patterns
and addressing them in certain physical or media contexts.[7] The main task of
the consumer engineer was to provide the business with consumers by insuring
that modern, distinct, and affordable goods made to suit their tastes and needs
were produced.[8]

In the postwar period, marketing-management ideas from the US were popularized in Germany. In the area of industrial-film production the leading figure
in these efforts was Friedrich Mörtzsch, chair of the Working Group on Industrial and Documentary Film of the National Association of German Industry as
well as author of two books, one on business PR, the other on industrial film.[9]
After making research trips to the US, Mörtzsch advocated the view that "trustworthy advertising" was absolutely essential in order to guarantee, in a time of
"far-reaching change in the forms of production" marked by greater division of
labor, that the social "schemata of order" could be maintained.[10]

The task of industrial film for him consisted in the first place of overcoming
the "problem of adaptation," in "sociocultural adaptation to new circumstances," for which a "mass means of information" like film seemed particularly
suitable.[11] Mörtzsch expressly positioned film in conjunction with other techniques of mass effect and PR practices. Inspired by the use of the medium by
General Motors,[12] he argued for the introduction of film during factory tours.
For Mörtzsch, it went without saying that trust in industrial production could

be made possible only by opening the factory gates, by freely providing information about the appearance of the factory halls, the atmosphere at the company, assembly, and the distribution of goods.[13] At the same time, the conventional factory tour seemed less appropriate for meeting these goals:

> No matter whether the factory facilities are too far apart from each other, the process
> of assembly is not easily comprehensible, or the factory halls are not entirely safe for
> lay visitors: film can help! It can explain the overall scheme of things, it can outline
> the meaning and purpose of the company through commentary far better than a tour
> leader can in a short visit. ... Even in those cases where a factory tour actually takes
> place, showing a film to the visitors at the start should be considered. It can express
> something about the history of the company in short scenes, it can reproduce the lay-
> out of the factory, and above all, by using animation effects it can convincingly repre-
> sent the flow of materials, from the incoming raw materials to the outgoing as-
> sembled product. With such preparation the visitor will be able to get much more
> out of the factory tour.[14]

Industrial film had to explain the what, how, and where of production, and in
doing so, represent what was not at all visible at the place of manufacturing
without further explanation. The factory-tour film was given the function of
demonstrating a systematic coherence of manufacturing, which had fallen out
of view over the course of industrial improvements; it was supposed to reconstruct a process for the spectator that had become "incomprehensible"[15]
through the increased speed of assembly, subdivision of the production process,
and automation. For Friedrich Mörtzsch, the factory-tour film needed to prepare the visitor for what he or she would see when finally entering the factory.
The factory is constituted cinematically through its history, though most importantly through the spatial and chronological organization of assembly: the "lay-
out," the overview of the space, is essential, because for the visitor, the logic of
the production process is abrogated in the spatial order.

   Mörtzsch saw film as the preferred representational technique of the factory.
Not because of the basic recording function of the film camera and the documentary possibilities that film offers, but precisely because of the techniques
that *distance* it from its function as simple recordings of existing events: slow
motion and micro-shots, rear-projection processes, and animation.[16] In industrial film, the film itself was supposed to be first of all visible as a representational technique, the analytical breakdown of a process, the movement, the
shaped image. Through these techniques, media like the factory-tour film also
made it possible to *not* show the real work being performed in the factory: work
at the level of personal interaction, social organization, company hierarchies.
The representational techniques of film, therefore, had the advantage of making
it possible to guide the visitor's journey through the factory to an extent not

Figure 2 The Volkswagen factory in Wolfsburg

Photo by Paul Wolff Tritschler, 1949 (Bildarchiv preussischer Kulturbesitz, Berlin)

possible in a conventional tour, and even streamline the tour itself. Finally, the film also permitted detachment of the tour from the place of production altogether; it "brings these experiences [in the factory tour] into the closed space, the movie theater, the factory screening room, or even the schoolroom."[17]

Factory tour in/on film

The influence of the very effective PR man Mörtzsch on industrial-film production during the postwar period can hardly be underestimated. Striking examples of visitor-instruction[18] films that correspond to the function of the medium he described can be found at the Volkswagen Group in the 1980s in particular.

Strictly speaking, the films produced at the time were manufacturing films that dealt with the construction of a new Volkswagen model in about 15 minutes and were shown to guests of the factory by the visitors' department before a two-hour tour. While these tours always showed only a small part of the assembly process, the film gave the impression that the viewer had received an overview of the entire process and its results.

The push to introduce visitor films at this point in time is a result above all of a change in marketing strategies. In the early 1980s, the automobile industry experienced a crisis in turnover. This necessitated a new, defensive marketing strategy that would allow it to tame the out-of-control market, regain a lost market position, and insure the profitability of the business.[19] The central factor in this strategy, today widely known as Customer Relationship Marketing, is the customer. Even Earnest Elmo Calkins understood the "desires" and "needs" of the consumer as the motor of economic stability, all the while keeping an eye above all on advertising agencies, which were supposed to deliver customers to the industry. Customer Relationship Marketing, on the other hand, sought and still seeks to regulate consumer behavior on the basis of voluntary cooperation. The relationship between the company and the customer should be insured through the quality and value of the product, with the goal of establishing long-term "cooperative behavior" between the parties, thereby enhancing the efficiency and productivity of the exchange.[20] Cooperation here means the way that the consumer processes the information the manufacturer provides through advertising or instructions, the act of buying itself, and the consumption of goods in accordance with the manufacturer's instructions. Here as well – to cite Mörtzsch again – it is a "problem of adaptation," to be overcome in an economic and social crisis situation through marketing-management measures.

The visitor films of the Volkswagen Group can be seen in this context. They served to insure the cooperation of potential consumers and secure it after the factory tour. How the visitor's experience was made productive for the goals of the company can be explained through three films from different years: EIN AUTOTAG (1980, gong-film bodo menck), BESUCH BEI VOLKSWAGEN (1985, Graf von Bethusy-Huc), and AUTOS AUS WOLFSBURG (1992, Peter W. Fera Film and Television Production).

EIN AUTOTAG, the first factory-tour film made for Volkswagen, follows the course that the visitor would be taken on later, beginning at the so-called transfer line. The film organizes manufacturing through the space, showing a process in which a car (in this case the Golf) is made from raw materials. The images of molds, dies, and assembly and painting processes are organized into three thematic complexes, which, in an interplay with voice-over commentary, are intended to engender trust in something that is not itself visible: the company's purpose. Initially, the factory's achievement is presented according to the

15-second rhythms of manufacturing, aided by a clock that fades in at the beginning and end while the speaker underscores the just-in-time logistics of production: "And that's the rhythm of the factory for 4,000 cars in two shifts. Need and consumption. Build and drive. Deliver and prepare. Come and go, twice every day." A second complex arises around the representations of automation. Few workers are seen; the "monotonous and dangerous" activities are left to automated machinery. The film actually represents all activity at the factory as a "program" that is checked and guided by the employees; automation is therefore accompanied by their "expertise and reliability." A third thematic complex revolves around the customer. The fact that high-volume manufacturing is programmed according to the "personal wishes" of individual consumers is made clear by the narrator in that the 23,000 variations of the Jetta are cited, set to images of women sewing seat covers. EIN AUTOTAG presents the rhythm of the factory, the automation, and the customer in a production context whose results, so it is claimed, are customized according to the wishes of individual buyers.

The film BESUCH BEI VOLKSWAGEN was used for tours of the external factory at Emden. This is also a process film, with representation concentrated on the process of manufacturing and material arranged around aspects of the assembly's speed (16 hours for one car), automation ("in order to reduce health risks to people"), and customization (seats "for every taste and every requirement"). In contrast to EIN AUTOTAG, this example of a factory-tour film accelerates the process; the result is presented more rapidly in that some of the assembly stations are eliminated. The film also frames the representation with commentary on the tradition of the original factory in Wolfsburg, accompanied by a helicopter flight around the building. Finally, it underscores the fact that "reliability" as a quality of the finished automobile depends essentially on human achievement: humans repeatedly perform "difficult jobs that machines cannot accomplish." We can recognize an attempt to anthropomorphize the production process here, an attempt that in the end even includes the automobile itself: from the assignment of the production code at the "christening point" until the moment that the car is filled with gas "and then drives under its own power for the first time."

Finally, AUTOS AUS WOLFSBURG functions almost identically. This film follows the change in model to the Golf 3 and is the company's last traditional visitor film. Scored with electronic mood music, this film emphasizes the coordination of robots and employees ("They remain in the wings, checking and maintaining the machinery") and expands upon the already familiar presentation with more current issues like environmental protection, the recycling of waste products, and health care for employees. Images of the painting line are highlighted with explanations of reduced environmental impact and, in an obviously staged scene, seamstresses are seen doing aerobics to loosen up.

Each of the three films follows the flow of materials from raw materials to end product, and each of them presents the stations of assembly in a larger systematic context of manufacturing that remains invisible and that is intended to attest to those qualities that are customized for each potential customer. With its causal connection of events in space and time, the representational technique of the film guarantees the logic and achievements of the factory. The films do the preliminary work of creating cooperation between the company and the visitors by instructing the latter in their role: by placing an order, the buyer gives the factory certain information that is fed into the assembly program and prefigures the production process. The customer is, according to the films, part of the control process, and as such, it can be expected that once the vehicle can drive "under its own power," he or she will remain loyal to it his whole life long.

If the era of visitor films had passed with AUTOS AUS WOLFSBURG, there were many reasons why. Producing a new film for every new model probably proved to be not cost-effective, given that it only be viewed by a limited public. Today, the situation is different. Product films are made available to journalists and employed as part of company presentations. Above all, however, the representational technique of the film occurs in a much broader cultural technique of touring, which was given a new form by Autostadt Wolfsburg in 2000.

Experiencing Autostadt Wolfsburg

The construction of Autostadt Wolfsburg was initially part of a rigid streamlining measure. In 1992/1993, the Volkswagen Group once again found itself in crisis. Demand fell sharply; by 1993, approximately 13,000 jobs had been eliminated, which had direct consequences for municipal finances in Wolfsburg.[21] In order to win back lost customers and employees in the motor-vehicle sector, the company turned to the concept of "Autovision," that is, the idea of making a large tourist attraction out of the factory and the city.[22] In this scheme, jobs were created outside the company to compensate for those that had been lost at the plant. With the help of Wolfsburg AG, to which the city of Wolfsburg contributed five million Deutsche marks of starting capital together with the Volkswagen Group, the company city was supposed to become a national tourist attraction, indeed the embodiment of a new service society.

Autostadt Wolfsburg is the expansion of a car-pickup center and was set up on the former eastern parking lot, that is, in the immediate vicinity of the original Wolfsburg factory. Autostadt is a theme park that entertains paying visitors

Figure 3 Flânerie, corporate style: Autostadt Wolfsburg

with driving-related attractions. Attractions like a training course, car exhibitions, widescreen films, and family restaurants quickly established its reputation as being symptomatic of a society in which "experience has become the dominant orienting principle."[23] The presumptive postmodern "experience boom," which the company park stands for, is to a large degree the result of an innovative marketing scheme, that of *experiential branding*. Attractions that focus on a certain brand name and experiences like Autostadt facilitate "psychographic alignment with, if not direct involvement by, the consumer."[24] Brand parks and corporate lands ally consumers with the product by first ascertaining their preferences and lifestyle with the aid of market research, and then addressing them through a tailor-made, emotional experience with the brand.

As a streamlining measure directed at the customer, Autostadt is, however, much less innovative than it initially appears to be. It's conception can be traced back to the idea of Consumer Engineering that Earnest Elmo Calkins promoted in the 1930s. More significantly, however, it expresses the all-encompassing market orientation of Customer Relationship Management. This too is a way of insuring the Group's productivity in a period of crisis regarding sales and world politics by stabilizing the relationship with the consumer – a relationship that should also depend on a consciousness of quality, and emotions and loyalty.[25] What is new here is the manner of touring made possible by Autostadt. If the tour can be understood as a cultural technique in which the experience of the consumer is made economically productive, then Autostadt Wolfsburg is an innovation in this sense: it opens up a space on the company grounds that had in the past been economically unexploited, making it accessible to the visitors passing through it. Much more than any individual film screened prior to a factory tour could ever do, Autostadt serves to instruct its visitor. It was created to prepare and control customer contact with Volkswagen products.

A moving sidewalk transports Autostadt's visitors over the canal that separates the city of Wolfsburg from the theme park. The movement of the sidewalk exposes them to the panorama of a cleaned-up industrial landscape, with the old original factory on the left and the imposing new gates of Autostadt on the right. After registering in the monumental reception hall, those who have come to pick up cars and other guests can stroll through the *Lagunenlandschaft* (lagoon landscape) to the *ZeitHaus* (time house) or the *MarkenPavillons* (brand pavilions); the *Autotürme* (car towers), where "their" vehicles will already be "waiting", are visible in the distance.[26] The primary attraction of the instruction course for visitors is the *WerkTour* (factory tour). For those who have to wait until the "big moment" of the "pickup experience" in the "customer center," there are two factory tours of different lengths available (60 and 90 minutes). The visitors themselves do not see anything during this tour that concerns the purpose of the business or the organization of work. This is made possible by the *dispositif* that carries the visitors through the space, a works railway with Golf cars that makes the tour completely controllable. The fastened-in visitor cannot influence the speed or the stops; the view outside is framed by small windows. Large parts of the trip entail crossing parking lots. Only small portions of the assembly lines are shown, for instance, in the moldings factory and the frame-construction area, while the facilities at hand tell laymen nothing about the quality and effectiveness of production.

In this context, the altered function of media representational techniques, like that of film, becomes clear. In fact, three media are employed to steer the spectator's gaze: the tour guide in the train, the DVD played over on-board monitors, and finally, graphs and photographs in the manufacturing halls. The three media work together to create redundancies of information, a discourse of repetition that demands attention and, at the same time, levels the information received. As such, the guide's commentary is limited, like in the early factory-tour films, to pointing out the factory's achievements by citing the size of the factory grounds, the amount of its capital investments, the number of employees, and similar statistics. Inside the factory, photographs show workers and assembly stations that viewers do not get to see themselves; they contribute to turning the factory into a museum, which will be expanded upon in the theme park's *ZeitHaus* in a glossed-over portrayal of history.[27] Finally, the DVD offers a modular form of advertising information that "fits like a glove," by means of which enthusiastic expectations are created at the beginning of the tour and empty moments while driving over the factory grounds are filled. Each of the approximately five-minute clips about the production of the Touran model is a kind of commercial that allows the experience in the factory to be carried over to the pickup of the waiting product. As the factory tour makes clear, the film (or rather, the DVD) is now just one representational technique among several, which is specifically introduced to give the impression of manufacturing which is not possible in the factory itself.

Conventions and "cooperative behavior"

Autostadt's factory tour stands in direct relation to the instructions of the factory-tour film as it was already employed at Volkswagen during the 1980s. As I have attempted to show, tours in the industrial context in general can be traced back to the large-scale advertising and industrial exhibitions of the late 19th century, which went on to include automobile exhibitions starting in the early 20th century. In the end, film was just one of many representational techniques that were introduced in the framework of organized tours to instruct potential customers.

As such, it would be problematic, starting from the example of the visitor film, to look for overarching formal patterns of industrial film. As Thomas Elsaesser, Yvonne Zimmerman, and others have made clear, industrial film is a phenomenon that constitutes an object of analysis only when its forms of production and use as well as the occasion of its creation are taken into account.[28] I would even go a step further and claim that industrial film as representational technique, even the *Medienverbund* or media mix into which it is usually integrated, should be viewed as a symptom of a general economic phenomenon. There is, as can be seen from the analysis above, something outside each of the representational techniques that has a retroactive effect on its implementation as a medium that facilitates visibility. This "something" can be described by the term *convention*. I borrow the expression from David Lewis, who employed it from the perspective of action theory and linguistic philosophy. Lewis understood conventions as the consequences of coordination problems.[29] Conventions are therefore regularities in the behavior of members of a society who act as agents in a recurring situation in which these disturbances in coordination appear. As internalized models of action that depend on shared knowledge about appropriate behavior in such situations, conventions contribute to the stabilization of these situations.[30]

As the crises in the automobile industry, the idea of "adaptation problems," the observed necessity of "cooperative behavior" in marketing and also the film examples themselves have shown, there are economic phenomena that can be explained through the term convention. Coordination problems can also arise in markets, for instance, when production is too fast for distribution,[31] or when it cannot keep pace with distribution.[32] In these historical phases, conventions contribute to economic stabilization and the mutual reliance of producer and consumer. In order to facilitate this shared knowledge on which the functioning of conventions is dependent, techniques of control are necessary, specifically techniques of business communication that advertise to the outside world, and those involving feedback from outside that are then integrated into the company's system.[33] Industrial films represent only one historical technique of business communication, just as Customer Relationship Marketing is only one of the many strategies that are employed in the basic processes of conventionalizing economic behavior. As this case study has made clear, it can therefore be instructive to describe industrial film as a partial aspect of an economic practice of development (like that of touring), a practice that for its part results from overarching business coordination problems.

Notes

1. I would like to thank Ria Kavemann and Manfred Grieger of the Volkswagen AG company archive for information on the production and distribution of the Group's films and for access to the archival holdings.
2. Having originated in the field of engineering, the term "cultural technique" is not a theoretical academic term, although in course of its renaissance in cultural criticism it has been used for activities as reading, writing, watching television, and engaging in sports.
3. Cf. Werberat der deutschen Wirtschaft (ed.), *Der Wille zur Motorisierung. Ergebnisse der Internationalen Automobil- und Motorradausstellung Berlin 1935. Durch Werbung zum Erfolg* (Berlin, 1935).
4. See DER KDF-WAGEN UND DAS VOLKSWAGEN-WERK, Mag. Nr. SP 18542, DAS VOLKS-WAGEN-WERK UND DIE ERÖFFNUNG DER INTERNATIONALEN AUTOMOBIL- UND MO-TORRADAUSSTELLUNG IN BERLIN 1939, Mag. Nr. SP 15657, AUTOBAHN UND VW-WERK IM BAU, Mag. Nr. 265, and TOBIS-WOCHENSCHAU 9, 1939, Mag. Nr. SP 18189, all in the Bundesarchiv-Filmarchiv Berlin.
5. Werberat der deutschen Wirtschaft (1935), p. 7.
6. Roy Sheldon, Egmont Arens, *Consumer Engineering: A New Technique for Prosperity* (New York: Harper Brothers, 1932).
7. Adam Arvidsson, "On the 'Pre-History of the Panoptic Sort': Mobility in Market Research," *Surveillance & Society* 1, 4 (2004), pp. 456-474, here p. 459.

8. See Earnest Elmo Calkins, "What Consumer Engineering Really Is," in Roy Sheldon, Egmont Arens, *Consumer Engineering: A New Technique for Prosperity* (New York: Harper Brothers, 1932), pp. 1-14 and Roland Marchand, *Advertising the American Dream: Making Way for Modernity, 1920-1940* (Berkeley, CA: University of California Press, 1985), pp. 130-132.
9. Moreover, Mörtzsch became the director of the press and PR department of the AEG in 1951 and was responsible in this function for the films the company commissioned. See Friedrich Mörtzsch, *Offenheit macht sich bezahlt. Die Kunst der Meinungspflege in der amerikanischen Industrie* (Düsseldorf: Econ-Verlag, 1956) and *Die Industrie auf Zelluloid. Filme für die Wirtschaft* (Düsseldorf: Econ-Verlag, 1959).
10. Mörtzsch (1959), pp. 21-22.
11. Op. cit.
12. Mörtzsch (1956), p. 63.
13. Mörtzsch (1959), p. 30.
14. Op. cit.
15. Op. cit., p. 31.
16. Op. cit., pp. 32-36.
17. Op. cit., p. 31.
18. The film's "instructions" are less a kind of discipline in the sense of the classic educational film than an offer of self-guidance in Foucault's sense; see Michel Foucault, *Sécurité, Territoire et Population* and *Naissance de la biopolitique* (Paris: Gallimard, 2004).
19. Gijsbertus Bernardus Willenborg, *An Integrated Conceptual Model of Cooperative Consumer Relationsships in Services, Development and Test* (Capelle: Labryrint Publications, 2001), pp. 255-257.
20. Willenborg (2001), p. 39.
21. Klaus-Jörg Siegfried, "Wolfsburg seit 1998. Autostadt und Erlebnisstadt," in Institut für Museen und Stadtgeschichte (ed.), *Wolfsburg – Zwischen Wohnstadt und Erlebnisstadt* (Wolfsburg: Institut für Museen und Stadtgeschichte, 2000), pp. 87-90, here p. 88.
22. Siegfried (2000), p. 90.
23. Hans-Jürgen Kagelmann, *ErlebnisWelten: Zum Erlebnisboom der Postmoderne* (Munich: Profil, 2004), p. 5.
24. Jack Yan, "Branding and the International Community. Foreign Policy with Commercial Lessons," *CAP Print* (Winter/Summer 2004), pp. 6-11, here p. 9.
25. Willenborg (2001), pp. 4-6.
26. Citations from the brochure.
27. In the *ZeitHaus*, the history of the Group is presented with the exception of 1939-1945; anyone who wishes to learn about the history of the factory's founding has to use a different entrance.
28. See Thomas Elsaesser, "Die Stadt von morgen: Filme zum Bauen und Wohnen," in Klaus Kreimeier, Antje Ehmann, Jeanpaul Goergen (eds.), *Geschichte des dokumentarischen Films in Deutschland. Band 2: Weimarer Republik 1918-1933* (Stuttgart: Reclam, 2005), pp. 381-409, as well as Zimmermann in this volume.
29. David Lewis, *Convention. A Philosophical Study* (Cambridge, MA: Harvard University Press, 1968), p.s42.
30. Lewis (1968), p. 83.

31. Cf. James Beniger, *The Control Revolution: Technological and Economic Origins of the Information Society* (Cambridge: Harvard University Press, 1986), p. 12.
32. Willenborg (2001), p. 2.
33. Beniger (1986), p. 243.

Corporate Films of Industrial Work

Renault (1916-1939)

Alain P. Michel

During the interwar period, Louis Renault's Motor Company became an emblem for the large French factory. The original small workshop from 1898 turned into a huge industrial complex covering 100 acres, with 33,000 workers producing 58,000 vehicles in a wide range of models.[1]

Figure 1 The development of the Renault plant, 1898-1908

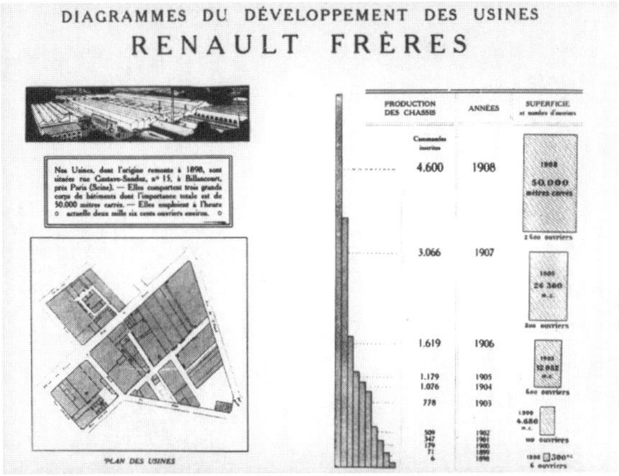

Promotion brochure 1909, SHGR Archives

Meanwhile, Renault produced many images of its activities that included films, photographs, posters, paintings, and industrial drawings.[2] On three main occasions – in 1920, 1930, and 1934 – the firm presented its successful development in full-length films, providing irreplaceable views of what was going on in the factories. These moving pictures show unedited aspects of the company's efforts to streamline car production. These industrial documentaries were targeted mostly at firm promotion, insisting on the founder's personal success story and using cinematographic techniques to give a proper vision of the working process. Images were used as "visual evidence" of what the firm wanted people to understand about its industrial activity. They represent a slanted representation of work and labor.

But in a micro-based historical approach, these images are also hints and traces of an industrial activity that not very many written documents mention. They are an opportunity to see details that no other records have kept. By analyzing the contexts of their visual discourse and questioning both the production and reception of these corporate images, these films can help us understand the way people actually worked. Cinema renews the technological, social, and cultural history of Renault and enriches our global comprehension of the industrial past.[3]

The aim of this essay is twofold. First, to show the way Renault's industrial motion pictures can be analyzed in series to compensate for the absence of written documents about their order, production, and reception (points 1 and 2). Also to point out – through the cinematographic study of the three major documentaries of the interwar period – the way the representation of industrial work evolved and how this reflected the changes in working conditions (points 3-5).

Figure 2 Shooting of a film in the Renault workshops, 1934

Production still, Picture Renault Communication/DR

I.   Industrial films with no concomitant records

Unfortunately, most of Renault's industrial films have to be interpreted without written, explicit records of their production details. In the interwar period, the company had no cinema department and did not keep records of their activities in the field. No motion pictures from this period can be found in the company's archives. At the time, films were ordered from external production companies like Gaumont or Pathé, who indeed have kept some footage, but no concomitant records concerning the commission, production, or utilization of those motion pictures. We have little information concerning the authors or their intentions, and little is known about what was expected of these films and how viewers reacted.

Written records would be of great help, but their absence does not compromise the documentary potential of the images. It compels us to make a deeper and more elementary analysis of the moving pictures themselves – exploiting any hints they may disclose or clues they may divulge. First, we must keep in mind that the ties between the client and the producer of images are implicit but essential. These films are part of a visual device that was commissioned for specific purposes (promotion, news, education, etc.) and produced using changing cinematographic techniques (sound, footage, supports, etc.). Thus, the interpretation of the record-less motion pictures necessitates a study from within the cinematographic archives they come from. The material characteristics of the footage kept are worth looking at. The way they (re)appear today and the condition of their conservation are major keys to understanding the views they offer. Films have to be (re)considered from the archives they come from.

Second, it must be remembered that industrial documentaries never appear alone. They are only a minor part of corporate films, which mostly presented the products in action rather than the production in progress. Films were only one part of the possible visual media used by the car company to promote its activities and encourage car sales. Each type of image offers a different vision of what was happening in the workshops. They show different aspects, follow specific rhythms of production, and tell their own story. Industrial films have to be compared to other documents, including visual documents, which help identify the vision they construct and the industrial situation they refer to. For that purpose – like with any other document – each film has to be critiqued and collated to other sources. They need to be (re)contextualized.[4]

Third, the effects of these industrial films are relatively discrete but determinant. None of these documentaries reached the wide audiences of classic commercial fiction productions. Being rather confidential and specialized items, they leave few if any traces in the public sphere. But an industrial documentary is commissioned by a firm and produced by a filmmaker only if the two expect to turn a profit from it and if they believe the subject can attract an audience. Efficiency is expected. Hints of this expectation are observed in the number of films produced during different periods of time. Are there specific moments when industrial films are made and others when the factory is not a cinematographic subject? What are the specific cinematographic means of communication that Renault used to present the industrial production of cars?[5]

Figure 3 From 1916 to 1938, 30 films showing the Renault plans add up to 210 minutes of industrial scenes

Synthesis of the Renault film corpus (1917-1938)

Subjects	Identification	Date	Title	Lenght	Nature	Support	Sound
	Pa	1917	Enterrement des victimes de l'usine Renault				mute
	Pb	1917	Usine Renault				mute
AROUND	Gh	1920	Aux Usines Renault	22 mn	mont.	b&w	mute
A WAR	Gc	1920	Rétrospective des usines Renault (1898 - 1920)	? mn	mont. ?	b&w	mute/insert
FACTORY	Ge	?	Les voitures Renault (usines)	? mn		b&w	
1920	Gf	?	Les voitures Renault (industrie automobile)	? mn		b&w	
	Gg	?	Renault, industrie automobile	? mn		b&w	
AROUND							
AN ECLIPSE	Pc	1926	Incendie des usines Renault			b&w	
1921-1929							
	C. FdA	1930	Fabrication d'une automobile	41 mn 14	mont.	b&w	mute/insert
	Gs	1930	Comment on construit une automobile	10 mn	mont.	b&w	mute/insert
AROUND	Gu	1930	Usine - machines - boulons	11 mn	mont.	b&w	mute
FABRICATIONS	Gl		Renault : Usine de fabrication	? mn		b&w	
1930	Gn		Renault : Vues générales des usines	? mn		b&w	
	Gm	1930	"Renault : Peinture et polissage"	? mn		b&w	sound
	Ga	1916	Visite des usines Renault par une délégation américaine			b&w	mute
	Gb	1917	Visite des usines Renault par Albert Thomas			b&w	
AROUND	Gd		Visite des us. R. par le ministre de la guerre de Pologne			b&w	
VISITES	Gi	1921	Visite des us. R. par le ministre de la guerre polonais			b&w	
1916/1933	Gk	1930	Cérémonie à Versailles puis visite des us. R.			b&w	
	Go	1933	Visite des usines Renault (XXVIIe Salon de l'Aut.)	8 mn 30	mont.	b&w	muet/intert.
	Gw	1933	Montage de voitures aux Usines Renault	55 s	mont.	b&w	mute
	Gv	1933	Visite des us. R. par des délégations belge et hollandaise	1 mn	séq.	b&w	mute
	P. AdF	1934	L'Automobile de France	80 mn	mont.	b&w	sound
AROUND	Gt	1934	Saint-Michel de Maurienne	8 mn	frag.	b&w	mute
AUTOMOBILE	Gp		Renault : "Centrale - Acier - Soudeur"	? mn		b&w	
INDUSTRY	Gq(1)	1934	Renault : "Fabrication de carrosseries" (1)	5 mn	frag.	b&w	sound
1934	Gq(2)	1934	Renault : "Fabrication de carrosseries" (2)	5 mn	frag.	b&w	sound
	Gj	1934	Renault : "Roulements à bille" (Vues int. des UR)	6mn 10	mont.	b&w	mute
	Gr	1934	Atelier de montage des automotrices	4 mn	frag.	b&w	mute
	SHGR	1936		15 mn 30		b&w	
AROUND	Brom.	1936	Grèves	10 mn		b&w	
STRIKES	Gx	1936	Grève chez Renault et autres	? mn		b&w	
1936	Pe	1936	Grèves			b&w	
	CGT	1938	Jacques LEMARE, Les métallos				

Source : Répertoires Gaumont, Pathé, Lobster-films, SHGR, CGT (Tangui Perron)

Alain P. Michel (2001)

2.   A corpus of 30 corporate films

More than 30 documentaries were shot inside the Renault factories between 1916 and 1940. The meticulous study of their origin, nature, and material characteristics can help define the aim and chronology of this specific film production.

Figure 4 During World War I, many scenes were shot in the Renault plants to show the efforts of female employees behind the lines in AUX USINES RENAULT (1917-1920)

Pathé-Gaumont Archives

The camera first entered the workplace during World War I. In 1916, just before the United States entered the war, an American military commission visited the Renault factory. The event was filmed by military film-service operators.[6] Many other scenes show women working in military production in order to promote the civilian effort as a way of supporting the soldiers on the frontlines. A visit by the Minister of War, Albert Thomas, on September 1, 1917, was also a subject of interest at a time when industry was being remobilized and the workforce galvanized for a battle that was being presented as the final one. These first industrial films worked as patriotic propaganda.

There are also other specific incidents when newsreels were shot at Renault factories. These broadcast documents show that film reporters followed a well-known visitor through the factory one day. But here the person is the focus rather than the workplace he is visiting. Outside scenes are favored over interior takes because daylight was essential for newsreel reporters who had no time to light the scene. Since short takes were preferable for newsreels, the footage is usually short and provides little information about the location. Other news reporters entered the factory after accidents (the collapse of a building in 1917, a fire in 1926, etc.). The factory was also highlighted during exceptional events such as the occupation by the Popular Front in June 1936. In these cases, the factory was not in operation, and very little was revealed about working conditions. These factory scenes are just a pretext, and these films serve news, not industry.

Figure 5 Visitors at a Renault facility, 1933

Picture Renault Communication/DR

Things were different in the early 1930s, because back then the camera followed tours of ordinary people visiting the Renault plants. During the annual Automobile Exhibition in October, films showed a short version of this factory tour as a substitute for an actual visit that only a few could actually experience. These brief industrial films focused on what were then considered the most important steps in automobile production. They work for the cinematographic presentation of factory work.

In contrast to these relatively numerous short documentaries, the corpus contains three medium and long films. The analysis of the more elaborate construction of these three films helps explain the logic of the entire corpus. The three titles clearly indicate their pedagogical and didactic aims. The point was to show how the Renault factory operated (AUX USINES RENAULT, 1920), how an automobile was produced (FABRICATION D'UNE AUTOMOBILE, 1930), or reveal the greatness of the French automobile industry (AUTOMOBILE DE FRANCE, 1934). The first was produced just after World War I, at a time when Louis Renault wanted to take advantage of the prestige his firm had gained through its commitment to the military effort, but did not want people to look too closely at how he benefited from it. The second documentary was made at the inauguration of a brand-new Renault factory on Seguin Island, as well as the Wall Street financial crash and the American economic crisis. The last film used the specific case of Renault to celebrate French industry in general at a time when France was suffering greatly from the global crisis. These long films construct a complex representation of the Renault factory, containing numerous and invaluable images of the work processes. Unlike military propaganda and newsreels, these three films were a result of direct and close collaboration between the automobile company and the film producer. These industrial films work for the firm.

3.   Celebrating victory AUX USINES RENAULT (1920)

In 1920, a film called AUX USINES RENAULT (*At the Renault Factory*) was made by the Gaumont film company to glorify Renault's effort during the war and promote the firm's reputation.[7] The Gaumont-Pathé archives possess a 14-minute film, silent of course, and also without intertitles. This documentary shows a succession of austere industrial scenes that are rather hard to identify and understand. The only written information we have about this film is the short notice in Gaumont's 1929 index,[8] which lists it along with the educational films. How could such complex and totally silent industrial scenes be used as a pedagogical aid? The answer lies in its description as a "22-minute" film; the documentary is now six minutes shorter than the 1929 version. It turns out that, in the 1990s, when the document was transferred from the original film version to a new video format, all the intertitles and texts were cut. Thus, an educational documentary had become a raw collection of industrial images.

But the written information on the original intertitles can be partly restored. Systematic identification of the scenes and technological analysis of the successive operations presented reveal a rather coherent picture of the 1920 Renault factory. The film is composed of 22 sequences showing scenes shot between

Figure 6 The analysis of Aux Usines Renault *reveals the film's scenario*

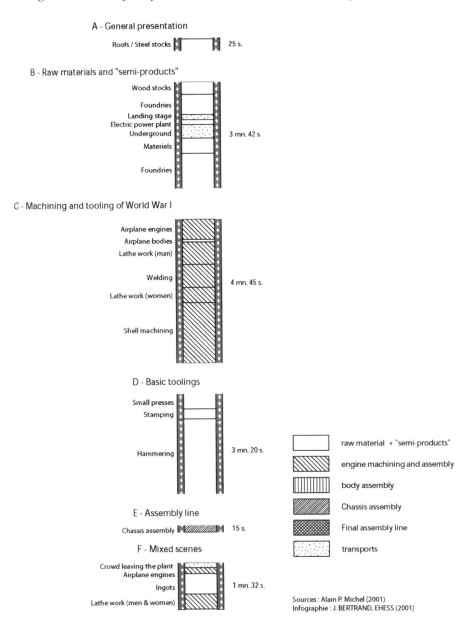

Sources : Alain P. Michel (2001)
Infographie : J. BERTRAND, EHESS (2001)

© Alain P. Michel (2001)

1916 and 1920. The scenario roughly follows the steps of automobile production. It starts with the delivery of the raw materials needed to build an automobile (sequences 1 to 7). It then shows the metallurgical activities (3, 8, 15, 16, 17, 20), a set of machining operations (11, 12, 13, 21), and a scene with workers leaving the factory (19). This discourse following the flow of production is disturbed by three sequences (9, 10, 14) shot during the war. Probably a well-introduced reminder – in the middle of the film – of Renault's participation in the military effort of World War I.

Figure 7 A short scene shows the chassis assembly line in
Aux Usines Renault *(1920)*

Some industrial scenes are spectacular and "speak" independently. For example, in the foundries (8) the impressive sparks and incandescence of molten iron do not need explanations to evoke power and glory. The lathe work of a man (11) and a woman (14) also provide a snapshot of a machining job. Even if the spectator does not know what they are manufacturing – that one is a skilled worker while the women is a (relatively) unskilled *munitionnette* hired during the war to produce bombshells – he or she has a clear idea of their activities. These scenes call to mind common representations of industrial action, but many other sequences are more disconcerting. For example, one shows a stamping operation (16). First smoke dissipates, then a worker puts an ingot of cast iron into a press. The ferrule drops and produces a circular piece of metal, which is rapidly hidden by a new cloud of smoke. This scene is neither expressive nor spectacular. What can this action tell students about industrial activity of the time? The action that is visible is of such short duration (less than 10 seconds) that the viewer has no time to understand what is going on. The smoke effect only hides the operation and it is not used aesthetically as a transition. The sequence could only work if introduced by a text explaining what was about to be shown. Indeed, technologically however, this scene shows an important innovation in production. Thanks to this rapid operation the wheel no longer had to be shaped with spokes by a trained worker. The stamping of a cast-iron wheel frame made it possible to lower production costs of mass-produced cars. At that time, Renault began producing a large series of common 10-horsepower cars on assembly lines.[9] Without written explanation or technological context, this brief stamping scene is incomprehensible. Only the intertitle and text can inform the viewer that this is a new and important innovation. The images serve only as an illustration of what the car producer and the filmmaker consider a scene worth showing.

Besides these recent innovations, the film also presents a short view of the chassis assembly line (18). A 15-second sequence shows a succession of five rows of frames being assembled on rolling trestles, guided by two rails on the floor. No real work is being done during the shot. The workers know they are being filmed; some act as if they are working, while others stare at the camera and pose as for a photograph. Meanwhile, no chassis are moving along the line and nothing is assembled. This sequence is nevertheless important because its background documents the successive operations accomplished by teams of workers. It is a manual assembly line similar to the first conveyors set up by Ford starting in April 1913, and rapidly mechanized at his Highland Park plant.[10] This type of assembly line was first adopted by Renault for the production of military vehicles in 1917. The short motion-picture sequence proves that the assembly line had been discreetly introduced in the Renault factory five years prior to 1922, the year often given as the firm's first use of an assembly line. Pierre Maillard's article[11] is the first public and explicit presentation of Renault's assembly line. As a written document, it is often used as evidence of Renault's delay in introducing assembly lines in his factory, whereas, their existence was in evidence at Citroën as early as 1919. This assertion is contradicted by photographs and motion pictures of Renault's factory. A series of pictures made between 1919 and 1921 of a plant inventory[12] provide other views of the same workshop and confirm the presence of this rudimentary form of assembly line.

The short 1921 crisis that occurred during the switch from war production to a peace-time economy postponed Renault's need to promote assembly-line production of its cheaper cars. Not being mechanized, this new assembly line was outdated compared to the Ford equivalent at the time. It had nothing spectacular to show in a movie. Photographs and drawings were preferred to give the proper vision of this industrial innovation. Thus, it is not through films but still images that the Renault firm chose to present its assembly lines in the 1920s.[13]

4.   Celebrating modernity in FABRICATION D'UNE AUTOMOBILE **(1930)**

Figure 8 In November 1929, Louis Renault invites reporters to visit his new plant on Seguin Island. The assembly line is not yet in operation here

SHGR Archives

On November 28, 1929, Louis Renault invited journalists from the sports press to visit his new factory on the island of Seguin, before the plant was actually finished. The American economic crisis had already begun to show its effects, and the new factory was meant to prove the continuing strength of the Billan-court plant. For journalists from auto magazines, Louis Renault's triumph proved that he was an astute businessman with foresight who had applied Ford's model with moderation. Louis Baudry de Saunier echoed this sentiment in July 1930 in the journal *Omnia*, which he directed:

> For some years now we have been familiar with a spontaneous fascination for what comes from America. We have been won over by the prestigious development of an industry that not only has enormous capital resources but that has also found, thanks to a large population with much purchasing power, a considerable and immediate market. The formula of production in "large series" appeared to be logic itself. The most audacious and enterprising were those to admire. At this time, then, it was as-tonishing that Louis Renault did not show his decisive spirit of conquest. Louis Re-nault did not succumb to influence; he remained himself. Years have passed, and to-day, we are able to see the results of his forsight, which have been consolidated into an organization perfectly adapted to the needs of the French market. To be concise, this is the magisterial and sovereign work of a great Frenchman whom we must all be proud of."[14]

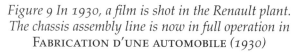

Figure 9 In 1930, a film is shot in the Renault plant.
The chassis assembly line is now in full operation in
FABRICATION D'UNE AUTOMOBILE *(1930)*

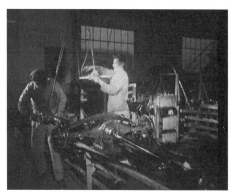

That same year, a silent documentary with intertitles called FABRICATION D'UNE AUTOMOBILE (*Making of a Car*)[15] presented the major stages necessary for the assembling of automobiles, from the raw materials to the final product. Henri Le Masson, director of the advertising department at Renault from 1928 to 1932, underlined what was exceptional in this type of cinematic promotional operation. Normally, a brand's reputation rests on the quality of its finished vehicles. Here, Louis Renault wanted a film to be made about the factories, not to promote the cars, but the modern methods of production:

> There were five weeks of hustle and bustle. It was December, which did not make things easier from the point of view of light and lighting. I visited the factory with specialists who wanted to do tests to determine the number of lamps that would be necessary to light up the workshops and assembly lines. These tests showed, especially in the foundry, that it would be necessary to start work very early (around six in the morning) so that the dust from the previous day had time to sink or dissipate and before new dust could pollute the atmosphere.[16]

A factory could not be filmed in just any conditions.

Renault had already become a vast industrial complex, dispersed over three factories, composed of some twenty sectors, each one in turn composed of approximately one hundred buildings and several workshops. As Marcel Béreux indicates in the January 1930 edition of his journal *Je Sais Tout*, a simple visit to Renault was no longer possible. "What are we going to see? Where to start? You have to choose, because if you want to see everything, it would take three to four days."[17] In relation to the complexity of the automobile production circuits, the 1930 film creates a triple illusion.

First, that of fluidity as the documentary presents a continuous – and artificial – succession of the different occupations that in reality are dispersed throughout Billancourt. The film would have one believe that the operations were in an unbroken chain, that the second group of operations were located directly after the first one, leading to the final assembly process. This, incidentally, is what Marcel Béreux believed: At Renault, "there is not *one* assembly line, but, starting from a certain stage of production, a veritable crow's foot, in which each branch turns out chassis ready to be fitted."[18] This image is analogous to that of water flowing from Ford's model.

Figure 10 The successive scenes of FABRICATION D'UNE AUTOMOBILE *(1930) do not follow the production flow or a visitor's steps*

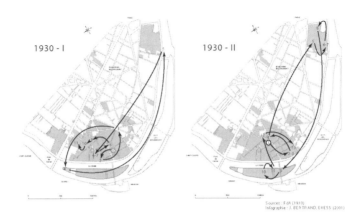

© Alain P. Michel (2001)

The second illusion is spatial. The editing presents production as a simple assembly of parts. Starting from the bare chassis, the film shows how assembly-line work can be summed up as the addition, one after the other, of all the organs which complete the automobile. Texts punctuate and comment on the successive stages. They follow the "linear path of rational organization."[19] By placing documentary sequences on the factory map, the film shows a very different path. The main activities (forges and foundries, mechanical motor, body work, assembly) are regrouped in distinct factories. The ubiquity of the film narrative erases the distances and the detours taken by the parts being manufactured. The film constructs an imaginary geography of the production process.

In the third place, the film proposes a symbolic representation of factory work. It limits itself to emblematic operations that give an account of the process in its totality. Certain positions in movement become symbols of the production work as a whole such as the installation of the engine, attachment of the wheels, joining of the body and the chassis, the car leaving the line, etc. Thus, in the early 1930s, while unforeseen delays meant that his modern factory was still being built, Louis Renault could still celebrate his triumph. All he needed to do was present a few notable workshops, such as the engine-testing room, the dynamo workshop, as well as the foundry lines. Such serialized work had become a guarantee of quality and a selling point. This is the third cinematographic illusion.

5. Celebrating industry: L'AUTOMOBILE DE FRANCE (1934)

According to L'AUTOMOBILE DE FRANCE (*The Car from France*) things only continued to get better at Renault.[20] This full-length sound documentary from 1934 was produced "for the glory of French industry" under the patronage of the Ministry of Commerce and Industry. It was directed by Jean Loubignac, editor-in-chief of the *Pathé Journal* and an enthusiastic defender of talking movies. Shown for the first time at the Gala de l'Opéra on October 2, 1934, it was then projected throughout France before being distributed, in several shortened versions, as a short film for the pre-feature program of the Pathé-Cinéma circuit theaters.[21] The reporting is particularly interesting since, four years after FABRI-CATION D'UNE AUTOMOBILE, a second documentary film showed the main Renault workshops in motion (if not at work). It is a propaganda film, and thus presents a distorted picture, albeit in the actual surroundings of the assembly lines at Billancourt.

A young employee in the advertising department, Paul Grémont, was put at the service of the shooting team for a period of three months. His role was primarily of a practical and economic nature. "It would have been unimaginable to stop an assembly line for several minutes to set up lights. We decided to shoot the scene on a Sunday morning, specially summoning all the necessary personnel so that the workshop didn't appear too deserted."[22] Industrial work can be compatible with the constraints of filmmakers only with some difficulty. The screenplay of this 1934 documentary minimizes this difficulty. It constructs the story of a factory visit in the style of a fiction film. In the first scene, the journalist calls the factory manager to organize the shooting. "It won't be an ordinary interview. We want to make a filmed report and we're simply asking for permission for our shots we take and our microphone. We are certain to discover some unexpected things to show the public thanks to the magical but impartial eye of the camera."[23] Convinced, the manager announces, "*Monsieur*, our factories are open to you."

The tour begins by presenting the great steel complexes at Hagondange and Saint-Michel-de-Maurienne. From the very beginning, the boundaries of Billancourt were crossed. The shots of provincial factories slowly reveal the spectacular operations such as the pouring of molten steel or the ballet of workers smoothing out an incandescent line. The tour guide asks us to "notice the fact that the materials are handled automatically," whereas what is shown is essentially manual dexterity and the metalworkers' virtuosity. This survey of the provincial factories underscores the high degree of integration at the Renault enterprise, set up to control every stage of production, from raw materials up to the automobile's exit from the line. The report then presents the main basic operations at Billancourt: "Let's go to the foundry, it's about time to pour the steel." It stops to show the powerful hammering machines and the immense presses for stamping out sheet metal. The report also depicts several precision operations such as cutting of gears, selection of ball bearings, and turning of bolts, which also provide occasions to show aesthetically pleasing long shots of sparkling machinery.

The first section of the film underlines the fact that a large part of automobile production was still done without assembly lines. The conveyors appear only during the finishing operations and installation of the engine, in particular, in a long traveling shot up the section of the mechanized assembly line for serially produced engines. This line is clearly "more feminine" than before. In the beginning, this was a relatively skilled and physical job since it demanded the maneuvering of heavy parts. Mechanization and the structures for handling materials allowed these constraints to be done away with and for numerous tasks to be consigned to women. They quickly adjust certain parts before mounting them, though while making the simple and rapid gestures of specialized workers. Dexterity and attention to detail have replaced qualification and professionalism. Women workers performed an increasing number of jobs, which increased their presence in the factories. The assembly line changed the nature of work and the composition of the manual labor force. In this traveling shot the impression of speed along the line is heavily accentuated by the movement of the camera. In fact, the engine did not move along the line as quickly, but the people had numerous tasks to fulfill, which forced them to work quickly, nonetheless. This shows that the assembly line, by mechanizing the handling of materials, reduced the burden of work, but not necessarily that of the operations to be accomplished. If the work pace was moderate, the quantity of work was heavy.

L'AUTOMOBILE DE FRANCE is a propaganda film. The fact that the French industrial sector was in crisis made the cinematic harmony of Billancourt suspect.

In fact, the images seem to contradict the words. In the course of the factory visit, the contrast between the reassuring tone of the commentary and the difficulty of the work is accentuated. While the guide praises the logical progression of operations, the camera shows a succession of ruptures in the flow, of manual transfers from one belt to the next, by carts, hoists, forklifts, and elevators. The editing, as was the case in 1930, takes us from one workshop to another with no concern for the itinerary or the geography of production. The filmed visit allows all the essential spaces of production to be viewed quickly without actually visiting all of the factories. Nevertheless, in 1934, it was no longer a matter of claiming it was an objective view of an industrial enterprise that went beyond the boundaries of Billancourt. The documentary praises the complexity of an extraordinary affair, bringing into play provincial factories, technological accomplishments and mysterious skills. The film does not explain, it fascinates the spectator by showing a multitude of operations, simultaneously beautiful and impressive. From this perspective, a scene of assembly-line work acquires a symbolic dimension that cannot be reduced to what is shown, but to what the image implies as the outcome of modern technological activity, and as a necessary stage in the production of an object that is itself emblematic. The assembly line has become a star.

Conclusion

There are times when documentaries showed the factory and other periods during which there were no industrial films being produced. The 1920s was a time of cinematographic eclipse of the Renault workshops. Apart from the Popular Front films of the summer of 1936 strikes, no industrial documentaries were made on the Renault premises from the second half of the 1930s until the 1950s. The doors of the factory remained closed to the filmmaker for the most part during this period. Work continued out of the camera's view. The most important factory motion pictures are represented by the three longer films, made during a period of cinematographic interest in industry. Newsreels sought to capture the events inside the factory while the firm was commissioning filmmakers to produce documentaries. This concordance is no coincidence.

The study of Renault's interwar industrial films also shows that only specific types of documentaries were made and that only specific filmmakers made industrial films.

The interwar corpus lacks "ergonomic" films on the work process. This type of motion study was undertaken away from the premises of industrial companies by streamliners like Etienne Marey and Frank and Lillian Gilbreth.[24] They both tried to combine the study of human movements with techniques of graphical visualization. By employing their cyclograph, the Gilbreth couple showed the invisible aspects of work so that workers could understand their mistakes and correct their movements. This use of cinema to help make work more efficient had no counterpart in French industry at that time, even though the question had been raised explicitly at the end of the 1920s.[25] This type of film was to make its first appearance at Renault only after World War II.[26] Thus, the factory's doors were closed to some types of films and open to others.

Motion pictures give a mediated account of the way work was performed in Boulogne-Billancourt in the first half of the 20th century. They do not present a direct vision of the material and practical processes at work in the Renault factories. These documents deal with a representation, an image of the production system. They produce a specific kind of discourse that makes it seem as if the work was actually being done as it should. But these manipulated images are constrained by the industrial scenery they are shot in, and by the evolution of the cinematographic instruments they are shot with. Although the work scene may have been arranged, the background was real. If the representation is a vision, it is confronted by the changing public imagery of what a factory was. Industrial documentaries serve history by comparing one period with another and films with other visual and written documents.

Notes

1. Patrick Fridenson, *Histoire des usines Renault, vol. I . Naissance de la grande entreprise, 1898-1939* (Paris: Le Seuil, 2nd edition, 1998); Jean-Louis Loubet, *Renault, cent ans d'histoire* (Boulogne-Billancourt: Éditions ETAI, 1998).
2. This contribution is drawn from my Ph.D. thesis dealing with the introduction of the assembly line at the Renault automobile factories (1917-1939), *Les images du travail à la chaîne dans les usines Renault de Boulogne-Billancourt (1917-1939). Une analyse des sources visuelles: cinéma, photographies, plans d'implantation* (2001, technical history thesis for the EHESS, under the direction of Patrick Fridenson). A revised version was published in Alain P. Michel, *Travail à la chaîne. Renault 1898-1947* (Boulogne-Billancourt: Editions ETAI, 2007).
3. In France, see Denis Woronoff, *La France industrielle. Gens des ateliers et des usines, 1890-1950* (Paris: Editions du Chêne-Hachette Livre, 2003) and Denis Woronoff, Nicolas Pierrot (ed.), *Les images de l'industrie, de 1850 à nos jours* (Paris: CHEF-CNRS-Université Paris I Panthéon-Sorbonne, 2002); see also Elspeth H. Brown, *The Corporate Eye: Photography and the Rationalization of American Commercial Culture, 1884-1929* (Baltimore: Johns Hopkins University Press, 2005).
4. In France, this historical approach was initiated by Marc Ferro, "Le film: une contre-analyse de la société," *Annales E.S.C.* (January-February 1973), pp. 109-124. This text has been published in Marc Ferro, *Cinéma et histoire* (Paris: Gallimard, 1993), pp. 31-

62. See also Pierre Sorlin, *Sociologie du cinéma: Ouverture pour l'histoire de demain* (Paris: Aubier, 1977) and Pierre Sorlin, *The Film in History: Restaging the Past* (Oxford: Basil Blackwell, 1980).

5.   Alain P. Michel, "Filmer le travail, les travailleuses et les travailleurs dans les usines Renault de l'entre-deux-guerres," in Patrice Marcilloux (ed.), *Le travail en représentations* (Paris: Éditions du CTHS, 2005), pp. 131-150.

6.   About the army's Photography and Cinema Service (SPCA), see Laurent Veray, *Les actualités filmées françaises de la Grande Guerre* (Paris: AFRHC-SIRPA, 1995).

7.   *Aux Usines Renault*, educational series, no. 5212 (Master 3037), Gaumont Actualité 1920, b&w, 22 min, silent.

8.   *Répertoire des films de l'encyclopédie Gaumont*, Société des Etablissements Gaumont, educational service, Imprimerie Gaumont, 1929. The film is presented as a 631-meter piece of footage.

9.   Alain P. Michel, *Travail à la chaîne. Renault 1898-1947*, op. cit.

10. David Hounshell, *From the American System of Production, 1800-1932* (Baltimore: Johns Hopkins University Press, 1984), p. 236. Hounshell analyzes the work of "dynamic assembly teams or gangs (who) moved from station to station down the row." For Peugeot, see Yves Cohen, "The Modernization of Production in the French Automobile Industry between the Wars: A Photographic Essay", *Business History Review*, volume 65, number 4 (Winter 1991), p. 756. He describes "the teams of specialized workers (who) passed from one fixed car to another."

11. Pierre Maillard, "Le montage à la chaîne de la 10 HP Renault," *Omnia*, 28 (September 1922), reprinted in *De Renault Frères, constructeurs d'automobiles, à Renault Régie Nationale*, 3, (December 1973), pp. 95-100. Anonymous, "Le montage à la chaîne," *L'Illustration* (October 4, 1924), reprinted in *Les grands dossiers de l'Illustration: l'automobile* (Paris: Le Livre de Paris, 1993), pp. 90-91. These articles are based on three photographic reports made by the Renault photographic service in the workshops: -1-Montage 10HP (2/27/22) SR(42) no. 12237/12252; 2-Montage 6HP (9/1/24) SR(53), no. 15854-15863; 3-Montage 10HP (7/1/24) SR(52), no. 15639/51 + 15703.

12. Chaîne de montage châssis (September 1919), SR(27), no. 7170, photograph published in the *Bulletin des Usines Renault*, 36 (January 15, 1920), SR(30) no. 8404/8408, 1920. Inventaire Plousey, archives of the SHGR. In 1921, the Renault firm was to change from a privately owned company (Automobiles Louis Renault) to a limited company (Société anonyme des usines Renault).

13. Alain P. Michel, *Travail à la chaîne chez Renault*, op. cit.

14. Louis Baudry de Saunier, "Le développement méthodologique et harmonieux d'un programme," *Omnia* (July 1930).

15. Fabrication d'une automobile aux usines Renault, Cinémathèque de la ville de Paris, 41 min. 14 sec. silent, insert titles in French, 1930, four parts.

16. Henri Le Masson, "Au service de la Publicité Renault (1928-1932)," *De Renault Frères, constructeurs d'automobiles, à Renault Régie Nationale*, 15 (December 1977).

17. Marcel Béreux , "Une usine française bat les records européens : avant d'admirer les américains... et si nous parlions un peu des français," *Je Sais Tout* (January 1930).

18. Ibid.

19. L. Danty-Lafrance, "Schéma de l'organisation d'une fabrication," *Bulletin de la Société pour l'Encouragement de l'Industrie Nationale* (May 1929), p. 384. Quoted by O.

Cinqualbre, "La mise en schéma de l'usine (1910-1930)," *Le Mouvement Social*, 125 (October-December 1983), p. 105.

20. Jean Loubignac, L'Automobile de France, Pathé Journal, produced by Pathé-Natan "sous le patronage de M. le ministre du Commerce et de l'Industrie," 1934, b&w, 35mm, 80 min.

21. Presented at the Gala de l'Opéra on October 2, 1934.

22. Paul Grémont , "L'Automobile de France," *De Renault Frères, constructeurs d'automobiles, à Renault Régie Nationale*, 18 (June 1979), pp. 285-286.

23. Jean Loubignac, *L'Automobile de France*, op. cit.

24. F. Gilbreth, L. Gilbreth, *Applied Motion Study* (Easton: Hive Publishing Company, 1973, first edition in 1917); S. Giedion, *Mechanization Takes Command* (New York: Oxford University Press, 1948).

25. E. Hymans, "Travail continu équilibré au lieu de 'travail à la chaîne artificiel'. Rapport au IVe Congrès International de l'OST, Paris, 19-24 juin 1929," *Bulletin du Comité National de l'Organisation Française* 3, 12 (December 1929).

26. Etudes du travail humain, Catalogue CEDIMAGES: *Renault: Liste des éléments du fonds audiovisuel*, edition dated July 16, 1993 (1149 titles).

Filming Work on Behalf of the Automobile Firm

The Case of Renault (1950-2002)

Nicolas Hatzfeld, Gwenaële Rot and Alain P. Michel

Because of their promotional function corporate films could be considered a mediocre source of knowledge about economic and social realities. At the same time, their apparent distance from the noble world of cinema disqualifies them in terms of cultural history. Doubly marginalized, this type of film would appear seriously biased. Nonetheless, the quantity and diversity of business films illustrate the importance that companies placed on cinema. Films were used as a tool of industrial streamlining or training, as a means of internal or external communication and mobilization, as a medium of information or debate. The plurality of their usage and the variety of their intended audience reflect the fact that industrial cinema is more complex and interesting than initially thought. The study of the technical and economic conditions of their production shows that these films cannot be completely dissociated from cinema as a whole: The borders between genres are porous, and usages are multiple. These films deserve to be reevaluated.

By working on the intersection of the two often-dissociated domains, the history of the company and the history of filmmaking, it is in fact possible to enrich the study of business. In this respect, the cinematic archives at Renault are a rich source of historical and social information. The automobile business has been a great producer of animated images, most of them advertisements and promotional documents for their cars. Others celebrate particular events like automobile races, long-distance treks, etc. Only a minority depict automobile production between 1950 and 2002, while some one hundred or so such films are still in existence. By analyzing this body of industrial films we can trace the evolving self-representation of an automobile maker. In this case, the study concerns how the Renault company has visualized assembly line work in its factories,[1] and more generally, the evolution of labor. The first part examines the rhythm of film production, which takes into account both the hazards of the business's history and the evolution of the cinematographic conditions of that production. Commissioned industrial images are therefore the reflection of a multitude of interrelated stakes. The second part deals with recurrent messages promoted by these films. We identify a few dominant themes whose meaning varies significantly from one period to another. Finally, the different forms of film narration used to represent work translate, in their own way, how the business sees itself in society, and more precisely, in relation to its own personnel.

1.   Connections between film and company history

An analysis of the industrial films collected by Renault's video library suggests that their production followed an irregular rhythm.[2] The number of films documenting their workshops vary according to the time period, but this variation does not correspond neatly to the stages of the company's history, to changes in industrial innovation, or even to the larger collection of Renault films.[3] The production of these factory films is linked to the adjustment between the evolution of the company's cinematographic structures (the staff, the professionals that were engaged, etc.), and the techniques that they used. With these factors as a starting point, two main periods can be distinguished.

The filmmakers' period (1950-1983)

At the end of World War II, Renault did not use cinema to celebrate the peace as it had done after the Great War.[4] At the beginning of Pierre Lefaucheux's presidency (1945-1955), the nationalized company only published the *Bulletin d'information* in order to create a new image of the business and to show the value of its national management.[5]

Internal production: the company's cinema department (1950-1961)

On March 27, 1950, Jean Farcy, a former student at the Institut des Hautes Études Cinématographiques (IDHEC), was hired to set up and direct a film department at Renault. He had been active since 1948 in the amateur *Caméra-club* created by the *Comité d'entreprise* (works council), which had brought together a team of self-taught filmmakers.[6] To fill out his department, Jean Farcy turned to other professionals who had also graduated from the IDHEC, such as René Vautier and Jean-Jacques Sirkis. The creation of this department, which suggests permanence, illustrates the company's interest in cinema. Films were to cover all aspects of car production, industrial, economic, and social, to play the exemplary role intended by Renault's management.

During this period of obsession with streamlining work and production,[7] business believed in cinema's capacity to improve industrial performance.[8] Farcy's first task consisted in shooting some 200 short analysis sequences for the department of ergonomics, assembled back to back in around 20 films entitled ETUDES DU TRAVAIL HUMAIN (*Study of Human Labor*).[9] Following the tradition of Gilbreth's studies,[10] they show the movements of men and women working in turn at the old job and then the new one. Jean Farcy stressed that these scenes were made outside the workplace:

> We didn't organize the shoot in the workplace where this operation was done, but in the rooms at the professional school, which we transformed into a studio. I had to be able to make shots in a set order, which would have been incompatible with the constraints of an active workplace. This technical argument obscured another one, which was psychological. The presence of a camera in a workshop, filming the workplace, would have been interpreted as a new method of keeping track of employees' time.[11]

In 1953, Renault's industrial film department began to reorient itself toward the production of films aimed at a larger audience. The cinema was a promotional tool that the company wanted to control directly. The advertising director asked the cinema department to make a film to enrich the traditional factory visits during the automobile trade fair.[12] A first attempt along 600 meters of the assembly line at the Flins plant proved to be unsatisfactory. Jean-Jacques Sirkis was given the task of redoing this traveling shot with all the necessary means. He reported: "It was winter, there was no light. Color film then only had a sensitivity of 35 ASA, far less than it has today. We had to use all the floodlights available. We 'ransacked' all the studios in Paris and borrowed from all the generating sets in France. Cables were led over the roofs. We needed a week just to set it up." In doing so, Renault filmed, according to its maker, "the most expensive shot in cinema."

Figure 1 Preparing for a traveling shot: 24 HEURES À LA RÉGIE (1957)

J.J. Sirkis Personal Collection

The films were often produced in several versions: French and foreign, short and long, original and updated, explicitly for Renault or altered for screening in cinemas and, as such, devoid of references to the company. Renault images were used for national propaganda, and their wider use went beyond borders.[13] Between 1953 and 1960, the cinema department also produced some 70 house magazines: the *Magazines de l'automobile*.[14] *At the same time, in 1954, the company ordered the 22-minute fictional documentary* CHAMPIONS JUNIORS *from an outside director*.[15] At this time, industrial cinema had no lack of means and could hire important filmmakers.[16]

Figure 2 The shooting of RENAULT DAUPHINE *(1959)*

Picture Société d'histoire du Groupe Renault/DR

External production (1961-1983)
Pierre Dreyfus (1955-1975) succeeded Pierre Lefaucheux and left the company's film structure in place. But in 1961, following the commercial failure of the Dauphine in America,[17] the film department was disbanded. During this time of rapid technical evolution in filmmaking, commissioning outside film producers

proved to be preferable. A second short period followed during which industrial cinema was abandoned altogether.

   Advertising basically became publicity in 1963. It was entrusted to Publicis, a
specialized partner that still does publicity for Renault. The documentary films
belonged to another circuit. The commercial director, Michel Rolland, ordered
them directly from other production houses, giving preference to former members or colleagues in the Renault film department. So, until 1975, Caméra Unit,
led by Guy Morance, made several industrial films in the same style as those of
the former Cinema Department.[18] This resumption of industrial-film production coincides with a change in the technical aspects of shooting. The introduction of the silent 16mm camera, lighter and easier to handle than the 35mm, as
well as the greater sensitivity of its film stock, allowed a reduction in the size of
film crews, lighting constraints, and more generally in the total cost of film production.

Figure 3 Cartoon of an assembly line from Made in Renault *(1983)*

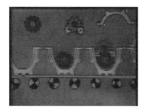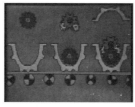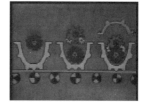

Jacques Rouxel and Georges Pessis

At Renault, however, the 1970s was a particularly poor period for commissioned films about the factories, and during this time, anti-establishment filmmakers took over the subject.[19] For the company this drop in interest in factory
films had no internal consequences, since the production of documentaries had
been externalized (shopped out) by then. In 1983, Georges Pessis filmed Made
in Renault on the introduction of robots and flexibility at Renault factories.[20]
The commission gave the director the autonomy and the time necessary to
shoot on location, do research, and write an original script. Animated sequences
by Jacques Rouxel – father of the Shadocks – gave a rhythm to the transitions.[21]
The filmmaker had the means to shoot a "real" cinema film on 16mm.[22] It was
one of the last Renault films. But the first signs of budgetary tightening also
began to appear. The shooting crew was reduced to three people, a cameraman,
a sound man, and a lighting engineer. The director negotiated with union representatives for permission for the crew to be in the factories. This film marks the
end of the first period.

The audiovisual period (1983-2002)

A triple upheaval was at work in the management and production of the Renault films. On the one hand, the film archives were entrusted to an external provider, Extension Vidéo, for servicing Renault's Communication Department.[23] On the other hand, a small team of a half dozen people, the Service des Moyens de Communication AudioVisuels (MCAV), was charged with coordinating the production of films by engaging outside directors.[24] Furthermore, some of the films were transferred from acetate to video. During this period there was a change in government in France and a change in the company's president.[25] With the organization of a system of film archiving and coordination by MCAV the production of images underwent a change in style. Film went from being in the service of commerce to that of communication.

Mobilizing film and video against the crises (1983-1992)

Numerous industrial films were made between 1983 and 1985, during which time Renault was undergoing the worst financial crisis in its history – accumulating a deficit of 12.5 billion francs. This period corresponds to the great period of business films and videos.[26] Film served to restore customer confidence, mobilize company personnel, or train workers in the "quality gesture," as was done in Sandouville in 1983: The filmed sequences show the proper way of working on an assembly line.[27]

Adapting the factories to the conditions of global competition was one of the things essential to the company's survival. The MCAV produced films that promoted the decentralized factories' contributions to the modernization effort.[28] These documentaries above all present intentions or anticipate results. With the *mallettes pédagogiques* ("pedagogical briefcases," starting in 1989) industrial film was mobilized explicitly in service of public education, and it still plays a role in the company's politics of global communication.

The specific problem of adapting the factory at Billancourt to the new conditions of production was a central theme during this period.[29] The obliteration of this "workers' fortress" gave rise to a number of films and "historical" documentaries charged with following the attempts at adaptation and then, starting in 1992, announcing the site's closure. The subject was delicate due to the importance of the industrial problem and the social and political implications. The Communication Department asked one director, Loïc Leguenedal, to film the last moments of the Seguin Island plant with his video camera (BetaCam) and make a short musical out of the last car to leave the assembly line.[30] Shooting conditions and industrial film production were thus transformed. It was no longer the same "job"[31] as it had been in the 1950s.

Diversifying film production through video and digital media (1993-2002)

Renault was no longer simply Billancourt, and its manufacturing plants were now spread across France and the world. These decentralized factories themselves now produced their own industrial films.[32] The local production of documentaries was facilitated by the wide availability of light cameras and the relatively low cost of video and digital cassettes. There was practically no need anymore for extra lighting when shooting an industrial scene. In this period of restrictions, film production was falling apart and becoming increasingly banal. At the same time, restrictions tended to reduce both time for conceiving films and money to make them. Each factory produced its own "business card" film, quickly, inexpensively, and along the lines of television and advertising culture.[33]

Starting in 1993 the maintenance of film archives had been reorganized. The film collection was entirely managed by a branch of Publicis – Global Event System[34] – which indexed the majority of the historical films and numbered them according to the requests for their images. At the same time, following a larger tendency, the legal department had become the pivot point for film production. The production of images was done through a contract that insured that the company could use them for their internal communication needs while respecting the rights of both the filmmakers and of the people filmed.

The distinction between films for internal use and those destined for a public audience was reinforced, diversifying the discourse on industrial work. In 1996, on the occasion of the Automobile exhibition at the Cité des Sciences et de l'Industrie, Renault had a big-budget film on the manufacturing of the Twingo made outside the factories.[35] One of the objectives was "to stay as pedagogical as possible, even if that means simplifying the stages of the process (that) will be restored thanks to special effects in post-production."[36] Furthermore, the collection possessed more and more films shot abroad – due to the internationalization of the Renault concern. These "transplanted" factory films served to transmit an image of specificity in the process of Renault manufacturing, raised to the level of the productive model, at a time when the group had developed a strategy of transnational alliance, first with Volvo, then with Nissan.

Several work-study films prolonged the initial experiences of the Film Department and those of the videos made in the 1980s. Thus, upon the initiative of the Flins factory, the movements of the workers in an elementary work team (UET) were filmed in 1997 in order to improve productivity. In 1999, MCAV produced a ergonomic film in order to make the study engineers more sensitive to the practical consequences of their conceptual work in the workshops.[37] Films were therefore a means of communication and a link between departments of the same company, and between branches of an international group. Renault had gone from cinema to audiovisual communication.

Figure 4 Activité de travail au montage *(1999)*

Renault Communication/Stéphanie Leloutre DR

2.   On recurrent subjects and changing messages

Having established the rhythm of the film productions commissioned or made by Renault, what about their content? On the one hand, the films tackle subjects in a recurring way. On the other, the treatment of these subjects varied considerably over time. Several themes, treated with particular importance, illustrate this duality. First of all, though, it is important to make some remarks about vocabulary. The firm did not always maintain the same language to designate people at work. The employees were first referred to as "workers," then as "operators" throughout the 1980s before the term "technician" appeared, albeit rarely, and then in some recent films the employees are identified by their first names or surnames. Because of these linguistic cosmetics, the specificity of the factory context becomes blurred.

Modernity: From new to obsolete

As one of the systematic stakes of film discourse, *modernity* illustrates the company's aptitude for facing the future. In the 1950s and 1960s, this word was synonymous with industrial power. A series of films in *Magazines de l'automobile* emphasized the means that were used in the service of mass production: "All the industrial potential of the factories, from the electromechanical heads down to the ultramodern assembly lines, all are used for the serial manufacture of a great car."[38] This potential was detailed machine by machine, workshop by workshop, and plant by plant, whether at the workshop or the factory. The same film lyrically evoked "the power of the company's enormous industrial machine. The Vulcan forges ring out day and night on Europe's loudest anvils. At Billancourt, the volcanoes free the metal by smelting it, showers of sparks flying out." Another insisted on the "console from which one orders the synchronous running of the assembly by pushing a button."[39] From potential to production, the slippage is barely noticed. The birth of the Dauphine was touted in a film that, from one shot to the next, seemed to send an unchanging series of vehicles from the end of the assembly line straight to the highway ramp: the fluidity of production was directly connected to the future of transportation.

Modernity was equally situated on the terrain of innovation. The theme appeared, here as well, during the presentation of the budding factory at Flins, praising "the most modern means," causing this plant "to prosper and the company to keep going."[40] One of these means is an aerial conveyor that lifts the cars up "to allow workers easier access," while at the press "the most modern safety measures allow the employees to work without danger." Modernity was therefore extended from industrial resources to working conditions. After the Flins factory, the opening of Sandouville in 1966 was widely celebrated, evoking the telex, kilometers of conveyors, and the painting equipment.[41] Starting in the late 1980s, the release of new vehicles had been the occasion to emphasize the investments made while modernizing the means of production in the new plants. Modernity was then often synonymous with the absence of people in the workplace. The same discourse that pointed out the modernization of the factory at Billancourt in 1985 had to resort to cinematic acrobatics: the camera avoided the dilapidation at the Seguin Island plant – as well as the age of the employees – and focused on the fresh paint job on the conveyors.[42]

Figure 5 MAGAZINE DE L'AUTOMOBILE, N° 15 *(1959)*

Renault Communication / DR

In this discourse of modernity, the representation of time played an essential role. Throughout this period, the films avoided a *before*, generally marked by defects and limits, in favor of a *now* that promised solutions and new possibilities, which then would become part of the future. This was the case for working conditions[43] and the organization of production.[44] The comparison of images representing the old procedures and the new ones accentuated the message.[45] Later, another representation of time accentuated the company's long history. Recycling images, in particular those of the founder's mythic shed, these films situate themselves in general between the serious crisis of the 1980s, which threatened Renault's future, and its 100-year anniversary in 1998. They celebrated a company always undergoing change, always innovative.[46]

Automation: From machine to robot

Automation plays a leading role in modernity. During the creation of new factories, the flow of conveyors and the large presses illustrated industrial potential.[47] The cinematic apogee of this particular image of automatic power was reached in two versions of Jean-Jacques Sirkis's film, 24 HEURES À LA RÉGIE, made in 1957 and 1961. During the 1980s, the theme returned to Renault's films, in which the automated synchronization of the production flow was emphasized.

In manufacturing, electromechanical groupings were used to produce motor units since the 4CV had been launched in 1947. It took several years before films began to deal with the subject. Since that time, starting in 1954, the machinery itself[48] had become a film "star" which the camera captured in great detail, showing the combinations of automatic procedures, of manufacturing in a strict sense, and of control, which could be observed in the impressive succession of vertical and horizontal movements in MACHINE TRANSFERT in 1956. For several minutes, chunks of metal are grabbed by large claws, carried off by conveyor belts, perforated by dozens of drills, or finished by cutters, all of this without visible human intervention, while learned commentators invite the uninformed spectator to survey this range of technical prowess. The high point of the genre was reached by the film U5, made in 1959 by André Cantenys, who uncompromisingly applied the exercise for more than 20 minutes. Then the machinery merged into images of generalized automation. Made in 1969 by the same director, AUTOMATIQUEMENT VÔTRE attempted to argue for the irrevocable generalization of the tendency: "Industrial production today anticipates the reality of the future. For the automobile it is inevitable. It will conquer Europe just as it has already conquered America."

The next image of automation was that of robots. Their presentation took time to settle in, and at the beginning of the 1980s, one spoke of an "arrival of new machines called robots" or of a "computer and its memory associated with a robot."[49] The films progressively insisted on the sophistication of the movement, speed, precision, and regularity of their actions, and therefore on the manufacturing flexibility that their programming permitted. They showed their spectacular interventions for the assembly of car bodies, for intricate soldering, painting, or the sophisticated application of putty. The robot took the inevitable leading role in the Renault films.

Quality: From best to better

Remarkable in its continuity, the theme of quality was used to gain the confidence of external spectators or mobilize personnel. Then again, the idea changed according to different themes which sometimes followed one another and at other times appeared simultaneously. On several occasions, filmmakers emphasized the rigor of the engineers who endlessly analyzed and developed the most effective, most beautiful, and most durable procedures and products: "a chain of attempts, of uninterrupted experiments, therefore a continually renewed and deeper knowledge of the primary matters, that's another aspect of the secret."[50] Fifteen years later, the message insisted on "researching the best manufacturing procedures and the development of new technologies."[51]

Automation was often presented as an essential factor in quality. While the machinery already mentioned allows for a "consistency in the quality of real work,"[52] a filmmaker in 1966 evoked workshops where "quality and precision are automatically achieved on the new soldering machinery."[53] Precision was frequently brought in to supplement regularity. The same assets were emphasized to praise the robot's contribution, "having become an essential factor in the improvement of quality and reliability."[54] Regular and untiring, the robot renewed the virtues of automated activity that could also be found in the conveyors: "As a guarantee of additional quality, all transfers and conveyance are entirely automated without any human intervention."[55]

But the company could not maintain this message without demoralizing its personnel, and therefore, it spoke highly of the employees, notably in those areas where manual labor was overwhelmingly predominant. As a commentator indicated, in the assembly areas, for instance, "quality is first and foremost a human matter."[56] The working body might be evoked: "The Clio benefits from a new quality control measure called stroking (*paluchage*). This is done by technicians capable of detecting any possible defect by touch."[57] Humans were then prized for their sensitivity in addition to their organizing skills in the frequency and variety of quality control: "There's no miracle. But there are two fundamental principles. The first, as you have seen, is quality control. Checking the metal at the beginning, checking every stage of production, and checking at the end of the production cycle."[58] After the crisis in the 1980s, the inversion of factors first of all presented quality as a question of mobilization, notably in films for internal use. In the "struggle for quality,"[59] everybody must remain vigilant, taking on their share of responsibility, to themselves and to others, up to the customer, who justified the following statement: "The hunt for the grain of sand is severe. Slacking off during surveillance is in nobody's interest. We work hand in hand."[60]

Men and machines, a fluctuating relationship

Throughout the often intricately intersecting themes of modernity, automation, and quality, the films outline a changing relationship between workers and machines. The emphasis on automatic facilities, on their speed, regularity, and precision, tended to obscure the employees. Reflecting this, activity was shown featuring no human presence in the workshop,[61] except for occasional slips of the camera.[62] These films from the 1950s and 1980s associated progress with a reduction in the number of employees, and they encourage the spectator to consider the workforce a factor of industrial imperfection and the weak link in production. In the films from the following period, the machine is the welcome assistant of the employees, in the sense that these "robots have permitted considerable progress in the ergonomics of the workplace."[63] The machine plays a subordinate role, classically represented as such following Lewis Mumford[64]: "But man in all this? He checks the work of his army of robots. In a certain sense he becomes the manager of the machines. A computer takes charge of data while man keeps the best for himself: quality control."[65] In the same year, another film took up a similar discourse: "Robots are machines... I would say much like other machines. They are much closer to machines than to men. Machines are incapable of working by themselves. Man is an element, he is the necessary link in a factory like ours and even more so in a robotic factory than a classical factory."[66] Filmmakers, however, sometimes mix up the roles to the point that it is no longer clear who is at the service of whom: "While the robot assembles the pieces loaded onto the consolidating platform, Monsieur Ziant can change the electrodes on the soldering tool. But he can also do quality control without slowing down production, having to reload the conveyor belt."[67-] Variations in the discourse, however, can coexist during the same period. Thus, starting in the 1980s, the company speaks simultaneously, but differently, to visitors, consumers, and employees.

3.   A diversity of cinematographic styles featuring work

Cinematic discourse has numerous ways of presenting industrial performance, of glorifying a business, of recounting its history, of announcing the industrialization of a vehicle, or of presenting new managerial methods. Between the linear representation of manufacturing and the use of stylistic procedures such as metaphors, pastiches, etc., the filmmakers' methods to film the factory, its production, and finally, *the work*, are borrowed from eclectic sources.

The narrative of production

Representing the process of manufacturing in its chronology, stage by stage, is one of the classic kinds of business film. This method of narrating occurs during all of the periods mentioned, from the 1950s[68] to the present day.[69] It stresses the techniques of manufacturing, and when celebrating the introduction of a new vehicle, attention is directed toward the car or one of its subgroups.[70] In these presentations of flow, the factory is presented as a well-oiled machine. A breakdown is never documented ,[71] and thus becomes an inconceivable event for the spectator. When one does appear on the screen, it is done deliberately to show the company's ability to react quickly.[72] Following the linear flow can, with regard to the passage of time, cover a production process in its entirety (as was accomplished at the Billancourt factory) or in a more limited way, notably when the factories shown have neither foundries nor power hammers (such as the sites at Flins and Sandouville). But the characteristics of the individual factories do not sufficiently explain the representational choice[73]: The places shown are selected very carefully. The films integrate the conception phase,[74] or they remain confined to the perimeters of certain workshops. In PROTO 117, the painting workshops are not represented, while in FABRICATION MÉGANE II DOUAI the stamping workshops are absent. Though it is difficult for the uninformed spectator to perceive, examples of gaps in the process are numerous. The workshops (or workplaces) that are given priority are very often those that have undergone modernization. Thus the detour into the sheet-metal workshop seems almost unavoidable when the multipoint welding machines arrive,[75] or more recently, with the latest generation of robots,[76] whose elegant dance has a fascination of its own. Aesthetic qualities of certain spaces can influence the cinematographic preferences. The shots of the entry into the light tunnels needed for quality control are shown regardless of the time period. If, on the one hand, filmmakers find their attention drawn to the agile and effective gestures of the workers, on the other hand, they avoid filming the most tiresome operations or those likely to tarnish the company's image.

The traveling shot seems to be unavoidable when representing a factory. What could be more natural than having the camera follow the movement of the rolling conveyor belt[77] to suggest the flow of production? The most remarkable one was made by Jean-Jacques Sirkis in 24 HEURES À LA RÉGIE RENAULT (1957). The traveling shot can even make a stopped line seem to be mechanically flowing along.[78] Thanks to the rolling bridges of the stamping workshop, the factory offers filmmakers the technical possibility of easily making traveling aerial shots. Charts or drawings are sometimes brought in to accentuate and accompany this presentation of flow and reinforce its scientific quality.

Another didactic interlude is the insertion of "past" images to underscore the modernity of the present. The play on the opposition between periods is even accentuated by showing the images in black and white (even if they were originally in color) and accompanied by sound that suggests the rough quality of earlier times. In these films, images are rarely sufficient: the sound and the commentary contribute to this narrative of flow. Aggressive sounds are reduced or even eliminated. Sounds are added, as in Sirkis's film (1957); to accentuate the effect of the machines' power the director inserted the sound of an air pump, though not without creating a certain anachronism![79] Music (classical music in the early productions, replaced by electronic music in the contemporary ones) also plays an important role in the construction of the narrative. Triumphant and alert, it serves to present grandeur in the 1960s films, when the company was in full expansion. The shift that it brings also allows the representation of the factory universe to be softened and reinforces the feeling of ease.[80] Another sonic element is the jarring *voice-over* that comes in to simply describe the images. In the 1950s, the monotonous male voice did not hesitate to describe, in very technical terms that recalled the language of engineers, what the spectator was supposed to appreciate. André Cantenys's aforementioned film, U5, is emblematic of this type of production. The accumulation of details serves to "prove" rationality, expertise, efficiency.[81] In more recent films, organizational aspects – such as the question of logistics or computer science – are equally in evidence.[82] This group of films, with standardized scripts, offers an entirely controlled industrial universe.

Visits, guides, and "witnesses"

In order not to lead the spectator through a disembodied production process, some filmmakers returned to the principle of the factory visit, led by "guides" who accompany them in their discovery of the factory.

By positioning themselves at the level of fiction, several of these films present outside characters, children who discover the factory and its manufacturing in an impromptu or programmed way. The spectator is invited to follow them in their initiatory journey. What does a child see? A world that, in principle, is forbidden to him (CHAMPIONS JUNIORS), or where access has been authorized as an exception (VISITEURS D'UN JOUR). A world of fascinating surprises, but which may also present certain dangers. The small size of the child contrasts with the immensity of the factory, which becomes a playground where the child can slip into the Fenwicks or hide there, play hide and seek among the machines, and lose him or herself in a place where everything is astonishing. Children make it possible for the film to be both pedagogical and playful at the same time. This meeting of two "foreign" worlds takes place in another cinematic genre: the "newsreels" made for a wide audience and screened in cinemas before the main features. Filming prestigious visitors raises the status of both the factory and those who work there. Thus, in the splendor of the 1960s, celebrities like Grace Kelly, Nikita Khrushchev, Queen Elizabeth, the emperor Haile Selassie, and certain African kings came to visit the Flins plant, as a symbol of the industrial grandeur of France.

Figure 6 Queen Elizabeth at the Flins plant (1957)

Société d'histoire du Groupe Renault / DR

The tour guide was associated with the company since he was an employee (worker or manager) who showed spectators the way. Upon entering, the focal point was delimited by the referential universe of the "hero" one will be following. The scale of representation was extended when the person being filmed was seen in several places. One could see the research department and various workshops while walking along with the head engineer or the manager.[83] When the guide was a worker it was above all his professional universe, that is, his work area that was being filmed.[84] Until the beginning of the 1980s,[85] the framework of the narrative was supported by voice-over commentary, which did not let the employee speak. By the end of this period, the humanization of the production universe, which meant taking an interest in the men who worked there, assumed a dimension both more collective and more direct. The perfecting of these procedures of sound and image recording, but also the renewal of the narrative's contours by mimicking television news reports, translated into a more systematic use of interviews in the workplace. The explanatory voice-over, however, was not abandoned; it was merely placed between two interviews[86] and even spoke from other sources, such as slogans embedded in the image.[87]

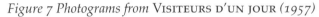

Figure 7 Photograms from VISITEURS D'UN JOUR *(1957)*

Renault Communication/Guy Cavagnac DR

Eclecticism, shifts, and imagination

Even when it concerned assembly-line work, the film often turned to the imaginary and the unexpected. Thanks to special effects and editing techniques, filmmakers could recreate the industrial universe. Techniques such as stop motion, superimpositions of images (posters, photos, etc.),[88] insertions of humorous cartoons, video animation, graphic processes, and graphic representations to suggest the flow of production were diverse and sometimes astonishing. The offbeat tone turned up again in the use of literary techniques. Thus, the commentary of MADE IN RENAULT in 1983 could avoid a boring demonstration thanks to a text rich in culinary metaphors, embellished with country music or a harp piece that could accentuate the impression of fluidity: "First you take a few hundred kilos of various metals and melt them in a very hot fire. Then you go to the mold ... sprinkle in some electronics and add four or five hundred other ingredients ... wrap it up in string, garnish it with leather, watch it while it's baking. After all is said and done, you have an automobile."

A living quality was evoked to embellish a universe of dead metal. The accent was on the magical and secretive side of production, the importance of the human factor, but also the "adding of the soul" located in the factory universe. Human groups could be associated with the factory: a football team, the orchestra,[89] or even the family,[90] or the army.[91] These, however, were not used to designate robots. The filmmakers employed fantasy when they evoked the "steel monsters" or the "mastodon" when referring to machines. Even the metaphor of voracity was employed: "Here, automatic mechanisms bring each machine its ration of metal."[92] But the steel monster also had a benevolent face, since "it does the taxing and dangerous work." The factory's vastness and its power are therefore suggested. In other films, it is the car that is presented as a living being. In the film RENAULT EXPRESS FABRICATION, the description of a utility vehicle's production process was accompanied by a languorous female voice. This voice, which was attached to a woman's face[93] between each presentation of a different workshop, gave a first-person account of the birth of this vehicle. The description was garnished with sexual allusions: "With agile and skillful movements, a robot accompanies me and decks me out with a perfect-looking, shiny coat of paint. Embellished in my most beautiful colors, they warm me up, check my outfit. I'm ready." Ten years later, a film promoting the introduction of a new model[94] took up the erotic metaphor again: "In the beginning, I was just a spool of steel, as round as a wheel. But be aware, not just any steel, but high-quality steel. No time to lose. I unroll myself like a rug so my metal can be carved up. But quickly they mold me, finally they end up giving me a shape." We should also mention that the vocabulary of the factory lends itself to this style of alluding to activities such as grooming and stroking (*paluchage*). Human properties are regularly attributed to the automobile: "Embryos of cars grouped into finished products, but they're still missing one thing they need to come alive: the engine."[95]

In the end, the categories chosen to represent assembly-line work all merge. As one advances in time, the combination of procedures becomes more systematic. The association of the insistent voice-over and interviews, falling back on special effects, and drawings are often put together in the same film. It is important to point out that one of the most significant evolutions was giving a voice directly to the people being filmed. In more recent films, it is rare that films do not appeal to the word "from below" (workers and supervisors on hand) to consolidate what the word "from above" (that of the voice-over) has said, at the very time the company has become more careful to praise the merits of participation. This could not have been done without the perfection of cinematic techniques that make it possible to conduct interviews using synthetic sound at the very locations where work is being performed.

4.   Conclusion

While business films could be considered an expression of management positions and an explanation of their strategy, studying these films reveals a more
complex and richer reality.

First of all, the history of corporate films translates the history of cinema in its
own terms. This is more than a simple tropism. To best utilize cinema, despite
the technical limitations of film stock and recording materials, the postwar
world of film relies on a heavily structured professional armada. Renault provided sizable funding for a permanent department of professionals from the
best schools who shared the progressive ideas of their generation. The breakup
of this cinema department in the early 1960s did not by itself change the way
films were made. What was more significant was the introduction of lighter
cameras, then videos, and finally digital media. There were also technical
changes in the evolution of film production, which related to the changing status of the films made, from auteur productions to communication products.
Throughout the postwar period, cinematic language developed a wide variety
of styles and was clearly a part of the history of cinema.

Moreover, these films illustrate the evolution of the modalities of business
communication. Even though we don't always know the target or actual audience of these films, it is obvious that the majority of those made between 1950
and 1960 "speak loud and clear" (to paraphrase a Gaullist formula) in the name
of a company, in a way that is sure of itself and triumphant. The global self-
representation of the firm has become blurred in recent film productions, promoting the cars themselves as much as the industrial establishments that produced them. In the 1980s, these films acquired a more focused message as they
were clearly addressing a more limited audience. They were even used as a
means for internal communications between industrial establishments or various services. The shift from periods of doubt and reform to times of confidence
invoked or rewarded was clearly reflected in these films. The voice of French
society was never far away in the tone these films adopted or the arguments
they employed, either as a source of the situations evoked or as a spectator the
films had to convince.

Ultimately, the images of work were variable. Until the end of the 1960s, work
was the exclusive subject of industrial films thought of as streamlining tools, or
was well founded in the lyrical images of industrial power. More recent films
have taken work as a problem to be resolved according to the individual case by
simply getting rid of it or making appropriate tributes, by promoting the solutions or making interjections. Thus, the Renault films constantly updated the
firm's relationship to its own workers.

Notes

1. This study was done as part of a project by the research group Nigwal, *"Quand la chaîne fait son cinéma. Regards sociologique et historique sur la représentation cinématographique d'une forme standard de travail industriel,"* Fonds national de la science, 2006.

2. Renault's media library has assembled a collection of numbered company films that have been listed in a database. While searching this database using terms like "work," "assembly line," and "factory," we identified some 100 documents, to which could be added several titles discovered in the course of meetings, readings, and conversations. In this corpus, we did not find any industrial films made during the 1940s. The following decade accounts for a dozen films. We located a half dozen from the 1960s and 1970s, another 20 from the 1980s and 1990s. Finally, our corpus includes approximately 15 films for the first two years of the 21st century.

3. Benoît Cadet, *Renault fait son cinéma. Le film d'entreprise de 1950 à nos jours*, memoir of DEA of social and cultural history under the direction of Myriam Tsikounas (Paris: Université de Paris I, 1998-1999), p. 44. In the works studied, we viewed very few advertising films.

4. AUX USINES RENAULT (Série enseignement n° 5212, Master 3037) and GAUMONT ACTUALITÉ (1920, 22 min., b&w, silent). On the postwar period see Alain P. Michel, above, and "Filmer le travail, les travailleuses et les travailleurs dans les usines Renault de l'entre-deux-guerres," in Patrice Marcilloux (ed.), *Le travail en représentations* (Paris: Éditions du CTHS, 2005), pp. 131-150.

5. Catherine Malaval, *Renault à la une. La presse d'entreprise Renault depuis 1945* (Paris: ClioMédia, 1992), p. 272.

6. Jean Farcy, "Renault et le cinéma d'entreprise," *Renault Histoire*, 3 (June 1991), pp. 21-68; Jean Beaupied, "Un ingénieur chez les saltimbanques," *Renault Histoire,*16 (June 2004), pp. 159-164.

7. Dominique Barjot, Christophe Reveillard (ed.), *L'américanisation de l'Europe occidentale au XXe siècle mythe et réalité* (Paris: Presses universitaires de Paris-Sorbonne, 2002), p. 280.

8. Jean Farcy was recruited by Jean Myon, then given the task by the personnel director to "make films for training purposes." His first "client" was Marcel Delfosse's department of organizational methods, which used cinema "to develop new working methods." Cf. Jean Farcy, "Renault et le cinema," op. cit.

9. André Lucas, "Les conséquences humaines de l'automation. L'expérience de la Régie Renault," *Economie et humanisme*, 112 (1958), pp. 246-256. Alain Wisner "Un exemple de laboratoire industriel. Les études physiologiques à la Régie Renault," *Le Travail humain*, 25 (1963), pp. 309-325.

10. Frank Bunker and Lillian M. Gilbreth, *Applied Motion Study* (Easton: Hive Publishing Company, 1973, first edition, 1917); Ernst Hijmans, CHRONOMÉTRAGES (1929), a film analyzing the movements of Dutch workers using office machines.

11. Jean Farcy, "Renault et le cinéma," op. cit., p. 51.

12. Jean-Jacques Sirkis, interview with Nigwal, April 6, 2006. This would be 24 HEURES À LA RÉGIE, made in 1957, then reedited for a second version in 1961. The film received first prize at the festival of business film.

13. Anonymous, TRAVAIL CHEZ RENAULT (1960, 6 min). This English report with commentary, dated September 1958, uses Renault images as political propaganda. Cf. Benoît Cadet, *Renault fait son cinema*, op. cit, p. 86.

14. Catalogue CEDIMAGES: *Renault: Liste des éléments du fonds audiovisuel* (July 16, 1993) (1,149 titles).

15. Films by Pierre Blondy on dialogues by Marcel Camus and Louis de Funès on his early acting career.

16. Jean Mitry, professor of the IDHEC, made SYMPHONIE MÉCANIQUE (1956), for Renault. This is the period when Alain Resnais made LE CHANT DU STYRÈNE (1958) for Péchiney.

17. Jean-Louis Loubet, *Renault, cent ans d'histoire* (Boulogne-Billancourt: Éditions ETAI, 1998), pp. 210-220.

18. Caméra Unit began producing the new magazine, *Renault Contact*, in 1965. It compiled a series of films (and not news features) meant to be produced in several foreign versions.

19. Cf. Nigwal, "Le travail en représentation dans les films militants. Caméras et micros dans les usines automobiles, 1968-1974," *Histoire et sociétés*, 9 (January 2004), pp. 117-131; as well as "Quand Louis Malle filmait le travail à la chaîne. *Humain, trop humain*, et les débats sur la représentation du travail," *Le Temps des médias*, 7 (October 2006); and "Humain trop humain. Le travail au premier plan," *Positif* (December 2005), pp. 96-97, all by Nigwal.

20. Georges Pessis, MADE IN RENAULT (1983). The film received first prize at the festival of commissioned film in Biarritz. The festival of business film was founded in 1959 in Rouen, then moved to Biarritz in 1972, until its demise in 1987. Today the festival of Creusot is its principal heir.

21. It experiments with computer-assisted drawings and introduces an audiovisual touch to the commissioned film.

22. Georges Pessis, interview with Nigwal, April 28, 2006.

23. Extension Vidéo was created in 1979. Its principal mission is to provide the media with appropriated images of the past that are free of copyright. It administers Renault's video stock and more generally the holdings of the commercial administration. The storage of industrial films is guaranteed by the CEDFI through a film and video library specially created in 1959, associated with the ministry of foreign affairs, which allows films on the French economy to be borrowed free of charge.

24. MCAV is an Economic Interest Group (GIE) that allows Renault to produce films itself. Benoît Cadet, *Renault fait son cinema*, op. cit., p. 20.

25. In May 1981, François Mitterand was elected president of France. The new socialist government appointed Bernard Hanon as the head of Renault in December 1981.

26. Georges Pessis, *Entreprise et cinéma – Cent ans d'images* (Paris: La Documentation française, 1997), p. 256. In France during the 1980s, 400 of the 2,000 documents made each year were presented at the Biarritz festival.

27. Gwenaële Rot, *La sociologie de l'atelier. Renault, le travail ouvrier et le sociologue* (Toulouse: Octarès Editions, 2006), p. 109.

28. L'EMPREINTE D'UN GÉANT (1983); BIENVENUE À CLÉON (1984); L'USINE DE MONTAGE À L'ÉTRANGER (1987).

29. Jean-Louis Loubet, Nicolas Hatzfeld, Alain P. Michel, *Ile Seguin. Des Renault et des hommes* (Boulogne-Billancourt: ETAI, 2004).

30. Loïc Le Guénédal, Dernier maillon (1992, 7 min); cf. Gwenaële Rot, *Sociologie de l'atelier*, op. cit., p. 64.
31. Jean-Charles Sirkis, interview with Nigwal, April 6, 2006.
32. Les coulisses de l'atelier (1995); Processus de fabrication à l'usine de Flins (1997); Cléon Passion (2000), etc.
33. Georges Pessis, interview with Nigwal, April 18, 2006.
34. Has since become Publicis Events France. A simple listing of films with contents depending on archivist knowledge has been followed by an indexed computer catalog.
35. Philippe Ros, Transfert mécanique automatisé (1996).
36. Cf. the study of accompanying documents in Benoît Cadet, *Renault fait son cinema*, op. cit., pp. 75-79.
37. Stéphane Leloutre, Activité de travail au montage (1999).
38. *Magazine de l'automobile*, 15 (1959).
39. *Magazine de l'automobile*, 8 (1957).
40. Flins (1952).
41. Naissance d'une usine (1966).
42. Nouvelles chaîne de production Renault 4 et Renault 5 (1985).
43. Montages en chaîne (1972); Conditions de travail (1980).
44. Made in Renault (1983); Histoire d'une porte (2000).
45. Conditions de travail (1980).
46. "Renault, one hundred years of innovation" was the formula in use during the centenary celebration in 1998.
47. Flins (1952).
48. Pierre Bézier, "Souvenirs d'un outilleur : de la 4 CV à la Dauphine (1)," *De Renault Frères, constructeurs d'automobiles, à Renault Régie Nationale*, 30 (June 1985), pp. 140-146; Alain Michel, "Un ingénieur-innovateur: Pierre Bézier," *Entreprises et histoire*, 23 (December 1999), pp. 117-120.
49. L'empreinte d'un géant (1983); Made in Renault (1983).
50. Supplices sur mesure (1969).
51. Made in Renault (1983).
52. Machine transfert (1956).
53. Naissance d'une usine (1966).
54. Made in Renault (1983).
55. Naissance d'une usine (1966).
56. Ibid.
57. Histoire d'une porte (2000).
58. Made in Renault (1983).
59. Gestes à temps (1987).
60. Ibid.
61. On the rushes of a 2000 film on the production of the Mégane, one hears the director suddenly becoming angry when he sees a worker enter the frame.
62. In the film Machine transfert from 1956, for instance, a worker with a cigarette dangling from his mouth can be seen making a furtive gesture.
63. Histoire d'une porte (2000).
64. Lewis Mumford, *Technics and Civilization* (New York: Harcourt Brace and Co., 1934).
65. Ibid.

66. L'EMPREINTE D'UN GÉANT (1983).
67. L'HOMME AU CENTRE DE LA PERFORMANCE (1998).
68. U5 (1959).
69. DOSSIER PÉDAGOGIQUE (1989) and L'AUTOMOBILE EN MUTATION.
70. U5 (1959); HISTOIRE D'UN MOTEUR (1997) and HISTOIRE D'UNE PORTE (2000).
71. The "snags" that nonetheless arise in reality can be accidentally filmed, as certain rushes testify.
72. Such is the case in a film from 1959, AUTONOMANU, where the attention given to a rapid resolution of an incident shows that the business knows how to react with the appropriate means.
73. In the Renault films of the 1930s, the editing constructs an "imaginary geography of the assembly line" and creates the illusion of linear production by placing scenes end to end that are in fact spread out throughout the factories at Billancourt. Cf. Alain P. Michel, *Travail à la chaîne. Renault 1898-1947* (Billancourt: éditions ETAI, 2007).
74. PROTO 117 (1969).
75. Ibid.
76. MÉGANE DOUAI (2002).
77. Often at a faster pace than the actual line to give an impression of speed.
78. LA NOUVELLE CHAÎNE DE PRODUCTION, ÎLE SEGUIN, BOULOGNE BILLANCOURT (1985).
79. Interview with Jean-Jacques Sirkis: "We recorded sounds separately since there's so much hubbub in the factory and if you want to have a particular sound you have to record it by itself, apart. We entertained ourselves... The famous U5 machine, we took pneumatic sounds from another machine. When we projected the film to the engineer, he said, 'Listen Sirkis, my machine isn't pneumatic, it's electric, it doesn't make any noise!' But the pneumatic sound is a great noise, it gives a really dramatic element to it!"
80. CONDITIONS DE TRAVAIL (1980).
81. "The drills have a maximum speed of 100 meters per minute and a forward motion that approaches two meters a minute... The tolerance is 02 millimeters... of fuel oxides, lubricated by a mist of petroleum, reaming the block at a pace on the order of 750 millimeters per minute... 540 different operations on each of [2,000] vehicles that come out each day."
82. For example, FABRICATION DE LA MÉGANE, STANDARDISATION DU PROCESS RENAULT MÉGANE (1996).
83. In UNE VOITURE EST NÉE (1956) the filmmaker describes the stages of production of a vehicle by following an engineer wandering through the factory, from the research office to the vehicle leaving the factory. In LA MODERNISATION DE L'USINE DE FLINS (1997), the "visit" is conducted mainly by an engineer, a member of the factory's management staff, who presents different modernized workshops in the framework of interviews.
84. LES COULISSES DE L'ATELIER (1995).
85. JOURNÉE D'UN MÉTALLO (1969); CONDITIONS DE TRAVAIL (1980).
86. BIENVENUE À CLÉON (1984); GESTES À TEMPS (1987); USINE VOIR ET SAVOIR N° 2 (1997).
87. For instance, the 13-minute film LES COULISSES DE L'ATELIER (1995) includes 14 panels inserted between two short interviews. They underscore the progress and the

socio-technical investments. "Here the operator checks his own mistakes"; "result on this line, four times fewer failures than two years ago"; "UET = Elementary Work Unit, 29 people on average"; "in one year the operators have made 30,000 suggestions. 90% of them have been implemented"; "each in their turn, the operators check and evaluate the level of efficiency in their UET"; "every day in the factory, 200 people are in training"; "the launch of the new Megane has required 400,000 hours of training."

88. IMAGES DE MARQUE (1970); HISTOIRE D'UNE PORTE (2000).

89. BIENVENUE À CLÉON (1984).

90. VISITEUR D'UN JOUR (1975).

91. MADE IN RENAULT (1957).

92. Op. cit.

93. Reminiscent of the actress Chantal Nobel, the lead actress in the successful television series, *Chateauvallon*, broadcast on TF1 in 1985-1986.

94. RENAULT DOUAI (1998).

95. VISITEURS D'UN JOUR (1975).

Eccentricity, Education and the Evolution of Corporate Speech

Jam Handy and His Organization

Rick Prelinger

Although the work of Jamison "Jam" Handy (1886-1983) and his multimedia production company, the Jam Handy Organization, have received almost no scholarly attention, both exerted a major influence on the development of the American sponsored film and the evolution of American corporate speech. During a production career that lasted almost 70 years, Handy's company produced some 7,000 motion pictures, many tens of thousands of slidefilms, thousands of mixed-media training products and innumerable live "industrial theater" shows. As interest in sponsored films grows and we begin to assess their influence upon 20th-century cultural and social spheres, it is high time to examine Handy's long career and come to terms with the vast number of works he left behind.

Jam Handy came of age in an era characterized by unprecedented industrial concentration and heightened class struggle, factors that encouraged corporations to develop communications strategies to address workers and the public. Fast-growing corporations engaged in the continuous rationalization of production processes turned their attention to rationalizing internal communication, training, and sales. New challenges led them to experiment with and embrace emerging media, including lantern slides, the phonograph, the slidefilm, the theatrical performance, and ultimately the motion picture. Handy became a communications consultant and service provider to large, decentralized enterprises.

Though an original and often idiosyncratic thinker, Handy had his antecedents. First among his direct influences was John H. Patterson, the charismatic, paternalistic, and autodidact head of National Cash Register. Patterson's passionate and very personal interest in the processes of production and selling led him to experiment with photography as a means of employee education. Initially turning to the inexpensive lantern slide, he organized a photographic department in 1896, building a glass slide collection that would ultimately total some 68,000 images, each depicting a particular moment of interaction between management and worker, sales trainer and salesman, and salesman and customer. Building a massive matrix of imagery that functioned as a semiotic dissection of everyday business activity, Patterson then assembled slides into training sequences. It was only a short step to the slidefilm (also known as a filmstrip), which combined still images onto a one-meter-long strip of film that could be shown with a pocket-size folding projector, and from the slidefilm a short step to the motion picture. Handy's career would follow a similar trajectory.

Jam Handy and his organization

"As a young man it seemed to me that the most important use I could make of my life was to find better ways for the transmission of instructions, and the transfer of experience. It seemed a shame that so many instructions were misunderstood, that information offered was so hard to understand, that the experience of my elders was so hard to get at, and so many good ideas lost."[1] Born to the eminent newspaperman Moses Purnell Handy on March 6, 1886, Henry Jamison Handy exhibited an interest in the media business and strategies of representation at an early age. At the age of seven, he asked and received permission from his father, then Chief of Promotion and Publicity for the World's Columbian Exposition, to miss school and instead spend his days at the Exposition. For two years, he regularly visited the fair and treated the exhibitors as his teachers while being exposed to the Exposition's celebration of industry and invention.[2]

Any detailed analysis of the rhetorical strategies employed by his films might well begin with an assessment of the rhetoric and the visual culture of the Exposition. He matriculated at the University of Michigan in 1902, hoping (by his own description) to agitate for the stronger presence of visual imagery in education, but his formal education ended when he was expelled for writing a freelance article for the *Chicago Tribune* which offended the professor whose class he described.[3] Offered a job by the *Tribune's* publisher, he worked as a journalist in every one of the *Tribune's* departments from 1903 to 1910, eventually leaving to work with the pioneer animator John R. Bray, who had begun a business focusing on the production of animated technical drawings and filmstrips. The exact chronology of his business involvements in the 1910s is difficult to pin down, and there was apparently a dispute concerning the invention and ownership of filmstrip technology. We do know that Handy gained experience in the production of animated training materials during World War I and that he served the US government as an "Americanization consultant," working under Franklin Lane, then Secretary of the Interior, advocating the wider use of visual material in textbooks and the news media so as to make them more accessible to illiterate Americans, which at that time were numerous.[4]

Working first through the Keeley-Handy Syndicate (which later evolved into the Newspapers Film Corporation, which later became the Jam Handy Organization [JHO]), Handy produced filmstrips and also worked with newspapers to release factual films in theaters. This media synergy does not at first appear to have been a wildly successful business, and it was not until the 1920s that his company seems to have achieved stability with the acquisition of a number of blue-chip clients, preeminently (in 1923) the Chevrolet Motor Company. After cementing his relationship with Chevrolet, Handy's company moved to Detroit, which would be its central headquarters for fifty years. Detroit's strategic location within 250 miles of most heavy manufacturing industries made it the host to two other large, industrial film producers, Wilding Picture Productions and the Metropolitan Motion Picture Company.[5] Handy's large, well-staffed, and vertically-integrated studio, less than a mile from the General Motors headquarters building, is said to have employed up to 600 people. Departments included slidefilm and motion-picture production departments, a full lab, an animation department, and, reputedly, two full orchestras. The Organization was not simply a producer of films, but also offered complete, vertically integrated media-production, distribution, and exhibition services to its clients. Handymen drove mobile projection vans across the country, presenting films at meetings, conventions, and public events; a complete Sales Manager's Service was offered to Chevrolet dealers, thus centralizing and standardizing the sales training curriculum; an almost incalculable number of training and marketing slidefilms were produced every month for their regular clients. Although Handy's multi-media pursuits have yet to be fully described, their existence and extent tell us that his motion pictures must be considered in the context of the other concurrent channels of communication that accompanied them. In fact, perhaps a majority of Handy films did not stand alone; they were probably coordinated with slidefilms, live shows, press articles, or training materials. Restricting historical and representational analysis to the films themselves falls short of a full assessment.

Handy films played in theaters before the main features, and in more specialized venues as commercially sponsored infotainment. Typically, several short subjects, often sponsored films, preceded the feature attractions in many theatres. In special cases, theaters were rented especially to premiere or showcase sponsored films. Newsreel theaters existed in many cities, showing newsreels, studio-produced and non-studio short subjects, and frequently sponsored films. Automobile industry films targeting consumers were projected on kiosks or in special rooms at auto dealerships. Many Handy films were either produced for school use or found their way into classrooms, often by way of the Association Films and Modern Talking Picture Service distribution channels, which distributed sponsored films to schools and non-theatrical venues under contract with sponsors, who paid fees based on the size of the audience that a particular film reached. MASTER HANDS (1936), for example, began its life as a theatrical film and later was channeled into trade schools as a "vocational subject" because it showed automobile manufacturing in detail. Educational venues were typically unfriendly to films containing explicit advertising, which likely influenced JHO to produce many films that simply mentioned sponsors' names and nothing more. Finally, world's fairs functioned as highly promotable frames for commercial speech, and as such were great showcases for sponsored films. JHO work was well-represented at both the 1939 and 1964 New York world's fairs.

JHO continued to produce carefully crafted industrials and sponsored films well into the 1960s. But as other companies modernized the appearance of their films, Handy's films remained stagey, formal and static, reflecting only superficially the visual culture's ferment during the late 1960s. Could JHO's founder, by then in his 80s, have successfully revitalized the look of its films? We will never know. In the summer of 1967, Detroit and many other American cities burned as economically and socially marginalized African-Americans took their anger to the streets. White people and the economic capital they controlled fled the city over the next several years, leaving behind a city that has lost half of its population since the 1950s. In 1972, JHO was sold to Reeves Teletape, a nationwide producer of industrial and training media, and became known as Teletape Detroit. This change of ownership did not last, and the company was divided into The Jam Handy Organization and Jam Handy Productions. The new JHO produced a number of little-known films, largely undocumented and using outside contractors, under the Jam Handy name. Bill Sandy, a Handy executive, turned Jam Handy Productions into a new company, The Bill Sandy Company (now Sandy Corporation), which managed to retain the Chevrolet business.[6]

Handy died in 1983, at the age of 97. Even before that the company, down to a staff of two, had already begun to contract and divest itself of its resources before that. Its Grand Boulevard studio building in Detroit, once the anchor of a six-building studio, became a religious television studio called Faith for Miracles. Most of its archives were dumped, although many of the films were recovered by scroungers and collectors. The studio building still survives, largely because of the depreciated value of Detroit real estate.

A brief assessment

Though the work of understanding JHO's vast body of film has only begun, it is possible to make a few preliminary statements.

First, JHO's work is remarkable for its longevity and quantity. Few if any production units in or out of Hollywood can boast of having produced so many films over such a long period of time under the supervision of just one person. For this reason alone, it would be worthy of a deeper and more thorough examination. Second, Handy cultivated relationships with many large corporations, including General Motors, DuPont, RCA, Dow Chemical, Xerox, IBM and National Cash Register. GM was especially active in a two-decade attempt to sway public opinion away from the New Deal and toward free-enterprise economics, and many of the key films made as part of this project are Handy films.[7] Handy often stated that he felt committed to bridging the gaps between corporations and the public, and between corporations and workers, and as such, his films deserve consideration as early articulations of corporate speech through emerging media. Third, the ubiquity and reach of sponsored films merit a more thorough investigation and analysis than has thus far occurred. With some films reaching an estimated 20 to 30 million viewers, it is clear that sponsored films constitute a mass-communications medium that has largely been ignored by scholars. While many members of the public age 40+ recall seeing sponsored films in school, on TV or elsewhere, for the most part they only remember specific titles and forget the ubiquity of these films, which were almost as widespread and ubiquitous in the culture then as corporate-image websites are today.

Stylistically, Handy's work is also *sui generis*. A detailed analysis of its representational strategies would have to consider such attributes as its frequent deployment of animation, including a number of striking stop-motion animation sequences that recall the work of Oskar Fischinger; its extreme concentration on visualizing the unseeable, as exemplified in the many scientifically oriented films that are part of the DIRECT MASS SELLING series; and the relation between narration and picture, considerably more hierarchical and ritualistic than many other sponsored films. Frequent viewing of his films also reveals a number of eccentric, almost fetishistic attributes, such as the use of the three primary colors red, blue and yellow in almost every scene of his late big-budget productions, including AMERICAN LOOK (1958), AMERICAN ENGINEER (1956) and AMERICAN MAKER (1960). It is hard to explain choices like this without attributing them to Handy's oft-expressed, unusual ideas about visual culture and the nourishment of viewer attention.

Finally, Jam Handy and his Organization are credited as formative influences by many who worked with them or who followed them in the industry. If we are to understand the influences that contributed to the growing commercialization of public discourse, I suspect that we can trace many of them back to Handy.

What should be done?

Sponsored film scholarship presently resides at an early stage which one might call the "summary level." Little in-depth work has been done on collections, subjects, or styles, and I am not aware of any analysis that dares to consider the entire oeuvre of a producer. There are probably some 800 to 1000 Handy films in various archives that are probably available for study. This is a scholarly opportunity that is probably unequalled anywhere in the US-sponsored film field. Almost every film is keyed to a specific conjuncture of corporate strategy and media tactics, and situating them historically will be a fascinating, if difficult, endeavor. Since the Jam Handy papers are primarily of biographical significance rather than business record, work needs to be done in the archives of corporations sponsoring Handy films to assess intentions and understand the business reasoning that motivated their production.

Reception poses difficult issues for the scholar of sponsored films, as we have little record of how audiences reacted, and trade press reviews and publicity releases provide little help. But the questions of reception continues to come up. Scholars who find and interpret records that illuminate this complex issue will make valuable contributions.

Finally, work needs to be done to preserve Handy's films and make more of them accessible to scholars and to a broad public audience. In theory, this should not be difficult because almost all of the Handy films are in the public domain. Funding to do this has not yet materialized, however, and then there is the matter of access to the works, an issue we hope will improve in the future.

Brief summary of Jam Handy Organization productions

The earliest identifiable JHO films known to survive date from approximately 1925 (though older films may exist without clear attribution), and I have been told by former employees that JHO produced films until the early 1980s, using contract employees hired for specific jobs. Production records that survive begin in approximately 1930 and end in 1968, and list approximately 7,000 distinct moving-image productions, though many productions are derived from previous works, while others represent projects such as contract shoots rather than finished films. The extant films represent a spectrum of genres and styles, ranging from motion slidefilms (motion pictures incorporating still images, some moving shots, narration and some sync sound) to full-blown, feature-length dramatic narratives; from single-strand Kodachrome industrial and process documentation films to high-end three-strip Technicolor productions; and animated technical diagrams to detailed cel-animated theatrical cartoons.[8]

Though it is risky to divide JHO's motion-picture production into chronological categories, it may be worthwhile to point out common characteristics of films made during different time periods.

1922-1934. Many films produced for Chevrolet and other divisions of General Motors, including Oakland (later Pontiac), Frigidaire, Delco Light; some work for National Cash Register, Ralston-Purina, Curtis Publishing and Coca-Cola. Key titles in this period include SAND ON THE SLIPPERY SIDEWALKS OF SALES (1925), a semi-dramatic film about the repair and maintenance of Frigidaire refrigerators; AROUND THE WORLD WITH G.M. (1927), a four-reeler depicting GM's decentralized management strategy under Alfred P. Sloan and their operations in many countries; and A CAR FOR EVERY PURSE AND PURPOSE (1926), a consumer marketing film showing GM's different product lines. Similar to films from other producers in this period, JHO's production combined silent-film dramatic style, technical animation, and relatively static views of cities, buildings, and machines. As far as is known, every film in this period was shot using the 35 mm negative-positive process.

1935-1941. The DIRECT MASS SELLING series, totaling 115 films (7 min. to 40 min.), was made for Chevrolet. Produced for theatrical exhibition, these films combined entertainment and instruction and directly addressed consumers. Some titles included MAGIC IN THE AIR (1941), showing the workings of television; BACK OF THE MIKE (1938), showing how sound effects were produced live in the radio studio; A COACH FOR CINDERELLA (1936), said to be the first Technicolor industrial cartoon; and PRECISELY SO (1936), on the technology of measurement, featuring a memorable Oskar Fischinger-style stop-motion march of compasses, slide rules and micrometer gauges. Also in this series was MASTER HANDS (1936), the Wagnerian "industrial symphony" showing all stages in the production of Chevrolets, the first sound industrial film to be named to the US National Film Registry. Like many sponsored films of the time, they contained no explicit advertising, in order to render their messages more palatable in theatres and schools, an attribute that would serve them well in the late 1930s when TV stations with experimental licenses, which were not permitted to run commercial materials, broadcasted these films. Other significant films of this period included To NEW HORIZONS, the part-Technicolor film version of Norman Bel Geddes' HIGHWAYS AND HORIZONS exhibit at the 1939-40 New York World's Fair, which documented the famous Futurama. During this time, JHO also produced Minute Movies, one-minute theatrical screen ads for a number of national clients, typically distributed through the General Screen Advertising Company, and a wide variety of sponsored films for other entities, including

Bayer Semesan, DuPont, Dow Chemical, and the Republican National Committee.

Beginning around 1936, JHO began to produce a few high-budget films in three-strip Technicolor, and in 1939-1940, started to experiment with the lower-cost 16mm Kodachrome process. Some early JHO Kodachrome films, such as To Market To Market (for General Screen Advertising, 1941), mix 35mm black-and-white photography with a single reel of Kodachrome, while others, including the tremendously successful We Drivers (for General Motors, 1935), mix 35mm Technicolor and black and white on a single reel. As an example of the reach of sponsored films of the time, We Drivers was shown in 7,000 theaters in 10 months and was also seen by an estimated 24 million viewers in non-commercial venues. The 1935 production was remade in 1947, 1955, 1962, and 1976.[9]

1941-1945. Like many other companies, JHO "went to war," producing several hundred training films and filmstrips for the military services (primarily the US Navy), many of which were restricted or classified. JHO also broke new technological ground in the development of what were euphemistically called "training aids," meaning simulators that permitted pilots and gunners to engage with virtual attackers and targets. After the war, this technology became the Cinesphere system, an immersive screening technology that projected images onto a half-dome above the audience.

While JHO continued to produce films for its prewar clients, its wartime films typically did not promote specific products, but rather depicted corporate activities in wartime or told stories designed to promote production or address specific corporate issues that arose. Typical titles from this period include These Are The People (for Kimberly-Clark Co., 1944), paying tribute to the paper-processing workers in Neenah, Wisconsin, the home of Kleenex products; To Each Other (for United States Steel, 1943), a widely shown dramatic film urging retired workers to rejoin the labor force; and The Open Door: The Story of Foreman Jim Baxter, His Family, and His Job (for General Motors Public Relations Staff, 1945), a lengthy film made to discourage factory foremen from joining unions.

1946-1968. Jam Handy films reflect the postwar industrial shift from military to consumer production, the outmigration from cities to suburbs, and the pro-free enterprise, anti-communist discourses of the period. During this period, JHO produced in many film formats, and also made films primarily intended to be shown on television, which in this period became one of the major distribution outlets for sponsored films. A few important titles from this prolific period include Looking Ahead Through Rohm & Haas Plexiglas (1947), in which Plexiglas serves as an example of economic reconversion to peacetime production; Unfinished Business (made for U.S. Steel, 1948), dramatizing the return of war veterans to the civilian workforce; AMERICAN HARVEST (made for Chevrolet, 1951), the first of five big-budget "American" films on the impor-tance of the automobile industry to the national economy; and OUT OF THIS WORLD (made for General Motors, 1964), which depicts a visit to the World's Fair Motorama exhibit, heir to the 1939 Futurama.

JHO production records from this period list innumerable films for large and small companies, including many titles intended for internal training and dis-cussion. Many of these films are extremely difficult to contextualize without knowledge of the specific corporate cultures in which they sought to intervene.

1968-1983. Aside from the ubiquitous training and management-orientation films produced for the automobile industry, I know little of JHO's production from this period.

Resources for the scholar

The largest single collection of JHO films resides at the Library of Congress, where it currently awaits a move to the new National Audiovisual Conserva-tion Center in Culpeper, Virginia. Until the collection is accessioned and opened, the primary access point remains the Prelinger Archives, which pre-sently holds 404 JHO titles that have been transferred to videotape. Most of these titles are available for free viewing and download as digital video files at the Internet Archive.[10] The Prelinger collection is represented by Getty Images for the sale of stock footage.[11] The collection of Handy films (mostly titles pro-duced for Chevrolet) given to the Bill Sandy Company is represented by His-toric Films for the sale of stock footage.[12]

Handy-produced slidefilms are frequently sold on eBay. The largest collection of them is held by a private collector, who also holds a portion of the still-photo-graph library used in the production of the filmstrips. Some production records, including checklists of films produced from ca. 1930-1968 and some JHO com-pany promotional material, are held by the author.

The Jam Handy Papers are housed at the Burton Historical Collection, Detroit Public Library, Detroit, Michigan; the collection illuminates Handy's early life but contains fewer documents related to JHO's film production from the 1930s on. John H. Patterson and NCR's glass slide collection is held by the Montgom-ery County Historical Society in Dayton, Ohio.[13]

Notes

1. Undated autobiographical fragment, Jam Handy Papers, BHC.
2. Mildred Handy Ritchie and Sarah Rozelle Handy Mallon (eds.) and Isaac W.K. Handy, *Annals and Memorials of the Handys and Their Kindred* (Ann Arbor, MI: William L. Clements Library, 1992), p. 669.
3. Linda Robinson Walker, "The Suspension of Jam Handy," *Michigan Today,* March 1995, at http://www.umich.edu/%7Enewsinfo/MT/95/Mar95/mt1m95.html; accessed January 28, 2008.
4. "Biographical Material – Mr. Handy," circa late 1940s, Jam Handy Papers, BHC.
5. Arthur Edwin Krows, "Motion Pictures – Not For Theatres," installment 16, *The Educational Screen* (February 1940), pp. 58-61. Published in 58 installments from September 1938 to June 1944, Krows's unfinished series recounts the fascinating (if sometimes less than accurate) story of early US industrial and educational film production.
6. Robert T. Eberwein and Bill Sandy, "The Contributions of the Jam Handy Organization to American Commerce and Culture," *Oakland Journal,* 4 (Spring 2002), pp. 82-92; Ray Pointer, posting in GAC Forums, at http://forums.goldenagecartoons.com/showthread.php?t=5779, accessed January 28, 2008.
7. For a detailed treatment of this corporate crusade, see William L. Bird, Jr., *Better Living: Advertising, Media, and the New Vocabulary of Business Leadership, 1935-1955* (Evanston, IL: Northwestern University Press, 1999).
8. Jam Handy Organization, *Motion Pictures: 1935-1968* (Detroit: Jam Handy Organization, n.d.), available at Prelinger Library, San Francisco. Typescript listing productions in production-number order.
9. Rick Prelinger, *The Field Guide to Sponsored Films* (San Francisco: National Film Preservation Foundation, 2007), p. 98.
10. http://www.archive.org/details/prelinger.
11. http://www.gettyimages.com.
12. http://www.historicfilms.com/library_pages/jamhandy.html.
13. http://www.daytonhistory.org/magiclantern.htm.

Centron, an Industrial/Educational Film Studio, 1947-1981

A Microhistory

Faye E. Riley

> Give them more than they expect and charge them less than they expect.
> *Russell Mosser*

At one time industrial/educational film studios were as prevalent in the United States as Hollywood studios. They employed hundreds of film technicians, actors, and directors. Thousands of industrial and educational films were created and widely distributed, and catalogues and archives probably contain more titles in this category than any other, including Hollywood's fictive features. These films impacted the lives of countless viewers, and yet, film scholars have so far largely neglected this important body of work. While the history of Hollywood cinema has largely been written in the last twenty or so years, the history of industrial and educational films remains as yet to be researched, both in terms of film styles and modes of production. Addressing this particular gap in film scholarship, this essay proposes a microhistory of one particular company, Centron, in an attempt to contribute toward a more comprehensive production history of industrial and educational films, which eventually will have to be written on an international level as well.[1]

Centron is of particular interest for a study of this type because of the company's relative longevity, and because it was a regional company that was able to compete on a national level during the heyday of industrial- and educational-film production in the US. Centron operated out of Lawrence, Kansas from 1947 to 1981. During that period, the company, founded by Art Wolf and Russell Mosser, produced approximately 500 industrial, educational, and government films.

Writing microhistory

My research into the company's history was guided by an interest in the key elements that allowed this relatively small regional company to compete on a national scale. I began without any real preconceptions as to what these "key elements" were. Instead, I was looking for clusters, patterns, what might be called particular motifs that aptly characterized the company. To this end, I interviewed Centron co-founders and staff and examined documents and films in the Centron Collection at the University of Kansas Kenneth Spencer Research Library. In addition, Russell Mosser's memoir, *Centron Remembered* (1999), was a valuable source of information.[2]

In my research, I examined small incidents within the Centron company, such as relationships between people, or identifying common patterns that evolved into "motifs." By motifs I mean some sort of pattern, some sort of theme, some sort of characteristic of Centron's way of doing things. When I found one of these characteristics that seemed to be woven through the history of the organization, I culled it out. During the course of the research, I found several motifs that characterized Centron. I did not consciously do this, but was drawn to recurring statements by Centroners themselves. I chose microhistory as the methodology for my research because I felt that the inner dynamics of the company were germane to the success of the company and its ability to compete within the larger industrial/educational-film industry. Perhaps the best explanation of microhistory is given by Giovanni Levi:

> Microhistory is essentially a historiographical practice whereas its theoretical references are varied and, in a sense, eclectic. The method is in fact concerned first and foremost with the actual detailed procedures which constitute the historian's work, so microhistory cannot be defined in relation to the micro-dimensions of its subject matter... In fact, many historians who adhere to microhistory have been involved in continuous interchanges with the social sciences and established historiographical theories without, however, feeling any need to refer to any coherent system of concepts or principles of their own. Microhistory, in common with all experimental work, has no body of established orthodoxy to draw on. The wide diversity of material produced clearly demonstrates how limited the range of common elements is. However, in my opinion, such few common elements as there are in microhistory are crucial and it is these that I will here attempt to examine.[3]

In addition, Levi states the following: "In microhistory ... the researcher's point of view becomes an intrinsic part of the account."[4]

As I began to go through my research, I realized existentially what Levi's final comment meant. I realized I could not separate myself from the data. Thus, as will be seen, my point of view as researcher had become an "intrinsic part of the account."

Centron: A history of motifs

Centron was an industrial/educational-film company which would come to the forefront of the industrial and educational film companies in the United States during its life from 1947 to 1981. Centron was incorporated on June 17, 1947. The founding partners were Arthur H. Wolf, president; Russell A. Mosser, secretary-treasurer; and Fred S. Montgomery, vice-president. Each purchased stock in the amount of $ 1,000. Later in the same year, when Centron needed more working capital, each partner bought an additional $ 1,000 of stock, bringing the initial investment to $ 6,000.[5] Montgomery was a silent partner who left the corporation in 1959. The first location of the company was 1107 Massachusetts Street.[6]

Figure 1 Wolf and Mosser on Centron Soundstage

Courtesy Russell Mosser

Wolf and Mosser had met in the third grade in Topeka, Kansas (around 1922) while living in the same neighborhood. They decided to start a club in a chicken house in Art's backyard. After cleaning the chickenhouse, they disagreed on who would be president and vice-president and the club broke up. The results of this argument proved significant during the formation of Centron when Wolf became president and Mosser vice-president. Their paths separated briefly when Mosser moved. Then they reconnected in junior high, only to again part and meet in 1938 at the University of Kansas (hereafter KU) Bureau of Visual Instruction. They would continue a relationship until Wolf's death in 2002.[7]

KU Bureau of Visual Instruction

The KU Bureau of Visual Instruction was one of the four largest and longest-established film libraries in the nation. As Mosser recalled in his memoir, *Centron Remembered*, the library was the only western distributor of films from the Museum of Modern Art (MOMA).[8] In an interview, Mosser talked about the reasons for MOMA's selection of the KU Bureau: "They wanted somebody in the west and we were located right and also we were one of the best distributors of educational film so we did the shipping. They did it to shorten shipping times."[9]

During his six years of association with the Bureau, Mosser viewed these classic MOMA films as well as previewing most of the educational films being produced, acquiring first-hand knowledge of a great body of work released in the audiovisual field.[10] It also gave him insight into the areas not being adequately supplied with audiovisual resources.[11]

Art Wolf again met Mosser at the Bureau of Visual Instruction in 1938, when Wolf came to the department and asked to use a camera to film an athletic contest. Although Wolf did not get the camera, Fred Montgomery asked Wolf to film a KU-Washburn game the next weekend.[12] Thus, Wolf began by filming athletic contests and doing clerical work for the Bureau. Wolf and Mosser would continue filming KU athletic contests until 1960.[13]

During World War II, both Wolf and Mosser went to work for Boeing, the aircraft company, in Wichita, Kansas. Wolf worked as a field engineer and Mosser worked in the personnel department. After the war, Mosser went to Chicago to work for an advertising agency and Art went to Kansas City to work for the Calvin Company. During this time, Art Wolf coined the word Centron in a letter to Russell Mosser written between 1945 and 1946. Recalling that letter, Mosser would write that, "The name was CENTRON which he [Wolf] said would work for most anything as we'd probably locate in the central part of the country, and it was the electronic age."[14]

In many ways, a study of the industrial/educational film-company, Centron, is a portrait of the lives of two men: Art Wolf and Russell Mosser. Their lives are inextricably woven into the fabric of the company. The meshing of their respective talents, skills, and abilities shaped the company and its growth.

Mosser handled the finances and personnel decisions. He instituted a cost accounting system, with expense categories for building overhead, payroll, film-shoot expenditures, and hired and fired personnel. He also watched the rough cuts of films.

Wolf wrote scripts, created original music scores, directed films, introduced technological advances and, as the company expanded, oversaw and signed off on scripts, rough cuts, and assignments of directors to film projects. He had final say on all projects. He also made sales calls, as did Mosser, during the company's initial stages of growth. Mosser and Wolf consulted with one another, with each making decisions in his own area.

Wolf was the more creative one, according to both Wolf and Mosser.[15] Wolf took up photography at the age of seven and edited his high school yearbook in Topeka. Mosser, on the other hand, studied personnel administration at KU and worked as the secretary for the Bureau of Audiovisual. Further, his experience as a personnel administrator for Boeing Aircraft prepared him to handle personnel management at Centron. Moreover, their work for large corporations informed their ability to understand and anticipate the challenges and politics involved in running their own company. They also understood that there was a client to please and they knew how to proceed in fulfilling this need.[16]

Together, Wolf and Mosser made the hard decisions of laying people off when the economy faltered and selling the company when they were both ready to retire. The synergy between the two kept the company afloat and energized during the intervening years. "We ran the place like a couple of brothers," Art Wolf said.[17]

When I met the two men for my initial interview in 1998, they said that after the chickenhouse conflict, they never had another fight. The mutual respect that I saw in them confirmed this statement. While they admitted to occasional bouts of disagreement, each had his area of expertise and each respected the other's boundaries.[18]

This respect carried over into their feelings about their employees. Generous profit-sharing plans motivated employees. Rushes of films were shown to everyone, with comments from all considered, but Wolf had the final say. Learning and experimentation were encouraged.[19] An atmosphere of camaraderie pervaded the company. Each employee's birthday was celebrated, often with limericks composed in honor of the person by employee Charles Lacey. Silly skits were presented. As a result, employees of Centron enjoyed their work. Very often, when I would ask a former employee of Centron what it was like working there, he or she would get a faraway look in his/her eye and say wistfully, "I had so much fun working there."[20]

This is not to say that things were always easy at the company. Standards were exacting; time schedules enforced; tempers sometimes flared. Careful documentation of time and equipment checkouts were kept; budgets were minimal; innovation was mandatory. As one Centron director said, "you either had the personality to work there or you didn't."[21]

Personnel

Centron personnel grew from two to approximately 10 during the initial phase of the company. In the beginning, employees came to Centron through recommendations from friends or serendipitously. As Centron grew, potential employees went through several interviews before a decision was made to hire. When questioned, Russell said they just talked to potential employees and tried to get to know them. In the initial 1998 interview, Wolf also stated:

> I mean, we were just very fortunate. I guess we were pretty picky who we hired but we got the kind of people who were happy to some degree that were happy at being here in Lawrence, Kansas and not in Chicago or New York and happy with what they were doing and for the most part content with the way the company was run and managed and so that was part of why we were successful.[22]

Figure 2 Trudy Travis and Norman Stuewe (foreground) on studio set of BEYOND THE TOWERS *(1949)*

Courtesy Norman Stuewe

Once hired, on-the-job training began with the new employee beginning at an entry-level job, then progressing toward more responsible positions when the first area had been mastered. Cross-training, with employees learning more than one job, was common. This practice allowed Centron to be responsive to changing demands, pursuing a wide variety of subject matter and location or studio shooting. The first four employees of Centron were Norman Stuewe, Charles Lacey, Margaret (Trudy) Travis and Harold "Herk" Harvey. These employees assisted with all of the tasks involved in production in the fledgling company.

Finances
Wolf and Mosser paid cash for everything but the mortgage, two IBM Selectric typewriters and Centron's Oxberry animation stand. Mosser said that this kept them from getting into a cash-strapped position, which would have made it very hard for Wolf to work because of the resulting stress.[23]

Their economic strategy was simple, yet effective. Mosser created a system of cost analysis per foot of film. Crews kept track of expenses. Mosser and Wolf evaluated the economy. If a recession were imminent, for example, they would know that the industrial-film companies would cut their budgets. Then, 18 months later, this cut would result in a cancellation of an industrial film contract. During economic recessions, educational-film contracts sustained the company.[24]

On the larger economic scale, Mosser and Wolf used the "Uncle Henry" method to decide what subject matter to film for the coming year. Mosser's Uncle Henry was a farmer. Every year he would visit his neighbors and ask them what crops they were planning to plant that year. When he had determined the predominant crop, perhaps wheat, he would plant a different crop, because the demand would be greater. Comparably, Mosser and Wolf would talk to other companies at trade shows to determine what subject area was in vogue that year, and offer films in subject areas that were different from that of the competition. For instance, in 1958, the year Sputnik was launched, Wolf and Mosser correctly assessed that because the market for science films would prove the most popular for the coming year, they would make geography films instead.[25]

Centron tried to satisfy the educational market first and then branched into the industrial market. The inclusion of the industrial market in Centron's marketing strategy came through word of mouth and contacts. Wolf and Mosser doggedly pursued potential clients for several years in some cases before they were able to secure contracts. Through these contracts, a loyal customer base evolved.

Location in the Midwest
Wolf related a story of going to New York to a film company to make a sales call and waiting for hours in the company's lobby. When he was finally ushered into the New York executive's office, the executive announced that he didn't have time to meet with him; rather he just "wanted to see what someone from

Kansas looked like."[26] The joy of having a film company in the Midwest often met with disdain from large companies on the coasts; however, when Centron began to win awards, the attitude toward it began to shift.

Indeed, Kansas was hardly considered a major industrial location during this postwar period, but the location was not without its many benefits. One advantage of having a company in the Midwest was cheap labor costs. Kansas was not unionized. A large university also provided a labor pool of actors and employees. Finally, the postal service from the Midwest to either coast created a competitive advantage for Centron.

Early clients
Centron made films for "organizations" as Russell Mosser labeled them in his memoir.[27] During this period between 1947 and 1981, these organizations included the University of Kansas, Kansas State University, the University of Mississippi, the American Medical Association (AMA), the American Hospital Association, Howard University, the Mott Foundation, the Kansas Children's League, the Topeka and Wichita Chambers of Commerce, the Kansas Economic Development Department, the Sears Foundation, the American Iron and Steel Institute, and the United Methodist Board.[28]

Centron also made films for industrial clients such as the Spencer Chemical Company, General Motors, General Electric, Exxon, Phillips Petroleum, Continental Oil, Skelly Oil, the Monsanto Chemical Company, Eli Lilly & Company, Hallmark, Sears-Roebuck, Caterpillar, John Deere, Tenneco, and Union Pacific and Company. Eventually, Centron acquired government clients, including the United States Navy and Air Force, for which they made training films.[29]

Wolf's strategy of cutting edge technology
In my initial interview in 1998, Wolf said that in order to compete with larger companies on both coasts, Centron needed to stay on the cutting edge of technology. Perhaps the best example of this is Centron's prescient purchase of the then revolutionary Nagra portable tape recorder, invented by Stefan Kudelski, a Polish inventor living in Sweden. Wolf traveled to Europe shortly after he learned that the device was available and purchased it in 1966. He elaborated on the need for cutting-edge technology in the interview.

> Well, I was always very interested in technical ways to either avoid work or get ahead. And I carefully watched everything that was going on and had the feeling all along that you had to get ahead. But we were particularly vulnerable, because here we were out in Lawrence, Kansas and we were facing the so-called big shots who had been established for years. People like Jam Handy and I can't think of all the names of various companies that we were actually in competition with and I speak more of the industrial things that we did rather than the educational.[30]

For Centron, the purchase of this device freed them from the confines of the studio and allowed them to do location shooting, not only in the United States, but throughout the world.

Competitors
Centron was in direct competition with industrial film companies: Corporate Productions of Toluca, Lake, California; Calvin Corporation of Kansas City; Bill Stokes of Dallas, Texas; Saul Bass of Los Angeles, California; Jack Hennessy of Pasadena, California, and Vision Associate of Nevada.[31] Educational-film corporation competitors of Centron included Churchill Films.[32]

Centron's success and standing in the industry brought it into revenue competition with most of the internationally famous industrial/educational-film companies.[33] For example, Tom Hope, editor of *Hope Reports* (a major industrial trade publication) created a custom analysis which compared Centron's revenue with that of other industrial- and educational-film companies for the year 1981.[34] Hope concluded that Centron ranked 10th nationally among educational producers with its revenue of $ 2.09 million. The largest competitor had revenues of $ 10.9 million while the smallest had revenues totaling $ 1.3 million. Further, Centron ranked 12th nationally among industrial film producers with a revenue of $ 0.925 million. The largest revenue it was competing with was with $ 17.6 million and the smallest was $ 0.9 million. Combining the two categories of producers, Centron ranked 13th out of 25.[35] The educational producers were Churchill; Coronet; Disney; Encyclopedia Britannica Educational Company; Film Fair; Films, Inc.; International Farm Bureau; Journal Films; Learning Corporation; McGraw-Hill; Phoenix; Prentice Hall; Pyramid, and Weston Wood. The industrial producers were Altschul, Comcorpos, Creative Visuals, Envision, Image Stream, R. Manning, Motivational Media, Fred Niles, Reeves, Sandy, Sorgel, and Tilton.

Revenue
In 1947, revenue was $ 4,000 and the staff numbered six. By 1954, revenue had risen to $ 162,164.[36] Meanwhile, the film production revenues had increased to $ 296,468 by 1960.[37] Personnel increased to some 15 during that six-year period.[38] Revenue from film production increased from $ 296,468 in 1960 to $ 1,050,001 in 1970.[39] Centron employed approximately 36 staff members in 1970.[40] Income from film production increased from $ 1,050,001 in 1970 to $ 3,005,486 in 1980.[41] In that year, the staff numbered approximately 49.[42]

The building of the studio
Eight years after Centron was founded, they had already acquired enough money to build a new studio. Thus, they bought a piece of property at 1621 W.

9th Street. At the time, the area was zoned for residential dwellings, but the owner of the property said he could get it zoned for business, so Mosser and Wolf bought it after it was rezoned.[43] The new property was located closer to the University, which made it convenient for KU actors. They paid $ 5,000 for the lot. Verner Smith, a KU architect, drew up the plans. Wolf visited an MGM studio and based the dimensions on the standard Hollywood sound stage. The Centron sound stage was 1/4 the size, to scale, of a standard Hollywood sound stage.[44] It was 60 feet by 40 feet with a 23-foot ceiling.[45] The building had 6,000 square feet of studio and 5,200 square feet of office space for a total of 11,200 square feet.[46] The cost for the new studio was $ 90,000, which they borrowed from the City National Bank in Kansas City for ten years at an interest rate of 5%.[47]

Economics

Ironically, concomitant to Centron's move into the new facility, the US experienced an economic contraction during 1957 and 1958. The industrial-film market was more sensitive to the economy than the educational-film market. Thus, Centron wisely relied on educational films, rather than industrial films, for their income. Centron's focus was educational films from the beginning and generally the educational films comprised 2/3 of total company income. Fewer industrial films were needed to make up the other 1/3 of income because of the different pricing structures.[48]

Centron stabilized its income with royalties from the educational films, while simultaneously trying to gain entry into the more lucrative, but volatile, industrial market. In contrast, revenue from industrial contracts was a larger amount paid in a lump sum upon the completion of a film.[49] In the economic recession of 1958, Centron's income was also bolstered by the Right to Work contract.

The films were part of a campaign to pass a constitutional amendment in Kansas to prevent unionization. The amendment was passed on November 4, 1958.[50] Centron created approximately 15 TV and radio ads and programs, newspaper ads, and billboards. Cecil B. DeMille appeared in SHOWDOWN (1958) for the committee. Wolf went to Hollywood to direct Mr. DeMille in his Hollywood office.[51] In a November 26, 1967 *Kansas City Star* newspaper article, Wolf commented on the experience: "Somehow, without anybody saying a word, everyone knew the second DeMille entered the building. Your backbone just stiffened. I've often wondered how he did it."[52]

Working at Centron

In the new building, adjustments were made by the entire staff. The larger physical structure created a separation between personnel, limiting the free communication they were used to when working in the smaller space. The Monday morning meeting was scheduled for 8:30 a.m. to provide cohesive communication regarding the status and assignment of projects.[53]

The need for communicating was satisfied in another way, informally dubbed "The Coffee Hour." Loren Dolezal, an animator, recalled in a September 16, 2000, interview that "at 9:30 or 10:00 the secretary would announce that coffee was ready. There would also be donuts and rolls. I thought, whoa, this is heaven."[54] At the dedication of the former Centron soundstage to Herk Harvey in 1996, Wolf said the gathering was like a homecoming that reminded him of the "coffee hour" in Studio B. It was named that because the 15-minute Centron coffee break turned into an hour. Many things were decided there. Wolf said, "We finally had to put a limit on it. There were many things decided and discussed around that coffee table. Management had to slow it down."[55]

Wolf said that there was spray painting done on the tables used for the "coffee hour." A design was left on a piece of wood on one of the tables. One of the employees said, "I'm going to enter that in Art in the Park." He framed it and it won first prize in the contest. Wolf said this example was meant to show how creatively this group worked.[56]

Creativity

When asked about things that were important about Centron, Dolezal said that the freedom to innovate was strong. Some directors would say exactly what they wanted done while others, like Herk Harvey, would say "here's some material and this is what I want to do and it's up to you to get it there..."[57] This extraordinary amount of freedom allowed Dolezal to create through trial and error.

This atmosphere of innovation combined with support affected the entire Centron organization. Centroners had autonomy and an encouraging atmosphere to test their ideas. Linda "Sam" Haskins, a director, confirmed this creative atmosphere in a March 8, 2001 interview:

> I just saw it all as a mechanical, you know, problem solving thing. And we can find creativity in the smallest things, you know what I mean? It was, everybody seemed to be into that and their little niche. They would find something creative, you know, a problem to solve. It was a creative thing and that was kind of nice to observe it. But everybody was doing that with whatever they were working on. They were putting everything into it, you know, and really just trying to do their best and try to come up with something that would be better than the average. So, right on down the line everybody was doing that, and we all felt we were working for ourselves because we were on a profit-sharing plan.[58]

Figure 3 Herk Harvey and Norman Stuewe preparing for a shoot

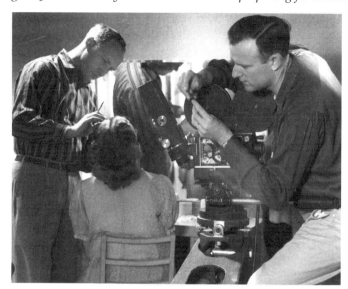

Courtesy Norman Stuewe

Sales

Centron was a complete production house from the concept to scriptwriting, to photography, to the casting of the actors, to editing and sound. The ability to throw out ideas and carry them from beginning to end was a great selling point. Other small production companies had to outsource or subcontract cinematography or editing, creating an uneven finished product in terms of quality.

Buck Newsom, vice president of industrial sales, stated in a sales memo of July, 1984, that "Centron is unique in this day because we are one of the few successful companies in the industrial/educational-film businesses exclusively that has a complete in-house staff."[59] The advantages of having their own crews were that they had a cohesive philosophy of quality, they had a staff at the ready for any project, and the quality of the product was consistent.

Production crews

During the 1960s, Centron truly hit its stride. At times, there were four or five production crews on the road, traveling across the United States, Europe, Latin America, and Canada, shooting industrial and educational films. Centron's small size and cross-training allowed them to be flexible. International projects involved a minimum of people and of cost. In Latin America, Harvey, Bob Rose, and a sound person shot footage for an award-winning geography series. In addition, a crew went to Canada to shoot footage of the dogsled races for John Deere.[60]

Conoco and Dennis Day

Centron was still using local people and KU actors, but they had reached a point of economic stability that allowed them to hire professional Hollywood actors, as well as actors from national television shows. For example, in 1962, they developed a sales meeting film, MORE STEPS UPWARD, for Conoco which employed the famous television actor Dennis Day. As part of this contract, Centron hired George Gobel, then one of the most-beloved television comedians. Other stars included Anita Bryant, Rowan and Martin, and Ed Ames.

SECRET TO THE 60S (1960)

SECRET TO THE 60S, a groundbreaking film, was made for the Phillips Petroleum Company in 1960 for a sales meeting. The film ran 96 minutes and included 250 slides at a total cost of over $ 100,000.[61] This was a multimedia presentation, incorporating three screens with slide shows running simultaneously at the edges of the frame, with some live action. This was one of the Centron's longest productions.

Phillips Petroleum wanted to begin the new decade with a revolutionary type of national sales program. Phillips 66 contracted Centron to create a special multimedia presentation that would combine live action and film action, giving a local touch to the program, though professional. It would consist of a "ribbon screen" (a screen that was slit vertically in several places) upon which an actress was projected before she walked through her own image. Afterwards, three un-slit film screens were erected with three synched film projectors that created a remarkable triptych effect of the subject filmed from three different angles. The screens imitated the aspect ratio of the then-current widescreen cinematography.[62]

Centron addition

Centron built a 18,200-square-foot addition onto the studio in 1965. The cost was equal to that of the original building – $ 90,000.[63] As they expanded and began to entertain high-level clients, they needed a nice office area for previewing films. Consequently, on the second floor, they added a conference room with an attached projection room and seven offices for more staff.

LEO

Centron's nomination for an Academy Award in 1970 in the Documentary Short Subjects category for the film LEO BEUERMAN (1969) stands as one of Centron's greatest achievements. Leo Beuerman, the main character in the film of the same name, lived on a farm outside Lawrence. He had been physically handicapped since birth. He drove a tractor to Lawrence, carrying his display of pencils and other items, which he would sell in front of the First National Bank at Eighth and Massachusetts Streets or in front of the Woolworth store in the 900 block of Massachusetts.[64]

Mosser and Wolf decided to shoot some footage of Leo in the late 1960s, without any specific plans in mind. After getting the initial footage, Wolf put a sequence together and assigned a writer to do a script. The sequence proved difficult to view because of the deformity of Leo's body and face, and Wolf shelved the piece for some time.[65] Then, a year or so later, Wolf gave Trudy Travis the project and asked her to rework the script. Additional footage was shot and was screened by Centron personnel, and Wolf said, "when we saw it in this room in the work print stage, it just made me feel this is something out of the ordinary."[66] Right from this point, Mosser and Wolf did everything possible to make Leo an outstanding film. Wolf planned to go to Vienna to write and record the music for an AC Spark Plug sales meeting film, so he decided to record the music for Leo in Vienna.[67]

A Hollywood writer, William Bowers, who had written the comedy Support Your Local Sheriff (1969) starring James Garner, visited the University of Kansas Speech and Drama Department and asked if he could tour Centron.[68] Bowers wanted to sample something that Centron had done. The film Leo wasn't finished yet, but they played the workprint on an interlock projector. After he had seen the film, Bowers said that it was Oscar material.[69] Wolf and Mosser were not convinced, but when Bowers returned to Hollywood he sent an entry blank to enter the film into the Academy Awards. Wolf, Mosser and the staff continued to work on the film, making a special 35mm print that was officially required to book Leo into a Los Angeles theater and then submit it to the Academy.[70] The Academy notified Centron of Leo's nomination on February 12, 1970. The credits for the film were: Ernie Johnson, production assistant; Bob Rose, cameraman; Mrs. Kenneth (Trudy) Travis, script writer; Gene Boomer, director; Dave Lutz, sound engineer; Art Wolf and Russell Mosser, producers. This was the first time that credits were added to a Centron film. The Academy required that all films nominated must include credits.

Centron did not win the Academy Award.[71] However, the film Leo did manage to win a total of 13 top awards in American and international festivals. To quote Russell Mosser, "The film was inspirational, it was motivational, it created sensitivity to others, it had a rather basic philosophy of life. In retrospect it spoke to each viewer [in] some special way and that was its genius."[72]

Leo's voice-over was translated into several languages, including Spanish, German, French, and Japanese, facilitating its international distribution. The film, released in 1969, was 11 minutes long with a production cost of $ 12,000.

By 1981, approximately 2,300 prints had been sold, generating estimated gross sales of $ 600,000. To put the film's success in perspective, an average of 300 to 500 prints of an educational film was considered a good sale at the time.

Centron Educational Films (CEF)

After LEO's Academy Award nomination, Wolf and Mosser took it to McGraw-Hill, their distributor, for distribution. However, there was a new vice-president who had replaced the one with whom Art and Russell had worked before. The new vice-president said it was a nice film but that she did not know where it fit and thus chose not to distribute it. The refusal by McGraw-Hill ironically created an opportunity for Centron to begin distribution of their own films and acquisition of other films to distribute. Wolf and Mosser formed Centron Educational Films (CEF). In time, Centron became known in educational markets as "the Leo company."[73] Moreover, the company did a complete sound reorganization in June, 1970, at a cost of $ 14,885, to upgrade the soundstage to state-of-the-art standards.[74] Ironically, however, at this pivotal point, the United States was suffering two pronounced economic contractions, and a powerful technological revolution began with the advent of videotape recording, which had been invented by Ampex in 1964. These forces would prove to be a harbinger of the company's eventual demise.

Potential sale of Centron

In 1972, Centron entertained an offer from the American Broadcasting Company (ABC) to buy the company. Representatives from the company came to Centron for a week to discuss details of the company's transfer to ABC. There was an educational convention in Las Vegas with Harry Reasoner as the guest of honor who was going to make the announcement. The sale had to be approved by the Board of Directors. Apparently, two vice-presidents presented two different projects, one being the acquisition of Centron, but in the end, the Centron project was not chosen. The entire staff was aware of the possible sale, which created a lot of tension and stress and drove productivity down.[75]

Chatsworth Distribution

In 1979, Malcolm Heyworth, of the British educational- and informational-film company in London, toured the United States to select a distributor for their films. He contacted Wolf and selected Centron. The association of Chatsworth and Centron was a profitable one for both companies. Heyworth wrote to Centron in a faxgram on November 4, 1980, that Centron had "exceeded the guarantee by a considerable margin" when revenues reached $ 1.3 million for the year.[76]

The 1970s saw Centron reaching its peak in achievement and recognition within the industry. At the same time, however, the rapid advancement of VTR and VHS technology from 1971 to 1978 led to the introduction of an extraordinary new technology. Wolf had anticipated this early development in the industry, just as he had foreseen other technological advances and used them to keep Centron competitive.

Corporate mergers swept the United States from 1975 to the late 1980s, and Centron was among the last wave of corporate mergers. In 1980 and 1981, there were two recessions. At this juncture, Wolf and Mosser decided to sell the company. When I spoke to Wolf in March of 2002 and asked him how technology had influenced Centron, he confirmed that technology was a great factor in Centron's success and in the eventual decision to sell the company:

> Greatly. As a matter of fact, that's one reason why we sold the business, because we were at the point where film production was probably not going to do it anymore and we faced the problem of investment of a million and a half at least to convert all this to video stuff – at least have that capability, and Russ and I were at retirement age anyway, and then we got this great offer from New York, and neither one of us had any children that wanted to be involved in this or were capable of it, and so we – placing all those things – we sold the company. But we were right there at that point where you no longer could just rely on the film business. I mean, I could see it coming. Russ could too. If you're going to be able to do something, you had to be in television of some sort in order to survive.[77]

Figure 4 Three-camera filming setup.
Left Jim Bird, middle John English, cameraman, right Ron Means

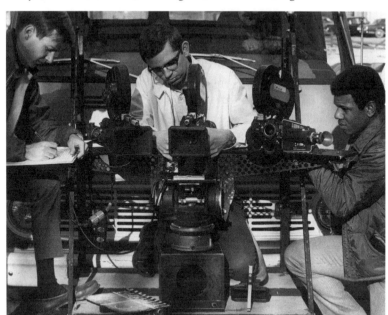

Courtesy John English

Wolf and Mosser received an offer from Esquire, Inc., parent company of Coronet Films, in July, 1981. The earlier unsuccessful sale to ABC had resulted in stress among the staff and management alike, which led Wolf and Mosser to negotiate the sale in secrecy. They flew to New York, where they reached an agreement and signed the contract to sell Centron. The company was sold on December 31, 1981. Mosser and Wolf continued to function as consultants for a year.

The entire staff was surprised by the sale of Centron.[78] Reactions varied from shock to acceptance to outright hostility. In a 2005 interview, Trudy Travis said that she knew that Wolf and Mosser were going to New York for a meeting, but did not know that the purpose was to sell Centron. Travis felt that even though it was time to sell Centron, Russell and Art were sad to see it come to an end.[79]

Although the sale of Centron was a blow to Centroners, for the most part, the family atmosphere that permeated and enhanced Centron continued. Centroners stayed in touch with one another, professionally and personally. In 2007, Centroners were still meeting at a local restaurant for coffee on the first Thursday of every month.

From commission to delivery

The process of gaining a commission of an industrial film from a company, creating the film and delivering it might end up taking weeks or months, depending on the scope of the film project. For example, a film such as Centron's SHAKE HANDS WITH DANGER (1980) was designed to illustrate the safety issues of Caterpillar tractors. The running time of the film was 23 minutes and featured several vignettes encompassing large-equipment safety issues. In the final sequence, a Caterpillar tractor overturns. SHAKE HANDS WITH DANGER received the Golden Eagle award from the prestigious Council on International Nontheatrical Events, Inc. (CINE) in 1980. Russell Mosser talked about the process in a 2005 interview.[80]

He said that initially, a representative of the company would call Centron and request a film. Art usually traveled to Caterpillar and met with representatives of the company to determine the content of the film, the budget, and the timeline. Next, Art would assign John Clifford to read through the research and write the script. A deadline would be established for delivery. Once the script was completed, Art would read it over and determine whether it met the company's expectations. If not, it would be returned for a rewrite and resubmitted to Art. According to Russell, Art was quality control; if the writer could sell Art on the script, then he or she could sell the client. After Art approved the script, either Art or the writer would travel to the company and read through the shooting script with company officials. The script was usually approved.

Art assigned Herk Harvey to direct the film. Art and Herk had a meeting to go over the script. If Herk had changes or questions, then the changes would be made. For instance, if the script called for 20 extras and the budget supported only six, then Herk would make changes in script to make it look like 20 extras to stay within the budget. The budget and time frame for shooting would be examined. Once the director and Art had come to an agreement, the director would pick his or her crew and schedule the location or the studio and proceed with filming. The director had complete control although Art was available for consultation if questions arose.

In SHAKE HANDS WITH DANGER, much of the film was shot on location in Pittsburgh, Kansas, at an old coal mining site. Hollywood stunt men were hired to execute the more hazardous and spectacular stunts. These included setting a person on fire, exploding a highly charged coil into a pickup truck window, and overturning a Caterpillar tractor. The three or four cameras used were operated by cameramen Robert Rose and John English.

After the shoot, the film was sent to the lab, and the editing process was begun when the print was returned. Herk met with the editor and explained what he was trying to do. The editor would edit the film and call Herk if there were questions.

Animation, sound, and music would be created. In SHAKE HANDS WITH DAN-GER, Jim Stringer, Centron's sound engineer, wrote and performed the music. Charles Oldfather performed the vocals. After the editing process, a rough cut was prepared. Art, sometimes Russell, the director, and anyone who wanted to watch would view the film and offer comments. Following the discussion, Art would usually be the one to take the print to the company for viewing, or the client would come to the Centron studio to view the rough cut. The client would generally approve the print.

After the rough cut was approved, the film would go to the lab for an answer print. From there, the company would determine how many prints they wanted and Centron would order them. The prints would be hand delivered to the company.

Payment from industrial clients usually came in the form of 10% upon signing of the contract, 30% upon approval of the shooting script, and 30% upon approval of the rough cut, with the balance upon approval of the answer print.[81]

Conclusion

Centron was unique in that it produced both educational and industrial films. The motifs that emerged were technological innovation, camaraderie, creativity, geography, and financial and economic structures. At this writing, I would posit that these five motifs are not intended as definitive characteristics, but provisional characteristics that were formed by the melding of my perceptions with extant data during my research. That is, while Centron shared much with its competitors, its curious combination of an awareness of technological innovation, of an almost family-like sense of camaraderie, exceptionally fertile freedom for individual creativity, its distinct location in the middle of America's Heartland, and its efficient business structure provides a fine example of an industrial/educational film studio.

Notes

1.   Production histories of industrial film companies have been proposed by Manfred Rasch and others in Germany. See Rasch's publications in the international bibliography at the end of this volume.
2.   Russell A. Mosser, *Centron Remembered*, (Lawrence, KS, n.p., 1999)

3. Giovanni, Levi, "On Microhistory," in Peter Burke (ed.), *New Perspectives on Histori-cal Writing*, 2nd ed. (University Park, PA: Pennsylvania State University Press, 2001), p. 95.

4. Levi, op. cit., pp. 109-110.

5. Mosser, op. cit., p. 6.

6. "Sound pictures are being made here by a new industry," *Lawrence Daily Journal-World* (September 15, 1947), p. 1.

7. Russell Mosser and Art Wolf, personal interview, November 21, 1998.

8. Mosser, op. cit., p. 15.

9. Mosser and Wolf interview.

10. Mosser, op. cit., p. 15.

11. *Who's Who in Filmmaking*, 38, pp. 1-2.

12. Mosser, op. cit., p. 2.

13. Maurice Prather, "Mosser-Wolf Shoot Official Football Movies," *University Daily Kansan* (December 1, 1952), p. 3.

14. Mosser, op. cit., p. 3.

15. Mosser and Wolf interview, op. cit.

16. Russell Mosser, telephone interview, 15 June 2001.

17. Mosser and Wolf interview, op. cit.

18. Mosser and Wolf interview, op. cit.

19. The significance of this action is the cost and time involved in reshooting a film. The fledgling director was given a second chance, instead of just summarily handing the film over to a more experienced director. Quality control of the finished product of a film for a client was very high and very exacting in order to satisfy the customer and to build a loyal customer base.

20. Linda "Sam" Haskins, personal interview, 8 Mar. 2001; John English, personal inter-view, 15 June 2001; and Norman Stuewe, personal interview, 2 Mar. 2001.

21. Haskins interview, op. cit.

22. Mosser and Wolf interview.

23. Mosser and Wolf interview.

24. Mosser and Wolf interview.

25. Mosser and Wolf interview.

26. Mosser and Wolf interview.

27. Mosser, op. cit., p. 33.

28. Mosser, op. cit., pp. 33-36.

29. Mosser, op. cit., pp. 31-33; pp. 39-42.

30. Art Wolf, personal Interview, 13 March 2002.

31. John W. "Buck" Newsom, personal interview, 8 June 2006.

32. Russell A. Mosser, personal interview, 8 May 2006.

33. In a June 26, 2001, interview with John "Buck" Newsom, Vice-President of Indus-trial Sales, Buck remarked that Centron competed directly with few of the industrial firms on this list.

34. Tom Hope, "1981 Media Production Companies," personal report, 30 Aug. 2000.

35. It is has been remarkably problematic to determine the exact sums of money. This organization publicly lists the companies in alphabetical order and will only dis-close that a given company falls in a range between x and y. But we do know that Hope's survey of more than 100 companies ranked Centron 13th.

36. Financial Binder, RH MS 541, Kenneth Spencer Research Library, University of Kansas.
37. Ibid.
38. "Personnel," Loren Dolezal private collection; John W. "Buck" Newsom private collection; Robert Rose private collection; Norman Stuewe private collection; RH MS 541, Kenneth Spencer Research Library, University of Kansas.
39. Financial Binder, RH MS 541, Kenneth Spencer Research Library, University of Kansas; "Centron Corporation, Inc. Statements 1960-1968," RH MS 541, Kenneth Spencer Research Library, University of Kansas; "Centron Corporation, Inc. Lawrence, Kansas Audit – 1969," RH MS 541, Kenneth Spencer Research Library, University of Kansas; "Corporate U.S. Income Tax 1970," RH MS 541, Kenneth Spencer Research Library, University of Kansas.
40. "Personnel," Loren Dolezal private collection; John W. "Buck" Newsom private collection; Robert Rose private collection; Norman Stuewe private collection; RH MS 541, Kenneth Spencer Research Library, University of Kansas.
41. "Corporate U.S. Income Tax, 1970-1979," RH MS 541, Kenneth Spencer Research Library, University of Kansas; "Financial Statements for the Years Ended December 31, 1980 and December 31, 1979," RH MS 541, Kenneth Spencer Research Library, University of Kansas.
42. "Personnel," Loren Dolezal private collection; John W. "Buck" Newsom private collection; Robert Rose private collection; Norman Stuewe private collection; RH MS 541, Kenneth Spencer Research Library, University of Kansas.
43. Mosser and Wolf interview.
44. Mosser and Wolf interview.
45. Mosser, op. cit., p. 12.
46. Mosser, op. cit., p.13.
47. Mosser, op. cit., pp. 12,13.
48. "Centron Sales," RH MS 541, Kenneth Spencer Research Library, University of Kansas.
49. Mosser and Wolf interview.
50. Mosser, op. cit., p. 27.
51. Mosser, op. cit, p. 27.
52. "Kansas – Mid-west Movie Capital," *Kansas City Star* (November 26, 1967), n.p.
53. Mosser, op. cit., p. 13.
54. Loren Dolezal, personal interview, 16 Sept. 2000.
55. "Dedication of 'Herk' Harvey Soundstage," videotape, Pauline Harvey private collection, 1996.
56. Ibid.
57. Dolezal interview.
58. Haskins interview.
59. John W. "Buck" Newsom, memo to J.D. "Dixie" Powers, 20 April 1982, John W. "Buck" Newsom private collection.
60. Dolezal interview.
61. "Contracts," RH MS 541, Kenneth Spencer Research Library, University of Kansas.
62. *Business Screen*, n.p.
63. Mosser, op. cit., p. 12.
64. Mosser, op. cit., p. 18.

65. Mosser, op. cit., p. 19.
66. Mosser and Wolf interview.
67. Mosser, *Centron*, op. cit., p. 20.
68. Ibid., op. cit., p. 21.
69. Mosser and Wolf interview.
70. Ibid.
71. Mosser, op. cit., p. 21.
72. Mosser, op. cit., p. 21.
73. Mosser, op. cit., p. 21.
74. "Centron Corporation Depreciation Schedule 1959-1977," RH MS 541, Kenneth Spencer Research Library, University of Kansas.
75. Mosser and Wolf interview.
76. Faxgram, Kenneth Spencer Research Library, RH MS 541, Kenneth Spencer Research Library, University of Kansas.
77. Wolf interview, op. cit.
78. Trudy Travis, personal interview, 8 Aug. 2005.
79. Ibid.
80. Russell Mosser, personal interview, c. 2005.
81. Russell Mosser, personal conversation, 8 May 2006.

Films from Beyond the Well

A Historical Overview of Shell Films[1]

Rudmer Canjels

Founded in 1907 and currently active in over 140 countries, Royal Dutch/Shell is one of the largest private-sector energy corporations in the world. Like other major companies, Royal Dutch/Shell, an Anglo-Dutch multinational, developed a keen interest in the moving image as early as the 1920s. Shell management recognized film as an ideal medium for reaching out and building public support for its activities. Over the years, Shell has produced hundreds of documentaries, many of them dealing with scientific and technological subjects. Beyond questions of scientific significance and educational value, the Shell films are of particular interest in that they reflect and serve to implement some of the company policies of a major global player in one of the key industries of the 20th century. Furthermore, in the case of Shell and particularly in the early films, company policies intersect with Dutch and British colonial interests, as they do with global geopolitical concerns in the later films, up to discussions of global warming in the films from the late 1990s. Accordingly, the Shell films may be read as exemplary media interfaces that tie some of the key economic and political discourses of the 20th century into a visual rhetoric which systematically links company interests to larger political and societal goals. While the limited scope of this contribution does not allow for a detailed discussion of the company's communication strategies, of how these relate to the film medium and how they evolved over time, I will provide a brief history of the production, use, and purposes of Shell films, with an eye to future research.

Cataloguing the world

Probably one of the earliest moving images of Shell employees in the Dutch East Indies can be seen in the BATAAFSCHE PETROLEUM FILM (1924). The three-hour documentary film was commissioned by the Bataafsche Petroleum Maatschappij, an operating company of Royal Dutch/Shell.[2] It was made in the Indies by well-known Dutch documentary filmmaker Willy Mullens in cooperation with C.W.A. Van Bergen, who worked for the Bataafsche marketing organization. The film premiered on June 18, 1924 at the majestic concert hall of the Kurhaus

in Scheveningen, near The Hague.[3] Many important representatives from the
government, the diplomatic corps, the business community, and the press were
present among the 1,600 invitees.

A classic example of both the "record" and "rhetoric" functions of industrial
films,[4] the film documents company activities with the aim of inducing cooperation from the public. Combining images of the colonies that exhibit exotic
nature with promotional sections that posit the company as an important player
on the world market, the film also had a clear educational function, displaying
the production of crude oil and oil products, and the uses to which they were
put. A review of the film in a Dutch newspaper seems to suggest that the strategy of the tactfully planned propaganda film paid off. The documentary
"taught us that the petroleum industry is not a money-making concern for
shareholders ... but it, wherever it goes, creates a prosperous colony, spreading
its benevolent influence far and wide."[5] After the premiere, the film toured the
Netherlands and was shown at various societies and associations.

As documentary films from a colonial viewpoint remained popular, in later
years, new films were made by reediting used and unused scenes from the material shot in 1924. In 1931, Van Bergen resigned from the Bataafsche marketing
organization and received a film camera as a farewell present. On a business
trip around the world, he produced several new films, creating an extensive
visual catalogue of all Royal Dutch/Shell activities.[6]

The beginning of the Shell Film Unit

The interest in film in the United Kingdom increased when, in 1933, the advertising policy of the Shell Group was under review and the influential John Grierson was asked to write a report on the potential use of film.[7] Grierson recommended the creation of a central film-production unit to serve all the areas of
the Group and to distribute the films mainly non-theatrically in cooperation
with educational and cultural organizations. Six types of production were suggested: general propaganda films that dramatized dominant themes in the oil
industry, sales-promotion films, popular-science films, technical films for specialized audiences, staff department information films, and a Shell newsreel. By
the end of the year, the managing directors had endorsed the plan for the Shell
Film Unit (SFU).[8]

On Grierson's recommendation, Edgar Anstey, one of the documentary filmmakers from the General Post Office Film Unit, became the first producer of the
SFU. The Unit's first film was AIRPORT (1935), documenting a "day in the life"

of Croydon Airport, at that time London's main airport and one of the world's busiest.

Figure 1 The first film of the newly formed Shell Film Unit was AIRPORT *(1935). Note that Shell is not mentioned anywhere on the leaflet*

The film linked Shell with the new glamour and excitement of flying while presenting a record of the air-transport infrastructure. Anstey, however, finding the slow rate of progress and political implications of working for an oil company difficult to endure, had by that time already left the Unit, though he would return a few years later.[9] As problems arose in connection with his departure, a new production policy was adopted. Though Shell had its own Film Unit, the planning and supervision of the films would be done by the Film Centre, set up by Grierson to function as a liaison between documentary filmmakers and sponsors.[10] It gave the films an appreciated sense of detachment from the Group, making them more universal. The arrangement of the Film Centre and Shell would last until the early 1970s.

Under the guidance of Arthur Elton, who until his death in 1973 would remain an important figure for the Unit, several other short documentaries were made during the 1930s. These 35mm films, usually lasting ten to twenty minutes, dealt with scientific and technological subjects related to Shell products and research. The innovative use of animated drawings or diagrams helped to explain difficult technical processes clearly. With a few exceptions, prestige was to be obtained through association instead of by clear propaganda. Shell's name appeared only in the credit titles. The SFU films, however, were not meant as an end in themselves, but were still considered in relation to other media and sales promotion to create goodwill, improve demand for Shell products, and improve efficiency and knowledge within Shell as well.[11]

New horizons

With the start of World War II, the Film Unit was closed down. This inactivity, however, did not last very long. In view of the likely shortage of film production, Shell decided in early 1940 to place the services of the Film Unit at the disposal of various government and national agencies that required films. During the war the Unit produced over 40 films to support the war effort, with such subjects as the production of Stirling bombers, malaria control, mobilizing procedures, debris tunneling, and confidential Admiralty training films on asdic and radar. Most of these were made for the newly formed Ministry of Information, which showed the films in theaters or lent them at no charge to schools and institutions. Films were also distributed to theaters in neutral countries through commercial and non-theatrical channels, carried out by the British Council.[12]

After the war, scientific subjects continued to be featured in SFU films. Technical, chemical, or physical processes that related to Shell products and research were shown. There were also the very popular films on the principles of flight, used as training films by the air forces of various countries, as well as several films on car and motorcycle racing. From that time onward, the Film Unit also became more international in its operations. More foreign language versions were made and Film Libraries were set up all over the world, loaning 16mm films at no charge to educational and technological institutions. Through the use of this non-theatrical distribution system, a Shell film was aimed at a specific, limited audience already interested in the subject. Shell subsidiaries, such as those in the Netherlands, France, Germany, or the US, continued to sponsor selected films that were to be made by local film companies, as they had done before the war. In most cases, this was done in consultation with the SFU during international film meetings. These locally produced films were intended for local distribution, but some of them were also distributed internationally through the SFU.

During this period it became clear that the SFU's films could aid host nations to see Shell as an interested and creative member of the community with a sympathetic understanding of their culture and a sense of public responsibility. This was especially important in countries where there was a threat of nationalist or political unrest. In 1947, Shell sent Anstey to Venezuela to devise a program of six films together with the 17 oil companies operating in that country.[13] Shell, one of the major foreign companies in Venezuela, sent a crew from the Unit to produce two films. Filming started in June 1948, but with an overabundance of locations to film, floods, a military coup, and a change of government, HORI-ZONTES NACIONALES (*New Horizons*, 1949) and LAS BASES DEL PROGRESO (*Harvest for Tomorrow*, 1950) were not released in Venezuela until 1950. Both films were designed to show the population the impact and development of oil on the Venezuelan economy, while at the same time stimulating the government to start gradually investing the proceeds of the oil in social services and industrial development.[14] Though it is not clear how these films were received or what impact they had on Venezuelan policy, the intention of oil companies to influence the population and the government through film is a striking and curious example of local involvement to say the least.

Creating an international audience

With the widening international interest in Shell films, influenced by the ever-growing global spread of the Group, additional Units were set up. They were manned initially by key creative and technical personnel from London, but designed to be taken over by trained local staff. The Australian Shell Film Unit was established in 1948, and Venezuela followed in 1952. Other Units were set up in Egypt, Nigeria, India, and Southeast Asia. In these regions, the films were often shown in a theatrical setting, but mobile units were sometimes also used. Although the films of the national Units were made for local consumption, some were distributed internationally, gaining fame and winning international film awards. With so much activity going on, it is perhaps no wonder that, during the 1950s, more than 130 Shell documentary films were made worldwide. In 1951, there were almost 160,000 screenings around the world with an audience of more than 8.5 million. In 1960, the international audience had grown to 45 million, and films were shown in some 30 countries.[15]

Shell's growing awareness of worldwide social and economic problems can first be seen with the SFU production THE RIVAL WORLD (1955), directed by the Dutch filmmaker Bert Haanstra, who had already made several sponsored films for the Bataafsche.[16] Shot in East Africa, Sudan, and Egypt, THE RIVAL WORLD shows man's battle against the insect as a pest and bearer of disease.

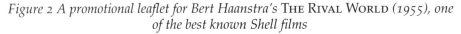

Figure 2 A promotional leaflet for Bert Haanstra's THE RIVAL WORLD *(1955), one of the best known Shell films*

A vital part of controlling the insect enemies was using chemicals and insecticide, relating to the business of Shell Chemicals, one of the sponsors of the film. With its mix of public relations, commercial interest, and social concern, THE RIVAL WORLD is a landmark among the Shell films. It was the Unit's first production in Eastman color and was produced in 27 languages. Its cinematography received a great deal of praise and won several international film awards. THE RIVAL WORLD is still one of the best known Shell films.

While producer Arthur Elton focused more on the technical aspects of Shell, it was Stuart Legg who, from THE RIVAL WORLD on, stimulated a new stream of films dealing with themes related to world health, food research, agrarian development, and environmental problems. Besides these social-issue films, many documentaries in the 1960s were also made that related to the Group's business. Films were made that dealt with modern refining processes, plastics and their place in modern industry, the history of motor racing, or the history of paint. In 1962, over 70 countries received films, while 4,500 prints were ordered for distribution by operating companies.[17] The audience numbers that saw an SFU film also continued to grow. In 1965, a total European audience of over 10 million had seen an SFU film (in 196,000 screenings), while in America the figure was nearly 18 million.[18] Approximately eight films were made per year.

Figure 3 National Shell companies also sponsored selected films; the documentary De lage landen *(1960) was made in the Netherlands*

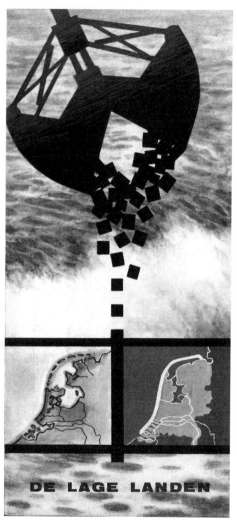

Offshore chances

In the 1960s, however, as the Group itself was still undergoing a thorough re-structuring in the interests of greater commercial efficiency, reduction in the volume of film production and the contracting out of technical facilities were deemed necessary.[19] The costly tradition whereby the director made a complete production, doing the research, scripting, shooting, and editing, was abandoned.[20] The SFU's permanent staff would gradually be reduced, working freelance on a film-to-film basis. At the same time, the difference between and use of "hard-sell" (sales promotion and advertising) or "soft-sell" (public relations, like most productions of the SFU) films was debated.[21] As economic pressures grew to provide guaranteed results in the years to come, it made public-relation films without a hard sell increasingly difficult to produce. One film, however, is considered to have managed this very successfully, creating a strong company image while keeping the direct link with Shell to a minimum.

As onshore concessions became more costly and harder to find, offshore became the new frontier in the 1960s. Oil was sought in ever-deeper waters, reaching depths of several hundred meters. As other international oil companies were also looking toward offshore production, Shell used film to prove its skill and expertise. Filming for THE UNDERWATER SEARCH (1965) took 18 months to make with scenes shot in nine countries, and the final product had (for an SFU film) the rather long running time of over 40 minutes.[22]

Figure 4 Director John Armstrong and cameraman Ron Bicker on location in the Louisiana swamps for THE UNDERWATER SEARCH *(1965)*

However, instead of putting the very expensive and prestigious film into worldwide distribution, the film was timed for limited release in relation to local developments in offshore legislation and applications for concessions. In the Netherlands, the film was shown at a time when a mining bill that addressed gas and oil extraction in the Dutch part of the North Sea was being discussed. Ministers, MPs, government officials, and the press were invited to the premiere.[23] The film was shown to the general public in cinemas as part of the regular program in The Hague, Rotterdam, and Amsterdam. How much THE UNDERWATER SEARCH indeed helped Shell worldwide is not known, but it must have been seen by many statesmen and ordinary people alike. The film was released in many countries, receiving much praise. John Chittock, industrial film correspondent for the *Financial Times*, was enthusiastic about the film, both for its creativity as well as for how it fulfilled its functional aim. "After seeing this, no one could ever doubt the supremacy of Shell."[24]

Repositioning film and new technologies

In 1973, Arthur Elton died, and not long afterwards the Film Centre closed its doors. For over 35 years the Film Centre had functioned as an independent advising body of the SFU. It had acted as a buffer between the interests of the Shell Group and those of the director, creating productions with a fair amount of artistic freedom while providing Shell with a positive corporate image. The SFU continued to make films, but more were being produced by external film companies and placed under the banner of the Unit.[25] Many of the films from this period were color remakes of the black-and-white classics of earlier days. The films on offshore production continued to be made as Shell's activities in the North Sea increased after the 1973 oil shock. These films blended drama with documentary to make it clear to the audience that Shell had the right technical means but also the right people to get the job done, often working in extreme weather conditions. Films on marine and offshore safety were also made for internal staff use, explaining subjects like offshore evacuation, first-aid duties, or how to handle oil spills.

   As the costs of film production rose considerably and the effectiveness of reaching a non-theatrical audience remained difficult to measure, budget cuts were also in order at Shell.[26] The number of productions declined, both for the SFU as well as regionally sponsored productions; national units had already stopped earlier. From the early 1980s onward, more productions were made, replacing 16mm or 35mm film with the cheaper video formats. However, screening the films remained popular at educational and technological institutions. In 1983, the Shell Film Library in the UK had roughly 40,000 16mm bookings per year, while France and the Netherlands each had loaned out some

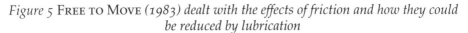

Figure 5 FREE TO MOVE *(1983) dealt with the effects of friction and how they could be reduced by lubrication*

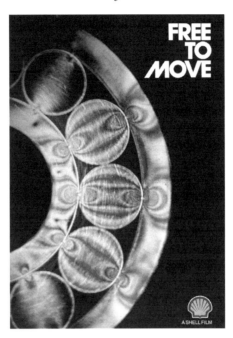

30,000.[27] In the years to come, videocassettes would slowly become the pre-ferred medium of distribution. Films that explained the use of petrochemicals, the working of the gasoline engine, or the formation of oil were popular. Social-issue films were also produced to show the causes and consequences of tropical deforestation, the attempt to provide water and food to the Third World, or the solutions to eradicate malaria. However, with continued budget cuts, many film libraries closed down.[28] At the same time, the Shell Video Unit that had been established at the start of the decade was now producing videos in ever-greater quantities for internal communication as well as promotional use. In 1986, the SFU was combined with the Shell Video Unit to form the Shell Film and Video Unit. With the merging of the Units the focus shifted from public affairs films to training, marketing, and internal communications programs.

In the 1990s, films were made on subjects such as the threat of global warm-ing, geology, and the search for new sources of energy. At the same time, more marketing-oriented films were also produced. Not unlike THE UNDERWATER SEARCH, the film EXPERIENCE IN DEPTH (1995) showed Shell's latest deep-water technology in offshore exploration and production. However, while the former showed Shell's expertise by indirectly referring to it, EXPERIENCE IN DEPTH used

Shell's name and the Pecten logo in the film. Other documentaries, such as those on the Gannet and Nelson oil and gas fields and the use of renewable energy, also used Shell's name and logo in a direct manner.

Today, dozens of training and marketing productions are made each year. Together with internal communications programs, these productions form the most important production function of the Shell Film and Video Unit. Through digital and web technology the videos are distributed worldwide in several foreign language versions in their efforts to create a strong positive image of Shell, showing the company's commitment, skills, and expertise.

Revealing the world

Ranging from the first films that had a strong cataloguing character linked with a colonial past, to the educational films showing the new promise of a technological and scientific world, to the training and promotional films of today, Shell's films show a history that is remarkable and perhaps unique in both its depth and its continuity. For over 80 years Shell has produced documentary films that have been seen all over the world by hundreds of millions of viewers. Other multinationals (including other oil companies) have also made use of sponsored films, but none had the global scope or the longevity of the Shell Film Unit. By setting up film libraries and other national film units around the world, films could be produced and consumed both locally and globally. Creative films with a sense of detachment from the Group were stimulated by key figures in British documentary history and were made by internationally renowned or up-and-coming directors. As the films were distributed mostly to non-theatrical venues like schools, societies, and associations, or shown during working hours to staff, trainees, and technicians alike, an already-interested audience was reached. By using impressive visuals, the latest techniques, and clear explanations, the films from the Shell Film Units gained a high reputation.

Further research on this unique corpus of films will further emphasize the Shell unit's important contribution to the development of the documentary film on an international scale, open up new angles on the role of cinema in modern society, and shed light on the dynamics of a global media discourse.[29] At the same time, the films document the cultural, social, economic, and environmental impact of the world's ongoing search for scientific and technological progress. As corporate films, they may easily be classified according to the three R's, "record," "rhetoric," and "rationalization," proposed in the functional heuristics of Hediger and Vonderau.[30] However, the Shell films also point to the fact that industrial organizations, particularly large ones like multinational energy corporations, always have to coordinate their goals and interests with broader cultural and societal concerns. In an exemplary fashion, the Shell film catalogue shows that corporate films are perhaps the most important among the multiple media interfaces where this negotiation takes place. Both in terms of the history of the documentary image in the 20th century and its impact as a medium of political and societal discourses, then, the Shell films warrant further research.

Notes

1. With kind permission from Royal Dutch Shell, this article is based on the more detailed "From Oil to Celluloid: A History of Shell Films," in Jan Luiten van Zanden (ed.), *A History of Royal Dutch Shell* (vol. 4, Oxford University Press, 2007). This volume also contains three DVDs that include several complete Shell documentary films. All illustrations with kind permission from Shell Photographic Services/Shell Int. Ltd.

2. The original credit title is OVERZICHT VAN DE BEDRIJVEN VAN DE BATAAFSCHE PETROLEUM MAATSCHAPPIJ IN NEDERL. OOST-INDIE. At the time, as well as later, the film was usually referred to as the BATAAFSCHE PETROLEUM FILM. Roughly 40% of the film survives and is preserved at the Filmmuseum, Amsterdam.

3. For a description of the journey to the Indies, the presentation of the film, and the response to it during the screening, see "Onze Indische Petroleumfilm," *Maandblad van het Personeel der Verbonden Petroleum-Maatschappijen*, 7, 8 (1924), pp. 114-119; and Willy Mullens, "Een film van onze film voor de Koninklijke," *Het Vaderland* (13 July 1924), pp. 1-2.

4. See Hediger and Vonderau, "Record, Rhetoric, Rationalization: Industrial Organization and Film," in this volume.

5. "De Petroleumfilm," *Het Vaderland* (19 June 1924), p. 3.

6. "Afscheid C.W.A. van Bergen," *De Bron*, 14, 1 (May 1931), pp. 90-91; "Personalia," *De Bron*, 14, 7 (August 1931), p. 204. These silent films, of uncertain date (such as KONING OLIE, AARDOLIE, VAN PUT TOT POMP, and DOING OILLAND IN AN HOUR) as well as several of the other Bataafsche films are preserved in the Filmmuseum, Amsterdam.

7. The films of Shell-Mex & BP that were made between the early 1930s and 1975 will not be discussed here. These films were intended for the English market only and consisted mostly of promotional films, unlike the SFU films that were meant for public relations and prestige purposes.

8. "The Record of the Film Unit" (1951), pp. 2-4. Shell Film & Video Unit archive. Unfortunately, Grierson's report and the various responses to it are lost.

9. Interview with Edgar Anstey, 10 February 1983, pp. 8-9. SFVU.

10. The initial advisory agreement was made in 1936 with the newly formed Associated Realist Film Producers. Two years later, the Film Centre emerged out of Associated Realist.

11. Memorandum, Alexander Wolcough, 15 February 1937, quoted in "The Record of the Film Unit," pp. 7-8.

12. H.D. Waley, "British Documentaries and the War Effort," *The Public Opinion Quarterly* 6, 4 (1942), pp. 606-8.

13. Interview Anstey, op. cit., p. 6.

14. "The Record of the Film Unit," 36. Promotional notes for *Harvest for Tomorrow* and *Venezuela Looks Ahead*. Shell Nederland Filmcentrale Archive.

15. John Drummond, "Shell Film Operations" (16 December 1960), p. 2. SFVU. Shell films were sometimes screened in their entirety on television, though mostly only an excerpt was shown. In this overview, Shell's interest in television could not be investigated.

16. DIJKBOUW (1952), and in 1954, ONTSTAAN EN VERGAAN (*The Changing Earth*), DE OPSPORING VAN AARDOLIE (*The Search for Oil*), DE VERKENNINGSBORING (*The Wildcat*), and HET OLIEVELD (*The Oilfield*).

17. *Films*, S.I.P.C., 1963, p. 4. SFVU.

18. Shell Oil to S.I.P.C, "Film Statistics for 1965." "Analysis of total film distribution of European countries in 1965," revised July 1966. Haanstra archive, 136 A 6-4, Filmmuseum Amsterdam. A very rough worldwide estimate of 75 million was also quoted, but this may have included television viewers. "Statement of Film Policy," 1965. SFVU.

19. John Drummond, "Shell Film Operations" (16 December 1960).

20. Interview with Alan Pendry, 18 May 1983, pp. 1-2. SFVU.

21. *The Film as a Medium of Communication*, The Royal Dutch/Shell Group of Companies, Public Relations, 1958, pp. 3-4. SFVU.

22. In the film, only the names of the Shell oil platforms, ships or tankers are mentioned; no Shell logos are shown.

23. Jean le Harivel, "Report on promoting 'Underwater Search,' " p. 4. Shell Nederland to BPM, "Promotion of 'Underwater Search' Film," SNF, April 22, 1966.

24. John Chittock, "Analysis of a good film," *Financial Times*, date uncertain. SNF.

25. Gordon, *Shell Films: The First Sixty Years*.

26. Films and Television Meeting, 10-11 October 1983. SFVU.

27. Ibid., pp. 15-28.

28. The film library in the Netherlands is the only one still in operation. A film catalogue in Dutch is available online at: www.shell.com.

29. Over three hundred Shell films were donated to the National Archive of the British Film Institute in 1999. However, most of the locally produced films as well as those from other national Shell Film Units are not included, making international research more difficult.

30. See Hediger and Vonderau, "Record, Rhetoric, Rationalization: Industrial Organization and Film," in this volume.

IV
See, Learn, Control

The Personnel Is Political

Voice and Citizenship in Affirmative-Action Videos in the Bell System, 1970-1984[1]

Heide Solbrig

In the period of the 1960s through the 1980s, the Bell System produced films and videos for use in implementing affirmative action programs. Affirmative-action plans at Bell recruited, trained, and sought to promote traditionally underemployed and segregated members of the community and the company, i.e., women and minorities. The Bell programs began in the early 1960s, in conjunction with President Lyndon Johnson's Plan for Progress, a voluntary plan for workplace racial integration signed by AT&T, Western Electric, and Bell Laboratories. This initial voluntary plan lead to aggressive recruitment, but was not successful in changing occupational segregation; despite the massive hiring of minorities in the 1960s, women and minorities remained in the lowest-paying jobs in the company.[2] This led the government to issue several EEOC (Equal Employment Opportunity Commission) consent decrees for AT&T and the Western Electric Company in the 1970s. The videos produced within the Bell System to implement affirmative-action management training provide a historical record of how media was simultaneously a part of institutional change and capitalist stasis.

Industrial media and the bell system

The Bell System and its subsidiaries (AT&T, Bell Labs, and Western Electric[3]) have been deeply involved in both the technological and ideological development of industrial media products since the 1920s. In 1928, Electrical Research Products Incorporated (ERPI), a research wing of Western Electric (initially established to develop sound products for the Bell Company) produced and distributed educational film products outside the Hollywood market. While this unit was dissolved in 1936 in Bell's first divestiture agreement, companies spun-off from the ERPI group went on to establish the core of postwar industrial film production and distribution, including Audio Productions and Encyclopedia Britannica Films. In the postwar era, along with other large industries, AT&T used industrial films to train managers in the principles of human-relations management theory. Both local telephone companies, Long Lines and Western Electric, created films that were shown both in-house and at high schools for promoting jobs and recruiting young people in the human relations-centered corporation. In the 1950s, many sectors of the giant corporation had their own production units as well as hiring independent producers to create narrative film products. These films by and large told stories of a self-conscious company man whose loyalties lay first with himself, and then with the company. As soon as television technology became available in the 1950s, AT&T began to experiment with the uses of closed-circuit corporate television communications. This new communication technology would become a critical tool in the implementation of affirmative-action programs, as it came to be used not simply to circulate ideology but also to document its circulation as a defense against legal action by the EEOC in the 1970s. Multiple divisions of the Bell System, along with other large corporations, were producing film documentaries and video instruction systems that sought to introduce new dialogues about gender and race within the corporation. The films were produced despite managerial resistance and were part of efforts to literally change corporate conversations about race and gender, albeit in limited, rationalized, and production-oriented ways.

The Bell Company's videos take some of the early practices of the 1950s human-relations management films and rid them of the familiar, cheerful-but-ideological story lines produced to emulate Hollywood. Early corporate video opted instead for strict and pedantic language instruction, case studies of manager-worker interactions, and first-person lectures produced with a low-tech televisual realism. In a sense, what this shift points out was the perceived limitations of ideology as an effective medium through which to change social organization. The switch from film to video was part of a shift away from a romantic ideology of the Hawthorne Effect – the idea that, if the proper attention is paid to a small group of workers or managers, they will create a reality that could supersede class loyalties. By the late 1960s and early 1970s, confidence in these mass-influence propaganda models had faded. Bell Company management needed media products that performed more concrete tasks and produced more quantifiable results. Videos were used to train employees in rational interactions within a newly diverse workforce. They gave clear instructions to white and male managers concerning how to talk to women and minority workers. Videos also taught women and minorities how to speak as managers (at times even giving minorities instructions on how to speak as white men). These videos taught corporate subjects the particular language permitted for speaking about race and gender within the workplace, delimiting the arena of work and economic productivity from that of social or political equity. In contrast to the public relations campaigns that presented the Bell Company as a partner in the civil-rights movement, the Bell Company and its subsidiaries, Western Electric, Long Lines, and Bell Labs, were focused on the bottom line. However, these videos clearly and repeatedly assert the *economic* importance of successful affirmative action within the Bell Systems over its *social* value, on the other hand, they did serve to open the discussion of social differences, inequality, and racism within the corporate culture, perhaps furthering that discussion in the broader culture – not an insignificant contribution. Video education at AT&T was a part of the complex discursive line walked between incorporating race, gender, and diversity while defending corporate governance and class hierarchy from both political and social realms.

"Plan for Progress": A community service proposal (1964), The Great Upheaval

It was in the early 1960s that the government began to implement various equal-opportunity initiatives through collaboration projects with business and government.[4] During that same period, AT&T, Western Electric, and a number of local Bell Companies signed voluntary Plans for Progress, a government-business initiative to integrate US workplaces. It is not surprising that, considering the special relationship that Western Electric and some AT&T Long Lines enjoyed with the US government, they were among the earliest to sign voluntary agreements to implement workplace integration. The 1961 Joint Statement for the voluntary Plan for Progress,[5] signed by Lyndon Johnson and Western Electric's president, H.I. Romnes, put the "Dissemination of Policy" as its first priority, which included both the distribution of information and discussion of the new equal opportunity policies at management seminars.

One of the earliest strategies for disseminating information about affirmative action was the production of films. A series of treatments in the development of the Plan for Progress film The Great Upheaval gives us some insight into the ways in which narratives about affirmative action and integration were negotiated between divergent interests:

> To accomplish these objectives the film will follow the course of the two revolutions that are simultaneously changing the face of America today: The revolution in civil and human rights and the revolution of modern technology and education... [I]t is a film utilizing this method that we propose to show to the Negro citizen in order to motivate him to enter the mainstream of American society and after having done so, allow the social revolution to complement and strengthen our technological revolution.[6]

There is some truth as well as a fair amount of bitter irony to the celebratory narrative connecting civil rights with the technological revolution. The entrance of African-American women into the Bell System, mostly as telephone operators, was indeed in response to both social and technological change. As postwar urban demographics changed and computer systems became increasingly significant in the workplace, the job of operator was rapidly de-skilled, and the Bell Company needed access to a low-wage workforce from the urban core. In October 1969, AT&T's vice president, Walter Straley, stated in a private meeting of company presidents:

> [We need skilled workers.] And from now on the number of such people who are available will grow smaller even as our need becomes greater. It is therefore perfectly plain that we need nonwhite employees. Not because we are good citizens. Or because it is the law as well as national goal to give them employment. We need them because we have so many jobs to fill and they will take them.[7]

As Venus Green recounts, corporate executives were in search of cheap, skilled labor. This was not so much a rights issue as it was an economic demand. However, it dovetailed with the demands of affirmative-action initiatives that offered tax breaks and other legal incentives for the company to bring more women and minorities into the workforce. By the end of the 1960s, the Bell System had drastically increased the demographic representation of women and minorities as they used affirmative-action initiatives to fill their own employment shortages. Workplace demographics changed significantly from 1960 to 1970, because the majority of black workers were operators, a corresponding change in *occupational* segregation did not take place.

Operators' jobs had become de-skilled because of Direct Distance Dialing (DDD) and Traffic Service Position Systems (TSPS) that changed the operator position to more repetitive, less skill-orientated labor, which also made the job increasingly stressful. With these changes in the job itself, and with new hiring practices, the traditional "white lady" image and actuality of the AT&T workforce was replaced in a matter of four or five years by an almost entirely African-American workforce. New female operators comprised the majority of black workers at the Bell System.[8] At the same time, the computerization of the operator's job meant that the numbers of jobs available in this position quickly dwindled from the 1960s to 1980s. Changing technologies had indeed opened opportunities for black women, but they closed them up again in a period of ten years.

These and other problems with the voluntary implementation of affirmative action led to legal action against AT&T in the early 1970s. The massive public-relations programs of the 1960s promoted AT&T as a great partner in the social changes of the era, but when the smoke cleared it seemed evident that these changes had yet to take place. In order for "equal opportunity" to be achieved new workers needed to be integrated into management. This was a change that required a change in AT&T's corporate culture, which was widely know for its rigid, hierarchical organizational structure. It was the failure to successfully break down occupational segregation, i.e., move African-Americans and women into management, that led to the EEOC ruling against AT&T in 1973.

It is in this context of an institutional change and social upheaval that affirmative-action training videos were introduced into the Bell Company culture. They are found in all of the company's divisions, Long Lines, local phone companies, Western Electric, and Bell Labs. The Corporate Education Center of the Bell System (in New Jersey) produced a significant amount of the corporate communication which was shown to large audiences of East-Coast workers during the 1970s and 1980s by way of closed-circuit corporate television systems.[9] At the same time, that these social changes needed to be implemented, corporate communications systems were undergoing dramatic changes internally, and by the time the consent decree demanded institutional change, video technology had become the dominant mode of internal visual communication at AT&T, with the Corporate Training Center producing a large number of video products from the 1970s onward.

The video produced for Bell was used for general communication between corporate executives and management groups, for small-group lectures on management behavior, and for inter-departmental communication. This video was a required dimension of training for lower, mid- and upper management in the expected communicative behavior in the affirmative-action context, and was used to facilitate dialogue between managers and workers in this charged setting. Video was able to communicate corporate public policy as well as fine-tuned instruction in terms of specific, individual behavior for various job categories. Video, shown on corporate closed-circuit television, became corporate public space where the rights, relationships, and duties of workers were defined, not in the cheery ideological narratives of the 1950s but clearly, point-by-point. The earliest Bell System video, titled simply AFFIRMATIVE ACTION,[10] SURVIVES SOLELY IN A FILM PRINT.[11] IN THIS FILM/VIDEO PRINT, RICHARD HOUGH, A SENIOR VP, CONNECTS THE PERSONNEL/PERSONAL WITH THE STATE:

[T]hat's the way I read the law of the land, more fundamentally that's the way I read our country's purpose, a purpose we have a responsibility to help fulfill, and furthermore that's what I personally believe is the right course for us, in short: affirmative action to achieve equal opportunity is a major factor in every Bell System Manager's job, a factor on which he can expect to be measured on the basis of the results that he achieves.

These video/films also contain warnings that, without compliance, the worst could happen, i.e., allowing the state to step in between white men and minority hiring. This prediction had some foresight, as in the next year, 1971, the FCC ruled that the Bell System had "systematically discriminated against women & minorities," and in 1973, AT&T signed a voluntary consent decree to "hire, transfer and promote a 'targeted' number of women and 'minorities' into higher-paying management and craft jobs, as well as to place men in some of the female dominated jobs" within six years of the EEOC agreement.[12]

Equal-opportunity policy and terminology

The video WESTERN ELECTRIC CO. EQUAL OPPORTUNITY POLICY AND TERMINOLOGY[13] gives a sense of how video differs from film narratives regarding corporate culture. First, the Bell System used video in an attempt to delimit the meanings of affirmative action with very explicit instructions, not stories. Video during this period often used a non-fiction style that simulated the television talk show, news hour and lecture series. This video defined the company's affirmative-action policy and, more specifically, the permissible speech according to this policy, in strict economic terms. In this video, M.D. "Mac" McDonald, Director of Corporate Equal Opportunity, defines the terms equal opportunity, anti-discrimination and affirmative action as specific parts of corporate policy. This video is designed very simply (cheaply, one might say), with two men seated next to one another in classic talk/news-show format. Each of the key words, as it is discussed, flashes across the screen over Mac while he explains its function in Western Electric policy.

> *Jack*: I guess the best place to start is with the term equal opportunity itself. How does the company define the term equal opportunity?
> *Mac*: Well, Jack. Equal means equal. Not more and not less. Opportunity means a chance. Access. Consideration. So equal opportunity means to be accorded an equal or fair chance. A fair shot at job and career opportunities based upon legitimate job factors and not on factors of classification unrelated to the performance of the job... [E]qual opportunity does necessarily mean the same treatment or the same outcomes or the same status. It's equality of opportunity not necessarily equality of condition. Equal opportunity is a neutral concept.

Figure 1 Equal Opportunity Policy and Terminology *(1975)*

AT&T Archives and History Center, Warren, NJ

Equal opportunity in this definition is essentially *economic* citizenship. Simply put, the right to work. Two hundred years after English serfs were allowed to move about freely to seek employment outside guilds or their social class, African-Americans and women were being afforded the same opportunity. However, the fundamental tenet of US affirmative-action legislation and programs was that this was an inadequate remedy in the face of these long historical inequities, affirmative action by necessity asked more of employers. The effort to improve African-Americans' self-esteem and bring them into the mainstream of American life represents an expansion of corporate goals and responsibilities far beyond human-relations theories of individualism and company loyalty. In this new environment corporate management had to create a hybrid between human-relations initiatives that encouraged empathy and compassion for the sake of small group and corporate identification, and a form of mental Taylorism in which identification needed to become intensely rationalized. In order to address these goals the company adopted language of sociological analysis to replace the political language of "civil rights," "racism," and "sexism." Mac explains the term "cultural bias":

> *Mac*: [C]ultural bias is the only term we'll be discussing that does not reflect the company position. Cultural bias is a term I use to shed light on what we're dealing with... [i]nstead of words like discrimination, prejudice, racism, sexism, and so forth, which can be emotionally charged words to some people... I'd like to try something with all of you: picture in your mind that you are taking a trip by air. Picture yourself boarding a plane: you walk up the steps and you glance to your left as you hand in your ticket and you notice a woman at the controls. Now be honest, what is your gut reaction? Neutral, comfortable, or slightly nervous and uneasy? In any case, the plane takes off, you get to your destination and it lands safely, as you get off you glance to your right. And there's that woman pilot. What is your feeling now? Is it "I guess I

was wrong about woman pilots, they're probably as good as men are," or was it "I sure am glad that trip is over, I hope I never get another woman pilot." Now those of you who were nervous getting on or off the plane should realize that that's cultural bias operating and that it's despite performance evidence to the contrary. The point is, when individual employment and placement decisions are made, none of us can be sure, not even the individual decision maker, the extent to which these cultural biases may be working.[14]

The corporation found itself charged with addressing that which it had always struggled to exclude from the workplace: the emotional, the unconscious, the cultural, and, most unnervingly, the political. The solutions at the Bell System were varied but predictable: more systems for regulating hiring in order to exclude bias, building in more standardized procedures for hiring based upon aptitude testing, and increased monitoring of the systems of hiring.[15] Increased emphasis on the strict adherence to "job-related selection criteria" was ideal for the purely *economic* citizen. Increased vigilance meant that work rules became more rigid, and informal affiliations and external group membership (nepotism, union affiliation, and so on) lost ground as a new kind of workplace governance emerged to renegotiate the categories of corporate citizenship for a new population of workers. As the human-relations paradigm was altered to relate to this new workforce, it used some of the theories of "humanizing" the workplace that were popularized in the 1950s and systematized them to increasingly rationalize basic modes of human communication, such as language, conversation, and self-image. This negotiation built new boundaries for corporate citizenship that helped to negotiate, but also limit, the demands of increased social equity – these careful linguistic tightropes were communicated through video.

Corrective action at Hawthorne: Getting feedback

The history of Western Electric's affirmative-action programs (beginning with the Plan for Progress) followed a track that was almost the exact opposite of AT&T. While Long Lines and the Bell Company subsidiaries had hired black women operators and promoted white women into careers in management, Western Electric was a model for the company development of minority business and the advancement of minorities into management positions.

> Those blacks who aspired to supervisory jobs realized that they would face considerable requirements beyond their job descriptions. At Hawthorne, a black engineer named Bill Alexander organized a support group. The group – four or five at first – met at Alexander's home or onsite to discuss what it took to succeed and how best to

bring about change. They decided that any gains they made had to come within the context of the company's success. The group grew rapidly in the late 1960s and needed more space. They finally became sufficiently established and well known that works manager Wyllys Rheingrover circumvented the line of command and met with them.[16]

Support groups had begun to take hold of the psyches of not only management, but also those groups who aspired to management. As minorities began to advance in the company, however, the opposite was true for women at Western Electric. A class-action suit brought by over two hundred women, won in 1979, accused Western Electric of "discrimination in promotion and access to training." The terms of the settlement required Western to develop women into positions of equal opportunity.[17]

Figure 2 CORRECTIVE ACTION PROGRAM (1979)

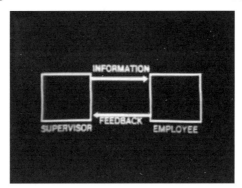

AT&T Archives and History Center, Warren, NJ

We find the same discourses of national and personal commitment to affirmative action in a video with much more specific intentions. Made ten years after AT&T's affirmative-action company communiqué, Western Electric's Corrective Action Program (CAP) training video was a response to an EEOC consent decree signed in 1979. The implementation agreement required, in the words of this CORRECTIVE ACTION (CAP) video, that Western Electric and the Hawthorne plant exhibit "real," "visible evidence" of the women factory workers being given opportunities to advance into managerial positions. Hovering between a mechanistic approach to interaction and the sort of immediacy of *Candid Camera*, the video's interaction between worker and manager appears partially scripted but still informal; the video first shows diagrams of communication/ information theory (information, feedback, noise) and then a manager explaining to a woman worker her options for advancement at the Hawthorne Plant in

a near cinéma-vérité style. The CAP video shows how personal interaction becomes "evidence" of compliance: the company talks to the state with images of
personal work review and advancement.

This was also one of many examples of the ways that interaction was broken
into specific skills that could be repeated and transferred and remain consistent
from manager to manager. In the conversation between Jessie and her supervisor, which lasted twenty minutes, the supervisor explains various job categories, and Jessie expresses interest and explains her qualifications. The video is
instructive in the specific types of behavior required for management interaction with employees, contributing to the various managerial and work skills
involved in the promotion and management of economic citizenship within the
company. And finally, with Jessie's quiet assertions of her right to participate,
and her interest in various categories of work that the CAP made available, her
presence in the video can be seen as an assertion, however docile, of her right to
social equity. Here, Jessie is both data for show and an actual person who appears excited to have an opportunity she did not have before. The sociological
diagram which begins the video frames Jessie's conversation about her rights as
literally another mechanical function in factory production, while her genuine
interest in new life possibilities seems to resist seeing this mechanical construction as the only aspect of a conversation about increased possibilities for women.

There are several reasons that the study of corporate media is especially suited to help us understand how US corporations have negotiated between the
economic, political, and social dimensions of citizenship during the implementation of affirmative action. The first is that films and videos constituted a con-
duit between both the company and the state, on the one hand, and the company and the workforce on the other. Films and videos were used as evidence to
demonstrate to the state the corporate commitment to, and specific implementa-
tions of, affirmative-action policies.[18] This also includes films that were used to
recruit a new workforce, in part through advertisement of the company's new
commitments and, early on, some films that documented particular policies
such as those produced by Plan for Progress committees.[19] The second reason
is that video shown on in-house corporate television systems was in some sense
creating a public space for communication about affirmative action within the
company.

Sometimes this tele-visual space was used for rigid instruction in relationships with minorities and women (such as SRT videos), sometimes it was used
as a place for employees to speak from their own positions so that the company
could communicate between multiple departments. This video pedagogy describes, acts out, and reiterates a variety of combinations of economic, political,

and social citizenship that converge to model a new rights conscious economic citizen in the Bell System.

Race and rights: The public, the private, and the therapeutic

Two contemporary books frame an ethical debate over the uses of social psychology in creating the (sometimes) coercive training programs for the expansion of rights and categories of "corporate citizenship" in this era. The first, *Race Experts* (2001) by Elizabeth Lasch-Quinn,[20] critiques the uses of social psychology, particular those forms of sensitivity, encounter groups, and work-diversity training that have produced a discourse of white guilt, racial identification, and a politics of racial anger. Quinn argues that this therapeutic approach to political problems has undermined the radical integrationist spirit of the civil-rights movement:

> Surprisingly, it turns out that our new rituals and rhetoric about race cannot be understood apart from the culture of therapy. The therapeutic sensibility, which interprets all of social and political life in terms of its relevance for individual "growth," emotional well-being, and gratification, has become deeply implicated in the way we view race.[21]

Lasch-Quinn argues that one of the profoundly disturbing problems of the discourses of race and therapy is how these systems have broken down distinctions between the public and the private in the political debate. Diversity is grounded in self-serving economic justifications, not social equity: what is good for the individual or the company is automatically what is good for society – sexual harassment will damage one's possibilities for career advancement, a diverse workforce will help in brokering international deals, etc. Lasch-Quinn points out that this is particularly evident in diversity training films.

> Like those of the diversity training films, these guidelines are predicated on the idea that the primary reason why an elaborate etiquette exists is that each group requires the other in order to fulfill its economic goals. Since workers and customers will be increasingly diverse, lack of tolerance will compromise profits. Mere tolerance is the only goal that remains – not an inspiring foundation for any social world.[22]

Corporate video is particularly effective for this therapeutic translation because it is able to turn the social/political meanings of affirmative action into rational language and the types of behavior that should be practiced by the individual. Reinterpreting the political meanings of ideological speech, for example, into the "value-neutral" categories of "equal opportunity" or even the sociological language of "cultural bias" turns the profoundly political moment of the civil-rights movement into a set of job skills to be learned by individual workers. For Lasch-Quinn, the divisions between the public and private are hard and fast barriers that, when breached, have led to political and personal demise: "The highly touted authenticity of behavior in actuality leaves individuals dry, since it fosters transitory emotional revelation rather than the richer expression that takes place only when private boundaries have been maintained."[23] Diversity training driven by economic goals in its various incarnations, while impoverishing the personal, also limits efforts at political discourse over social inequity.

On the other hand, Cynthia Estlund argues in *Working Together* (2003)[24] that it is in fact the workplace (which I argue here is fundamentally shaped by social psychology and its attendant media tools) where integration and diversity has become the most functional in the United States. Estlund writes that

> the very involuntariness of interactions within the workplace turns out to play a curiously constructive role in making possible the extraordinary convergence of close and regular interaction and a relatively high degree of demographic diversity. Both the external law governing workplaces and the constraints that operate within workplaces help to make the often-troubled project of racial integration work relatively well there. People can be forced to get along – not without friction, but with surprising success.[25]

Estlund argues that the ability of the state to regulate workplaces along with the ability of workplaces to coerce workers is a necessary function in the creation of a diverse society. While Lasch-Quinn laments diversity training's coercive reduction of rational civil discourse, Estlund argues that coercion, from both state and business, is necessary for the functional production of a diverse society. Estlund's argument carries more nuance here: workplace diversity is a difficult problem when "'the preponderance of empirical evidence suggests that diversity is most likely to impede group functioning,' unless steps are taken to address these problems."[26] Estlund writes that when the law has a limited ability to address the "cultural bias" that research has shown still predominates in the workplace, it does not seem unreasonable that interpersonal training approaches, however imperfect, could conceivably be a part of the solution.[27]

Both Lasch-Quinn's critique of invasive and politically compromising methods of psychological training and Estlund's argument that certain forms of coercion at work can be socially and politically productive, provide two poles from which to understand the problems and possibilities for notions of citizenship framed by corporate media. Private business's obvious commitment to economic productivity above general social equity raises some of the fundamental questions about the uses of media communication for the promotion of rights consciousness. A new rights consciousness emerged from the civil-rights legislation implemented in the 1960s, and many new legislative demands were put into practice using new interactive technologies of communication and social psychology. As Michael Schudson points out, many areas of life that had never before been a part of public culture or government now came under state jurisdiction:

> Today, terms like "date-rape," "marital rape" and "battered women" are familiar. "Deadbeat dads" is a political rallying cry, a nominee to the Supreme Court has been publicly embarrassed by charges of sexual harassment, and state policy about women's decisions on abortion has fueled the most extensive populist movement of our time. The notions of representation, justice, and political participation have extended far beyond the sphere of conventional politics into "private" life.[28]

The videos I discuss here can be understood as early communication tools for the translation of the private into the public. A range of communicative strategies were marshaled for implementing affirmative action and "equal opportunity." Some of these were quite intimate, some quite political, and all were designed to serve the company's economic demands. Videos, shown in the public space provided by in-house corporate television, played a role in influencing the opinions of managers about integration and their behavior toward a new population of employees brought into the company. The uses of film and video for shaping beliefs and behavior, in particular as they relate to rights, occurred in the critical juncture between the civil-rights movement and Reagan's initiation of an ongoing roll-back of the welfare state. This brings us to the questions raised in the early years of film research: To what degree can democracy be shaped, or reshaped, through the applications of social science embedded in visual communication technologies?

As the "silent rights revolution" of legislation that had accompanied the social movements of the 1960s were put into affect, corporations needed ways to incorporate difference into the corporate structure in ways that they had never done before. And in many cases, video's much touted "immediacy" supported the requirements of corporate management to make the real changes (or at least "real" evidence of changes) in employee "consciousness" deemed necessary for these demographic changes to be effective. Corporate television and video management systems could amplify the group dynamics and sensitivity training that film training had embraced in the 1960s. Video was ideal for showing extremely specific types of relationship changes that could be incorporated into the workplace.[29] Corporate consciousness-raising systems in the 1970s congealed into video training that showed employees and managers highly mechanized systems for emotional relationships, and introduced the skills necessary for their economic citizenship (i.e., the skills required to keep their jobs) through detailed models of psychological behavior.

Supervisory Relationship Training: New technologies for new citizens

The technology of video allowed for the production of very simple examples of relationships for in-house audiences, emphasizing simple dyadic (two person) interactions, rather than either fictional or documentary narrative styles.

These videos had lower production costs and values than television; they were characterized by their poor lighting and continuity, their simple graphics, their use of employees as actors and their limited narrative structures, which, in the case of both Supervisory Relationship Training (SRT) and CAP, relied entirely upon a set of behavior instructions combined with examples of conversations between two people. Unlike the producers of many industrial films, the producers of these videos were often not related to the Hollywood industry at all, but instead were educational technologists, psychologists, and corporate media managers. SRT videos are good examples of how race and therapy meld. Managers are instructed in listening when encountering discrimination complaints, in sympathizing with workers who do not want to work for a woman, etc. Political solutions such as disciplinary or legal action are replaced with consideration, understanding, and *an increase in work rules*. It is probably not surprising that the narrative uses of video were limited in this early video period. While the film producers of the Plan for Progress committees had attempted to construct large social overviews of technology and civil rights, video programs from the 1970s focused upon a technology of personal interaction. Video dyads began with a corporate narrator, whose pedantic voice recalled the earliest ERPI educational voice-over, who laid out the main points of the directive with the aid of simple graphics. Despite this apparently stripped-down simplicity, the video intensified the ways in which this technology was able to address workers and managers in an intimate way. Television viewing is more personalized than film because it is easily viewed by a single individual, or a small group.

Corporate video spoke from the position of individual (corporation) to individual (manager, worker, governmental official). Television, with its location in our homes rather than theaters, has historically claimed a greater intimacy and immediacy with the viewer. In the case of the corporate video, this intimacy is both shown on the screen – managers speaking candidly to employees and one another about personal relationships, problems on the job – and also replicated by the sometimes more personalized viewing experience between worker and monitor. Video communication itself reproduces a dyadic quality between viewer and monitor that was different from the viewing of large, dramatic narratives about productivity shown in cafeterias with other employees that was the standard viewing practice for the classic industrial film. Corporate television was able to address problems within the corporation quickly, specifically, and with a basis in company policy and current political mandate, even as these conditions changed throughout the 1970s.

Videos engaged the vocabulary of company policy (as we have seen) and trained managers to subsume both political and personal discourse within economic mandates.

The voice of the manager

Supervisor Relationship Training (SRT) was a large-scale video training program for management used at both AT&T and Western Electric. This 1974-1978 program used video vignettes to illustrate a wide number of dyads described as "supervisory relationships." The wide range of job categories represented in these productions suggests that the program was used extensively throughout the Bell company.[30] Each interaction is introduced with a series of "learning points" and is then followed by an interaction between a manager and a supervisor, both roles performed by members of AT&T's public-relations group.[31] The videos illustrated how issues perhaps once deemed too personal or private for such public discussion, such as hygiene, resistance to female supervisors, fear about aging and discrimination, and complaints about racism, could be talked about in managerial terms. The types of interactions featured in the programs are numerous and yet of a specific, recognizable form. For example, one of the videos explains and illustrates a white manager suggesting to one of his black foremen that the manager would like the foreman to attend SRT training. The manager explains to his employee that he might be having trouble working with a woman on his crew and that SRT, a training program offered one day a week over a series of weeks, might give him some skills for working with her. The video's "learning points" encourage the manager to observe his foreman as the foreman attends the seminar. The videos purport to teach the standard skills of therapy: listening, observing oneself and others, and sensitivity.

The video training sometimes deals with mundane issues of authority and reprimand, while using African-Americans or women as either manager or employee without comment as to their non-traditional roles. In one particularly telling example, the manager uses the Supervisory Relationship Training itself as a tool for increased employee supervision. This video turns the very raw conflict of racial division in the workplace into a problem that can be solved through increased management, while at the same time fostering interactive skills and bringing legitimacy to the discussion of feelings about race and the experience of racism within the workplace. That the introduction of race into the workplace led to increased work rules is evident in this interaction; this is also consistent with Venus Green's report of the deep levels of contention between older white workers and newer black workers as older values of group affiliation and social support were replaced by rules that circumvent informal relationships.

Figure 3 SUPERVISORY RELATIONSHIP TRAINING *(1976-1978)*

  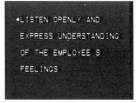

AT&T Archives and History Center, Warren, NJ

Discrimination complaint against a peer

Joan (manager): Shirley, I know that you wanted to talk to me today.
Shirley (worker): Yes, Joan, I'm very upset about what's happening on the job.
Joan: Well, I'm certainly sorry about that. What seems to be going on?
Shirley: Well, I think the other girls are making my work harder, and I think its [sic] because I'm Black. And I just can't take it anymore and I had to talk to you about it.
Joan: Well, I'm very glad you came into see me about it and I suppose there is the possibility, though we don't like to admit it, that someone would feel that way about you because you're Black, but there's also, I guess, the possibility that some of the problems come from just being new on the job and…
Shirley: Well, I'm the only Black in the office and Sheila's newer than I am and she doesn't have that kind of problem.
Joan: Well, tell me how it came about. Probably something must have happened today to make you especially concerned and upset. …
(Shirley then explains being excluded, ostracized, and not getting assistance in her daily work requirements.)
Joan: Shirley, might there be anything that I've done to contribute to this situation?
Shirley: Well, I don't know if you've done anything, directly, but maybe you could have some more formal meetings, for example with the communications thing? Tell-

ing us where things are in the file, and how we go about getting them so I wouldn't have to rely on someone telling me where the information in the file is.

Joan: That's a good point. In other words, something like a short meeting on a series of maybe Friday mornings when we're not quite as busy as usual, and exchange information, whose [sic] getting what data, what is already in the file, where do you get material, would this help?

Shirley: Yeah, that would be really good. I think that would help me a whole lot. A great deal.[32]

Shirley's discrimination complaint and Joan's "sensitive listening" lead to an increase in the various forms of bureaucratic work rules. Instead of reprimanding or disciplining employees for making Shirley's job more difficult, Joan proposes more meetings, a system for formalizing procedures that were previously informal, and a way to oversee these new systems in order to make Shirley less dependent upon social supports deemed both hostile and unchangeable. For this video, the "learning points" encourage the supervisor to acknowledge workers' feelings and find a solution. These are certainly fine goals. Joan's sympathetic but pragmatic approach to racism shows viewers how to be efficient and rational about race and gender and other issues of a "personal" nature. The positive affirmations of the discrimination complaints are coupled with a response to problems on the job, however, that *ignores* racism as either a social or a legal issue, only to address it in terms of productivity. Joan at one point comments, "I can see how that might be upsetting, particularly if it affects your job," opting instead for the implementation of rules and hierarchies that *reduce* worker autonomy on the job. In the case of management, video interactive technologies involving sociological communication actually circumvent emotional relationships through bureaucratic practices.

We should remember that this transference of social difference into work rules was practiced in the context of efforts to internally promote minorities and women into the managerial ranks. The training session of this video program was to teach minorities and women to speak from a position that was unidentified with their race or gendered position. One SRT video has a woman manager speaking to a subordinate about his difficulties in being managed by a woman. As the learning points instruct, the woman sympathizes with the man who tells her, "I just can't get used to the fact of you being a female." The manager goes so far as to agree with the employee's sentiment by noting that she too is not comfortable with her new authority. This sequence concludes with a less cut-and-dried rule-making conclusion, but with the employee agreeing to try harder. The moral of an exchange like this seems to be simply not to take social difference seriously, only performance difference.

The SRT videos highlight how media is useful for asking questions about the political problems and possibilities with engineering social change. They are the largest collection of these types of videos in the AT&T collection, with dozens of vignettes that direct diverse managers in how to speak to workers and vice versa. While their effectiveness is not documented, their structure and intent is apparent. All of these videos rationalize and oversimplify human relationships, breaking them into certain component parts, language, speech, identification, and most importantly productivity. The premise of productivity is a powerful goal, allowing diverse worker identity to be integrated in to this greater goal. By streamlining interaction through the logic of productivity – but in a language of intimacy, i.e., personal interaction on a television screen – industry has been able to meaningfully impact diversity consciousness while limiting any meaningful change in the social structure of capitalism.

"Unseen and unnoticed": COMMUNICATION OBSTACLES FOR WOMEN AND MINORITIES

The final video I would like to examine in some detail was written and narrated by an engineer who worked at Bell Laboratories. This video shows a level of theoretical sophistication concerning the experience of race and gender within an engineering population that reflects a critical self-awareness, and still remains strictly within the goals and limitations of corporate identification and the logic of productivity. COMMUNICATION OBSTACLES FOR WOMEN AND MINORITIES[33] is essentially a lecture by one engineer who explains his personal experiences of discrimination in the upper echelons of the Bell Company as a prototype for others. John Pan's narrative is sociologically informed and uses both popular how-to-succeed texts and social critiques of what he describes as "the dominant white society."

Pan presents the experience of being an "other" in the workplace in four stages: exhilaration about success, self-doubt when confronted with a variety of slights and insults, anger that accompanies the realization that these are phenomena related to being of a different race than the "dominant white-male culture," and finally, acceptance, when he recognized these problems as "communication obstacles" that could be addressed with a variety of coping strategies that will increase the possibilities of being understood, accepted, and successful. Pan is both critical and assimilationist, arguing that certain skills and behaviors are necessary for functioning within the dominant culture. The focus of his presentation is on speaking at meetings.

Figure 4 COMMUNICATION OBSTACLES FOR WOMEN AND MINORITIES *(1983)*

AT&T Archives and History Center, Warren, NJ

John Pan: After I make an important statement at the meeting, the conversation could go on as if I never existed. The humiliation of being unseen and unnoticed is that later another person could say the same thing, sometimes word for word, and that would be greeted with general enthusiasm. Even now, sad to say, I still encounter this.

One can certainly imagine a conversation like this taking place in Western Electric's support group for developing managers, as early as the 1960s. This kind of personal testimonial video was a lesson in economic citizenship or the primacy of productivity over social change. Pan's presentation is practical and compelling in its own right; however, it brings to light many of the strange marriages between the rights of a citizen made possible with broader social changes and the limitations to those rights within the demands of capitalism. It is also a critique that takes into account a broad range of differences from both women and minorities, even as he provides personal stories and specific skills. Women, Pan notes, were fortunate for having the tools from feminist popular culture, such as BETTY HARIGAN'S GAMES MOTHER NEVER TAUGHT YOU. Also, African-Americans developed the skills to dress necessary for corporate power brokering. Power was cultural, and Pan, in this video, addressed minorities and women, but also occasionally included white men in the audience. With this mix-and-match approach to power behaviors at Bell Labs (attempted with much less appeal and nuance in SRT videos), Pan provides a socially constructed model of "whiteness," "maleness," and "Americanness" as a set of learnable skills, and understands them specifically as body and language behaviors.

John Pan: Body language, the gestures and facial expressions that accompany speech, is also culture dependent and sex dependent. The speaker uses body language to supplement what is said, but the listener sees body language as confirmation of what is heard. When a style is different, for example saying "Yes" when shaking my head, unconscious suspicion sets in because the confirmation has failed. How often have you heard the remark "Something about him I don't trust" [sic]. Now why would I send a signal to nullify what I said? ... What I do now is I stand still and let the other person approach me until he or she becomes comfortable and conversation flows freely. Invariably, I become uncomfortable but I realize that better to communicate than to be comfortable myself. Eye-movement [sic] and eye-contact is another example. I consciously maintain continuous eye contact. My reward is the trust and attention I would not otherwise get. Would I be a less truthful person if I reverted to my old habit of averting others' gaze?

The uses of the instructional video to shape the working body have come full circle, as a manager of color explains the language codes of whiteness to other colleagues of different races, genders and ethnicity. "Cultural bias" is not longer the problem but the solution, as long as everybody knows the code. Still, learning to behave in white, male, American corporate culture is not without its price. Pan does not minimize the cost, but argues that there is no other option. White male culture at Bell Labs is not changing anytime soon, as he states simply:

> *John Pan*: I sympathize with the notion that the dominant culture should change to accommodate to the culture of minorities and women for the benefit of everyone as well as the company. To think that this will happen however is to ignore reality.

Economic citizenship, as Pan recognizes here, as black Western Electric employees recognized years earlier, was about productivity. The degree to which it was about civil rights, or at least equity, was limited. The central crux of Pan's discussion addresses learning the skills of a white speaker in a meeting. The central argument of the video is that it is necessary to learn to speak "white," and to speak it with a particular physical style and presence, within an environment that favors white men speaking – specifically the meeting culture of the Bell Labs. He begins with a story of silence, how he was ignored, patronized, and dismissed when he spoke at meetings. He then explains these painful moments with a discussion of "ritual," animal-dominance behavior, and costume, and American dismissiveness of those who do not display this same behavior. In order to be heard, to eliminate the "communication obstacles," one must learn to imitate these rituals of dominance. That these rituals often include offensive behavior must be critiqued and analyzed, but for the sake of communication accepted – *and emulated*:

> *John Pan*: I also follow rituals practiced by most white males before a meeting. In brief I make sure that I arrive early, preferably with a supportive friend. Then I engage in

some animated conversation with other early arrivals. I exaggerate my body move-ments. If I was scheduled for a presentation, I parade back and forth near the podium as if to set things up. This ritual serves to create an identity for me, and to expose my accent, my language style, my gestures. The importance of these rituals was brought home to me when I realized the relationship between the pre-meeting discussions and the discussions during the meeting proper. As white males stand in clusters to talk about sports or to exchange ethnic or sexist jokes they are establishing the right to speak later... I now join in the telling of bad jokes as important placeholders for more important contributions to follow.

These are disturbing results for those involved in diversity training, and it may be concluded that citizenship within the corporation was (in fact, still is) a vio-lent process. Corporate citizenship at the Bell Labs required a kind of double consciousness that saw both social inequity and social benefit. The corporate video was especially suited to the creation of this double consciousness through a kind of intimate, yet public, space. In the semipublic-yet-personal setting of managerial meetings and diversity training difference was translated into an explicit performance of whiteness and capitalist productivity was maintained. While, as Estlund has argued, this approach has served to make the workplace one of the preeminent arenas for integration, it also has set a high price for this mix.

Conclusion

To miss the bargaining over social organization that occurs in therapeutic med-ia and other means of diversity training means to miss many of the ways that contemporary US corporate culture has disseminated models of laissez-faire ci-tizenship throughout popular culture. Private media narratives have become a part of public discourse as well, informing how contemporary popular culture has learned to narrate itself in the therapeutic mode. Affirmative-action videos have been used to set the boundaries of change for corporate as well as a larger part of US culture. AT&T videos have been part of the rationalization of human interaction in such a way that the economic is privileged over the social. They can also be seen to have popularized a therapeutic, sociological imagination. In addition to video training that strictly delimits interactions we also find training videos produced by minority employees that show the degree to which these sociological skills of observation have become skills of assimilating oneself within the corporation. Psychological tools found in the media products I am discussing, as well as other forms of human-relations training, have become a part of explaining and governing difference inside organizations. The general familiarity of a management class with these tools, as well as their academic legitimacy, can potentially be understood to have created a space for at least a discussion of economic citizenship for women and minorities. In an era where economic segregation has taken the place of legal segregations, this is an important accomplishment. However, this raises questions about the degree to which this partial, limited economic citizenship may indeed legitimize social segregation. There are no large-scale studies about the circulation of management ideology in public discourses at this time, but it seems reasonable to suppose that, when integration requires such substantial sacrifices of the self, it has limited appeal as a solution to larger social or political inequities.

All of these videos have concentrated on language systems and speech. They have played within the common context of the Bell System and its initiative to implement affirmative action in response to federal regulation stemming from the Equal Opportunity Act of 1964. I am mostly concerned with presenting these products as moments of corporate speech that impact citizenship. This is certainly not because they are moments of liberating speech, but precisely because they are not. Citizenship and the public speech that often contributes to its construction is not always the product of a public sphere of free and non-coercive speech. An examination of the Bell System's industrial media does expose the limitations of leaving the governance of social relationships to corporations who are deeply and finally committed to the economic, rather than the political citizen. It also shows how the political interventions into the corporations influence the creation of the economic citizen along the way to the social citizen.

Lasch-Quinn's anger about these practices is not without its appeal. But has public debate ever been as bloodless as her alternative of rationally considered political debate implies? We currently speak to each other almost perpetually, on cell phones, the Internet, voice mail, television, talk radio, audio books, and so on. These intimate but technological talk systems are also part of the contemporary political discourse.

Training in self-analysis, ritual, and discursive conformance may support larger goals of citizenship as it serves to create certain sociological skills of the self. Still, the video indoctrination products discussed in this article illustrate that these are not fundamentally liberating skills and that they are skills for participation in a corporate rather then a civic public.

Notes

1. I would like to acknowledge Matthew Stahl's suggestion of this title.
2. See Phyllis A. Wallace (ed.), *Equal Employment Opportunity and the A.T.&T. Case* (Cambridge, Massachusetts: MIT Press, 1976); Venus Green, *Race on the Line: Gender, Labor and Technology in the Bell System, 1880-1980* (Durham, NC, and London: Duke University Press, 2001).
3. The Bell System was the largest corporation in the world for much of the 20th century, this was possible because of the depth and breadth of their monopoly over telecommunications, with Western Electric as their manufacturing division, Bell Labs as the research division, and the Long Lines and local companies cooperating on the maintenance of the legally established "special relationship," or legal monopoly, with the US government. The company's status was legitimated through the logic of "natural monopoly" when particular services are considered so necessary to infrastructure and basic public utilities which would not be as well produced through unfettered competition.
4. Michael Schudson, *The Good Citizen: A History of American Civic Life* (New York, etc.: Martin Kessler Books, The Free Press, 1998), pp. 265-266.
5. Western Electric, *Joint Statement on "Plan for Progress." Plan for Progress. E. E. Opportunity* (unpublished manuscript, Western Electric: 3, Corporate Film Collection/AT&T Archives, 1961).
6. AT&T, "Audio Productions" treatment for THE GREAT UPHEAVAL, p.2.
7. Green, op. cit., p. 212.
8. See Green, op. cit.
9. John Brooks, *Telephone: The First Hundred Years. The Wondrous Invention That Changed a World and Spawned a Corporate Giant* (New York: Harper & Row, 1975/1976), p. 326.
10. AT&T Long Lines/Richard Hough, AFFIRMATIVE ACTION, US Corporate Communication, AT&T Corporate Collection, Archives, 1969-1970: 20:00.
11. According to the film narration it was originally "recorded on tape The fact that there is a film record of this video, which includes a very brief descriptive voice over added to the original video that indicates how and where it was used, is in itself significant: the film clearly exists to document the videotape and the efforts of the company in order to limit legal liability – the presence of a film copy also shows how at this time video was still a very new technology, with film still the preferred and more accessible form of documentation. So, while video was used to speak to an audience of upper-level management, the film would possibly be shown to federal EEOC officials.
12. See Green, op. cit.
13. Western Electric Corporate Education Training Center, WESTERN ELECTRIC CO. EQUAL OPPORTUNITY POLICY AND TERMINOLOGY, Western Electric Collection/AT&T Archives, 1975: 10:00.
14. AT&T Long Lines/Richard Hough, Affirmative Action, US Corporate Communication, AT&T Corporate Collection, Archives.
15. Wallace, op. cit.
16. Stephen B. Adams, Orville R. Butler, *Manufacturing the Future. A History of Western Electric* (Cambridge: Cambridge University Press 1999), p. 181.

17. Adams, Butler, op. cit., p. 182.

18. Visible in the video Western Electric, Hawthorne's Corrective Action Program-CAP, The Hawthorne Works, Hawthorne Collection/AT&T Archives, 1979: 21:00.

19. Western Electric, *Assorted Documents related to the Plans for Progress: Letters from W.E. President to President Johnson, Plan for Progress, Joint Statement, Memo to Supervisors from H.I. Romnes*, Corporate Film Collection/AT&T Archives, 1961-64.

20. Elizabeth Lasch-Quinn, *Race Experts: How Racial Etiquette, Sensitivity Training, and New Age Therapy Hijacked the Civil Rights Revolution* (New York and London: W.W. Norton & Company, 2001).

21. Lasch-Quinn, op. cit., p. xi.

22. Lasch-Quinn, op. cit., p. 191.

23. Lasch-Quinn, op. cit., pp. 108-109.

24. Cynthia Estlund, *Working Together: How Workplace Bounds Strengthen a Diverse Democracy* (Oxford/New York: Oxford University Press, 2003).

25. Ibid., pp. 4-5.

26. Ibid., p. 78.

27. Ibid., p. 81.

28. Michael Schudson, *The Good Citizen: A History of American Civic Life* (New York, etc.: Martin Kessler Books/Free Press, 1998), p. 241.

29. John M. Stormes, James P. Crumpler, *Television for Communications Systems for Business and Industry* (New York, etc.: Wiley-Interscience, 1970).

30. Personal observation from the archival material in which SRT videos outnumbered other affirmative-action training significantly

31. This is indicated at the end of each video, and although it is not completely clear, it is common for these kinds of productions to be performed by employees. Also, general acting style/ability indicates amateur performers with managerial experience.

32. AT&T/Western Electric, S.R.T. Supervisory Relationship Training, Western Electric, AT&T, and The Bell System, Corporate Education Center: Western Electric/AT&T Corporate Archives, 1976-78.

33. John Pan/Bell Laboratories, Communication Obstacles facing Minorities and Women, Merrimack Valley Affirmative Action Advisory Committee, Bell Laboratories/AT&T Archives, 1983.

Behaviorism, Animation, and Effective Cinema

The McGraw-Hill INDUSTRIAL MANAGEMENT Film Series and the Visual Culture of Management

Ramón Reichert

After the end of World War II, new media representations of industrial work were created in the US. A new genre of industrial educational film was developed in the areas of military strategy, operations research, organization theory, and cybernetics:[1] the management film.[2] Based on the assumption that industrially disciplined work in the production process had long been established, indeed, had already become a *sui generis* social model, the management film focused instead on another aspect of productivity in industrial work: its functional and abstract regulation. Unlike other forms of the industrial film like the work-study film, the management film did not concentrate on optimizing physical processes and worker performance, but on establishing and stabilizing its functional contexts.

For this reason, conventional photographic recording methods are not dominant in management film, as are film techniques that had previously been used infrequently in industrial film, namely those of animation.[3] In order to investigate the specific visual knowledge that these films produce, it will be necessary to examine their methods of producing images and detailed communication in images. In the following essay, I would like to develop certain theoretical reflections on media and representation in management film using three theses as a guide. Central to my reflections is the film series INDUSTRIAL MANAGEMENT, which was produced by the textbook publisher McGraw-Hill and was also distributed in Europe. The theses cover the following three fields:

1. *Production context and reception history.* Taking the specific historical and media production contexts of McGraw-Hill's management films as an example, one can see the political development and historical importance of a new media format. The example chosen here is ideal in that the films of the INDUSTRIAL MANAGEMENT SERIES were not only used to educate American college students. They also made significant contributions to the importation of American management methods to Europe in the postwar period, as well as to the success of the European Recovery Program, which the US government carried out from 1947 to 1952. The program was initiated by US Secretary of

State George C. Marshall, whose name it bore in the end ("Marshall Plan"). The legal basis of the European rebuilding program was shaped by the Economic Cooperation Act, which the US Congress replaced on April 3, 1948 with the Foreign Assistance Act. Sixteen countries, Belgium, Denmark, Great Britain, France, Greece, the Netherlands, Iceland, Ireland, Italy, Luxembourg, Norway, Austria, Portugal, Sweden, Switzerland, Turkey, and beginning on June 30, 1949, West Germany also, received aid of approximately $5.3 billion until 1952. The signing of the Economic Cooperation Act required each of the European participants to put certain measures in place to raise production: the creation of internal financial stability, close economic and political cooperation with the European Duties Union, as well as the balancing of the trade deficit with the US by simultaneously raising export quotas.

2. *Effective cinema, optimized view.* If we want to elucidate film's media productive power as well as the specific structural qualities that distinguish it from other media, it serves well to work out its *rules of showing*. Seen superficially, nothing happens in the management film without cause and effect, without linear succession and continuity. The management film is an instrument of the cinematic popularization of knowledge, and if animation techniques are employed in such films for tables, registers, maps, organizational diagrams, cyclograms, and graphs, this is not only intended to construct an epistemic object, but more importantly a pedagogy of images. But what is the scope of this difference between epistemic object and the imperatives of a pedagogy of images? Films about organization and management require that abstract contents be translated into moving images, which necessitates the development of specific film strategies and narratives to generate knowledge. Namely, the spectator's attention must be drawn to decisive points, with the goal of transmitting work knowledge effectively. It was therefore necessary to develop a professionalized viewing technique, one which would have the task of directing – and controlling – the gaze. To achieve this, a procedure was borrowed from the cartoon. What in the cartoon is a technique for the entertainment of an audience of children becomes in the management film a social technique, a technique of direction and control. The pioneer of color and sound cartoons, Walt Disney, was the first to make such use of cartoon techniques when he produced educational films for the US government in the 1940s.[4]

Like the industrial educational film,[5] the management film took a behaviorist approach and then set out to condition the audience's behavior.[6] In terms of their cinematic form, however, two subspecies of industrial films can be fundamentally distinguished. The dominant means of style in the management film are animation, special effects, zooms, and wipes; they serve to direct the spectator's gaze. In the end, then, what the management film contributed to industrial pedagogy is a surplus of theatricality.

3. *Intermediality and intertextuality.* The use of established non-cinematic repertories of images like those of the allegory, the memory card, the circuit diagram, etc. as well as media formats from outside cinema such as diagrams, maps, pictograms, etc. prove to be central to the cinematic methods of the management film, particularly in serving the goal of controlling vision. At any rate, it will be shown that the film image, due to its unavoidable multiplicity of meaning and the fact that it contains multiple intertextual references and works in complex visual traditions, in the end evades the intended effect of controlling efficient readings.

Production context and reception history

In 1945, the McGraw-Hill Company, a New York-based publisher that specialized in educational materials, published the book *Industrial Organization and Management.* Two years later, in order to advertise its own textbooks and further the company's image, McGraw-Hill commissioned Transfilm Inc. to make a film version of the textbook.[7] This film was finally finished in 1951 as part of a new series. Entitled INDUSTRIAL MANAGEMENT, production began in 1950 in cooperation with leading representatives of business-management and private companies. According to the existing archival reports, the series contains 17 films made between 1950 and 1954.[8] Managers such as Lawrence L. Bethel (director of New Haven YMCA Junior College), Franklin S. Atwater (industrial engineering manager, Fafnir Beavy Company), and Harvey A. Stockman Jr. (personnel administrator, Scovill Manufacturing Company) served as regular consultants.[9] With a company history that dates back to 1888, McGraw-Hill still serves as a global provider of information services, publishing, among other things, textbooks in the areas of finance, education, and business information, as well as the most commonly used introductory work to film studies, Bordwell and Thompson's *Film Art: An Introduction.*[10] The publisher's current form is the result of the publishing houses McGraw and Hill merging in 1909, and since then it has concentrated on textbooks for college students, above all in the core areas of engineering and science. In the 1930s and 1940s, McGraw-Hill expanded into the areas of economics, management, and the social sciences. In order to reach a wider audience the publisher also invested in the production of educational films on industrial management, beginning in 1947.[11] After World War II, McGraw-Hill's textbooks were also integrated into the lesson plans of elementary and high schools. With the acquisition of the Gregg Company (a publisher of trade school textbooks) and the California Test Bureau (a developer of testing systems), the company managed to establish itself at all levels of educational publishing, from pre-school to 12th grade. In 1947, a department was founded for the internal production of educational films, McGraw-Hill Textfilms; it was placed directly under the business department of "economy and management." In this same year, the first films were also created.[12] These initial films were versions of the company's textbooks, made to reach a wider audience.[13] During World War II, McGraw-Hill cooperated with the War Department, the United States Information Service/Visual Media Section and the United States Office of Education/Division of Visual Aids.[14] These close contacts also laid the ground-work for the McGraw-Hill Company to make their educational films conform to the needs of the Marshall Plan Aid, thereby making a significant contribution to the economic Americanization of Europe.[15] As a result, the publisher was able to establish itself quite early in the European market as a provider of multimedia information in the area of industrial knowledge.

The films of the INDUSTRIAL MANAGEMENT SERIES reached a wide audience in Europe and contributed considerably to the introduction of American management methods at European companies.[16] Together with Marshall Plan Movies, they were distributed in numerous participating countries in the ERP by the European Film Unit of the Economic Cooperation Administration (ECA), located in Paris. Along with the America Houses and the Information Centers, the national productivity centers represented one of the most important institutions in the comprehensive import of American-style management.

Leading firms in the US included McGraw-Hill films in their archives and organized company screenings, which were then discussed in training courses.[17] In the Europe of the Marshall Plan, films from the INDUSTRIAL MAN-AGEMENT SERIES were introduced into various social situations. In the German-speaking context, for example, they were presented as "educational films" and "training films."[18] In general, they were used for training and further education of (future) workers. The differentiation of "education" and "training," reflected different social usages. One spoke of "educational goals" when the films were screened in schools, trade schools, and universities, and of "training goals" when the films were placed in companies, unions, and other business-related institutions. Finally, the term "further education" was used when the films were shown by non-profit organizations.[19] The same films were shown in concrete situations using different terminology; the various categories like further education and training, however, signified a different social context in each case.

Although the films of the INDUSTRIAL MANAGEMENT SERIES are not industrial films per se, produced under commission from a company, they were regularly shown at companies and business-related organizations.[20] The management films were added to a communications framework that arose from a genuine interest on the part of various businesses. As such, a film screening always initiated an attempt at social organization as well. The social and communicative setting specified learning strategies and tactics that were geared toward utilizing the film to achieve the goals of the given situation. Private companies such as Böhler, Andritz, Siemens, and Elin, for instance, started renting management films from the film service of the Austrian Productivity Center in 1951, and they were then screened in wider contexts. In discussion groups, questions that radically called the usefulness of the management principles into doubt often arose.[21] And the screening of brand new, English-language US management films during factory tours and general company meetings always produced a new social situation, through which the management tried to create social distinctions: the company presented itself as being an advanced organization at which such films were shown.[22] The creation of a company's own film archive, the acquisition of the company's own projector, the provision of a (temporary) space for the screening, as well as competent and knowledgeable assistance by a projectionist and personnel director, play an important role in the process of differentiating industrial forms of organization.

Effective cinema, optimized view

The use of films to optimize company operations can be traced back to the early 1910s and the work-study films of Frank Butler Gilbreth.[23] Study films intended to optimize industrial work are, as a rule, *films of observation*. For this reason, even after 1945 they remain closely bound to the method of the "time and motion studies" that Gilbreth had developed. Management films, on the other hand, radically break with the empirical field. The films do not examine and present physical operations, but rather the structures and formal criteria of industrial organization. While the work-study film focused on what happens on the factory floor, the management films focus on administration. Both types follow leading theories of industrial organization, if in different ways. The work-study film based its position on a project of disciplining the "individual worker" (Taylorism) with the goal of ergonomic optimization of individual production operations, and thereby also managed to contribute to the integration of individual workers into the "collective worker" (Fordism).[24]

Essentially, McGraw-Hill's management films build on Max Weber's concept of bureaucracy and classical teachings on organization.[25] In terms of film technique and cinematic stylistics, this difference is shown most noticeably in that management films are *abstract films*, in which geometric rather than organic bodies are animated. A new media apparatus for presenting and observing the company was established with the management film. There was a transition from a concrete, physical rationalization of the body on the "factory floor" to a systematic view, produced within the management film itself. In the framing story we see the disciplined worker; the actual core of the film consists in making the company's organizational structures visible. As early as the 1920s, for example at Krupp, films were produced to introduce the Hollerith Method[26] with the intention of making the administrative structures transparent to an internal audience. Even so, it was only with the massive popularization of methods and operational practices from American business in the framework of European reconstruction aid that films on industrial planning, organization, and administration were screened to a wider audience.[27]

The difference between the work-study film and the management film can also be seen in their reception and desired effect. The observation-oriented study film is intended to make the workers' bodies "motion minded":[28] In Frank and Lilian Gilbreth's films on optimizing work, this had primarily been a matter of internalizing *physical* movement. In contrast, the management film was presented in small circles of industrial and academic elites.[29] Like the study films, there was also an economy of attention; at any rate, the film took on the goal transforming the basic "attitudes" of its addressees.[30] In the management film, it was namely a matter of presenting the successful organization as being transparent and easy to organize. The appropriate methods here proved to be imaging and mapping[31] the company by means of special effects and animation. The basic profile of business pedagogy was altered through the introduction of certain animation techniques intended to reduce complexity.

The functional distinction between the goal of disciplining individual workers on the factory floor and that of normalizing administrative operations in the business then demands that the business be represented in various ways. Documentary shots of the concrete industrial location only provide the background in the industrial-management film. They serve to present the object of the administration and the industrial organization, to whose construction and stabilization the film is meant to contribute, to position it in a concrete social and historical field. The prime task of the INDUSTRIAL MANAGEMENT SERIES, in any case, consisted of bringing abstract data and contexts of business management into a graphic form that was easy to understand visually. For this reason, the dominant representational forms in the film are those drawn from the graphic visual techniques of the textbook (that is, tables, diagrams, maps of visual statistics, diagrams, organizational diagrams, descriptions of workplaces, isotype tables, matrix plans, pictograms, etc.).

I would like to clarify the specific methods of mental and visual pedagogy in the management films by analyzing an example. The film INTERNAL ORGANIZA-

TION (USA 1951) seeks to put into practice administration and management teachings that had been developed in the US and Great Britain in the 1930s and 1940s. Questions of task and department education, of administration, and problems of the business leadership and its coordination occupy the foreground. A central part of the film is dedicated to visually presenting a catalog of management functions like preliminary planning, organization, delegation of duties, coordination, and follow-up. INTERNAL ORGANIZATION consists of a framing story and a main story. The framing story shows external and internal shots of a large company, not mentioned by name, and workers punching in at a time clock. The main story consists exclusively of sketches and animated special effects. In the first part of the film, basic leadership structures are made visible, in the second the typologies and criteria of efficient personnel leadership are represented differentially, and the systematic archiving of company knowledge is discussed.

Figure 1 INTERNAL ORGANIZATION *(1951)*

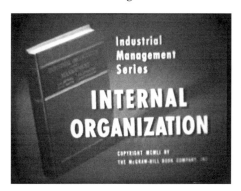

The opening title credits of INTERNAL ORGANIZATION show a book. An insert indicates that it is the source text on which the film was based. The book itself is out of focus, which provides the advantage, in terms of production and distribution, that the image of the book need not be altered when the language of the insert is changed, which happened when the film was distributed in Europe.

At the same time, however, the lack of focus also produces a symbolic charge. The fact that the book remains the same from version to version also means that it is a universally valid text, independent of specific cultural contexts. The credits are followed by four scenes of workers entering the factory. There is an establishing external shot of an unnamed factory as well as scenes showing forms of the division of labor and the smooth operations inside the factory. The visual material was drawn from archival material or found footage shot in documentary style. In the images' interplay, the male voice-over establishes the univers-

ality of the topics "management" and "organization" and refers to the "necessity" of modern organizational culture. This is followed by a caesura, which is
announced by a cartoon. The commentary presents the programmatics of the
film and turns to the question of how people and things can be regulated and
administered and how these elements can be made operable in the space of the
company. We see an animated sequence of images which establishes a recording matrix and creates the possibility for administration and regulation, a space
that is particularly well suited to the representation of administration and personnel management. The structure of the matrix forms a line diagram, arranged
in a pyramid: a small leadership staff oversees many workers, and communication proceeds from the top down. The presentation therefore follows the rules
that have been put forward in the McGraw-Hill guidelines, which are geared
toward a cinematic *Verlebendigung des Lehrbuchs* (bringing the textbook to life
with cinematic means).[32] Seen pedagogically, the methods direct the gaze and
shut out alternative readings. One could speak in this context of a social technique of "correct" memory training which makes use primarily of two cinematic
methods:

1. *The successive construction of images*. The animated diagram of the company's
    hierarchy comprises elements, fields, and vectors.[33] The tableau is set up suc-
    cessively and, as a rule, opened with an element (e.g., General Manager) or a
    field (e.g., Management, consisting of the Advisory Board and the General
    Manager). The commentary prepares the subsequent visual statement (ele-
    ment/field) immediately beforehand. Then the element or field is put into a
    relationship with another element or field, as a rule by means of a vector that
    ties both visual statements together. Additionally, a continuous deficit of in-
    formation is generated through the unchanged camera position and the si-
    multaneous reduction of the image (cut in). Control of the gaze here means
    that the recipient's should not "wander around" the table, but should be led
    in a step-by-step method.[34]

2. *The zoom*. A second relevant method of directing the gaze is the zoom to a
    certain detail in the table. The zoom is a gestural method of emphasis: an
    element is placed in the midpoint, giving it special meaning. What is signifi-
    cant here is that in the film examined, zooming only occurs on the upper
    level of the hierarchy (Manager). The "worker," located in the lower third of
    the table, does not receive such treatment. The zoom is also usually used to
    prepare the exit from the table. The zoom, for example, goes from a box en-
    titled Advisory Board into a cartoon that shows top management gathered
    around a table. The spectator may recognize him or herself and the wider
    circles of the film's addressees in those represented, which we could call a
    kind of identificatory viewing.

Such cinematic methods of directing the gaze, as could be maintained in relation to Bruno Latour's reflections on viewing in the sciences, add up to a reading apparatus, aimed as a whole at controlling the gaze.[35] The McGraw-Hill films use techniques like the successive setup of the image and the zoom as *cinematic gestures of showing*. In the guidelines, it is noted that "the spectator should only perceive what is relevant for him in each situation."[36] In addition to directing the gaze, the management film also makes use of strategies like introducing overly clear distinctions, concentrating on the most essential and most easily comprehensible, while all these strategies make graphic representation – as opposed to photographic "illustration" – the starting point of the pedagogical argument.[37] Like all graphic devices,[38] *how* they can be viewed or perceived is precisely established through the construction of the organizational diagrams. At this point, another genuine cinematic technique comes into play, namely special effects. They transform the multidimensionality of the organizational diagrams and tables into a precise representation of speech, that is, they translate the linear succession of spoken arguments into an interplay of image and voice-over commentary. This means that, at first, we never see the entire table, just a portion of it. Every subsequent and additional visual element is simultaneously commented upon by the voice-over: *Image*: Manager – *Voice-over*: "The tasks of the manager are..." – *Image*: arrow vector – *Voice-over*: "The leadership of..."

The coordination of animation and commentary is meant to prohibit the graphics from being read in different ways. In the second part of the film, lists of categories are introduced in order to arrange the decisive criteria of linear organization according to their relevance. The table of categories is also intended to generalize the characteristics of effective organization and contribute to the further abstraction of the company. This table is a representational method that belongs to the technique of synopsis. It makes hierarchies comprehensible and, in the case of the example examined here, gives the viewer an overview of all types, methods, and solutions in question. The stylistic table of the management film corresponds completely to the Taylorist workplace. The superfluous does not appear; the visual tools are organized by goal; the way film methods are utilized target the optimization of performance exclusively, in this case conveying knowledge, and the spectator is directed by the film in a similar way to the work-study film, which contains concrete references to optimization. So, in the visual pedagogical succession, for example, ([close up] gaze toward A [pan] follow the arrow to B [zoom] watch B).

According to information provided in Internal Organization, the exemplary business can be recognized above all by a working hierarchy of command. This is presented in line and hierarchical diagrams.[39] Its Lines of Responsibility[40] mean that each spot arranged in a hierarchy can receive instructions from a higher authority only. The elements, therefore, are always arranged from the bottom up or rather from the top down. The construction of this organizational diagram is strictly symmetrical in the horizontal direction and strictly asymmetrical in the vertical direction (top down). In the course of legitimizing clear chains of command, "clear" leadership is in the end distinguished from "unclear" leadership. This qualitative difference is made visible through meandering curves ("ineffective") and straight lines ("effective"). What is most noticeable in this context is the wide use of elementary graphic techniques: lines and arrows have varying widths, making self-evident statements – the difference in their intensities remains limited to speculations such as "important/less important" or "main/secondary direction." The linking of linear and circular ideas that double back (which are generally presented by McGraw-Hill by a dotted line) connotes ideas of the methodic, the successive, and the ability to program operations, also creating the image of a perpetual circulation of work.

The medium of animation unites the expressive means of the most varied art forms: painting, literature, graphics, and typography. If film is the medium of moving images in their temporal succession, then animation is perhaps the sub-species in which the possibilities of the medium can be used most consistently, since the filmmaker who works in animation – at least in manually produced animation as was common until the mid 1990s – works on each individual image personally. He or she can therefore achieve such precision in detail and has so much control over representation that, in educational films in particular, a thought can be brought to an exact point, which the use of conventional photographic images does not allow as easily. It is precisely these factors that make animation the preferred stylistic and communicational method of management films concerned with efficiency, and it is precisely these factors that explain why even INDUSTRIAL ORGANIZATION employs a great deal of animation effects.

The cinematic management discourse makes extensive use of the principle of modeling and simulation, and therefore anticipates *scientific modeling*, that is, the *computer-generated visualization* of digital data.[41] As is the case with virtual simulation, management films focused not on illustrating the business world, but putting a normative model of the business organization into play and of making it manifest and useful through modeling. The simulation then creates affirmations in cinematic management discourse, not of what it is, but in view of what it could become.

It is then only to be expected that, in management films like INTERNAL ORGANIZATION, the classic dichotomies of distinguishing the form of content and expression, or of a discursive formation like the language of efficiency and a visible, physically material space of reference like the factory building, would tend to disappear. The manager, as he appears in the management film, is oriented toward the table and does not phenomenologically make a distinction between the behavior of the workforce and the mathematical optimizing functions of the organizational planner. In the course of a development that began in the middle of the 19th century with the introduction of media technologies like the telephone, the telegraph, and the typewriter,[42] the space of business and ultimately of political decisions was also provided with a new symbolic foundation. The ideal of realtime modeling of all business operations soon formed the horizon more than it corresponded to the requirements of a running evaluation of company performance, which had previously been the domain of the financial markets.

Figure 2 Effective leadership in INTERNAL ORGANIZATION

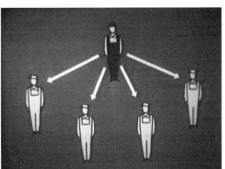 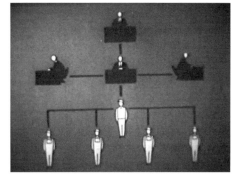

Decisions were therefore not oriented to the "material substance" of company operations, but instead to their media modeling, to relational elementary time functions, efficiency coefficients, and performance indicators, whose standardization, on the other hand, requires a complete statistical investigation of elementary operations and the company's micro-relationships. In order to organize and predict production in the most efficient way, it is no longer enough to merely arrange, classify, or sound out a company's empirical data. The data must be brought into numerically legible form, mutually comparable, which makes possible a form of relations, only expressible and visible within this symbolic space of numbers, which can be used as the basis of business leadership. In the end, the business is organized as a form of relations; the stock of machines, tools, the warehouse stock, and the production waste, the gestures, body language, and reaction time of the workforce, up to the monetary flow of sales, income, and of accounts receivable, all of this finally creates – in representation and in a "reality" that can no longer be separated and divided from this – a singular functional ensemble of relationships.

Intermediality and intertextuality

As was made clear in the previous section, the animated tables from INTERNAL
ORGANIZATION are responsible for putting into play *the necessary succession of the
argument in images*. In order to increase, first, the iconic representation of sug-
gestivity and, second, the ability to remember the material taught, every visual
multiplicity was to be avoided wherever possible. In this central point of their
image pedagogy, McGraw-Hill and Transfilm make explicit reference to the
"speaking signatures" developed by Otto Neurath in his visual statistics.[43] In
the "guidelines for the correct use of the teaching material" from McGraw-Hill,
Manager and Worker are also called "speaking figures."[44] Animation filmmakers and engineers modeled these visualizations of "behavior in social roles"
on the "common experience that we have today in the cinema."[45] The development of a social typology according to models borrowed from the cinema is,
however, in no way new. Otto Neurath himself had established a close connection between cinema and visual pedagogy as early as 1925. He derives his visual pedagogical method from the premise that the "modern man is very
spoiled by cinema and illustrations": the advantages of "optical impressions"[46]
should be exploited to popularize social topics. The visual language developed
by Neurath in his Vienna Method served the iconic transmission of sociological
data and was therefore meant to increase the visibility of visual argumentation.
How can visual pedagogy solve the problem that a few managers must deal
with a large number of workers in industrial production? In INTERNAL ORGANI-
ZATION, the larger number of workers is not represented by a larger figure; the
figures are instead multiplied. Furthermore, one can speculate about whether
political concerns played a role in this decision. Undoubtedly, "the worker"
would have been more significant politically if the mass of workers were represented by a figure, larger in both scale and volume. That such an effect was not
necessarily desirable in the US in the 1940s and 1950s goes without saying.

   McGraw-Hill's visual pedagogical program, however, proves to be contradictory in several respects. On the one hand, the film is meant to speak without
words, that is, to create unmediated evidence, on the other, the deciphering of
images that channel understanding buries, through the commentary that
McGraw-Hill provides, precisely this demand for unmediated understanding.[47]
The fact that the images always contain text and are also described in a voice-
over is not least an indicator of the equally unwanted and unavoidable multiple
meanings of visual symbols. An efficient cinema for managers can obviously
not be satisfied with the fact that images are seen any old way. It does not get
by without a "literal" codifying of the film image, as is intended in INTERNAL
ORGANIZATION. The intention is to add visuality to a "readable text."[48] The

images should be read *correctly*, and to ensure this, the eye must be given in-structions. Walter Benjamin described captions as "directives"[49] that stipulate how the viewer should receive the image. At any rate, the multiple meanings in visual language cannot be so easily eliminated by a simply authorial gesture. Visual signs constantly refer to symbolic and allegorical fields of meaning, which, for their part, are interwoven into certain historical and cultural contexts. Paradoxically, however, the gesture of unified meaning alone is what introduces multiple meanings into the field of visual pedagogy.

An aperçu of Rebis Debray's may clarify this: "When the mediologist meets someone who's pointing to the moon, he does not look at the moon, but at the finger and the gesture of showing."[50] The gesture of directing attention always implies, in other words, that directing the eyes *toward* something simulta-neously entails directing them *away* from something else. In its attempt to do-mesticate the visual potential for meaning, business visual pedagogy becomes the showplace of a cultural transformation. Ideals of business efficiency run up against the borders of culturally sanctioned methods of evidence, on which they still rely for their transmission.[51]

The structurally determined precariousness of the correct coding of the film image can be seen from the following observations. The voice-over in INTERNAL ORGANIZATION insistently claims that a successful organizational theory must take into account every concrete and individual view of its objects and subjects. But the attempt to put the film image into such a programmatic is itself avoided by the visual. Let us attempt, then, to "describe" the image differently, in a way that takes into account the excess of the visual. The visual shape of INTERNAL ORGANIZATION has a leitmotiv: workers are consistently presented as faceless figures; while male management staff, on the other hand, have faces. Further-more, the manager appears as an active figure in the diegesis of the film, and he is given his own gaze, as is typical for film characters. This is managed by means of a media caesura. The narration privileges the manager by having him appear in a cartoon as a singular figure. In contrast to the faceless workers, this figure has a comparatively distinguishable psychology. This is shown in a med-ium shot and expressed mimetically and gesturally. The manager is persona-lized, as opposed to the workers. At the same time, he becomes part of a com-plex staging of gazes. The task of the narrative is, as has been indicated above, directing and channeling the manager's gaze, that is, the gaze of the intended audience. In the film, the figure of the manager is accompanied by his gaze, what is directed toward the image is now inside the image. The spectator is duplicated in the film via the narrating figure of identification, which strength-ens the attachment to the spectator and, at the same time, legitimizes narrative authority: indeed, it speaks through the spectator to the spectator, or rather through his animated representative, the cartoon manager.

The guidelines of the McGraw-Hill films, consistently following commercial interests, are marked by an attempt to legitimize and increase the social value of the management film: "The management film is a medium of culture. Its mission is to create an image of modern management according to which man and machine are equally important as factors of the successful enterprise."[52] In other words, the management film takes on the goal of anchoring the premises of organizational theory that had been formulated since the twenties in a general discourse of business culture. Along with this profession of business culture there is also a hidden dimension in the image that is only implicitly communicated: in the cinema for the manager, disciplining the film image necessarily means concealing social power relationships. In INTERNAL ORGANIZATION, the static organizational diagram is dominant. Nothing, or so it seems, disturbs the unified linear order that was determined by invisible demiurges. An intertextually motivated examination, however, can problematize the unspoken subtext of the images, which seem not to allow any further explanation in their evidence.

Let us begin with the matrix of forms of expression in INTERNAL ORGANIZATION. Here the symbolic language of forms is limited to a few geometric figures. There is the rectangular, the regular and the irregular, the linear, the open, and the closed. The elements are the rectangle, the line, the speaking figure, as well as various forms of written commentary in the image. How elementary connotations are established by means of simple geometric figures is decisive here:

1. The *stable* and *unchanging* is shown in square frames. This framing stands for a firm position in business practice and marks a logical point. It presents the determinant from which a dynamic is developed that can most likely be modeled theoretically and is expressed within the framework of the film's representational system. The symbolic form of the rectangle, on the other hand, is intended to create the impression of closure and completeness.

2. The *vague* and *undetermined* is marked by round forms. Serpentine lines resemble mythological images of nature (snakes) and code them as ambiguous and potentially harmful.

Using this visual formal canon, which runs through the entire matrix, the film establishes a world of order, connection, and working together, of the consequential and the continuous.

In the tables, the basic pattern of the pyramid-shaped order of organization is dominant. The film image is therefore positioned fundamentally: the vertical lines code the social superiority of the Manager over the Worker. The Worker can be found at the bottom of the vertical line, above him the Foreman, Plant Manager, and others. Still higher is the President, and above the Board of Directors. In other tables of linear organization in the same film, the positions are even more radically situated: a lone, ruling General Manager has a Superintendent and three Foremen under him, and there are three Workers beneath each of the individual Foremen. The distinction between Manager and Worker is reflected in a subtly formed, unnoticeable difference in the fades. A slow, faint fade is used when leadership tasks are discussed, a jumpy hard fade is employed when the "lower" duties of subordinate workers are dealt with.

Difference is also created by means of posture: The Worker symbol shows a figure in the posture of someone receiving a command, the demanded attention to the superior's instructions being presented as a constant given.[53] The Manager, on the other hand, is shown sitting with another attribute of power and rights over the workforce placed beneath him, namely the desk. In this way the dichotomy of tasks involving mental and physical labor reflects the spatial hierarchy of everything in the tables, that is, its matrix. The ruling relationships in the business are also depicted abstractly: Vertical relationships (e.g., the Leadership Lines between Foreman and Worker) are represented by even, thick lines. Horizontal relationships, termed Cooperation, are drawn as dotted lines. These so-called Lines of Participation signal an open channel of communication. What is decisive, however, is that the vertical, constant lines suggest a stronger bond by virtue of their shape. The line diagram itself is by no means free of historical requirements. Namely, it presents the business within a visual rhetoric of origin, adaptation, and evolution. The simple experience of workers form something like the organic foundation of the business, which grows steadily through the mental achievements of the well-educated leadership, who translate the workers' experiential knowledge into intellectual achievements. But there is yet another visual tradition that should be more closely examined here: the technical drawing. The linear organizational diagrams in INTERNAL ORGANIZATION suggest an ideal totality, regularity, and simultaneity of all aspects and functions of the business. A central part of this control fantasy is the assumption of the universal, normative effectiveness of suggestive images, which seems to be presented by the animated tables. Their power of suggestion relates these images not least to the fact that they use the style of technical designs. They map out the social relationships within the business according to the model of a circuit diagram or blueprint, which also makes sense because, in a world of circuitry symbols, creating order must be possible at any time, as would be the case with a real circuit. Due to this coding of the business as serially produced software, INTERNAL ORGANIZATION connects in large part to a visual tradition of the all-knowing gaze, a tradition which includes the blueprint of the ideal city as much as the tree chart or even the technical drawing of circuitry.[54] In organization theory, questions regarding systems and models, regulation, circular causality, feedback, equilibrium adaptation, and control have been rampant since the 1920s – questions that should have become problems of action-oriented cybernetics.[55] Long before the use of the information theories of cybernetics, systems analysis, and operations research, an increasing methodologization, technologization, and concretization of knowledge and activity took place within organization theory. With the codification of business organizational units not only was a rational model of business put in place, there was a similar attempt to direct the reception of the films by drawing figures that were "correct" and "conformed to regulations." Information that gets lost or falsified during a film viewing should be integrated into the information process by means of redundant feedback loops (overviews by the projectionist, distribution of questionnaires after the screening, discussions led by experts, requests for suggestions for improvement, etc.).

Conclusion

As I have attempted to show, it is no coincidence that the management film systematically uses animation effects to represent business. Through the stylistic means of camera work and animation techniques used in McGraw-Hill films, the tendency toward abstraction of business operations, which has increased since the middle of the 19th century, has been modified in reception and aesthetics. The use of animation effects suggests an omnipotent ability to plan and administer all possible resources without going into the actualities of a concrete, individual business.

Furthermore, however, it proves to be the ideal cinematic means of realizing the project of an actual "Taylorization of the gaze," which can be detected throughout the INDUSTRIAL MANAGEMENT SERIES. The visual pedagogy of films like INTERNAL ORGANIZATION is oriented toward a particular goal: rationalizing the cinema experience. At the same time, however, the graphic language of forms in the management film furthers and transforms a series of cultural oppositions that draw on the visual pedagogical codification of educational films and undermine the informationally and organizationally strategic placement of goals at many points. Or, turning once more to a formulation suggested above: the ideal of business efficiency in the management films, as is the case elsewhere in business communication, is limited by the culturally codified representational methods on which it relies for its transmission.

Notes

1. Cf. Agatha C. Hughes, Thomas P. Hughes (eds.), *Systems, Experts, and Computers: The Systems Approach in Management and Engineering, World War II and After* (Cambridge: MIT Press, 2000); see on the historical debate Stafford Beer, *Cybernetics and Management* (New York: John Wiley & Sons, 1959); Stafford Beer, *Decision and Control: The Meaning of Operational Research and Management Cybernetics* (London and New York: John Wiley & Sons, 1966).
2. Cf. Robert A. Reiser, "A history of instructional design and technology. Part I: A history of instructional media," *Educational Technology Research and Development*, 49, 1 (2001), pp. 53-64.
3. See Michael Eraut, "Educational technology: Definition and conceptual background," in Tjeerd Plomp, Donald P. Ely (eds.), *International Encyclopedia of Educational Technology* (Oxford: Pergamon, 1996), pp. 1-17.
4. Cf. Lisa Cartwright, Brian Goldfarb, "Cultural Contagion: On Disney's Health Education Films for Latin America," in Eric Smoodin (ed.), *Disney Discourse* (New York and London: Routledge, 1994), pp. 169-180; on visual pedagogy in general, see Brian Goldfarb, *Visual Pedagogy: Media Cultures of Education in and Beyond the Classroom* (Durham, NC: Duke University Press, 2002).
5. Gottfried Boehm's classification of the images of science as "performative and utility images" represents, in my opinion, the common characteristic of the educational film. Cf. Gottfried Boehm, "Zwischen Auge und Hand: Bilder als Instrumente der Erkenntnis," in Bettina Heintz, Jörg Huber (eds.), *Mit dem Auge denken. Strategien der Sichtbarmachung in wissenschaftlichen und virtuellen Welten* (Zurich and New York: Springer, 2001), p. 53.
6. John K. Burton, David M. Moore, Susan G. Magliaro, "Behaviorism and instructional technology," in David H. Jonasen (ed.), *Handbook of Research for Educational Communications and Technology* (New York: Macmillan, 1996), pp. 46-73; Peggy Ertmer, Timothy J. Newby, "Behaviorism, Cognitivism, Constructivism: Comparing critical features from an instructional design perspective," *Performance Improvement Quarterly* 6, 4 (1993), pp. 50-71. Paul Saettler, *The Evolution of American Educational Technology* (Englewood: Information Age Publishing, 1998), pp. 268-317.
7. McGraw-Hill (ed.), *Index to 16mm Educational Films, National Information Center for Educational Media* (University of Southern California, New York: McGraw-Hill, 1967), p. 7.
8. McGraw-Hill (ed.), *McGraw-Hill Films: Film Catalog of Motion Pictures including Selected Releases from Contemporary Films* (New York, n.d.), p. 47.
9. Credits, INDUSTRIAL MANAGEMENT SERIES.
10. Gary J. Anglin, *Instructional Technology: Past, Present, and Future* (Englewood: Information Age Publishing, 1968), p. 189; David Bordwell, Kristin Thompson, *Film Art. An Introduction* (10th edition, Boston: McGraw-Hill, 2008).
11. Charles F. Hoban, *The State of the Art of Instructional Films* (Stanford: ERIC Clearinghouse on Media and Technology, 1971), p. 157; Edward B. Van Ormer, *Instructional Film Research, 1918-1950* (New York: Arno Press, 1972), pp. 274 f.
12. The first film series was called ENGINEERING DRAWINGS SERIES and began with the film ENGINEERING DRAWING (US 1947, b&w, 15 min., 16mm).

13. Saettler, op. cit., p. 179.

14. Ibid., p. 44.

15. McGraw-Hill Films (ed.), *Guidelines*, n.d., p. 6.

16. Film Section, Information Division, Special Representative in Europe (ed.), *Catalogue of Information Films Produced in Europe for the Marshall-Plan 1948-1953* (Washington, D.C., 1954), pp. 167 f.

17. Paul Saettler, *The Evolution of American Educational Technology* (Englewood: Information Age Publishing, 1998), p. 180.

18. McGraw-Hill Films (ed.), *Guidelines*, n.d., p. 6.

19. Ibid.

20. Cf. the results of audience research in Austria in the period from 1951-1953 in Ramón Reichert, "Die Popularisierung der Produktivität. Die Filme des Österreichischen Produktivitätszentrums 1950-1987. Ein Beitrag zur Diskussion um den Film als historische Quelle," in Österreichische Akademie der Wissenschaften (ed.), *Relation. Medien, Gesellschaft, Geschichte* 2, 7 (2000), pp. 105-08.

21. Österreichisches Produktivitäts-Zentrum (ed.), *Produktivität. Mitteilungen* 6, 3 (1952), p. 3.

22. See the regularly printed readers' letter and reports about the film screenings of INTERNAL ORGANIZATION (1951), PHYSICAL FACILITIES (1951), METHODS ANALYSIS (1951), JOB EVALUATION (1952) and MATERIAL CONTROL (1952) in Österreichisches Produktivitätszentrum (ed.), *Der Schlüssel*, vols. 1951-53.

23. In *Motion Study* (1911), Gilbreth proposed the use of steroscopic and cinematographic cameras for the first time; see Frank B. Gilbreth, *Motion Study: A Method for Increasing the Efficiency of the Workman* (New York: D. van Nostrand, 1911); Marta Braun, *Picturing Time: The Work of Etienne-Jules Marey (1830-1904)* (Chicago: University of Chicago Press, 1992), p. 341.

24. On the differentiated representation of Taylorism and Fordism, see Alfred Kieser, "Managementlehre und Taylorismus," in Alfred Kieser (ed.), *Organisationstheorien* (Köln: Kohlhammer, 1995), pp. 75-78. On the differences between Taylorism and the work of Frank B. Gilbreth, see Philip Sarasin, "Die Rationalisierung des Körpers. Über 'Scientific Management' und 'biologische Rationalisierung,'" in Philip Sarasin (ed.), *Geschichtswissenschaft und Diskursanalyse* (Frankfurt am Main: Suhrkamp, 2004), pp. 61-99. As Sarasin explains it, Taylor's problem was the "laziness" of the worker, who had to be kept on the track toward achievement, while Gilbreth's attention was primarily devoted to ergonomic questions, namely the avoidance of damage from wear and tear. Gilbreth accordingly worked on the optimization of procedures, whose construction was no longer problematic.

25. Max Weber, *Wirtschaft und Gesellschaft* (Tübingen: Niemeyer, 1922); Henri Fayol, *Administration Industrielle et Génerale* (Paris: Dunod, 1916).

26. See Vinzenz Hediger and Patrick Vonderau, "Record, Rhetoric, Rationalization: Industrial Organization and Film," in this volume.

27. Cf. Jacqueline Mac Glade, "The US Technical Assistance and Productivity Program and the education of Western European managers 1948–58," in T.R. Gourvish, N. Tiratsoo (eds.), *Missionaries and Managers: American Influences on European Management Education 1945–1960* (Manchester: Manchester University Press, 1998).

28. See Gilbreth, op. cit.; Frank. B Gilbreth, Lilian M. Gilbreth, *Angewandte Bewegungsstudien: Neun Vorträge aus der Praxis der wissenschaftlichen Betriebsführung* (Berlin:

Springer, 1920), p. 39; Frank B. Gilbreth, *Das ABC der wissenschaftlichen Betriebsfüh-rung* (Berlin: Springer, 1917), p. 52.

29. See footnote 16.

30. McGraw-Hill Films (ed.), *Guidelines*, n.d., p. 7.

31. See on *cognitive mapping* Donna J. Peuquet, *Representations of Space and Time* (New York: Guilford, 2002), pp. 58 ff.

32. McGraw-Hill Films (ed.), *Guidelines*, n.d., p. 11.

33. The successive setup of images is also dominant is the films METHODS ANALYSIS (1951) and JOB EVALUATION (1952).

34. Ibid., p. 10.

35. Bruno Latour, *Laboratory Life: The Construction of Scientific Facts* (Princeton: Princeton University Press, 1986).

36. McGraw-Hill Films (ed.), *Guidelines*, n.d., p. 17.

37. Arrow vectors and flow charts are used in an analogous way in PHYSICAL FACIL-ITIES (1951) and MATERIAL CONTROL (1952), two other films from the McGraw-Hill series.

38. See Denis Bayart, "How to Make Change Manageable: Statistical Thinking and Cognitive Devices in Manufacturing Control," in Miriam Levin (ed.), *Cultures of Control* (Amsterdam: Harwood, 2000), pp. 153-176.

39. Line diagrams represent the development of a series of values in the form of a steady line; hierarchical diagrams picture a functional overview in the branches of a hierarchical tree.

40. According to the voice-over commentary in INTERNAL ORGANIZATION.

41. Cf. Heiko Neumann, Siegfried H. Stiehl, "Modelle der Informationsverarbeitung zur frühen visuellen Wahrnehmung. Eine interdisziplinäre Synopse der Paradigmen: Von Helmholtzschen Tiefenhinweisen zur Neuroinformatik," Klaus P. Dencker (ed.), *Interface 2: Weltbilder – Bilderwelten: computergestützte Visionen* (Hamburg and Baden-Baden: Nomos, 1995), pp. 86-95.

42. See JoAnne Yates, *Control Through Communication: The Rise of System in American Management* (Baltimore: Johns Hopkins University Press, 1989).

43. Cf. Otto Neurath, "Statistische Hieroglyphe," in Rudolf Haller, Robin Kinross (eds.), *Gesammelte bildpädagogische Schriften*, vol. 3 (Vienna: Hölder-Pichler-Tempsky, 1991), pp. 40-50.

44. McGraw-Hill Films (ed.), *Guidelines*, n.d., p. 17.

45. Ibid., p. 24.

46. Cf. Otto Neurath, "Gesellschafts- und Wirtschaftsmuseum in Wien," in Rudolf Haller, Robin Kinross (eds.), *Gesammelte bildpädagogische Schriften*, vol. 3 (Vienna: Hölder-Pichler-Tempsky, 1991), p. 1.

47. On the process of the uselessness and inefficiency of knowledge, cf. Klaus Amann, Karin Knorr-Cetina, "The fixation of visual evidence," in Michael Lynch, Steve Woolgar (eds.), *Representation in Scientific Practice* (Cambridge: MIT Press, 1990), pp. 85-122.

48. Roland Barthes, *S/Z* (New York: Farrar, Straus and Giroux, 1974), p. 8.

49. Walter Benjamin, "The Work of Art in the Age of Mechanical Reproduction," in Hannah Arendt (ed.), *Illuminations* (New York: Schocken, 1968), p. 226.

50. Régis Debray, *Vie et mort de l'image* (Paris: Gallimard, 1992), p. 142.

51. This transformation was examined in the example of the medical educational film by Cartwright 1995, op. cit.; cf. in particular Chapter 6, "Women and the Public Culture of Radiography," pp. 43-171.

52. McGraw-Hill Films (ed.), *Guidelines*, n.d., p. 11.

53. "Den Managementfilm verstehen wir als Kulturträger, seine Mission ist es, ein Bild des modernen Managens darzustellen, das Mensch und Maschine als gleichberechtigte Faktoren eines erfolgreichen Unternehmens ansieht." Thus, social work already figured as an industrially disciplined subject, as was noted in the first paragraph of this text.

54. Cf. Thomas Jantschek, "Bemerkungen zum Begriff des Sehen-als," Ralf Konersmann (ed.), *Kritik des Sehens* (Leipzig, 1997), pp. 299-319; on the genealogy of the model of circuitry as a visual strategy, see also Friedrich A. Kittler, "Die Stadt ist ein Medium," in Gotthard Fuchs, Bernhard Moltmann, Walter Prigge (eds.), *Mythos Metropole* (Frankfurt am Main: Suhrkamp, 1987), pp. 228-244.

55. In 1910, the American engineer Robb Russel had already transferred the old analogy between the activity of the ship's helmsman (*kybernetos*) and the activity of the political leader and compared the company with a ship, which a manager would navigate through the universe of statistical figures. Cf. Robb Russell, *Lectures on Organization* (Boston: published by the author, 1910), pp. 44 f.

Technologies of Organizational Learning

Uses of Industrial Films in Sweden during the 1950s

Mats Björkin

By 1945, industrial films had been produced in Sweden for more than 20 years. Following rapid growth during the mid-1920s, the practice of commissioning industrial films had become common among many larger companies in what were later regarded as the core industries of Sweden: mining, steel, wood, and paper. Industrial films, taking their lead from the dominant industrial-film production company of the 1920s, were primarily seen as suitable for public relations and documentation.[1] Those interwar period films were made along the lines of the typical documentary films of the time, with a straight narrative structure, authoritative narrator (or intertitles), and, in the films of the 1930s and 1940s, dramatic music. Even though they could also be screened at the companies themselves, which they were, they were obviously made as "stand-alone aesthetic objects," though with an informational or sometimes even didactic purpose.

During the 1950s, industrial films began shaping the theoretical discussion on corporate communication, organization, corporate learning, human resources, public relations, etc., albeit from the margins. Technologies created a bit more than theory could describe uses for, while theory demanded a slight bit more from technology than it could provide.[2] It is important, I will argue, to consider the films as the results of the theoretical debates of the time. Industrial films were not only part of developments in corporate communication, organization, and learning, but soon became part of what could be described as a whole system of theories or, perhaps more in keeping with its cybernetic foundation, a "theory machine," where different technologies, methods, and theories worked together, reacted to each other, and helped each other develop, at least as long as the postwar economic boom continued.

My own research of 1950s discourse in Sweden, or the "theory machine," has shown that it is a case of a more or less closed system, not to be understood as insular or provincial, but auto-referential. This makes the system closed to a certain extent, and dependent on constant, reasserting communications, similar to Herbert A. Simon's theories concerning the importance of relying on enough information.[3]

Sweden in the 1950s constitutes a useful case for understanding this process. It is small enough to grasp, not in its entirety of course, but satisfactorily. After

World War II, Sweden was also extremely open to an influx from other countries, especially the US, but also England, France, Italy, and the Netherlands, as
well as its old business partner and ever-present source of inspiration, Germany.
When an idea emerged in any of these countries it was immediately taken up in
Sweden. This is particularly true for industrial film. In the British journal *Industrial Screen*, Sweden was described in 1959 as well organized and having an
infrastructure for industrial films that they, in the UK, could only dream of.[4]

Another reason for studying Sweden is its political situation, with a business
world that still considered itself a natural part of the Western capitalist system
(and with a similar legal framework to other Western democracies) and a social-
democratic government that was determined to strengthen Sweden's exceptional way. Therefore, I think that what disappears in many other discourses,
such as in the US or Germany, can be singled out in Sweden as more clear-cut,
"cleaned up" examples of corporate communicative behavior. Despite later
high-profile engagement in the UN and EU, Sweden has never been as international as it was concerning business-development discourses during the 1950s.

After World War II, different media produced new values by transforming
information into economic assets. When face-to-face interaction was no longer
the only way of communicating, either in politics or at companies, and conceptual, psychological, and physical distance had to be overcome, modern media
determined the characteristics of that distance.[5] These theories of information,
which came out of the war apparatus, made this new economy possible.[6] In this
quest for the new, an old medium like film was redefined for new purposes.
Industrial film did not become a "new medium," but it was treated as if it were
new. Not because its uses were new, but because they were inscribed in new
fields of knowledge, theories, and practices, primarily concerning the embodiment of knowledge and the visualization of capital.

Efficiency and contact

Soon after 1945, new uses for industrial films were already being discussed
within companies and branch organizations. In 1946, Einar Förberg, a leading
advertising agent and industrial film producer, published his book *Att sälja med
film* ("Selling by Means of Film"). The purpose of the book was to "translate"
and adapt methods from other countries, meaning the US, for Swedish business
and industry and the Swedish market. However, he structured the book in a
manner well known to discourses on industrial film at the time – by emphasizing film's usefulness as propaganda (i.e., public relations) and documentation.[7]

Förberg provides a background to industrial films and filmmaking in Sweden. His main argument, though, is the *efficiency* of films. Here he enters into in an ongoing debate on streamlining and efficiency within the industry. By using films instead of oral presentations, nothing gets lost going from producer to consumer, despite all the agents involved in marketing, distribution, and selling. Film should be used to help salesmen improve the *contact* between producer and consumer. Even so, it is the salesman who does the selling, not the film. His conclusion was that industrial films, more than advertising films, are especially suited for goodwill and long-term effects rather than direct effects on the sale of individual products. It could be argued that Förberg's book was more related to his own interests in production than representative of most uses of film during the late 1940s and early 1950s. The book was, by and large, a tool for selling his services and films. On the other hand, this makes it even more interesting, because Förberg represented a new profession in Sweden, the information and communication consultant. All this considered, Förberg pinpoints two important discourses: the strong concern for the streamlining of production, administration, and selling, and a widespread belief in the economic value of using films for many purposes in business and industry.

The latter was something that was discussed in many different contexts. Audiovisual media were said to have a strong, direct, emotional impact on people. This was seen as useful for selling specific products. Audiovisual media were also discussed as having long-term effects, especially useful for creating goodwill for individual companies, kinds of products, or branches of industry. To achieve these long-term goals another dimension was added: *contact*. When films were used to enhance human interaction, directly or indirectly, their content could be understood more thoroughly. Therefore, a systematized composition of individual films and entire programs, together with systematized film screenings, would be the most effective sales machines.[8] This discourse would be elaborated upon in the following decade, but the basic idea remained the same.

This becomes evident a few years later. In May 1954, the Swedish Center for Business and Policy Studies, founded in 1949 to promote interdisciplinary research in business, economics, and society, arranged a conference for the top managers in Sweden's industries under the title Business and Industry Plan for the Future at the summer resort of Tylösand (in southwestern Sweden). The conference focused on automation, atomic energy, game theory, operation research, cybernetics, and the social, economic, physiological, and psychological consequences of automation.[9] Automation in production was already well established and had for some decades proved to be important for the development of Swedish industry and a key component in the economic progress of postwar Swedish society.

During the two or three years preceding the conference, many new theories
and methods of communication were discussed and often implemented, especially at companies aiming for international markets. Ideas regarding cybernetics, systems analysis, new accounting practices, and budgetary principles as
well as theories of information, communication, marketing, public relations,
and organization were discussed at conferences, seminars, and courses, and in
articles and books. At the same time, new technologies changed corporate communication, from a loose-leaf accounting system to mechanical and electronic
business machines,[10] from written texts and oral presentations to slide shows,
audio tapes, films, and television.

The interest in the social, economic, physiological, and psychological consequences of automation has often been regarded as an ideology of engineering or
a technocratic and inhuman way of thinking. Even if some psychological research was quite behavioristic, it does not follow that all thinking about human
behavior lacked other dimensions. This is particularly evident when looking at
contemporary discussions on modern management, as well as on some psychological discourses.[11]

Some cybernetic concepts, particularly feedback, were included in the predominant behavioral perspectives on organizational and educational psychology
of the time. According to psychologist Ernest Kramer, cybernetics and General
Systems theory helped to make "purpose" respectable among psychologists,
even among those "psychologists who took pride in their tough-mindedness."[12]
If that is correct, it would mean that cybernetics helped to establish "softer"
perspectives on the human mind.[13] This helps explaining the otherwise contradictory co-presence of interests in cybernetics and human resources.

On a superficial level, most discourse on psychology, sociology, economics,
etc. of the time seems to describe and analyze totalities and systems. Expressions like "patterns of behavior" had become more and more common even in
public debate. Interest in large-scale systems required theoretical discussions on
the importance of scale, which becomes evident in most sectors of society from
changes in local governance and industrial organization, as well as localization
issues. The key questions were how to handle organizations spread over large
areas, how to communicate over long distances, and the most important question, how to organize management in large and spatially scattered organizations?

The medialization of contact, or connectiveness, as Stafford Beer described it
in April 1958 in a speech on cybernetics and industry at the Royal Swedish
Academy for Engineering Sciences,[14] was transferred to the field of communication and learning very early on. Although many attempts were made to measure the effects of audiovisual aids, they were, a decade later, summed up as
follows: "In general, it has been concluded that graphic-verbal means of com-

munication are better than verbal alone, and that in some cases an appropriate film is equivalent to an average teacher."[15]

A basic presumption here is that, although many contacts seem to happen at random, there is some level of regularity or some kinds of patterns that can be discerned to form a basis for a systematic understanding of the "social life" of an organization. These aspects of an organization's social framework describe the context of industrial films' functions quite well. It is not possible to understand the function of instructional film in terms of workplace safety without knowing the functions and chains of contacts involved, for example, in job requirements and systems of sanctions. This is not only a question of context, but of the mechanisms of feedback between the different parts within the system. A consequence of this approach is that industrial films, perhaps more than other types, are more difficult to treat as stand-alone objects. Of particular importance is the process of visualizing flows of capital, as well as communicating values.

Information and learning

Other schools of thought contested audiovisual media, or rather unreflective uses of them, and focused on the cybernetic concept of feedback. Sten Rosell's 1957 *Återkopplad pedagogic* ("Feedback Pedagogy"), a communication handbook and promotional piece for the courses at the KVE school of information and communication (a private company specializing in adult education in economics), argued intensively against certain uses of film. Rosell's idea of education was a modern version of the object lessons of the late 19th century: seeing, listening, and doing. His understanding of the communicative moment in education was shared by many commentators on the uses of audiovisual media, who stressed the importance of verbal explanations and discussions both before and after any use of film.[16] Films were not just primarily vehicles for information, but were also means for improving and creating contact between people as well as contact between companies and society. Here, the links between different contact-creating techniques are important.

Annual reports were one of the mandatory phenomena that were seen as having the potential for making contact with society. Although the law stated that annual reports must contain certain information, the discussion of additional uses for it started around 1950. It was argued that it could, and should, be used as a contact-promoting medium. It was not enough to just discuss what was in the report, but also how that information was communicated, and, most importantly, how it could build up trust.[17]

In a 1956 Swedish book on annual reports, author Gustaf Bondeson pointed out that modern companies have to be able to communicate with the surrounding society as well as customers, suppliers, shareholders, and employees. He labeled this "public relations" (English in original) and translates it as "society contact."[18] Today, it is part of what is called corporate responsibility. The three-part socioeconomic system that was developed in Sweden at the beginning of World War II, the "Swedish model," presupposed that employers and labor unions settled as much as possible between themselves. The state provided the infrastructure and, what would become more apparent later, maintained strong control through legislation.[19] The 1950s in Sweden saw the rapid development of a more controlling state apparatus: public spending increased, taxes were raised, the social-welfare system developed rapidly, and the state also increased the amount of control it had over information, especially in print and broadcast media,[20] knowledge, education, and research.[21] In an era when visual media were being discovered as tools for information on "invisible" or intangible assets, film became more important than ever before. Even the contemporary struggle over television was not only a matter of commercial versus public service television; it was a struggle over the system of organizing knowledge and information.

Bondeson presented some general principles – objective and commented fact, comparability, clarity, circumstantiality, validity, and a fair overall presentation.[22] He argued for using images, preferably of people, but also of plants and processes. For spatial information, Bondeson advised using cartograms, process charts, organizational charts, concern charts, etc.[23] New uses required new methods of distribution. The distribution list had to mirror the strategies for contact. Bondeson did not go into detail, but emphasized that the decision of distribution was important.[24] When looking at annual reports from the mid- and late 1950s, it is obvious that Bondeson's recommendations were followed by many companies, particularly those that employed new means of communications.

For these new, expanded uses of the annual report it was crucial to supplement it with other forms of communication. This was specified in the 1946 agreement concerning *företagsnämnder* (works councils) between the state, employers, and trade unions.[25] Other measures were dedicated informational meetings or using employee publications in particular. During the 1950s, most of the larger companies, as well as many mid-sized companies, produced or commissioned films for the works councils. Starting in 1947, every Swedish company above a certain size had to create a works council where representatives of the employees had the right to obtain information about the company and also comment on these issues. When films started to be made for the works councils, traditional modes of narration seem to have become insufficient.

Although entertaining aspects were recognized, the films no longer had to be "closed" in the sense that they were independent of the viewing context. Rather, all of the materials used in council work were discussed in relation to each other, and were regarded as part of what could be called an information system.[26]

After World War II, there was a new demand for making contact with shareholders. The older means of contact were no longer useful with most of the shareholders, who were, for the most part, smaller. With a more even distribution of capital and income and greater investments in plants and machines, industry needed more capital. Subsequently it had to be better in the communication of economic issues. As was often the case, inspiration for new methods came from the US, where the responsibility clearly was that of top management. This may explain why meetings and courses on the uses of film and other communication technologies even attracted the top managers at many of the larger companies. Bondeson regarded personal contact as one of the most important means of communicating with the financial market, and it was important to make it clear who at the company was responsible for this contact.[27] Other ways to encourage shareholder participation, and where film could be used, were annual meetings or specific shareholders' meetings and company demonstrations (on location). Here Bondeson uses a quote in English: "No decision is better than the information upon which it is based."[28]

Films were also made to provide new employees with background information. What was new were the many films that provided training for specific moments in the industrial production process. Again, the basic idea was the pedagogical model of seeing, listening, and doing. But these films were not just training tools. They were presented together with the films for works councils and others dealing with individual companies, industrial branches in Sweden, and Swedish industry as a whole. This demand seems to have created, or at least supported, an increasing trade in moving images within Swedish business and industry, which demanded fairly sophisticated information activities, education, and film catalogues.[29]

The links between information and learning have already been described by Förberg. When describing film exhibition, especially those traveling sales shows that were quite common during the late 1940s, Förberg discussed how to sell industrial films to schools. Interest in using films as pedagogical tools in schools was high, and since so many of the films available were made during the 1920s and 1930s, it was easy to sell new productions to schools. This gives us one clue as to why Förberg argued for goodwill films rather than advertising films. Films for goodwill purposes were of more "general interest," and were therefore made available for rental or purchase by schools. At schools, the audience was prepared to receive important information, which is the key to his argument. A site for learning was a good site for selling. It could even be better than tradi-tional advertising.[30] On the other hand, we have to remember that the book itself was an instrument for selling – selling the production of films. But recruit-ing large numbers of people to the industry was a key concern of the time – as was the general interest in making the industry attractive, especially to young people. So, all means of making contact with people had to be explored.

During the 1950s, advertising, marketing, and management literature and journals made references to many American, British, and German studies on media, marketing, pedagogy, and psychology that seemed to confirm Förberg's ideas. That was certainly not surprising, since Förberg made use of the latest information in the mid-1940s. What is interesting is that the widespread idea that audiovisual media in combination with human contact were the most effec-tive means possible of both learning and selling. Another outcome of this is that issues of learning and selling were regarded as an organizational problem, or even a spatial problem: the best place to sell something was where people were prepared to learn things.

Accounting practices and information strategies

One example of the often complicated relationships between different commu-nication links would be the attempts to make financial details more visible. In-terest in relationships between information and capital, for example, required new accounting methods. As in other areas of society, even accounting became increasingly inspired by American standards after World War II, replacing two traditions, one German and one British. In practice, the differences at the end of the 1940s and early 1950s seem minor. The American tradition of budget and budget accounting was introduced in Sweden (and other European countries) by way of the so-called M-chart. Budget accounting meant that revenues and costs were budgeted for every cost center, something that, at least in Sweden, was rarely applied during the 1930s. In spite of its German origin, the M-chart became standard practice after the war. In 1948, at a conference on accounting practices, one of the largest Swedish companies, Svenska Cellulosa AB (SCA), a major commissioner of industrial films, explained that they were using the M-chart, and that it was especially appropriate for them, since they used punch-card machines for their bookkeeping. The uses of punch cards and the M-chart made it easier for SCA to make a distinction between sectors, like sulfite-pulp factories, sawmills, paper mills, etc., rather than individual companies.[31] As a result, they developed a system that was suited to their actual relation to differ-ent groups of shareholders, plus it facilitated communication. When looking at

SCA's communication practices in the 1950s – films, publications, traveling exhibitions (which often included films), etc. – a more sector-oriented perspective is visible, a result of general trends, but also, most likely, of a better overview of the company's financial situation and better methods of communicating this knowledge.

This interest in and understanding of the technological conditions for efficient communication explains to a large degree SCA's interest in computer technology and new media.[32] According to other companies, the major advantage of a combined use of M-chart and bookkeeping machines was flexibility, which was good for a company facing big changes. It was also easy to use by people within the company who did not work with bookkeeping, but who needed to understand business reports.[33] This shows that the connection between accounting practices and information strategies during the mid-1940s had spread even to mid-sized companies. It also indicates that economic information had become available to a larger group of employees, that is, middle and lower management. And finally, it indicates the influence exercised by the Swedish system of works councils for which many of the films were made.

Conclusion

Debates on relationships between streamlining, efficiency, and information were sometimes confusing, but the initial process is not without relevance. For some time, the focus was on the development of technological systems. But before that, during the first half of 1950s, the debate still concerned the need for new information, which earlier systems could not provide. Traditional histories of accounting are therefore missing the key issue: how accounting could be employed as an information system that, with the aid of films and posters, ensured wider dissemination, both inside the company and out, than earlier forms of accounting.

In Sweden, the works council system forced companies not only to simplify accounting and financial information, but also to create a new, "total" system for company information. Industrial films could be used for this purpose, and were, as an efficient tool for contact. The key challenge was the development of transparent flows – of information and money. This resulted in an increased interest in pedagogy, advertising, and public relations with methods that increased transparency, or at least gave the appearance of transparency. The latter was the case because the aspects being made transparent were often not otherwise visible, though making them visible was necessary. This was not a tendency to reveal matters previously hidden, but to visualize abstract processes needed for a better understanding of the new economy.

Notes

1. Mats Björkin, "Industrial Greta. Some Thoughts on an Industrial Film," in John Fullerton, Jan Olsson (eds.), *Nordic Explorations: Film Before 1930* (Sydney: John Libbey, 1999), pp. 263-268.
2. Karl U. Smith, Margaret Foltz Smith, *Cybernetic Principles of Learning and Educational Design* (New York: Holt, Rinehart and Winston, 1966).
3. Herbert A. Simon, *Organizational Behavior* (New York: Macmillan, 1947).
4. "300 Swedish firms now employ executives trained in audio-visual communications," James Platt, "Audio Visual Aids in Management Training," *Industrial Film and Photography* 3, 5 (1959), p. 216.
5. It is of course possible to see it the other way around, that media filled the gap, but I prefer a more "active" view of media.
6. See, for example, Eric P. Rau, "The Adoption of Operations Research in the United States during World War II," in Agatha C. Hughes, Thomas P. Hughes (eds.), *Systems, Experts, and Computers: The Systems Approach in Management and Engineering, World War II and After* (Cambridge: MIT Press, 2000), pp. 57-92.
7. Einar Förberg, *Att sälja med film* (Stockholm: Förlags AB Affärsekonomi, 1946).
8. See, for example, L. Bn. [Lennart Bondeson], "Modern aktivitetspedagogik kräver förkortad 'hanteringstid' för idéer," *Arbetsgivaren* 12, 1 (June 18, 1955), p. 7, a text that summarizes some ideas regarding industrial films from the beginning of the 1950s.
9. Hans B. Thorelli (ed.), *Automation. Ny teknik - nya perspektiv i ekonomi och arbetsliv. Del I. De tekniska utsikterna* (Stockholm: SNS Studier och Debatt, 1954), and *Automation. Ny teknik - nya perspektiv. Del II. De ekonomiska och sociala framtidsutsikterna* (Stockholm: SNS Studier och Debatt, 1954).
10. For an interesting British comparison, see, for example, Jon Agar, *The Government Machine: A Revolutionary History of the Computer* (Cambridge: MIT Press, 2003). In 1949, two studies, in Swedish, had already been published on the principles and functions of computers. *Siffermaskiner*, literally translated "number machines," that is, calculators and punch-card machines: Carl-Erik Fröberg and Göran Kjellberg, *Siffermaskiner* (Lund: Elementa, 1949); and Olof Boivie, *Hålkortsmaskiner* (Lund: Elementa, 1949). Fröberg and Kjellberg spent one year, 1947-48, in the US with a stipend from the Swedish Academy of Engineering Sciences to study mathematical machines, Fröberg at the Institute for Advanced Study at Princeton, studying John von Neumann's work, and Kjellberg with Prof. H.H. Aiken at Harvard. Both were later at Matematikmaskinnämnden, a government agency responsible for the development and uses of computer technology.
11. This can be seen in studies like F.L.W. Richardson, Charles R. Walker, *Human Relations in an Expanding Company* (New Haven: Labor and Management Center, Yale

University, 1948), p. 5. A more theoretical approach can be found in Stafford Beer, *Cybernetics and Management* (London: English Universities Press, 1959).

12. Ernest Kramer, "Man's Behavior Patterns," in *Positive Feedback: A General Systems Approach to Positive/Negative Feedback and Mutual Causality* (Oxford: Pergamon Press, 1968), p. 140.

13. Kramer already refers this approach to the work of E.C. Tolman long before systems theory and cybernetics, in a 1925 article, Kramer, p. 140.

14. Stafford Beer, "Cybernetics and Industry," unpublished paper delivered in Stockholm on April 26, 1958, Royal Swedish Academy for Engineering Sciences/The United Steel Companies Limited, 1959, p. 7.

15. Karl U. Smith and Margaret Foltz Smith, *Cybernetic Principles of Learning and Educational Design* (New York: Holt, Rinehart and Winston, 1966), p. 140.

16. Sten Rosell, *Återkopplad pedagogic* (Solna: KVE förlag, 1957).

17. Sven Andrén, *Om förvaltningsberättelsen ett led i svenska aktiebolags årsredovisning* (Göteborg, 1955); P.V.A. Hanner, *Årsredovisning i praktiken* (Stockholm, 1953).

18. Gustaf Bondeson, *God årsredovisning – goda relationer* (Stockholm: Studieförbundet Näringsliv och Samhälle, 1956).

19. R. Freeman, R. Topel, B. Swedenborg (eds.), *The Welfare State in Transition: Reforming the Swedish Model* (Chicago: University of Chicago Press, 1997).

20. Karl-Hugo Wirén, *Kampen om TV: svensk TV-politik 1946-66* (Stockholm: Gidlunds, 1986); Stig Hadenius: *Kampen om monopolet: Sveriges Radio och TV under 1900-talet* (Stockholm: Prisma, 1998).

21. A. Nilsson, *Visions and Labour Demand. The Planning of Vocational Education for the Swedish Manufacturing Industry 1950-1993* (Lund: Lund Papers in Economic History, 39 (1994).

22. Bondeson, op. cit., pp. 9-14.

23. Bondeson, op. cit., p. 35.

24. Bondeson, op. cit., pp. 55 ff.

25. Bondeson, *Aktiebolagens årsredovisning* (Stockholm: LO, 1956).

26. Bondeson, *Företagsnämnden och årsredovisningen* (Stockholm: SAF, 1951).

27. Bondeson, op. cit., p. 66.

28. Bondeson, op. cit., p. 68.

29. Most importantly, the Swedish Employers Association's work on developing an infrastructure for educational and informational tools, primarily films and sound slides.

30. Förberg, op. cit., p. 64.

31. Leif Carlsson, *Framväxten av intern redovisning i Sverige 1900-1945*, dissertation (Uppsala University, Department of Business Studies, 2001), p. 237.

32. See, for example, *Arbetsgivaren* 1955, 21; 1956, 4, 5; 1956, 8, 6; 1956, 18, 3; 1958, 21, 2; 1958, 22, 6.

33. Carlsson, op. cit., p. 338.

The Central Film Library of Vocational Education

An Archeology of Industrial Film in France between the Wars

Valérie Vignaux

The Central Film Library of Vocational Education constitutes one of the first attempts to rationally organize industrial film in France. Affiliated with the Office of Technical Education of the Ministry of Public Instruction, it was created in 1925 within the framework of wider reforms encouraging the use of visual images in teaching. The institution's principal objective was to direct individuals toward occupations or activities consistent with the modernization of the country. To this end, it commissioned films from Jean Benoit-Lévy, a director renowned as a specialist in educational cinema. The catalogue, published in 1934, almost ten years after the institution's creation, shows that despite its intentions, its means remained meager. By studying the process that led to the emergence and then the disaffection of a public policy in favor of industrial film, we can examine the ideological foundations of the cinematic representation of work in France between the wars.

The Central Film Library of Vocational Education

The Central Film Library of Vocational Education was officially established on December 14, 1925, although it stems largely from previous reflections or legislative measures. The institution is inscribed, in effect, in a wide-ranging movement that, together with reforms in favor of "educating the people," encouraged the use of visual images in education. At the turn of the century, legislators attempted to establish the most complete educational system possible. They promulgated laws instituting public, civil, and obligatory education, and regulated adult education. A decree on January 11, 1895, placed "popular education," previously left up to private initiatives, under the supervision of the Ministry of Public Instruction, which was now charged with organizing "further" education. Recognizing the fact that working-class children were expected to start earning a living as soon as possible and therefore only received a

general education at primary school, the politicians reformed vocational education. Complementary programs of two or three years were defined according to
their placement in either cities or the country, and girls were integrated into the
system thanks to the inclusion of home economics in education. Three kinds of
education – primary, further, and vocational – were entrusted to people already
working in institutions throughout the country. In order to aid them in their
functions, a commission was named to "research means for facilitating the initial work of novice lecturers." It proposed subjects, determined which books
were useful in preparation, and above all examined the use of "projectors and
collections of photographic views for adult courses and public lectures."[1]

The reformers, taking their inspiration from experimental methods that were
popularized during the 19th century, encouraged teaching "by aspect," i.e., the
illustration of books and the use of wall murals or a magic lantern to project still
images, among other things. An image service was then instituted at the Pedagogical Museum, which was founded in 1879 under the supervision of the Ministry for Public Instruction in order to provide teachers with the technical or
intellectual means to reflect on the exercise of their profession. Noting that the
most experienced lecturers or the most prestigious societies of popular education had rapidly begun to combine animated images with still views, the legislators created an "extra-parliamentary commission" on March 23, 1916, which
was entrusted with "researching the best means of generalizing the use of the
cinematic in the different branches of teaching." Its conclusions were published
in 1920,[2] the same year that films were first placed in the Pedagogical Museum.

The Central Film Library of Vocational Education was created because of this
context of reform. However, it also evolved out of initiatives that were specifically Parisian. Indeed, starting in December 1919, the municipal council,
wishing to contribute to the movement for educational cinema, commissioned
Léon Riotor, a member of the Commission on Education and the Fine Arts, to
carry out a study to define the modalities of introducing moving images into
Parisian schools.[3] Léon Riotor was aided in this task by Adrien Bruneau[4] who,
as inspector of artistic and vocational education for the city of Paris, had the
schools of Boule (furniture), Estienne (typography and printing), Fondary and
Jacquart (fashion), etc. within his jurisdiction, that is, precisely those schools
which had been instituted under the reforms. Bruneau, who was also director
of the School of Art and Advertising, put in a bid for a projector for the Boulle
school in 1920 and confirmed the lack of films adapted to vocational education.
The municipal council heard his request, and in 1921 they allotted him a grant
of 40,000 francs targeted for use in two films: "the one relative to work at the
wrought-iron works, the other to the history of costume." He entrusted their
direction to Jean Benoit-Lévy, who at the time was simply the nephew of Edmond Benoit-Lévy,[5] one of the influential protagonists of educational cinema

and a member of the extra-parliamentary commission named to further the educational use of cinema.

The films that were made pleased the commissioners, who gladly projected them for members of the government to show off the vocational training in the Parisian schools. They were shown in April 1922 at the National Conservatory of Arts and Professions (CNAM) during a conference dedicated to the use of cinema in teaching, inaugurated by Léon Bérard, Minister of Public Education and Gaston Vidal, Undersecretary of State for Technical Education.[6] The municipal council allocated new funds, and Jean Benoit-Lévy made Les Beaux métiers du livre: École Estienne; Comment on fabrique un siège à l'École Boulle; La Fleur artificielle telle qu'on l'enseigne à l'École professionnelle de la rue Fondary, à Paris et La Ferronnerie d'art. An exposition entitled Art in French Cinema, which took place in October 1924 at the Galliera Museum, one of the municipal museums of the city of Paris, provided the occasion to present Jean Benoit-Lévy's latest commissioned works to M. Vincent de Moro-Giafferri, Undersecretary of State for Technical Education. All of the films were projected again in 1925 at the International Exposition of Decorative Arts. Édouard Herriot, commenting on the event, underlined the involvement of the vocational schools:

> The entire exposition has been dominated by the intimate connection between art and the technical. This could be seen not only by the proximity of the works, but also the cooperation of the schools in the same groupings; you translated it into public formulas: one of you stated that it was "a living reality."[7]

The Parisian initiatives clearly influenced the creation of a national film library dedicated to vocational education. Several months after the CNAM convention, Edmond Labbé, director of technical education, took up the conference's position and on September 26, 1922, proclaimed cinema to be "useful in the career placement of youth."[8] Then, on May 14, 1923, the General Office of Technical Education announced the creation of a committee of cinematography concerned with vocational teaching within the Ministry of Education and the Fine Arts. The committee brought representatives of the state together with members of the Parisian municipality such as Léon Riotor and Adrien Bruneau. On December 14, 1925, after two years of work, they confirmed that they could not undertake anything without "a central service" which would provide access to the films. Léon Riotor then proposed the constitution of an administrative service, part of a municipal institution, in this case the School of Art and Advertising directed by Adrien Bruneau. His proposal satisfied the representatives of the state, Edmond Labbé, but also Julien Fontègne, director of professional orientation services to the Undersecretary of State of Technical Education. Thus, on 14 December, 1925, the committee officially ratified the creation of the Central Film

Library of Vocational Education, to be directed by Adrien Bruneau, with its initial holdings being the films made by Jean Benoit-Lévy.

Vocational-education films

The film library was placed under the authority of the committee which "had its seat in the general assembly, in the examination section for equipment, and in the examination section for film." The film section was charged with the creation of films, and Adrien Bruneau was designated "to generate scenarios and achieve [their] execution."[9] In 1926, the committee agreed on the relevance of certain titles, so that one of the officiating members received private funding, according to G.-Michel Coissac:

> It was decided that films should be made, for example, for agriculture, and there are numerous employers' federations, such as the Entrepreneurs of Masonry, Cement, and Reinforced Concrete of the city of Paris and of the Department of the Seine, the Entrepreneurs of Roofing and Plumbing of Paris, the Department of the Seine and Seine-et-Oise, which have already collaborated on the production of career orientation films. Therefore, thanks to the initiative of the permanent commission, the following films are currently being made: Les Beaux métiers du bâtiment: le maçon et le tailleur de pierre; La Couverture et la plomberie; La Machine humaine (physiological examination in view of career placement); Le Fonctionnement d'un Office d'orientation professionnelle (Nantes); Le Métier de fondeur; Les Ateliers-écoles préparatoires à l'apprentissage de la Chambre de commerce de Paris; L'orientation professionnelle par l'école pratique (Tourcoing, etc.).[10]

The section dedicated to film thus established a rapport with trade groups, with production companies, and with technicians and their teachings, in order to arrive at the most adequate solution possible. The use of properly cinematic technical means, like slow motion and fast motion, was recommended, as was the integration of diagrams or static shots showing details or articles in their entirety. The films obey an officially defined protocol, and they were obliged to bring together "an elite practitioner, a professor, and an artist":

> The practitioner brings his profound knowledge of the profession... He gives an impression of mastery, of self-confidence, and also of the satisfaction that he experiences at a job well done... But with all his professional skill, he might not possess the pedagogical sense that remains the teacher's prerogative. He is the processor, required by very definition to observe, decompose, arrange, and organize by level in order to teach better... As for the artist, his role is that of the director, his responsibility is the whole, the groupings, the evaluation, concerning the surroundings as much as the

characters themselves... An artist will know how to choose the framing, set up the lighting, place the characters, rectify certain attitudes, make good use of certain oppositions in order better to bring out the things that should be featured and foregrounded.[11]

The committee examined the edits and could demand changes. It then submitted the films to the Secretary of Technical Education, who granted the financial means, reimbursing the costs of production and funding the purchase of prints that were then distributed to the 15 film libraries and the deposit offices. These were essentially offices of educational cinema[12] in the big cities such as Paris, Bordeaux, Clermont-Ferrand, Lille, Lyon, Marseille, Nancy, Nîmes, Poitiers, Rennes, and Saint-Étienne, to which can be added three centers of career placement located in Nantes, Strasbourg, and Toulouse. For the Paris area, the General Office of Technical Education, in agreement with the Office of Primary Education of the Seine, delegated screenings to the Parisian circle of the League of Education starting in 1930. The films were accompanied by notices drawn up by the committee and made available free of charge.

Despite its stated goals, the Central Film Library of Vocational Education possessed a very limited catalogue. The 44 titles in the 1934 inventory included 23 films commissioned by the committee, all of them general documentaries made by Jean Benoit-Lévy. In order not to overly tax the spectators and at the same time create programs of appropriate length, the educational films were each augmented with a documentary and an entertaining short film. The films commissioned by the film library for the most part have to do with professions related to the "industry of art," that is to say, artisanal or urban small industry, while the locations featured were those of the firm or the workshop. In compliance with the directives formulated by the committee, the films were conceived in two principal categories, according to which they were geared either toward career placement or technical education.

The earliest films, which were career-placement films, were made in the Parisian schools under the supervision of Adrien Bruneau. With the creation of the film library the credits specified that the films had been "approved by the committee of cinematography applied to vocational teaching." The story lines try to convince young people and their parents that it is in their best interests to be educated in a school environment rather than entering an apprenticeship at a workshop. Whether for the boys' schools (LA FERRONNERIE D'ART (1924); ÉCOLE BOULLE: LES ARTS ET INDUSTRIES DU MEUBLE (1924); LE MÉTIER D'ÉBÉNISTE [1924]) or the girls' schools (LA FLEUR ARTIFICIELLE À L'ÉCOLE DE LA RUE FONDARY (1924), HISTOIRE D'UN CHAPEAU DE PAILLE - LA MODISTE (1925), PETITS DOIGTS DE FÉE (LA LINGÈRE - ÉCOLE JACQUARD [1925], UN BEAU MÉTIER MÉCONNU: LE REPASSAGE [1925] et LA BRODERIE [1925]), the cinematic strategies used are identical. We first see the school buildings and the classes where the theoretical teaching is conducted, then on to the tidy workshops where the students test out their knowledge, done under the vigilant watch of a professor. Finally, after having exchanged their overalls for dress clothes, the students present the objects they have made, set off by dark backgrounds and appropriate lighting. The repetition of the discursive modalities of the film within a film was desirable certainly because it facilitated the transmission of information by recognition. The vocational schools clearly made use of the appropriate locations, and the instruction, while it favored the practice of the profession, did not, for all that, neglect knowledge with strong scientific content. The school sometimes received contracts from industry, and then the students were paid for their work. The apparently didactic discourse of the films voluntarily took on a moralizing tone through the intermediary of short fictional sequences. In order to scare the "lazy," DES MÉTIERS POUR LES JEUNES GENS (1928) shows a young man diverted from his work and sent shopping by the not-very-affable workers. The dirty atmosphere in the workshop suggests that they sent him to a café to get alcohol. Emphasis is provided by a title card: "A resourceful apprentice at school never gets diverted from his work." DES MÉTIERS POUR LES JEUNES FILLES (1928) warns families: "Giving them a profession that allows them to live honorably, makes them learn to do housework, keeps them in good health, this is the gift that parents can give their young daughters."

In order to extend the range of the work and to enlarge its audience the committee commissioned Jean Benoit-Lévy to produce a feature-length film touting the building trades. According to the credits, it was funded by a donation from the Masonry Employers' Federation. LA MAISON (c. 1930), due to its length and narrative structure, constitutes an entirely different spectacle. The story is acted out by reputable actors whom the spectators probably recognized, having already seen them in educational hygiene films[13] or agricultural propaganda[14] made by Jean Benoit-Lévy and screened in similar contexts. LA MAISON compares and evaluates the fates of two childhood friends. Jean-Pierre (Jimmy Gaillard) gets good grades in school, but to help out his mother (Andrée Brabant), who is raising him by herself, he chooses to study a trade. Paul is directed toward office work, and his parents discourage him from associating with his friend, whose educational plans they disapprove of. Jean-Pierre, who is in love with Paul's sister Jeannette, plunges into despair. After having gotten a job as an apprentice, he is rewarded with his certificate of professional aptitude, while Paul is getting bored in his office. The former, having gotten a job in a warehouse, is given a raise while the latter gets fired from his job and then turns to drink and gambling. Forced to sell the family home because of his debts, Paul gets a job at the same warehouse where Jean-Pierre works. Despite their past differences, the latter decides to help his friend and advises him to take evening courses. Thanks to his savings, Jean-Pierre has bought a plot of land and they construct a house there for his loved ones: Jeannette and his mother. The story, praising technical education to the detriment of the administrative route, was therefore able to satisfy the commissioners. Indeed, the education given to the working classes provided them with a better material existence without modifying structures or social hierarchies in the process.

The earliest films on technical education were made together with the career-orientation films. LE FER FORGÉ (1922), for example, is the "technical-education" version, feature-length and didactic, of LA FERRONNERIE D'ART (1922), a short film with more evocative editing. With the creation of the Central Film Library of Vocational Education, technical films seemed to gradually displace the career-orientation films. The presentation of schools is then abandoned in favor of showing industrial sites. Technically proficient, these films could be shown to young people during their schooling or to adults in the framework of further education. The activities of the trades are precisely described, whether determined by tools (APPRENTISSAGE DU TOURNEUR SUR MÉTAUX [1926], L'ÉBÉNIST-ERIE [1930]; LA PLOMBERIE [1930], LA FABRICATION DU PAPIER PEINT [c. 1935]) or by machines (LA FILATURE DU COTON [1930], LA FABRICATION MÉCANIQUE DE LA DENTELLE [c. 1935]). Close-up shots supported by animated sections allowed for technical procedures to be explained and sometimes shot in real time.

ÉCOLES NATIONALES PROFESSIONNELLES (c. 1930) is at one and the same time a career-orientation film and a medium-length film about technical education. Intended to provide information about the schools (Armentières, Epinal, Nantes, Vierzon, Voiron, and Tarbes), the story centers on trades (ironworks, fitting, electricity, smelting works, cabinet making) and favors the description of job activities. The film exists in two versions of different lengths, and the credits of one call it an "excerpt of the film made by Jean Benoit-Lévy under the direction of M. Druot, General Inspector of Technical Education." The two versions have preserved the intertitles of the presentation, which underline the historical origin of the schools:

> The first three (Armentières, Vierzon, and Voiron) were founded almost a half century ago by the great minister Jules Ferry, and each one occupies an area of four hectares. Since their creation, they have continued to be model establishments.

Made under the direction of a specialist and conforming to the directives of the committee, the film seems intended to create interest in industrial careers among the middle classes:

> The schools serve to recruit for middle management in industry (foremen, shop leaders, etc.) and the numerous technical positions demanded by the new rational organization of work. Other than the regular section, each school possesses a preparatory section for the schools of arts and professions.

While the film attempts to promote management ideas consistent with the modernization of society, the story paradoxically draws its arguments from references borrowed from the 19th century. Such paradoxes suggest the difficulties that ideologues have in thinking or transmitting new paradigms, despite the fact that they may help and favor social changes.

Cinematic representations of work

In 1934, the Central Film Library of Vocational Education published its first, and probably only, catalogue. It was compiled under the supervision of Adrien Bruneau by the students at the Estienne school, which specialized in the book-related arts and professions. It is very carefully designed, illustrated with numerous photographs, and the director's preface includes a number of documents along with the inventory of titles, such as the official texts that had ratified the institute's creation. Despite the evident care taken with the catalogue, the institution's shortcomings are obvious. It only possessed about 40 titles, while the two other ministerial film libraries, those of Agriculture[15] and of Social Hygiene,[16] at the time already had over 200 educational titles each at their disposal. Adrien Bruneau borrowed certain titles from the collections of the city of Paris's film library, for which he was also responsible, and reedited them. There was no attempt to conceal this process, as G.-Michel Coissac pointed out in his work on educational cinema: "Under M. Bruneau's care, some films ... released by the industry and the city of Paris have been adapted in view of the role that they have had to play in career placement";[17] this was confirmed by Adrien Bruneau himself:

> The Film Library [of the city of Paris] is also the seat of the film service of the General Office of Technical Education for career placement and vocational teaching. To fill the needs of this service it has produced about twenty films relative to the trades. Sixteen copies of each have been made, which have been sent to the provincial career-placement offices and some regional offices.[18]

The double administrative supervision could have inhibited its functioning. Indeed, the institution was dependent on both the Parisian municipality and the Ministry of Public Education. Promoted to the level of national film library, it was charged with distributing films throughout France that had specifically Parisian content, since they were made at the schools in the capital. Moreover, its director was responsible for the city of Paris's film library, housed within the same buildings. It seems, however, that the progressive disengagement of the state was above all tied to discrepancies related to the stakes of the cinematic representation of work. Adrien Bruneau, in his preface to the catalogue, confirms having a "doctrine." He wrote:

> All of this results in the fact that the administration of technical education not only
> has a doctrine, but, in fact, a policy of educational cinema, and that it deserves perhaps
> more than timid references in the public conversations that relate to it.[19]

Adrien Bruneau borrowed his theoretical models from encyclopedias, and some of the shots for LA FLEUR ARTIFICIELLE, for example, obviously refer to plates in such works describing a practice, while the subheading underlines the significance of the profession in the capital since the 18th century. The reference to the Lumière brothers motivates him to affirm a close relationship between art and technology, imagining that a short training period could elevate the artisan to the level of artist and the unskilled laborer to that of qualified worker. The analogy is justified by bringing in the idea of the hand, and it leads him to vindicate artisanal activity and practice in accord with the theories of the historian Henri Focillon. Focillon, former educator at the Universités populaires[20] and member of numerous commissions interested in educational cinema, had presided in September 1931 over the national convention of educational cinema organized by Adrien Bruneau under the title The Film Library of the City of Paris and of the Undersecretary of State of Technical Education.[21] For Henri Focillon, the work of the artists could not be understood until one had reconstructed the genealogy of the technical process that had led them to express, by means of the hand, the spirit in the material.[22] POÉSIE DU TRAVAIL: DOIGTS D'OUVRIÈRES, MAINS DE FÉES (1930) seems to be an illustration of his position, since the film is exclusively composed of close-ups of women's hands: hands embroidering at a frame and crocheting, folding, ironing, and making artificial flowers, while the beauty of the gestures is underscored with very literary declarations. The opening title card compares the gestures of the artisan to those of the artist: "The sculptor kneads the formless clay with his hands and makes a statue out of it. Intelligence and taste guide the fingers at the same time." And the final card equates manual and intellectual work: "The labor of the hands has its virtue and nobility just like that of the mind, since it also creates beauty."

These are theories that, in those times of increasing industrialization, must have seemed quite obsolete and which furthermore ignored the difficult physical conditions for the workers. Adrien Bruneau wanted to make propaganda, and he did not hesitate to affirm this:

> Their [the films] goal was to favor the recruitment of our Parisian vocational schools
> above all by making known the preponderant role of artistic education in the practice
> of the occupations and industries of art. The attraction produced by these films in
> favor of our schools should encourage the elite of our primary schools to gravitate
> toward the trade schools instead of running to the liberal professions.[23]

Now the training given at the schools was not exempt from criticism. In 1909, Claire Gérard commented on the activities of the schools of artificial flower making in the MÉMOIRES ET DOCUMENTS of the Musée social,[24] a review of experts, stigmatizing them as follows:

> As for the vocational schools in the city of Paris... Apprenticeship is free of charge there and lasts three years, during which time the student learns to make a few flowers... but since she receives varied instruction at the same time, she has not been taught her profession sufficiently, and she will never acquire the suppleness necessary to earn a living from it. Education is not practice and work is often done in competition, that is to say for the benefit of the teachers.[25]

The director of the film library expressly wanted to work on the minds to orient adolescents towards occupations "that are difficult to recruit for" in order to guarantee them work. He neglected the fact that these adolescents, who had been improperly trained, fed the pool of unneeded workers. The Office of Technical Education, in the person of Julien Fontègne, disavowed the process, which no doubt led to the progressive substitution of technical-education films for career-orientation films. According to Fontègne, the task of the career-orientation film was to inform, but not to influence:

> The details do not matter much: what matters is getting a view of the whole picture, of major traits, in such a way that the child, coming out of a screening, can, in all freedom, express his point of view...]. The career-orientation film must be impartial, true, that is to say it must not knowingly hide certain difficulties of the occupation, and it must also not exaggerate certain of its beauties.[26]

The dissensions were so numerous that the state withdrew its support. The institution, however, in legitimizing the introduction of cameras into the workshop or the factory, contributed to the development of industrial film in France.

Confronted with a low number of commissions, Jean Benoit-Lévy solicited private interests, and the films were thereafter a matter of "industrial propaganda." Indeed, conforming to the transformations that were altering the social body in this period, the activities related to artisanal practice were replaced by industry, and films geared toward business communication replaced the mass-education films. The filmmaker abandoned the worker for the movement of machines, preferring to describe the mechanics put in place to raise productivity rather than the poetry of hands. Industrial propaganda films were long, almost an hour, while the editing and the music, most often written by Jean Wiener, confirmed the lyrical ambitions underscored by the lack of title cards.

Jean Benoit-Lévy made LA PIERRE QUE L'ON TISSE (1932) about asbestos, and LE CHANT DE LA MINE ET DU FEU (1932) about metallurgy. CONSTRUIRE (1934) describes the entire construction process of the Muette housing project in

Drancy. Symphonie du travail (1934), commissioned by the Larousse Society, sang the praises of the encyclopedia. Le port de Paris (1932) was a commission from the Paris chamber of commerce. Notre pain quotidien (c. 1934), on the other hand, was a montage film comparable in form to Poésie du travail: doigts d'ouvrières, mains de fée. The film was a meditation on the human condition, and the story opens and closes on images of an infant suckling in rural surroundings, the image of an eternally new beginning. This was chosen to illustrate the first title card: "After the first feeding in its life...," while the second, "The law of work," introduces shots borrowed from films made on industrial sites and edited to rhythmic chords in music written by Édouard Flament. The lyric film, much more than discursive, attests to the aesthetic ambitions in agreement with the filmmaker's assertions:

> Propaganda, whether made with smoke signals, printed characters, or images, is above all: A SIGN OF WORK. This general incomprehension of propaganda translates into a mistrust of the propaganda film. For a good many aesthetes it is the lowest manifestation of cinema from which all art must necessarily be excluded.[27]

Thus, this study of the work films of Jean Benoit-Lévy has shown how a genre was codified in the period between the wars. The three typologies evoked, career orientation, technical education, and industrial propaganda, put back into their context of production, have been shown to be genetically connected. They have conferred on industrial film the narrative or visual resources that would then constitute it.

Conclusion

The Central Film Library of Vocational Education probably constitutes one of the first attempts at a rational organization of industrial film in France. Created in 1925 within the framework of reforms encouraging the use of visual images in teaching, the institution commissioned the production of films, the direction of which was given over to Jean Benoit-Lévy, a filmmaker known as one of the specialists in educational cinema. Its catalogue, published in 1934, almost ten years after the institution's creation, shows the meager means that the film library had at its disposal. The study of this process, however, leading to the emergence and then disaffection of a public policy in favor of industrial film, permits an examination of the ideological foundations of a cinematic representation of work in France between the wars.

Notes

1. Maurice Pellisson, *Les Œuvres auxiliaires et complémentaires de l'école en France* (Paris: Imprimerie nationale, 1903, publication of the office of information and studies/ Musée pédagogique), pp. 25-26.

2. Cf. Auguste Bessou, *Rapport général commission extraparlementaire, chargée d'étudier les moyens de généraliser l'application du cinématographe dans les différentes branches de l'enseignement* (Ministère de l'Instruction publique et des beaux-arts, Paris: Imprimerie nationale, 1920).

3. Cf. Emmanuelle Devos, "La cinémathèque de la Ville de Paris, les idées et les faits (1906-1938)," master's thesis, in Michel Marie (ed.), *CFR Cinéma & Audiovisuel*, (Paris III, 1996); Emmanuelle Devos, Béatrice de Pastre, "La cinémathèque de la ville de Paris," Thierry Lefebvre (ed.), *Images du réel la non-fiction en France (1890-1930), 1895*, 18 (summer 1995).

4. Cf. Béatrice de Pastre, "Adrien Bruneau," François Albéra, Jean A. Gili (eds.), *Dictionnaire du cinéma français des années vingt, 1895*, 33 (June 2001).

5. Cf. Jean-Jacques Meusy, "Qui était Edmond Benoit-Lévy?," in Jean Gili, Michèle Lagny, Michel Marie (eds.), *Les Vingt Premières Années du cinéma français* (Paris: Presses de la Sorbonne nouvelle, 1995), pp. 115-43.

6. *Catalogue for Exposition du cinématographe, Conservatoire national des arts et métiers, April 20-23* (Paris: éditions Louis Mestre, 1922).

7. Letter from Édouard Herriot, Minister of Public Education, to Paul Léon, director of the fine arts, and Labbé, General Director of Technical Education, *La pédagogie de l'enseignement technique, recueil de circulaires, instructions et documents*, preface by Edmond Labbé (Paris; Librairie de l'enseignement technique, Léon Eyrolles éditeurs, 1927), p. 56.

8. G.-Michel Coissac, "Le 10e congrès de l'Art à l'école, le cinéma appliqué à l'enseignement," *Le Cinéopse*, 33 (May 1922), pp. 421-68.

9. G.-Michel Coissac, *Le cinématographe et l'enseignement*, new practical guide, approved and adopted by the Ministry of Public Education, the Ministry of Agriculture, the Office of Technical Education, the city of Paris's film library (Paris: Librairie Larousse, éditions du Cinéopse, 1926), p. 38.

10. Ibid., p. 40.

11. Paul Bénazet, "Le cinéma et l'enseignement professionnel," directive sent to the head of the Ministry of Public Instruction and the Fine Arts, the Undersecretary of State for Technical Education, dated December 19, 1925, and reproduced in an annex in G.-Michel Coissac, "Le cinématographe et l'enseignement," op. cit., p. 186.

12. Cf. Raymond Borde, Charles Perrin, *Les offices du cinéma éducateur et la survivance du muet, 1925-1940* (Lyon: Presses universitaires de Lyon, 1992).

13. Cf. Valérie Vignaux, "Jean Benoit-Lévy: l'ignorance est une maladie contagieuse ou le cinéma auxiliaire de la science," in Thierry Lefebvre, Jacques Malthête, and Laurent Mannoni (eds.), *Sur les pas de Marey, science (s) et cinéma* (Paris: L'Harmattan/ Semia, Les temps de l'image, 2004).

14. Cf. Valérie Vignaux, "Cinéma, éducation de masse et propagande agricole: les films de Jean Benoit-Lévy pour la cinémathèque du ministère de l'Agriculture (1924-1939)," *Archives*, February 2006.

15. Cf. *Catalogue de la cinémathèque du ministère de l'Agriculture* (1934).
16. Cf. *Catalogue des imprimés et films de propagande antituberculeuse*, published by the Propaganda Office of the National Committee against Tuberculosis, q.v.
17. G.-Michel Coissac, *Le cinématographe et l'enseignement*, op. cit., p. 41.
18. Adrien Bruneau, *Catalogue cinémathèque centrale d'enseignement professionnel* (Paris: édition de l'Ecole Estienne, 1934), p. 97.
19. Ibid., p. 8.
20. Cf. Annamaria Ducci, "Entre art et politique. La formation parisienne, 1881-1913," in *La vie des formes, Henri Focillon et les arts*, exhibition catalogue at the Musée des beaux-arts in Lyon, from 22 January to 26 April 2004 (Ghent: éditions Snoeck, 2004), p. 49.
21. Cf. *Cinédocument*, 1 (January 1932).
22. Cf. Henri Focillon, *Vie des formes* (Paris: Presses universitaires de France, 1943, re-printed 1984).
23. Adrien Bruneau, "L'orientation professionnelle, conférence du Musée Galliera," *Le Cinéopse*, 65 (January 1925), p. 35.
24. Cf. Janet Horne, *Le Musée social, aux origines de l'État providence* (Paris: Belin, 2004).
25. Claire Gérard "Condition de l'ouvrière parisienne dans l'industrie de la fleur artificielle," in *Le Musée social, Mémoires et documents* (1909), p. 15.
26. Julien Fontè "Le film d'orientation professionnelle," in *Catalogue cinémathèque centrale d'enseignement professionnel*, op. cit., p. 16.
27. Bordeaux Conference, 21 June 1932, private archives of Jean Benoit-Lévy.

"Reality Is There, but It's Manipulated"

West German Trade Unions and Film after 1945

Stefan Moitra

Industrial films shape ideas and knowledge about industrial trades, production operations, and economic processes using a wide variety of stylistic forms. They can be seen as part of both internal and external communication strategies within companies. If the image of industry, however, is based solely on the self-representations of companies, a central feature in the structure of industrial production is disregarded: that of labor and the perspective of the workers. Within the system of industrial relations their image has been represented traditionally by the counterpart to the employer and entrepreneur perspective – by the trade unions as institutions of the organized workforce. The German labor movement – the trade unions as well as the Social Democrat and Communist parties – took up the new medium of film rather early on. Until 1933, however, with certain exceptions, the filmic representation of workers in relation to industrial production was not emphasized as often as political confrontation or the documentation of working-class or labor movement culture.[1]

Outright labor movement feature films such as Phil Jutzi's MUTTER KRAUSENS FAHRT INS GLÜCK (1929) or Slatan Dudow's KUHLE WAMPE (1932), which are considered classics today, barely present any depictions of work as such, emphasizing instead unemployment and the wretched living conditions of the (sub)proletariat, to which a rhetoric of organization and solidarity is counterposed. Not only features but also documentary films by both directors from the same period were dedicated to the subject of working-class misery, political culture and party organization – taken as a sign of the fight against these conditions – as can be seen in Dudow's WIE DER BERLINER ARBEITER WOHNT (1930) and Jutzi's DIE ROTE FRONT MARSCHIERT (1927), about a meeting of the Communist Red Front Fighters' Association (*Rotfrontkämpferbund*) in Berlin.

More direct representations of industrial conflict were exceptional, such as Werner Hochbaum's BRÜDER (1929) about a strike of Hamburg dock workers which resulted from the – visibly explicit – discrepancy between the hard work of unloading the ships and the inadequate wages and living conditions. Whether in such Social Democratic films or rather Communist-oriented ones, the rhetoric of class solidarity and the necessity of fighting for social change were always at the ideological core of filmic representation. Starting in 1933 at the latest, National Socialist films attempted to counter this visual discourse with a rhetoric of desolidarization and individualization.[2]

Against this background, a break seems to have taken place in trade union films of the postwar period in comparison to those of the Weimar Republic. The representation of living conditions and the necessity of system change took a back seat to the representation of labor and industrial conflicts. The trade union film was narrowed to industrial film from a different perspective. This line of development, however, has so far enjoyed little attention or research. Historians as well as film scholars have mainly examined the connection between trade unions/labor movements and film for the period of the Weimar Republic.[3] The film work of trade unions after 1945 has gone fairly unnoticed, by both film scholars and historians of the period.[4] The interests of both these disciplines overlap, especially with regard to the functions of the unions' media practices. In particular, analyzing of the continuity of employing film as a means of propaganda and legitimization from the Weimar Republic to the early phase of the German Federal Republic requires the reconstruction of historical contexts of communication as well as the analysis of cinematic strategies of representation.

In fact, along with the trade union film's generic shift towards industrial film, a change in the self-perception of the workers' organizations took place. In this respect, cinematic representational strategies eventually had symptomatic value. The image of a social movement aiming at system transformation disappeared – initially and at least at the level of film – and was replaced by a more limited framework of industrial relations and social politics. Here, as in the broader union discourse, the term "work"/"labor" (*Arbeit*) began to take the place of "class" as a key term of identification. Annual union conventions, for instance, were called "parliaments of labor" – not the least to emphasize the place of trade unions in the new democracy. Similarly, the shift from "class" to "labor" was continually represented in the discussions of the union press. Their coverage included articles on the iconography of labor in the visual arts, and reporting on cinematic representational forms of labor and the workforce was a standard part of the postwar unions' cultural debate.[5] Special emphasis was placed on the discussion of industrial films produced by the companies and the "correct" form of representing the social conditions of industrial production. For instance, one article from 1961 observed the following with regard to two mining films:

> Both directors joyfully show the sparkling machines that are intended to make the miner's life easier, but they are silent about the fact that he still has a lot of hard physical work to do. Reality is there, but it's manipulated... Industry is valorized at the costs of the working man's interests. It is a similar case with the steel industry films. TECHNIK – DREI STUDIEN IN JAZZ (shot at and also financed by Krupp) would have us believe that the same rhythms are at work in the blast furnace and in impro-

visational jazz. The editing gives an even stronger impression of man adjusting to a rhythm. A degraded workhorse! ... The industrial firms that finance these films ... are only interested in advertising, social problems are of no concern here.[6]

Instead of "singing the praises of the machine age," as another article stated, the aim had to be to "let man stand up to the machine."[7] With this pathos of the exploited working-class hero the trade unions of the postwar years connected their discourse to the rhetoric of the Weimar period as well as to the aesthetic frameworks of the socio-critical realist novel of the 19th century and its associated visual program.[8] It remains to be seen, however, how far the unions' own film practices corresponded to this rhetoric.[9] What kind of measures did they employ to counter the business slant of industrial films? How much did their own film productions provide an alternative image of broader economic structures, workplace conditions, and production processes? A comparison of the filmic strategies reveals a series of both overlaps and differences between trade union films in the postwar years and industrial films of company provenance. Like the company films, trade union films present no consistent picture. Instead, the structuring of form and content depends on the occasion and the relevant institutional contexts; in both types of film the form is determined by three "A" factors: *Anlass* (occasion), *Adressat* (audience), and *Auftraggeber* (commissioning body).[10] It is particularly significant that a radical stylistic and thematic break with the conventions of the company film was not intended, as had been the case of the German labor movement films of the 1920s or even those of the early Soviet Union. The following article on the film practices of the West German trade unions in the 1950s and 1960s attempts, in the first part, to reconstruct the uses and functional integration of trade union films. Special attention is paid to the internal film discourse on the varying organizational levels as well as to the specific contexts of film screenings. In the second part, selected trade union films are examined and investigated with regard to their image of the workforce and the trade unions themselves and with respect to specific, situation-based forms of representation.

Trade union film discourse and screening contexts

In the discussion of trade union film practice, two recurring lines of approach can fundamentally be distinguished: on the one hand, the sheer attraction of the medium is relied upon to draw members and audiences; on the other hand, the effectiveness of film to convey political and ideological positions is trusted. These arguments hold true as much for the use of all kinds of narrative and non-fiction films at trade union events as they do for the production and use of films commissioned by the unions. However, the actual functional integration of films can only be understood by placing the unions' media practice in a wider historical context. Their employment of film during the period has to be seen with regard to their specific position in the early German Federal Republic. Hence, a series of features which are significant for the relation between the union movement and the wider public are reflected as much in the uses as in the content of the films.

A focal point in this respect is the unions' self-conception during the period and the position they claimed within the new democracy. The reestablishment of union work after 1945 reflected manifold stages of the labor movement's ideological and organizational development – from the time of the Empire through the Weimar Republic, up to complete suppression under National Socialism.[11] One of the most distinctive consequences that is derived from these experiences was the overcoming of political factions along party lines as they had existed until 1933 – additionally signifying the sharp disintegration of Weimar society. Now, after the end of the war, wage earners of all political affiliations – Social Democrats, Christians, and at first even Communists – were supposed to find a common representative under the slogan of a "united trade union" (Einheitsgewerkschaft). The German Federation of Trade Unions (DGB) established itself as the unitary organization; distinctions between unions were no longer made in relation to political leanings, only according to trade sector. The largest of the 16 individual trade unions affiliated with the DGB in 1949 were the IG Bergbau und Energie (Industrial Union of Mining and Energy Workers), the IG Metall (metal workers), IG Chemie (chemical workers), and the ÖTV (public-service and transportation workers).

Although formally overcoming party political divisions, strong personal continuities in union work prevailed. Officials who had already been active in the Weimar Republic often remained influential, and the social milieu structures in which the unions had been rooted continued to exist. Thus, at multiple levels of union engagement traditional lines and concepts from the Weimar period – above all of Social Democratic origin – were pushed forward or at least continued in a modified form.[12] In this respect, the main issues of continuity related to the classic fields of union activity, in particular the demands for workers' participation in decision making, be it on the shop floor, in the company management, or even in macroeconomics on a government level. Continuities, however, also emerged in the area of cultural education as the unions adhered to some extent to the principles of Weimar labor movement culture. It was particularly in this context that film came into discussion.

What was significant, apart from establishing the new political unity of the trade union movement and stressing lines of continuity, were the unions' attempts to position themselves within the young republic. Despite the endeavors to overcome political frictions, the union movement soon found itself involved in the Cold War. Communist trade unionists were caught in a constant tug of loyalties between the East German party line and the West German concept of labor unity. On the other hand, the Social and Christian Democratic majorities in the DGB unions made great efforts to distance themselves internally and externally from socialist ideas of the "eastern" type and to force the Communists, wherever possible, out of their functions.[13] At the same time, this conflict served as a contribution to the unions' integration into the new West German democracy. When accusations were made by conservatives and company owners that unions' demands for socialization and codetermination were colluding with GDR socialism, West German unions could respond by citing their clearly visible anti-Communism. This made the unions seem even more legitimate in their demands, indeed as much in relation to the economy as to a democratic influence on society at large. It is notable that, in the course of the 1950s and 1960s, the unions' ambitions to exert influence on society as a whole, instead of being limited to the improvement of working conditions, were abandoned. Nevertheless, on a basic level, elements of a traditional leftist working-class culture continued to exist.[14]

Apart from merely social and economic issues, postwar union debates continued to encompass questions of education and culture as means of emancipating the working class from the restraints of the capitalist consumer system. The discussion of film use within the framework of trade union activities and long-term goals principally belongs in this area. With regard to feature films, the unions took part in the contemporary debates about cultural quality and replicated the common distinction between entertainment and high culture. In general, feature films were included in the category of entertainment. At the same time, there were demands for alternative "realistic," socio-critical, and enlightening film. Labor press organs posed questions such as: "Why doesn't anyone work in film?", "Where is the worker's film?", and "Why not films about reality?" These questions did not refer solely to feature films; they were also directed at industrial films, which in the classification scheme of entertainment vs. high culture tended to find its place in the area of culture (and indeed, they usually belonged to a whole genre of the so-called *Kulturfilm*).[15]

Unions published film recommendations and reviews in their press organs. But from quite early on, they also established their own film screenings, through which they sought to meet their own cultural demands. The DGB, as the central union organization, and the large individual unions, such as IG Metall and IG Bergbau, however, took precautions not to leave the choice of films solely to local union officials. In order to make film use more effective, the supply of "appropriate film material" was centralized.[16] The usual procedure for film shows at union events was to put together mixed programs, in which a feature film was screened along with a "cultural film" or "supporting film" (*Beifilm*), as it was called by the miners' union. While particular attention was paid to ensure that the features corresponded to the cultural and ideological principles of the organization, the supporting films usually dealt with explicit union themes or topics relevant to union work. But these films were by no means restricted to the unions' own productions. The miners' union catalogue, besides films by the DGB and its affiliated member unions, also listed films by occupational-insurance institutions, the European Coal and Steel Community, the United Nations, the federal government's department for political education, and even the allied postwar re-education institutions.

Due in part to the centralized organization, the films screened at local union events reached a notably wide audience. The DGB, to which the local officials of all trades could turn, as well as the single unions that had set up their own film offices, e.g., IG Metall and IG Bergbau, built up distribution networks that covered the entire Federal Republic. Film screenings were included at the most diverse types of union gatherings, at cultural evenings on a local level, in youth work, at so-called housewives' afternoons, at seminars and training sessions, etc. DGB, IG Metall, and the Union of Gardening and Agriculture also introduced mobile traveling cinemas in order to establish a presence in provincial settings and in the countryside. The available audience figures clearly show that up until the establishment of television, film remained a central medium, capable of attracting large numbers of people. In 1954, the DGB's local and regional committees recorded 499,191 visitors at 5,817 events; in 1958, there were 767,341 attendees counted at 8,594 events. IG Metall held fewer events and therefore reached fewer spectators: 250 events with 28,574 attendees in 1959. The average number of spectators, however, at about 100 per screening, was higher than that of the DGB. Similar figures can be found for the miners, which, after establishing a centralized film distribution system, could count 35,000 spectators at 310 film screenings in the first six months of 1956 alone.[17]

In addition to their educational value, the film screenings were seen as an important occasion for public self-representation. In 1956, for example, the executive board of the miners' union wrote the following to the local administrative offices:

> Since film events are usually attended by a large number of colleagues and their family members, they are a good occasion to convince the attendees of the importance and the goals and tasks of our union. ... Film events should not be thought of as pure entertainment; we want to reach a wider audience to publicize all of our union activities and address those members and their families who otherwise never or rarely turn up at gatherings.[18]

Along with the regular screenings, film shows were given a prominent place in public conflict situations, both during campaigns, such as the coal crisis of 1959, and during strikes. After the six-week strike at the Bremen shipyard in 1953, a union official stated that the 41 film shows integrated into the other protest activities had "contributed significantly to the success of the strike." During the strike, free film screenings, held in the morning in various parts of the city, were put on for the striking workers and their wives. They consisted of feature films, trade union industrial films and cultural films, as well as newsreels.[19]

While mere "entertainment" was initially rejected, by and by, a tendency to include popular feature films into programs could also be noted. In the immediate postwar period, pure "cultural film" screenings with an entirely educational content were still able to draw a large audience. Demand, however, continually shifted in the direction of feature films. As early as 1957, an official of the miners' union complained that "unfortunately very little use" was being made of non-feature films, which was regrettable, since "the projectionist could easily put together an interesting program of the supporting films, especially for smaller groups and educational evenings." Nevertheless, supporting films were screened at 300 events with an average audience of 100.[20] Indeed, an important forum for non-fiction films was maintained in a variety of educational courses as well as in youth work until the end of the 1960s and early 1970s, when both the DGB and the affiliated trade unions suspended their distribution activities. Before then, a significant drop in audience numbers had been observed, which the miners' union, like the film industry itself when confronting the problem of declining audiences, initially tried to counter by introducing more entertaining films. The discontinuation of unions' film activity, however, can also be explained by the fact that the self-perception of the union audience had changed. For both union members and officials, maintaining a separate, independent labor movement culture had become an anachronistic goal. The specific educational task of union film work was no longer relevant.

The image of unions and workers in trade union film productions

The labor press turned their attention to film shortly after the unions were newly constituted in the first postwar years and published reviews and articles about union film work. However, the first films were not produced immediately. The DGB initially considered becoming active in the restructuring of the German film industry after the liquidation of UFA, but quickly abandoned these ideas. Filmic coverage of union activities was limited to cooperation with various newsreel producers.[21]

The unions' own productions can be divided into two basic periods. In the first phase at the beginning of the 1950s, productions which mainly served the purpose of general self-representation were commissioned. This phase begins with the first film produced by the DGB in 1951, HANS BÖCKLER, about its recently deceased first postwar chairman, and also includes various reports on conventions of the DGB, the affiliated unions and their individual subdivisions like the union youth, along with longer "cultural films" that combined a documentary style with feature-film elements to narrate the organizations' history and tasks and explain the benefits of union membership. A second phase becomes apparent in the mid-1950s, when a thematic distinction can be discerned, with much greater attention being paid to individual aspects of labor activity. These films, for example, targeted the recruitment of young people or office workers, who were traditionally difficult to organize. There was also a series of quickly produced films dealing with current conflicts and campaigns. IG Bergbau, for instance, released two films at the beginning of the coal crisis of 1958/59 to support and widen effective forms of public protest: SCHON VERGESSEN? (*Already Forgotten?*), which briefly sketched the background of the crisis; and GEWERKSCHAFT IN AKTION (*Union in Action*), which documented a mass demonstration of miners in Bonn.[22] Similarly focusing on current political affairs, EIN GEFÄHRLICHES EXPERIMENT (*A Dangerous Experiment*), produced in 1960 by the DGB, attacked plans by the government to limit the self-administration of health-insurance companies. The film was immediately taken out of circulation when the government altered its plans. IG Metall, IG Chemie, and the DGB additionally produced a series of short animated films, starting in 1957, that were used in the campaign to reduce working hours and shown before features in commercial cinemas.[23] Finally, the unions produced their own *Monthly Newsreel* on labor issues in cooperation with Deutsche Wochenschau newsreel production, which provided the necessary film material. Starting in 1955, these initially circulated under the title WELT DER ARBEIT (*World of Labor*) and from 1957 as PERSPEKTIVEN.

All of the films sketched here ultimately served the goal of conveying the internal and external public positions of the DGB and its member organizations. In all of the themes they treated, these films were, as expressed in the initial title of the monthly newsreels, presented and understood as commentaries on the world of labor and the industrial system and as a contribution to their progress and reform. Using examples of union film production, I will now consider different cinematic variations on a central motive of postwar labor discourse: the presentation of the worker and his (the use of the masculine pronoun is appropriate here, since the films during the period under consideration as well as the discourse at large mainly addressed the prototype of the male industrial worker) representation in the union organization. I will try to show, on the one hand, that union strategies indeed rested on the representational form of the "heroic worker," representing an iconic figure in the class struggle between the militant proletariat and the exploitative capitalists. But I will also argue that this figure, on the other hand, only appeared as a semantic trace determined within a rhetoric of social integration.

Two films by IG Bergbau will serve as initial examples: KAMERADSCHAFT (*Comradeship*, 1953) and SCHON VERGESSEN? (1959).[24] KAMERADSCHAFT was the union's first longer representation film, and it outlines the fields of activities and duties of the union with a mixture of narrative and documentary forms. At the center of the story line is an old coal miner who performs his duties as a union contribution collector after his shift. Various problems of the postwar period, both general and specific to mining, are illustrated through his example – e.g., lack of housing, occupational safety, accident and health insurance, co-determination, and pay rates. The representation of mine work follows the classic pathos of the male industrial worker. But what is articulated here is signified as pride in a distinct industrial trade and craft, rather than radical class consciousness. The beginning of the film is marked by an elegiac description of the coal-mining region: The Ruhr is the "land between dusky rivers and canals," that "has become our homeland and our destiny," as the commentator declares. Chimneys and engine gears are the "symbols of work" in the coalfield in which the mining tools (*das Gezähe*), are passed on over generations of men to their sons.[25] The images that accompany this narrative completely correspond to the figure of physically taxing manual labor: Men with bare torsos and mining hammers are seen in front of a coal face, the coal that has already been hewn is being transported away in trucks. The commentary elaborates on the images with a discourse of sacrifice: Above all, in the "decisive years" of postwar destruction, "the miner" always "stood at the head of the line" and "did the hard work." For, as we hear at another point, "their work is hard everywhere, but coal is necessary," it "is at the heart of a modern economy."

Despite this dramatic connection between the role of sacrifice and hard labor, the image of the miner is not presented in a combative or confrontational context, but is integrated into a civil discourse of shared responsibilities: work is performed for the good of society as a whole, and anyone who wants a change in the economic situation must not "gripe and nag" but should instead "participate equally." Anyone who "wants to have a say must also take responsibility," as two shop stewards maintain. The representation of union activities – the commitment to democracy inside the companies and to the betterment of the workers' living conditions, the improvement of educational and leisure opportunities for the youth, etc. – always has a triple meaning. Primarily, it shows how the organization is tangibly improving the social conditions of the miners. In addition, the images address the integration of the miners and their representatives into West German society. They are not exploited workers who are seeking a confrontation with the mining companies in order to pursue their own interests. Instead, they sacrifice themselves "at the heart of modern economy" for the sake of the common good. The union is also shown as the responsible representative of workers' interests, for instance, in the images of youth work and the quest for greater democratic progress in West German society.

The theme of consensus in KAMERADSCHAFT was clearly overturned during the mining crisis in SCHON VERGESSEN? The latter film was produced in 1959 – at the beginning of a crisis situation that would last until 1969 – at a time when a mass protest by the miners' union was in full swing.[26] In May 1959, every district office received a copy of the film and was encouraged to screen it at events over the coming months.[27] SCHON VERGESSEN? is 12 minutes in length and essentially uses the same footage as KAMERADSCHAFT, but in contrast to the previous half-hour film, it is much more committed to the depiction of the actual working process. The editing and music alone confer a contrasting style to the earlier film. Initially, images of the production process underground are shown in a long sequence set to dramatic music at a fast rhythm, reminiscent of Hanns Eisler work from the Weimar period. A narrator explains the following at the same rhythm:

> Day and night the fires blaze, the wheels turn, the chimneys smolder, the pulleys turn at the pit head. Day and night men travel underground to dig the coal. Every day hundreds of thousands do their work at a tireless rhythm, for – the Ruhr is the source of power for our people.

After that, coal mining is placed in the same historical context as it was in KAMERADSCHAFT: Coal production is the backbone of economy and ensures everyday survival after the war, the miners are sacrificing themselves for the social good. However, this narrative then takes a confrontational turn. The music, provocative commentary, constant movement of the image, rhythmic editing, and the use of sounds from the workplace create a dramatic presentation of work that stands in stark contrast to the images of the West German postwar boom that follow.

We see images of modern apartment buildings, rows of houses, cars, and window displays accompanied by light and lilting music. The climax, then, is reached with shots of a beauty contest. The commentator notes: "All too quickly we forgot about grievances (*Miss-stände*) and put on beauty contests (*Miss-Wahlen*). Everything was glittering in the light of the German economic miracle." By these polemic means, the sequence aims to recreate notions of class division. But the conflict is portrayed in an utterly cinematic way by employing specific body

Figure 1 Girls and grievances: SCHON VERGESSEN? *(1959)*

politics and viewing structures. A close-up of one underground worker's masculine body, with which the film has established its iconography, is juxtaposed with the gaze of the middle-class man at a beauty contest, who for his part is assessing the female bodies presented there. The objectifying, power-oriented male gaze at the female body is, as has frequently been stressed in film theory, a classic figure of cinema. But in the case of SCHON VERGESSEN?, the male gaze is not only used to mark a difference in gender, but also of class. The bourgeois man depicted is an idle beneficiary of obtained wealth in very different ways, who lets his gaze wander self-indulgently while the others (the mine workers, the women) use their bodies to accomplish hard work – to serve him and his gaze, respectively.

While the image of the worker in KAMERADSCHAFT was constructed within a discourse of integration, SCHON VERGESSEN? reactivates an almost forgotten potential for confrontation. In the context of contemporary West German debates, the film's confrontational demand for justice denotes a threatening gesture which references the common fear of a political radicalization of the miners.[28] Thus, an older, more aggressive tone is consciously taken up in the film to warn against the miners' exclusion from society and their expulsion from the Federal Republic's civil democratic consensus. The fact that the use of this image was short-lived and intended as a ritualistic, threatening gesture is demonstrated by the second film from the period of the coal crisis, the 1959 GEWERKSCHAFT IN AKTION. It documents a series of protests in the Ruhr that led to a mass demonstration of miners at the seat of the West German government in Bonn. In this film, no opposition is created, on the visual level, between the working and the middle classes. The usual underground scenes, which typically mark the place of the worker, are entirely absent. In appearance, the miners – in suits and coats – cannot be distinguished from other people, and the commentary places a great deal of emphasis on proving the well-organized and orderly nature of the demonstrators. The protesting miners are no threat, and are instead part of a civil, respectable, bürgerlich democracy.

A position between the image of the "threatening" and the "civil" worker is occupied by HIER WIRD GESTREIKT (There's a Strike Going On), produced by IG Metall in 1957.[29] It describes a six-week strike by engineering workers in Schleswig-Holstein in the winter of 1956/57 for equality between blue-collar and white-collar workers in sickness pay and for an increase in holiday pay. As in GEWERKSCHAFT IN AKTION, a dramatic image of a worker's body and a threatening tone are avoided, despite the fact that the film describes the most classic form of labor struggle. References are indeed made, above all on a musical and rhetorical level, to the tradition of the labor movement of the Weimar period, but this continuity appears entirely within the framework of a West German political consensus. Two main levels of representation can be distinguished in the film. On the one hand, the strike is shown as part of a democratic practice derived from the traditions of the labor movement. On the other hand, the film refers to a civil consensus within which the strike is presented as a legitimate, and above all mature, limited form of conflict within the mainstream of society.

The tradition of the labor movement is present from the start. We see a factory gate closing while the soundtrack presents the tune of an old labor movement song, "Brüder, zur Sonne, zur Freiheit" ("Brothers, to the Sun and to Freedom"). Played by a jazz group, this musical theme becomes a leitmotiv in the film. The initial cause of the strike, the demand for equality between blue-collar and white-collar workers, is only briefly explained by the narrator. Emphasis is instead placed on the fact of work stoppage. The entire opening sequence is committed to the immediate results of the strike – quiet shipyards, empty harbors, and picket lines in front of factory gates. This impression of a deadlock is juxtaposed in the second part with issues of strike organization and measures of support given to the workers and their action. Emphasis is placed on the centrality of decision making in terms of carrying out and ending the conflict. The commentary connects these activities with the traditional values of solidarity, discipline, and strength. The position of work and the production process, which is set at the center of conventional industrial film, is occupied here by the effectiveness of union organization – a cinematic assertion of equivalency that is used as a rhetorical tool. This thematic shift of strike activity taking the place of workplace activity is established from the very beginning and provides a leitmotiv throughout the entire film. From the strike ballot – accompanied by images of a torchlight procession to which the participants sing another song from the labor movement's traditional repertoire, "Mit uns zieht die neue Zeit" – to the detailed depiction of support, like the distribution of Christmas packages and solidarity telegrams from the DGB, from other IG Metall divisions and American steel workers, and the production of strike newspapers: All of these activities are part of a rich organizational repertoire that allows the union to wage the conflict and that, according to the rhetoric of equivalency, temporarily replaces industrial production, not least of which because the union's efficient organization is up to the task in every way. This image of a work process is complemented by an emphasis on democratic practices as part of the structure – in particular, the detailed presentation of meetings, decision making, debating, voting, and ballot counting, which also provide moments of suspense on a narrative level.

On the other hand, the confrontational tone of a depiction of union efficiency is diluted by the narrator's explicitly genial tone and a series of narrative inserts in the course of the action. What is happening here is a struggle between strikers and bosses, not a conflict with the general public as in SCHON VERGESSEN? This is especially vivid in one small scene, when a group of pickets are seen enjoying a glass of rum to fend off the cold and the commentator says, "Rum is not at all bad as a remedy for thirst, cold, or rheumatism. Let's try a little: not bad, my friend, not bad." In another scene, a worker is seen grinning as he polishes the company sign at the factory gate, which the speaker narrates with the comment, "We'll give them a wipe." In the same tone, the image of the workers' steadfastness is integrated into a notion of civil order: "No strike can work without discipline and order. Anyone who pickets will want to have a stamp [of official endorsement] as well." This narrative strategy of removing a potential division between workers and the rest of society culminates in two sequences in which the consciousness of responsibility for public order and the ideal of the respectable family is stressed. Two examples are shown: in the first, the strikers temporarily suspend their action in order to protect "life and property wherever possible"; in the second, we see a Christmas party where the unpacking of DGB presents is celebrated as "a good deed for a housewife at Christmastime." With such assurances of the socially integrated position of the workers and their organization, it is made clear that these strikers are solving a specific problem, and that they were not, as was often feared by the political establishment, seeking to bring about far-reaching and radical changes in society.

Conclusion

HIER WIRD GESTREIKT alternates, like other trade union films, between the reaffirmation that the workers and their organizations no longer posed any threat to social order, and the legitimization of its own actions in conflict situations. Often enough, the trade union films place the depiction of organizational activities in the foreground to convey an impression of order and transparency and provide a guarantee that unions are as organized as the industry itself instead of questioning the existing social order. The trade union film takes up the central motive of the industrial film to project it onto the trade unions, and it does so with the political goal of creating a consensus that will stay the ground in the case of conflict.

In light of these findings, the question of the multiple functions of the organizations' film activities can be posed again. Given that a large portion of union productions are still awaiting full examination, what has gone particularly unnoticed are films that, in a formal sense, cannot easily be categorized among the normal propaganda functions of union events and which were directed at a more specific audience. This is especially the case for work-study films commissioned by the DGB and occasional films, i.e., the private footage of youth leisure activities or celebrations, which were only seen in local circles.[30] Just as work-study films served as part of streamlining measures at industrial companies and private souvenir films helped to create group identities and the establishment of memories,[31] it seems worthwhile to examine the alternative or corresponding union films covering similar specific functions and involvements in order to assess their value in the unions' organizational structure.

Furthermore, an exciting change in the way unions saw themselves is visible in the aesthetic of trade union film productions in the first two decades after the war. Trade union films indeed proposed an alternative image of the industrial system by making the workers – rather than the machinery or industrial organization – the central factor in the industrial creation of value. At the same time, they depict a transformation of the unions, from a group anchored in a historically aspiring social and cultural milieu to an organization that is almost exclusively limited to representing their members in the field of social policy and industrial relations. Union-produced films communicated this transformation to a wider, partly non-union, audience, thus functioning both as depiction and mediator of union change. Indeed, as before, the worker "still had to do hard physical labor," as one film review put it, but the image of the alienated proletariat standing outside society had almost completely disappeared from cinematic representation. Even with regard to film style, the unions attempted to "conquer the center" of society.[32] In a formal sense and in its generic modes, the labor union film could barely be distinguished anymore from the companies' industrial films. One could speak of an aesthetic strategy of consensus. When this consensus was transgressed, such as in Schon vergessen?, it was merely to make a cinematic gesture of threat.

The aesthetic consensus between the union and the industrial film further raises the question of a long-term development in the labor unions' visual self-representation. In the end, it corresponds to the way the unions positioned themselves in the early Federal Republic, in which they paid for social political compromise by giving up more far-reaching demands. The greatest success of the unions was the establishment and legal foundation of co-determination (*Mitbestimmung*), of workers' and trade union representation on the shop floor as well as – in the coal and steel industries, and later in all large companies – on the directorial boards. A further examination has to ask for the degree to which the early cinematic reflections of co-determination/participation, as focal points of identification in the 1950s and 1960s, led to a unique "aesthetic of *Mitbestimmung*" in the 1970s, when the trade unions' impact in West Germany was at its peak. If such an aesthetic existed, this would cast an interesting spotlight on the face of the old Federal Republic.

Notes

1. As an overview of, above all, Communist film work, see Gertrud Kühne et al. (eds.), *Film und revolutionäre Arbeiterbewegung in Deutschland 1918-1932. Dokumente und Materialien zur Entwicklung der Filmpolitik der revolutionären Arbeiterbewegung und zu den Anfängen sozialistischer Filmkunst in Deutschland* (Berlin: Volk und Welt (1975); cf. also Dieter Langewiesche, "Das neue Massenmedium Film und die deutsche Arbeiterbewegung in der Weimarer Republik," in Jürgen Kocka et al. (eds.), *Von der Arbeiterbewegung zum modernen Sozialstaat* (Munich: Oldenbourg, 1994), pp. 114-30 and Hans-Joachim Teichler, "Arbeitersport im Film. Notizen zur filmischen Werbe- und Lehrtätigkeit des Arbeitersports in Deutschland. Mit einer Filmographie archivierter und verschollener Filmdokumente zum Arbeitersport vor 1932," *Internationale*

wissenschaftliche Korrespondenz zur Geschichte der deutschen Arbeiterbewegung, 17 (1981), pp. 361-378.

2. Cf. Thomas Meyer, " 'Gesichtsverlust' versus Resemantisierung. Überlegungen zum Gesicht des Arbeiters im Nationalsozialismus anhand einiger Filme von Walther Ruttmann," *Montage AV* 13, 2 (2004), pp. 75-91.

3. Along with the titles mentioned in footnote 1, cf. especially the work of the Dutch film historian Bert Hogenkamp: Bert Hogenkamp (ed.), *Bergarbeiter im Film* (Oberhausen: Westdeutsche Kurzfilmtage im Auftrag der Stadt Oberhausen, 1982) and *Deadly Parallels: Film and the Left in Britain, 1929-1939* (London: Lawrence & Wilshart, 1986).

4. Exceptions include Uli Veith, *Gewerkschaftliche Medienpolitik und Filmarbeit. Am Beispiel des DGB und der IG Metall* (Cologne: Pahl-Rugenstein, 1984), Stefan Moitra, *"Wo bleibt der Arbeiterfilm?" Die Auseinandersetzung der IG Bergbau und Energie mit dem Medium Film in den 1950er und 1960er Jahren* (Bochum: Institut für soziale Bewegungen, 2004) and Bert Hogenkamp, *Film, Television and the Left in Britain*; cf. also Peter Stead, *Film and the Working Class: The Feature Film in British and American Society* (London and New York: Routledge, 1989).

5. Cf. "Die Arbeit in der bildenden Kunst," *Bergbau und Wirtschaft. Informationsblatt der IG Bergbau für Mitarbeiter und Betriebsräte* (1953), pp. 546-548. On the changes in the labor discourse in the early Federal Republic, cf. Barbara M. Kehm, *Zwischen Abgrenzung und Integration. Der gewerkschaftliche Diskurs in der Bundesrepublik Deutschland* (Opladen: Westdeutscher Verlag, 1991).

6. "Wohin geht der Dokumentarfilm? Bericht über die Internationalen Filmtage in Mannheim," *Bergbau und Wirtschaft Jg. 1961*, pp. 584f. The mining films treated are the German production BERGMANN AM HEBEL by Bert Brandt and the French film SURVOL by Guy Gillet. On TECHNIK – DREI STUDIEN IN JAZZ cf. Herwig Müther, "Technik – Drei Studien in Jazz," in Manfred Rasch et al. (eds.), *Industriefilm – Medium und Quelle. Beispiele aus der Eisen- und Stahlindustrie* (Essen: Klartext, 1997), p. 225-232.

7. "Warum wird im Film nicht gearbeitet? Filmkritiker und Filmfachleute diskutierten in Recklinghausen," in *Bergbau und Wirtschaft Jg. 1961*, pp. 430f.

8. Cf. Klaus Türk, *Bilder der Arbeit. Eine ikonografische Anthologie* (Wiesbaden: Westdeutscher Verlag, 2000), pp. 202-204.

9. In the following, the term "film practice" is used to cover both union organized film screenings as well as union film production.

10. Cf. Thomas Elsaesser, "Die Stadt von Morgen: Filme zum Bauen und Wohnen in der Weimarer Republik," Klaus Kreimeier, Antje Ehmann, Jeanpaul Goergen (eds.), *Geschichte des dokumentarischen Film in Deutschland, Vol. 2: Weimarer Republik (1918-1933)* (Stuttgart: Reclam-Verlag, 2005), pp. 381-410.

11. Cf. in general Klaus Schönhoven, *Die deutschen Gewerkschaften* (Frankfurt am Main: Suhrkamp, 1987); Hans-Otto Hemmer, Kurt Thomas Schmitz (eds.), *Geschichte der Gewerkschaften in der Bundesrepublik Deutschland. Von den Anfängen bis heute* (Cologne: Bund-Verlag, 1990).

12. Karl Lauschke (ed.), "Die Gewerkschaftselite der Nachkriegszeit: Prägung, Funktion, Leitbilder," *Mitteilungsblatt des Instituts für soziale Bewegungen*, 35 (2006).

13. Till Kössler, *Abschied von der Revolution. Kommunisten und Gesellschaft in Westdeutschland 1945-1968* (Düsseldorf: Droste, 2005).

14. Langewiesche 2003 uses the term *Weltanschauungskultur*; Dieter Langewiesche, "Zur Geschichte der Arbeiterkultur in Deutschland," in Dieter Langewiesche, Friedrich Lenger (eds.), *Liberalismus und Sozialismus. Ausgewählte Beiträge* (Bonn: Dietz, 2003), pp. 249-264. Cf. also Wolfgang Kaschuba (ed.), *Arbeiterkultur seit 1945. Ende oder Veränderung?* (Tübingen: Tübinger Vereinigung für Volkskunde, 1991).

15. "Warum wird im Film nicht gearbeitet? Filmkritiker und Filmfachleute diskutierten in Recklinghausen," *Bergbau und Wirtschaft*, 14 (1961), pp. 430-431; "Wo bleibt der Arbeiterfilm?," *Die Bergbauindustrie*, 3 (1950), p. 12; "Wann Filme aus der Wirklichkeit? Einige Betrachtungen zum Verhältnis von Bergbau und Film," *Bergbau und Wirtschaft*, 14 (1961), pp. 227-229.

16. IG Bergbau (ed.), *Jahrbuch 1952*, p. 193.

17. Figures according to Veith (1984), p. 257; Moitra (2004), p. 37.

18. Rundschreiben des geschäftsführenden Vorstands der IG Bergbau nr. 36/56, 02.05.1956, Archiv für soziale Bewegungen, Bochum, Bestand IGBE, 12320.

19. Friedrich Düßmann, "Der Film im Dienste der Gewerkschaften," *Metall. Zeitung der IG Metall für die Bundesrepublik Deutschland*, 8 (December 23, 1953), p. 6.

20. IG Bergbau (ed.), *Jahrbuch 1957*, p. 1046; Moitra (2004), pp. 39f.

21. Cf. the summaries in Geschäftsberichte des Bundesvorstandes des Deutschen Gewerkschaftsbundes, 1950-1951ff.

22. On the mining crisis, see Christoph Nonn, *Die Ruhrbergbaukrise. Entindustrialisierung und Politik 1958-1969* (Göttingen: Vandenhoeck und Ruprecht, 2001).

23. Cf. Veith (1984), pp. 310-312.

24. All of the films discussed in the following can be found in the Archiv für soziale Bewegungen, Bochum.

25. Unless otherwise noted, this and all subsequent citations are from the films discussed.

26. The crisis was caused by the fact that cheaper imports of coal and oil were increasingly being introduced. Apart from growing coal stocks, the most visible effect was work reduction or mine closures. Cf. Nonn 2001 and Karl Lauschke, *Schwarze Fahnen an der Ruhr. Die Politik der IG Bergbau und Energie während der Kohlenkrise 1958-1968* (Marburg: Verlag Arbeiterbewegung und Gesellschaftswissenschaft, 1984).

27. Rundschreiben des geschäftsführenden Vorstands der IG Bergbau nr. 16/59 (May 19, 1959), Archiv für soziale Bewegungen, Bochum, Bestand IGBE, 12320.

28. Cf. Nonn (2001), pp. 63-65.

29. Cf. also Veith (1984), pp. 366-368.

30. On the work studies, see Veith (1984), p. 276; Geschäftsberichte des Bundesvorstandes des Deutschen Gewerkschaftsbundes 1959-1961, p. 77. Examples of private 'occasional films' in the appendix of Moitra (2004), 69f.

31. Cf. Hediger and Vonderau, "Record, Rhetoric, Rationalization: Industrial Organization and Film," in this volume.

32. Kehm (1991), pp. 137-139.

V
Urbanity, Industry, Film

Modernism, Industry, Film

A Network of Media in the Baťa Corporation and the Town of Zlín in the 1930s

Petr Szczepanik

Zlín is a typical example of a town closely related to one multi-industrial company and not just one industry. Until World War I, it was a small Moravian town in a rural area, but after the local shoe company Baťa rapidly expanded and became a multinational corporation with many branches in the 1920s and 1930s, the town developed dramatically, its population increased by a factor of almost ten (from approximately 4,000 to 40,000),[1] and it was totally rebuilt into a highly modern urban complex, which was to serve as a functional extension of the factory. The founder of the company, Tomáš Baťa, was the mayor during the important period 1923-1932, and was succeeded in this function by his key collaborator. The symbiotic relationship between the company and the town deeply affected the economic, social, and cultural life of its inhabitants. Baťa built standardized family houses for the workers, a new transport system, key public buildings, and last but not least, the new complex network of media.

Since his pragmatism and rationalism corresponded with the new principles of functionalist architecture, Baťa engaged some of the leading Czech architects of the time – Jan Kotěra, František Lydia Gahura, Vladimír Karfík, etc. – and Zlín became what was probably the first project of functionalist city planning ever implemented, the first "functionalist city," partly corresponding to the Athens Charter of the CIAM (Congrès Internationaux d'Architecture Moderne), issued later in 1933.[2] Baťa's main architect and urban planner, František Lydie Gahura, described the basic architectural principle of Zlín simply as a direct extension of an industrial standard, the variation and combination of a basic structural unit originally used for factory buildings – the 20x20-foot box.[3] The key term that describes the symbiosis of the town and company and promotes this concept as a universal formula for building similar urban complexes was the "Ideal Industrial City." In 1937, Jan Antonín Baťa, the stepbrother of founder Tomáš, who became the head after Tomáš's death in 1932, commissioned an extremely detailed and practically oriented book entitled *Ideal Industrial City*, prepared by a diverse team of Baťa's collaborators. The book, with over 400 pages, was never published, but its manuscript can be found in Baťa's archive in Zlín.[4] An ideal industrial city was supposed to have about 10,000 inhabitants and be an organic structure of interconnected spheres of production, recreation, and housing. Communication, one of the key functions and necessary conditions of the Ideal Industrial City, was to be provided by a network of telephone lines, teletypewriting equipment, radio telegraphy, and even television broadcasting.[5] The main areas of enterprise listed in the manuscript included film studios, movie theaters, and the production of radio receivers.[6] It is interesting to note that cinema was considered one of the major divisions of the industrial city, operating on the same level in the hierarchical scheme as, for example, the tannery or power plant, and the movie theater on the main map was in the virtual center of the city. The movie theater for 1,000 spectators was supposed to present a new program each day: nine screenings every week, including six new features, one film for children, two newsreels, and four short films.[7]

Figure 1 The main urban plan by architect R.H. Podzemný

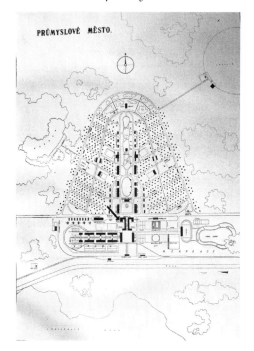

from: *Ideální průmyslové město*, 1937

According to the ideas from *Ideal Industrial City*, the model should be (and, indeed, partly was) used as a universal formula for building a series of industrial towns around the world. The role of media in this process was both internal and external: they were supposed to enable better standardization by explaining the key principles of production to the employees, promote Baťa's social security system, secure the communication networks between the satellites and the center, and also establish an inner coherence of the individual towns and industrial production. In this paper, I will analyze the network of media in Zlín and its satellites in terms of the communicational and representational functions that it performed in the service of industrial production, with the company films preserved in the National Film Archive in Prague and company journals and other records kept in the archive of the Baťa corporation in Zlín as the main sources.[8] The media will be considered not just the instruments of documentation, promotion, and instruction, but above all the means of production: the conditions that enable the efficient functioning and development of industrial production and the industrial city.

1.   Medienverbund

Most of what has so far been written about media and Baťa in Zlín concerns film production at Baťa's own film studios in terms of the artistic values and authorial approaches of the Zlín filmmakers. The involvement of the industrial company, as the body that commissioned the films, was considered nothing more than the inevitable prerequisite for the emergence of a unique island of cinematic creativity which surpassed most of the conventional feature production in Prague. Zlín cinema was thus incorporated into the history of Czechoslovak national cinema as an individual step in the general progress towards a higher professional and artistic level, especially in the fields of documentary and animation film.

My approach is different in terms of the logic of industrial production and international business as the primary sources and subjects of media infrastructure, of which cinema was just one part. Film has to be reincorporated into the complete network of media, which were used by the company to record, archive, and teach its production techniques and promote its developments, products, public services, and the social welfare it provided its employees, though mainly to build a system of internal and external communication integrating the employer and the workers, customers and the brand, the parent industrial branch and affiliates, as well as the center of Zlín and dozens of satellite cities, subsidiaries at home and abroad, and hundreds of shops worldwide as well. Thomas Elsaesser, Vinzenz Hediger and Patrick Vonderau have proposed calling this kind of chain or network of media a *Medienverbund*: the media are interconnected around certain urban or industrial complexes and are employed as the components of a broad and effective multimedia strategy to complement each other and fulfill different functions for different occasions and at different moments.[9]

The coordination of different media within one strategy of publicity could be presented through the example of trade fairs and exhibitions, which Baťa perceived as extremely important in building its public image. It used film in its first important trade-fair exhibit in 1924: within the exhibit itself there were three projectors constantly showing "images of our products, life, and production techniques."[10] But the film medium was also used to record the first day of Baťa's exhibition and to play this movie the following day at the theaters in all of Czechoslovakia's larger cities, but also in factory courtyards.[11] As early as 1929, Baťa presented statistics of how many thousands of meters of film were screened and for how many viewers, and at the same trade fair it distributed 92,000 copies of its factory journal, 50,000 advertising postcards, and 200,000 leaflets; offered free telephone usage to 3,500 visitors, and played 3,180 gramophone discs.[12] In 1934, Jan Baťa commissioned a special screening space next to the pedicure section of an exhibition so that visitors could watch his industrial films and advertisements while they were getting a pedicure.[13] This perhaps inspired Le Corbusier, who – in his unrealized project for Baťa's trade-fair pavilion, proposed during his visit to Zlín in 1935 – designed special chaise lounges for a pedicure salon from which the visitors were supposed to watch films projected onto the ceiling.[14] At the World Exhibition in Paris in 1937, where Alexander Hackenschmied and Elmar Klos's advertisement for Baťa's tires, THE HIGHWAY SINGS, won a special prize, Baťa started experimenting with a series of slides or photos supplemented by Baťa's slogans and arranged according to the principles of cinematic montage – the technique called "suggestive exposition montage."[15] At another exhibition that same year, it installed endless-loop 16mm projectors that could be activated by the visitors themselves.[16] And finally, in 1938, it organized a special exhibition of its own electrical department, presenting the newest media apparatuses of the time: noise meters, sound generators, oscillographs, the Blattnerphon, teletypewriters, new telephone and sound-recording systems, projection devices, radio transmitters, etc.[17]

The media network used by Baťa in its factories included print, telegraphy, telephone, photography, slide projections, cinema, gramophone, radio, teletypewriter, phototelegraphy, pneumatic tubes, and potentially television as well. If we decide to also list non-technical media, we could add theater, popular music, and the plastic arts – but I will stick to the first group here. Although not all of these media were organized by one department and integrated into one system in a strict sense, carrying out different functions, they can still be considered components of a whole – if we focus on industrial production as their main source and subject. Many other intersections and links existed among these media besides the exhibition strategies mentioned above: quotations and cross-references between media texts (radio inviting listeners to the cinema, industrial or advertisement films referring to radio and telephone, the company's journal

publishing Baťa's radio programs, gramophone apparatuses recording important telephone exchanges, gramophone discs being played on the company
radio, etc.), multimedia seasonal advertisement campaigns, education (film,
slides, journals in schools), and archiving (special archives of written documents, photographs, films), all working together in a centralized communication network.

Figure 2 Broadcasting studio at Baťa

Apart from this, all the media were closely related to the logic of industrial production: the structural ties between media usage and the assembly line in Baťa's
factories could be illustrated by the terminology used to describe and evaluate
the functioning of media. The efficiency of production, distribution, as well as
the exhibition of films was analyzed in terms of meters produced, rented, or
screened, often without listing any concrete titles, in the same purely quantitative way that the company talked about the production of shoes or tires: "The
efficiency of the film department could be demonstrated by the fact that, since
May 1st of this year, it shot 30,000 meters of film, of which 20,000 are still being
exhibited at 1,100 theaters around the Republic."[18] Dozens of articles written
about radio and telephone also focused on statistical data like the numbers of
radio listeners, speakers, telephone numbers, and calls connected inside the factory, within the country, and between Baťa and its branches abroad:

> Fifteen hundred telephones have been installed in our factory and they are used for
> 200,000 calls every day! If only one minute were wasted during each individual call,
> the total loss would reach 3,000 minutes per day, which means 138 days, i.e., more

than a quarter of the year. What the extent of the losses would be in terms of money is impossible to calculate.[19]

These statistics were used to promote exceptional progressiveness at the factory: Baťa's main company journal was the biggest in Europe; more prints of its film newsreels were distributed than all of the rest of the newsreels in the country combined; it had the first private automatic telephone exchange office in the country, the first private telephone lines, the biggest movie theater in Central Europe, the first company radio in the country, the first private teletypewriter connection, etc. Media did not only advertise the company as channels for the transmission of promotional content, they themselves became advertisements.

Nonetheless, the more appropriate way to describe the interdependence of factory, city, and media in the case of Baťa would be to foreground the communication processes connecting different components of the corporation with the center and the company with the public, as well as the functioning of media in a broader *dispositif* of industrial production in the sense of a spatiotemporal regime creating certain positions for each member of this communication network.

2.   Media in a *dispositif* of serial production

The *dispositif* of Baťa's production was a highly sophisticated and complex disciplinary system based on the precise division of time and space, high levels of specialization, measurement, and surveillance, with its main goal being to set everybody at their proper place and rhythm in relation to the overall organization of work. But, at the same time, it included certain structural components that exceeded the classical disciplinary mode: it aimed to give everybody a feeling of being a potential shareholder or even self-sufficient entrepreneur who did not need to be watched because he watched himself for his own benefit. Subordination to the discipline of the assembly line was translated into the idea of sharing the company's lifestyle and benefiting from the social services it offered. In this way even private life and leisure time became functions of the factory that were organized and controlled by the company. This position, based on a subtle interplay between emancipation and homogenization, could be illustrated by Baťa's insistence on building family houses instead of apartment buildings (or even "collective houses", as Le Corbusier proposed to Baťa unsuccessfully) as the main strategy for rental housing. Comfortable family houses arranged within wide strips of greenery functioned as a means of control because they separated and localized the workers in their leisure time; gave them a sense of comfort, which made them more loyal, and above all prevented them from forming disruptive political bodies in pubs or on the streets. As Baťa claimed, "Every worker should feel like a servant collectively, but like a king individually."[20] This position is strikingly similar to the one described in classic theories of cinematic *dispositif*: a fixed position ascribed to the spectator, who is optically and socially isolated from the community and who undergoes the process of psychic regression, which decreases his or her critical ability to test reality, but who simultaneously adopts the privileged position of the central vantage point. Thus, it is worth stressing the key spatial position of the movie theater in Baťa's industrial city and in Zlín itself, where the so-called Big Movie Theater with its 2,500 seats occupied the center of Labor Square, the main part of the "new" Zlín, just opposite the factory's main entrance.

Figure 3 Jan Baťa's movable office, 1940

The *dispositif* had a radial structure, with the center occupied by the "chief" (the term used by employees to address or refer to Baťa), who not only supervised the factory, but also the town and its inhabitants, like a master helping the masses of peasants become modern industrial citizens. The central position of the *dispositif* had a special medial arrangement: it was not static or bound to one place (as in Bentham's panopticon), but rather mobile and potentially omnipresent. Jan Baťa's famous movable office was placed in a special elevator that could move among 15 floors in his largest skyscraper, the main administration building. Tomáš and Jan Baťa were also famous promoters of aviation, and the former built his own private airport. The quasi-cinematic vertical and horizontal movement of the optical point of view was combined with concentric communication channels: not only telegraph, telephone, radio, and teletypewriter, but also a system of light and sound signals and special instruments of surveillance. Using radio, Baťa could address all the workers at once. But he could also eavesdrop on his employees' telephone calls by means of a gramophone and penalize them if their communication was not efficient enough.

Baťa's desire to control all the communication channels can clearly be seen in the long-term campaign against non-efficient telephone communication, which strove to discipline the behavior of all telephone users according to the principles of the rationalization of production. At Baťa the telephone was considered a highly beneficial medium which saved a lot of time and helped coordinate and control the synchronous actions of the employees, and the company invested big sums of money in building private telephone lines. The campaign, which focused on eliminating any redundant or disturbing elements, is evidence of the importance Baťa ascribed to media communication. By the early 1920s, Baťa had already forbade the use of the word hello, which was (and still is) commonly used as the first phatic signal to start a conversation.[21] Numerous articles from company journals and transmissions from the company radio system through the 1920s and 1930s analyzed improper telephone behavior and criticized users for being too loud, too fast, too repetitive, talkative, incoherent, for pressing the telephone cradle excessively, forgetting to hang up, etc.[22] The most extreme method of controlling telephone usage was a gramophone recorder installed in the telephone exchange that could deliver evidence of telephone misuse. The elaboration of the telephone campaign is documented by Baťa's plan to establish special school lessons of telephony[23] and also a film about proper telephone techniques, characteristically entitled TIME IS MONEY (1938).

Figure 4 Workers in front of the radio speaker 1940,
cinema at the Baťa exhibition 1934

The media were responsible for building channels for feedback between factory work, education, housing, shopping, social welfare, and amusement. Everything became part of one complex, and with industrial production at its center, the town became an industrial garden city and the citizens became the "industrial men". The main example of this function is radio and cinema. Daily broadcasting was established in 1938, and a typical program consisted of two parts. The first was usually a rhythmic march played from a disc from 6:30 to 6:45, when workers were arriving for work. The second, the main 10-minute program, started at 9:00 during the break and was composed of short musical fragments, followed by news from the factory and city life, educational slogans, and finally a lecture about the organizational and ethical problems of work in factories, about security issues, health care, or an advertisement for Baťa's movie theater. Both of these regular broadcasts served the function of regulating and coordinating the masses of workers at the moments when they assembled in one place and there was a risk that their movements could become chaotic. Up to 2,000 speakers were installed in all the factory's workshops and departments, the main satellite town of Baťov, and also the largest hotel in Zlín, in the hospital, dormitories, community center, department store, and at times at the city's main square also.[24] Jan Baťa attempted to extend the simultaneous address even further: he tried to establish an international company broadcast addressing his satellites, shops, and employees abroad. He called this idea "export radio," the title corresponding to his conviction that exports were his main financial source. In 1938, he arranged a joint Czech broadcast with Radio Luxembourg so that he could inform his collaborators in America, Africa, and Asia about selected events in the center of Zlín and greet them at Christmas.[25]

Baťa's methods concerning the rationalization of production and the division of labor were inspired by Taylorism and Fordism, but, at the same time, they differed from classic mechanistic models by providing the workers higher standards of social welfare, stressing their continuous education and mobility, dividing the factory into semi-autonomous economic units, giving selected employees a "share of profits," and also by the rhetoric of cooperation used between employees and employer, which was similar to Fayolism.[26] This strategy demanded special industrial psychology of work or "psychotechnique" to measure the abilities and skills of the workers and their dispositions regarding certain jobs. In 1938, the following was claimed in the company's journal in an article entitled "The Future of Industrial Man": "The good worker should be educated technically and morally: this purpose is accomplished by psychotechnique in the service of industry. The proper assignment of the proper man to the proper task is the main principle of all work."[27] The media played a central role in this process of creating the new industrial man. The person responsible for the psychological state of the workers and for transfers from one to another workplace was the so-called "social inspector." The social inspector used the company's journals and radio to deliver educational lectures and warnings concerning not only professional affairs, but also private problems involving housing, family finances, health care, etc.

The social services provided by Baťa were also promoted in numerous exhibitions and especially industrial films in which the whole city, rebuilt by Baťa, served as a showcase of successful production methods. Instead of exploiting a cheap labor force, Baťa decided to educate the local people not only in new production methods, but also in a new lifestyle, and pay them above-average wages, which would help establish closer ties between them and the company. Film production, radio, and journals were the tools of fast transformation from "old" village peasants into new citizens, a more efficient labor force with specific skills and ambitions like flexibility and entrepreneurial spirit. Therefore, the company needed to extend the scope of its films from internal issues to broader social and cultural contexts and later even to the production of feature fiction films, which would promote the company's lifestyle and morality more indirectly. The company's film studio was built in 1936, when Jan Baťa started his campaign to gain more skilled workers for his advertising department and provide Zlín with the feeling of real city culture by establishing a new infrastructure of cultural life: a gallery, a public educational institute, a community center, an art school, etc.[28]

Until 1945, Baťa produced and commissioned approximately 170 films plus three periodical newsreels and many versions in foreign languages.[29] The films can be roughly divided into four main groups according to their function:

1. advertisements promoting concrete products, often part of a seasonal campaign;
2. industrial films: representation or image films showing a broad range of company activities, the individual steps in production from raw material to final product, or the growth of the town of Zlín, the social welfare of the employees, and the general philosophy and lifestyle of the company; instructional films for re-qualifying the employees or as a teaching tool at the special schools;
3. school films used as pedagogical devices in Baťa's and other primary and secondary schools;
4. documentary, fiction, and animation films that were only indirectly related to the factory and the company's industrial production (e.g., by promoting Baťa's work ethic or "optimistic spirit").

Each of these categories could fulfill various functions for the company, were commissioned on different occasions and exhibited under different conditions, and could address the target audience both inside and outside factory in different ways. The most important group for our purposes here are the representation or image films showing the production processes and social life at the factories and in the town of Zlín. This was the largest group and also includes two special periodical film series, the quarterly BAT'A NEWSREEL (BAT'ŮV ŽURNÁL, 1927-1931) and the weekly WINDOW ONTO THE WORLD (OKNO DO SVĚTA, 1937-1938), and annual documentaries of the May Day celebrations (1928-1937).

Some of the industrial films fulfilled a primarily internal function, others an external one, many of them served both functions simultaneously or in succession. The internal function was explicitly defined in a compilation film about the history of Baťa's film production called WE WILL SAY IT THROUGH FILM (ŘEKNEME TO FILMEM; dir. Bořivoj Zeman, 1941):

> They [the films intended for internal purposes at the factory] illustrated the advantages of newly designed machines, or showed the work techniques in slow motion. Thus, they solved the problem of maintaining the same pace of technological modernization at different plants, the problem of training new employees, and the coordination of work processes under the conditions of high decentralization at the company, which has been building new branches in other, often unindustrialized regions.

The internal functions of industrial films, circulating on the inner routes within factories and between branches and satellite towns, were above all information, training, and standardization. Many that might be considered purely internal by today's viewers were nevertheless used for external promotional purposes as well.

The first surprising fact about the circulation of these films was that they were distributed in far larger numbers than usual for features and newsreels in the former Czechoslovakia – in the peak years of 1937 and 1938, it was usually 100 to 150 prints. They reached most domestic movie theaters and were often exhibited in foreign versions in many other countries, including in Asia, the Americas, and Africa. Moreover, they were also presented on many special occasions, like world exhibitions and trade fairs, film festivals organized by the Baťa company in Zlín, free screenings for the workers during lunch breaks, and on a more regular basis, at non-theatrical sites like shops, schools, and the weekly internal meetings of company representatives.[30]

The second periodical newsreel mentioned above, the weekly 16mm WINDOW ONTO THE WORLD (1937-1938), in particular, deserves closer attention. One hundred twenty prints, Czech or German versions, were regularly sent to 800 of Baťa's shops. The newsreels were exhibited via special self-service endless-loop projectors with rear projection, activated by the customer pushing a button. The 60-meter reels contained reports on the factory's progress or life in Zlín and advertisements, but also general information about current technological inventions, economic affairs, social and sporting events (the clips were often bought from another newsreel producer).[31] The periodical newsreel was unique in the way that it built a dense network of exhibition points connected to one center, sometimes including Zlín's satellites abroad also: British Tilbury, Dutch Best, French Hellocourt, Croatian Borovo, Swiss Möhlin, etc.[32] It also succeeded in competing with normal newsreel productions because it had a much larger number of prints and faster distribution, even to the small towns. The strategy of simultaneously addressing as many people as possible and using seemingly neutral informative messages like world news or surveys of new inventions for publicity purposes was a common denominator of Baťa's films, radio, and journals, although each of them differed in their concrete techniques of distribution and the way they targeted the audience.

The industrial image films strove to present shoe production as part of the broader project of technological, economic, and social modernization, of demographic and urban planning with a wide national and international impact; in contrast, these broader social contexts then served to advertise for shoe production. The constant linking of social and industrial issues, of working time and leisure, of the efficiency of the machines and aesthetics of the workplace is not a matter of connecting two separate and distinct spheres, but instead social matters – the "production" of "new industrial men" – are considered to be an integral part of the production process. One example is MODERN PRODUCTION OF SHOES (MODERNÍ VÝROBA OBUVI; dir. Otakar Vávra, 1930), a typical industrial film depicting the entire process of shoe manufacturing, from processing of the raw material, through cutting and sewing, to final packaging and distribution. But between the stages of sewing and inspection of the finished shoes we see detailed descriptions of the workplace and living conditions, which are clearly incorporated into the manufacturing process. The film montage itself thus expresses the thesis that social service functions as an integral step in industrial production and that the automation of an assembly line is socially beneficial. The relationship between man and machine is not necessarily of a fragmentary and alienating nature, then, although this is often the case in the industrial films as a generic category: A man is pictured as a creative individual, with his entire body being visible, capable of his or her own facial self-expression.

Like the functionalist architecture in Zlín, Baťa's films from the late 1930s provide an example of a symbiosis between avant-garde form, the rationalism and positivism of industrial production techniques, and the educational discourse: a complex overall structure based on repetition and variation, rhythmic montage and varied framing (from the excessive use of aerial shots to macro details), clear composition and often complicated camera movements – all of them corresponding to Baťa's sense of the organization of space; distribution of light; taste for movement, change, and speed, or more concretely, to devices of motorized workshops, conveyors, high-rise factory buildings, or a passion for aviation.

Figure 5 Tomáš Baťa in his office, 1931

To summarize the arguments about the *dispositif* of industrial production and the related *Medienverbund,* we could claim that Baťa's organization of work and the respective media infrastructure were not typical examples of a disciplinary *dispositif* of surveillance in the Foucauldian sense, just as they were not a pure application of mechanistic models of management (Taylor and Ford). Baťa was already partly exceeding the disciplinary mode and moving toward what Deleuze called "societies of control."[33] He successfully replaced the factory with the corporation, and the subject of his *dispositif* was supposed to be mobile in space, flexible in time, highly adaptive to new technologies and techniques, exposed to permanent training and retraining (via journals, film, and radio), able to cross the borders between traditional spaces of enclosure, and thus become a student (or spectator) at work and a self-sufficient worker at school (or the cinema).[34] At the same time, this regulated emancipation was counterbalanced by new strategies of controlling minds and bodies in a much more precise and extensive way than before, transforming everything into functions of the factory, including families and houses – something that would be unacceptable in the age of control societies that we live in. The media technologies of mass address or synchronous communication, be it telephone, radio, or film, enabled the coordination and regulation of these moving subjects and helped construct the ideal industrial cities and ideal industrial men without being bound to any concrete enclosed place or branch. In terms of the media themselves, this tendency toward control meant a new level of multi-functionality of all media content:

the industrial film could become an educational film if it crossed the border between factory and school, a newsreel could turn into an advertisement if it crossed the border between cinema and shop, etc. Baťa's media strategy was an extreme example of the broader tendency in media industries in the late 1920s and early 1930s: horizontal integration of all possible channels within multimedia corporations, leaving passages open for media content and formats to travel from one channel to the other, using one to advertise for the other.

A brief chronology of Baťa's *Medienverbund*

Print (journals)
1918 – Founding of the weekly *Sdělení* ("Message"), which became the company's main journal
1926 – Establishment of the joint-stock company Tisk (Print), whose main goal was to print and publish journals, books, and advertisement posters, and run a cinema
1930 – *Sdělení* renamed *Zlín*
1932 – *Zlín* published three times a week
Besides this, Baťa also published approximately 15 other, more specialized journals, some of them in foreign languages

Telephone
1925 – Fully automatic telephone exchange office (Western Electric, for 300 numbers)
1929 – Two private telephone lines connect Baťa factories in Zlín with Brno and Prague
1929-1930 – Baťa uses free telephone service for promotional purposes in its Prague shop as well as at its trade-fair exhibit
1933 – Telephone exchange for 1,000 numbers
1938 – Conference call system for 10 simultaneous callers
1938 – Baťa's film about proper telephone usage, Time Is Money

Film
1928 – Establishment of the film unit (as a part of the advertising department) to commission, copy, and distribute films, though not produce them
1927-1931 – Baťa Newsreel – the first of Baťa's periodical films, usually released quarterly
Beginning of 1930s – Separate film department, which began to produce some of its own films

1928-1937 – The second periodical newsreel: regular reports on the May Day celebrations

1932 – Construction of the Big Movie Theater in Baťa with 2,500 seats

1935 – New team of young filmmakers, including avant-gardist Alexander Hackenschmied; adoption of the new film-production plan

1936 – New sound-film studio and laboratory

1937-1938 – The third periodical newsreel, the weekly Window onto the World is distributed mainly to Baťa's shops

1939-1940 – Rental of HOST studios in Prague for the purpose of producing feature fiction films

1940 – The first Czech film festival, Film Harvest, in Zlín

1941 – Film Harvest II

1941 – Beginning of animation film production

1942 – Takeover of Baťa's studio by the German company Descheg

1945 – Film studio taken over by the state (as a part of nationalization of the Czechoslovak film industry)

Phototelegraphy

1930 – The first radiotelegraphic transmission of a picture

1936 – The first phototelegram

Teletypewriting

1931 – Teletypewriting connection between Zlín (Baťa factory) and Prague

Gramophone

1930 – Baťa's inexpensive gramophones put on the market (this information was confirmed by some sources but questioned by others)

1932 – Production of a special sound recording which included sound montage of aviation noises in memory of the death of Tomáš Baťa in an airplane crash

1938 – Implementation of gramophone systems for recording telephone calls and broadcasting music via company radio

Pneumatic tube

1934 – Installation of the tubing and the central office of a pneumatic-tube system

Radio

1931 – Radio broadcasting used at Baťa's airport

1937 – Film about the joint advertising campaign of Bata and Czechoslovak radio station, 999 999

1938 – Commencement of daily radio broadcasting at Baťa's factory

Television

1936 – Attempts made to buy a television system in the US and Great Britain
and to install it in one of the administration buildings

1937 – Jan Baťa orders the construction of a TV transmitter (which never happened).

General chronology: Building activities in Zlín related to the development of the Baťa company, 1900-1945 and beyond[35]

The southern Moravian town of Zlín has existed since at least the 13th century.
Beginning in the 16th century it was termed a city; in the early 17th century it
comprised approximately 200 city houses and homesteads. Heavily damaged
during the Thirty Years' War and having lost half its population, it then stag-
nated throughout the 17th and 18th centuries. Long before Baťa, it was known
for its annual fairs and regionally strong contingent of craftsmen, mainly pot-
ters, cloth workers, and shoemakers. Development picked up again in the 19th
century, with the first shoe factory being founded there in 1870. In circa 1900,
when Tomáš Baťa moved his plant into the new factory building, Zlín entered
the turning point in its development and slowly began changing into an "industrial city," although the overall impression was still strongly rural, with its sky-
line dominated by a castle and a church. Until then, its population had not risen
significantly, but it shot up by 60% between 1900 and the early 1920s (3,000 in
1900, 4,700 in 1921), and, during the 1920s and 1930s, it increased another ten-
fold. After the city's boundaries were expanded in 1938, the population reached
44,000 in 1940. The number of Baťa's employees rose from 120 in 1900 to 5,200 in
1925, 17,400 in 1930, 28,700 in 1932, 43,000 in 1935, and 65,000 in 1938 (42,000 in
Czechoslovakia and 23,000 abroad; 16,000 at shops). The factory's output grew
even faster: 2,200 pairs per day in 1905, 10,000 in 1917, 100,000 in 1930, 58 million per year in 1936 (30 million of those for foreign markets). In the 1930s, it
built dozens of subsidiaries, satellite towns, and factories, and thousands of
shops both inside the country and internationally. Thanks to Baťa, Czechoslovakia became the world's largest exporter of leather shoes.

1894-1914: Slow, gradual growth and modernization of a still partly rural town

1894 – Tomáš Baťa (1876-1932) founds a shoe factory together with his siblings
Anna and Antonín. They make use of the experience gained in their father's

small operation. In the early days, they only have a few manual sewing machines and rely heavily on handwork and home workers.

1895 – T. Baťa takes over management of the company

1896 – Baťa studies shoemaking machines and organization of work in Frankfurt's Moenus A.G. factory with the intention of modernizing his equipment and rationalizing production.

1897 – Introduction of the *baťovka*, the first type of inexpensive fabric shoe, and its new mechanized production

1898 – The first railway connection in Zlín links it indirectly with Vienna

1900 – T. Baťa moves manufacturing to the new factory building close to the train station and introduces steam engines to power his sewing machines.

1904-1905 – T. Baťa's first trip to the US to learn about the American system of production. He works in Lynn, Massachusetts, a shoe production center, as an ordinary worker.

1906 – The first strike of Baťa's workers, who protest against recently implemented American-style rationalization of work, raising demands, a system of penalties, and low wages. Despite the high costs involved, Baťa successfully suppresses it by employing new, unskilled workers. This experience leaves him vehemently opposed to trade unions.

1906-1910 – A number of other, competing shoe factories were founded in Zlín, some of them by former Baťa's employees. Baťa remains the biggest manufacturer with the fastest growth rate.

1909 – First export sales and first sales agencies abroad

1911 – A second trip to the US to buy new cutting tools and facilities for the mechanical engineering workshop for the production of shoemaking machines

1912 – Construction of Zlín's telephone network

1913 – Construction of Zlín's power station

1914 – With 400 employees, Baťa is the 7th largest shoe factory in Austria-Hungary, but its productivity of 3,600 shoe pairs per day makes it the leader.

1914-1923: World War I and postwar stagnation

1914-1918 – Soon after the outbreak of World War I, Baťa starts to receive government commissions to produce shoes for the Austro-Hungarian army. The commissions are so large that they outsource some of the work to Baťa's competitors. Baťa also hires thousands of new employees (their total number reaches 4,000 in 1918), who thus escaped being drafted into the army. Its production probably covered approximately 50% of the monarchy's consumption of military footwear. His company's net profit reaches 12.6 million crowns during the war, 10 times his registered capital in 1914. However, the new workers still do not have adequate permanent housing in Zlín.

1914 – Establishment of the company's construction division, which commences construction of a series of four-story factory buildings during the war

1915 – The first urban plan for a worker's colony by the architect Jan Kotěra; he presumes that factory workers would live like small farmers, which proves to be wrong, because the factory work is too demanding; the colony is only partly completed, the plan was later reworked by F.L. Gahura.

1917 – Baťa starts to open his own shops in Czech cities, which totaled 18 by 1918.

1918-1923 – Postwar crisis (collapse of market and leather shortage after the breakup of Austria-Hungary); some of the wartime commissions go unpaid; the number of Baťa's employees drops from 4,000 in 1918 to 1,800 in 1923.

1918 – Construction of the first workers' housing colony for Baťa's employees: single-family houses with gabled roofs, consisting of three rooms, kitchen, and bathroom (cost: 90,000 Czechoslovak crowns). Other colonies followed in the early 1920s: two or four family houses with gabled or flat roofs, most apartments have a separate entrance, one room, kitchen, and toilet (cost: 80-130,000 Czechoslovak crowns).

1918-1919 – Political radicalization of Baťa's workers, who protest and organize small-scale strikes because of complaints regarding overtime, low wages, insufficient health protection, and frequent dismissals. Baťa is forced to make compromises, but he later often breaks the agreements; new conflicts follow in 1922 (after Czechoslovak Communist Party is founded in 1921).

1919 – T. Baťa's third trip to the US. At the Ford factory, he sees the assembly line; at the Endicott-Johnson shoe factory, he observes how the owner ensures his workers' social welfare.

1922 – Baťa reacts to the currency revaluation by lowering prices by 50%, which proves to be an extremely successful strategy.

1922 – The manor house of Zlín's most powerful aristocrat, Baron Haupt Buchenrode, is purchased by Baťa and in part made public (some of the Baron's estates have already been purchased). This helps Baťa prepare new space for the construction of worker's colonies and transform the city's medieval center.

1923-1939: Symbiosis of the city and factory, transformation into a multinational corporation, Zlín is transformed into a "functionalist industrial city"

Since 1923 – Intense production and international expansion boom: from export turnover of 23 million Czechoslovak crowns in 1923 to 36 million in 1925 and 77 million (= 2 millions shoe pairs) in 1927, when Baťa was already responsible for almost half of Czechoslovakia's total shoe exports. Investments in new factory buildings, highly modern machines, transport infrastructure, and power engineering reaches 34 million Czechoslovak crowns in 1924 and 1925 alone.

T. Baťa (and later his successor J.A. Baťa) starts more systematic cooperation with some of the key representatives of modern Czechoslovak architecture on construction, land use, and urban planning: first Jan Kotěra and his pupil Jiří Gočár, later several others, including Vladimír Karfík, Emanuel Hruška, Vladimír Kubečka, Richard Hubert Podzemný, Jiří Voženílek, Miroslav Lorenc, etc. However, the most important among them is a former Baťa worker, František Lydie Gahura; Baťa finances his study of architecture, and Gahura becomes the city of Zlín's main architect (1924-1946) and planner of most of the standardized factory buildings and the key urban development plans in Zlín (in 1921, 1927, 1931, and 1934).

1923 – T. Baťa runs in the local elections with his own party and is elected mayor of Zlín, marking the end of Communist dominance (1921-1923) and the beginning of mutual coordination of the city's and factory's development. He remains in this position until his death in 1932. This gives him the authority to control city planning and construction. He becomes the main (although not the only) investor in the building activities in Zlín and its surroundings.

1924-1925 – Renovation of the plant: construction of the new complex of factory buildings in western Zlín based on a standardized structural unit (the "cell"): modules or boxes measuring 20 x 20 feet, or 6.15 x 6.15 meters, with visible reinforced-concrete or steel skeletons (2-5 stories) with red bricks or windows. The dimensions of the typical factory building are 13 x 6.15 meters lengthwise and 3 x 6.15 meters wide, plus an attached vertical core with stairs, elevators, and some auxiliary rooms. Conforming to the ideals of universality, repeatability, variability, and flexibility, the factory building module enables extremely fast and efficient construction and becomes a leitmotif for all of Zlín architecture, including public-use buildings, giving it a uniform style. Such buildings are arranged in a checkerboard pattern, forming larger functional groups surrounded by greenery.

1924 – Introduction of the system of economic "autonomy" for individual factory sections and of a "profit-and-loss-sharing" system (applies to the section heads). However, the workers have to deposit approximately 50% of the premiums into their "personal bank accounts" (with 10% interest), which are controlled by the company, so that Baťa can potentially use the funds for investments and as a guarantee to cover any losses caused by individual workers.

1924 – Introduction of conveyor belts, which streamline work by 20 to 30 percent, eventually leading to an enormous increase in output. To deal with the necessary reorganization of the work processes, Baťa commissioned Taylor-

style time and motion studies of individual operations to eliminate all ineffi-
cient physical movement.

1925 – Foundation of Baťa School of Work to train young workers from the age
of 14. The working students – so-called elite workers referred to as "young
gentlemen" and "young ladies" – live in Baťa's dormitories and are subjected
to special discipline.

1926 – Electrical motors are attached to individual machines instead of shafts
and driving belts, which make the machines easily movable. This enables
Baťa to reorganize production processes at the workshops.

1927 – Introduction of assembly lines with mechanical conveyors capable of
changing speed. Total production increases by 75% in 1927, and the average
productivity of one worker per day rises from two pairs of shoes in 1924 to
10 in 1927.

1927 – Introduction of the most typical standard of workers' housing for the
serial production of family houses over the next years: double-family house,
"type 1927." There are two basic variants, with flat and gabled roofs, two
stories, each apartment with 45 square meters of usable space, plus a base-
ment. The houses are arranged in a checkerboard pattern surrounded by
greenery, according to the principles of English garden cities, and in harmony with the hilly terrain of the Zlín valley. Approximately 2,000 of these
standardized houses are built during the company's existence in Zlín, plus
hundreds in satellite cities. They are all rented to employees at a very low
price.

1927 – While the average salary per day in the country is 27 Czechoslovak
crowns, Baťa pays approximately 39.

1928 – Baťa's relief fund is financed with fines paid by employees and from the
company's grants.

1927-1937 – Construction of the dormitory district (supplemented with parks
and "study institutes") for young workers and students. As in many other
cases, F.L. Gahura adopts standardized factory frames and boxes for public
buildings.

1927-1936 – Construction of the hospital complex (called the Health Center)

1927-1935 – Planning and construction of the complex of standardized school
buildings (M. Lorenc, F.L. Gahura, V. Karfík)

Late 1920s to early 1930s: Initial reaction to the Depression (import duties and
quotas in many foreign countries): The company starts to become an international corporation, founding dozens of foreign affiliates for both production
and sales (the first one of them was Deutsche Schuh A.G. Bata in Ottmuth,
then Germany, in 1929). These affiliates start to establish an extensive international network of shops (in 1932, there were already 666 in 37 countries
around the world).

1930 – Baťa founds affiliate joint-stock company Zlín as a construction firm responsible for all new Baťa buildings in Czechoslovakia.

1930 – Architect Vladimír Karfík – who had studied and worked in Le Corbusier's atelier in 1925-1926 and Frank Lloyd Wright's atelier in 1927-1929 – moves to Zlín, becomes the head of Baťa's architectural office, and receives some important commissions in the 1930s (the community center, evangelical church, film studio, schools, swimming pool, a series of standardized shops around the country and abroad, a 15-story administrative building, etc.).

1930 – Introduction of the 45-hour, five-day workweek – a first in Czechoslovakia.

1930 – Baťa's first factory complex and attached satellite city, Baťov, is built outside Zlín in the nearby town of Otrokovice. Others soon follow in both Czechoslovakia and abroad. Each estate is carefully chosen according to its potential for further economic, social, and cultural development: inexpensive (often unsuitable for farming) land, conditions for developing transportation and energetic infrastructure, access to raw materials, demographic and social characteristics of the local population, tax laws, etc. Each of these cities imports not only industrial know-how from Zlín, but also common architectural and urban-planning principles, as well as specific ideals about social organization and work ethics. The most important foreign satellites (autonomous towns or urban complexes) are: Ottmuth/Otmęt, built in 1931 (German Silesia, now Poland, near Opole), Borovo (1932, Croatia, near Vukovar), Chelmek (1932, Poland, near Auschwitz), Möhlin (1932, Switzerland, near Basel), Hellocourt, Bataville (1932, France, near Strasbourg), East Tilbury (1933, United Kingdom, suburbs of London), Best (1933, the Netherlands, near Eindhoven), Batanagar (1934, India), Alexandria (Egypt; Baťa's factory in 1930, settlement in Alexandria in 1936), Belcamp (1938, US, near Baltimore), Batanagar (1938, India), Martfű (1941, Hungary).

1930: Baťa's airport in nearby Otrokovice, with approximately 20 planes in 1934, international flights, an aviation school, production of its own type of plane beginning in 1935.

1931 – Change from partnership, T. A. Baťa, to joint-stock company, Baťa a.s., for the purpose of lowering its tax burden. However, T. Baťa keeps the entire share. In the same year, its stock reaches 175 million Czechoslovak crowns, and the company gets rid of all of its bank credits and becomes financially fully independent.

1931 – T. Baťa reorganizes the ownership of all of his foreign affiliates through the Leader A.G. holding company, located in St. Moritz, Switzerland, which becomes their majority owner. With help from his Swiss lawyer Georg Wettstein – who formally subscribed the holding's capital – he manages to hide his financial control over these companies and thus avoid protests over his expansionism in various foreign countries. Moreover, Leader A.G. enables him to safeguard a large amount of capital in neutral Switzerland in the event of another war.

Early 1930s – A new city center, Labor Square, is set up in front of the main gate to Baťa's factory, thus embodying a symbiosis of company and city. Among its dominant buildings were the Baťa department store (F.L. Gahura, 1932), the Big Movie Theater Baťa (F.L. Gahura, 1932), and the 11-story community center (including a hotel, restaurants, cafés, clubrooms, and conference rooms; V. Karfík, 1933). Zlín is changing into a functionalist city, i.e., an organic structure of interconnected functional zones: factory, colonies of family houses, dormitories, social and medical service centers, and cultural and educational centers, all supplemented with large strips of greenery and rationalized transportation, energy, and communication infrastructures.

December 10, 1931-February 14, 1932: T. Baťa's business flight "around the world" (from Zlín to India via Italy, Tunis, Libya, Egypt, Palestine, Iraq, and Iran) in a Fokker plane. Baťa starts to shift its export focus from Europe to Asia, the US, and Africa.

1932 – After Baťa's death, and in accordance with his will, his stepbrother and inheritor Jan Antonín Baťa (1898-1965) assumes the position of company owner and head of all of the Czechoslovak and foreign affiliates. The position of mayor goes to one of his key executives, Dominik Čipera. Čipera and J. A. Baťa continue to realize T. Baťa's plans for building the industrial garden city of New Zlín, which turns into a plan to populate the entire Zlín valley with 200,000 inhabitants.

Around 1932 – The company responds to the delayed effects of the Depression with a broad diversification of production and expansion into other industries (rubber making, tanning, chemicals, textiles, mechanical engineering, building, electrical engineering, paper, film, etc.). Among the most typical products, besides shoes and shoe production machinery, were stockings, floor coverings, tires, and toys.

1933 – Gahura builds Tomáš Baťa's Memorial, a huge concrete and glass building, using the factory skeleton, but wrapping its frame entirely in glass and reworking the principles of Gothic architecture.

1934 – Introduction of the 40-hour workweek thanks to further increases in productivity. The average age of Baťa's workers is 26.

1934 – F.L. Gahura creates a key urban plan for the future of Zlín with 100,000 inhabitants, elaborating functional relationships between the factory and the city as well as between the city and the region.

1935 – Zlín is established as a county seat, administrating the affairs of 56 villages.

1935 – International architecture competition for new standardized family house. In the same year, several winning projects are built in a special proto-typical colony. Le Corbusier presents his housing project outside the competition, but it is never realized.

1935 – Plan for the city's layout by Le Corbusier, who spends six weeks in Zlín. The plan is eventually rejected because it ignores certain basic requirements of the commissioner (individual housing, zoning determined by the shape of the valley).

1935-36 – Construction of the sound film studio and laboratory.

1937 – Like his predecessor, J. A. Baťa takes a business trip "around the world" to analyze new potential export markets. The company successfully launches a new wave of expansion to foreign, mostly overseas, markets and reaches a new peak of production and profits; it represents 6/7 of the total Czechoslovak shoe production, 9/10 of Czechoslovak shoe exports, and 1/8 of total world shoe exports; the total turnover of the central company reaches 1.8 billion Czechoslovak crowns.

1937 – Completion of the unpublished manuscript "Ideal Industrial City"; in subsequent years, three satellite towns are constructed according to the principles formulated in the book: Baťovany/Partyzánske, Zruč nad Sázavou, and Sezimovo Ústí (the first in Slovakia, the other two in the present-day Czech Republic).

1937 – Construction of Evangelical church (V. Karfík)

1938 – Baťa's skyscraper (Building No. 21), a 15-story, 77.5-meter administrative building in the Zlín factory complex, which has the famous movable office in the elevator (V. Karfík). At the time, it was the tallest building in Czechoslovakia.

1938 – Expansion of the city's borders, connecting it with several villages, thus establishing what is called Greater Zlín.

1939-1945 (and afterward): Limited business activities during World War II; nationalization in Czechoslovakia; postwar reconstitution in Canada

1938-1939 – After the Munich Agreement (when the company lost many of its facilities in the Sudetenland) and then during the beginning of the German occupation, J. A. Baťa organizes transfers of money and transport of some of the key production units, raw materials, and approximately 2,000 experts to the UK and US to avoid their exploitation by the Germans. Some of them are sent to Belcamp, Maryland, to help in the establishment of a new factory and satellite town there.

1939 – The company tries to prepare for the coming German occupation, and T. Baťa's son, Tomáš J. Baťa (born 1914, J.A. Baťa's nephew), is sent with some important business documents to Canada via Switzerland to negotiate with its government and arrange a new base there. He registers Bata Shoe Company Canada in Toronto and establishes the corporation's management center there.

1939 – After German occupation begins, J.A. Baťa flees to the US, where he supervises the construction of the factory in Belcamp, the American Zlín. But he is blacklisted by the US and UK as a Nazi collaborator. However, as some key testimonies and recent investigations have shown, J.A. Baťa probably never collaborated with the Nazis.

1940 – J.A. Baťa transfers 60% of his share of the central Zlín company to T. Baťa's widow and some of his Zlín executives to protect the company from being confiscated by the Germans (because the owner had fled to an enemy country).

During World War II, the Zlín factory continues reduced production under German supervision, with some military commissions. While shoe production decreases, mechanical engineering booms because the Baťa factory produces many weapon components (parts of antiaircraft guns, submarines, V1 and V2 rockets, etc.). In total, the Baťa factory in occupied Czech territory (protectorate) shows a profit and is expanded further. Protectorate officials install special supervisors as the members of the board of trustees.

1940 – Under the supervision of T.J. Baťa, a factory is built together with a satellite town named Batawa near the Canadian cities of London and Toronto. A group of Zlín specialists and a series of consignments for key machinery follow young Baťa to Batawa. He becomes the boss of a key part of the company, which flourishes thanks to the increased wartime demand. After some time, the Batawa factory expands to include mechanical engineering and starts producing machinery for military purposes: anti-aircraft machine guns, components for torpedoes, etc. The Canadian government provides the company with subsidies, which aids the expanded construction of housing colonies.

1941 – J.A. Baťa moves to Brazil and founds a shoe factory and a small town named Batatuba (1941-1943) in São Paulo province. In Brazil, during the 1940s and 1950s, J.A. Baťa shifts from the shoe industry to agricultural colonization projects, acquiring large estates and the Viação-Mato Grosso colonization company. He founds a group of towns: Mariapolis (1944) in São Paulo province, and Bataypora (1953) and Bataguassu (1954), both in Mato Grosso do Sul province. Later, he builds a huge bridge across Paraná River, thus connecting the provinces of Mato Grosso and São Paulo.

1944 – US bombing of Zlín destroys or damages large parts of Baťa's factory, dozens of houses, and the movie theater.

1945 – Nationalization of Baťa's factories in Czechoslovakia, followed by similar moves in other countries that would soon become Communist. The company has to rebuild itself with the aid of its facilities outside Eastern Europe, where many were destroyed or nationalized.

1947 – J.A. Baťa is busy with lawsuits with the Czechoslovak state and later a long series of international suits (1947-1962) in the US against his step-brother's son, T.J. Baťa, and his mother, widow of the founder T. Baťa, who want to change his will, as he had bequeathed all his shares to J.A. Baťa. They also wanted to gain control of the 41% share in Leader A.G. and thus over Baťa's international empire. J.A. Baťa eventually loses both at home (1947) and in the US. He receives no compensation for his nationalized properties, is declared a Nazi collaborator in a Czechoslovak trial, and given a 15-year sentence in absentia; T.J. Baťa becomes the major owner of the international corporation. Recent investigations have shown that the charges were manipulated by the Communists. The Czechoslovak state also influences the international lawsuits indirectly, because its officials intentionally withhold some key documents proving J.A. Baťa's claims; as a result, the state is not liable to pay compensation for the nationalized factories in Czechoslovakia. For a long time, J.A. Baťa's Brazilian family, joined recently by the city of Zlín, has tried to reopen the case and rehabilitate his name.

1949 – Zlín renamed Gottwaldov (after Czechoslovakia's first Communist president Klement Gottwald); Baťa Company renamed Svit. Some of the urban-planning and architectural tendencies persist after World War II, but many are rejected (e.g., individual housing standards, principles regarding urban greenery).

1960s – The company headquarters is officially relocated to Toronto under the leadership of Tomáš J. Baťa (Thomas J. Bata).

At present, with Baťa still a successful multinational corporation, neither T.J. Baťa nor J.A. Baťa's families have regained control over any of their former major holdings in former Czechoslovakia.

Filmography

Baťa Newsreel (Baťův žurnál; 1927-1931; series; usually quarterly)
Modern Production of Shoes / Moderne Schuherzeugung (Moderní výroba obuvi; dir. Otakar Vávra, 1930; 20 min.)
999 999 (1937; 1.5 min.)
The Highway Sings / Die Strasse singt (Silnice zpívá; dir. Elmar Klos, 1937; 4 min.)
Time Is Money (Čas jsou peníze; dir. František Gürtler, 1938; 3.5 min.)

WINDOW ONTO THE WORLD / FENSTER IN DIE WELT (OKNO DO SVĚTA, 1937-1938; weekly
per 3 min.)
WE WILL SAY IT THROUGH FILM / DURCH DEN FILM GESPROCHEN (ŘEKNEME TO FILMEM;
dir. Bořivoj Zeman, 1941; 21 min.)

Notes

1. See Zdeněk Pokluda, "Přerod venkovského města v průmyslové centrum – lidna-
    tost Zlína 1900-1940," in Ludvík Ševeček (ed.), *Zlínský funkcionalismus. Sborník přís-
    pěvků sympózia pořádaného u příležitosti 100. výročí narození Františka Lydie Gahury a
    90. narozenin Vladimíra Karfíka* (Zlín: Státní Galerie ve Zlíně, 1993).
2. Comparable in some repects perhaps only to several American, German, or Soviet
    industrial towns like Alfred Krupp's colonies built in Essen in the second half of the
    19th century (the social-security system for the workers), to so-called "garden cities"
    planned according to the principles of Ebenezer Howard in Great Britain in the
    early 20th century and later in the US, or to Magnitogorsk in the USSR in the 1930s
    and 1940s (city as an emanation of the factory).
3. F.L. Gahura, "How Zlín Was Built," in Josef Setnička (ed.), *Urbanismus – architektura
    závodů Baťa a. s. ve Zlíně* (Prague: Časopis Stavitel), p. 6.
4. Moravský zemský archiv, pracoviště Zlín, fond Baťa, a.s. Zlín [MZA, BA], II/6, k. 56,
    "Ideální průmyslové město."
5. Ibid., p. 281.
6. Ibid., p. 6.
7. Ibid., pp. 256-57.
8. I would like to thank the director of NFA, Vladimír Opěla, for making Baťa's films
    accessible to me; Eva Pavlíková, a historian of documentary cinema in NFA, for
    providing me with important filmographic information, and Vladimír Štroblík
    from the Zlín archive for his great help while I was searching in Baťa's files.
9. Thomas Elsaesser, "Die Stadt von Morgen: Filme zum Bauen und Wohnen in der
    Weimarer Republik," in Klaus Kreimeier, Antje Ehmann, Jeanpaul Goergen (eds.),
    *Geschichte des dokumentarischen Film in Deutschland, Band 2: Weimarer Republik (1918-
    1933)* (Stuttgart: Reclam-Verlag, 2005), pp. 381-410; see also Hediger's and Vonder-
    au's contributions in this volume.
10. Pag., Naše firma na P. V. V, September 21-28, 1924, *Sdělení* 7, 39 (September 27,
    1924).
11. Pag., Naše firma na P.V.V, September 21-28, 1924 (pokrač.), *Sdělení* 7, 40 (October 4,
    1924).
12. Baťovy závody na výstavě moderního obchodu, *Sdělení* 12, 32 (August 10, 1929).
13. V., Pražské vzorkové veletrhy otevřeny. Pavilon Baťových závodů na veletrhu, *Zlín
    páteční* 17, 10 (March 9, 1934).
14. Vladimír Karfík, *Architekt si spomína* (Bratislava: Spolok architektov Slovenska
    1993), p. 122.
15. Zlín na světové výstavě v Paříži, *Zlín pondělní* 7, 10 (March 8, 1937).

16. Zlínská exposice na výstavě Slovácka. Exposice města Zlína, firmy Baťa a.s. a zlínského regionu, *Zlín pondělní* 7, 25 (June 21, 1937).

17. Elektřina svátečním dnům. K výstavě elektrooddělení Baťových závodů, *Zlín pondělní* 8, 19 (May 9, 1938).

18. Filmové oddělení Baťových závodů. *Zlín páteční*, vol. 13, October 4, 1930, no. 39.

19. *Zlín páteční* 21, 13 (April 1, 1938).

20. Josef Setnička, Stavební činnost a bytová péče Baťových závodů, *Stavitel*, 11-12 (1928), p. 5.

21. Jak telefonovat, *Sdělení*, 4 (6 August 1921); Jak se správně telefonuje, *Sdělení* 6, 36 (September 8, 1923).

22. See clippings in MZA, BA, II/8, k. 165, 166, Telefon – telegraf – rozhlas.

23. M. Škoda, Strach z telefonu, *Zlín páteční* 14, 2 (January 9, 1931).

24. Denní rozhlas pro naše spolupracovníky, *Zlín páteční* 21, 12 (March 25, 1938); 1800 amplionů pro přenos. Závodní rozhlas Baťových závodů, *Národní kovodělník* (January 22, 1941); J. Handzel, Závodní rozhlas v Baťových závodech, *Organisace* (February 15, 1941).

25. Radio Luxembourg vysílá český pořad, *Zlín středeční* 7, 36 (1938); Baťa Radio Luxembourg bude vysílati každé pondělí, *Zlín pondělní* 8, 36 (September 12, 1938).

26. Henri Fayol (1841-1925) stressed the organic harmonization of the relationship between capital and labor, and coordination and communication between individual departments of the company. He also promoted the idea of profit sharing. For period comment on Baťa and Fayol, see Stanislav Jandík, *Železní tovaryši. Sociologická reportáž o zrození nového věku* (Prague: Volné myšlenky, 1938), pp. 280-303. For recent analysis of Fayol's management principles in contrast to the classical mechanistic theories of Ford and Taylor, see David Boje and Robert Dennehy, *Managing in the Postmodern World* (1999), Chapter 2: Planning Stories. Online: http://cbae.nmsu.edu/~dboje/mpw.html, accessed in January 2008.

27. Nová tvář zlínského pracovního máje. Budoucnost průmyslového člověka, *Zlín*, 18 (2 May 1938).

28. See memories of Elmar Klos, one of the key Baťa's filmmakers, in Elmar Klos, Hana Pinkavová: *Historie gottwaldovského filmového studia v pohledu pamětníků, očima současníků a v dokumentech* (Texty Čs. filmového ústavu, no. 22; Prague: ČFÚ 1984), p. 38.

29. See Jiří Stejskal, *Zlínská filmová výrobna*, Ph.D. thesis (Brno: FF UJP 1972).

30. See Jiří Novotný, Zapomenuté šedesátiny, *Prostor Zlín* 1, 7-8 (1993), p. 4; Stejskal, *Zlínská filmová výrobna*, p. 56.

31. Elmar Klos, "Kronika Kudlovské stodoly," Elmar Klos, Hana Pinkavová, *Historie gottwaldovského filmového studia v pohledu pamětníků, očima současníků a v dokumentech* (Texty Čs. filmového ústavu, no. 22; Prague: ČFÚ 1984), p. 5; Stejskal, *Zlínská filmová výrobna*, p. 57; Zdeněk Štábla, *Data a fakta z dějin čs. kinematografie 1896-1945*, vol. 3 (Prague: ČSFÚ 1990), p. 492.

32. MZA, BA, I/4, k. 45 – Příkazy J. A. Bati, D. Čipery, J. Hlavničky.

33. Gilles Deleuze, "Postscript on the Societies of Control," *October*, 59, (Winter 1992), pp. 3-7.

34. I am referring not only to the practice of using different media as a means to inform and train the workers, even if they are in a hospital or on the street, or the practice of frequent transfers of employees to other positions or the satellites abroad (often very quickly and by plane), but also Baťa's strategy of employing the students of his

training institutions to make them economically self-sufficient and thus more sub-
missive to his ideology and less to that of their families.

35. This chronology is not based on independent research, but on a compilation from
     various secondary sources. Since there is no serious historical research on the Baťa
     Company available, it was difficult to prove the credibility of these sources; there-
     fore, it should be considered a provisional overview for orientation. See Stanislav
     Jandík, *Železní tovaryši. Sociologická reportáž o zrození nového věku* (Prague: Volné my-
     šlenky, 1938); Bohumil Lehár, *Dějiny Baťova koncernu (1894-1945)* (Prague: Státní
     nakladatelství politické literatury, 1960); Miroslav Ivanov, *Sága o životě a smrti Jana
     Bati a jeho bratra Tomáše.* 2nd ed. (Vizovice: Lípa, 2000).

A Modern Medium for a Modern Message

Norsk Jernverk, 1946-1974, Through the Camera Lens

Bjørn Sørenssen

The industrial film genre has so far been a neglected field in Norwegian film studies. One of the main reasons for this may be that there has been very little discussion of the genre as such in Norway. The most comprehensive Norwegian film bibliography[1] contains no entries related to "film and industry" or "industrial film." In spite of this, there has, over the years, been a steady output of what could be defined as "industrial film" in the form of information and educational films sponsored by industrial companies and corporations, in addition to films produced for public-relations purposes and outright advertising. Some of these films have, however, been discussed and described in a historical context, for example in Diesen[2] (about Norwegian educational film) and Skretting[3] (about Norwegian advertising film).

That being said, the sporadic examples of films made for, by, or in connection with industrial enterprises are so few and far between as to warrant the exclusion of the generic concept of this kind of film from the annals of Norwegian non-fiction film. Nevertheless, there are interesting single cases to be found, and the present article will focus on three films made at different points in time – 1952, 1958, and 1974 – in the history of what was undoubtedly the major industrial undertaking in postwar Norway: the state-owned iron production company Norsk Jernverk A/S in Mo i Rana. These films are interesting inasmuch as they may be said to mirror the expectations, the reality, and, finally, the disillusionment that met this great social and industrial experiment.

Norway 1945-1963: Reconstruction and industrialization

Prior to the outbreak of World War II in 1940, Norway had been an independent nation-state for only 35 years and was in the process of developing from an agricultural to an industrial economy. Although Norway had escaped the five years of war and occupation with far less devastation than other European nations, German occupation had nonetheless inflicted great damage on the fledgling national economy. Apart from German war-related industry there had been no new investment in industry, great resources had been taken out of the country, and the German retreat in 1944 from Finnmark, using the "scorched earth" tactic, had left that part of the country in ruins, with thousands of people left homeless.

The task at hand was formidable, and it is not difficult to see why reconstruction became a prominent word in the official vocabulary of the period, indeed, the keyword of the time. In this extraordinary situation there was a national political consensus to empower the central government with broad powers regarding economic policy, allowing for a large degree of state intervention to this end.

Several factors made this possible. On the ideological level, the war had had a mitigating effect on the main political contradictions in Norway. A pre-war political climate dominated by class conflict had given way to a situation where the resistance to Nazi occupation instigated close cooperation among former political enemies. The Norwegian government in London was a coalition of socialists and non-socialists, and the same constellation was found in Norway's resistance movement, leading to a situation where the desire for national unity was a political aim.

The parliamentary situation also provided a favorable context for a consistent and unified policy. During the general elections of October 1945, the Labor Party achieved a majority in the Norwegian Storting and was thus able to present a unified policy and put it into effect, with an emphasis on a planned economy and a pronounced ambition to work with the other parties. The long-term aims were radically different, however with Labor working toward a socialist Norway. Meanwhile, the non-socialist parties favored various degrees of a free-market economy. Both sides agreed, however, that central regulation and state intervention were appropriate tools in the existing situation.[4]

Given this political climate, central ideological positions of the postwar reconstruction period can be summed up as *national pride and self-reliance, economic growth, and technological optimism*. The first pair of concepts had to do with the immediate task at hand and was closely related to the new sense of national cohesion that the war had provided the Norwegian people. While nationalism had been conceived as a basically conservative sentiment in the twenties and thirties and identified with right-wing causes like the movement to annex East Greenland, nationalistic slogans began appearing in the May Day speeches of prominent labor leaders.

Closely related to this new nationalistic tendency was an emphasis on national self-reliance. This was manifested, for instance, in the Norwegian attitude toward the Marshall Plan. This American financial support program was initially viewed somewhat skeptically by the Labor government for fear it might tie Norway too closely to the United States (this was before Norway decided to join NATO). Norway had applied for $100 million in currency support from the

United States, and had assumed, as the sole receiver among West European nations, that the aid was to be paid back in full. Eventually, Norway received $400 million as a gift, but Marshall Plan aid still only accounted for 8.8% of net investments in the Norwegian economy.[5]

The task of reconstruction was coupled with a stated wish to advance further. Norway was emerging from the economic depression when the Germans attacked in 1940. Unemployment was still high, and it was important for the Labor government to exorcise the "spirit of the thirties" by securing full employment. The key was economic growth, and economic growth was based on increased productivity – the entire industrial system of Norway needed an overhaul.

The third factor can be found in this "spirit of reconstruction," which I have chosen to call *technological optimism*. With the expansion of the industrial sector and the opening up of Norway after five years of isolation under German rule, the war also marked a technological divide. The war effort had, however, brought technological innovation, and the application of war technology to civilian ends was an international trend that inevitably came to influence the Norwegian industrial effort.

The construction of the Norsk Jernverk iron and steel works in Mo i Rana

The establishment of Norsk Jernverk was based on these three initial concepts that governed the development of postwar Norway. One of the first acts of the free Norwegian government in July 1945 was to establish a state commission for steel and iron production. The need for national self-reliance became clear during the inter-war and World War II periods, and the creation of a national steel and iron industry based on Norwegian resources was considered an absolute necessity for the reconstruction and development of a strong Norwegian national economy. In 1946, the commission suggested that a large iron and steel production facility be erected in Mo i Rana in northern Norway, just below the Polar Circle.[6]

The choice of this location was largely determined by existing natural resources in the area. The rich deposits of iron ore in nearby Dunderlandsdalen had been utilized since the turn of the century for export purposes and were considered the obvious source for raw materials. Rich natural resources for the development of a giant hydroelectric power plant were utilized by damming and controlling the Røssåga river in the vicinity, the existence of an ice-free deep-water harbor – these factors were favorable for establishing the first site of

large-scale integrated industrial production in Norway. Mo i Rana was to become the Norwegian equivalent of the Ruhr or Magnitogorsk, with the emphasis on *Norwegian*.[7]

The national aspect was further accentuated by the choice of technology. Because of the abundance of hydroelectric power in Norway, engineers and industrialists had been looking at alternatives to the coal-based blast furnace technology normally used in steel and iron production. In the 1920s, the Norwegian
engineers Georg Tysland and Ivar Hole patented an electric smelting furnace
and the 1946 commission recommended that the planned iron and steel works
in Mo i Rana be based on this technology. However, there was still a need for
coke in the production process, and in 1964 a state-owned coke factory – Norsk
koksverk A/S – was established in Mo i Rana to process Norwegian coal from
the mines in the Svalbard archipelago.

There were also two other significant factors in the Mo i Rana undertaking –
the question of *regional politics* and *national infrastructure*. These two factors were
strongly intertwined with the planning of the Mo i Rana industrial complex. On
the one hand, it was a project based on utilizing existing local resources to supply and strengthen the national market, avoiding further pressure on the import
of foreign goods. On the other hand, the very fact that it was located in northern
Norway meant there was a will to maintain and develop a region that had been
hardest hit by the war. As mentioned above, the entire province of Finnmark
had been torched by the retreating Germans in 1944, and the burden of reconstruction was heavy throughout the region, especially in the area of employment.

And the regional consequences of Norsk Jernverk were indeed great. When
the iron works were fully operative by the mid-1960s Norsk Jernverk and its
associated activities represented more than 4,000 jobs in Mo i Rana. In addition
to this figure of employees directly involved in steel and iron production, there
were also many jobs to be had in the related infrastructure, with the result that
the population in Mo i Rana increased from 9,000 in 1946 to 25,000 by the mid-
1960s.

Seen in relation to these numbers, Mo i Rana emerged as a typical *company
town* during the 1950s and 1960s, with most of its economic and social activities
centered around the iron and steel industry and Norsk Jernverk. A study from
2003[8] exemplifies how the state iron company dominated the town's cultural
and social life, from the social organization of housing (villas for the administrative elite, semi-detached houses for administrative functionaries, housing
projects for the workers) to politics, environmental problems, culture, and leisure time, and to the effects on the communities in the vicinity of the great industrial locomotive.[9]

Figure 1 The construction of Norsk Jernverk in Mo i Rana in
JERNVERKET REISER SEG *(1952)*

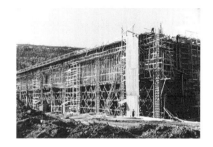

A 2003 study emerged from a historical research project originally titled A Society Between Dream, Steel and Reality, indicating a clash between the so-
cial-democratic vision (dream) of a postwar society which was industrially developed and the real events following the establishment of a Norwegian steel
industry in Mo i Rana. And the reality was harsh. One of the project's assumptions was that it would take a very long time for the German steel industry to
get back to pre-war production levels and that the iron and steel works in Norway would become a strong player on a free international market for steel and
iron. It was also assumed that the price of coal would go up, giving an edge to a

steel industry based on subsidized electricity. As it turned out, none of these predictions were right. The German steel industry was soon back on track, coal prices went down, and the European Coal and Steel Union – the precursor to the EU – made it difficult to compete on the international market. Moreover, there was an abundance of internal problems: construction took longer than expected, the utilization of local iron ore was postponed by a decade, meaning that ore had to be brought in from other Norwegian mines, the electric furnaces did not produce the expected quality, and the coke production unit ran into problems, triggering a national political crisis. Furthermore, Mo i Rana profoundly experienced one of the inevitable side effects of large-scale industry – pollution. In 1988, after struggling for nearly 35 years, Norwegian steel and iron production based on national resources came to an end, and the long and troublesome process of dismantling Norsk Jernverk began.

The editors of the 2003 study concluded:

> The history of Mo i Rana during the time of the iron and steel works can, in many ways, be regarded as a compressed version of general Norwegian history following World War II, a variation on the theme "growth and dismantling of the social-democratic order."[10]

Norsk Jernverk in film: Three industrial films, 1952-1974

A monumental industrial undertaking like Norsk Jernverk is, of course, thoroughly documented – by contemporary sources in the form of press coverage, political debate, and commentary, as well as retrospectively by historians. The project has also, fortunately, resulted in a number of audiovisual artifacts, sources that tend to be overlooked by historians working with that historical source material in connection with Norsk Jernverk.

The material in question consists of three documentaries made during different stages of the short history of this industrial and social experiment, in 1952, 1958, and 1974. Each of the films represents and reflects the dominant discourse in relation to the Mo i Rana industrial complex and society at the time.

JERNVERKET REISER SEG. SMÅ GLIMT FRA ET STORT ANLEGG
("The Building of Norsk Jernverk. Small Glimpses from a Great Undertaking") (1952)

The first film, produced by Bjørset-Film in 1952, is a compilation with an additional interesting aspect, as it points out another postwar phenomenon in Norway – the Norwegian newsreel FILMAVISEN.

The first postwar Norwegian newsreel was produced by Norsk Film a/s, the municipally owned Norwegian film production company, and shown in Oslo (May 21) and Trondheim (May 29) in the days immediately following the German capitulation in Norway in the spring of 1945. Prior to the war there had been no Norwegian newsreel for national distribution, although the municipal cinema organization in Oslo had been inserting locally filmed news in a weekly newsreel program consisting of various international newsreels.

During the war, the Nazi-controlled Film Directorate had decided that Norsk Film should produce a weekly Norwegian newsreel in conjunction with the German WOCHENSCHAU, and a subdivision of Norsk Film was organized in 1943 to start production in January 1944. The newsreel was given a synchronizing studio by the Germans, and production of a weekly newsreel continued until the end of the war. The newsreel was "force fed" to unwilling Norwegians by being shown as a compulsory first attraction at all cinemas, but the production facilities were excellent, and it became the foundation upon which Norsk Film based its national newsreel service after the war.

According to Erik Hurum, chief editor of FILMAVISEN from 1954 to 1963, the stated aim of the postwar newsreel was to mirror the reconstruction and growth of modern Norway.[11] A look at the contents for the various yearly volumes seems to confirm this. In the 1950 edition, there is at least one item in each one of the 50 newsreels that pertains to rebuilding, construction of new homes, new industry, new technology, ships being launched, new Norwegian inventions, etc. Special emphasis is also placed on the revenue-producing activities of whaling and shipping, the development of Norwegian hydroelectric power stations, and the sizable investments in the new aluminum industry. Given all of this, it is obvious that the construction of Norsk Jernverk would be given special treatment by the national newsreel. From the first inspection tours of the chosen location and then throughout the entire construction period, the newsreel regularly reported on the progress in that enthusiastic rhetorical style that would become the trademark of the newsreel, which is still being parodied today, more than 40 years after FILMAVISEN ceased to exist.[12]

The importance placed on this development is reflected by the fact that FILMAVISEN regularly produced reports concerning the construction process during this period. These reports fit into a permanent category of newsreel reports, that of the reconstruction and modernization of Norwegian society. In the 1950 edition, there is at least one item in each of the 50 newsreels that pertains to rebuilding, construction of new homes, new industry, new technology, ships being launched, new Norwegian inventions, etc. Special emphasis was also placed on the currency-making activities of whaling and shipping, the development of Norwegian hydroelectric power stations, and the sizable investments made in the new aluminum industry, and – of course – the first large-scale industrial enterprise in the Norwegian industrial economy, the construction of Norsk Jernverk.

THE BUILDING OF NORSK JERNVERK: SMALL GLIMPSES FROM A GREAT UNDER-TAKING is a compilation film made by one of the FILMAVISEN newsreel reporters, based on material shot for the newsreel produced during construction. The film was commissioned by Norsk Jernverk and was obviously produced to counter criticism related to the prolonged period of construction at Mo. After some panoramic shots of the area prior to construction, the voice-over states:

> Many people are asking questions: What is really going on with this iron works business? Will we ever see a return on the millions of taxpayer money allocated? These are the questions that this brief film will attempt to answer.

This is followed by a chronological recapitulation of the construction period, from the initial inspections of the building site by the building committee in 1946, through the clearing of the forest, the digging of the foundations, and the erection of the first structures in circa 1950, which are all taken from earlier FILMAVISEN newsreel reports. The camera and voice-over generally emphasize the magnitude of the building project. Following this are shots from a later stage covering the construction of the workers' homes, scenes with a great symbolic importance in Norway at a time when the housing shortage was one of the most deeply felt problems in the population.

In conclusion, there is a series of shots obviously made explicitly for the film at the end of 1952. Besides the steel-processing mill, the main buildings are also in place, as are the monumental electric furnaces and steel converters. The Norwegian people are going to be richly rewarded for their patience, explains the voice-over commentary:

> This short film has taught us that *steel* is of central importance for all construction work. Thousands and thousands of tons in all forms have been used. ... All of this steel has had to be imported, costing the country valuable assets. And it is exactly this kind of product that the new iron and steel works will now deliver to the world markets.

The film in general is deeply influenced by the FILMAVISEN newsreel style, with upbeat music and an enthusiastic commentary voice belonging to one of the FILMAVISEN people.

A/S NORSK JERNVERK (1958)

The next two films commissioned by Norsk Jernverk were both produced by the small film production firm Vitek-Film and, despite apparently having two directors, they are the work of one person, O. Wulff Johansen, who later changed his name to Wulff Yljo. It is characteristic of the time and the situation of freelance Norwegian film workers (this was a year before television was introduced into Norway) that, when it became known that Vitek-Film had been contracted to make the film for Norsk Jernverk, the matter was taken up at a meeting of the national film workers' union. It was assumed that the contract was lucrative, and one member voiced the fear that Wulff Johansen would capitalize on this by performing several functions, thus barring other film workers from taking part in the film. Although this fear later seemed to be substantiated, with Wulff Johansen being credited as the cameraman as well as the editor and the director, the union officials decided that it would be impossible for the union to intercede on behalf of its members.[13]

The contrast to the earlier film is manifested by the first color images (the 1952 film had been shot in black and white) of liquid iron pouring out of the furnaces in Mo i Rana, accompanied by orchestral fanfare by Gunnar Sønstevold, a prominent composer of music for fiction film. While the tone of the first film was defensive, targeted, as it was, at appeasing a perceived impatience regarding the construction of the iron and steel works using taxpayers' money, the 1958 film is a triumphant presentation of the accomplished feat, announcing great expectations for the future.

After the opening audiovisual fanfare, the film continues with background information about the motivation behind Norsk Jernverk. Norway is presented as a country rich in natural resources and with a strong need to utilize these resources in the modernization process. Over a map of Norway with Mo i Rana at its center, the voice-over explains:

> Mo i Rana was chosen as the place to build a Norwegian steel- and iron-processing plant. Here, just below the Arctic Circle, we find the largest deposits of iron ore, abun-

Figure 2 "When the worker's family is well provided for, the worker thrives, performing his best in his workplace": A/S NORSK JERNVERK *(1958)*

dant hydroelectric power, and an excellent harbor. Few places in the world are more suited to the establishment of a modern iron and steel plant.

The triumphant tone is enhanced in the next shots, starting with a panorama of the newly constructed factory buildings and steel being loaded onto ships in the harbor.

> Norwegians have made iron and steel since the Vikings, but one hundred years ago, the last iron furnaces closed down, and since then, Norway has been dependent on foreign markets for its steel. Today, hundreds of thousands of tons of raw materials and finished steel products are shipped from the Norsk Jernverk harbor every year.

This is followed by a sequence that shows the process of Norwegian iron ore being transformed into iron, steel, and finished steel products. This is an established genre in the *view aesthetic* tradition,[14] with the logical progress of the work process providing the choreography and with an explanatory voice-over, giving the filmmaker ample opportunity to excel in dramatic images of liquid steel pouring out of furnaces, glowing ingots being pounded into profiles, stretched into wire, and rolled into steel plates. Finally Norwegians were able to see the modern technical wonder of Norsk Jernverk for themselves.

This process-dominated sequence is literally at the heart of the film. A conclusion was added in the form of a sequence that points out the importance of the iron works in the creation of a new modern society in Mo i Rana. After a few shots of the new houses, the emphasis falls on presenting Mo i Rana as a young society, a society for the future, by showing young skiers on a local ski slope and a dance at the new city hall, where young men with ducktail hairstyles swirl their girls to rock 'n' roll rhythms. A shot of a family idyll with a worker surrounded by his family is accompanied by the comment: "When the worker's family is well provided for, the worker thrives, performing his best at his job."

For its final images, the film returns to the captivating shots of torrents of Norwegian steel flowing from the converters, assuring the Norwegian public that the mission defined in 1945 has been accomplished. Norway can finally utilize her rich resources and thus proceed on its way to prosperity and social welfare.

Norsk Jernverk (1974)

When Vitek-Film was again commissioned to make a film about Norsk Jern-verk in 1974, more things had changed than the director's name. While the community of Mo i Rana had played a marginal role in the 1952 and 1958 films, it was at the very heart of the 1974 film. Following a dramatic shot of an explosion in the open-pit mine in Dunderlandsdalen, the film starts chronicling the rise of Mo i Rana's society from a tiny market village in the 19th century to the modern, 20th-century industrial town, with its hotels, restaurants, a shopping center (with escalators!), and modern homes, which all signaled a high standard of living. In addition to these modern comforts, the film conspicuously dwells on the rich variety of outdoor activities enjoyed by the citizens of Mo at their very doorsteps. A sequence shows how the workers from the iron and steel works enjoy skiing and ice fishing in winter, lake fishing, sea fishing, and hunting in summer and fall. The commentary emphasizes the value of a clean environment.

Then the film goes into *process* mode, very much like the 1958 film, but this time on a larger scale. By 1974, two more of the original conditions of the 1946 plan had been fulfilled. As mentioned above, the existence of rich iron ore deposits in the Dunderlandsdalen valley nearby was one of the reasons for building the iron and steel works in Mo in the first place. However, developing these resources took far more time than anticipated, and when Norsk Jernverk finally started production in 1956, it had to utilize iron ore transported from other mines in Norway. The processing of local ore had to wait until 1965, by which time the coke factory in Mo i Rana had been established, thus fulfilling the idea of Norsk Jernverk as a fully integrated production system for steel and iron. The 1974 *process film* is intended to show it as a well-functioning system.

By the early 1970s, however, Norsk Jernverk had ceased to be the shining example of Norwegian industrial policy in the public eye, and had turned into a political liability. The enterprise had tried to transcend its problems that came as a result of the gap between expectations and preconditions on the one side and the actual development on the other by extending its production capacity. By this time the undertaking had become an economic liability, causing serious questions about the Labor party's economic policies. The coke factory in Mo was considered a political scandal even before production had begun, and the attitude toward the whole undertaking had changed considerably since the optimism of the early 1950s.

Furthermore, during the 1960s, environmental problems began to be taken into consideration. When, in 1962, furnaces for melting scrap steel were installed at Norsk Jernverk, the community became all too acquainted with the red dust that resulted from the so-called LD process, in which oxygen was blown into the steel converters, resulting in small red, magnetic particles escaping from the converters with the smoke. This dust would cling to surfaces wherever it landed, and in a short period of time Mo i Rana would earn its nickname "the red town" for more than just its traditional left-wing politics. In 1968, eight housewives initiated a petition demanding that action be taken, collecting more than 1,000 signatures.[15] Although a filter system had been planned during the installation of the new converters, it was still not in place four years later, as the allocated money was used for other purposes. The 1968 housewives' petition came at a time when awareness of environmental problems had started to emerge as a political movement in Norway, and the leaders of the petition drive obviously felt that in the current situation they had to act. After some unsuccessful attempts, they managed, in 1970, to bring the level of dust back down to pre-1962 conditions. This background information presented in the 1974 film would explain the sequences underlining the value of unpolluted nature that open it, as well as the emphasis on the new cleaning systems attached to the converters.

Produced at a time of crisis for Norsk Jernverk, this film emphasizes the function of the iron and steelworks in Mo as a guarantee for the continued welfare of a new and growing modern generation. Environmental problems are countered with images of the unspoiled nature that the workers in Mo can potentially enjoy.

The role of the film medium in the Norwegian public discourse on Norsk Jernverk

The three films on Norsk Jernverk testify to the importance attached to audio-visual information about this greatest of all industrial undertakings in postwar Norway. In conclusion, it would seem appropriate to place the films in their institutional context.

The 1952 film is closely linked to the position of the Norwegian national newsreel FILMAVISEN during the first decade after World War II. As mentioned above, one of the explicit aims of this newsreel was to report and record the reconstruction and growth of modern Norway, and, through its distribution system and the system of municipal cinemas, it was to be regarded as an important and powerful mass media agent in postwar Norway.

The compilation film made in 1952 from the newsreel material was distributed through another important channel for non-commercial film distribution in Norway, Statens Filmsentral – the State Film Central – established in 1948 to coordinate the use of educational films in the comprehensive school system and for other organizations. Statens Filmsentral thus became an important factor in the organized use of educational film. In addition to the consolidation of the municipal cinema system, this established a public service system for the use of film as a medium for education and enlightenment, fulfilling ideas initiated during the 1920s and 1930s. There were also, of course, the postwar initiatives to create a system of financial support for Norwegian fiction film.

The film medium was now clearly regarded as an important part of public discourse, and this newfound respect for a medium that had thus far primarily been seen as mere entertainment in turn made it natural for a major industrial undertaking like Norsk Jernverk to spend money on publicity films like those produced by Vitek-Film in 1958 and 1974, thus achieving the perceived effect of mirroring the process of modernization and industrialization through the modern medium of film and cinema.

Norsk Jernverk chronology

1946: Parliament decides to establish a state-owned iron and steel plant in Mo i Rana. Construction of plant and infrastructures begins.

1955: Operation begins.

1963: Economic crisis and pollution problems – massive new state investments.

1964: Coke production starts in Mo i Rana – Norsk koksverk.

1978: Economic problems exacerbated by the international steel industry crisis.

1988: Norsk Jernverk ceases iron and steel production based on local iron ore. Norsk koksverk closes.

1990: Norsk Jernverk is privatized, reopens to manufacture steel from scrap metal.

1996: Norsk Jernverk is sold to the Finnish steel company Rautaruukki.

Notes

1.   Odd Heide Hald, *Norsk filmbibliografi. Litteratur om norsk film og norske filmforhold* (KULTs skriftserie no. 13, Oslo: Norges forskningsråd, 1993).
2.   Jan Anders Diesen, *Eit hugtakande læremiddel? Undervisningsfilmen i norsk skole.* Ph.D. dissertation (Trondheim: University of Trondheim, 1995).
3.   Kathrine Skretting, *Reklamefilm: norsk reklame i levende bilder 1920-1990* (Oslo: Universitetsforlaget, 1995).
4.   Fritz Hodne, *Norges økonomiske historie 1815-1970* (Oslo: J.W. Cappelen, 1981), pp. 532-562.
5.   Hodne, op. cit., pp. 552-557.
6.   Anne Kristine Børresen, *Drømmer av stål. A/S Norsk Jernverk fra 1940-årene til 1970-årene* (no. 10 Skriftserie fra Historisk institutt, Trondheim: University of Trondheim, 1995), pp. 65-67.
7.   Håkon With Andersen, et al. *Fabrikken* (Oslo: Scandinavian Academic Press, 2004).
8.   Per Maurseth, Håkon Andersen, Anne Kristine Børresen, *Jernverk og samfunnsendring. Tretten bidrag til historien om jernverket og Mo i Rana* (no. 40 Skriftserie fra Institutt for historie og klassiske fag, Trondheim: NTNU, 2003).
9.   Ibid.
10. Ibid., p. 7, my translation.

11. Bente Sellereite, *Filmavisen 1945-1963 – Folkeopplyser med levende bilder*, M.A. thesis (Trondheim: University of Trondheim, 1984), p. 62.

12. Bjørn Sørenssen, "The Voice of Reconstruction: the Norwegian Post-war Newsreel," in Roger Smither, Wolfgang Klaue (eds.), *Newsreels in Film Archives* (Trowbridge, UK, and Cranbury, US: Flicks Books/Associated University Presses, 1996) pp. 44-56.

13. According to the protocols of Norsk filmforbund of 1958. The author wishes to acknowledge Mr. Ivar Hartviksen of Mo i Rana for this and other information on Wulff Johansen/Wulff Yljo.

14. Tom Gunning, "Before Documentary: Early nonfiction films and the 'view' aesthetic," in Daan Hertog, Nico de Klerk (eds.), *Nonfiction in the Teens* (Amsterdam: Nederlands Filmmuseum, 1994), pp. 9-24.

15. Maurseth, op. cit., pp. 181-183.

Harbor, Architecture, Film

Rotterdam, 1925-1935

Floris Paalman

Between 1925 and 1935, there was a great deal of interaction between avant-garde cinema and architecture. This is exemplified by the Dutch cinema club *Filmliga* (1927-1933), founded in Amsterdam by the literary critics Henrik Scholte and Menno ter Braak.

Branches were quickly formed in other cities. The ones in Rotterdam, Utrecht, and The Hague were all initiated by architects.[1] Moreover, a close connection existed between the *Filmliga* and the architecture associations *De 8* and *Opbouw*. Why were these architects so committed to film? Set design might have been a reason,[2] but the *Filmliga* mainly showed films without spectacular sets. Architects were also interested in designing cinemas, whose numbers were growing exponentially. The architects of the *Filmliga* realized some, but relatively few. It seems more important that many avant-garde films dealt with architecture, like Joris Ivens's DE BRUG (*The Bridge*, 1928), which follows the logic of its subject: Trains cross the bridge, a train waits while the bridge is raised, ships pass by, and finally, the train continues on its way. The movements are shown from different angles and broken apart in the editing. There are numerous other examples, such as Ivens's NIEUWE ARCHITECTUUR (*New Architecture*, 1930), which was part of WIJ BOUWEN (*We Are Building*, 1930) and included images of the Van Nelle factory in Rotterdam, or MODERNE NEDERLANDSCHE ARCHITECTUUR (1930) by Mannus Franken. The question then could also be reversed: why were filmmakers interested in architecture? Bert Hogenkamp (1988: 49) remarked that New Building lent itself well to experiments in image composition. Tom Gunning[3] went a step further by arguing that there were intrinsic relationships between architecture and cinema. Comparing DE BRUG with the architectural theories of Siegfried Giedion, Gunning notes that Ivens came close to the architectural ideal of "visual simultaneity."

> Using the railway bridge in Rotterdam as a base, Ivens explores the reorganization of space, but he also shows its functioning, its processes and rhythm through cinematic time. Until then, no other avant-garde film had researched the visual characteristics of one location so profoundly.[4]

According to Gunning, both film and architecture framed the world anew. DE BRUG is then not so much about architecture as about a changed vision of the world, made possible by new technological constructions. In this paper, I will examine the broader conditions in which such relations came about, the way that architecture has been studied, explained, exhibited, modeled, and promoted by film. This examination links up with an argument made by Elizabeth Lebas[5] with respect to municipal filmmaking in Britain between the wars.

> Films could show both procedure and progress in ways that were practical, succinct and even entertaining. In turn, by showing the *actual sites and settings* of procedure and progress to inhabitants who were called upon to visit them and in the case of new housing estates, actually occupy them, they played a vital role in assigning and re-designating new spaces for another way of living (italics F.P.).[6]

Lebas makes two main points. Firstly, "these were not films *about* modern living, but *for* modern living" (p. 141). Secondly, they were not part of a regular distribution system, but shown free of charge in town halls, clinics, schools, clubs, etc. (p.140), as well as at large exhibitions and fairs.[7]

Their function can be understood in light of Thomas Elsaesser's three great "A factors": the *Auftraggeber* (commissioning body), the *Anlass* (occasion), and the *Anwendung* (use).[8] These factors will be examined in the case of Rotterdam to understand film in relation to urban development.

The image of the city

It has been said that, even before World War II, Rotterdam was the most modern city in the Netherlands.[9] Moreover, its harbor was one of the largest in the world. This affected all businesses in the city and made Rotterdam a city of labor, which also had political consequences. In 1919, after general suffrage was introduced, the socialists won the elections in Rotterdam. The conservative mayor A.R. Zimmerman was compelled to install two socialist aldermen, in social-service positions, such as the Municipal Housing Department, and Education, including the *Gemeentelijke Schoolbioscoop* (Municipal School Cinema).[10] While the department of housing directly improved everyday living conditions, educational films did so by providing the means to understand them. The first achievement of the housing department, directed by August Plate, was the Spangen quarter, the location of the exemplary *Justus van Effencomplex* (1919-1922, Michiel Brinkman). It was followed by the projects of J.J.P. Oud (Witte Dorp, Hoek van Holland, Kiefhoek), which became paradigms of social housing worldwide. The school cinemas, on the other hand, were an institution established in several cities, first in The Hague in 1918 by the socialist David van Staveren,[11] and soon after that in Rotterdam by A.M. van der Wel.[12] Unlike the others, the one in Rotterdam produced its own films – more than 30 in total. Similar to the case referred to by Lebas,[13] these films were not *about*, but *for* modern living, and they dealt with many subjects: One of the first ones (1920) is about milk products, the subject of the last one (1933) is a "school for women's labor." The latter encouraged working-class girls to continue their education while promoting a modern style of housekeeping; architect Han van Loghem did the same by designing the renewed school building, including a model kitchen and two model dwellings.[14] The school cinema and the housing department fell victim to the economic crisis and to political reforms, but construction of social housing continued; August Plate continued this work with his private firm, Volkswoningbouw Rotterdam, which built the first high-rise housing projects in Rotterdam.[15]

Figure 1 Ship in the dock

Photo by Andor von Barsy, 1930

Besides housing projects the most important example of modernist architecture in Rotterdam, and one that resulted from the trade in the harbor, is the Van Nelle factory (1925-1931), which was commissioned by Kees van der Leeuw and built by Jan Brinkman, Leen van der Vlugt, and Mart Stam. With its concrete columns and glass-and-steel façade, it became an icon of the modern movement, which was heralded by Le Corbusier and others. Other functionalist industrial complexes were built, such as the cooperative HAKA factory (1931-1932, Hermann Mertens). Along with architecture, Rotterdam became a stage for industrial and graphic design and indeed a center for avant-garde cinema. Besides Ivens's DE BRUG, other famous examples include the film HOOGSTRAAT (*High Street*, 1929), about the main shopping street in Rotterdam, made by the Hungarian filmmaker Andor von Barsy, and MAASBRUGGEN (*Maas Bridges*, 1937), by Paul Schuitema.[16]

The image of Rotterdam was also shaped by a number of feature films, several of which used Rotterdam as a stage of modern urbanism and industry.[17] One of them is LENTELIED (1936, Simon Koster), an early example which was shot on location. Archaic images of the countryside make Rotterdam, in contrast, look even more modern. The film contains a montage sequence with icons of modern Rotterdam that were located in different parts of the city. Although it was still an old city, with alleys, canals, and old warehouses, the sequence suggests that it is utterly modern, which was reinforced by emphasizing the harbor and its industry. LENTELIED provided a frame of reference for how to perceive and envision the city. From that perspective we might also consider a particular documentary genre, that of "construction films," which also emphasized the promise of modernity.

Construction film

In the late 1910s, Dutch film pioneer Willy Mullens documented the construction of the garden village Vreewijk. Later on, he also made a film about the construction of the Van Nelle factory. Other filmmakers started making similar films, which are more than simply records of new construction. They are celebrations of progress and urban development, characterized by an optimism that the future can be built. Notwithstanding this common goal, these films were made for different reasons, depending on the factors mentioned above of commission, occasion, and use.

A particular case is that of the department store chain De Bijenkorf. In the late 1920s, it commissioned architect Willem Dudok to build a modern department store with a glass-and-steel façade. In the ten years of its existence – it was destroyed during World War II – it became a symbol for modern Rotterdam, to which many films contributed.[18] One that is particularly worthy of a closer look is the construction film GROEI (*Growth*, 1928-1930, J. De Haas), produced by Polygoon. The film makes use of modern aesthetics, mobile framing, superimposition, rhythmic editing, and special compositions. There is, for example, a shot from the roof, showing a construction elevator coming up, while down in the street a tram comes into the film image from top to bottom. This "three-dimensional graphic" of double movement, seen from an unusual perspective, distorts the viewer's perception by using opposed movements and depth, resulting in "cinematic plasticity." It establishes an analogy between tram and elevator, and at the same time between urbanism and architecture. Other images show ram machines and cement transporters, followed by informal shots of workers having lunch and then workhorses eating and drinking in a similar way – a humorous example of associative filmmaking. At the conclusion, the completed building is shown. The architectural composition, with a tower and a large rectangular building, is transferred into a cinematic composition. The camera frames the tower diagonally, then moves to the right along the building so that the top corner of the rectangular building is shown diagonally. The building has changed into a floating architecture of moving graphics. Finally, the film shows the opening, with about 70,000 people attending. They had been waiting for this moment for two years, and were regularly kept informed by the Polygoon newsreels made from the footage. In this way De Bijenkorf bought itself into the news, or rather, it took advantage of an occasion (*Anlass*), similar to what commercials would later do.[19] Thus, GROEI expressed the identity of the store. The construction, as a seemingly functional concern, was above all a way to show modernity, progress, hence "growth," as the title notes. Functionalism dictated style and fashion, and style and fashion were the trade of De Bijenkorf. Trade, architecture, and film reinforced each other.

Whereas GROEI was based on modernity as trend, similar films like Ivens's WIJ BOUWEN (1930), on building in the Netherlands, and the related film BETONARBEID (1930, Ivens),[20] on the construction of embankment walls in Rotterdam, had other goals. Since they were commissioned by the Union of Construction Workers (ANBB), they above all promoted the building industry and its workers. Different cases again show different reasons, like the Polygoon film DE COOPERATIEVE PRODUCTIE GROEIT (*The Cooperative Production Grows*, 1932), about the new cooperative HAKA factory. The film presents manual labor and mechanical production as extensions of each other, the individual engagement and collective force of the workers, and, as the title also suggests, the very idea of progress and growth. BOUW MAASTUNNEL (1937-1941, Dienst Gemeentewerken), a film about the construction of a tunnel under the Maas River, takes the viewer along the design and engineering process in order to gain support for the project from both professionals and citizens.

Industrial film

The construction film is a variant of the industrial film. In total more than 200 industrial films were made in Rotterdam between 1925 and 1935. Willy Mullens

and Polygoon were among the first to make such films, which were often related to enterprises in the harbor, like Steenkolen Handels Vereeniging and Hol-
land-Amerika-Lijn. After the mid 1920s, other producers came to the fore, like
the Rotterdam-based Transfilma, which made many industrial films, for example about the municipal electricity and gas works, and about food production.[21]
In these films, raw materials (e.g., coal, barley) are brought into the harbor,
transported through the city to the plant, processed there, and brought into the
city again. The end of the gas film shows how the product is enjoyed by two
fashionably dressed women in a kitchen, who move elegantly about the heated
room; a man with snow on his coat entering a house, and a young girl playing
in a light, spacious bathroom. Other images show a big bakery, a hotel kitchen,
and an ironing workshop. They either promote the idea of modern housing or
frame the places as extensions of the factory and a continuation of the production process. The flow of energy relates all (modern) environments. Other productions by Transfilma include the feature film DE MAARSCHALKSTAF (The Marshal's Baton, 1929, Luc Willink), commissioned by the Centrale Bond van
Nederlandsche Verbruikscoöperaties (Central Union of Dutch Consumer Coop-
erations), which promotes a socialist production model disguised as a love story
and, despite its fictional character, exhibits a common agenda with certain industrial films.

Besides films for private firms, we might also consider documentaries about
the city in general, and which promoted the urban economy as a whole. In 1926,
for example, businessmen collaborated and commissioned FILM OVER DE ROT-
TERDAMSCHE HAVEN EN PLAATSELIJKE INDUSTRIE EN HANDEL (1927, Th. Güsten),
produced by Germania-Film. As it only summed up a number of firms, it was
generally considered a failure, except for its cinematography,[22] which was the
work of Andor von Barsy. After that he and Transfilma were asked to make
eight short films for companies in the harbor. Additionally, the municipality
commissioned a feature-length documentary on Rotterdam DE STAD DIE NOOIT
RUST (The City that Never Rests, 1928, Andor von Barsy).[23] The film starts with
the historical growth of Rotterdam, using maps and animation, followed by an
overview of the city and the harbor. The film is a whirlpool of movement, with
rushing traffic, including trains, cars, trams, trucks, airplanes, and ships, while
the camera itself is mounted on vehicles. The harbor gets special attention and is
shown as a highly dynamic city in itself with "moving architecture" – vessels
that are state of the art in terms of industrial design and engineering, and barges
that turn the harbor into a Waterstad. Porters carry heavy loads, while cranes
make a veritable choreography out of unloading all kinds of cargo. Besides
overviews, including shots taken from an airplane, von Barsy also had an eye
for detail: a pedlar takes orders on a victualling boat, a man washes his hair
over the railing of his fast-moving ship.

Figure 2 At the harbour

Photo by Andor von Barsy, 1930

Nico Brederoo,[24] writing on the influence of the *Filmliga*, remarked that the film is less experimental than von Barsy's HOOGSTRAAT. Nevertheless, it was shown by the *Filmliga Rotterdam*, though under a different name (VAN VISSCHERSDORP TOT WERELSTAD[25]). It is unclear which version Brederoo referred to, since the film was reedited and shortened several times due to ongoing changes in the harbour.[26] In Germany, it was even cut into three different films, with titles like WELTHAFEN (*World Harbor*), ROTTERDAM, and KANÄLE UND GRACHTEN (*Canals and Waterways*).[27] Moreover, Albrecht Viktor Blum subsequently "recycled" the material into five short educational films, which also included images shot in Rotterdam for his feature film JENSEITS DER STRASSE (1929). Thomas Tode[28] classifies the recycled work as "a rather conventional cultural film series," while Bert Hogenkamp[29] views the original film as a progressive step in the Dutch documentary tradition. Instead of categorizing this and other films as experimental, educational, or documentary, it makes more sense to frame the circumstances and reasons of this film, hence Elsaesser's three A's.

Industrial exhibition

In 1928, when the Olympic Games were held in Amsterdam, Rotterdam sought to profit from it by organizing the *Nenijto* international trade and industrial exhibition (*Nederlandsche Nijverheids Tentoonstelling*). *Nenijto*, with exhibitors from the Netherlands, Belgium, Germany, Great Britain, France, Denmark, and Austria, was a heterogeneous combination of product information and entertainment. Its actual purpose was to promote the city and its industry. The event attracted almost 1.5 million visitors in four months.[30] During this period *Nenijto* became part of big city life, at the expense of other entertainment in the city, especially the cinemas.[31]

According to Marlite Halbertsma,[32] *Nenijto* was the beginning of a city marketing strategy that highlighted modern architecture and the harbor. The exhibition itself was a showcase of contemporary architecture, with pavilions in the modernist style, designed by the young architect C.B. van der Tak. The entrance of *Nenijto* consisted of a large semi-circular building flanked by two monumental towers. This provided access to an avenue with more than twenty kiosks, each six meters tall, in Cubist style, and four large halls made of iron with wooden panels and white plaster. They offered space to all kinds of firms, many of which were related to the harbor. This strategy was most noticeable in the Rotterdam Pavilion by the architect Adrianus van der Steur, which presented a huge scale model of Rotterdam and its harbors, with the Maas River as a walkway.

Halbertsma[33] argues that *Nenijto* made use of tactics from theater and advertising. It even encompassed one of the biggest amusement parks in Europe,[34] while across the exhibition a small steam train ran over a 2.5-kilometer railway track. The Oranjeboom brewery set up the Ober-Bayern beer hall, with drinking, singing, and games, next to the attraction of an African village where one could observe the daily life of a hundred Senegalese people. Andor von Barsy wittily referred to both, though implicitly, in his film ORANJEBOOM, HET BIER-BROUWERIJBEDRIJF (*The Oranjeboom Beer Brewery*, 1927) by showing a Bavarian, an African, a Dutchman, and a Chinese man[35] uniting the world at the end by drinking beer together. A variety of media were introduced at the exhibition: design, architecture, performance, print media, photography, film, and sound. This reflects Thomas Elsaesser's notion of the *Medienverbund*, that is, strategies in which different media are used to promote a social, political, or economic agenda.[36]

Several activities were organized during *Nenijto*. John Logie Baird presented his invention of television,[37] and Philips installed loudspeakers all over the exhibition, which surprised journalists with violin music and other sounds.[38] The press was highly involved in the exhibition. *Rotterdamsch Nieuwsblad* published a daily *Nenijto* paper, while *Nieuwe Rotterdamsche Courant* published a weekly *Nenijto* edition. In addition, the event was covered by newsreels, in particular those by Polygoon. *Nenijto* also concluded an agreement with the distribution company Haghe-film to arrange ongoing film screenings.[39] Some of von Barsy's films were made for this reason, like those commissioned by "harbor baron" Daniël van Beuningen,[40] the main financial backer of *Nenijto*, as well as the film ORANJEBOOM.[41] In view of these and other films, the municipality realized that the city as a whole needed a film too; DE STAD DIE NOOIT RUST was commissioned just before the beginning of *Nenijto*, with the requirement that it be ready within only two and a half months, so that it could be shown during the event.[42]

A promotional booklet designed by Piet Zwart was published for the exhibition under the title "Visiting Rotterdam." It is likely that this booklet and Andor von Barsy's film went together. This idea seems to be confirmed by looking at the world exhibition in Antwerp in 1930, for which von Barsy was commissioned to make both the film ROTTERDAM (1930) and a promotional booklet. Its cover was designed by Hendrik Wijdeveld, the architect of the Dutch pavilion. According to Halbertsma, the book was created "in a newly objective language of forms which underscored the modern character of Rotterdam."[43] The most appropriate description of von Barsy's films would in fact be that of "functional cinematography," analogous to functionalism in architecture. This is also true of his other films, such as TUSSCHEN AANKOMST EN VERTREK (*Between Arrival and Departure*, 1938), that present similar perspectives, possibly in connection to the World's Fairs such as the one in Paris in 1937 and the one in New York in 1939.

Institutions and networks

The cross-disciplinary development of cinema and architecture has been largely directed by three structuring powers: industry and trade, the municipality, and the press. In concordance with the network theory of Ulf Hannerz,[44] these powers might be embodied in particular organizations, which, moreover, operate in different capacities, as institutions, associations, and individuals. Networks are formed across institutional borders in environments where formal and informal activities take place simultaneously. New organizations can thus emerge.

The first power, industry and trade, played a pivotal role by commissioning films and buildings and by shaping organizations through membership and support. Of special importance were the shipping companies Steenkolen Handelsvereeniging and Holland-Amerika Lijn, the financial firm of Mees & Zoonen, and most importantly, the coffee, tea, and tobacco factory of Van Nelle, directed by Kees van der Leeuw. He and his industrial designer, Willem Gispen, actively supported the *Filmliga*, while the factory's architect Jan Brinkman was a member of the board in Rotterdam.[45] Van Nelle was already using film for publicity purposes at an early stage, for example, there is the film DE THEE, VAN PLANTAGE TOT HET PAKJE (*Tea: From the Plantation to the Package*, 1920) by Willy Mullens, who also filmed the construction of the factory: BOUW VAN DE VAN NELLE FABRIEK (*Construction of the Van Nelle Factory*, 1930). Later the factory commissioned Polygoon to make the diptych ACHTER GLAS (*Behind Glass*, 1931), a film which celebrated both coffee and tea production as well as the new factory's operation. A more experimental film was made for the *Filmliga*, DE GEBOUWEN VAN DE ERVEN WED. J. VAN NELLE (*The Buildings of De Erven Wed. J. Van Nelle*, 1931, Jan Teunissen[46]), showing the factory from different perspectives, shot with a mobile camera, so that it seemed to defy gravity. Van der Leeuw also supported the architectural organization *Opbouw*, while its head of publicity, Jacob Jongert, was active in the *Volksuniversiteit*, which was supported by Van der Leeuw, and organized presentations on architecture, painting, film, theatre, and more.

The second structuring power was the municipality. The Department of Public Works (Dienst Gemeentewerken), directed by Willem Witteveen, constructed many public buildings, like those by city architect Adrianus van der Steur.[47] The Municipal Information Service commissioned films to promote the city and its harbor. The municipality also encompassed the Housing Department, for which J.J.P. Oud worked, who at the same time was active in the *Filmliga*, *Opbouw*, and the *Volksuniversiteit*. In comparison, director A.M. van der Wel of the municipal Schoolbioscoop, collaborated with different organizations, such as the production company Polygoon, which resulted in DE RIJN VAN LOBITH TOT AAN ZEE (*The Rhine from Lobith to the Sea*, 1922), for example, and, among others, the Municipal Traffic Department, which is reflected by the film VEILIG VERKEER (*Safe Traffic*, 1930). Furthermore, Van der Wel was a member of the Association for Educational and Development Films, with *Filmliga* programmer Mannus Franken as its chairman.

The third power was the press, such as the weekly *Groot Rotterdam*,[48] the newspapers *Nieuwe Rotterdamsche Courant* and *Rotterdamsch Nieuwsblad*, as well as the publishers Brusse and Nijgh & Van Ditmar, which promoted new forms of design and publicity. *Groot Rotterdam* also commissioned a feature-length documentary, GROOT ROTTERDAM (1930, Co van der Wal), about journalists working in the city. The film makes it clear, through a double self-reflective move, that events become important when the media is present.

The newspapers were of general importance, for city reports, for their support of events like *Nenijto*, and for architecture and film criticism. *Nieuwe Rotterdamsche Courant* even had its own architecture editor, Han van Loghem, while it had also its own film section. The latter was headed by Coen Graadt van Roggen, who edited a series of ten monographs on film, published by Brusse between 1931 and 1933. Among the journalists contributing to the film section were the foreign correspondent and filmmaker Simon Koster and editor Johan Huijts, who was the chairman of the *Filmliga Rotterdam*. This commitment to film is articulated by a short ironic fiction film, REDACTEUREN ZIEN U AAN (*Editors Watch You*, 1933, anonymous), about *Nieuwe Rotterdamsche Courant* editors. In this "practical joke" in avant-garde style, an editor (Victor van Vriesland) goes crazy: the atmosphere in the office is too poor, the pressure too great, the pay too low. He tries to commit suicide, but does not succeed. In 1935, *Nieuwe Rotterdamsche Courant* opened its own cinema, Cineac, which showed newsreels, documentaries, and cartoons and linked the newspaper directly to the film industry.[49]

Economically and politically, the powers of industry and trade, the municipality, and the press exercised a great deal of influence on organizations and studios involved with film and architecture. A further structuring power can be seen in the socialist movement, including organizations such as Links Richten and IVAO/Ons Huis, but in Rotterdam, it was partly institutionalized by its role in the municipality. Notwithstanding the importance of the three main powers, we can see other forces, of individual and social nature at work as well. We can, for example, note the films that were initiated by filmmakers themselves, like Ivens' THE BRIDGE and von Barsy's HOOGSTRAAT, which at the same time offer possibilities for drawing extensive social networks. In the case of Ivens, we could, first of all, look at the role played by women (such as his wife Germaine Krull). Meanwhile, we can observe the Hungarian connections in the case of von Barsy. Professional ties are also important here, which is illustrated by von Barsy's industrial film ORANJEBOOM (1927), of which parts were used for the avant-garde film and stage play NUL UUR NUL (1927, Simon Koster), being an instance of the "functional" meeting the "experimental." Similar arguments could be made for others, in particular, Kees van der Leeuw, not just as a representative of Van Nelle, but as an influential individual.

Whereas the main powers largely directed the cross-disciplinary development of cinema and architecture, a number of individuals certainly offered, in their turn, new (organizational) perspectives. They were supported in these efforts by international organizations and networks such as *C.I.C.I.* (cinema) and *C.I.A.M.* (architecture), whose members also visited Rotterdam.[50]

The intention of this article has been to trace some of the links found between film and architecture. Starting from Thomas Elsaesser's three A factors, I have come to three C factors, *content, conditions,* and *connections*. The creation of industrial film has shown itself to be framed by social-order networks, but also by a cultural and aesthetic order. There are also clusters within the network that, in turn, create networks within the network.[51] The foremost factor here has been how the network relates to its environment, in this case Rotterdam, whose films and buildings can be seen as its "fixation points." This network has determined both the infrastructure through which the buildings and the films are produced, and the frame of reference for what they show. As my case study has demonstrated, the emergence of an image of the city can be described in terms of such communication processes and sociocultural forces that constitute a complex of similarities and differences, of common goals and contrasting movements.

Notes

1.   J.J.P. Oud was the founding chairman of *Filmliga Rotterdam*. As such, he also signed its manifesto together with journalist J. Huijts and architect J. Brinkman, etc. The chairman and secretary in Utrecht were S. van Ravesteyn and G. Rietveld, in The Hague architect C. van Eesteren and designer V. Huszár. See T. Gunning, C. Linssen, H. Schoots (eds.), *Het Gaat Om De Film! Een Nieuwe Geschiedenis van de Nederlandsche Filmliga, 1927-1933* (Amsterdam: Bas Lubberhuizen / Filmmuseum, 1999), pp. 183-185.

2.   Such as for architect H. Wegerif who designed the sets for 19 feature films. Cf. Kathinka Dittrich, *Achter het doek, Duitse Emigranten in de Nederlandse Speelfilm in de Jaren Dertig* (Houten: Het Wereldvenster, 1987).

3.   T. Gunning, C. Linssen, H. Schoots, pp. 256-257.

4.   Ibid., p. 257.

5.   Elizabeth Lebas, "The Clinic, the Street and the Garden Municipal Film-making in Britain Between the Wars," in M. Kostantarakos (ed.), *Spaces in European Cinema* (Exeter: Intellect, 2000), pp. 138-51.

6.   Ibid., p. 140.

7.   Cf. Thomas Elsaesser , "Die Stadt von Morgen; Filme zum Bauen und Wohnen," in Klaus Kreimeier et al. (eds.), *Geschichte des dokumentarischen Films in Deutschland 1919-1933* (Stuttgart: Reclam, 2005), p. 400.

8.   Ibid., p. 383.

9.   Roman Koot, in Marlite Halbertsma and Patricia van Ulzen (eds.), *Interbellum Rotterdam, kunst en cultuur 1918-1940* (Rotterdam: NAi, 2001).

10.   A. Heijkoop, A. De Zeeuw, resp.

11.   Bert Hogenkamp, "De Schoolbioscoop," *Skrien 140* (February/March, 1985), pp. 42-45.

12.   Cf. Marcel Westhoff, *Levensgangen, biografische data over 30 cineasten* (SFW-werkuitgave, no. 9, Amsterdam: St. Film en Wetenschap, 1995), p. 78.

13.   Lebas, op. cit.

14. Cf. also W. van Gelderen, "Scholenbouw. School voor Vrouwenarbeid," *De 8 & Opbouw* 6, 9 (1935), pp. 95-97.

15. Bergpolderflat (1932-1934, Van Tijen, Brinkman, Van den Vlugt); Kralingse Plaslaan (1937-1938, Van Tijen, Maaskant).

16. Other examples include Nul Uur Nul (1927, S. Koster), Verkeer (1929, Polygoon), Groei (1930, J. de Haas), Van Nelle (1930, J. Teunissen), De Steeg (1932, J. Koelinga), Rotterdam (1935, M. de Haas), Tusschen Aankomst en Vertrek (1937, A. von Barsy).

17. For example, Jenseits der Strasse (1929, A.V. Blum), Een Lied van den Arbeid (1929, W. Jansen), The Marshal's Baton (1929, L. Willink), Boefje (1939, D. Sirk), Ergens in Nederland (1940, L. Berger).

18. For example, Moderne Nederlandsche Architectuur (1930, M. Franken), the Bijenkorf commercial Dreams (1931, Alsem), De Steeg (1932, J. Koelinga), Lentelied (1936, S. Koster).

19. Droomen (1931, H. Alsem), Herfstmode (1932, A. von Barsy), Tafeltje Dekje (1933, A. von Barsy).

20. Alternative title: Caissonbouw.

21. Het Gemeente Electriciteitsbedrijf, Het Gemeente Gasbedrijf Rotterdam, Oranjeboom, Hygiënische Melkstal de Vaan, and Modelbedrijven der Volksvoeding (1927-1928); directed by Von Maydell, camera by von Barsy, script by von Reitzenstein.

22. E.g., "Een Film van Rotterdam," *NRC*, 1927/01/12.

23. F.C. von Maydell was officially the director, but von Barsy was the actual "author" of this and other Transfilma films, cf. also, e.g., "Filmkritiek, Rotterdam als Film-Epos," *Het Vaderland* (August 16, 1928); "Van Visschersdorp tot Wereldhavenstad," *Rotterdamsch Nieuwsblad* (August 16, 1928).

24. Nico Brederoo, "De Invloed van de Filmliga," pp. 183-228; K. Dibbets and F. Van der Maden (eds.), *Geschiedenis van de Nederlandsche Film en Bioscoop tot 1940* (Houten Het Wereldvenster, 1986), p. 201.

25. Cf. *Het Gaat Om De Film!*, p. 288.

26. Cf. "Een Nieuwe film over de Rotterdamsche haven," *Nieuwe Rotterdamsche Courant* (May 1, 1938).

27. Cf. Thomas Tode, "Dossiertes Muskelspiel," Klaus Kreimeier, et al. (eds.), *Geschichte des dokumentarischen Films in Deutschland 1919-1933* (Stuttgart: Reclam, 2005), p. 549.

28. Thomas Tode, "Albrecht Viktor Blum," Hans M. Bock (ed.), *Cinegraph Lexikon*, Lg. 29 (Munich: Text + Kritik, 1997), p. B8.

29. Bert Hogenkamp, *De Nederlandsche documentaire film, 1920-1940* (Amsterdam: St. Film en Wetenschap / Van Gennep, 1988), p. 21.

30. Marlite Halbertsma and Patricia van Ulzen (eds.), *Interbellum Rotterdam, kunst en cultuur 1918-1940* (Rotterdam: NAi, 2001), p. 209.

31. *Interbellum Rotterdam* , p. 209. Cinema revenues that year were 90,000 guilders less than the year before.

32. Ibid., p. 211.

33. Ibid., p. 214.

34. Cf. Peter de Winter, *Evenementen in Rotterdam, Ahoy', E55, Floriade, C70* (Rotterdam: Uitgeverij 010, 1988), p. 4.

35. Rotterdam at that time had a significant Chinese community.

36. Cf. Elsaesser in Kreimeier, loc.cit., p. 391.

37. Jan Wieten, "Televisie is omroep," *Informatie & Informatiebeleid*, I&I, 3 (1994), http//www.cram.nl/ieni, last accessed June, 2006.

38. *Nieuwe Rotterdamsche Courant* (June 1928) (week after opening), front page of Nenij-to special edition, GAR XX C48.

39. Ibid.

40. Cf. "Bedrijfsfilm D'Oranjeboom," *De Maasbode* (January 14, 1928).

41. Cf. "De Steenkolen Handelsvereeniging," *Nieuwe Rotterdamsche Courant* (March 2, 1927); *De Maasbode* (January 14, 1928).

42. Cf. "Van Visschersdorp tot Wereldhavenstad," *Rotterdamsch Nieuwsblad* (August 16, 1928).

43. *Interbellum Rotterdam*, p. 215.

44. Ulf Hannerz, *Exploring the City: Inquiries Toward an Urban Anthropology* (New York: Columbia University Press, 1980).

45. Johan Huijts, "Filmliga Rotterdam (1927-1933)," in *Rotterdams Jaarboekje 1975* (Rotterdam: W.L. & J. Brusse, 1975), p. 266.

46. Cf. Bert Hogenkamp, *De Nederlandsche documentaire film, 1920-1940* (Amsterdam: St. Film en Wetenschap/Van Gennep, 1988), p. 146.

47. *Interbellum Rotterdam, p. 233.*

48. Ibid., p. 23.

49. Cf. Henk Berg, *Over Stalles en Parket, Rotterdam en het Witte Doek, een populair-historisch overzicht van de Rotterdamsche en Schiedamsche bioscopen (1896-1996)* (Rotterdam: Ad. Donker, 1996); Frans Blok, *Rotterdamse Bioscopen voor 1940*, scriptie architectuurgeschiedenis TH-Delft, afd. Bouwkunde, 1985 (unpublished – library Gemeentearchief Rotterdam no. XVI B41).

50. Bert Hogenkamp, "De Russen komen! Poedowkin, Eisenstein en Wertow in Nederland," *Skrien*, 144 (November/December 1985), pp. 46-49. – *Interbellum Rotterdam*, ibid.

51. Hannerz, p. 201.

Industrial Films

An Analytical Bibliography

Anna Heymer and Patrick Vonderau

I.   Introduction

The following bibliography covers scholarly as well as archival and practical writings on industrial and commissioned film. This overview of the international literature is intended to open up the field of "industrial film" within the field of film and media studies by making the focal points and desiderata of research more accessible. It proceeds "analytically" in two ways. In the first section, it proposes a systematic that compiles criteria inductively with the goal of isolating, as far as possible, the larger specific areas. In the second section, it provides a means of retracing the state of the research in individual examples through commentary on selected texts from all the subject areas. By taking on the goal of opening up the field analytically, the following bibliography covers new territory, since to date only smaller, usually subject-specific or nationally defined lists of the relevant literature exist.[1]

The lack of a comprehensive bibliography can be explained above all by the fact that "industrial film" has not previously constituted a significant research field within film and media studies. Research fields arise from communications between researchers and are distinguished by the fact that they can be conceived as a whole, distinct from wider research, through an internal cohesion and points of reference between individual works. Indeed, since the 1990s, utility film in general and industrial film in particular have become the subject of scholarly interest. This interest is still, however, primarily due to the initiative of individuals.[2] Among these individual pioneers are archivists and collectors, without whom the material would not be available to research at all. One important figure to be mentioned here would be Rick Prelinger, who was already making his collection of "ephemeral films" accessible during the 1980s, initially through an edition of CD-ROMs (New York: Voyager), later through his own web repository, the contents of which have been placed in the Library of Congress and made accessible at no charge through the Web site www.archive.org. Business archivists such as Paul Hofmann and Horst Wessel should also be mentioned here. With their first collection list (Hofmann 1994), they encouraged research on industrial film in the Ruhr region in Germany (cf. Rasch 1997 ff). The research on industrial film is not only determined by the productivity of individual authors among archivists and collectors, but also within the humanities and social sciences, as can be seen in section 4 of the bibliography. The contribution made by this volume, the conference that instigated it, and this bibliography therefore also serve to coordinate such individual activities and, in doing so, constitute the research field of "industrial film" within film and media studies.

The literature on industrial film – and more generally, on visual media in business communication – is characterized by a close relationship to issues of practice, whether this is due to the "applied" character of the scholarly work, or because the work itself is practice-oriented as in the case of handbooks or first-hand reports. The considerably smaller number of primarily academic writings come from the fields of technical, business, or social history, from communication studies and sociology, and also from film and media studies. Surprisingly, interest in industrial film or instrumental film has so far remained marginal even in film and media studies. Even a cursory examination of the literature makes this clear. As we have mentioned, bibliographies are largely lacking excepting individual cases like the selected, annotated French bibliography in Chémery (1991, pp. 20-31). Hans Jürgen Wulff's *Bibliographie der Filmbibliographien* (1987) lists only a single entry on "industrial film" (Gordon 1961), that being a practical manual, while the editors of *Film – An International Bibliography* (2002) include industrial film as a "Special Subject" along with "Advertising Film," and only two of the nine titles listed are dedicated primarily to industrial film – though with very varied goals (Rasch 1997, Schaller 1997).[3] As these and older, national bibliographies of film literature make clear, the problem already exists at the level of terminology, namely in the fact that "industrial film" is usually subsumed under other headings.[4] This tendency toward insufficient systematization can also be clearly seen in a wide variety of film encyclopedias, which do not even include industrial film as a category,[5] or that understand it as a subcategory of the documentary.[6] Even if many industrial films do fit into the wider body of documentary films, such a practice overlooks the characteristic forms of production and use in industrial film, its responsibility to the *commissioning body*, and its close connection to its *use* for the company. The typology of industrial film has also always included representational and public-image films, and these do not (at least officially) belong within the canon of the documentary (cf. Zimmermann 2006a).

Finally, film history has made the least contribution to finding a way out of this dilemma, and this applies to older, classic studies as well as newer, "revisionist" ones.[7] The lack of interest in instrumental and industrial film is due to the fact that film studies was and is understood as the study of feature films.

Film histories focus on the cinema as an institution of entertainment, they are lists of names and places, of works, authors, and nations. They write a history of film as event, which narrates the evolution of styles and "movements" as the great biography of cinema. Industrial films on the other hand, are often nameless, have no place and no life other than the task at hand, particularly none that can be represented in the form of financial statements and marketing figures. They seem, like memos, company brochures, and other forms of "grey literature," ephemeral to media studies – and this despite the fact that the industrial-film sector, as an institution, particularly in the US in the 1960s and 1970s, took on characteristics much like Hollywood, with its own journals, festivals, meetings, and production methods set out in manuals. Industrial films – and this they have in common with the no less neglected documentary film, in which they are often included – rarely form part of the cinematic experience, they are the "most sober" characteristic imaginable of a "discourse of sobriety" (Bill Nichols), in that they create forms in which the discursiveness, the directedness of communication becomes the most recognizable factor.

Industrial film is marginal within film and media studies not only because bibliographies, encyclopedias, and film history have largely ignored it. It remains so also because a large part of the research remains unpublished, which can be clearly seen in the dissertation section of the bibliography, of which very few have found a wider audience. Under the circumstances, it is very difficult to summarize the international state of research. This can only be achieved for partial areas of the literature or scholarly practice. It should therefore be taken in light of the essay by Ralf Stremmel, included at the end, which outlines the state of research from the perspective of a regional business archive. Nevertheless, three tendencies became clear during the preparation of this bibliography. The first marks the majority of practical manuals, which were put together by industry insiders, mostly producers or commissioners, and a portion of the "applied" research from communications studies. These texts often present film as a universal audiovisual medium that can aid in the transmission of any kind of data. Central to this position is the criterion of efficiency, which is attributed to industrial film in the competition between the various communications media. Starting from (socio)psychological premises, management theories, and cybernetic ideas, industrial film appears in this section of the literature as a guidance tool, not only for business processes, but also for overriding social ones. The second impulse is of a different nature altogether and consists of the need to maintain and develop industrial films as aesthetic artifacts. Represented in archive directories and registers as well as historical outlines of the history of sponsored film, the authors that argue according to this tendency have contributed to the historical-empirical fixation of the object, while the disciplinary contexts and questions are very diverse. A third tendency can be seen in more recent, American research, usually aligned with cultural studies. It sees industrial film primarily as one facet of a media epistemology and analyzes it accordingly in connection with the reconstruction of general, historical arrangements of knowledge and processes of knowledge production. Between these roughly sketched tendencies in the approaches to the subject area, there are a large number of individual studies dedicated to the history and theory of individual subgenres, directors, and films that open up production and evaluation contexts, reflect the perspectives of the commissioning bodies, or generally respond to related areas such as industrial photography or business communication. The essays collected in this volume bear witness to the variety of these approaches.

2.   Notes on systematics

The initial impulse for this bibliography was to make it easier to understand the terms used for "industrial film" in general. This means that all terminologically related expressions were taken into account in the research, including common synonyms like "corporate film," "non-theatrical film," "sponsored film," or "business film," but also the description, once common in Germany, of "technical film." But film-specific publications were not the only sources included; the availability of technical visual media in a company context was also crucial for the research. Publications on related subject areas like advertising films, documentary films, and training and educational films as well as industrial work in film (and other media) were considered, but only partially included. Not listed were texts that engage in a broader discussion on industrial film, primarily in the field of cultural studies, that however show no clear relation to questions of media.[8] In order to determine the "core" and "marginal" areas of this bibliography, the criterion of scholarliness was taken as decisive: publications that contribute to scholarly discussions were included as much as possible, while practice-oriented writings were considered, but not thoroughly researched. This was done by using the available international registers and catalogues as a basis, with special attention paid to texts from English, French, German, and Scandinavian origins.

Despite all these attempts to identify the term "industrial film" and the typology of its forms, it was only possible to systematize the writings to a limited degree because of the lack of a larger research field within film and media studies on this topic. In order to make the texts easier to locate, no detailed subgrouping of the list was attempted. The conventional division into sources and literature was discarded as well, since part of the scholarly literature is itself primarily valuable as source material. As such, the categories are essentially limited to the division between practice- and research-related writings, aside from categorization according to the form of publication (essays, books). Such a process is certainly no less problematic, for the reasons listed above, because of an often practice-oriented scholarship, a general preponderance of practice-oriented texts, and also because the purpose of the publications is not always clearly recognizable. The advantage of the process, however, is the division into two mutually exclusive fields of discussion. The annotated portion, on the other hand, includes practically all types of writings in a wider overview, though it had to be limited to commentary on scholarly monographs due to the workload. The choice of annotated texts therefore does not reflect the need for representation, but rather the goal of being able to get an overriding impression of the state of the research "at a glance." The bibliography does not so much have the goal of being exhaustive as of being exploratory.

II. Systematic section

I. Filmographies, registers, and archive guides

Association of Documentary Film Producers (1940) *Living Films: A Catalog of Documentary Films and Their Makers*. New York: Association of Documentary Film Producers.

Catalogue of Technical and Scientific Films: International Film Reference Library of the Organisation for Economic Co-Operation and Development (OECD), 1966. Paris: Film Section of the Information Service of OECD.

Center for Mass Communication (1954) *1954 Sales and Rental Catalog*. New York: Center for Mass Communication, Columbia University Press.

Cook, Dorothy E., and Eva Rahbek-Smith (1936-1943) *Educational Film Catalog* 5 vols. New York: H.W. Wilson Co.

Denmark. Ministeriet for handel, industri og søfart (1957) *Produktivitetsudvalget. Katalog over film og billedbånd for industri, handel og håndværk*. Copenhagen.

Department of Audio-Visual Instruction, National Education Association (ca. 1951) *Guide to Films in Economic Education*. Washington, DC: National Education Association.

Department of Public Relations, General Motors Corporation (1943) *GM Film Catalog, 1943-1944*. 5th ed. Detroit, MI: General Motors Corp.

Deutsche Industriefilm-Zentrale (ed.) (1963) *Filmkatalog der DIZ*. Cologne.

Deutsches Industrieinstitut (ed.) (1958) *Der deutsche Wirtschaftsfilm*. Cologne: Deutscher Industrieverlag.

Deutsches Industrieinstitut (ed.) (1959) *Der deutsche Wirtschaftsfilm*. Cologne: Deutscher Industrieverlag.

Deutsches Industrieinstitut (ed.) (1962) *Der deutsche Industriefilm*. Cologne: Deutscher Industrieverlag, 1960-1962.

Dörnemann, Astrid (1996) Erläuterungen zur Filmverzeichnung und zum Filmbestand der Thyssen Still Otto Anlagentechnik GmbH im Archiv der Thyssen AG. *Archiv und Wirtschaft*, 29, pp. 183-188.

Dörnemann, Astrid (2003) Zur Filmsammlung im ThyssenKrupp Konzernarchiv. *Industriefilm 1948-1959. Filme aus Wirtschaftsarchiven im Ruhrgebiet*. Manfred Rasch, Ulrich Berendes, Peter Döring, et. al. (eds.). Essen: Klartext, pp. 54-56.

Eastman Kodak Company (1957) *Industrial Motion Pictures*. Rochester, NY.

Educational Film Guide. 10 vols. New York: H.W. Wilson Co., 1945 62.

Educational Film Locator of the Consortium of University Film Centers and R.R. Bowker Company. New York and London: R.R. Bowker Co., 1978.

Farrenkopf, Michael and Przigoda, Stefan (2003) Das Bergbau-Archiv Bochum. *Industriefilm 1948-1959. Filme aus Wirtschaftsarchiven im Ruhrgebiet*. Manfred Rasch, Ulrich Berendes, Peter Döring, et. al. (eds.). Essen: Klartext, pp. 58-60.

Günther, Walther (1927) *Verzeichnis deutscher Filme. Grundausgabe. I. Lehr- und Kulturfilme. Bearbeitet im Archiv für Lichtbild- und Filmwesen des Deutschen Bildspielbundes*. Berlin: Bildwart-Verlags-Genossenschaft.

Hanson, Patricia and Alan Gevinson (eds.) (1988) *The American Film Institute Catalog of Motion Picture Films Produced in the United States: Feature Films, 1911-1920*. Berkeley, CA: University of California Press, 1988.

Hofmann, Paul (1994) *Filmschätzen auf der Spur. Verzeichnis historischer Filmbestände in Nordrhein-Westfalen*. Düsseldorf: Selbstverlag des Nordrhein-Westfälischen Hauptstaatsarchivs (= Veröffentlichungen der staatlichen Archive des Landes Nordrhein-Westfalen, Reihe C: Quellen und Forschungen; 33).

Industrie Film Produzenten. Mitgliederverzeichnis. Verband deutscher Filmproduzenten. Wiesbaden: Verband deutscher Filmproduzenten.

Katalog Filmów Oswiatowych. Warsaw: Filmos, 1962.

Lichtwarck, E.W.M. (1948) *Kulturfilm-Almanach*. Hamburg: Hermes.

Lüken, F.W.: *Filmographie: Planen-Bauen-Wohnen Berlin*. Berlin: Technische Universität: unpublished manuscript.

Paparoni, Luigi (1988) *Nuovo repertorio del film industriale*. Rome: Editore SIPI.

Przigoda, Stefan (2002) Bergbau auf Zelluloid. Die Filmsammlung des Bergbau-Archivs Bochum. *Archiv und Wirtschaft*, 35, pp. 9-18.

Przigoda, Stefan (2005) *Bergbaufilme. Inventar zur Überlieferung in Archiven, Museen und anderen Dokumentationsstellen in der Bundesrepublik Deutschland*. Bochum: Deutsches Bergbau Museum.

Rasch, Manfred, Berendes, Hans Ulrich, Döring, Peter, et. al. (eds.) (2003) *Industriefilm 1948-1959. Filme aus Wirtschaftsarchiven im Ruhrgebiet*. Essen: Klartext.

Reichsfilmarchiv. Spielfilme, Kulturfilme, Werbe- und Industriefilme, politische Filme. Berlin: Reichsfilmarchiv.

Savada, Eli (1995) *The American Film Institute Catalog of Motion Pictures Produced in the United States: Film Beginnings, 1893 1910*. Metuchen, NJ and London: Scarecrow Press.

United States Dept. of Labor, United States Employment Service (1946) *Occupational Analysis and Industrial Services Division*. Washington, DC.

United States. Employment Service (1946) *Industrial Films: A Source of Occupational Information*. Washington, DC.

Weaver, Gilbert Grimes and Ericsson, Eric Sigurd (1934) *Bibliography of Technical and Industrial Motion Picture Films and Slides*. New York: New York State Department of Industrial Teacher Training.

Werbefilme für den Spargedanken. Berlin: Deutscher Sparkassenverlag.

Wessel, Horst A. (1997) Das Mannesmann-Archiv/Filmarchiv. *Industriefilm – Medium und Quelle. Beispiele aus der Eisen- und Stahlindustrie*. Manfred Rasch, Karl-Peter Ellerbrock, Renate Köhne-Lindenlaub and Horst A. Wessel (eds.). Essen: Klartext, pp. 59-81.

2. Specialized periodicals

Audio-Visual: Use of All Forms of Audio-Visual Media in Industry, Commerce, Higher Education and the Public Sector. Croydon: McLaren, 1972-1995.

Audiovision in Wirtschaft und Bildungswesen. Munich, 1969, etc.

Business Screen Magazine. *Chicago, 1938-1968*.

Dein Film. Fachblatt für den 16-mm-Schmalfilm in Gewerbe, Industrie und Verbänden. Essen.

Der Deutsche Industriefilm. Cologne, 1959-1992.

Der neue Film. Fachorgan für die Filmindustrie. Wiesbaden-Biebrich, 1947, etc.

Eastman Kodak Company: Radiography and Clinical Photography. Rochester, NY, 1930-1946.

The Educational Film Review and Industrial Cinematography. London: George Newness, April-October 1935.

The Educational Screen. Chicago, 1922-1956.

Film World: Non-Theatrical Film Magazine. Los Angeles: Ver Halen Publications, 1945, etc.

Industrial Photography: The Workbook of Visual Communication, Reproduction and Instrumentation. New York, 1952-1995.

Industrie-Film Magazin – Film und Fernsehen im Dienste der Industrie und Wirtschaft. Berlin.

3. Practically oriented publications: Reports and instructions

3.1 Articles

Anon. (1934) "More Sales in Business Films." *Printers' Ink Monthly*, 28, 6, p. 55.

Anon. (1977) "Directing sponsored film offers opportunity to show creativity." *Business Screen*, p. 24.

Anon. (1978a) "Sponsored films in theatres: a million theatre showings each year." *Business Screen*, 40, p. 28.

Anon. (1978b) "Sponsored film saga: MTPS update." *Business Screen*, 40, p. 30.

Anon. (1978c) "MTPS spotlights corporations' role in sponsored films." *Independent Film Journal* 81, p. 12.

Anon. (1978d) "High potential seen for sponsored films." *Boxoffice*, 112, p. 4.

Anon. (1979) "Commission is attracting filmmakers but effort is weak, says consultant." *Boxoffice*, 114, p. S-4.

Anon. (1981) "NFB out of sponsored films by 1986." *Cinema Canada*, 77, p. 4.

Anon. (1985) "Sponsored films: alternative cinema." *Movie Maker*, pp. 48-49.

Anon. (1985) "Production focus: corporate filmmakers shoot for the top." *Millimeter*, 13, pp. 290-91.

Anon. (1985) "Allo! le film d'entreprise." *Banc-Titre*, 47, pp. 14-15.

Appleton, Stuart (1992) "Those little training programmes..." *Eyepiece*, 13, pp. 48-50.

Bettin, Sandra (1988) "SAG & AFTRA approve new industrial film contract." *Screen Actor*, 27, p. 8.

Brodsky, Bob (1981) "Corporate update on super-8." *Filmmakers Film & Video Monthly*, 14, pp. 28-31.

Cappa, Marina (1990) "Narrazione industriale d'autore." *Rivista del Cinematografo*, 60, p. 22.

Chittock, J. (1980) "The Changing Sponsored Film Scenario." *Screen Digest*, July 1980, pp. 127-129.

Collins, J.K. (1910) "Advertising via the moving picture." *The Nickelodeon*, 2, 3, p. 207.

Darvell, Michael (1977) "'Movie Maker's' guide to sponsored films 1977." *Movie Maker*, 11, pp. 738-739.

Darvell, Michael (1983) "Sponsored film guide." *Movie Maker*, 17, pp. 529-532.

Dasques, Francoise (1985) "L'image des images industrielles." *Banc-Titre*, 53, pp.14-15.

Dellwig, Friedrich (1923) "Industrie und Kino. Werkschul-Lichtspiele der GBAG." *Das Werk*, 3, pp. 34-36.

Deriaz, Philippe (1994) "Internationale Leistungsschau des Wirtschaftsfilms." *Film & TV Kameramann*, 43, pp. 66-70.

Deriaz, Philippe (1995) "Film im Industrierevier." *Film & TV Kameramann*, 44, p. 90.

Deriaz, Philippe (1998) "Die Schönheit einer Maschine." *Film & TV Kameramann*, 47, pp. 34-37.

Dicks, Hans-Guenther (1990) "Starke Kamera, oft schwache Regie." *Film & TV Kameramann*, 39, p. 68.

Farrell, Rena M. (1924) "Originating and Distributing the Industrial Motion Picture." *Printers' Ink Monthly*, 9, 5, p. 62.

Fillinger, P. (1973) "Diary of an Around-the-World Corporate Film." *American Cinematographer*, 54, 4, April 1973, pp. 430-433 and 485-491.

Finehout, Robert (1978) "Sponsored film: talking pictures to satellite transmission." *Business Screen*, November 18-19, 1978.

Frances, Jack (1976a) "Sponsored films: the Barry Wiles 8mm sponsored film." *Film Making*, 13, pp. 33-35.

Frances, Jack (1976b) "Sponsored films: the best sponsored films of all times." *Film Making*, 13, pp. 15-18.

Frances, Jack (1976c) "Sponsored films: watch the message." *Film Making*, 13, pp. 43-46.

Frances, Jack (1976d) "Sponsored films: travels of a film making man." *Film Making*, 14, pp. 26-27.

Frances, Jack (1976e) "The pick of sponsored movies: British Sponsored Film." *Film Making*, 14, pp. 32-33.

Frances, Jack (1976f) "Sponsored films: the making of a sponsored film." *Film Making*, 14, pp. 35-37.

Frances, Jack (1976g) "Sponsored films: which type of director are you?" *Film Making*, 14, pp. 39-40.

Frances, Jack (1976h) "Sponsored films: a film man for all seasons." *Film Making*, 14, 45-46.

Fritze, G.A. (1913) "Herstellung kinematographischer Bilder in Fabriken." *Zeitschrift des Vereins Deutscher Ingenieure*, 57, pp. 454-461.

Goetz, Hans (1914) "Kinematographie und Wissenschaft." *Zeitschrift des Vereins Deutscher Ingenieure*, 58, pp. 268-272.

Holz, Günther (1954) "Der Film im Dienste der Rationalisierung." *Dein Film*, 2, pp. 2-4.

Hope, Adrian (1976) "Hunting ground: the British Sponsored Film Festival." *Times Educational Supplement*, 3181, p. 95.

Jones, Clive (1979) "Sponsored film is alive and well and living..." *Audio Visual*, 8, pp. 102-104.

Kayser, Ulrich (1924) "Industriefilme." *Das Kulturfilmbuch*. E. Beyfuss and A. Kossowsky (eds.). Berlin: Carl P. Chryselius'scher Verlag, pp. 157-159.

Klein, W.J. (1976) "Making $$$ in filmmaking: sponsored films: A producer/distributor partnership." *Filmmakers Newsletter*, 10, pp. 52-54.

Kleinfield, N.R. (1982) "New style in corporate films." *New York Times*, 131, pp. D1-D3.

Kühnemann, Arnold (1924) "Landwirtschaft im Kulturfilm." *Das Kulturfilmbuch*. Ed. by E. Beyfuss & A. Kossowsky. Berlin: Carl P. Chryselius'scher Verlag, pp. 152-156.

Lassally, Arthur (1924) "Berufsfilme." *Das Kulturfilmbuch*. Ed. by E. Beyfuss & A. Kossowsky. Berlin: Carl P. Chryselius'scher Verlag, pp. 166-173.

Lebegott, Martin (1913) "Kinematographische Aufnahmen aus der Technik." *Mitteilungen aus den Gesellschaften Siemens & Halske und Siemens-Schuckertwerke*, November 1913, pp. 79-81.

Leuthner, Josef (1923) "Der Werbefilm." *Zeitschrift für Handelswissenschaft und Handelspraxis*, 16, pp. 7-13.

Lloyd, H. (1974) "Portrait of a Railroad." *American Cinematographer*, 55, 7, July 1974, pp. 834-837 and 848-851.

Meyer, Herbert E. (1966) "Kunst und Kalkül. Über die Gestaltung von Industriefilmen." *Der Industriefilm*, 2, September 13, 1966.

Minas, Guenter (1995) "Maschinenträume – Industriefilme in Oberhausen." *EPD Film*, pp. 8-9.

Murphy, Philip (1976) "Women and sponsored films." *Business Screen*, 37, pp. 18-21.

Noel, Daniel C. (1990) "SAG organizing new industrial jobs at corporate video trade shows." *Screen Actor Hollywood*, 11, p. 3.

Overend, K. (1978) "Film finance 2: the sponsored film." *Film Making*, 16, 34-35.

Peragine, Marcel (1992) "Post-production in Switzerland: courting the corporate client." *On Production and Post-Production*, 1, pp. 42-43.

Pfeiffer, Günter (1966) "Der Industriefilm sucht seine Form. *Der Industriefilm*, 1, July 6, 1966.

Pinschewer, Julius (1924) "Reklamefilme. *Das Kulturfilmbuch*." E. Beyfuss and A. Kossowsky (eds.). Berlin: Carl P. Chryselius'scher Verlag, p. 204.

Puttnam, D. (1995) "The Growing Importance of Education in the Information Society and puts in a Plea for the Development of a New Film Audiovisual Industry in the UK." *Television: The Journal of the Royal Televison Society*, 32, 3, p. 11.

Ratz, Josef (1928) "Der technische Film." *Spannung*, July 1928, pp. 324-325.

Rodman, Howard A. (1985a) "The world of sponsored films." *Millimeter*, 13, 122-127.

Rodman, Howard A. (1985b) "Distributing sponsored films." *Millimeter*, 13, p. 127.

Rottmann, Gert (1978) "Erfahrungen mit industriellen Auftragsfilmen aus unternehmerischer Sicht." *Film im Auftrag: Industrie-Informations-Wirtschaftsfilm. Ein Wegweiser für alle, die mit einem der wirksamsten Kommunikationsmedien arbeiten wollen.* Ed. by Wilfried von Tresckow. Stuttgart: Kodak, pp. 150-159.

Splunteren, Bram Van (1978) "Sponsored films: production/distribution update." *Business Screen*, July 29, 1978.

Stein, Th. (1928) "Das Bild der Technik im Unterbewussten." *Spannung*, September 1928, pp. 353-357.

Tillotson, Jery (1983) "Tirage 16: du cinema rural au film industriel." *Banc-Titre*, 34, October 1983, pp. 34-35.

Tonndorf, Käthe (1924) "Hauswirtschaftliche Filme. *Das Kulturfilmbuch.*" Beyfuss and A. Kossowsky (eds.). Berlin: Carl P. Chryselius'scher Verlag, pp. 174-177.

Treadway, T. (1980) "Superserious-8: super-8 at work in business." *Filmmakers Film & Video Monthly*, 13, pp. 43-46.

Trevelyan, J., Thomas, H. and Chittock, J. (1973) "The State of the Art." *American Cinematographer*, 54, 9, September 1973, pp. 1122-1125, 1170, 1191-1197.

Wagner, Josef (1953) "Der Film im Dienste der Wirtschaftswerbung." *Filmkunst* (Special Issue), March 1953, p. 10.

Wagner, Karl (1996) "Trockene Inhalte spannend vermitteln." *Film & TV Kameramann*, 45, pp. 106-108.

3.2   Individual publications

Absil, Daniel and Gilles Ades (1979) *L'audiovisuel sur mesure. Guide pratique*. Paris: La Documentation Francaise.

American Management Association (1922) *Industrial Motion Pictures: How to Circulate them and a few Cautions Regarding their Manufacture and Distribution*. New York: National Personnel Association.

Anciaux, Jean-Pierre (1992) *La présentation orale es ses suppuorts visuels*. Paris: Les Éditions d'Organisation (= Les règles d'or de la communication).

Anciaux, Jean-Pierre (1995) *L'entreprise apprenante. Vers le Partage des savois et des savoir-faire dans les organisations*. Paris: Les Éditions d'Organisation.

Anon. (1960) *Le cinéma dans L'entreprise. Livre publié en supplément à la revue Cinéma TV promotion. Centre d'études et de diffusion du film d'information*. Paris.

Anon. (1986) *Vidéo et communication d'entreprise. Étude sur le rendement et l'efficacité*. Paris: CNPF.

Association of National Advertisers Films Committee (1946) *New Horizons for Business Films. A Report of the A.N.A. Film Study*. New York.

Association of National Advertisers Films Steering Committee (1954) *The Dollars and Senses of Business Films: A Report on the Production and Distribution Costs of Representative Advertising and Public Relations Motion Pictures*. New York: Association of National Advertisers.

Bachmann, Philippe and Schultz, Marie-Claude (1994) *Concevoir et produire un audiovisuel d'entreprise. De la vidéo au multimédia*. Paris: CFPJ.

Bélanger, Jean (1975) *Les films au service des entreprises. Comment les faire réaliser. Comment les réaliser*. Paris: Éditions Eyrolles.

Berne, Edouard (1992) *Pratique du film de commande*. Paris: Dujarric.

Berriet, Yann and Leblanc, Pierre (1968) *L'audiovisuel et l'entreprise*. Paris: Éditions Technique Relations.

Borzeix, Anni (1997) *Filmer le travail: recherche et visualisation*. Paris: L'Harmattan (= Collection: Champs Visuels; 6).

Bourgault, Pierrick (1993) *La communication audiovisuelle: Guide pratique pour les entreprises et collectivités*. Paris: Dunod.

Brepohl, Klaus (1966) *Der Deutsche Industriefilm. Eine Analyse.* Cologne: Institut der deutschen Wirtschaft.

British Iron and Steel Federation (ed.) (1954) *Films on Electric Furnaces: Notes for Instructors.* London.

Brugger, A. and Sommerfeld, K. (ed.) (1936) *Jahrbuch für deutsche Filmwerbung 1936.* Berlin: Haude & Spenersche Buchhandlung.

Brysch, Helmut (ed.) *Der deutsche Industriefilm. Im Auftrag des Instituts der deutschen Wirtschaft, Köln, zusammengestellt und bearbeitet von der Deutschen Industriefilm-Zentrale (DIZ).* Cologne: Institut der deutschen Wirtschaft.

Burder, John (1973) *The Work of the Industrial Film Maker.* New York: Hasting House Publishers.

Chamont, Yves (1990) *Les Techniques de la vidéo institutionelle en 10 questions et 69 remarques pratiques.* Paris: Les Éditions d'Organisation.

Cernavin, Oleg and Keller, Stefan (1998) BIA-Report 3/98. Prävention und Neue Medien. Eine Untersuchung zur Mediennutzung in Kleinunternehmen von Sicherheitsfachkräften. Wiesbaden: Verlags- und Mediengesellschaft.

Coböken, J.: *Der Film in der Werbung.* Füssen: J. Iversen (Deutscher Werbe-Unterricht; 13).

Cohen-Séat, Francois and Falconnet, Anne-Marie (1987) *L'audiovisuel d'entreprise. Film et vidéo.* Paris: Dixit (= Collection: Le Guide du producteur).

Croussy, Guy (1990) *La communication audiovisuelle. En 6 questions, 23 exemples, 160 exercices, 51 conseils pratiques.* Paris: Les Éditions d'Organisation.

De Witt, Jack (1968) *Producing Industrial Films. From Fade in to Fade Out.* South Brunswick, NJ: Barnes.

Der Film im Dienste der Wissenschaft. Festschrift zur Einweihung des Neubaues für das Institut für den Wissenschaftlichen Film. Göttingen: IWF.

Der Film in der Wirtschaft. Landesfilmdienst für Jugend und Volksbildung Hessen & Dagmar Zitelmann (eds.). Frankfurt am Main: Landesfilmdienst.

Deutsche Industriefilm-Zentrale (ed.) (1964) *Blick in die deutsche Wirtschaft.* Cologne: Deutscher Industrieverlag.

Deutsche Lichtbildgesellschaft e.V. (ed.) *Der Film im Dienste der Industrie.* Berlin.

Dumas de Rauly, Thierry (1987) *Choisir et utiliser les support visuels et audiovisuels.* Paris: Les Éditions d'Organisation.

Eastman Kodak Company (1974) *Clinical Photography and Basic Police Photography.* Rochester, NY.

Festival of Technical Films (1970) *Final Report: The Role of Scientific and Technical Films in the Industrial and Scientific Progress.* Budapest: Hungarian Central Technical Library and Documentation Centre/Information Centre for Technical Films.

Gordon, Jay E. (1961) *Motion Picture Production for Industry.* New York: MacMillan.

Halas, John (1978) *Audiovisual Techniques for Industry.* New York: United Nations.

Hansell, Peter and Ollerenshaw, Robert (1969) (ed.) *Longmore's Medical Photography* (8. ed.). London and New York: Focal Press.

Herbin, P. and Gaumont, Ph. (1960) *Le film 16 mm au service de l'entreprise et des collectivités. Préface par Marcel l'Herbier.* Paris: Éditions Arts et Sciences Appliqués.

Herman, Lewis (1965) *Educational Films: Writing, Directing, and Producing for Classroom, Television, and Industry.* New York: Crown Publishers.

Ignatus Paul R. (1949) *The Film in Industrial Safety Training.* Boston: Harvard University.

Kaplan, Daniel (1993) *Les médias électroniques. Vidéotex, audiotex, multimédias: connaître et exploiter les nouveaux outils de communication de l'entreprise.* Paris: Dunod.

Kempe, Richard: *Der Industriereklamefilm.* Dresden: Eichgrabenverlag.

Klein, Walter J. (1976) *The Sponsored Film.* New York: Hasting House.

Kleinhaus, R. (1925) *Der Film und seine Bedeutung für die Landwirtschaft. Praktischer Ratgeber in allen Film-Apparate- und Vorführfragen.* Berlin: Parey.

Loosey, Mary (1948) *A Report on the Outlook for the Profitable Production of Documentary Films for the Non-Theatrical Market.* New York: The Sigar Research Foundation.

Lowry, Stewart M. and Maynard, Harold B. and Stegemerten, G.J. (1940) *Time and Motion Study and Formulas for Wage Incentives* [1927]. New York and London: McGraw-Hill.

Martin, Antoine: *La Vidéo d'entreprise.* Paris: Chotard.

Matrazzo, Donna (1985) *The Corporate Scriptwriting Book: A Step-by-Step Guide to Writing Business Films, Videotapes, & Slide Shows.* Portland: Communicom.

McGuire, Jerry (1934) *How to Write, Direct & Produce Effective Business Films & Documentaries.* Blue Ridge Summit: Tab Books.

Mercer, John (1981) *The Informational Film.* Carbondale: Stipes Publishing Company.

Mörtzsch, Friedrich (1956) *Offenheit macht sich bezahlt. Die Kunst der Meinungspflege in der amerikanischen Industrie.* Düsseldorf: Econ.

Mörtzsch, Friedrich (1959) *Der Industriefilm auf Zelluloid. Filme für die Wirtschaft.* Düsseldorf: Econ.

Olsen, Walter R. and Sommers, William A. (2006) *Energizing Staff Development Using Film Clips: Memorable Movie Moments that Promote Reflection, Conversation, and Action.* Thousand Oaks: Corwin Press.

Raffard, Jean-Philippe and Cumet, Michel (1993) *L'audiovisuel des entreprises et des collectivités. Le guide de l'audiovisuel et de la communication.* Paris: Dixit.

Rationalisierungs-Kuratorium der Deutschen Wirtschaft (ed.) (1955) *RKW-Filmdienst. Erfolgreich bleiben durch Bild und Ton.*

Rigg, Robison Peter (1974) *L'Audiovisuel au service de la formation. Méthodes, matériels.* Paris: Entreprise moderne d'éditions.

Ring, Ragnar Lasse (1928) *Kallprat om film.* Stockholm: Tullberg Films Förlag.

Roeber, Goerg and Jacoby, Gerhard (1973) *Handbuch der filmwirtschaftlichen Medienbereiche: die wirtschaftlichen Erscheinungsformen des Films auf den Gebieten der Unterhaltung, der Werbung, der Bildung und des Fernsehens.* Munich: K.G. Saur.

Rohwedder, Detlev Karsten (1971) *Ansprache von Staatssekretär Dr. Detlev Rohwedder anlässlich des 3. Deutschen Industriefilm-Forums 1971 am 2. Juni 1971* (BMWI-Texte; 136).

Sewell, George H. (1933) *Commercial Cinematography for Business and Commerce Using Substandard Film.* London: Putnam.

Spooner, Peter (1959) *Business Films: How to Make and Use Them.* London: Batsford.

Steele, William Paul (1994) *Acting in Industrials: The Business of Acting for Business.* Portsmouth, NH: Heinemann.

Stork, Leopold (1962) *Industrial and Business Films: A Modern Means of Communication.* London: Phoenix House.

Tresckow, Wilfried von (ed.) (1978) *Film im Auftrag: Industrie-Informations-Wirtschaftsfilm. Ein Wegweiser für alle, die mit einem der wirksamsten Kommunikationsmedien arbeiten wollen.* Stuttgart: Kodak.

Ulbing, Rolf B. (1991) *Movie. Handbuch für den Wirtschaftsfilm. Was ein Auftraggeber wissen muß.* Wien: Hofstätter.

United Nations Educational, Scientific and Cultural Organization (1977) *The Economics of the New Educational Media: Present Status of Research and Trends*. Paris: UNESCO.

Westphalen, Marie-Hélène (2004) *Communicator. Le guide de la communication d'entreprise*. Paris: Dunod.

Wilson, William H. and Haas, Kenneth B. (1950) *The Film Book: For Business, Education, and Industry*. New York: Prentice-Hall.

Wolfe, John Leslie (1999) *You Can Work On-Camera!: Acting in Commercials and Corporate Films*. Portsmouth, NH: Heinemann.

4 Specialized publications

4.1 Essays and special sections in journals

The Arts Enquiry: The Factual Film special issue. London, New York and Toronto, 1947.

Baldizzone, Jose (2000) "Des approches multiples..." *Les Cahiers de la Cinémathèque*, 71, December 2000, pp. 3-6.

Bennett, James R. (1983) "Corporate Sponsored Image Films." *Journal of Business Ethics*, 2, pp. 35-41.

Biering, Carsten (1992) "Tre videoprogrammer om teglproduktion og teglværkshistorie." *Årbog for Arbejderbevægelsens Historie*, 22, pp. 135-156.

Bird, William (1989) "Enterprise and Meaning: Sponsored Film, 1939-1949." *History Today*, 39, 12, pp. 24-30.

Björkin, Mats (1999) "Industrial Greta: Some Thoughts on an Industrial Film." *Nordic Explorations: Film Before 1930*. John Fullerton and Jan Olsson (eds.). Sydney and London: John Libbey, pp. 263-268.

Björkin, Mats and Snickars, Pelle (2003) "1923 | 1933 – on the Production, Reception, and Cultural Significance of Swedish Nonfiction Film." *Triumpf der Bilder. Kultur- und Dokumentarfilme vor 1945 im internationalen Vergleich*. Peter Zimmermann and Kay Hoffmann (eds.). Stuttgart: UVK Medien, pp. 272-290.

Björkin, Mats (2004) "Industrifilm som dokument och kommunikationsmedium." *Det förflutna som film och vice versa. Om medierade historiebruk*. Ed. by Pelle Snickars & Cecilia Trenter. Lund: Studentlitteratur, pp. 245-258.

Brickman, William (1939) "The Talking Film as a Medium of Instruction in Modern Languages." *Modern Language Journal*, 24, p. 498.

Buchanan, David and Huczynski, Andrzej (2004) "Images of Influence: 12 Angry Men and Thirteen Days." *Journal of Management Inquiry*, 13, 4, pp. 312-323.

Caron, Estelle, Ionascu, Michel and Richoux, Marion (1998) "Le cheminot, le mineur et le paysan." *L'âge d'or du documentaire. Europe: Années cinquante. France, Allemagne, Espagne, Italie*. vol. 1. Roger Odin (ed.). Paris: L'Harmattan, pp. 63-98.

Champoux, Joseph E. (2004) "Commentary on 'Filmmaking and Research' and 'Images of Influence.' " *Journal of Management Inquiry*, 13, 4, pp. 336-340.

Davis, K.D. (1993) "The Virtual Body and the Imaginery Subject in Corporate Videocommunication." *Afterimage*, 21, 1, pp. 6-9.

Dimendberg, Edward (2005) " 'These are not exercises in style.' Le Chant du Styrène." *October* 112, pp. 63-88.

Dohnhauser, Peter (2004) "Musik, Ton und Sprache im Industriefilm." *Ferrum. Nachrichten aus der Eisenbibliothek*, 76, pp. 14-23.

Elsaesser, Thomas (with Malte Hagener) (2002) "Walter Ruttmann: 1929." *1929. Beiträge zur Archäologie der Medien*. Stefan Andriopoulos and Bernhard Dotzler (eds.). Frankfurt am Main: Suhrkamp, pp. 316 349.

Elsaesser, Thomas (2005) "Die Stadt von Morgen: Filme zum Bauen und Wohnen in der Weimarer Republik." *Geschichte des dokumentarischen Film in Deutschland, Vol. 2: Weimarer Republik (1918-1933)*. Klaus Kreimeier, Antje Ehmann and Jeanpaul Goergen (eds.). Stuttgart: Reclam-Verlag, pp. 381-410.

Goodman, Paul S. (2004) "Filmmaking and Research: An Intersection." *Journal of Management Inquiry*, 13, 4, pp. 324-335

Guillory, John (2004) "The Memo and Modernity." *Critical Inquiry*, 31, pp. 108-131.

Gunning, Tom (1994) "The World as Object Lesson: Cinema Audiences, Visual Culture and the St. Louis World's Fair 1904." *Film History*, 6, 4, pp. 422-444.

Hediger, Vinzenz, Gertiser, Anita, Jaques, Pierre-Emmanuel and Zimmermann, Yvonne (2003) "Views and Perspectives: Studies on the History of Non-fiction Film in Switzerland to 1964." *Cinema & Cie: International Film Studies Journal* (*Early Cinema, Technology, Discourse, Cinéma des premiers temps* special issue), 3, Autumn 2003, pp. 124-126.

Hediger, Vinzenz (2005) "Prumyslova produkce jako medialni praxe. Kvyznamu prumysloveho filmu na priklade podniku Fried." Krupp and Essen. *Iluminace*, 16, 4, 2005.

Hediger, Vinzenz (2006) "Visible Calculations. Computing in German Industrial Films, 1928-1963." *Entreprise et histoire*, 44, pp. 43-54.

Hediger, Vinzenz (2007) "Die Maschinerie des filmischen Stils. Innovation und Konventionalisierung im Industriefilm." In *Filmische Mittel, industrielle Zwecke. Das Werk des Industriefilms*. Ed. by Vinzenz Hediger and Patrick Vonderau. Berlin: Vorwerk 8.

Heller, Steven (1988) "Ephemeral films: the Prelinger collection." *Print*, 42, pp. 122-128.

Hogenkamp, Bert (1982) "Zur Dramaturgie des Bergarbeiterfilms." *Bergarbeiter im Spielfilm*. Ed. by Bert Hogenkamp. Oberhausen: Westdeutsche Kurzfilmtage, pp. 39-59.

Hortzschansky,Werner (1955) "Unterrichtsfilm, Lehrfilm, Industriefilm, populärwissenschaftlicher Film, Dokumentarfilm. Versuch einer Begriffsbestimmung." *Deutsche Filmkunst* (supplement), 1.

Huczynski, Andrzej and Buchanan, David (2004) "Theory from Fiction: A Narrative Process Perspective on the Pedagogical Use of Feature Film." *Journal of Management Education*, 28, 6, pp. 707-726.

Jaques, Pierre-Emmanuel (2003) "Aspects documentaires: Charles-Georges Duvanel (1906-1975)." *Décadrages*, 1-2, Autumn 2003, pp. 163-172.

Jaques, Pierre-Emmanuel (2004) "Les Seuils du film documentaire. *Liminia. Le soglie del film – Film's thresholds*. Ed. by Veronica Innocenti and Valentina Re. Udine: Forum, pp. 255-263.

Jaques, Pierre-Emmanuel and Haver, Gianni (2004) "Le cinéma à la Landi: le documentaire au service de la Défense nationale spirituelle." *Le cinéma au pas: les productions des pays autoritaires et leur impact en Suisse / sous la dir*. Gianni Haver (ed.). Lausanne: Antipodes.

Jaques, Pierre-Emmanuel (2005a) "Explorations documentaires: étapes pour un travelogue helvète." *Cinéma et voyage: Imaginaires et figures du voyage*. René Gardies (ed.). Aixen-Provence.

Jaques, Pierre-Emmanuel (2005b) "L'Ovomaltine et un cinéaste d'avant-garde: Hans Richter et le film de commande en Suisse." *Décadrage* (Cinéma, à travers champs), 4-5, Spring 2005, pp. 154-166.

Jaques, Pierre-Emmanuel (2006a) "Werben, zeigen oder verbergen? Zum Tourismusfilm in der Schweiz." *Montage/AV. Zeitschrift für Theorie & Geschichte audiovisueller Kommunikation*, Gebrauchsfilm special issue (2), 15, 1, pp. 91-107.

Jaques, Pierre-Emmanuel (2006b) "Un cinéma national?" *Film Distribution from 1895 to the 1910s*. Frank Kessler (ed.). Bloomington: Indiana University Press (in preparation).

Kammel, Rudolf (1990) "Wirtschaftsfilm und/oder Industriefilm in Oesterreich." *Filmkunst. Zeitschrift fuer Filmkultur und Filmwissenschaft*, 124, pp. 3-8.

Kinter, Jürgen (1992) " 'Durch Nacht und Licht' – Vom Guckkasten zum Filmpalast. Die Anfänge des Kinos und das Verhältnis der Arbeiterbewegung zum Film." *Kirmes – Kneipe – Kino. Arbeiterkultur im Ruhrgebiet zwischen Kommerz und Kontrolle (1850-1914)*. Dagmar Kift (ed.). Paderborn, pp. 119-146.

Kremski, Peter and Bosshard, Robert (1995) " 'Industrie ist kulturlos.' Gespräch mit dem Soziologen Robert Bosshard zum Industriefilm." *Agenda*, 18, pp. 46-48.

Lackner, Helmut (2004) "Die Selbstdarstellung der österreichischen Eisen- und Stahlindustrie im Film." *Ferrum. Mitteilungen aus der Eisenbibliothek*, 76, pp. 70-77.

Lagny, Michèle (2000) "Documentaire et commandite: consequences pour le cinéma ouvrier." *Les cahiers de la Cinémathèque*, 71, December 2000, pp. 35-40.

Lathrop, C.W. (1953) "Contributions of Film Instructions and Film Summaries to Learning from Instructional Films." *Journal of Educational Psychology*, 44, p. 343.

Leblanc, Gérard (1979) "Rhône-Poulenc: Une firme et ses films dans le secteur industriel de l'audiovisuel." *Du cinéma selon Vincennes*. Paris: L'herminier éditeur.

Leblanc, Gérard (1999) "La télévision face au travail." *Dossiers de l'audiovisuel*, no. 84, March/April 1999.

Linse, Ulrich (1988) " 'Technische Kulturdenkmäler im Laufbild.' Über die Anfänge der filmischen Dokumentation industriearchäologischer Denkmäler." *Technikgeschichte*, 55, pp. 323-337.

Mauranen, Tapani, Niemi, Erkki and Varho, Esko (1993) "Puu Pääosassa: Piirteitä 1930-luvun teollisuuselokuvasta (Wood in the starring role: aspects of industrial film in the 1930s)." *Historiallinen Arkisto*, 1993, 100, pp. 126-161.

Meusy, Jean-Jaques (1986) *CinémAction, La science á l'écran* special issue. *Dossier réunis par Jean-Jacques Meusy.*

Meyer, Erich (2004) "Die Stahlindustrie im Unterrichtsfilm." *Ferrum. Nachrichten aus der Eisenbibliothek*, 76, pp. 42-49.

Mittell, Jason (1997) "Invisible Footage: Industry on Parade and Television History." *Film History*, 9, 2, pp. 200-219.

Montage AV. Zeitschrift für Theorie & Geschichte audiovisueller Kommunikation. Themenhefte *Gebrauchsfilm*, 14, 2, 2005 and 15, 1, 2006. Ill. Marburg: Schüren.

Navratil, Josef (1990) "Historische österreichische Industriefilme aus der Werkstaette von Ing. Karl Koefinger." *Filmkunst. Zeitschrift fuer Filmkultur und Filmwissenschaft*, 124, pp. 33-38.

Neumann, Peter (2004) "Die Symbolik von Bildern aus der Eisen- und Stahlindustrie in Spielfilmen." *Ferrum. Nachrichten aus der Eisenbibliothek*, 76, pp. 34-37.

Nohr, Rolf F. (2004) " 'Denken mit dem Auge.' Der Trick im Industriefilm unter der Perspektive der Wissenskommunikation. *Ferrum. Nachrichten aus der Eisenbibliothek*, 76, pp. 24-33.

Novak, Lars (2000) "Motion Study/Moving Pictures. Die Anfänge des tayloristischen Arbeitsstudienfilms bei Frank B. und Lilian M. Gilbreth." *Kintop. Jahrbuch zur Erforschung des frühen Films*, 9, pp. 131-149.

O'Quinn, Kimberly (1996) "Industrial and Urban Discourses in Die Poldihütte." *A Second Life: German Cinema's First Decades*. Amsterdam: Amsterdam University Press (= Film Culture in Transition), pp. 192-204.

Perkins, Daniel J. (1982) "The Sponsored Film: A New Dimension in American Film Research?" *Historical Journal of Film, Radio and Television*, 2, 2, pp. 133-140.

Pessis, Georges (2000) "Les archives du film d'entreprises." *CinémAction*, 97, 4, pp. 99-105.

Prelinger, Richard (1986) "Industrial jeopardy films." *Re/Search*, 10, pp. 169-70.

Przigoda, Stefan (2004) "Vom Bergbauarbeiter zum Bergtechniker. Zum Wandel des Arbeiterbildes in Industriefilmen des Bergbaus von den 1930er bis zu den 1990er Jahren." *Ferrum. Nachrichten aus der Eisenbibliothek*, 76, pp. 50-59.

Rasch, Manfred (1997a) "Der Industriefilm begann mit fliegenden Geschossen in Zeitlupe." *Jahrbuch Ruhrgebiet 1996/97*. Kommunalverband Ruhrgebiet (ed.). Essen: Standorte, pp. 589-591.

Rasch, Manfred (1997b) "Von der Kinoempfehlung zum firmeneigenen, prämierten Dokumentarfilm." Über die Anfänge des Industriefilms auf der August Thyssen-Hütte AG. *Industriefilm – Medium und Quelle. Beispiele aus der Eisen- und Stahlindustrie*. Manfred Rasch, Karl-Peter Ellerbrock, Renate Köhne-Lindenlaub and Horst A. Wessel (eds.) Essen: Klartext, pp. 82-97.

Rasch, Manfred (1997c) "Zur Geschichte des Industriefilms und seines Quellenwertes. Eine Einführung." *Industriefilm: Medium und Quelle. Beispiele aus der Eisen- und Stahlindustrie*. Manfred Rasch, Karl-Peter Ellerbrock, Renate Köhne-Lindenlaub and Horst A. Wessel (eds.). Essen: Klartext, pp. 9-23.

Rasch, Manfred (1999) "Filme als technikgeschichtliche Quelle und ihre Erschließung. Das Beispiel: Nur der Nebel ist grau. Impressionen aus dem neuen Werk der August Thyssen-Hütte." *Innovationen einst und jetzt. Einblicke in die Montangeschichte des Ruhrgebietes. Technikgeschichtliche Vortragsveranstaltung des Geschichtsausschusses des Vereins Deutscher Eisenhüttenleute. Duisburg 14.-16. Oktober 1999*. Manfred Rasch (ed.). Düsseldorf, pp. 101-114.

Rasch, Manfred (2003) "Film ab! Zum Industriefilm des Ruhrgebiets zwischen 1948 und 1959." *Industriefilm 1948-1959. Filme aus Wirtschaftsarchiven im Ruhrgebiet*. Manfred Rasch, Hans Ulrich Berendes, Peter Döring, et. al. (eds.). Essen: Klartext, pp. 11-49.

Rasch, Manfred (2004a) "Mehr als nur Werbung! Zum Industriefilm der rheinisch-westfälischen Stahlindustrie von den Anfängen im Wilhelminischen Kaiserreich bis zu den Wirtschaftswunderjahren der jungen Bundesrepublik Deutschland." *Ferrum – Nachrichten aus der Eisenbibliothek*, 76, pp. 78-91.

Rasch, Manfred (2004b) "Düsseldorf, ein Neu-Babelsberg? Westdeutsche Industriefilme der 1950er-Jahre. *Geschichte im Westen*, 19, pp. 84-92.

Reichert, Ramón (1996) "Die Arbeitsmaschine. Dokumente zu Sozialtechnologie und Rationalisierung." *Wunschmaschine – Welterfindung*. Ed. by Brigitte Felderer and Herbert Lachmayer. Vienna: Kunsthalle Wien, pp. 119-145.

Reichert, Ramón (1998) "Effizienzfieber. Profitable Bilder im Film." *Effizienzfieber. Die Rationalisierung des Alltagslebens*. Ramón Reichert (ed.). Vienna: Technisches Museum, pp. 3-12.

Reichert, Ramón (2000a) "Schöne neue Arbeit. Ästhetik, Politische Ökonomie und Kino." *Schöne neue Arbeit. 2. Internationale Filmtage Politischer Film.* Ramón Reichert (ed.). Vienna and Linz: Talheimer Verlag, pp. 2-11.

Reichert, Ramón (2000b) "Die Popularisierung der Produktivität. Die Filme des Österreichischen Produktivitätszentrums 1950-1987. Ein Beitrag zur Diskussion um den Film als historische Quelle." *Relation. Medien, Gesellschaft, Geschichte,* 2, 7, pp. 69-128.

Reichert, Ramón (2000c) "Die Poren der Zeit. Industrielle Zeitökonomie in der Angewandten Psychologie Hugo Münsterbergs." *Zeit. Phantom, Mythos, Realität.* Wolfgang Müller-Funk (ed.). Vienna: Springer, pp. 207-219.

Reichert, Ramón (2001) "Film und Rationalisierung. Die Produktivitätsfilme des ÖPWZ während des European Recovery Program." *Blätter für Technikgeschichte,* pp. 45-111.

Reichert, Ramón (2001b) "Nützliche Bilder. Film als Instrument der Arbeitsrationalisierung." *Diagonale 2001. Festival des österreichischen Films,* pp. 123-128.

Reichert, Ramón (2001c) "The Popularization of Productivity. The Industry Films of the Austrian Productivity Center 1951-1959." *Conference Proceedings: The Seventh Biennial National Labour History Conference.* Canberra: Canberra Australian National University, pp. 209-215.

Reichert, Ramón (2002) "Der Arbeitsstudienfilm. Eine verborgene Geschichte des Stummfilms." *Medien und Zeit,* 4, pp. 29-43.

Reichert, Ramón (2004) "Film und die Rationalisierung der 'Arbeitskraft' 1880-1918." *Ferrum, Nachrichten aus der Eisenbibliothek,* 76, pp. 38-42.

Reichert, Ramón (2005) "Marshallplan und Film: Intermedialität, narrative Strategien und Geschlechterrepräsentation." *Kino und Film in der Besatzungszeit.* Filmarchiv Austria (ed.) (in print).

Schenk, Irmbert (2004) "Walter Ruttmanns Kultur- und Industriefilme 1933-1941." *Mediale Mobilmachung I. Das Dritte Reich und der Film.* Harro Segeberg (ed.). Munich: Wilhelm Fink (= Mediengeschichte des Films; 4), pp. 35-58.

Schuchnig, Josef (1990) "Die Reise ins Unmoegliche: über die Magie von Eisenbahnfilmen." *Filmkunst: Zeitschrift fuer Filmkultur und Filmwissenschaft,* 124, pp. 39-44.

Sørenssen, Bjørn (1996) "The Voice of Reconstruction: The Norwegian Post-War Newsreel." *Newsreels in Film Archives.* Roger Smither and Wolfgang Klaue (eds.). Trowbridge and Cranbury: Flicks Books/Associated University Presses, pp. 44-56.

Sørenssen, Bjørn (1999) "Travel Films in Norway. The Persistence of the View Aesthetic." *Nordic Explorations: Film Before 1930.* John Fullerton and Jan Olson (eds.). Sydney and London: John Libbey, pp. 102-113.

Stäheli, Urs und Dirk Verdicchio (2006) "Das Unsichtbare sichtbar machen: Hans Richters Die Börse als Barometer der Wirtschaftslage." *Montage AV,* 15, 1, pp. 108-122.

Tardy, Daniel (1991) "Scenario et film de commande." *CinemAction,* 61, pp. 196-201.

Tenfelde, Klaus (1997) "Der Industriefilm als Quelle für die Sozialgeschichte." *Industriefilm: Medium und Quelle. Beispiele aus der Eisen- und Stahlindustrie.* Manfred Rasch, Karl-Peter Ellerbrock, Renate Köhne-Lindenlaub and Horst A. Wessel (eds.). Essen: Klartext, pp. 258-263.

Terveen, Fritz (1960) "Der Film als Hilfsmittel für Firmengeschichte und Unternehmerbiographie." *Tradition,* 5, p. 135.

Töteberg, Michael (1992) "Schokolade, Waschpulver und Politik." *Das Ufa-Buch.* Hans-Michael Bock and Michael Töteberg (eds.). Frankfurt am Main: Zweitausendeins, pp. 284-286.

Van Rens, Noël (1998) "Les films du plan Marshall: 1948-1952. La naissance de l'Europe moderne dans l'image." *L'âge d'or du documentaire. Europe: Années cinquante. Grande-Bretagne, Belgique, Pays-Bas, Danemark, Norvège, Suède.* Roger Odin (ed.). Paris: L'Harmattan, pp. 187-226.

Veeder, Gerry K. (1990) "The Red Cross Bureau of Pictures, 1917-1921: World War I, the Russian Revolution and the Sultan of Turkey's Harem." *Historical Journal of Film, Radio and Television*, 10, pp. 47-70.

Vonderau, Patrick (2007). "Die Besichtigung als Kulturtechnik. Besucherfilme und die Autostadt Wolfsburg." In *Filmische Mittel, industrielle Zwecke. Das Werk des Industriefilms.* Vinzenz Hediger and Patrick Vonderau (eds.). Berlin: Vorwerk 8, pp. 201-213.

Weber, Wolfgang (1997) "Der Industriefilm als technikgeschichtliche Quelle. *Industriefilm: Medium und Quelle. Beispiele aus der Eisen- und Stahlindustrie.* Ed. by Manfred Rasch, Karl-Peter Ellerbrock, Renate Köhne-Lindenlaub and Horst A. Wessel. Essen: Klartext, pp. 251-257.

Wiatr, Elizabeth (2002) "Between Word, Image, and the Machine: Visual Education and Films of Industrial Process." *Historical Journal of Film, Radio and Television*, 22, 3, pp. 333-351.

Wilharm, Ingrid (1995) "Die Döring-Film. Oberingenieur Dreyer und die Ozeanriesen." *Wir Wunderkinder. 100 Jahre Filmproduktion in Niedersachen.* Hannover, pp. 35-48.

Zeppenfeld, Burkhard (2004) "Die Werksfotografie der Gutehoffnungshütte. Ein bisher kaum beachteter historischer Fotobestand." *Technikgeschichte im Ruhrgebiet. Technikgeschichte für das Ruhrgebiet.* Ed. by Manfred Rasch and Dietmar Bleidick. Essen: Klartext Verlag 2004, pp. 219-231.

Zimmermann, Yvonne (2004a) "Bilder von Arbeit und Interesse: Zur (Selbst-)Darstellung der Eisen- und Stahlindustrie im Industriefilm aus der Schweiz." *Ferrum: Nachrichten aus der Eisenbibliothek, Stiftung der Georg Fischer AG.* no. 76. Schaffhausen: Georg Fischer AG, pp. 60-69.

Zimmermann, Yvonne (2004b) "Jak zkoumat průmyslové filmy: metodologická úvaha / How to Deal With Industrial Films: Methodological Approach." *Illuminace*, 16, 4 (56), pp. 5-23.

Zimmermann, Yvonne (2005a) "Schweizer Industriefilme 1910-1970: Anders Reisen ins Landesinnere." *9. Internationale Kurzfilmtage Winterthur.* Festivalkatalog. Winterthur: Internationale Kurzfilmtage, pp. 69-79.

Zimmermann, Yvonne (2005b) "Der Industriefilm erzählt mehr, als man denkt: Neue Aufmerksamkeit für die verborgenen Qualitäten des Auftragsfilm." *Neue Zürcher Zeitung*, no. 169, 22. July, p. 41.

Zimmermann, Yvonne (2006a) "Vom Lichtbild zum Film: Anmerkungen zur Entstehung des Industriefilms." *montage/av*, 15, 1, pp. 74-88.

Zimmermann, Yvonne (2006b) "Maggis Wandervortragspraxis mit Lichtbildern: Ein Schulmädchenreport aus der Schweiz von 1910." *KINtop*, 14, 15, pp. 53-65.

Zimmermann, Yvonne (2006c) "Auftragsfilm versus Autorenfilm: Zur Geschichte einer Beziehungskiste." *Cinema* (Erotik), 51, pp. 109-118.

Zimmermann, Yvonne (2006d) "Les films d'entreprise de Maggi: image d'entreprise et identité nationale." *Entreprises & Histoire*, 44, September, pp. 9-24.

Zimmermann, Yvonne (2007) "Heimatpflege zwecks Suppenpromotion: Zum Einsatz von Lichtbildern und Filmen in der Schweizer Lebensmittelbranche am Beispiel von Maggi." *Zeitschrift für Unternehmensgeschichte*, 52, 2 (in print).

Zimmermann, Yvonne and Jaques, Pierre-Emanuel (2009a) *Schaufenster der Nation: der nicht-fiktionale Film in der Schweiz 1896-1964.* Zurich: Limmat (in preparation).

Zimmermann, Yvonne and Jaques, Pierre-Emanuel (2009b) *Vitrine de la nation: le film documentaire en Suisse 1896-1964.* Lausanne: Editions d'En bas oder Antipodes (in preparation).

4.2 Monographs, edited collections, and dissertations

Allègre, Evelyne (1991) *Le film d'entreprise.* Marseille: Université de Provence Aix-Marseille.

Argenti, Paul A. (2003) *Corporate Communication.* New York: McGraw Hill.

Auster, Donald (1959) *The Role of Business and Labor Sponsored Films in Education: A Study in Mass Persuasion.* Dissertation. Indiana University.

Beniger, James (1986) *The Control Revolution. Technological and Economic Origins of the Information Society.* Cambridge and London: Harvard University Press.

Bird, William L., Jr. (1999) *"Better Living": Advertising, Media, and the New Vocabulary of Business Leadership, 1935 1955.* Evanston, IL: Northwestern University Press.

Bouillot, René (1978) *L'objet et son image. Photographie industrielle et publicitaire.* Paris: Publications photo-cinéma Paul Montel.

Bourron, Yves (1980) *Audiovisuel, pédagogie et communication.* Paris: Les Éditions d'Organisation.

Bourron, Yves (1995) *Pédagogie de l'audiovisuel et du multimédia. En 68 fiches, avec 11 diapositive.* Paris: Les Éditions d'Organisation.

Brazelton, John Henry (1981) *A Critical Analysis of the Sponsored Film as a Promotional Instrument for the Southwestern United States Tourism Industry.* Dissertation. University of Texas at El Paso.

Braun, Marta (1992) *Picturing Time: The Work of Etienne-Jules Marey (1830-1904).* Chicago: University of Chicago Press.

Broult, Lionel (1992) *La Dom. La communication d'entreprise au-delà du modèle publicitaire.* Paris: Dunod.

Brown, Elspeth H. (2005) *The Corporate Eye: Photography and the Rationalization of American Commercial Culture, 1884-1929.* Baltimore: John Hopkins University Press.

Brownlow, Kevin (1992) *Behind the Mask of Innocence: Sex, Violence, Crime; Films of Conscience in the Silent Era.* Berkeley: University of California Press.

Bub, Gertraude (1938) *Der deutsche Film im Weltkrieg und sein publizistischer Einsatz.* Dissertation. Berlin.

Cartwright, Lisa (1995) *Screening the Body: Tracing Medicine's Visual Culture.* Minneapolis: University of Minnesota Press.

Chemery, Philippe (1989) *Genèse et état des films d'entreprise en France.* Dissertation. Paris.

Clark, John Bruce (1972) *An Analysis of the Marketing of 153 Sponsored Films.* Dissertation. Texas Technical University.

Comité pour l'historie économique et financière. Ministère de l'Économie, des Finances et de l'industrie (ed.) (2002) *Les images de l'industrie. De 1850 à nos jours. Actes du colloque tenu à Bercy, les 28 et 29 juin 2001.* Paris: Comité pour l'histoire économique et financière.

Czapek, K.C. [= Wolf-Czapek, K.W.] (1909) *Angewandte Kinematographie in Wissenschaft und Technik.* Dresden: Appolloverlag.

Czapek, K.C. (1911) *Die Kinematographie. Wesen, Entstehung und Ziele des lebenden Bildes.* Berlin: Union Deutsche Verlagsgesellschaft.

Dahms, Erich (1925) *Film und Filmindustrie in ihrer volkswirtschaftlichen und kulturellen Bedeutung.* Dissertation. Universität Greifswald.

Davies, Sue and Collier, Caroline (ed.) (1987) *The Industrial Image: British Industrial Photography 1843-1986.* London: Photographers Gallery.

Dewulf, Yves (1991) *La communication audiovisuelle au service des entreprises.* Paris: Eyrolles (= Collection "Communication").

Ducom, Jacques (1930) *Le cinématographe scientifique et industriel. Son évolution intellectuelle, sa puissance éducative et morale.* Paris.

Eberwein, Robert (1999) *Sex Ed: Film, Video, and the Framework of Desire.* New Brunswick, NJ: Rutgers University Press.

Eckardt, André (2004) *Im Dienst der Werbung. Die Boehner-Film 1926-1967.* Berlin: Cinegraph-Babelsberg (= Filmblatt Schriften).

Ende, W. (1930) *Der Film als Forschungsmittel der Technik.* Berlin: J. Springer (= Forschung und Technik).

Ewert, Malte (1998) *Die Reichsanstalt für Film und Bild in Wissenschaft und Unterricht (1933-1945).* Hamburg: Kovac (= Schriften zur Kulturwissenschaft; 15).

Forster, Ralf (1999) *Sparkassenfilme im Nationalsozialismus.* Frankfurt am Main, Berlin and Bern: Lang (= Europäische Hochschulschriften, Reihe 3; 842).

Freeman, Frank N. (1924) *Visual Education. A Comparative Study of Motion Pictures and Other Methods of Instruction.* Chicago: University of Chicago Press.

Fuchs, Otto (1909) *Theoretische und kinematographische Untersuchungen von Dampfhämmern mit selbsttätiger Schiebesteuerung.* Berlin 1909.

Gaines, Jane M. and Renov, Michael (ed.) (1999) *Collecting Visible Evidence.* Minneapolis: University of Minnesota Press.

Geimer, Peter (ed.) (2002) *Ordnungen der Sichtbarkeit. Fotografie in Wissenschaft, Technologie und Kunst.* Frankfurt am Main: Suhrkamp.

Gilbreth, Frank Bunker (1911) *Motion Study.* New York: Van Nostrand Co.

Gipson, Henry Clay (1947) *Films in Business and Industry.* New York and London: McGraw Hill.

Gnam, Arnulf (1930) *Der Film in seiner Bedeutung als Werbemittel.* Munich.

Goergen, Jeanpaul (1989) *Walter Ruttmann. Eine Dokumentation. Mit Beiträgen von Paul Falkenberg, William Uricchio und Barry A Fulks.* Berlin: Freunde der Deutschen Kinemathek.

Goldfarb, Brian (2002) *Visual Pedagogy. Media Cultures of Education in and Beyond the Classroom.* Raleigh, NC: Duke University Press.

Goodman, Michael B. (ed.) (1994) *Corporate Communication: Theory and Practice.* New York: State University of New York Press.

Grau, Hermann (1932) *Technik und Film. Die Filmkamera im Dienste der Technik und Wissenschaft.* Stuttgart: Dieck.

Guckes, Emil (1937) *Der Tonfilm als Werbemittel in Deutschland.* Dissertation. Innsbruck: University of Innsbruck.

Günther, Walther (1928) *Städtefilme.* Berlin: Bildwartverlagsgenossenschaft (= Bildwart-Flugschrift; 3).

Günter, Roland, Hoffmann, Paul and Günter, Janne (1978) *Das Ruhrgebiet im Film,* 2 vols. Oberhausen.

Guyot, Jacques (1992) *L'écran publicitaire. Idéologie et savoir-faire des professionnels de la publicité dans l'audiovisuel 1968-1992*. Paris: L'Harmattan (= Collection Logiques sociales).

Guyot, Jacques (1997) *Les techniques audiovisuelles*. Paris: Presses Universitaires de France.

Habel, Ylva (2002) *Modern Media, Modern Audiences. Mass Media and Social Engineering in the 1930s Swedish Welfare State*. Stockholm: Aura.

Hébert, Nicole (1987) *L'entreprise et son image. La publicité institutionnelle, pourquoi, comment?* Paris: Dunod.

Hediger, Vinzenz and Vonderau, Patrick (eds.) (2007) *Filmische Mittel, industrielle Zwecke. Das Werk des Industriefilms*. Berlin: Vorwerk 8.

Heller, Thomas (1990) *La communication d'entreprise. Le discours des apparences*. Paris: Les Éditions d'Organisation.

Hertogs, Daan and De Klerk, Nico (eds.) (1994) *Nonfiction from the Teens. The 1994 Amsterdam Workshop*. Amsterdam: Stichting Nederlands Filmmuseum.

Hessler, Martina (ed.) (2006) *Konstruierte Sichtbarkeiten. Wissenschafts- und Technikbilder seit der frühen Neuzeit*. Munich: Fink.

Hogenkamp, Bert and Stallaerts, Rik (1983) *Le Borinage. La grève des mineurs de 1932 et le film de Joris Ivens et Henri Storck*. Brussels: Revue Belge du Cinéma

Hogenkamp, Bert and Stallaerts, Rik (1986) *Pain Noir et Film nitrate. Le mouvement ouvrier socialiste belge et le cinéma durant l'entre deux guerres*. Brussels: Revue Belge du Cinéma.

Hogenkamp, Bert (1986) *Deadly Parallels. Film and Left in Britain 1929-39*. London: Lawrence and Wishart.

Holtzmann Kevles, Bettyann (1997) *Naked to the Bone: Medical Imaging in the Twentieth Century*. New Brunswick, NJ: Rutgers University Press.

Horak, Jan-Christopher (ed.) (1995) *Lovers of Cinema: The First American Film Avant-Garde, 1919 1945. Madison, WI: University of Wisconsin Press*.

Hovland, Carl and Lumsdaine, Artur (ed.) (1949) *Experiments in Mass Communication*. Princeton: Princeton University Press.

Jacquinot, Geneviève (1977) *Image et pédagogie. Analyse sémiologique du film a intention didactique*. Paris: Presses universitaires de France.

Jarmer, Martin (1986) *Der Industriefilm: Einsatzmöglichkeiten und bedingungen im Marketing für Investitionsgüter*. Dissertation. Berlin: Freie Universität (microfiche).

Kalbus, Oskar (1956) *Pioniere des Kulturfilms. Ein Beitrag zur Geschichte des Kulturfilmschaffens in Deutschland*. Karlsruhe: Neue Verlags-Gesellschaft.

Kinsky-Weinfurter, Gottfried (1993) *Filmmusik als Instrument staatlicher Propaganda. Der Kultur- und Industriefilm im Dritten Reich und nach 1945*. Munich: Ölschläger (= Kommunikation audiovisuell; 9).

Kühn, Michael (1998) *Unterrichtsfilm im Nationalsozialismus. Die Arbeit der Reichsstelle für den Unterrichtsfilm/Reichsanstalt für Film und Bild in Wissenschaft und Unterricht*. Mammendorf: Septem Artes.

Lambert, Guy and Lioult, Jean-Luc (2003) *Filmer le travail. Stratégies de recherche et réalisation*. Dissertation. Marseille: University of Provence.

Lambert, Jacques (1979) *L'information ascendante dans les entreprises*. Paris: Entreprise Moderne d'Édition.

Lambert, Jacques (1981) *Politiques globales de communication interne: douze études de cas d'entreprise*. Paris: Entreprise moderne d'éditions.

Lassally, Arthur (1919) *Bild und Film im Dienste der Technik. Erster Teil. Betriebskinematographie*. Halle and Saale: Wilhelm Knapp.

Leblanc, Gérard and Ferro, Marc (1982) *Le cinéma industriel. La cinémathèque de Rhône-Poulenc*. Paris: École des hautes études en sciences sociales.

Leblanc, Gérard (1983) *Quand l'entreprise fait son cinéma. La médiathèque de Rhône-Poulenc (1972-1981)*. Paris: Cinéthique P.U.V.

Leblanc, Gérard (1997) *Scénarios du réel*. 2. vols. Paris: Éditions l'Harmattan.

Leopard, Danny Ray (2005) *The Teacher and the Teaching Screens: Transformations of Instructional Practice through Film, Television, and New Media*. Dissertation. Los Angeles, CA: University of Southern California.

Liesegang, Paul F. (1920) *Wissenschaftliche Kinematographie einschliesslich der Reihenphotographie*, 6th ed. Leipzig: Ed. Liesegang's Verlag.

Loiperdinger, Martin (1999) *Film & Schokolade. Stollwercks Geschäfte mit lebenden Bildern*. Frankfurt am Main: Stroemfeld/Roter Stern (= Kintop Schriften; 4).

Low, Rachael (1998) *Documentary and Educational Films of the 1930s: The History of the British Film, 1929-1939*. London: George Allen & Unwin.

Lüken-Isberner, Folckert (1988) *Der städtebauliche bedeutsame Lehr- und Informationsfilm 1946-1960*. Pfaffenweiler: Centaurus.

Marchand, Roland (1985) *Advertising the American Dream: Making Way for Modernity, 1920-1940*. Berkeley, CA: University of California Press.

Marchand, Roland (1998) *Creating the Corporate Soul: The Rise of Public Relations and Corporate Imagery in American Big Business*. Berkeley, CA: University of California Press.

May, Mark A. and Lumsdaine, Arthur A. (1958) *Learning from Films*. Yale University Press.

McCauley, Elizabeth A. (1994) *Industrial Madness: Commercial Photography in Paris, 1848-1871*. New Haven and London: Yale University Press.

Michel, Alain P. (1997) *L'introduction du travail à la chaîne aux usines Renault: 1917-1939*. Paris: Éditions JCM-SHGR.

Michel, Alain P. (2003) "Les images du travail à la chaîne dans les usines Renault de l'entre-deux-guerres: entre l'attestation d'une activité laborieuse et la representation d'une forme de production emblématique." *Études photographiques*, 13, pp. 12-28.

Michel, Alain P. (2002) Filmer le travail, les travailleuses et les travailleurs dans les usines Renault de l'entre-deux-guerres. Unpublished paper, *Congrès national des sociétés historiques et scientifiques. Le travail et les hommes*, Nancy, April 2002.

Michon, Roland C. (1988) *Esthétique du film d'entreprise*. Dissertation on microfiche. Paris III.

Möslein, Kathrin M. (2000) *Bilder in Organisationen. Wandel, Wissen und Visualisierung*. Wiesbaden: Gabler.

Musser, Charles (1990) *The Emergence of Cinema: The American Screen to 1907*. Berkeley and Los Angeles: University of California Press.

Normann, Ingrid (1979) *Der Industriefilm, ein Medium der Öffentlichkeitsarbeit von Unternehmen*. M.A. Study. Institut für Publizistik, Freie Universität Berlin.

Novak, Lars (2000) Motion Study/Moving Pictures. Die Anfänge des tayloristischen Arbeitsstudienfilms bei Frank B. und Lillian M. Gilbreth. *KINtop. Jahrbuch zur Erforschung des frühen Films, 9 (Lokale Kinogeschichten)*, pp. 131-149

Nowlin, Eric Guy (1976) *A Survey of the Develoment of the Business and Industrial Film*. Dissertation. Evanston, IL: Northwestern University Press.

Nye, David E. (1985) *Image Worlds: Corporate Identities at General Electric, 1890-1930*. Cambridge: MIT Press.

Nye, David E. (1990) *Electrifying America: Social Meanings of a New Technology.* Cambridge, MA: MIT Press.

Pastre-Robert, Béatrice de (2004) *Cinéma pédagogique et scientifique: à la redécouverte des archives.* Lyon: ENSÉ.

Perriault, Jacques (1989) *La logique de l'usage. Essai sur les machines à communiquer.* Paris: Flammarion.

Pessis, Georges (1989) *Film et vidéo: miroir de l'entreprise.* Paris: Les Éditions d'Organisation.

Pessis, George (1991) *L'oevre audiovisuelle de commande. Miroir de l'entreprise.* Paris: Les Éditions d'Organisation.

Pessis, Georges (1993) *L'entreprise et son double. Enjeux, choix et paris de la communication audiovisuelle institutionnelle.* Paris: Dunod.

Pessis, Georges (1997) *Entreprise et cinéma. Cent ans d'images.* Paris: La Documentation Francaise.

Peters Van Deinse, Sophie (1992) *Les Supports d'information dans l'entreprise.* Paris: CFPJ.

Posner, Bruce (ed.) (2001) *Unseen Cinema: Early American Avant-Garde Film, 1893-1941: A Retrospective of Restored and Preserved Films Detailing the Unknown Accomplishments of American Pioneer Filmmakers.* New York: Black Thistle Press and Anthology Film Archives.

Przigoda, Stefan (ed.) (2005) *Bergbaufilme. Inventar zur Überlieferung in Archiven, Museen und anderen Dokumentationsstellen in der Bundesrepublik Deutschland. Bearbeitet von Stefan Przigoda unter Mitarbeit von Holger Menne.* Bochum: Deutsches Bergbau-Museum (= Veröffentlichungen aus dem Deutschen Bergbau-Museum Bochum, 130; Schriften des Bergbau-Archivs, 16).

Rasch, Manfred, Ellerbrock, Karl-Peter, Köhne-Lindenlaub, Renate and Wessel, Horst A. (eds.) (1997) *Industriefilm: Medium und Quelle. Beispiele aus der Eisen- und Stahlindustrie.* Essen: Klartext.

Rembert, Susan Macmillan (1981) *Components of an Industrial Film: The 1980 United Way Campaign Film.* Dissertation. Greensboro: University of North Carolina.

Rosart, Jean-Paul (1992) *L'entreprise et les médias.* Paris: Armand Colin.

Ross, Steven J. (1998) *Working-Class Hollywood: Silent Film and the Shaping of Class in America.* Princeton, NJ: Princeton University Press.

Rumpff, H. (1920) *Die wissenschaftliche Photographie als experimentelle Grundlage des Geschützbaues.* Düsseldorf.

Sainderichin, Sven (1972) *L'audiovisuel. Collection: Comment informer.* Paris: CNPF.

Schaefer, Eric (1999) *"Bold! Daring! Shocking! True!": A History of Exploitation Films, 1919-1959.* Durham, NC: Duke University Press.

Schaller, Hans (1997) *Der Industriefilm schrieb Geschichte, 1895-1995: Hundert Jahre Industrie- und Wirtschaftsfilm.* Dortmund: PR Trend Agentur.

Schiltz, Jacques (1970) *Le cinéma au service de l'industrie.* Paris: SDAC.

Schmacke, Ernst (ed.) (1994) *Industriebilder. Gemälde einer Epoche.* Münster: Ardey.

Slide, Anthony (1992) *Before Video: A History of the Non-Theatrical Film.* Westport, CT: Greenwood Press.

Smith, Ken (1999) *Mental Hygiene Classroom Films 1945-1970.* New York: Blast Books.

Solbrig, Heide Frances (2004) *A History of Industrial Motivation Film.* Dissertation. University of California at Berkeley.

Standal, Jerry Thor (1967) *The Effect of Style Difficulty on Information Communication by an Industrial Film*. Dissertation. University of Washington.

Tedlow, Richard S. (1979) *Keeping the Corporate Image: Public Relations and Business, 1900-1950*. Greenwich, CT: Jai Press Inc.

Tenfelde, Klaus (2000) *Bilder von Krupp. Fotografie und Geschichte im Industriezeitalter*. Munich: C.H. Beck.

Thomas, Ann (ed.) (1997) *Beauty of Another Order: Photography in Science*. New Haven and London: Yale University Press.

Thun, Rudolf (1925) *Der Film in der Technik*. Berlin: V.D.I.-Verlag.

Tröhler, Margit (1996) *Le produit anthropomorphe ou les figurations du corps humain dans le film publicitaire*. Lille: Atelier National de Reproduction des Thèses.

Tucker, Charles Lee (1989) *Industrial and Technical Photography*. Englewood Cliffs, NJ: Prentice-Hall.

Tufte, Edward (1997) *Visual Explanations: Evidence and Quantities, Evidence and Narrative*. Cheshire, CT: Graphics Press.

Verdone, Mario (1962) *Cinema del lavoro*. Rome: Realtà.

Vogels, Jonathan B. (2000) *"Outregeous Acts of Faith." The Films of Albert and David Maysles 1962-1986*. Dissertation. Boston: Boston University.

Wehlau, Karl (1939) *Das Lichtbild in der Werbung für Politik, Kultur und Wirtschaft. Seine geschichtliche Entwicklung und gegenwärtige Bedeutung*. Würzburg: Triltsch (= Zeitung und Leben; 64).

Weiße, Johannes (1970) *Wirkungsmöglichkeiten und Gestaltungsmittel im Industriefilm vorwiegend abgehandelt an Filmen des DEFA-Studios für Kurzfilme*. Dissertation. Potsdam-Babelsberg.

Westbrock, Ingrid (1983) *Der Werbefilm. Ein Beitrag zur Entwicklungsgeschichte des Genres vom Stummfilm zum frühen Ton- und Farbfilm*. Hildesheim: Olms.

Williams, Jon M. and Muir, Daniel T. (1984) *Corporate Images: Photography and the Du Pont Company, 1865-1972*. Wilmington, DE: Hagley Museum and Library.

Willsher, Adrian Alexander (1996) *"Where are the Roads?" The Tourist and Industrial Promotion Films of the Nova Scotian Film Bureau, 1945-1970*. M.A. Dissertation. Canada: Dalhousie University.

Wolbring, Barbara (2000) *Krupp und die Öffentlichkeit im 19. Jahrhundert. Selbstdarstellung, öffentliche Wahrnehmung und gesellschaftliche Kommunikation*. Munich: Beck (= Schriftenreihe der Zeitschrift für Unternehmensgeschichte; 6).

Yates, JoAnne (1989) *Control Through Communication: The Rise of System in American Management*. Baltimore: Johns Hopkins University Press.

Yates, Jo Anne and Van Maanen, John (eds.) (2001) *Information Technology and Organizational Transformation. History, Rhetoric and Practice*. Thousand Oaks, CA: Sage Publications.

Yates, JoAnne (2005) *Structuring the Information Age: Life Insurance and Information Technology in the 20th Century*. Baltimore: Johns Hopkins University Press.

Zimmermann, Peter (ed.) (2003) *Triumpf der Bilder. Kultur- und Dokumentarfilme vor 1945 im internationalen Vergleich*. Konstanz: UVK (= Close Up; 16).

Zipfel, Astrid (1997) *Public Relations in der Elektroindustrie. Die Firmen Siemens und AEG 1847-1939*. Cologne, Weimar and Vienna: Böhlau (= Public Relations; 3).

III. Annotated section

Agde, Günter (1998) *Filmmernde Versprechen. Geschichte des deutschen Werbefilms im Kino seit 1897*. Berlin: Verlag Das neue Berlin.

> The first comprehensive historical presentation of German cinema advertising films between 1900 and 1980, including films made in the GDR. Agde also writes at length about industrial film pioneers like Julius Pinschewer and the advertising films made at Ufa. Includes an index of persons, film titles, film companies, and brand names.

Amsler, André (1997) *"Wer dem Werbefilm verfällt, ist verloren für die Welt." Das Werk von Julius Pinschewer 1883-1961. Texts and tables by André Amsler*. Zurich: Chronos.

> Amsler's study is devoted to the "inventor" of the advertising film, Julius Pinschewer, who produced over 700 films of all types between 1910 and 1960, including numerous industrial films. Pinschewer worked in Germany and Switzerland as a producer, but was also active in distribution. The book is divided into two sections. The first section is a dossier of texts and materials, with a biography of Pinschewer and biographies of companies and collaborators. The second part consists of a comprehensive, chronologically organized filmography.

Argenti, Paul A. (2003) *Corporate Communication*. New York: McGraw Hill.

> In this textbook, Paul A. Argenti develops a theory of communications based on the work of Marshall McLuhan, and drawing on Aristotle's art of rhetoric and the strategies of management communications pro Mary Munter, with whom Argenti directs the Management Communication department at the Tuck School of Business at Dartmouth College. The case studies discussed in the book refer to well-known firms like Disney or Dell Computer Corporation. According to Argenti, a decisive step in the planning of an individual communications strategy is choosing the channel of communication. He distinguishes between "old" (writing, speaking) and "new" channels (fax, e-mail, voice mail, electronic meetings, video telephone conferencing).

The Arts Enquiry (1947) *The Factual Film*. London, New York and Toronto: Oxford University Press.

> This overview of films belongs to a series of reports on the cultural sector, sponsored by Dartington Hall Trustees. The term "factual" refers to documentary films, industrial films, and training films. The report concentrates on the use of these films during World War II and the role of large companies in the production of such films.

Association of National Advertisers Films Steering Committee (1954) *The Dollars and Senses of Business Films. A report on the production and distribution costs of representative advertising and public relations motion pictures*. New York: Association of National Advertisers.

The editorial team of this book consisted of specialists from large firms like Shell and Ford Motor Company. An overview of production costs, audience figures, and types of industrial film production is given with a wide variety of tables and graphs. Sixty-seven firms were questioned and 157 films were evaluated. The authors show that industrial film's characteristics and advantages make it an indispensable corollary medium.

Bachmann, Philippe and Schultz, Marie-Claude (1994) *Concevoir et produire un audiovisuel d'entreprise: De la vidéo au multimédia*. Paris: Les Éditions du CFPJ, 1994.

Given multimedia technological development and progress in the area of audiovisual media, the authors start from the assumption that a precise knowledge of the possibilities and limits of their use is necessary for business communication ends. The handbook therefore targets commissioners and producers of industrial films and offers step-by-step instruction on the production of an audiovisual product in the service of industry. From project planning to screening, from script through shooting to editing, this manual covers the important steps in production. Innovations due to multimedia usages are also treated. Includes a small bibliography on industrial film and audiovisual business communication as well as a list of related addresses.

Bélanger, Jean (1975) *Les films aus service des entreprises. Comment les faire réaliser. Comment les réaliser*. Paris: Eyrolles. Ill.

This book gives an overview of the essential working steps in the production of an industrial film, in which organizational as well as technical requirements and processes are explained. It is conceived as a practical handbook, meant to make the medium of film less daunting for companies.

Beniger, James (1986 [1946]) *Control Revolution: Technological and Economic Origins of the Information Society*. Cambridge and London: Harvard University Press.

This landmark study concerns the "control revolution, a complex of rapid changes in the technological and economic arrangements by which information is collected, stored, processed, and communicated, and through which formal or programmed decisions might effect societal control." (p. vi). Beniger's book begins by looking into the reasons behind the prominent position of the computer in modern society. The author sees the historical origins of this development in the last decades of the 19th century. At that time there was a "crisis of control," since the economic and social changes of the industrial revolution had come so quickly and so thoroughly. Beniger locates the establishment of the paradigm for today's information society in the period between 1880 and 1920. The author configures cybernetic epistemes in which he sees the principle of regulating observation implied in all life and human activity. Includes a comprehensive bibliography.

Beyfuss, Edgar and Kossowsky, A. (ed.) (1924) *Das Kulturfilmbuch*. Berlin: Carl P. Chryselius'scher Verlag.

> One of the most important sources on the history of non-fiction film in Germany in the 1920s. The authors conceive of the *Kulturfilm* as an important term, in the broadest sense including all those films "that carry an ethos," that have an educational effect. The volume's program is correspondingly broad: it attempts to create a survey and prognosis of the "educational" film, be it in the non-fictional or fictional area. The volume contains numerous shorter first-hand reports, for example on business and industrial film, such as those by Curt Ascher, general director of the Industrial Film Corporation (pp. 160-165) on the use and dissemination of industrial film, or by Arthur Lassally on the occupational film (pp. 166-173). Furthermore, the book briefly isolates a series of problem areas that are informative for *Kulturfilm* as a whole, from manuscripts, distribution, and pedagogical goals through the relation to state and politics up to screenings in cinemas and private events. The collection also includes historical overviews, such as that of Oskar Kalbus (pp. 1-13). Also includes a small advertising section.

Braun, Marta (1992) *Picturing Time: The Work of Etienne-Jules Marey (1830-1904)*. Chicago: University of Chicago Press.

> Marta Braun's achievement consists in having assembled step-by-step the many individual puzzle pieces of Etienne-Jules Marey's life and work: letters, films, and negatives from his partially forgotten estate. Braun provides the evidence that Marey is not only relevant to the history of photography, but also that it is important to place his work within the spirit of scientific positivism of the 19th century in order to understand it. Marey's interest was scientific, and his photographs, unlike Muyerbridge's artistic ones, function as scientific tools. Marey's photographic techniques developed out of his deep interest in movements, his specific medical knowledge and physical techniques. Marta Braun demonstrates that Marey saw the human body as an animated machine and wanted to make its mechanisms, such as walking and jumping, visible.
>
> Along with numerous graphics of movement, the book also contains descriptions and drawings of Marey's early work from ca. 1870. The comprehensive appendices include two catalogs with a compilation of more than 1,355 negatives on glass and flexible film plates and a third catalog with a list of Marey's films. Some of the negatives were discovered in 1979 and are here listed with their current locations and sorted by period. Moreover, there is also a bibliography of Marey's many articles written for various scientific publications.
>
> Marta Braun is professor of "technology in practice" at the Ryerson Polytechnic University in Toronto. Her main areas of research are early film and the history of photography as well as scientific photography.

Brown, Elspeth H. (2005) *The Corporate Eye: Photography and the Rationalization of American Commercial Culture, 1884-1929*. Baltimore: John Hopkins University Press.

> In this book, Elspeth Brown shows how American companies began to introduce photography to various ends toward the end of the 19th century, from studies of movement, advertising and up to control measures. Her research concerns the production of visual texts, using the examples of Edward Muybridge, Frederick Taylor, Frank Gilbreth, and Lewis Hine. Brown contextualizes these four case studies and positions the rise of photography as a mass medium in a context with the business goals of raising efficiency and boosting public image. She concludes that it was not only industrial production that was streamlined and reshaped, but also the modern subject.

Burder, John (1973) *The Work of the Industrial Film Maker*. New York: Hasting House Publishers.

> "An industrial film can prove a first class investment if it is properly planned, competently produced and efficiently used." In this manual, John Burder describes the benefits and advantages of industrial films and their production techniques. He attempts to convince corporate managers that the production of an industrial film is a reasonable and necessary investment. The author conducted research in Great Britain, the US, and Germany, and therefore has numerous examples to draw on. Burder also addresses the issue of television as a means of distribution for industrial films, although he does indicate that it is difficult to place a company-sponsored film on publicly funded television stations. Industrial film is defined as a public image tool, well suited to address both potential customers and employees.

Business Screen Magazine. Chicago, Illinois, Monthly, 1938-1968, 8 issues annually.

> "World Trade is a two way street. As the United States reaches the hour of decision on liberalized trade registration, the common market countries come aggressively forward. At this decisive period in world trade affairs, we bring our readers background on several international film programs, which conclusively point to the film medium as the one 'universal language' which can prove a decisive means of communication among all nations." (vol. 23, no. 3, 1962, Editorial). *Business Screen Magazine* was the most influential industrial film trade journal in the US and appeared from 1946 to 1968. It contains film reviews, book reviews, and reports on conferences and workshops. The magazine gave special notice to elaborate shoots and unusual locations. It was meant to bring producers together with the users of the films, in order to optimize the efficiency and effectiveness of industrial film. The focus clearly lies with corporate management and public-image films. The authors understand film primarily as a tool to be used in the framework of modern management theories. Film is constantly referred to as an international language that makes it possible for compa-

nies to find customers and partners abroad. A film is presented as a great success if it has "functioned" in several countries, that is, has been exported and taken up enthusiastically by foreign audiences. Although complete collections of the journal can only be found in certain libraries in the US, even individual issues offer a glimpse into the field of industrial film and its practices.

Cartwright, Lisa (1995) *Screening the Body: Tracing Medicine's Visual Culture.* Minneapolis: University of Minnesota Press.

"My object here is the cinema as an institution and an apparatus for monitoring, regulating, and ultimately building 'life' in the modernist culture of western medical science." Lisa Cartwright, a professor in the Communications Department at the University of California, San Diego, examines the discourse of the cultural and technological intersections of cinema and medical recording techniques. She shows that the breaking up and reshaping of the body done by technical viewing instruments is closely aligned with a markedly modern way of representing western scientific and public culture. At the same time, however, this is closely connected with the control and regulation of the body in the Foucauldian sense of discipline. Lisa Cartwright elucidates and connects the various historical lines and developments of the physiological gaze and its cultural implications.

Chémery, Philippe (1991) *Genèse et état des films d'entreprise en France.* Dissertation. Université Paris I – Panthéon Sorbonne. Microfiche.

The goal of this work is to explain and show the "essence" of industrial film and the corresponding social and economic realities. In an introductory chapter, the author places industrial film in the context of French film production. In the first large section, he outlines the state of industrial film in France (pp. 61-230), taking up the history of the category as well as – in the sense of marketing analysis – the demand and supply for/of industrial film as well as the situations of 14 different producers and finally the significance of the festival in Biarritz. The second part is devoted to the creation process of industrial film, which covers the choice of director and sponsorship as well as the whole production process from conception to post-production; finally he examines the legal issues concerning the broadcasting of industrial films on television. Includes an annotated, selected bibliography (pp. 20-31) as well as a comprehensive appendix that, along with a list of sources and literature, contains a series of documents on industrial film in France.

Dahms, Erich (1925) *Film und Filmindustrie in ihrer volkswirtschaftlichen und kulturellen Bedeutung. Inauguraldissertation zur Erlangung der staatswissenschaftlichen Doktorwürde der Rechts- und Staatswissenschaftlichen Fakultät der Universität Greifswald.* Greifswald: unpublished manuscript.

Dahms's study is valuable for research on industrial film in that it describes film as a "cultural and economic medium" and contains an outline of the history of the German educational film movement (pp. 29-50).

Davis, K.D. (1993) "The Virtual Body and the Imaginary Subject in Corporate Videocommunication." *Afterimage*, 21,1, pp. 6-9.
In this essay, the author examines the use of information technologies in corporate communication through an analysis of the Bank of America's internal video production. Davis begins her argument with the thesis that the development of information technologies is closely connected with a fundamental separation of text from context. Analyzing the content and style of the film materials, she shows how a virtual corporate body is constructed. Internal video communication is positioned as a key medium in the translation and transference of the information and data that steer a company.

Deutsches Industrieinstitut (ed.) (1959) *Der deutsche Wirtschaftsfilm*. Cologne: Deutsche Industrieverlags GmbH.
An overview of the available German films as of 1959, intended as information about the German business film. It is interesting today as a filmography divided into industrial branches, but also because of the introduction by Friedrich Mörtzsch (pp. 9-14), the chairman of the working group on industrial and documentary film within the National Association of German Industry and author of two books on the topic (included in this bibliography), which makes clear the then current understanding of the goals of industrial film production.

Deutsches Industrieinstitut (ed.) (1969) *Jenseits von Skandal und Krise*. Der deutsche Industriefilm 1959-1969.
Small brochure, printed in typescript, that answers the question of what industrial film is for the time period 1959-1969, in reference to German institutions and films. Includes a filmography and a list of prizewinners.

Dewulf, Yves (1991) *La communication audiovisuelle au service des entreprises*. Paris: Éditions Eyrolles.
This book is conceived as a practical guide for effective communication within a company with and through audiovisual media. It seeks to offer companies concrete tips on how to make use of the possibilities and advantages of audiovisual communication; industrial film is only one part of this audiovisual communications strategy. The starting point is the idea that the audiovisual media play an important role for the optimization of (potential) target groups/audiences and can significantly contribute to a company's public image.

Eckardt, André (2004) *Im Dienst der Werbung. Die Boehner-Film 1926-1967*. Berlin: Cinegraph Babelsberg (= Filmblatt-Schriften. Beiträge zur Filmgeschichte; 2).

A company biography of the medium-sized advertising-film company Boehner, founded by Fritz Boehner in Dresden in 1926. Along with educational and cultural films and advertising films, the company also produced industrial films. Industrial film is frequently addressed in the book; in the company's early days and in the 1950s, in particular, it played an important role in its production. The author first presents data and facts on the company's history (pp. 11-20), then takes up individual aspects like Fritz Boehner's profiling strategies, the internal organization of work, and technological development (pp. 21-57) before writing about development tendencies in content and form (pp. 58-103). An appendix contains a list of employees of Boehner-Film, a source list of available copies, a bibliography, and an index of films.

The Educational Screen. Chicago, vol. 1, no. 1 (Jan. 1922) – vol. 35, no. 6 (Summer 1956).
The monthly magazine *The Educational Screen*, at only 30 pages, is significantly less comprehensive than *Business Screen Magazine* and *Educational Film Review*, and it also has significantly fewer authors. According to its own advertising ("The only magazine devoted to the new influence in national Education") it is the first magazine in the US specifically devoted to training and educational films. It is the sequel to the magazine *Visual Education* (1920-1924). Along with information specific to educational film, *The Educational Screen* contains information relevant to the general film business and short reviews of normal entertainment films. Each issue has an evaluation scale for these films for educational purposes. Moreover, each issue offers a list of new book publications and newspaper articles on the topic of educational film and a few reviews.

Ewert, Malte (1998) *Die Reichsanstalt für Film und Bild in Wissenschaft und Unterricht (1933-1945)*. Hamburg: Verlag Dr. Kovac.
This dissertation looks at the institution in which the German school-film movement was organized. It is strongly focused on personal histories with the goal of evaluating and, to a certain degree, apologizing for the ideological-propagandistic role of the RWU in the context of National Socialism. The author only marginally treats the actual RWU films, including research films and training films found in commerce, agriculture, and other areas. Includes list of sources and literature.

Festival of Technical Films (1970) *Final report: The Role of scientific and technical films in the industrial and scientific progress*. Budapest: Hungarian Central Technical Library and Documentation centre and Information Centre for Technical Films.
In April 1970, one of the many conferences on the subject of industrial film that were common in the 1950s and 1960s took place in Budapest. Experts from 16 countries and seven international organizations took part. One of the main positions of all the lectures is that industrial films are a necessary means for scientific and technological

advancement. The various speakers discussed how films are used to exhibit and present objects researched. Due to the increasing complexity of the fields it is argued that film can assist in the development of knowledge. All the experts are also convinced that not all of the possibilities of film have been exhausted. A list of all participants and their institutions and addresses is included.

Forster, Ralf (1999) *Sparkassenwerbefilme im Nationalsozialismus*. Frankfurt am Main, Berlin and Bern: Peter Lang (= Europäische Hochschulschriften, Reihe III; 842).

> Forster takes on the task of the new film history in his dissertation, to view films "in a cultural historical framework, indeed as a reflection of a certain politics, of an economic framework as well as of concrete everyday social life" (p. 9). He focuses on the short advertising films on savings banks, in order "to show the special ways that National Socialist propaganda worked and its functioning in the social environment" (p. 10). The thesis of the volume is that savings-bank films have "the sole intention of getting capital from the population for the armament of the German army and later for the 'silent financing of the war'" (ibid.). The author discusses the contents of the savings bank films that have been passed down and places than in historical, cultural, and social contexts. A section on economic history provides information about the mechanisms and background of war financing. Appendix with comprehensive filmography and current archival locations. Cf. Forster (2005).

Forster, Ralf (2005) *Ufa und Nordmark. Zwei Firmengeschichten und der deutsche Werbefilm 1919-1945*. Trier: Wissenschaftlicher Verlag.

> This book also began as a dissertation on the advertising film during National Socialism (cf. Forster 1999). The author here writes two company biographies to work out the national (UFA) and local (Nordmark) specificities of the German advertising film in two social cultures. The main focus is on the production history and the films themselves. What is especially interesting is the historical presentation of business advertising terminology in the introduction, as well as the typology of the advertising film according to distribution and forms of presentation. A detailed study, rich in sources, including a CD-ROM with an overview of German short advertising films in the period 1919-1945 in European archives as well as an appendix with lists of literature and sources, film titles, and index of names.

Freeman, Frank N. (1924) *Visual Education: A Comparative Study of Motion Pictures and Other Methods of Instruction*. Chicago: University of Chicago Press.

> This publication is the final report of a large empirical study from the 1920s on the use of films in education, financed with with assistance from the Commonwealth Fund. The overall study is divided into many individual projects, each of which compares the effectiveness of various conventional teaching methods with that of educational films. There is an attempt to use scientific methods and their evidence to support the

effectiveness of film. The use of films in education at the time was involved and expensive, so it was feared that the economic interest of the producers was the central issue. There is no attempt, however, to measure the educational success of the films solely in comparison with oral teaching methods, as well as with other conventional means of visual education like slides or wall charts. The individual studies each compare two or more groups of students in Illinois.

Gaines, Jane M. and Renov, Michael (ed.) (1999) *Collecting Visible Evidence.* Minneapolis: University of Minnesota Press.

"The documentary horizon is a virtual terra incognita, studded with promise and peril for resourceful analysts" (Michael Renov). The essays published in this collection represent a selection of texts that were given as lectures at the *Visible Evidence* conferences. This is a series of interdisciplinary conferences that are among the most important places for academic discussion of all non-fictional or documentary forms. Taken as a whole, the authors represent a significant reorientation of documentary film theory. A rewriting of the history(ies) of documentary film can be found for example in observations on historical phenomena like the detective camera (Tom Gunning) or techniques like film x-rays that can be used for empirical evidence (Akira Mizuta Lippit). Eithne Johnson contributes to the literature on the utility film with her essay on self-help advice films for women. The authors of the volume work within a discourse of knowledge that thinks cultural representation together with social and political forces.

Geschichte des dokumentarischen Films in Deutschland
Vol. 1: *Kaiserreich 1895-1918*. Ed. by Uli Jung and Martin Loiperdinger. Stuttgart: Reclam, 2005.
Vol. 2: *Weimarer Republik 1918-1933*. Ed. by Klaus Kreimeier, Antje Ehmann and Jeanpaul Goergen. Stuttgart: Reclam, 2005.
Vol. 3: *„Drittes Reich'*. Ed. by Peter Zimmermann and Kay Hoffmann. Stuttgart: Reclam, 2005.

This first German standard work on documentary film contains a broad panorama of cinematic forms, including nature and animal films, portraits of cities, amateur films, artist portraits, missionary films, ethnographic and archaeological films, marine films, and expedition films. The numerous contributions to the volumes deal with the great formal wealth and the functional variety of the documentary before 1945. They not only deal with the films themselves, but also their production circumstances, distribution methods, their screening and reception, and the wider societal context. The volumes are supported by an appendix that could have been a valuable publication in its own right, consisting of a comprehensive bibliography, a filmography with sources, short biographies of filmmakers, and an index of various people. Furthermore, the book is supported by a database that is accessible on the homepage of the Haus des Dokumentarfilms, as well as by the collection *Triumph der Bilder*, which appeared in 2003 in the Close-Up series of the UVK-Verlag and which advanced a comparative examination of German documentary film history with international examples of the cultural film. Industrial film is also taken up by various authors in the three volumes. Topics include industrial images (vol. 1, pp. 324-332, by Martin Loiperdinger, also in this collection) from Imperial Germany before 1918; the workings of propaganda during World War I (ibid., p. 437); industrial film in the Weimar Republic, for instance, in reference to a context of the belief in progress, and industrial advertising film (vol. 2, pp. 364-380 by F.T. Meyer); as well as a methodical essay by Thomas Elsaesser on "Die Stadt von morgen. Filme zum Bauen und Wohnen" (pp. 381-410). The treatment of industrial films during the time of National Socialism is particularly thorough, with contributions on individual directors like Walter Ruttmann, Svend Noldan, and Willy Zielke (vol. 3, pp. 110-132; 231-241), the intersections of industrial modernization, mobilization, and film (pp. 231-308), industrial and advertising film from the state railway, by Boehner Films, the films of the German Workers' Front (pp. 242-256), and on advertising film (pp. 257-265). Volume two also contains a very useful research overview on industrial and advertising film (pp. 33-37) by Jeanpaul Goergen.

Gipson, Henry Clay (1947) *Films in Business and Industry.* New York and London: McGraw-Hill.

"This book is designed not only to tell when and how to use films but to give a basic understanding of the grammar of the screen – the how and why of film production ... to form the most potent medium for the transmission of thought since the invention of the printing press." This practical book is based on observations that the authors made in various organizations that produce industrial films. First, Gipson briefly sketches the history of moving images and explains why film can be so effective. Then, he traces the course of the utility film back as far as the 1940s. Along with the "universal" comprehensibility that constitutes a film, Gipson stresses the possibility of making visible what is otherwise invisible. Industrial film is above all used in the area of "training," for instance, for health and safety, but also in public work. One of the goals of the films discussed by Gipson is the "indoctrination" of employees. Examples of scripts and descriptions of film screenings are also provided. Furthermore, the book contains an extensive list of a wide variety of production companies, as well as a group of newspapers on the topic.

Goergen, Jeanpaul (1989) *Walter Ruttmann. Eine Dokumentation. Mit Beiträgen von Paul Falkenberg, William Uricchio, Barry A. Fulks.* Berlin: Freunde der Deutschen Kinemathek.

An annotated filmography (pp. 97-158) supplemented by a compilation of Ruttmann's unfinished films and projects and other films that he probably or certainly worked on (pp. 159-170). The filmography is framed by two very useful sections: essays (pp. 17-72), including Goergen's portrait of Walter Ruttmann, and an essay by

Uricchio on Ruttmann after 1933. The volume also contains texts and conversations with Ruttman (pp. 73-96) as well as comprehensive lists of literature and sources.

Goodman, Michael B. (ed.) (1994) *Corporate Communication: Theory and Practice.* New York: State University of New York Press.

The book contains an introduction by editor Michael B. Goodman on the various subjects that are expanded upon by the essays, case studies, and commentaries. The subject area of business communication is divided into the following subcategories: the practice of business communication, the company's social activity, company identity, business culture, publicity work, use of the media, crisis management, and communication strategies for the world market. Goodman describes the rapid changes in world markets since the 1990s as the instigation for the book. Technology has been modernized at a fast pace in many different areas, so that management techniques have been significantly transformed into High Speed Management. The media that Goodman and his colleagues draw on in the various essays are the following: corporate television, video, radio, film, company newspapers, computer networks, e-mail, posters, and displays. The main focus of the publication therefore lies not only in the *one-to-many* media, but rather in the network character of media. This is developed with descriptions based on cost/use factors through case studies that show how efficiency can be raised by changing the communication structure. Each of the chapters is supplemented by a small bibliography on the subject.

Gordon, Jay E. (1961) *Motion-Picture Production for Industry.* New York: Macmillan.

"The motion picture is industry's most convincing medium of expression." The author, a professor at Fullerton College in California, views industrial film in light of its forms of representation and communication in the industry as well as in the educational sector and in government. First he traces a history of the industrial film, which begins in the 1910s and reaches its highpoint in the 1960s. Gordon describes industrial film as the "best tool" to win over both customers and employees, but only if high quality can be assured. For this reason, he argues that it is up to production techniques to insure the interplay of "authenticity and authority." The author stresses the strengths of film as a medium, which is in many cases superior to the book. An appendix contains a list of industry newspapers and industrial film festivals.

Grau, Hermann (1932) *Technik und Film. Die Filmkamera im Dienste der Technik und Wissenschaft* (3rd ed.). Stuttgart: Dieck & Co. and Franckh's Technischer Verlag.

Grau begins with a historical outline that takes the history of industrial film "after the war" as its theme, along with the appearance of businesses that were particularly dedicated to the production of industrial film (p. 11). The author refers to industrial film as "technical films" or even as "technical advertising films," and in the second chapter, he describes their meaning, production, and presentation (pp. 14-25). This is followed by a small practical section on what to be aware of in production (pp. 26-33) and, after these introductory sections, he presents thorough observations on the technique of technical films: Grau takes up the subject of camera and recording techniques (pp. 34-49), slow-motion/time-lapse photography, and micro-cinematography (pp. 50-62) before speaking of "Film and Medicine" (pp. 63-72) and "Sound Film" (pp. 73-80) in two further chapters.

Guillory, John (2004) The Memo and Modernity. *Critical Inquiry*, 31, pp. 108-131.
The subject of this essay is memos, those short reminders from everyday (office) life that are meant to ensure and efficiently convey information. For Guillory, the practice of memos is an example of the organization of information and dates in a complex linguistic structure. Guillory develops an epistemological axis between three coordinates *literary/journalistic – informational – scholarly/scientific*. His hypothesis maintains that all information genres developed since the beginning of newspaper printing have been based on writing. The author attempts to show how exemplary the establishment of memos is for (business) communication in modern times. He stresses the technical aspects of this special form of communication and, in the end, poses the question of why the transmission via writing remain indispensable in a time of medialized information.

Gunning, Tom (1994) The World as Object Lesson: Cinema Audiences, Visual Culture and the St. Louis World's Fair, 1904. *Film History*, 6, 4, pp. 422-444.
Tom Gunning's article concerns the phenomenon of the visual spectacle of modernity, using the example of the St. Louis World's Fair. Gunning points out that film had no central role there as an exhibition object itself, rather it represented a "backstage technology" for other attractions of the modern period. The author distinguishes the new form and style of visual exhibitions, which are closely tied to modern consumer culture. The term "object lesson" is taken from the context of the discourse on the duty of educating society, a very prevalent idea at the turn of the century. This "lesson on the object" was direct and visual persuasion, and therefore, a predecessor phenomenon of the conveyance of evidence by photos and film.

Hansell, Peter and Ollerenshaw, Robert (1969) (eds.) *Longmore's Medical Photography* (8th ed.). London and New York: Focal Press.

This textbook on medical photography was originally put together by one of the pioneers of the field, Thomas Albert Longmore (1905-1957). Longmore was the head trainer in x-ray technology in the British Army medical corps, and member of the Society of Radiographers starting in the 1920s, of which he was later president. The book first appeared in 1944 and is the first important publication on the topic of medical photography. The 1969 edition, revised by Hansell and Ollerenshaw, contains revised chapters and updated information, while certain chapters from the original edition, such the one on cardiography, were left out entirely. The theoretical bases of photography are thoroughly examined. The second part of the book treats the individual possibilities of using medical photography, such as, for example, photography in the operating room, endoscopic photography, and also photography with infrared and ultraviolet rays. The largest chapter is concerned with radiography. All of the chapters are purely medical-technological, the patient appears only as the object of the technical apparatus.

Hébert, Nicole (1987) *L'entreprise et son image. La publicité institutionnelle: pourquoi, comment?* Paris: Dunod.

The publication arose in the framework of a discussion of the competitiveness of French companies. Its goal is to present the development and meaning of product advertising and takes up the question of what role advertising plays in the representation of a company. The starting point of the book is the conviction that advertising strategies represent an essential factor in relation to customer loyalty and a positive company image. According to the author, advertising makes a fundamental contribution to the construction of an international reputation and can also have economic consequences. She orients herself above all toward American and Japanese examples, but also German, British, and a few French ones, pointing out specific national characteristics in the process. Each chapter treats numerous examples, taking examples from a large variety of ad campaigns.

Heller, Thomas (1990) *La Communication audiovisuelle d'entreprise. Le discours des apparences.* Paris: Les éditions d'organisation.

Heller discusses the use of audiovisual means in industry, specifically addressing students of communications. First he describes aspects of audiovisual communication in the service of business: what it is about (typology), what its goals and effects are, what belongs to production, what genres (like reportage and documentation) there are. Then he more thoroughly treats the communicative function of the audiovisual for companies and evaluates them in light of changes in society. With a bibliography and a brief video- and filmography.

Herman, Lewis (1965): *Educational Films: Writing, Directing, and Producing for Classroom, Television, and Industry.* New York: Crown Publishers.

This book distinguishes itself from other manuals by focusing on textual contents. Film technique is only briefly mentioned. Each individual step of the development of a pedagogically valuable narration is precisely described. The excursus on propaganda films and persuasion films, which treat Nazi and Soviet propaganda films, is of particular interest.

Hillyer, Minette (2006) *Making Home: Film and the Modern American Everyday.* Dissertation. University of California at Berkeley.

This dissertation studies the making of the home through film in postwar America between 1945 and the early 1960s. It analyzes a group of films and related texts that attempted to understand and analyze "home" within a homemaking culture. The study encompasses socio-scientific research that made use of films to delimit a culture of home, either via the textual analysis of feature films or the more literal re-editing or remaking of ethnographic film footage; sponsored films that show real or model homes in which the home space was remade in the image of an idea of homeland; and home movies made within the discursive, affective, and material space of home.

Hofmann, Paul (1994) *Filmschätzen auf der Spur. Verzeichnis historischer Filmbestände in Nordrhein-Westfalen.* Düsseldorf: Selbstverlag des Nordrhein-Westfälischen Hauptstaatsarchivs (= Veröffentlichungen der staatlichen Archive des Landes Nordrhein-Westfalen, Reihe C: Quellen und Forschungen; 33).

The first comprehensive German-language index of archives in the German state of Nordrhein-Westfalen that have holdings of industrial films, edited by Paul Hofmann, who was the director of the Duisburg-based Kinemathek des Ruhrgebiets and contributed significantly to the organization of the archival exchange in the area of industrial film. The volume contains descriptions of public and private collections throughout the state as well as those from local city and club archives, media centers, and educational film centers, as well as a concise overview of industrial film holdings in associations and business archives, with an introduction by Horst A. Wessel of Mannesmann (pp. 143-148).

Hogenkamp, Bert and Storck, Henri (1983) Le Borinage. La grève des mineurs de 1932 et le film de Joris Ivens et Henri Storck. *Revue Belge du Cinéma*, Winter 1983/Spring 1984, 6/7.

Documentation of the film BORINAGE and of the strike that is its subject in a special number of the *Revue Belge du Cinéma*, consisting of a dossier in which Storck reproduces the history of the production, a report by Hogenkamp on the film, its reception in the press, its place in the history of documentary film, and a shot sequence of the film with stills. Furthermore, there are factory photographs and accompanying texts by Joris Ivens (reprinted from *The Camera and I*) and Jean Fonteyne. Includes a bibliography and list of sources.

Holtzmann Kevles, Bettyann (1997) *Naked to the Bone. Medical Imaging in the Twentieth Century.* New Brunswick, NJ: Rutgers University Press, Sloan Technology Series.

The book covers the history of medical images from the invention of the x-ray in 1865 to the latest developments in visualizing technology. In the first section, Holtzmann Kevles concentrates on the history of the development of the x-ray during World War II. She examines how this new technology changed the practice of medical diagnosis. In the second part of the book, the author takes up the effects and influences of medical-imaging technology on culture and society and integrates newer developments like ultrasound into this discourse. Holtzmann Kevles concentrates on the change from a culture of the opaque in the 19th century to a culture of the visible in the 20th century. The idea of seeing-through is presented as essential to a general cultural shift. In this context, she points to avant-garde artists and even to H.G. Wells (*The Invisible Man*, 1897). Additionally, she attempts to trace the question of why x-rays, unlike any other medical tool, is associated not only with great curative powers, but also has the reputation of being an extremely dangerous, sinister technology.

Jacquinot, Geneviève (1977) *Image et pédagogie. Analyse sémiologique du film a intention didactique.* Paris: Presses universitaires de France.

For a long time, this was the only work that analyzed utility films in any depth, even if it does not deal with industrial film, but with education and training films. Written in the 1970s, the book belongs to a tradition of genre analysis, which is stressed in the text. Jacquinot attempts to uncover their semiotic origins, how training films make use of *langage cinématographique*. She sees her task as questioning the structure of audiovisual messages with didactic intentions. Cf. also the essay by Eef Masson in the Utility Film special issue of *Montage/AV* 15,1, 2006.

Jarmer, Martin (1986) *Der Industriefilm. Einsatzmöglichkeiten und -bedingungen im Marketing für Investitionsgüter. Inauguraldissertation zur Erlangung der wirtschaftswissenschaftlichen Doktorwürde des Fachbereichs Wirtschaftswissenschaft der Freien Universität Berlin.* Microfiche. Berlin.

This is the single most comprehensive German publication on industrial film to date, looking at the subject from the perspective of communications theory. It is divided into three parts: "Industrial film presented in outline" (pp. 4-89), "Foundations in decision and communications theory in industrial film planning and formation" (pp. 90-164), and "Industrial film conception on the basis of the findings of decision and communications theory" (pp. 165-238). The book's chief interest lies in its examination of the possibilities of industrial film for use in the area of capital-goods marketing, from a psychological viewpoint, and on the basis of decision-process orientation. The dissertation deals with the area of marketing research, in which industrial film normally plays no role at all due to its focus on consumer-goods marketing. The author sees industrial film as an independent marketing instrument in its own right, one that can exercise political control functions over decision-making processes in commercial organizations. Includes a bibliography.

Kaplan, Daniel (1993) *Les Médias électroniques. Vidéotex, audiotex, multimédias: connaître et exploiter les nouveaux outils de communication de l'entreprise.* Paris: Dunod, 1993.

> A handbook on the use of electronic media as a means of communication in industry. Given advanced technical development, the author believes that these media represent some of the most important means of communication for the future. The term electronic media is here used for all those media that work are based on electronic data processing and telecommunications. The publication is aimed at a professional readership, but it is also conceived as introductory reading in the field of business communication. Taken as a whole, it has two goals: first, to offer a broad overview of the field of electronic media and to present their function, use, and market; second, to provide a methodological guide. The publication also provides a view of French information technology and media use in the 1980s and 1990s and their special forms such as the information platform Minitel.

Kennard, Margot Elizabeth (1989) *The Corporation of the Classroom: The Struggles Over Meanings of Menstrual Education in Sponsored Films, 1947-1983.* Dissertation. University of Madison-Wisconsin.

> For over 40 years, schools across the United States have relied on films sponsored by manufacturers of menstrual products to teach young women about menstruation. This dissertation investigates the menstrual-education discourse that was produced and represented in two educational films sponsored by one of the leading manufacturers of menstrual products. Using a cultural-studies framework, the textual practices of these films and the contextual practices of various groups and institutions that struggled over meanings of menstrual education produced and circulated in these sponsored films are examined. The primary conclusion of this study is that the sponsoring corporation does not simply impose meanings of menstrual education that best serve its economic interests. Rather, the menstrual-education discourse produced in both sponsored films, *The Story of Menstruation* and *Julie's Story,* is a product of struggles and negotiations among various groups and institutions with different interests in the meanings of menstrual education.

Kinsky-Weinfurter, Gottfried (1993) *Filmmusik als Instrument staatlicher Propaganda. Der Kultur- und Industriefilm im Dritten Reich und nach 1945.* Munich: Ölschläger.

> This dissertation in the field of music pedagogy works through the documents left by Viennese composer Viktro Hruby (1894-1878), which contains autographs, sketches, notes, and other types of texts on Hruby's work in the area of the cultural film, supplemented by presentations of the composers Erich Markaritzer and Paul Kont, both

of whom also wrote "media music." The starting point is the hypothesis that the state-sponsored, public education-oriented cultural film before and after the National Socialist era conveyed political values and ideologies that can be traced back to the official conception of propaganda. The cultural film represents this ideology of public or semipublic institutions, in which film music provides "ideological help." The author takes up the industrial film of the silent era (pp. 27-28), the industrial film work of the Austrian Productivity Center (pp. 81-82), and additionally delivers a case study on a short industrial film from 1952 entitled *The Twentieth Century, Century of Electricity* (pp. 276-315), produced by Rondo-Filmproduktions GmbH as a film to instill public trust in the construction of power plants. Includes a bibliography (with interviews).

Klein, Walter J. (1976) *The Sponsored Film.* New York: Hasting House.

In the 1970s, the Walter J. Klein Company produced various kinds of sponsored films. These were commissioned by various private companies as well as governmental organizations. The company left behind a large collection of over 1,000 films, which are held at the archive of the North Carolina School of Arts.

The firm's founder and author of this book wants to proclaim his practical experience in the field of industrial film production and to clear up certain prejudices. With an ironic journalistic writing style he tries to provide observations of industrial-film production. Like other authors, Klein divides utility films (non-theatrical) into three categories: television spots, sponsored films, and training films. The author presents the effects of public relations on the conception of industrial films and shows the coherency between industrial film and other advertising media. In this way, Klein makes a case for a wider acceptance of commercial film. The specific practical tips that Klein gives are supplemented by, among other things, examples of production contracts and a list of distribution centers.

Kühn, Michael (1998) *Unterrichtsfilm im Nationalsozialismus. Die Arbeit der Reichsstelle für den Unterrichtsfilm/Reichsanstalt für Film und Bild in Wissenschaft und Unterricht.* Mammendorf: Septem Artes.

The study focuses on the central facility for production and distribution of educational media in Nazi Germany. Subjects treated are the development of school and classroom movies, the founding phase of the institution for classroom films and their framing conditions, the structure and the field of duties of the RWU, the educational film center during World War II, the further use of RWU films, and the development of classroom movies in the first postwar years. Industrial films are not separately thematized. An appendix contains extensive lists of RWU productions with further data on individual films and their use, as well as a list of sources and literature.

Lambert, Jacques (1979) *L'information ascendante dans les entreprises*. Paris: Entreprise moderne d'édition.

> The book thematizes the area of internal business communication, especially the way that upper echelon employees, that is, those "ascending" in the hierarchy, communicate. The publication offers an initial, foundational analysis of this phenomenon, supported by numerous questionnaires, statistics, and concrete examples. Essentially, the author seeks to methodically compile the distinct elements of the ascending information and the effects it has on the company's internal labor relations. The conviction that an appropriate communication system forms the prerequisite for clearing up problems and "humanizing" the company in general is fundamental to the book. Therefore, it is conceived as a guide and practical manual for those responsible for such development.

Lambert, Jacques (1995) *Le journal d'entreprise*. Paris: Eds. du Centre de Formation et de Perfectionnement des Journalistes (CFPJ).

> Guidebook on creating a company newspaper. The book/work is conceived as a practical guide and concentrates on questions around the institutional framing conditions as well as the editorial conditions of such a publication. Subjects such as work organization, editorial procedures, going to press, and journalistic reliability are treated. The author starts from the conviction that the newspaper represents one of the most significant forms of internal business communication, in order to develop the medium into a place of (idea) exchange.

Lassally, Arthur (1919) *Bild und Film im Dienste der Technik. Zweiter Teil: Betriebskinematographie*. Halle: Wilhelm Knapp (= Enzyklopädie der Photographie; 91).

> One of the first and most important German sources on industrial film, this follow-up book to Lassaly's slim volume on industrial photography from the same year takes on the task of describing film photography in its execution, that is, the use of images and film in industry and to industrial ends. The author begins with a typology, a systematization of "technical film" according to use, for instance, for trade fairs, movement studies, training, or even as a sales tool. He then examines the special conditions of shooting film in a factory (pp. 101-164) and finally thoroughly describes the production of film in view of technical apparatuses and the processing of materials (pp. 165-237). Includes an index.

Leblanc, Gerard (1983) *Quand l'entreprise fait son cinéma. La médiathèque de Rhône-Poulenc (1972-1981)*. Paris: Cinéthique Presses Universitaires de Vincennes.

> The film collection of the French Chemical and Pharmaceutical Concern Rhône-Poulenc forms the basis for this film-studies work. This collection is interesting because the corporation showed a great affinity for cinematic representation from the beginning. The company was involved in the production and distribution of industrial film extensively and with great variety; the wide variety of forms becomes apparent in the analysis of films. The goal of the book is to work out one of the fundamental specifi-

cities of industrial film despite its diverse characteristics. The author starts from the thesis that its particularity lies in harmonizing the interests of (potential) commissioners, or of customers and companies. He analyzes the commitment of each individual film in comparison to the wider development of the company. Leblanc's book is an attempt to incorporate industrial film in media theory within the wider field of other audiovisual areas like the scientific film or the entertainment film.

Liesegang, Paul F. (1920) *Wissenschaftliche Kinematographie einschliesslich der Reihenphotographie*. Leipzig: Ed. Liesegang's Verlag (M. Eger).

A revised version of the second part of the fifth edition of Liesegang handbook of practical cinematography. Its main value, along with the commentaries on cinematographic recording and reproduction, on screening, on camera technique, and on the special use area of film recording, lies in its thorough treatment of the ways of using the movie camera as a research tool (pp. 261-296) as well as in teaching (pp. 297-310). Includes a bibliography.

Loiperdinger, Martin (1999) *Film & Schokolade. Stollwercks Geschäfte mit lebenden Bildern*. Basel and Frankfurt am Main: Stroemfeld/Roter Stern (= Kintop Schriften).

This work of media history analyzes the distribution and screening contexts of films in a commercial sense, which previously had been largely neglected. This seminal book is also interesting for industrial-film research because it focuses on the business of the brothers Stollwerck, Germany's leading chocolate manufacturers. Loiperdinger looks at Stellwerck's business relations with a number of film pioneers in Europe and America during the period of 1892-1897. The first part covers Stollwerck's business ventures with photo booths and the use of Cinématographe Lumière in Germany. In the second part of the book, 34 German recordings, which are included in the Société Lumière's film catalog, are documented and placed in their historical context. Also includes a chronicle of the locations of the Lumière *cinématographes*, a list of the Lumière scenes shot in Germany, and extensive notes.

Lüken-Isberner, Folckert (1989) *Der städtebaulich bedeutsame Lehr- und Informationsfilm 1946-1960*. Pfaffenweiler: Centaurus.

The author examines a body of training, teaching, explanatory, advertising, and informational films in view of how they thematize questions of urban planning and how these cinematic treatments relate to a more general discussion in the field of urban development. Its interest is not specifically in film studies, but rather in following the discussion in urban planning about using film "sources." With lists of sources and literature, filmography, indexes of film titles and persons, film transcripts.

Martin, Michelle Holley (1997) *Periods, Parody, and Polyphony: Ideology and Heteroglossia in Menstrual Education*. Dissertation. Illinois State University.

A comparative, critical analysis of sponsored educational menstruation films and girls' fiction on menstruation, this project explores the incorporation of fiction into school puberty-education programs. Using the Disney and Kimberly-Clark 1947 film *The Story of Menstruation* as a standard for comparison, this study analyzes several subsequent films through a Bakhtinian lens with the purpose of uncovering the heteroglossia in these works.

Le Media Entreprise. Sous la direction de Nancy Angel. *Dossiers de l'audiovisuel*, 8, July/August 1986.

The fourth edition of this French periodical concerns the relations between (industrial) businesses and media. The 32-page dossier section brings together various texts on the subject. The majority of the texts, which are made up of essays, studies, and case descriptions, were originally published in newspapers and journals; there are, for instance, articles taken from *Le Figaro* and *01 Informatique*. In her introduction, Angel clarifies the point of the collection: the entry of computer technology into the business sector has brought with it profound changes in trade. In light of innovations in information technology and their consequences for the definition of work and the meaning of people in relation to it, a business is no longer defined by its economic power alone. Communication as such occupies the foreground. It plays an essential role both in the sense of belonging that employees have to the company as well as for the transmission of public image to the outside. Communication therefore encourages trust and creates the basis for legitimation.

Mercer, John (1981) *The Informational Film*. Carbondale: Stipes Publishing Company.

The main appeal of this textbook is the fact that the author categorizes utility films according to schemata from educational theory. Mercer places skill films in the psychomotor domain, whereas record films and informational films, in which one learns by watching, are placed in the cognitive domain. As the sole industrial-film category, he categorizes persuasive films in the affective domain, along with dramatic films and experimental films. Psychomotor films work, above all, with imperative address and commentary on the work processes shown. Mercer dismisses a categorization of films at the level of context, which would involve the films' use. In the historical part of the book, he concentrates primarily on the development of educational film, especially on the history of various associations and institutions in the US like The Educational Film Library Association. In the final chapter, the author finally ventures a glimpse into the future possibilities of utility-film distribution. He takes up both the role of television as well as the possibilities of new storage media such as the CD. An appendix includes an Informational Film Analysis Sheet. Furthermore, there is a list of associations, producers, archives, research centers, competitions, and festivals in the area of training and utility films and a very extensive bibliography with 190 entries.

Michon, Roland (1988) *Esthetique du film d'entreprise.* Dissertation on microfiche. Paris III.

Michon addresses the neglected but important social, economic, and cultural factors of French industrial film, or more precisely those films that were screened between 1977 and 1986 at the Festival National du Film d'Entreprise in Biarritz. He uses semiological and sociological approaches in order to work out the structure of the films and the ways that they organize meaning, and in order to find a functional model for them. Starting from this analysis, he seeks to characterize this kind of film by defining nine figures and to formulate a specific "grammar" for the industrial film as a genre. The functional model is important for him in order to show what kind of services industrial films can render together with a company's communication strategies. Includes a bibliography and an extensive appendix with a filmography and shot protocols, as well as extracts from scripts from the films covered.

Mittell, Jason (1997) Invisible Footage: Industry on Parade and Television History. *Film History,* 9, 2, pp. 200-219.

In this article, Jason presents his case study on a television production from the 1950s, Industry on Parade. This NBC television program was produced by one of the biggest industrial film producers in the US, the National Association of Manufacturers (NAM), and it consisted of short clips on specific branches of industry, companies, employers, and industrial technology. By working through this source, which he discovered in the archive of the National Museum of American History, the author thematizes the practices of historiography as well as the ideological implications of historical television material.

Mörtzsch, Friedrich (1959) *Die Industrie auf Zelluloid. Filme für die Wirtschaft.* Düsseldorf: Econ-Verlag.

Mörtzsch was chairman of the Industrial and Documentary Film working group at the National Association of German Industry, made study trips to the USA, learning the craft of PR there, and starting in 1951 was director of the Press and PR department of AEG. In this function, he was also responsible for the company's commissioned film production. His book focuses on the economy in order to clarify the fact that film, as a means of communicating information, is based on certain formal rules that must be taken into consideration when making a commission. Moreover, film, as a means of mass communication, performed an important social task in postwar Germany. Film served to publicize the advances of industrial production and was meant to guarantee retention of the social systems of order despite changes in production forms brought about by the more strict division of labor (p. 21). The task of industrial film for Mörtzsch consists above all in overcoming the "problem of adaptation." He sees film as one of several techniques and practices of PR, effective on a mass scale, which he described in his earlier book *Offenheit macht sich bezahlt* (Düsseldorf 1956). An appendix includes examples of budgets and data sheets for commissioning bodies of film.

Montage AV. Zeitschrift für Theorie & Geschichte audiovisueller Kommunikation. Special issue *Gebrauchsfilm*, 14, 2, 2005 and 15, 1, 2006. Marburg: Schüren.

Under the name utility film or instrumental film, the editors collect a body of films that have largely been neglected in film studies, including industrial film, educational film, and scientific film, "which are not primarily aesthetic-artistic artifacts, but were understood by their producers as instruments, that is, as a means to specific, clearly defined ends, which are followed in organized processes in the manufacture of various kinds of knowledge, goods, and social relations" (p. 4). The special issue connects with the general cultural-studies debate about educational theory and the production of knowledge, making a special contribution to this debate from within the field of film studies. The goal of both special issues is to construct an initial topography for the field of research: to discuss methodological problems that come up in relation to the utility film, analyze the different types of utility film, and present important contexts in the use of the films. The first issue deals with the scientific film that deals with laboratory practice and the popularization of scientific knowledge, in which various disciplines such as physics, ethnology, and social psychology are discussed. The second issue takes on films that have pedagogical goals or that were introduced into the economy. Among the most significant contributions on industrial film are Scott Curtis's essay in the first issue, which examines the role of film for research practices in the natural sciences, and, above all, contributions in the second issue, including Yvonne Zimmermann's text on the historical genesis of industrial film (pp. 74-90), Pierre-Emanuel Jaques's essay on tourism films in Switzerland (pp. 91-107), as well as an essay by Florian Hoof, who examines the work-study films of Frank B. Gilbreth (pp. 123-138).

Nye, David E. (1985) *Image Worlds: Corporate Identities at General Electric. 1890-1930.* Cambridge: MIT Press.

"This book is about ideology and art, capitalism and photography" (p. xi). During the course of his research, David Nye discovered General Electric's forgotten photo collection in 1977. This collection is one of the largest in the world, even if collections like the National Archive or the George Eastman House are much more specific and systematically organized. The photographs date from the period 1892-1965. Precisely because the collection lacked any previous structure, Nye was able to discover thematic, stylistic, and technical development. Nye developed a method for his analysis that is not only based on concepts from cultural studies, but also takes into account the use of socio-historical aspects of culture as a whole. The author uses the photos to investigate the ways a large company like General Motors not only had an influence on social and economic developments, but could also develop its own symbolism. For this reason Nye is initially interested in what type of photos these are, whom they are intended to address, and to what ends they were made. Using these images as a starting point, he infers a functioning method of (business) ideology. As a result of his analysis, David Nye comes to the conclusion that the symbolic construction of a social world is necessary to the life of a corporation.

L'oeuvre audiovisuelle de commande. Sous la direction de George Pessis. *Dossiers de l'audiovisuel*, 61, May/June 1995.

This dossier is concerned directly with industrial film, or rather audiovisual media in the service of industry. The special issue includes essays by Gérard Leblanc and Thomas Heller, who performed important initial research on French industrial film. Noting that industrial film has belonged to cinema since the beginning of film history (LA SORTIE DES USINES LUMIÈRE) and has developed into a significant factor of business leadership, but has nonetheless remained largely unnoticed, the issue takes up the question of definition. What is industrial film and where can it be located in the field of corporate promotion and publicity? The collective starting point of the essays is the idea that industrial film or commissioned film has gone through decisive processes of change in the last decades. Technological innovation in the 1980s led to the disappearance of industrial films from movie theaters, and they were thereafter restricted to the business world, developing into one of its most important communications tools. As a cinematic phenomenon, it lies outside typical film categorization and is usually characterized by anonymous authorship.

Perkins, Daniel J. (1982) The Sponsored Film: a new dimension in American film research? *Historical Journal of Film, Radio and Television*, 2, 2, pp. 133-140.

"This article seeks to establish a rationale for the study of the sponsored film by discussing its nature and scope, its availability, its relevance to traditional film methodologies, and finally its parallel importance to the Hollywood film based upon traditional assumptions historians have made about film." Perkins provides an overview of the research situation on industrial film in 1982 and cites a group of projects, institutes, and publications that took on the subject in various ways. In the end, Perkins offers practical advice for industrial film research and names some of the relevant journals and archives. His starting point is a critique of the history of films according to the inventor or star, which overlooks the industrial film and more generally the "factual film."

Prelinger, Rick (2006) *The Field Guide to Sponsored Films*. San Francisco: National Film Preservation Foundation.

The best-informed and most extensive guide to sponsored, industrial and more generally, "ephemeral" films to date. "The *Field Guide to Sponsored Films* is a first effort to review and assess the thousands of industrial and institutional films sponsored by

American businesses, charities, educational institutions, and advocacy groups over the last century. In the tradition of the naturalist's field guides, it describes examples discovered by patient observation and points out their identifying characteristics. In so doing, The *Field Guide* calls attention to historically significant but neglected titles, makes an argument for reclaiming their rightful place in film history, and suggests directions for scholarship" (from the Introduction, p. vi). With indices of subjects, places and organizations, and personal names.

Przigoda, Stefan (ed.) (2005) *Bergbaufilme. Inventar zur Überlieferung in Archiven, Museen und anderen Dokumentationsstellen in der Bundesrepublik Deutschland. Bearbeitet von Stefan Przigoda unter Mitarbeit von Holger Menne.* Bochum: Deutsches Bergbau-Museum.

> The goal of this extensive bibliography, created by archivists at the Bochum Mining Museum, is to make film available as a source for historical research (above all on mining). Feature fiction films, newsreels, television productions, and television clips are not taken into account. The bibliography is divided up according to mining sectors and offers the most comprehensive information possible on contents, year of production, commissioning body, production, script, direction, camera, editing, sound, music, cast, language, shooting location, speakers, and further aspects for each sector. The mining archive was founded in 1969, by the end of the project the collection contained 1,200 film titles on approximately 2,500 rolls of film and almost 500 videos; more than 1,000 films were viewed for the bibliography. The appendix include a list of abbreviations, literature, and aids (pp. 801-804), and index by film title, person, business/institution, professional term, and geography (pp. 805-922).

Rasch, Manfred, Ellerbrock, Karl-Peter, Köhne-Lindenlaub, Renate and Wessel, Horst A. (eds.) (1997) *Industriefilm – Medium und Quelle. Beispiele aus der Eisen- und Stahlindustrie.* Essen: Klartext-Verlag.

> The occasion of the 100th anniversary of film in 1995 also drew more public attention to industrial film. At Thyssen AG initiated a presentation of films that was organized in Essen with the participation of industrial archivists and historians in the field as well as filmmakers. This collection documents this event in three sections. First, there is an introductory text by Manfred Rasch, who outlines the problem with a history of early industrial film and its historical source value (pp. 9-21). A second section deals with films being passed down into the individual archives and with company film production, which is presented through individual examples. Particular stress is given to the contents of the films, supplemented by the history of how they came to be and what affect they had (pp. 108-234). In the third section historians contribute shorter observations, for instance from a socio-historical perspective. The films documented include classics like Ruttmann's MANNESMANN (1936/37) and Robert Menegoz's NUR DER NEBEL IST GRAU. IMPRESSIONEN AUS DEM NEUEN WERK DER AUGUST THYSSEN-HÜTTE (1965) along with other less well-known films, each being presented

with brief filmographic information, in part even text documents from archives of written materials.

Rasch, Manfred, Berendes, Hans Ulrich, Peter Döring, et. al (2003) *Industriefilm 1948-1959. Filme aus Wirtschaftsarchiven im Ruhrgebiet.* Essen: Klartext-Verlag.

The point of this anthology is to encourage the use of industrial film during the period 1948-1959 as a source for the social sciences. The volume documents the current state of the participating archives' holdings and the industrial work of the time, for both film and cultural history. The largest portion of the book consists of a filmography (pp. 84-436), organized by a commissioning body. Along with the usual filmographic information, versions, literature, sources, current locations and archives, and even short descriptions of content are also listed. The films included come from the Archive of the Ruhr Region, among them RWE, St. Antony Steelworks Archive-Rhenish Industrial Museum, Bochum Mining Archive, Marl der Degussa AG Archive, Aral Historical Archive, Historical Archive of the RWE AG, Krupp Historical Archive, HOCHTIEF Business Archive, Hoesch Archive, Mannesmann Archive, VDEh Steel Institute, Westphalian Business Archive Foundation, and the ThyssenKrupp Group Archive. The film descriptions are preceded by essays on the archives and the formation of their holdings as well as an introductory essay by Manfred Rasch (pp. 13-48) in which industrial film is described as a barely researched field of study. Appendix with film titles, commissioning bodies, lists of sources and literature, index.

Rennkamp, Alexandra (2005) *Ein halbes Jahrhundert Werbegeschichte: Einsatz filmischer Stilmittel von 1950 bis 2005 am Beispiel der ARAL AG.* Dissertation. Ruhr-Universität Bochum, Department of Film and Television Science. Bochum.

The author examines audiovisual business advertising through the example of selected advertising films made for Aral AG in Bochum. The work consists of an analysis of six advertising spots from the 1950s to 2005. Includes a bibliography.

Riley, Faye E. (2006) *Centron: An Industrial/Educational Film Studio, 1947-1981. A Microhistory.* Dissertation. University of Kansas.

This dissertation is a microhistory of Centron, an industrial/educational film studio that operated in Lawrence, Kansas from 1947-1981. Special attention is given to oral history interviews with the co-founders, Art Wolf and Russell Mosser, as well as the Centron employees. Further, the Spencer Archive of the University of Kansas now houses a vast collection of Centron documents and films. This data allowed more public historical components to be interwoven with the very personal oral histories. The composite result reveals several "motifs" which help explain Centron's successful competition with larger industrial/educational film companies in other parts of the United States. These motifs include Centron's central location, the special sense of camaraderie among its employees, its constant concern with the technological changes that marked the motion-picture industry during Centron's 30-year history, and a special blend of economic and business structures that enabled a remarkable freedom of creativity.

Rumpff, Hans (1919) *Die wissenschaftliche Photographie als experimentelle Grundlage des Maschinenbaus. Dissertation zur Erlangung der Würde eines Doktor-Ingenieurs.* Düsseldorf.

> Written by a chief engineer with a military background and director of the department of business technology at the Rhein Metal and Machine Factory in Düsseldorf, this dissertation is concerned with new possibilities for using scientific photography in weapons construction. Written in light of the practice of machine construction, it examines the relevant literature of the time on photographic measuring procedures that employ the Ernemann camera, which was used to make serial shots of a mortar.

Scodari, Christine Ann (1985) *The Rhetoric of Mass Intercultural Identification: A Burkeian Study of the New Australian Film Industry.* Dissertation. Ohio State University.

> The study examines the rhetoric involved in the Australian government's effort to sponsor a cinema industry geared toward producing indigenous Australian films. A systematic framework is adopted and Kenneth Burke's dramatic method of rhetorical criticism is applied to determine the interrelationships between variables in the system. Burke's concept of the "representative anecdote" is used to synthesize the messages of the sponsored films in light of their response to Australia's need for a sense of cultural "selfhood." It is found that Australia is attempting to communicate within a context of "mass intercultural identification," in that the films are meant to express a uniform sense of Australian cultural identity to Australians as well as to audiences elsewhere.

Slide, Anthony (1992) *Before Video. A History of the Non-Theatrical Film.* Westport, CT: Greenwood Press.

> As the title implies, Anthony Slide's book is a chronicle of the utility-film industry. In the author's definition, there are two main categories for "non-theatrical films" before the introduction of video technology: 1) short films and presentations, shot on 35mm and not shown in regular cinemas; 2) films that were shot for utilitarian purposes, for example, training, and 3) those financed by the industry, especially industrial films. The sources for Slide's inquiry were all issues of the trade journals *Educational Screen, Business Screen, Film News, Sightlines,* and *Film Library Quarterly.* The historical overview of utility film in the US begins with the first forays into film in the late 19th century and ends with the arrival of video in the 1980s. Slide is mainly concerned with the early years, from 1900 to 1950. He cites several film producers, highlights their networks and cooperation and identifies Chicago as the center of the industry. An industry "with its own trade papers, its own trade organizations, and even its own award ceremonies" (p. 6). Furthermore, the author lists a number of archives,

film festivals, and other institutions associated with industrial film. At the end of the book, Slide provides a brief introduction to the state of industrial-film research in the US. The publication contains an appendix listing the largest utility-film distributors in the 1920s, 1930s, and 1940s, as well as several valuable addresses for further research.

Smith, Ken (1999): *Mental Hygiene, Classroom Films 1945-1970*. New York: Blast Books.

While working at the US Comedy Channel looking for funny material for the show, Ken Smith came across the *Mental Hygiene Films* in Rick Prelinger's archives. Smith decided to examine these films to see whether they influence the consciousness of their viewers. In his book, Smith shows that the *Mental Hygiene* films were produced as a kind of preventive medicine. Young people were to be shown the way into society by internalizing the dogmatic rules of adult society. Smith demonstrates that *Mental Hygiene* films were typical of the social climate of the 1950s in the US and that they were directly influenced by the aftermath of World War II. The middle section of the book is concerned with various related genres and he cites examples for each case from the Prelinger Archives. Moreover, Smith also describes the working practices of various producers and institutions. The largest part of the book consists of a long list of 285 *Mental Hygiene* film with brief descriptions of their content and information on producer, year, and length.

Solbrig, Heide (2004) *Film and Function: A History of Industrial Motivation Film*. Dissertation. University of California at San Diego.

Heide Solbrig's dissertation concerns the history of motivation films from the 1920s to the 1980s, combining approaches from the history of communications as well as those from film studies and sociology. The author therefore seeks to examine not only the development of the role of the motivation films, but also to uncover the different discourses and schools of thought behind the films. Solbrig places a great deal of importance on the role of instruction films in the creation of the contemporary media network. After presenting the basic concepts important to her work, Solbrig then describes the history of industrial-film production and research in the 1920s and 1930s, in which the Visual Education Movement laid the foundations for later development in the utility film. She demonstrates how, in the 1950s, the early "How to do" instructional films became increasingly "How to be" films. To illustrate the setting and scope of industrial film, Solbrig, on the one hand, uncovers the connections between industrial-film production and the big Hollywood studios, and, on the other, shows how the industrial-film industry gradually established itself. Solbrig clarifies how, little by little, a mix of current events, reality, and narration became typical for the industrial film and how individual genres were formed out of this.

Spooner, Peter (1959) *Business Films: How to Make and Use Them.* London: Batsford.

> The author of this manual set out to clear up some of the misunderstandings about industrial film production and clarify both the relations of production and the use of the films. Spooner points out that industrial film is by no means limited to public-image and advertising films. He also shows that producing industrial films need not always be relegated to professionals, that even smaller companies can have their own film-production units. Spooner provides information for companies wanting to produce their own films about the materials needed as well as the costs. In addition to instructions on equipment, production, and post-production, the book contains a great deal of information on distribution paths and possibilities.

Stork, Leopold (1962) *Industrial and Business Films: A Modern Means of Communication.* London: Phoenix House.

> The author aims to give those responsible in industry an idea of how film as a media can be introduced into business life and industrial production. The book targets both management and PR and marketing personnel. The manual is divided into three parts: In the first part, Stork cites the reasons that film can be seen as a means of communication; in the second part, there are practical instructions on film production; while in the third part, he offers help in the economic planning of a production. Along with a list of addresses of trade journals and production companies, the book also contains photos of industrial-film sets and an extensive glossary.

Tedlow, Richard S. (1979) *Keeping the Corporate Image: Public Relations and Business, 1900-1950.* Greenwich, CT: Jai Press Inc.

> The initial thesis of Tedlow's work is the assumption that contemporary society – especially American society – is determined by the art of selling. The author takes up the topic of corporate public relations in particular, which he sees as one of the basic principles of the economic wellbeing of America. He argues that the existence of a politically free public sphere is the basis for business publicity that works, and this liberal foundation has more tradition in the US than any other country. He traces a line from Benjamin Franklin by way of John Adams to modern managers. According to Tedlow, businessmen, like politicians, must also generate trust and faith to convince the public. From this perspective, the selling of products through public relations is a purely democratic process. Tedlow values the question of whether industry produces its own public image democratically or manipulatively, but he does not offer a definitive answer to this question.

La télévision face au travail. Sous la direction de Gérard Leblanc et Catherine Pozzo di Borgo. *Dossiers de l'audiovisuel*, 84, March/April 1999.

> Depsite the fact that work is one of the central aspects of human life, it is relatively underrepresented on television. Television's timidity, in this respect, seems to be based on, among other things, the traditional separation of work and leisure. For this

reason, work is mainly seen on television in the context of daily events. The authors of this issue take this conclusion as their starting point and call for a new level of consciousness concerning television's task of social education. Making sense of modern life is one of television's responsibilities. The starting point of the work is therefore the idea of television as a social agent. Industrial film is not addressed directly.

Thomas, Ann (ed.) (1997) *Beauty of Another Order: Photograph in Science*. New Haven and London: Yale University Press.

The essays in this volume trace the interwoven influences of photography with scientific goals and aesthetic expression. The five authors take up works from such varied photographers as Mandé Daguerre, William Henry, Fox Talbot, and Edward Muybridge. The volume provides a historical overview of the contexts and discourses of art and science in order to be able to understand the current aesthetic practices of photographers as a resulting phenomenon. The authors look at the history of these photographic works and their predecessors, their technical origins, and pose questions regarding form and manner of representation.

Tresckow, Wilfried von (ed.) (1978) *Film im Auftrag: Industrie-Informations-Wirtschaftsfilm. Ein Wegweiser für alle, die mit einem der wirksamsten Kommunikationsmedien arbeiten wollen*. Stuttgart: Kodak.

Thirty-five essays explain the advantages of film as an advertising tool, covering costs and distribution. The book is conceived as a as a reference work and guide for business and film commissioners. It attempts to explain the business film to commissioners in business, defining it and its technology, evaluating its innovation and functionality, but also distinguishing it form older forms like the newsreel. Sponsored by Kodak, this volume is a kind of advertisement for business advertising itself. At the same time, the practical reports contained in the book provide information in the form of a historical document about the relations between businesses and film production. Includes a glossary for non-professional readers and various templates and formulas, plus a list of addresses.

Tucker, Charles Lee (1989) *Industrial and Technical Photography*. Englewood Cliffs, New Jersey: Prentice-Hall.

Charles L. Tucker based this guidebook on his ten years of teaching experience in the area of industrial photography. According to Tucker, such a guidebook was needed because of the boom and demand for industrial photography in the 1990s, along with the appearance of many technical innovations. The 16 chapters cover the basic areas of industrial photography such as architectural and factory photography, aerial photography and product advertising. In each case, Tucker provides an introduction and further explanation of the uses and the necessary technical equipment. In the last chapter, he turns to creativity and artistic form to fulfill the promise of the book's opening statement: "Photography! It is both science and art."

Wehlau, Kurt (1938) *Das Lichtbild in der Werbung für Politik, Kultur und Wirtschaft. Seine geschichtliche und gegenwärtige Bedeutung. Inauguraldissertation zur Erlangung der Doktorwürde der Philosophischen Fakultät, 1. Sektion der Ludwig-Maximilians-Universität zu München.* Würzburg: Konrad Triltsch.

> An interesting source, especially regarding the history of photography, which presents a history of the photographic media that have been used internationally for "propaganda" purposes in both political and business and product advertising. The author treats the "photograph in business advertisement" (pp. 125-155), by which he basically means product advertising, for instance, in the automobile industry.

Westbrock, Ingrid (1983) *Der Werbefilm. Ein Beitrag zur Entwicklungsgeschichte des Genres vom Stummfilm zum frühen Ton- und Farbfilm.* Hildesheim, Zurich and New York: Olms (= Studien zur Filmgeschichte; 1).

> A study of the history of German advertising from around 1900 to the end of the 1930s, concentrating on technical and aesthetic innovation. The advertising film as "genre" is the central focus: its production techniques, pioneers, its new means of expression, the specifics of the conditions of production, the relationships between commission and avant-garde. The authors explicitly distinguish their subject from industrial film. (pp. 7-9).

Wiatr, Elizabeth (2002) "Between Word, Image, and the Machine: visual education and films of industrial process." *Historical Journal of Film, Radio and Television*, 22, 3, pp. 333-351.

> The subject of this article is the training and industrial films of the late 1910s and 1920s and the discourse associated with them, which posited the advantages of film as a medium to convey information. The historical materials for Wiatr's examination are trade journals and books like the *Educational Film Magazine* and selected films. The author shows how the hope of making knowledge comprehensible through visualization was closely related to the modernization and regulation of general perception patterns. In the end, Wiatr hypothesizes that, through this change in visual perception, the path was paved for the abstract visual propaganda of the 1930s.

Williams, Jon M. and Muir, Daniel T. (1984) *Corporate Images: Photography and the Du Pont Company. 1865-1972.* Wilmington, Delaware: Hagley Museum and Library.

> In this slim volume, Williams and Muir tell the history of the photographic archive at the DuPont Company, which is housed in the Hagley Museum in Delaware. The DuPont Company is today one of the largest chemical concerns in the world and has become famous for, among other things, the invention of nylon and Teflon. The firm was founded in 1802 in Wilmington, Delaware. The amount of visual documentation, beginning in the very first days, has been extensive. The company's entire history has been extensively recorded, in drawings and paintings at first, then, after 1865, in photographs. The Hagley Museum houses these images in the buildings of the origi-

nal DuPont factory and published this volume as a guide to its collection. There is some basic documentation of the very first years up to the public image photos that were produced later for the company's own magazines *DuPont Magazine* and *Better Living*. The authors draw particular attention to the notably artistic form of many of the pictures. The more than 80,000 photos in the Hagley Museum collection are archived at various locations, a selection of which are presented at the end of the book.

Willsher, Adrian Alexander (1996) *"Where Are the Roads?" The Tourist and Industrial Promotion Films of the Nova Scotian Film Bureau, 1945-1970.* Dissertation. Dalhousie University, Halifax, Canada.

This thesis examines the tourist and industrial films produced by the Nova Scotia film bureau from 1945 until 1970. About half of the films were short tourist promotions, examining Nova Scotia's history, culture, and recreation. The industrial-promotion films were produced for various provincial government departments, usually Lands and Forests or Agriculture and Marketing. This thesis asserts that the films were usually able to adhere to the basic political goals established by the government, but that the nature of films, in this case the integration of dissimilar themes, frequently meant that unintended messages and values were conveyed.

Wolf-Czapek, K.W. (1911) *Die Kinematographie. Wesen, Entstehung und Ziele des lebenden Bildes.* Berlin: Union Deutsche Verlagsgesellschaft.

According to its objective, which is primarily the "practical exercise of cinematography", this volume is divided into explanations on film recording, copying, and screening. The chapter on "Uses of the Living Image" (pp. 110-135) is particularly interesting, covering the areas of technology, training, and promotion.

Yates, Jo Anne and Van Maanen, John (ed.) (2001) *Information Technology and Organizational Transformation: History, Rhetoric and Practice.* Thousand Oaks, CA: Sage Publications.

The main interest of the collection deals with the interplay of information technologies and social processes in larger organizational structures. The term information technologies here means those mechanisms used for organizing, storing, reworking, representing, conveying, and calling up information. The term therefore covers not only modern computer technologies, but is also extended to refer to various means of human communication. The essays in the book take up the idea that social structures, communication practices, systems of meaning, and information technologies are intimately interconnected and that sensitivity to their connections has so far been lacking. The first part of the book pursues the question of historical connections. The essays in the second part contain analyses of rhetoric and organizational transformations. The last part deals with the practices that arose in response to new information technologies.

Ziegler, Reiner (2003) *Kunst und Architektur im Kulturfilm 1919-1945*. Konstanz: UVK (= Close Up; 17).

> This volume is concerned with the reception of the *Kulturfilm* through Nazi propaganda, and shows, through a comparison with films from the Weimar Republic and the example of architecture, how films changed in both content and form. Ziegler concretely examines filmed construction projects and building planning in the cultural film sector after 1933, including the films about the Autobahn (pp. 188-226). Extensive appendix with biographies and filmographies.

Zimmermann, Peter and Hoffmann, Kay (ed.) (2003) *Triumph der Bilder. Kultur- und Dokumentarfilme vor 1945 im internationalen Vergleich*. Konstanz: UVK (= Close Up; 16).

> As a supplement to the three-volume history of documentary film (2005), this collection focuses on the *Kulturfilm*. It brings together essays in both German and English on subjects such as Walter Ruttmann's industrial films (Heinz B. Heller, pp. 105-120) and on industrial-compilation films from Sweden (Pelle Snickars, Mats Björkin, pp. 272-290). Includes an index of persons and films.

Zipfel, Astrid (1997) *Public Relations in der Elektroindustrie. Die Firmen Siemens und AEG 1847 bis 1939*. Cologne, Weimar and Vienna: Böhlau Verlag (= Public Relations; 3).

> This book contributes to historical PR research. The author seeks to clarify the details of PR in Germany prior to World War II, arguing against the prevailing notion that PR only emerged after the war and was then based on American models. The book is interesting not only because it treats Friedrich Mörtzsch as a key figure in the German industrial film movement at AEG, but also because AEG already had its own film department as early as 1917. Extensive appendix with data on the history of the company, including short biographies, documents on PR work at Siemens and AEG, a list of sources and literature, and an index of persons and topics.

Notes

1. Cf. for instance for Germany Jeanpaul Goergen's concise overview of industrial and advertising film in *Geschichte des dokumentarischen Films in Deutschland* (vol. 2, p. 33-37).
2. One exception is the Swiss project "Ansichten und Einstellungen: zur Geschichte des dokumentarischen Films in der Schweiz 1896-1964" at the Seminar für Filmwissenschaft at Zurich University, where Yvonne Zimmermann, Pierre-Emmanuel Jaques and Anita Gertiser have all examined central issues in industrial film.

3. Cf. Hans Jürgen Wulff (ed.), *Bibliographie der Filmbibliographien* (Munich, New York and London: K.G. Saur, 1987) as well as Malte Hagener, Michael Töteberg, *Film – An International Bibliography* (Stuttgart and Weimar: J.B. Metzler, 2002).

4. Cf. Hans Traub, Hanns Wilhelm Lavies (eds.), *Das deutsche Filmschrifttum. Eine Bibliographie der Bücher und Zeitschriften über das Filmwesen* (Leipzig: Karl W. Hiersemann, 1940). The authors of this otherwise very comprehensive bibliography do not differentiate between industrial and advertising film and furthermore conceive of advertising film as a subgroup of the 'Kulturfilm', which is primarily equated with the literature on training and educational film.

5. Cf. for example Ephraim Katz, *The Film Encyclopedia*, 5th edition (New York: Collins, 2005) or *Dictionnaire théorique et critique du cinéma* by Jaques Aumont and Michel Marie (Paris: Nathan, 2001), which is aimed at an entirely different audience, or finally even *Metzler Lexikon Medientheorie Medienwissenschaft. Ansätze-Personen-Grundbegriffe* (Helmut Schanze (ed.), Stuttgart and Weimar: Metzler, 2002).

6. *The Film Studies Dictionary* (Steve Blandford, Barry Keith Grant and Jim Hillier (eds.), London: Arnold, 2001) describes industrial film as "a form of documentary made to provide information about a company or industry. Often sponsored by the company that is its subject, they may be promotional films designed to sell or promote the company or industry, or may be intended as in-house training for employees" (p. 132). Cf. Thomas Koebner (ed.), *Reclams Sachlexikon des Films* (Stuttgart: Philipp Reclam jun., 2002), p. 271-272.

7. Cf. among others Mauriche Bardèche, Robert Brasillach, *Histoire du Cinéma*, 2 volumes (Paris: André Martel, 1953/54); Gerald Mast, *A Short History of the Movies*, 2nd edition (Indianapolis: Bobbs-Merrill, 1976); John L. Fell, *A History of Films* (New York: Holt, Rinehart and Winston, 1979); Jean Mitry, *Histoire du cinéma. Art et Industrie*, vol 4., 1930-1940 (Paris: Jean-Pierre Delarge, 1980); Douglas Gomery, *Movie History: A Survey* (Belmont, CA: Wadsworth Publishing, 1991); Jerzy Toeplitz, *Geschichte des Films. Achter Teil 1945-1953* (Berlin: Henschel, 1991); Geoffrey Nowell-Smith (ed.), *The Oxford History of World Cinema* (Oxford: Oxford University Press, 1996); David Bordwell and Kristin Thompson, *Film History: An Introduction* (New York: McGraw-Hill, 2002).

8. German examples of such thematically relevant texts that fall outside the field of media studies include Olaf Breidbach, *Bilder des Wissens. Zur Kulturgeschichte der wissenschaftlichen Wahrnehmung* (Munich: Fink, 2005) or Klaus Türk (ed.), *Bilder der Arbeit. Eine ikonographische Anthologie* (Wiesbaden: Westdeutscher Verlag, 2000).

The Desiderata of Business-Film Research[1]

Ralf Stremmel

"There is an answer to every question about German film..." In 2004, visitors to the central Internet access page of German film, filmportal.de, were welcomed with this phrase. To every question? Well, in *one* area of film research at least – that of business-film research – there were and are more questions than answers. In the following paper, I will limit myself to the situation in Germany, using films from the Krupp Historical Archives as concrete examples.

The questions begin at the most basic level, that is, with the very term business or industrial film. If we look at the approximately 450 film titles in the Krupp Historical Archives, we immediately encounter difficulties in definition, and the question of which categorical designations should be used. The archive contains the oldest film sequence from the Ruhr, a short scene showing Kaiser Wilhelm II in the funeral procession for Friedrich Alfred Krupp in 1902. But aside from the fact that this piece is contained in a later business film, can it really be called an industrial film? And what about a film shot by Arndt von Bohlen while on a business trip with his father, Alfried Krupp von Bohlen und Halbach, in Japan?

The first research desideratum is therefore to establish the very object of research. No generally accepted definition has yet been established in the literature. The term "industrial film" is controversial; some prefer the more general term "business film," and I think with good reason, since it makes sense for research to take economic areas outside industry into consideration, that is, the areas of raw materials, the agrarian economy, trade, commerce, service industry, and banking. Films have been produced in these areas as well, and they can and should be examined using the same methods and questions used for films made by industry.

Whether they are business films or industrial films, the term is only of analytical, heuristic value if it can be precisely and therefore narrowly contained. In my view, two criteria must come together: Business films are films that – firstly – are commissioned or greatly influenced by businesses or business associations and that – secondly – deal with the world of business, that is, companies and associations, their business connections and products. A travel film like the one mentioned above does not fall within this definition. A movie about Alfred Krupp planned by Tobis, to be produced in connection with Fried. Krupp AG and starring Emil Jannings, would not be a business film either.

Anyone wanting to name the concrete desiderata of business-film research easily runs the risk of making sweeping, even boundless statements. I will concentrate on four core areas, each of which I would like to collect under a pair of terms: *1. overview and availability, 2. motivations and creators, 3. histories and forms, 4. resonance and reception.*

Overview and availability

Anyone who researches, interprets, and, if possible, also applies theoretical rigor to business films needs a sound basis, namely an overview, along with a consideration of their availability. Concretely, which business films have been produced and where are they held today? Wide-ranging projects to produce such a catalog obviously exist, especially online at filmportal.de, a cooperative effort of Cinegraph (Hamburg) and the Deutscher Filminstitut (Frankfurt am Main). As worthy as this approach is, it does concentrate on the area of fiction film.

There are indeed numerous titles from the area of business listed, but the level of completeness remains unclear and only rarely does one find further information, for example on sources or literature on business films, especially about whether they are kept anywhere or are even available. Contextual information is even lacking on the multiple prize-winning Mannesmann film by Walther Ruttmann from the 1930s. And the project by the Haus des Dokumentarfilms (Stuttgart), funded by the DFG, has not led to a complete documentation of business film. In the three-volume *Geschichte des dokumentarischen Films* (2005) business film plays a subordinate role, and the authors limit themselves to the analysis of individual examples, without thematizing whether or not they can be taken as representative.

So far, the starting position even for individual commissioning bodies has been rather desolate. Not even for Krupp, which maintained a cinema department, i.e., its own central production office, between 1913 and 1945, is there a complete overview of the films produced and their physical fate. The only information on certain films occasionally mentioned in the research – for instance, BLECHWALZWERK (1916) or VOM ERZ ZUM EISEN (1917) – is the title and a short summary. In the case of other films, we are not even aware of the fact that we do not know anything about them. I fear that the situation is similar at Siemens, AEG, BASF, Bayer, Thyssen, Mannessmann, and other companies.

There is no lack of places to start on an overview and assessment of availability. We could point to contemporary newspapers – both film and business papers – official registration lists, inventory overviews, and catalogs from archives, although the latter were only rarely published. An exception is the recently published book *Industrial Film 1948-1959*,[2] which provides a survey full of information on 1950s business films in the Ruhr. Other publications like *Filmschätzen auf der Spur* (1997) do not concretely address individual titles.

On the basis of such catalogs one could get significantly closer to a typology of the business film and could even make efforts toward periodization. Concretely: When was the boom in business film, and when did it fall into crisis?

Motivations and creators

Borrowing from communications theory, one could say that the research on business film has to go beyond pure information, i.e., the film, but must turn to the "transmitters" and the "receivers." Regarding the film's creators and commissioning bodies in particular, there seems to be a pronounced need for research. Biographical reference works on directors, camera operators, film composers, etc. are lacking; interviews and memoirs of contemporaries are extremely rare, and only the (film) biographies of important individual business-film pioneers like Oskar Messter and Walther Ruttman are dealt with in the research. The mass of "nameless" producers has not been given any notice at all. In the previously mentioned book, *Industrial Film 1948-1959*,[3] Manfred Rasch tried to put together a great deal of individual biographical information. Such efforts must be taken up by the research so that they can ultimately result in collective biographical assertions.

Furthermore, it would be particularly interesting to trace the constellation of materials and ideal interests of the creators, or uncover the conflicts between financial and artistic aspects. Many motivations for producing business films come to mind: conveying a generally positive image of the business; representing the branch as particularly effective, solid, and/or innovative, conscious of tradition, and/or future oriented; recruiting employees; supporting the sales of particular products, or even evoking emotions by mythologizing.

Many of those files that could offer precise information on the motives and interests of the commissioning bodies have not survived. The papers at Krupp's cinema department were lost in World War II, and there is an equal lack of information on the strategic motivations of the company's management and the department responsible for advertising prior to 1950. The situation involving the actual producers is similar: all too little proper documentation or "archives" of production companies are known. For example, it is not known what happened to the files of the Hamburg company Porta-Film, which produced numerous business films for Krupp and other industrial businesses under the direction of Herbert Obscherningkat between the 1950s and 1980s.

It remains a rare stroke of luck when files containing the correspondence be-tween commissioning body and producer, which indicate deliberations and changing plans, survive. The Krupp short film TECHNIK – DREI STUDIEN IN JAZZ (1961) can, for example, be reconstructed, and the same goes for the Thyssen film NUR DER NEBEL IST GRAU (1965). Both movies make it clear, by the way, how much can be gleaned through conventional social-science research on the creators and motives of cultural-historical findings, that is, about mechanisms of experience and perception typical of the time.

Histories and forms

In this rubric the desiderata is the analysis of the contents and forms of business films, or, put more simply: what is shown and how is it shown? Very simple questions still remain unanswered: what was the first sound business film, what was the first color business film? Research must advance beyond such facts and beyond the pure narrative into the analytical, and must turn to the causes of the established events. This would provoke a particularly significant *comparative* perspective.

Business-film research has so far concentrated all too often on a few indivi-dual films, without clarifying whether these films are typical or whether they represent exceptions. Comparisons should not only be made of films from indi-vidual business sectors, but also of business films on the one hand and enter-tainment/fiction films on the other. This could result in statements about whether and at what periods the business film was especially innovative or backward in the context of wider film history, whether there was any interplay between business films and fiction films and why. Was the film made for the 125th anniversary of the Krupp factories, PIONIERE DER DEUTSCHEN TECHNIK from 1935, groundbreaking because of its animated sequences, fictional scenes, or use of music? Did it display or incorporate an artistic impulse? Only by com-paring it with other business films of the time and the development of fiction film – one thinks of names like Leni Riefenstahl – can these questions be an-swered.

It is therefore obvious that the form – that is, image (color), sound and music, camera movement, use of fictional scenes and animated techniques – should be taken into account as much as the contents, and that this can be analyzed with an extremely wide variety of methods and questions, such as social, technical, cultural, etc. Recently there has been a good deal of research on "histories and forms," but serious gaps still remain. Much more serious, however, are the desiderata in the last complex, circumscribed here under the heading "resonance and reception."

Resonance and reception

Here as well there are initially quite tangible, even quantitative data that research should cover: where were business films shown in the first place? Who were the addressees, the target groups, and how did they react? In which festivals were German business films represented and what kinds of success did they enjoy there?

A concrete example of such an analysis of reception and effect: did the accident-prevention film DER UNBEKANNTE ("The Unknown"), produced by Krupp's film department in 1940, actually increase workplace safety and decrease the number of accidents? The answers to such questions are undoubtedly difficult to determine, since a direct correlation between cause and effect is hardly possible, meaning that changes are always based on many causes and cannot be traced back to a single factor or event. Nonetheless, at the very least an effort must be made to find answers.

Finally, interactions of another kind would be of interest, namely those between the artistic claims of a film and its practical uses. Did the audience value artistic genius and aesthetic power in business films, or did these special target groups for business films contribute precisely to rather conventional uses of the image?

So far, the sources of information concerning resonance and reception have hardly been taken up in the research at all. Memoirs, letters, or other expressions of the spectators' opinions are rare; it is much easier to find reports in the press, files from film festivals, documents from governmental film review boards, and so on. Systematic research of such sources, however, let alone their evaluations, are unknown to me.

Conclusion

It is clear from the roughly sketched desiderata here what kinds of problems business-film research faces, and the fact that business-film researchers require multi-disciplinary skills: the media historian who only takes up the aesthetics of the film language comes up as short as the technical historian who limits him or herself to the working processes and functioning methods of machines, thereby running the risk of taking what is presented as reality. The films never speak for themselves. That is perhaps a banality, but it has consequences for research that should not be underestimated. It remains a matter for the non-cinematic, and above all written and photographic sources.

In 1997, the reader of a standard work would come across the formulation that the history of German industrial film must still be written.[4] This statement is still true today, although the foundational research has made certain advances, even if the gap between well-researched objects and less well-researched ones has grown. Research on business films dealing with the Ruhr and the coal and steel industries have advanced the furthest. It is to be hoped that research will soon take up other regions and branches, indeed with a comparative perspective.

Selected bibliography (chronological)

Der deutsche Wirtschaftsfilm, ed. Deutsches Industrieinstitut, Cologne, 1959 (catalog of business films of the period).

Der deutsche Industriefilm, ed. Deutsches Industrieinstitut, Cologne, 1960-1992 (annual catalog of business films of the period).

Friedrich Mörtzsch. *Die Industrie auf Zelluloid. Filme für die Wirtschaft*, Düsseldorf, 1959 (report by someone involved in film production).

Klaus Brepohl. *Der Deutsche Industriefilm. Eine Analyse*, Cologne, 1966 (on the history of the business film which reflects the rather insufficient state of research at the time).

Roland Günter, Paul Hofmann, and Janne Günter. *Das Ruhrgebiet im Film*, 2 vols., Oberhausen, 1978 (first groundbreaking attempt at a sociologically inspired regional film history).

Martin Loiperdinger (ed.). *Oskar Messter – Filmpionier der Kaiserzeit*, Basel and Frankfurt am Main, 1994 (exemplary approach to the biography of a business-film pioneer).

Filmschätzen auf der Spur. Verzeichnis historischer Filmbestände in Nordrhein-Westfalen. 2nd expanded edition, edited by Paul Hofmann, Düsseldorf, 1997 (inventory with reports on availability at numerous archives).

Manfred Rasch, Karl-Peter Ellerbrock, Renate Köhne-Lindenlaub, and Horst A. Wessel (eds.). *Industriefilm – Medium und Quelle. Beispiele aus der Eisen- und Stahlindustrie*. Rev. by Manfred Rasch, Essen, 1997 (contains overviews of the history of industrial film and availability at various business archives of the Ruhr, in addition to comprehensive individual analyses of 16 business films).

Hans Schaller. *Der Industriefilm schrieb Geschichte. 1895-1995. 100 Jahre Industrie- und Wirtschaftsfilm. Eine Chronik*, Dortmund, 1997 (eyewitness reports rather than a comprehensive academic presentation).

Manfred Rasch et al. (ed.). *Industriefilm 1948-1959. Filme aus Wirtschaftsarchiven im Ruhrgebiet*. Rev. by Silke Heimsoth, Essen, 2003 (inventory with thorough descriptions of the films).

Peter Zimmermann, Kay Hoffmann (eds.). *Triumph der Bilder. Kultur- und Dokumentarfilme vor 1945 im internationalen Vergleich*, Stuttgart, 2003 (overview of the development in individual regions, without concentrating on business film).

Ferrum. Nachrichten aus der Eisenbibliothek, Georg Fischer AG Foundation, no. 76, 2004 (contains contribution to the conference Das Unternehmen im Bild – das Bild vom Unternehmen. Zum Industriefilm der Eisen- und Stahlindustrie).

Peter Zimmermann et.al. (eds.). *Geschichte des dokumentarischen Films in Deutschland*, 3 vols., Stuttgart 2005.

Notes

1. This is a revised version of a short lecture given at the international conference *Filme, die arbeiten* (*Films that Work*) in Bochum on December 9, 2004. The spoken style of a lecture has been retained.
2. Manfred Rasch et al., ed., *Industriefilm 1948-1959. Filme aus Wirtschaftsarchiven im Ruhrgebiet*, rev. by Silke Heimsoth (Essen: Klartext, 2003) (inventory with thorough descriptions of the films).
3. Ibid.
4. Manfred Rasch, Karl-Peter Ellerbrock, Renate Köhne-Lindenlaub, Horst A. Wessel (eds.), *Industriefilm – Medium und Quelle. Beispiele aus der Eisen- und Stahlindustrie*, rev. by Manfred Rasch (Essen: Klartext, 1997), p. 9.

Contributors

Mats Björkin holds a Ph.D. from the University of Stockholm and is senior lecturer in film studies in the Department of Culture, Aesthetics and Media at the University of Gothenburg. He is also co-founder of the University of Gothenburg Television Studies Centre. His main research interests concern the economic and organizational aspects of television as well as practice-based research in audiovisual media. He is currently finishing a project on audiovisual media and corporate communication in Sweden during the 1950s.

Rudmer Canjels received his Ph.D. at Utrecht University for a study on the international distribution and cultural transformations of silent film serials, and he has published various articles on silent-film serials and seriality. He has also collaborated on the production of several documentaries for *A History of Royal Dutch Shell* (Oxford University Press, 2007) and done extensive research on Shell and other industry-sponsored films. He is currently a lecturer in Comparative Art Studies at Vrij Universiteit Amsterdam.

Scott Curtis is associate professor of Radio/Television/Film at Northwestern University. He has published on a wide range of topics, including animation, medical imaging, and early cinema. He is primarily interested in cinema and modernity at the turn of the century, and his current projects are *Managing Modernity: Art, Science, and Early Cinema in Germany* and a history of scientific and medical cinema.

Thomas Elsaesser is professor in the Department of Media and Culture and director of Research Film and Television at the University of Amsterdam. His most recent books as (co-)editor include: *Cinema Futures: Cain, Abel or Cable?* (1998), *The BFI Companion to German Cinema* (1999), *The Last Great American Picture Show* (2004) and *Harun Farocki – Working on the Sightlines* (2004). His books as author include *Fassbinder's Germany: History, Identity, Subject* (1996), *Weimar Cinema and After* (2000), *Metropolis* (2000), *Studying Contemporary American Film* (2002, with Warren Buckland), *Filmgeschichte und Frühes Kino* (2002), *European Cinema: Face to Face with Hollywood* (2005), *Terror und Trauma* (2007), and *Filmtheorie zur Einführung* (2007, with Malte Hagener).

Nicolas Hatzfeld is Maître de conférences en histoire at the University of Evry, Laboratoire LHEST. His publications include *Les gens d'usine. Peugeot-Sochaux, 50 ans d'histoire* (Paris, 2002). His research areas include the history of labor, the history of car factories, the history of labor institutions and unions, as well as the cinematic representation of labor.

Vinzenz Hediger is the Alfried Krupp von Bohlen und Halbach Foundation professor for the history and theory of documentary forms at Ruhr University, Bochum. His publications include *Nostalgia for the Coming Attraction: American Movie Trailers and the Culture of Film Consumption* (forthcoming).

Anna Eva Heymer received a master of arts in Media Studies at the Ruhr University of Bochum and is a Ph.D. candidate in Media Studies. She is presently working on a dissertation entitled *Creative Output in Television Industries: Terms, Patterns, and Practices.*

Frank Kessler is professor and chair of Film and Television History at Utrecht University. His research focuses on early cinema, in particular early non-fiction films, and the genre of *féerie*. Together with Nanna Verhoeff he co-edited *Networks of Entertainment: Early Film Distribution 1895-1915* (2007). He is a co-founder and co-editor of *KINtop. Jahrbuch zur Erforschung des frühen Films* and the *KINtop-Schriften* series.

Gérard Leblanc is professor at the École nationale supérieure Louis-Lumière in Paris, France. A specialist in film history, his publications include a monograph on industrial films, *Quand l'entreprise fait son cinéma* (Paris, 1983) as well as books on documentary film and major directors, such as *Scénarios du réel* (2 volumes, Paris, 1997), *Le double scénario chez Fritz Lang* (with Brigitte Devismes, Paris, 1991), *Georges Franju, une esthétique de la déstabilisation* (Paris 1992) and, most recently, *Presque une conception du monde* (Paris, 2007).

Martin Loiperdinger is professor of Media Studies at the University of Trier, Germany. From 1993 to 1997, he was deputy director of DIF, the German Film Institute, in Frankfurt. He has made several television features and exhibitions on film history and has published widely on early cinema and Nazi film propaganda. His publications include *KINtop*, the German yearbook of early film (as co-editor), *Film & Schokolade* (1999), on the beginnings of German film business in the 1890s, *Celluloid Goes Digital: Historical-Critical Editions of Films on DVD and the Internet* (ed., 2003), *Geschichte des dokumentarischen Films in Deutschland 1895-1918* (ed. with Uli Jung, 2005), and *Travelling Cinema in Europe* (ed., 2008).

Eef Masson teaches at the department of Media and Culture Studies at Utrecht University. Meanwhile, she is finishing her PhD. She has published articles on non-fiction film and archival issues, among others, in journals such as *The Moving Image*, *Montage AV*, and *Film History*.

Alain P. Michel is Maître de conférences en histoire, Université d'Evry, Laboratoire LHEST. His publications include *Travail à la chaîne, Renault, 1898-1947* (Boulogne, 2007). Among his research areas are the history of technical industries, the history of images and representations of work.

Stefan Moitra is Marie Curie Fellow at the University College London. He works on the history of the labor movement and the social history of cinema. He is currently completing a Ph.D. project on working-class culture and cinema in Britain and West Germany after 1945. His publications (as co-editor) include *Stimmt die Chemie? Mitbestimmung und Sozialpolitik in der Geschichte des Bayer-Konzerns* (Essen, 2007).

Floris Paalman is a Ph.D. candidate at the Department of Media Studies at the Universiteit van Amsterdam. He has a background in cultural anthropology and filmmaking, and is currently finishing his dissertation on film, architecture, and urbanism in Rotterdam (1920s-1970s). He has published various articles in these fields. At present, he is the curator of the *Rotterdam Classics* film program (Gemeentearchief Rotterdam, Lantaren/Venster).

Rick Prelinger (http://www.prelinger.com) is an archivist, writer, and filmmaker. He founded the Prelinger Archives in 1982. With the Voyager Company, he produced 14 laserdiscs and CD-ROMs with material from his archives, including *Ephemeral Films*, the *Our Secret Century* series and *Call It Home: The House That Private Enterprise Built* (co-produced with Keller Easterling). He has taught in the MFA Design program at New York's School of Visual Arts and lectured widely on American cultural and social history and issues of cultural and intellectual-property access.

Ramón Reichert is assistant professor at the Department for Media/Media Theories at the University of Arts Linz and has been lecturing and researching at many other institutions both in Austria and abroad. His research interests include the historiography of media and technology, the impact of new media and communication technologies such as the Internet, film history and film analysis, history of science, and identity politics. His many publications include *Im Kino der Humanwissenschaften. Studien zur Medialisierung wissenschaftlichen Wis-*

sens (2007), *Effizienzfieber. Zur Rationalisierung der Alltagskultur* (1998), and *Schöne neue Arbeit. Ästhetik, Politische Ökonomie und Kino* (2000).

Faye E. Riley is instructor in the Media Arts program at the University of South Carolina. She is a guest co-editor for the 2009 theme issue of the *Journal of Popular Film and Television* "Orphans No More: Ephemeral Films and American Culture." She currently creates documentary and experimental film shorts.

Gwenaële Rot is Maître de conférences en sociologie, Université de Paris X Nanterre, Laboratoire IDHE CNRS. Her publications include *Sociologie de l'atelier, Renault, le travail ouvrier et le sociologue* (2006). Her main research areas are the sociology of labor and the history of sociology.

Heide Solbrig is assistant professor of Media and Culture at the English Department at Bentley College in Boston and is an internal fellow of The Valente Center for the Arts & Sciences. She writes about the history of industrial management film and video training and is currently working on a documentary about Henry Strauss, a preeminent industrial film producer from 1950 to 1970. She is also editing "Orphans No More: Ephemeral Films and American Culture," a special issue of the *Journal of Popular Film and Television*, along with Elizabeth Hefflefinger, scheduled for publication in 2009.

Ralf Stremmel is professor and head of the Krupp Historical Archive at the Alfried Krupp von Bohlen und Halbach-Stiftung in Essen. His research area is the social and economic history of the 19th and 20th centuries. His many publications include *Modell und Moloch. Berlin in der Wahrnehmung deutscher Politiker vom Ende des 19. Jahrhunderts bis zum Zweiten Weltkrieg* (1992) and *100 Jahre Historisches Archiv Krupp. Entwicklungen, Aufgaben, Bestände* (Munich and Berlin, 2005).

Bjørn Sørenssen is professor of Film and Media at the Department of Art and Media Studies, the Norwegian University of Science and Technology (NTNU) in Trondheim. His main research interests focus on documentary film and new media technology. He has published on these and other film-related subjects in numerous international journals and anthologies. He has also published books in Norwegian, most recently *Å fange virkeligheten. Dokumentarfilmens århundre* (*Catching Reality: A Century of Commentary*, 2nd edition, Oslo, 2007).

Petr Szczepanik is assistant professor at the Department of Film and Audiovisual Culture, Masaryk University, Brno, and researcher in the National Film Archive (NFA), Prague. He has published essays in Czech, English, and German on the introduction of film sound in the context of broader media culture in the 1930s, the history of movie-going, and the history of industrial film, and he edited or co-edited several books on the history of film thought and film historiography including *Cinema All the Time: An Anthology of Czech Film Theory and Criticism, 1908-1939*. He is an editor-in-chief of *Iluminace*, a film-studies journal published by NFA. In 2005-2006, he was a post-doc member of the Graduiertenkolleg Mediale Historiographien in Weimar.

Valérie Vignaux is Maître de conférences in film studies at the University François-Rabelais in Tours, France. Her research focuses on the relationship between the archive (film, paper, and material objects) and the writing of film history. Her publications include *Jacques Becker ou l'exercice de la liberté* (Liège, 2000), *Suzanne Simonin, la Religieuse de Jacques Rivette* (Liège, 2005), and *Jean Benoit-Lévy ou le corps comme utopie* (AFRHC, 2007). She has edited a special issue of the film-history journal *1895* on archives (October 2003) and another issue on animation pioneer Emile Cohl (December 2007).

Patrick Vonderau is assistant professor at the Department of Media Studies at the Ruhr University, Bochum. He has published on the cultural history of film distribution (*Bilder vom Norden. Schwedisch-deutsche Filmbeziehungen, 1914-1939*, Marburg, 2007), on film marketing (*Demnächst in Ihrem Kino. Grundlagen der Filmwerbung und Filmvermarktung*, Marburg, 2005, with Vinzenz Hediger) and on YouTube (*The YouTube Reader*, Stockholm 2009, with Pelle Snickars). He is currently writing two books, on the media history of audience research in the American film industry, the other one on the aesthetics of production (to be published in 2010).

Yvonne Zimmermann is assistant professor at the Department of Film Studies at the University of Zurich. She is author of *Bergführer Lorenz: Karriere eines missglückten Films* (Marburg, 2005) and has written a number of articles on industrial and sponsored films (i.e., "Negotiating Landscape: Engineering Consent on the Exploitation of Water Power in Swiss Corporate Films," which was published in *Cultural Heritage and Landscapes in Europe. Landschaften. Kulturelles Erbe in Europa*, Bochum, 2008). She is also the editor of a DVD series of 1939-1959 sponsored films from Switzerland (Praesens Film, 2007).

Index of Names

Adorno, Theodor 141
Agricola, Georg 44
Altman, Rick 83n
Anstey, Edgar 244-245, 247, 254n-255n
Arnold, Martin 30

Baird, John Logie 398
Barnum, P.T. 86
Barthes, Roland 301n
Bass, Saul 229
Bat'a, Tomas 349, 356, 363-364, 370-371, 373
Baudry de Saunier, Louis 177, 184n
Bel Geddes, Norman 217
Benjamin, Walter 295, 301n
Benoît-Lévy, Jean 315-321, 324-325, 326n-327n
Bérard, Léon 317
Blum, Albert Viktor 397, 403n
Boehm, Gottfried 299n
Bourdieu, Pierre 40, 48n
Brabant, Andrée 320
Braune, Willhelm 85, 97n
Bruneau, Adrien 316-319, 322-323, 326n-327n
Burke, Kenneth 41-42, 48n

Calkin, Elmo 155, 158, 161, 165
Campen, Hans-Heinrich 131-132, 147
Canguilhem, Georges 16n, 147n
Cartwright, Lisa 299n, 302n
Churchill Films 229

Decroly, Ovide 81, 84n
De Haas, J. 394
Deleuze, Gilles 361, 375n
Delpeut, Peter 30
Deutsch, Gustav 30
Diderot, Denis 44, 48n

Dimendberg, Edward 15n
Disney 229, 284, 299n
Dressler, Werner 112
Dreyfus, Pierre 190
Dudow, Slatan 329
Duvanel, Charles-Georges 110

Eisenstein, Sergej 22, 26, 404n
Elton, Arthur 245, 249, 251
Encyclopedia Britannica 229, 259
Estlund, Cynthia 270, 279, 282n

Farcy, Jean 188-189, 205n
Farocki, Harun 30, 33n-34n
Fischer, Otto 85, 97n
Fischinger, Oskar 215, 217
Focillon, Henri 323, 327n
Fontègne, Julien 317, 324
Förberg, Einar 304-305, 309-310, 312n-313n
Forgacs, Peter 30
Foucault, Michel 12, 16n, 165n
Franken, Mannus 391, 400, 403n
Fridenson, Patrick 183n
Früh, Kurt 112

Gahura, Frantisek Lydia 349, 366-368, 370, 374
Gaillard, Jimmy 320
Giedion, Siegfried 185n, 391
Gilbreth, Frank Butler 13, 39, 46, 85-86, 88-96, 98n-99n, 103, 139, 147, 182-183, 185n, 189, 287-288, 300n-301n
Gilbreth, Lilian 85, 88, 93, 97n-99n, 182-183, 185n, 205n, 288, 300n
Gispen, Willem 400
Godard, Jean-Luc 10
Goldfarb, Brian 299n
Gottwald, Klement 373

Grémont, Paul 180, 185n
Grierson, John 42, 76, 83n, 112, 244-245,
    254n
Gunning, Tom 390n, 391, 402n

Hackenschmidt, Alexander 23
Haanstra, Bert 247, 255n
Handy, Jam 14, 57-61, 211-219, 220n, 229
Hanon, Bernard 206n
Harvey, Herk (Harold) 59, 227, 231, 233,
    238
Hegel, G.W.F. 132, 148n
Hennessy, Jack 229
Herzog, Werner 31
Hitler, Adolf 28
Hochbaum, Werner 329
Hogenkamp, Bert 84, 344n, 391, 397,
    402n-404n
Hollerith, Hermann 128, 132-140, 145,
    147n-148n, 288
Huijts, Johan 401, 404n

Iros, Erich 111, 116n
Ivens, Joris 23, 391, 394-395, 401

Johnson, Lyndon B. 259, 261, 282n
Jutzi, Phil 329

Karfík, Vladimir 349, 367-371, 374n
Kelly, Grace 201
Kessler, Frank 13, 73n, 75, 83n-84n
Kestner, Max 31
Khrushchev, Nikita 201
Kipp, Rudolf 140
Kittler, Friedrich 40, 47n, 94, 99n, 131-
    132, 147n-148n, 302n
Klos, Elmar 352, 375n
Knies, Karl 40, 45, 47n
Koster, Simon 394, 401, 403n
Kotěra, Jan 349, 366-367
Krupp, Alfred 374n
Kudelski, Stefan 228

Labbé, Edmond 317, 326n
Lacan, Jacques 146

Lacey, Charles 225, 227
Lagny, Michèle 37, 47n, 326n
Langlois, Henri 29
Lasch-Quinn, Elizabeth 269-270, 280,
    282n
Le Corbusier 352, 354, 369, 371, 393
Le Guénédal, Loïc 207n
Lefaucheux, Pierre 188, 190
Leloutre, Stéphane 207n
Le Masson, Henri 178, 184n
Levi, Giovanni 222, 240n
Lewis, David 163, 165n
Loubignac, Jean 180, 185n
Lumière, Louis 9, 67, 78, 101, 145
Lumière brothers 323

Malle, Louis 206n
Manovich, Lev 20, 33n
Marey, Etienne-Jules 85-86, 94, 96, 97n,
    182, 300n, 326n
Marx, Karl 128, 141, 144, 148n
May, Ernst 24
McGraw-Hill 14, 229, 235, 283, 285-287,
    290-292, 294, 296, 298, 299n-302n
Mitchell & Kenyon 78, 84n
Mitry, Jean 206n
Mitterand, François 206n
Menegoz, Robert 43
Messter, Oskar 24, 27, 69
Mol, J.C. 23
Montgomery, Fred 223-224
Mörtzsch, Friedrich 108, 116n-117n,
    155-158, 165n
Mosser, Russell 221-225, 227-228, 230,
    234-238, 240n-242n
Mullens, Willy 243, 254n, 394-395, 400
Müller, Matthias 116n
Mumford, Lewis 198, 207n
Münsterberg, Hugo 136, 148n
Muybridge, Eadweard 89, 96

Neurath, Otto 294, 301
Nielsen, Asta 27
Noldan, Svend 21, 23

Olson, Mancur 15n, 144, 148n

Pal, George 23
Painlevé, Jean 23
Pessis, Georges 191, 206n-207n
Peters, John Durham 137, 148n
Prelinger, Rick 10, 13-14, 16n, 29, 31, 34n, 51, 57, 211, 219, 220n

Queen Elizabeth II 201

Rammert, Werner 47n
Rappaport, Mark 30
Rasch, Manfred 47n-48n, 115n, 148n, 240n, 344n
Renault, Louis 167, 173, 177-178, 180, 184n
Renoir, Jean 26
Resnais, Alain 10, 15n, 125n, 206n
Richter, Hans 21, 102, 114n, 147n
Riefenstahl, Leni 22
Rikkli, Martin 23
Riotor, Léon 316-317
Rolland, Michel 191
Romnes, H.I. 261, 282n
Ros, Philippe 207n
Rotha, Paul 76, 84n
Ruttmann, Walter 22-23, 47n, 102, 112, 117n, 344n

Schuitema, Paul 394
Schumpeter, Joseph 127, 146n
Seiler, Alexander J. 101-102, 114n
Selassie, Haile 201

Sekula, Alan 48n
Sheeler, Charles 43, 84n, 95
Simon, Herbert A. 303, 312n
Sirkis, Jean-Jacques 188-189, 196, 199-200, 205n, 207n-208n
Straley, Walter 262
Stringer, Jim 239

Taylor, Frederick Winslow 39, 85, 88, 92, 97n-98n, 130, 139, 147n, 265, 287, 291, 298, 300, 357, 361, 367, 375n
Tenfelde, Klaus 46n, 48n,

Van Bergen, C.W.A. 243-244, 254n
Vautier, René 188
Vavra, Otakár 360
Vidal, Gaston 317
Vierny, Sacha 43
Von Barsy, Andor 20, 22, 394, 396-399, 401, 403n
Von Maydell, F.C. 403n

Ward, Tracy 58
Weber, Max 287, 300n
Wettler, Peter 102, 113, 114n, 116n
Willink, Luc 396, 403n
Wolf, Art (Arthur) 221, 224-228, 230-231, 234-237, 240n-241n
Wolf, Gotthard 49n, 98n
Wood, Ed 59

Yates, JoAnne 16n, 38-39, 45, 47, 301n

Zielke, Willy 22, 102

Index of Film Titles

A Car for Every Purse and Purpose (USA 1926) 217

Achter Glas (Behind Glas, NL 1931) 400

A Coach for Cinderella (USA 1936) 217

Activité de Travail au Montage (F 1996) 207n

Affirmative Action (USA 1970) 263

Airport (GB/NL 1935) 244

Alpsegen im Glarnerland (CH 1930) 110-111

American Harvest (USA 1955) 60, 219

American Engineer (USA 1956) 60, 215

American Look (USA 1958) 60, 215

American Maker (USA 1960) 60, 215

American Thrift (USA 1962) 60

Angestellte unserer Zeit (D 1963) 142

Apfelsinen-Industrie (Orange Industry, D 1906) 66

Apprentissage du tourneur sur métaux (F 1926) 321

Arbeitende Elephanten (Working Elephants, 1909) 66

Around the World with G.M. (USA 1927) 217

A/S Norsk Jernverk (N 1958) 385

Aus dem früheren und heutigen Rechnungswesen eines Werkes (D 1928) 134

L'Automobile de France 180-181

Autos aus Wolfsburg (D 1992) 158-160

Ein Autotag (D 1980) 158-159

Aux Usines Renault (F 1920) 173, 205n

Back of the Mike (USA 1938) 217

Las Bases del Progreso (Harvest for Tomorrow, NL/VZ 1950) 247

Bataafsche Petroleum Film (NL 1924) 243

Les Beaux Métiers du Livre (F 1922) 317

Besuch bei Volkswagen (D 1985) 158-159

Berlin. Die Symphonie der Grossstadt (D 1928) 117

Betonarbeid (NL 1930) 395

Bienvenue à Cléon (F 1984) 206n, 208n-209n

Blick in eine Automobilfabrik (Look in a Car Factory, D 1910) 69-70

Bouw Maastunnel (NL 1937-1941) 395

Bouw van de Van Nelle Fabriek (Building of the Van Nelle Factory, NL 1930) 400

La Broderie (F 1925) 319

Brüder (D 1929) 329

The Building of Norsk Jernverk: Small Glimpses from a Great Undertaking (N 1952) 384

Champions Juniors (F 1954) 190, 200

Le Chant de la mine et du feu (F 1932) 324

Le Chant du styrène (F 1957) 15n, 206n

Cléon Passion (F 2000) 207n

Comment on Fabrique un Siège à l'École Boulle (F 1922) 317

Communication Obstacles for Women and Minorities (USA 1983) 276

Conditions de Travail (F 1980) 207n-208n

Construire (F 1934) 324

CORRECTIVE ACTION PROGRAM (USA 1979) 267, 281n
LES COULISSES DE L'ATELIER (F 1995) 207n-208n

THE DANUBE EXODUS (H 1998) 30
DATING DO'S AND DON'TS (USA 1949) 59
DEFOURNAGE DU COKE (F 1896) 65
DE BRUG (NL 1928) 391, 394
DE COOPERATIVE PRODUCTIE GROEIT (THE COOPERATIVE PRODUCTION GROWS, NL 1932) 395
DE MAARSCHALKSTAF (NL 1929) 396
DE STAD DIE NOOIT RUST (THE CITY THAT NEVER RESTS, NL 1928) 396, 399
DE THEE, VAN PLANTAGE TOT HET PAKJE (TEA: FROM PLANTATION TO PACKAGE, NL 1928) 400
DERNIER MAILLON (F 1992) 207n
DES METIERS POUR LES JEUNES FILLES (F 1928) 320
DES METIERS POUR LES JEUNES GENS (F 1928) 320
DIENSTBARE KRAFT / FORCES DOMPTÉS (CH 1937) 110-111
DIJKBOUW (NL 1952) 255n
DIRECT MASS SELLING (USA 1939-1941) 215, 217
DIVA DOLOROSA (NL 1999) 30
DOSSIER PÉDAGOGIQUE (F 1989) 208n
DREAMS (NL 1930) 403n
DREI IN EINEM BOOT (CH 1950) 108
DROOMEN (NL 1931) 403n

L'ÉBÉNISTERIE (F 1930) 321
ÉCOLE BOULLE: LES ARTS ET INDUSTRIES DU MEUBLE (F 1924) 319
ÉCOLES NATIONALES PROFESSIONNELLES (F 1930) 321
EEN LIED VAN DEN ARBEID (NL 1929) 403n
L'EMPREINTE D'UN GÉANT (F 1983) 201n, 207n-208n

EQUAL OPPORTUNITY POLICY AND TERMINOLOGY (USA 1975) 264, 281n
ERGENS IN NEDERLAND (NL 1940) 403n
DIE ERNTE DES ZUCKERROHRS (HARVESTING SUGAR CANE, 1910) 66
ERNTE UND ZUBEREITUNG DER ANANAS ZUR HERSTELLUNG VON KONSERVEN (D 1910) 67
ETUDES DU TRAVAIL HUMAIN (STUDIES OF HUMAN LABOR, F 1950) 189
EXPERIENCE IN DEPTH (GB 1995) 252

FÄCHERINDUSTRIE IN JAPAN/L'INDUSTRIE DES ÉVENTAILS AU JAPON (1907) 66
FABRICATION DE LA MÉGANE, STANDARDISATION DU PROCESS RENAULT MÉGANE (F 1996) 208n
LA FABRICATION DU PAPIER PEINT (F 1935) 321
FABRICATION D'UNE AUTOMOBILE (MANUFACTURING A CAR, F 1929) 173, 177-178, 180
LA FABRICATION MÉCANIQUE DE LA DENTELLE (F 1935) 321
FABRICATION MÉGANE II DOUAI (F 2002) 199
FABRIKATION DES PAPIERS (MANUFACTURING PAPER, 1911) 67
DIE FABRIKATION DER SCHWEIZERKÄSE (THE MANUFACTURE OF SWISS CHEESE, 1913) 67
FABRIKATION VON KUNSTBLUMEN (MANUFACTURING ARTIFICIAL FLOWERS, 1911) 66
FABRIKATION VENETIANISCHER SPITZEN (MANUFACTURING VENITIAN LACE, 1906) 66
LE FER FORGÉ (F 1922) 321
LA FERRONNERIE D'ART (F 1924) 317, 319, 321
LA FILATURE DU COTON (F 1930) 321
FILMAVISEN (NORWEGIAN NEWSREEL) 383-385, 388
FILM IST (A 2001) 30

FILM OVER DE ROTTERDAMSCHE HAVEN EN PLAATSELIJKE INDUSTRIE EN HANDEL (NL 1927) 396

LA FLEUR ARTIFICIELLE TELLE QU'ON L'ENSEIGNE À L'ÉCOLE PROFESSIONELLE DE LA RUE FONDARY À PARIS (F 1924) 317, 319, 323

FLINS (F 1950) 40n, 207n

FLYING TRAIN (D 1901) 65

GEFÄHRLICHES EXPERIMENT (D 1960) 336

HET GEMEENTE ELECTRICITEITSBEDRIJF (NL 1927-1928) 403n

HET GEMEENTE GASBEDRIJF ROTTERDAM (NL 1927-1928) 403n

GESTES À TEMPS (F 1987) 207n-208n

GEWERKSCHAFT IN AKTION (D 1959) 336, 340

THE GREAT UPHEAVAL (USA 1964) 261, 281

GROEI (GROWTH, NL 1928-1930) 394-395, 403n

HÄNDE UND MASCHINEN / HOMMES ET MACHINES (CH 1938) 112

HAWTHORNE'S CORRECTIVE ACTION PROGRAM CAP (USA 1979) 281n

DIE HERSTELLUNG EINER WACHSFIGUR (THE MANUFACTURE OF A WAX FIGURE (1911) 67

DIE HERSTELLUNG KÜNSTLICHER ROSEN (THE FABRICATION OF ARTIFICIAL ROSES, 1910) 66

DIE HERSTELLUNG VON BAMBUSHÜTTEN (THE FABRICATION OF BAMBUS HUTS, 1909) 66

HERSTELLUNG VON FÄSSERN DURCH MASCHINEN/LA FABRICATION MÉCANIQUE DES TONNEAUX A CETTE (1911) 71

HERSTELLUNG VON HOLLÄNDISCHEM KÄSE/COMMENT SE FAIT LE FROMAGE DE HOLLANDE (1909) 66

HIER WIRD GESTREIKT (THERE IS A STRIKE GOING ON, D 1957) 340, 342

THE HIGHWAY SINGS (CZ 1937) 352, 373

HISTOIRE D'UN CHAPEAU DE PAILLE – LA MODISTE (F 1925) 319

HISTOIRE D'UN MOTEUR (F 1997) 208n

HISTOIRE D'UNE PORTE (F 2000) 207n-209n

HOOGSTRAAT (NL 1930) 394, 397, 401

L'HOMME AU CENTRE DE LA PERFORMANCE (F 1998) 208n

HOPFEN UND MALZ, GOTT ERHALT'S! EIN RUNDGANG DURCH DIE BRAUEREI BINDING IN FRANKFURT (GOD SAVE HOPS AND MALT! A TOUR OF THE BINDING BREWERY IN FRANKFURT, D 1910) 71

HORIZONTES NACIONALES (NEW HORIZONS, NL/VZ 1949) 247

HYGIËNISCHE MELKSTAL DE VAAN (NL 1927-1928) 403n

INDUSTRIAL MANAGEMENT (USA 1950-1954) 14, 283, 285-286, 288, 298, 299n

INDUSTRIE IN VENEDIG (1909) 66

INDUSTRIE UND SPORT IN BURMA (1909) 66

INTERNAL ORGANIZATION (USA 1951) 289, 291-292, 294-298, 300n-301n

JENSEITS DER STRASSE (D 1929) 397, 403n

JOB EVALUATION (USA 1952) 300n-301n

JOURNÉE D'UN MÉTALLO (F 1969) 208n

KAAS (CHEESE, NL 1943) 81-82

KAMERADSCHAFT (D 1953) 337-338, 340

KUHLE WAMPE (D 1932) 329

LENTELIED (NL 1936) 394, 403n

LEO BEUERMAN (USA 1969) 234

LOKOMOTIVBAU BROWN BOVERI & CIE (CH 1939) 111

LYRICAL NITRATE (NL 1991) 30

MAASBRUGGEN (NL 1937) 394

MACHINE TRANSFERT (1956) 196, 207n
MADE IN RENAULT (F 1983) 191, 202,
    206n-207n, 209n
THE MAELSTROM (H 1997) 30
MAGIC IN THE AIR (USA 1941) 217
LA MAISON (F 1930) 320
MANNESMANN (D 1937) 112
MASTER HANDS (USA 1936) 214, 217
MAX BY CHANCE (DK 2004) 31
METALL DES HIMMELS (D 1935) 112
METHODS ANALYSIS (USA 1951) 300n-
    301n
LE MÉTIER D'ÉBÉNISTE (F 1924) 319
MILCHERZEUGUNG IN DER SCHWEIZ/PRÉ-
    PARATION ET EXPORTATION DU LAIT
    PAR LA STÉ LATIÈRE DES ALPES BER-
    NOISES (MILK PRODUCTION IN SWIT-
    ZERLAND, 1909) 68
MODELBEDRIJVEN DER VOLKSVOEDING
    (NL 1927-1928) 403n
MODERNE NEDERLANDSCHE ARCHITEC-
    TUUR (NL 1930) 391, 403n
MODERN PRODUCTION OF SHOES (CZ
    1930) 360, 373
MONTAGES EN CHAÎNE (F 1972) 207n
MORE STEPS UPWARD (USA 1962) 233
MUTTER KRAUSENS FAHRT INS GLÜCK (D
    1929) 329

NAISSANCE D'UNE USINE (F 1966) 207n
NIEUWE ARCHITECTUUR (NL 1930) 391
NORSK JERNVERK (N 1974) 387
NOTRE PAIN QUOTIDIEN (F 1934) 325
NOUVELLES CHAÎNES DE PRODUCTION RE-
    NAULT 4 ET 5 (F 1985) 208n
NUL UUR NUL (NL 1927) 401, 403n
NUR DER NEBEL IST GRAU (ONLY THE
    FOGS ARE GREY, D 1964) 43-44

HET OLIEVELD (THE OILFIELD, NL 1954)
    255n
ONTSTAAN EN VERGAAN (THE CHANGING
    EARTH, NL 1954) 255n
DE OPSPORING VAN AARDOLIE (THE
    SEARCH FOR OIL, NL 1954) 255n

ORANJEBOOM, HET BROUWERIJBEDRIJF
    (NL 1927) 398-399, 401, 403n
OUT OF THIS WORLD (USA 1964) 219

PANORAMA EPHEMERA (USA 2004) 51-
    52
PANORAMA VON ALGIERS (D 1906) 66
PERSPEKTIVEN (D 1959) 336
PETITS DOIGTS DE FÉE (F 1925) 319
LA PIERRE QUE L'ON TISSE (F 1932) 324
PIONIERE DER DEUTSCHEN TECHNIK (D
    1935) 266
LA PLOMBERIE (F 1930) 321
POÉSIE DU TRAVAIL: DOIGTS D'OUVRIÈRES,
    MAINS DE FÉES (F 1930) 323, 325
LE PORT DE PARIS (F 1932) 325
POUSSIÈRES (F 1954) 13, 119, 121
PRECISELY SO (USA 1936) 217
PROCESSUS DE FABRICATION À L'USINE DE
    FLINS (F 1997) 207n
PROTO 117 (F 1969) 199, 208n

REDACTEUREN ZIEN U AAN (EDITORS ARE
    WATCHING YOU, NL 1933) 401
RENAULT EXPRESS FABRICATION (F) 203
THE RIVAL WORLD (NL 1955) 247-248
DIE ROTE FRONT MARSCHIERT (D 1927)
    329
ROTTERDAM (NL 1930) 397, 399, 403n

SAND ON THE SLIPPER SIDEWALKS OF
    SALES (USA 1925) 217
SCHINDLER'S LIST (USA 1993) 27
SCHON VERGESSEN? (D 1958) 336-341,
    343
SEILFABRIKATION IN KENT (MANUFAC-
    TURING ROPE IN KENT, 1911) 71
SHAKE HANDS WITH DANGER (USA 1980)
    238-239
SHOWDOWN (USA 1958) 231
SIAMO ITALIANI (WE ARE ITALIANS, CH
    1964) 101
SORTIE D'USINE (F 1895) 78, 101
DE STEEG (NL 1932) 403n

Supervisory Relationship Training (USA 1976-1978) 282n
Supplices sur mesure (F 1969) 207n
Symphonie du Travail (F 1934) 325
Symphonie Mécanique (F 1956) 206n
Das Stahlwerk der Poldihütte während des Weltkriegs (A 1916) 24

Technik des Glücks (2000-2003) 31
Technik – Drei Studien in Jazz (D 1961) 330, 344n, 466
Thompson's Dressierte Elefanten (Thompson's Trained Elephants, D 1908) 66-67
Time is Money (CZ 1938) 356, 362, 373
Die Tomaten (Tomatoes, D 1908) 67
Transfert Mécanique Automatisé (F 1996) 207n
Travail chez Renault (F 1960) 206n
Tusschen Aankomst en Vertrek (NL 1937) 399, 403n

Un Beau Métier méconnu: Le Repassage (F 1925) 319
Der Unbekannte (D 1940) 467
The Underwater Search (GB/USA 1965) 250-252
Der Untergang (2004) 27
Unsichtbare Kraft / Puissance Invisible (CH 1933) 111

L'Usine de Montage à l'Étranger (F 1987) 206n
Usine voir et savoir No 2 (F 1997) 208n

De Verkenningsboring (The Wildcat, NL 1954) 255n
Verkeer (NL 1929) 403n
24 Heures à la Régie Renault (F 1957) 199
Visiteurs d'un Jour (F 1957) 200, 209n

Was Geschieht mit alten Eisen- und Blechabfällen (D 1911) 67
Welt der Arbeit (D 1957) 336
Der Werdegang Eines Daimlermotors (The Development of a Dailmer Engine, D 1912) 69
Werdegang einer Kamera (Development of a Camera, 1909) 69
We Will Say it Through Film (CZ 1941) 359, 374
Wie der Berliner Arbeiter Wohnt (D 1930) 329
Wie eine elektrische Glühbirne entsteht (How and Electric Light Bulb is Made, 1911) 67
Wij Bouwen (NL 1930) 391, 395
Window onto the World (CZ 1937-1938) 359, 363, 374
White Diamond (2004) 31

Index of Subjects

Academy Award 234-235

Accounting 132, 134-138, 145, 224, 306, 310-311

Accounting Machines 133

Advertising 19-23, 31-32, 39, 46, 51, 60, 70, 81, 102, 104-106, 109-110, 140, 153, 155, 158, 163, 178, 180, 189, 191, 193, 205n, 214, 217-218, 244, 250, 304-305, 309-311, 316, 352, 358, 362-363, 377, 398

AEG 69, 109, 165

Aesthetics 27, 30, 52, 102, 141, 148n, 298, 360, 394

Aesthetics of Destabilization 121

African-American 214, 262-263, 265, 273, 277

Affirmative Action 14, 259-269, 271, 279-280, 281n-282n

Amateur film 31, 51, 77, 101

American Medical Association (AMA) 228

Animation 14, 21, 23, 145, 156, 202, 213, 215, 217, 227, 239, 283-285, 287-289, 291-295, 297-299, 351, 358, 363, 396

Architecture 15, 21, 349, 360, 367, 370-371, 391-401

Archive 10-15, 17, 19, 24-27, 29-31, 33, 34n, 35-37, 40-42, 46, 51-52, 54-57, 61, 78, 111, 114n, 134, 137, 169, 173, 184n, 187, 192-193, 214, 219, 255n, 286, 351

Archiving 13, 26, 42, 51, 61, 192, 289, 353

Assembly 69-71, 98n, 153, 156, 158-160, 162, 179, 195, 197, 318

Assembly line 162, 176, 178-183, 187, 189, 192, 194-203, 205n, 208n, 353-354, 360, 366, 369

Association Film 213

Astonishment 145

ATAuteur 10, 13, 15, 20, 23-24, 28-29, 57, 101-102, 111-112, 125n, 204

Automation 81, 115n, 156, 159, 196-198, 305-306, 360

Automobile 14, 45, 58, 60, 67, 69, 71, 127, 154-155, 158-159, 163, 172-173, 178-181, 183n-184n, 187, 189, 193, 196, 202-203, 214

Automobile industry 155, 158, 164, 173, 184n, 213, 219

Autostadt Wolfsburg 13, 153, 160-162

Avant-Garde 19, 21-23, 25, 28, 30, 32-33, 33n, 47n, 52, 58-59, 65, 102, 112, 114n, 117, 360, 391, 394, 401

Bärenmarke (Condensed Milk) 70

BASF 22

Bauhaus 22

Bat'a Shoe Factory 14, 364-365, 372

Bayer Chemicals 35

Behaviorism 14, 283, 299n

Bell Laboratories 259, 276, 282n

Billancourt (factory plant) 177, 179-184, 192-193, 195, 199, 206n, 208n

Bill Sandy Company 214, 219

Body 20, 33n, 36, 46, 71, 92, 109, 119-120, 130, 134, 137-139, 142-144, 180, 197, 234, 277-278, 288, 324, 339-340, 351, 360

Body language 277-278, 293

Brown Boveri & Cie (later Asea Brown Boweri/ABB) 111

Buick 59

Business History 113

Business Practice 129, 134, 296

Business Propaganda 68

Business Network Switzerland 105, 110, 112-113

Cadillac 59

Camera 28, 37, 41, 45, 46n, 65, 69-72, 76, 79, 88-89, 96, 156, 171, 181-182, 189, 191-192, 196, 224, 244, 298, 300n, 324, 360, 377, 384, 395-396, 400

Capitalism 40, 102, 127, 144, 146n, 276-277

Career placement film 319

Car Industry 59

Cartoon 202, 217, 284, 290, 295, 401

Catalogue 21, 25, 33n, 77, 82, 221, 244, 254, 255n, 309, 315, 319, 322-323, 325, 327n, 334

Caterpillar 228, 238-239

Cinematic Discourse 198

Central Film Library of Vocational Education (France) 14, 315, 316, 319, 321-322, 325

Centron 14, 58-59, 221-239, 240n-242n

Chevrolet 59, 213, 214, 217, 219

Children 58, 81-82, 200-201, 237, 284, 315, 350

Citroën 176

Cold War 32, 333

Communication 37-40, 45, 47, 48n, 104, 106, 110, 112, 128, 132, 134, 137-139, 142-143, 148n, 164, 169, 187, 192-194, 204, 211, 213, 231, 243, 253, 255n, 260, 263, 266-268, 270, 271, 273, 275-276, 278, 281, 283, 287, 290, 297-298, 301n, 303, 305-311, 324, 329-330, 350, 353-354, 361, 370, 375n, 402

Communism 333

Communist Party 366

Computer 11, 39, 45, 127-133, 140-144, 146, 148n, 196, 198, 200, 206n-207n, 262, 292, 311, 312n

Condor Film 102, 114

Congrès Intérnational d'Architecture Moderne (CIAM) 24, 349

Construction film 394-395

Consumer Engineering 155, 161, 164n-165n

Control 11, 14, 16n, 33n, 39, 41, 47n, 55, 58, 60, 125, 127-130, 139, 141, 143-144, 155, 160, 164, 189, 196-200, 238, 240n, 257, 284, 290, 292, 297, 300n-301n, 308, 354, 356, 361, 373, 375n

Convention 37, 43, 46, 78, 80, 125, 143, 154, 163-164, 165n, 336

Corporate film 13-14, 101-104, 107-108, 111, 113, 134, 138, 142, 167, 169, 171, 187, 204, 253-254

Corporate speech 14, 211, 215, 280

Creative destruction 127-129, 131, 141, 144-146, 148n

Crisis, Crises 13, 48n, 107, 128, 131, 133, 137, 139, 145, 154, 158, 160-161, 164, 173, 176-177, 181, 192, 196-197, 335-336, 338, 340, 345, 366, 382, 388-389, 393

Cultural Technique 13, 153, 160, 162, 164n

Customer Relationship Management 161

Cybernetics 43, 283, 298, 299n, 305-306, 313n

Cyclegraph 94, 96, 99n

Dadaism 23

Data processing 133-134, 136-139, 142

DEHOMAG 132-133

Detroit 39, 57-59, 213-214, 219, 220n

Deutscher Gewerkschaftsbund (DGB Union) 128, 140

Digital 19, 36, 131, 193, 219, 253, 292

Digital Media 19, 28, 193, 204

Digitization 54-55, 61

Discipline 165n, 283, 341, 354, 356, 368

Discrimination 264-265, 267, 272-276

Dispositif 11, 16n, 28, 162, 354-355, 361

Distribution 24, 37, 61, 70, 77, 82, 86, 109, 137, 156, 164, 213, 218, 235-236, 246, 249-250, 252, 255n, 259, 261, 289, 298, 305, 308-309, 334-335, 341, 353, 360, 383, 388, 392, 399

Diversifying, Diversification 193, 370

Documentary 13, 19, 30, 46, 76, 83n-84n, 87, 91, 96, 98n, 111-112, 117n, 119-121, 125n, 155-156, 169, 173, 178-180, 182,

191, 234, 251-254, 272, 288-289, 319, 336-337, 351, 358, 374n, 390, 394, 396-397, 400
Documentary film 21-23, 32, 42, 98n, 105, 243-247, 253, 254n, 303, 329
Dupont 60, 215, 218
DVD 31, 56, 61, 101, 162-163, 254n

Eclipse 65-66, 71
Economics 72, 230, 285, 305-307, 316
Economic Citizenship 265, 268, 272, 277-278, 280
Economic Miracle (Germany) 14, 43, 338
Educational Films 11, 14, 57, 59, 66, 68, 75, 90-91, 110, 134, 173, 221, 224, 230, 233, 235, 253, 284-286, 292, 298, 319, 377, 388, 392
Efficiency 13, 63, 79-80, 85-88, 92-99, 114n, 169, 200, 209n, 246, 249, 292-293, 295, 298, 304-305, 311, 341, 353, 360
Electrical Research Products Incorporated (ERPI) 259, 272
Emergence 11, 16n, 19, 38-39, 48n, 75, 115n, 128-130, 132, 315, 325, 351, 402
Emerging media 211, 215
Encyclopédie (Diderot and D'Alembert) 44-45, 48n
Engineering 21, 155, 161, 164n, 276, 285, 306, 312n, 340, 365, 367, 370, 372, 395-397
Ephemeral Films 13, 29, 51-53
Epistemic image 146
Epistemology 12, 16n, 129, 139, 145, 147n
Ergonomic film 182, 193
Ergonomics 189, 198
Ernemann 68
Equal Employment Opportunity Commission (EEOC) 259-260, 263-264, 267
Equal Opportunity Act (1964) 280
Evolution 14, 120, 132, 146n, 183, 187-188, 190, 203-204, 211, 297, 407
Exhibition 24, 27-28, 33n, 68-69, 78, 102, 104-112, 153-155, 163, 172, 193, 213,

217, 309, 311, 352-353, 358-360, 398-399
Experiential Branding 161
Expressionism 23
Exxon 228

Factory floor 39, 88-89, 130, 139, 141, 287-288
Factory gate 9, 78, 340-341
Factory gate films 78, 84n
Factory tour 153-159, 162-163, 172, 287
Filmliga 391, 397, 400-401, 402n
Film screening 16n, 287, 300, 305, 331, 333-335, 344n, 399
Flexibility 191, 196, 311, 358, 367
Football 96, 203
Ford 39, 59, 361, 366, 375
Fordism 287, 300n, 357
Found Footage 30, 289
Frankfurter Küche 24
Frankfurt School 141
Functionalist architecture 349, 360

Gaumont 65-66, 169, 173, 184n, 205n
Gebrauchsfilm 19, 30, 32, 47n
Gender 53, 58, 133, 136, 138, 260-261, 275-276, 278, 281n, 339
General Electric 52, 228
General Motors 59-61, 155, 213, 215, 217-219, 228
General Post Office Film Unit 244
Genre 10, 20, 28, 30, 46, 52, 54, 71, 75, 77-78, 83, 102, 111, 129, 145, 187, 196, 201, 216, 283, 325, 333, 377, 386, 394
Gesture 92, 112, 181, 192, 199, 207n, 277, 279, 291, 293, 295, 323, 340, 343
Goodyear Rubber 59
Government 24, 26-27, 32, 35, 60, 114n, 192, 206n, 212, 221, 228, 244, 246-247, 251, 259, 261, 271-272, 281n, 283-284, 304, 312n, 317, 332, 334, 336, 340, 365, 372, 378-379
Gutehoffnungshütte 69

Hawthorne Effect 260

Historical Pragmatics 75
Hollywood 13, 44, 58, 101, 113, 215, 221,
    230-231, 233-235, 239, 259-260, 272
Home Movies 28, 30, 42
Howard University 228
Human Locomotion 85, 94
Human Zoo 67

IBM 132-133, 215, 227
Ideal Industrial City (Zlín) 349-350, 371
Ideology 12, 260, 280, 306, 376n
IG Bergbau und Energie (Industrial Union
    of Miners and Energy Workers) 332,
    344n-345n
IG Metall (Industrial Union of Metal
    Workers) 332-334, 336, 340-341,
    344n, 345n
IG Chemie (Indutrial Union of Chemical
    Industry Workers) 149n, 332, 336
Indexical image 146
Industrial organization 9, 11-14, 35, 38-
    40, 44-47, 75, 127-132, 134, 139, 141,
    143-145, 253, 285, 287-288, 306, 342
Industrial production 11, 13, 16n, 35, 39-
    40, 47n, 59, 67, 71, 79, 127-130, 132,
    137-138, 140, 143, 145-146, 155, 169,
    196, 294, 306, 329-330, 341, 351-354,
    357-358, 360-361, 380
Industrial Screen (British Trade Publica-
    tion) 304
Industriebild 65, 72n, 105
Industry 10, 21, 32, 37, 39-40, 44-45, 47n-
    48n, 56, 66, 75, 77-78, 85, 96, 102, 106,
    108-109, 113, 114n, 117n, 120, 122,
    140-142, 147n, 155, 158, 164, 171-173,
    177, 180, 182-183, 212-213, 215, 219,
    222, 229, 236, 244, 249, 272, 276, 304-
    306, 309-310, 319-322, 324, 329, 330,
    335, 342, 349, 357, 363, 372, 377, 379-
    384, 389, 394-395, 398-399, 401
Information 11, 20, 29, 38, 41-42, 44-45,
    53, 57-58, 68, 70-71, 78, 90, 92, 96, 104,
    110, 114n, 127-133, 139, 144-145, 146n,
    156, 158, 160, 162-163, 173, 187, 212,

    222, 244, 246, 261, 267, 275, 285-286,
    298, 304, 306-311, 320, 326n, 377, 388
*Institut des Hautes Études Cinématographi-
    ques* (IDHEC) 188
*Institut für Film und Bild in Wissenschaft
    und Unterricht* (FWU) 66
*Institut National de Recherche sur la Sécur-
    ité* 119
Institutional Memory 11, 40-41
Instruction 81-83, 105, 110, 158, 162, 212,
    217, 224, 260, 263, 268, 315, 320, 324,
    351
Instructional video 278
Internationale Automobilausstellung (Inter-
    national Automobile Exhibition) 154
Internet Archive 51-52, 55-56, 61, 219
Jam Handy Organization 57-58, 60, 211,
    213-214, 216, 220n
John Deere 228, 233
KdF-Wagen (*Kraft durch Freue* Vehicle)
    155
Knorr Food Corporation 108, 116n
Knowledge 10-13, 16n, 49n, 57, 82, 91,
    102, 105, 127-131, 139, 142, 145-147n,
    284, 291, 297-298, 304, 311, 408
    – production of 91
    – consumption of 91
Kulturfilm 21, 23, 44, 77, 109, 333

Labor 11, 72, 78, 85, 90-91, 97, 127, 155,
    167, 181, 187, 197, 262, 289, 297, 323,
    329-330, 333, 336-337, 340, 344n, 357-
    358, 375n
Labor movement 329-332, 335, 340-341,
    378, 392-393, 395
Labor Unions 14, 97, 308, 343
Leadership 25, 289-293, 297
Learning 14, 81, 225, 273, 275, 278, 287,
    303, 306, 309-310
Library of Congress 51, 55, 219
Louisiana Purchase Exhibition 78

Management film 11, 260, 283-285, 287-
    288, 291-292, 296, 298
Management theory 13-14, 260

Manufacturing 65, 67, 70, 72, 77, 105, 108, 115n, 124, 153-156, 158-160, 162-163, 175, 193, 196-197, 199, 214, 281n, 360, 365
Market 31, 80, 127, 132, 134, 158, 161, 177, 227, 230, 235, 259, 286, 304, 309, 366, 371, 380-382, 384
Marshall Plan 284, 286, 378-379
Marxist critique 128, 142
Media network 22, 352
Medienverbund 22-23, 38-40, 104, 163, 351, 361-362, 398
MGM 230
Microhistory 221-222
Military 28, 77, 171, 173, 175-176, 218, 247, 283, 365, 372
Mitchell & Kenyon 78, 84n
Mode of production 128, 141, 144
Modern Talking Picture Service 213
Modernity 79, 137, 177, 194-196, 198, 200, 394-395
Monsanto Chemical Company 228
Motion pictures 85, 90, 168-169, 176, 182-183, 211, 213, 216
Motion Study 39, 85-86, 90, 92, 94, 182
Museum of Modern Art (MoMA) 29, 224
Music 113, 159, 200, 202, 234, 239, 303, 324-325, 338, 352, 363, 385, 398
Mutoscope and Biograph Company 65, 78

Nagra (film sound tape recorder) 228
National Cash Register 211, 215, 217
National Socialist films 330
NATO 378
Nazi 21, 372-373, 378, 383
Newsreel 21, 31, 59, 61, 76, 155, 171-173, 182, 213, 244, 335-336, 350, 354, 358-360, 362, 383-385, 388, 395, 399, 401
New York World's Fair (1939, 1964) 214, 217
Nominalism 131
Non-Visible 124-125

On Film, Inc. 58
Ontology 131-132
Opel 69-71, 75
ÖTV (Union of Public Service Workers) 332

Painting 9, 155, 158-159, 167, 195, 197, 199, 231, 292, 400
Panorama 65, 78, 129, 147n, 162, 386
Pathé 65-66, 77-81, 91, 169, 173, 180
Péchiney 206n
Pedagogical 173, 192-193, 201, 291, 294, 298, 309, 316, 318, 358
Pedagogy 268, 284-285, 288, 294-295, 298, 299n, 310-311
Performance 40-41, 45, 49n, 72, 92, 96, 98, 103, 128-129, 139, 143-144, 147n, 188, 198, 211, 275, 279, 283, 291, 293, 398
Philips 228, 233
Philosophy 124, 132, 163, 233, 235, 258n
Photography 9, 14, 20-21, 23, 28, 35-36, 40-41, 45, 68, 82, 88, 104, 129, 133-134, 141-142, 211, 218, 225, 232, 352, 398
Plant (factory) 9, 24, 160, 172, 176-178, 189, 192-193, 195, 201, 227, 267, 350, 367, 396
Polygoon (Dutch film company) 394-396, 399-400
Pontiac 59, 217
Popular Front 172, 182
Porsche 155
Poster 133-134, 155, 167, 202, 311
Precisionists 95
Preservation and Presentation 25, 31
Problem-solving 91-93
Process Film 13, 35, 43-45, 75, 78-81, 105, 153, 159, 387
Productivity 46, 85-86, 91, 104, 127-128, 130, 137, 139, 141, 158, 161, 193, 236, 260, 270, 273, 275-279, 283, 286, 324, 365, 368, 370, 379
Promotion 167, 169, 246, 267-270, 351

Propaganda 19, 21-22, 24, 76, 110, 155,
    171, 173, 180-181, 190, 244, 246, 260,
    304, 320, 323-325, 337, 342
Psychotechnik / Psychotechnics 136-137
Public Relations / PR 78, 218, 248, 250,
    254n, 260, 273, 303-304, 306, 311, 377
Purchasing power 177

Quality 44, 53, 61, 70, 79, 110, 113, 158,
    161-162, 178, 180, 197-200, 203, 233
Quality Testing 45

Race 260-261, 269, 272, 274-278
Railway 22, 65, 110-111, 133, 162, 365,
    391, 398
Rationalization 11, 40, 45-46, 85, 96, 104-
    105, 127-128, 130, 133, 137-138, 144-
    145, 147n, 211, 253, 279, 288, 356-357,
    365
Raleigh & Robert 65
RCA 60, 215
Regimes of knowledge 127-131
Regimes of visibility 129
Reichsverband der Automobilindustrie (Na-
    tional Automobile Industry Associa-
    tion) 155
Republican National Committee 218
Research film 41, 49n, 90-92, 105, 153
Rhetoric 41-46, 52, 85, 90, 91, 96, 104-
    105, 108, 112-113, 128, 134, 143, 212,
    243, 244, 253, 297, 329-331, 337, 341,
    357
Robot 43, 138, 159, 191, 196-199, 203
Rockefeller 60-61

Scènes d'art et d'industrie 65,
Science 43, 87-88, 97n, 123, 285, 291,
    299n
Scientific Management 39, 85, 88, 92,
    97n
Sears-Roebuck 228
Serial Film Analysis 102, 104, 112
Shell / Royal Dutch/Shell 14, 243-253,
    254n-254n
Shell Film Unit / SFU 244, 247, 253, 255n

Slide Show 13, 134-135, 233, 306
Social Democrats (Germany) 144, 332
Spectator 91, 109-110, 119, 121-122, 124-
    125, 156, 175, 182, 196-201, 204, 284,
    290-291, 295, 355, 361
Sponsor 31, 106, 109, 214, 245, 248
Sponsored film 54, 57-58, 86, 96, 101,
    112, 114n, 211, 213-220, 247, 253, 407-
    408
Sputnik (Sovjet Satellite, 1958) 227
Stichting Nederlandse Onderwijs Film / N.
    O.F. 81-82
Standardization 37, 91-92, 293, 350, 359
Streamlining 153, 160-161, 187-188, 204,
    276, 305, 311, 342
Supervisory Relationship Training (SRT)
    268, 272-273, 275-277, 282n
Swiss Central Office for Cultural Film
    Production 111
Swiss National Exhibition (*Schweizerische
    Landessaustellung*, 1939) 110, 112,
    117n

Tabulating Machines 45, 127-128, 132-
    138, 140, 145
Taste 110, 155, 323, 360
Taylorism 265, 287, 300, 357
Technicolor 217-218
Technology 10-11, 21, 32, 39, 40, 47n, 54,
    108, 129, 217-218, 228, 236, 272, 303,
    323, 380-384
Telegraph 38, 45, 293, 356
Television / TV 19, 28, 31, 193, 272-273,
    280, 306, 308, 334, 352, 364, 385, 398
Thyssen Steel 35, 43
Time Study 85, 92, 94, 98n
Trade Fair, Fair 24, 37, 41, 45, 68, 78, 105,
    107, 109, 113, 134, 139, 352, 359, 362
Training Films 20, 60, 82, 218, 228, 246,
    269, 286
Tullberg Film (Sweden) 111

Union Pacific 228
United States Air Force 228
United States Census 133

United States Navy 228
University of Kansas (KU) 222, 224-225, 228, 230, 233

Verein Deutscher Motofahrzeugindustrieller (German Association of Automobile Industrialists) 154
Video-on-demand 61
Visibility 13, 36, 124, 127-140, 143-145, 163, 294
Visitor film 13, 153, 158-160, 163
Visual Simultaneity 391
Visual Rhetoric 128, 143, 243, 297
Visualization 91, 93-94, 183, 292, 294, 304
Vitek-Film 385, 387, 389
Volkswagen 13, 140, 153-155, 157-160

Wage 72, 262, 329, 332, 341, 358, 365
Weimar period 331-332, 338, 340

Western Electric 259-267, 273, 277-278, 281n
Westinghouse 78
World War II 28, 134, 140, 144, 183, 188, 224, 246, 283, 285-286, 304, 308-310, 372-373, 377-379, 382, 388, 392, 394
Work, Representation of 167, 315, 323, 325, 329
Working class 315, 321, 329, 331, 333, 344, 393
Work-study film 46, 130, 139, 147n, 193, 283, 287-288, 291, 342

Union 9, 41, 85, 128, 141-145, 149n, 218, 286, 330, 332-338, 341-344, 385
Utility Film 10-11, 13, 19, 30, 36, 47n, 101-102, 104, 106, 109-112, 117n

Xerox 215

Film Culture in Transition

General Editor: *Thomas Elsaesser*

Thomas Elsaesser, Robert Kievit and Jan Simons (eds.)
Double Trouble: Chiem van Houweninge on Writing and Filming, 1994
ISBN paperback 978 90 5356 025 9

Thomas Elsaesser, Jan Simons and Lucette Bronk (eds.)
Writing for the Medium: Television in Transition, 1994
ISBN paperback 978 90 5356 054 9

Karel Dibbets and Bert Hogenkamp (eds.)
Film and the First World War, 1994
ISBN paperback 978 90 5356 064 8

Warren Buckland (ed.)
The Film Spectator: From Sign to Mind, 1995
ISBN paperback 978 90 5356 131 7; ISBN hardcover 978 90 5356 170 6

Egil Törnqvist
Between Stage and Screen: Ingmar Bergman Directs, 1996
ISBN paperback 978 90 5356 137 9; ISBN hardcover 978 90 5356 171 3

Thomas Elsaesser (ed.)
A Second Life: German Cinema's First Decades, 1996
ISBN paperback 978 90 5356 172 0; ISBN hardcover 978 90 5356 183 6

Thomas Elsaesser
Fassbinder's Germany: History Identity Subject, 1996
ISBN paperback 978 90 5356 059 4; ISBN hardcover 978 90 5356 184 3

Thomas Elsaesser and Kay Hoffmann (eds.)
Cinema Futures: Cain, Abel or Cable? The Screen Arts in the Digital Age, 1998
ISBN paperback 978 90 5356 282 6; ISBN hardcover 978 90 5356 312 0

Siegfried Zielinski
Audiovisions: Cinema and Television as Entr'Actes in History, 1999
ISBN paperback 978 90 5356 313 7; ISBN hardcover 978 90 5356 303 8

Kees Bakker (ed.)
Joris Ivens and the Documentary Context, 1999
ISBN paperback 978 90 5356 389 2; ISBN hardcover 978 90 5356 425 7

Egil Törnqvist
Ibsen, Strindberg and the Intimate Theatre: Studies in TV Presentation, 1999
ISBN paperback 978 90 5356 350 2; ISBN hardcover 978 90 5356 371 7

Michael Temple and James S. Williams (eds.)
The Cinema Alone: Essays on the Work of Jean-Luc Godard 1985-2000, 2000
ISBN paperback 978 90 5356 455 4; ISBN hardcover 978 90 5356 456 1

Patricia Pisters and Catherine M. Lord (eds.)
Micropolitics of Media Culture: Reading the Rhizomes of Deleuze and Guattari, 2001
ISBN paperback 978 90 5356 472 1; ISBN hardcover 978 90 5356 473 8

William van der Heide
Malaysian Cinema, Asian Film: Border Crossings and National Cultures, 2002
ISBN paperback 978 90 5356 519 3; ISBN hardcover 978 90 5356 580 3

Bernadette Kester
*Film Front Weimar: Representations of the First World War in German Films of the
    Weimar Period (1919-1933)*, 2002
ISBN *paperback 978 90 5356 597 1*; ISBN *hardcover 978 90 5356 598 8*

Richard Allen and Malcolm Turvey (eds.)
Camera Obscura, Camera Lucida: Essays in Honor of Annette Michelson, 2003
ISBN paperback 978 90 5356 494 3

Ivo Blom
Jean Desmet and the Early Dutch Film Trade, 2003
ISBN paperback 978 90 5356 463 9; ISBN hardcover 978 90 5356 570 4

Alastair Phillips
City of Darkness, City of Light: Émigré Filmmakers in Paris 1929-1939, 2003
ISBN paperback 978 90 5356 634 3; ISBN hardcover 978 90 5356 633 6

Thomas Elsaesser, Alexander Horwath and Noel King (eds.)
The Last Great American Picture Show: New Hollywood Cinema in the 1970s, 2004
ISBN paperback 978 90 5356 631 2; ISBN hardcover 978 905356 493 6

Thomas Elsaesser (ed.)
Harun Farocki: Working on the Sight-Lines, 2004
ISBN paperback 978 90 5356 635 0; ISBN hardcover 978 90 5356 636 7

Kristin Thompson
Herr Lubitsch Goes to Hollywood: German and American Film after World War I,
    2005
ISBN paperback 978 90 5356 708 1; ISBN hardcover 978 90 5356 709 8

Marijke de Valck and Malte Hagener (eds.)
Cinephilia: Movies, Love and Memory, 2005
ISBN paperback 978 90 5356 768 5; ISBN hardcover 978 90 5356 769 2

Thomas Elsaesser
European Cinema: Face to Face with Hollywood, 2005
ISBN paperback 978 90 5356 594 0; ISBN hardcover 978 90 5356 602 2

Michael Walker
Hitchcock's Motifs, 2005
ISBN paperback 978 90 5356 772 2; ISBN hardcover 978 90 5356 773 9

Nanna Verhoeff
The West in Early Cinema: After the Beginning, 2006
ISBN paperback 978 90 5356 831 6; ISBN hardcover 978 90 5356 832 3

Anat Zanger
Film Remakes as Ritual and Disguise: From Carmen to Ripley, 2006
ISBN paperback 978 90 5356 784 5; ISBN hardcover 978 90 5356 785 2

Wanda Strauven
The Cinema of Attractions Reloaded, 2006
ISBN paperback 978 90 5356 944 3; ISBN hardcover 978 90 5356 945 0

Malte Hagener
*Moving Forward, Looking Back: The European Avant-garde and the Invention of Film
    Culture, 1919-1939,* 2007
ISBN paperback 978 90 5356 960 3; ISBN hardcover 978 90 5356 961 0

Tim Bergfelder, Sue Harris and Sarah Street
*Film Architecture and the Transnational Imagination: Set Design in 1930s European
    Cinema,* 2007
ISBN paperback 978 90 5356 984 9; ISBN hardcover 978 90 5356 980 1

Jan Simons
Playing the Waves: Lars von Trier's Game Cinema, 2007
ISBN paperback 978 90 5356 991 7; ISBN hardcover 978 90 5356 979 5

Marijke de Valck
Film Festivals: From European Geopolitics to Global Cinephilia, 2007
ISBN paperback 978 90 5356 192 8; ISBN hardcover 978 90 5356 216 1

Asbjørn Grønstad
Transfigurations: Violence, Death, and Masculinity in American Cinema, 2008
ISBN paperback 978 90 8964 010 9; ISBN hardcover 978 90 8964 030 7